D1521030

Management of Technology:
Growth through Business Innovation and Entrepreneurship

Selected Papers from the Tenth International Conference on Management of Technology

Management of Technology:
Growth through Business Innovation and Entrepreneurship

Selected Papers from the Tenth International Conference on Management of Technology

EDITED BY

Max von Zedtwitz
IMD – International Institute for Management Development, Lausanne, Switzerland

Georges Haour
IMD – International Institute for Management Development, Lausanne, Switzerland

Tarek M. Khalil
University of Miami, Florida, USA

Louis A. Lefebvre
ePoly, Ecole Polytechnique de Montreal, Quebec, Canada

2003

PERGAMON
An Imprint of Elsevier Science

Amsterdam – Boston – London – New York – Oxford – Paris
San Diego – San Francisco – Singapore – Sydney – Tokyo

ELSEVIER SCIENCE Ltd
The Boulevard, Langford Lane
Kidlington, Oxford OX5 1GB, UK

First edition 2003

Library of Congress Cataloging in Publication Data
A catalog record from the Library of Congress has been applied for.

British Library Cataloguing in Publication Data
A catalogue record from the British Library has been applied for.

ISBN: 0 08 044136 X

♾ The paper used in this publication meets the requirements of ANSI/NISO Z39.48-1992 (Permanence of Paper).
Printed in The Netherlands.

PREFACE

Max von Zedtwitz, IMD, Lausanne, Switzerland[*]
Georges Haour, IMD, Lausanne, Switzerland[**]
Tarek Khalil, University of Miami, Florida, USA[***]
Louis-A. Lefebvre, École Polytechnique de Montréal, Canada[****]

The International Association for Management of Technology (IAMOT) conferences are designed as a forum and meeting place to exchange best practices and novel concepts of managing innovation, technology and R&D. The 10th International Conference held in Lausanne, Switzerland in March 2001 focused on "Growth through Business Innovation and Entrepreneurship."

This book is a selection of papers representing the best thinking of leading researchers and practitioners in the field of Management of Technology. More than 260 abstracts were received during the call-for-papers, of which 156 were submitted as full papers, reviewed and accepted for presentation at the conference. It is indicative of the quality of some of the original conference papers that they have since been published in leading journals; in such cases a reference to published papers is given.

The Scientific Committee of IAMOT and the editors selected papers for inclusion in this book according to the following set of criteria:

[*] Dr. Maximilian von Zedtwitz is Professor of Technology Management at IMD-International Institute for Management Development in Lausanne, Switzerland. Email: zedtwitz.imd.ch.

[**] Dr. Georges Haour is Professor of Technology Management at IMD- International Institute for Management Development. Email: haour@imd.ch.

[***] Dr. Tarek M. Khalil is the Founder and current President of the International Association for Management of Technology. He is Professor of Industrial Engineering at the University of Miami, Florida, USA.

[****] Dr. Louis Lefebvre is Professor in the Mathematics and Industrial Engineering Department at the École Polytechnique de Montréal, Canada.

- They fit with the theme of the conference of business innovation and entrepreneurship;
- They reflect future trends and streams in the field;
- They are original and relevant contributions to the on-going debate of management of technology;
- They are the most solidly researched and presented contributions to the conference.

Many excellent conference papers were eliminated in due course of review for not meeting the set criteria. Thirty papers were finally selected and their authors were then invited to update their manuscripts and resubmit them. The contributions are arranged according to three burning issues of our times:

1. Entrepreneurship and venture creation;
2. Knowledge management;
3. Multi-actor innovation.

Since the underlying theme of the book deals with entrepreneurial energy, the conditions for its appearance and its success, the first section includes papers covering a wide range of *entrepreneurship and venture creation* issues: start ups and venturing activities. Ventures emanating inside companies are discussed by Katzy et al. for Siemens' entreprise network division, by Yamada et al. in the case of Mitsubishi Electric and by Christensen, who contrasts the approaches of Danfoss and Grundfos. Some of the paths innovations are taken to market have been studied by Ruping and Zedtwitz on incubators, by Kondo on start ups in China, by Cloutier and Boehljie on trade offs in investing in the biotechnology sector, and by Dellepiane on bio-start ups. The role of the investors' community is the object of papers by Lange et al. on angel investors, by Christensen and Christensen on venture capital in Denmark, and by and Henderson and Leleux on service for equity arrangements, while the valuation of start ups by investors is indeed perceived differently from that of entrepreneurs, as found by Micol and Rabassa.

The second section is composed of articles addressing various issues of *knowledge management*. The papers are organized in a macro to micro perspective. The first three articles focus on competition in turbulent environments. Praest looks at competence groups and links the ability to develop and manage technological capabilities with economic performance. Munir and Phillips reconsider the concept of industry and suggest substituting this concept with the notion of the 'activity network'. Kuivalainen et al. study the effects of internationalisation of a firm on managing knowledge and learning. The next three papers focus on process-related perspectives of knowledge management. Schulze provides insights into the management of knowledge creation in innovation processes. Baroni de Carvalho and Ferreira describe taxonomy for knowledge management tools, and Albors gives an example of how knowledge tools and knowledge processes can be developed and applied in an SME context. The last two papers in this section are concerned with the integration of knowledge in and across projects. Hunt et al. discuss the benefits and approaches to technology re-use, and Alderman et al. study customer requirements in long-term engineering projects from a knowledge management point-of-view.

The third theme discusses the trend towards a *multi-actor innovation* process, according to which developments are carried out by several organizations, firms or otherwise, each contributing a piece of the innovation puzzle. Several sub-themes have been identified. The first one deals with the actual implementation of collaborative developments, involving various types of partners: a) university-industry, with the issues of licensing, presented by Hoye and Roe, or joint development, as discussed by Leo and Zuppiroli; b) firm-laboratories, by Francisco et al. and; c) multi-firm collaborations with regards software development, as explained by McLoughlin and Koch, product architectures and the design of modular lifts, as studied by Hsuan-Mikkola and Gassmann, or R&D project selection, by Torkkeli et al. Another group of papers deals with the supply and demand chains: Zawislak and de Borba Vieira look at General Motors, Brazil, and Heikkilä and Suolanen study Nokia Networks. A last group of papers focuses on the interplay between technology and its societal context, at the level of the firm, with distant workers, as described by Buser and Koch, and at the level of the country: clusters in Korea presented by Chung, and relocations of manufacturing facilities studied by de Bruijn and Steenhuis.

We would like to acknowledge the generous support of IMD-International Institute of Management Development in the preparation of this book as well as its involvement in the IAMOT conference. Other institutions and companies have also contributed to the quality and relevance of the included articles here, mostly with their support of the IAMOT conference: Nestlé, Bobst, Nokia, ABB, Möwenpick International, Sulzer, Kudelski, Swissair, EPF-Lausanne, Ecole Polytechnique de Montréal, Unido, The State of Vaud, and the City of Lausanne. We are happy to see our publishing relationship with Elsevier and Pergamon flourish with this next volume in a series of IAMOT publications. Last but not least, our gratitude goes out to the participants of the conference whose constructive criticism improved the quality of the papers included in this book, and the authors who put in tremendous efforts to comply with the high expectations of the editors.

IMD, Lausanne, Switzerland, July 2002

Max von Zedtwitz
Georges Haour
Tarek Khalil
Louis Lefebvre

LIST OF CONTENTS

SECTION II – KNOWLEDGE MANAGEMENT

SECTION III – MULTI-ACTOR INNOVATION

CONTRIBUTORS

José Albors Garrigós

Dr. José Albors is Professor of Project Management and Organizational Behaviour at Universidad Politecnica de Valencia (UPV), Spain. He holds PhD. and lic. Industrial Engineering degrees from the Universidad Politecnica de Madrid where he also obtained an MBA in 1986. As an engineer he has twenty years experience in international project management. He has worked with ICI Ltd., Foster Wheeler and Fuller Corp. Since 1987 he works in the technology management field being the Eureka program Director in Spain and later a consultant with various organizations including UNIDO and the European Commission. His field of specialization is the SME having ample consultancy practice there. In 1994 he joined UPV to teach Business Management. He has published numerous papers on innovation management and leaded more than five international research projects.

Neil Alderman

Dr. Neil Alderman is a Principal Research Associate in the Centre for Urban and Regional Development Studies and recently appointed to a senior lectureship in the University of Newcastle upon Tyne Business School. He holds a BSc in social sciences degree in geography from the University of Bristol and a PhD from the University of Newcastle upon Tyne. His current research concerns the management of complex projects, knowledge management, innovation and supply chain networks in the low volume capital goods industries, the product development process in engineering, and the implications of project-based activity for regional innovation systems, clusters and knowledge processes. He has held both ESRC and EPSRC research grants and acted as a consultant to the European Commission DGXIII, as well as carrying out studies for a number of UK government departments and agencies. He has published widely in both geographical and management journals.

Thaís de Azevedo

Thaís de Azevedo is an undergraduate student at Management School of the University of Rio Grande do Sul State (UFRGS). She worked at NITEC as a Research Assistant in 2000.

Jun'ichi Baba

Dr. Jun'ichi Baba holds B.Eng., M.Eng., and Ph.D. degrees all from the University of Tokyo, Tokyo, Japan. He joined Mitsubishi Electric Corporation, Tokyo, Japan in 1952. His career in the company is outlined as follows: 1973-1977, general manager of Planning Department, Power & Industrial Systems Division (Tokyo, Japan); 1977-1981, general manager of Central Research Laboratories (Hyogo, Japan); 1981-1985, director and general manager of Corporate Engineering and Manufacturing (Tokyo, Japan); 1985-1996, advisor to the Board of Directors (Tokyo, Japan); 1996-present, consultant to Mitsubishi Electric Corporation (Tokyo, Japan). He received the Prize of Progress from the Institute of Electrical Engineering of Japan for "Research on Interconnection Equipment for Power Systems" in 1980 and received the Best Chairman of the Year Award from the IEEE EMS in 1998. He lectured at the Department of Business Administration, Kobe University, in 1997. He is a senior member of IEEE and founding chairman of the IEEE Japan Chapter of EMS. He was a member of the Board of Directors of the Academic Association for Organizational Science, now he is a member of this association. He was also a member of the Board of Directors of the Japan Society for Science Policy and Research Management (JSSPRM) and now senior councillor of JSSPRM. His recent interest is on the management of R&D from the corporate governance's view.

Michael D. Boehlje

Michael D. Boehlje, Ph.D. is a professor of Agribusiness Management in the Department of Agricultural Economics, Center for Agricultural Business, at Purdue University. His research focuses on the impacts of innovation in agribusiness management, agricultural finance, value chain coordination, and the economics of commercial biotechnology.

Franziska Blindow

Franziska Blindow holds a PhD in Technology Management from the University of St. Gallen (HSG) and an MBA in Finance and Accounting from the same institution. She is with EIM, a pioneer in Delegated Investment Management with more than USD 7 billion allocated assets, as a Board Member and Manager for the structuring of tailor-made Hedge Fund-of-Fund Portfolios. Before joining EIM, Franziska has been working at the University of St. Gallen as a Senior Researcher, Project Manager and Head of Competence Center. Prior to that, she has been in Corporate Finance for eight years, most recently as a CIO for a multinational automotive supplier. Franziska is a lecturer at the University of St. Gallen and a Reviewer for the Academy of Management.

Erik Joost de Bruijn

Erik Joost de Bruijn is Professor of Business Management in Developing and New Industrialising Economies at the Faculty of technology and Management of the University of Twente, Enschede, Netherlands. He holds a Ph.D. and M.Sc. degree in Mechanical Engineering of the University of Twente and a M.Sc., Operations Research and Industrial Engineering of the University of Massachusetts, USA. Currently he is the chairman of the Technology and Development Group of the University of Twente. He worked as a research coordinator of an international project team for development of the metal industry in Indonesia, and as a consultant for various projects of the World Bank, The Directorate for International Development Cooperation of the Netherlands and commercial enterprises in Asia, Africa and South America. He published books and articles on Transfer of Technology, Joint Ventures, and Business Management in Developing Countries.

Martine Buser

Martine Buser is sociologist; she is working as scientific collaborator at the Institute of Logistic, Economic and Management of Technology at the Swiss Federal Institute of Technology in Lausanne. Her research interests have focused mainly on changes introduced by information technologies in organisations and work practices. She has conducted a study on the development of mobile work in Switzerland for the centre for Technology Assessment of the Swiss Science and Technology Council. Other research activities include transports in relation to new technologies and tele-teaching. She has taken part in several national projects and three European in the TSER programme. She is currently doing a Ph.D. on management of knowledge in engineering companies.

Rodrigo Baroni de Carvalho

Rodrigo Baroni de Carvalho is a Professor of Computer Science at Fumec University Center. He holds a master degree from School of Information Science at the Federal University of Minas Gerais (UFMG), Brazil. He graduated in Computer Science from UFMG. He also works as a system analyst for the Development Bank of Minas Gerais (BDMG). He is now a doctor degree student at School of Information Science at UFMG. He is interested in the following areas: information systems, software engineer, object-oriented system, data bases and knowledge management. He can be contacted by e-mail at baroni@bdmg.mg.gov.br.

Claus E. Christensen

Claus E. Christensen has been working in the Danish Ministry of Economic and Business affairs (former Ministry of Trade and Industry) since 1998. His area of responsibility in the ministry has mainly been venture and risk capital markets. In particularly, economic impacts of venture capital and the government's role in promoting well-functioning risk capital markets. In 2001 he was co-writer on a research project analysing seed capital markets in the Nordic region with a specific focus on the role of government in the seed capital segment. The project was carried out by the independent research institute Centre for Economic and Business Research (www.cebr.dk) on the behalf of the Nordic Industrial Fund.

Jens Frøslev Christensen

Jens Frøslev Christensen is Professor of Management of Technology at Department of Industrial Economics and Strategy , Copenhagen Business School. He is the coordinator of the master of science programme in Management of Technology at Copenhagen Business School and teaches courses in Innovation and Technology Strategy. He is director of CISTEMA, a research consortium dedicated to inter-disciplinary studies in Management of Technology and member of the board of DRUID, a Danish-based global research network within the field of industrial dynamics. His research focuses on three issues: (i) Management of Innovation, (ii) the strategy and structure of corporate R&D, and (iii) the industrial dynamics of 'New Economy' sectors such as Internet consulting services. He has published several books and numerous articles in, among other journals, Economics of Innovation and New Technology, Industrial and Corporate Change, Research Policy and Managerial and Decision Economics.

Jesper L. Christensen

Jesper L. Christensen has been a member of the IKE-research group of Aalborg University since 1989. As an associate professor at Department of Business Studies he is teaching at both the business administration education and the economics education. His research includes various aspects of innovation theory and -practice. He has a broad knowledge on innovation and innovation policy, and has specialized in financial aspects of innovation. He is currently investigating Danish business angels, the Danish venture capital market, development in financial systems and inter-firm collaboration. Among previous projects should be mentioned that he was the daily coordinator of a 3-year research project on the Danish Innovation System in Comparative Perspective ("DISKO"). In addition, he was conducting some of the analyses in this project including an analysis on the collaboration between industrial firms and technological institutes and an analysis of the role of business angels in Denmark.

Sunyang Chung

Dr. Sunyang Chung is Professor of Technology Management and Director of Institute for Technological Innovation (ITI) at Sejong University, Seoul, Korea. He holds Ph.D. degree from the University of Stuttgart, Germany and MBA and B.Sc. degrees from Seoul National University, Seoul, Korea. During his study in Germany, he carried out several research projects at the Fraunhofer-Institute for Systems and Innovation Research (FhG-ISI) in Karlsruhe. He had worked for 13 years at a Korean governmental research institute, Science and Technology Policy Institute (STEPI), as a senior research fellow. He joined Sejong University in March 2000 to teach technology management and policy. His research areas are technology management and policy, regional innovation strategies, environmental management and policy, and the integration of the South and North Korean innovation systems. He has published several books in Korea and Germany and has written many articles for Korean and international journals.

L. Martin Cloutier

L. Martin Cloutier, Ph.D. is a professor in the Department of Management and Technology at the University of Quebec at Montreal. His research includes the design of system dynamics models and simulations to characterize the decision-making processes in value chains associated with economic, managerial, and regulatory dimensions of technology and biotechnology development and diffusion. His teaching program includes courses in dynamic modeling and simulation both at the undergraduate and graduate levels.

Nicola Dellepiane

Nicola Dellepiane received an Italian engineering science doctor's degree, cum laude, in chemical engineering, and an M. Sc., with congratulations, in industrial management, from Columbia University, New York, where he was a Fulbright and an Institute of International Education student. After managing a small electric company until all such companies were nationalized in Italy, he served as director of operations research and integrated planning at Shell Italy and as director of interfunctional planning at the Italian National Steel Company Italsider. He has lectured in the internal management training programs of large corporations including IRI and the Royal Dutch Shell Group. He is presently professor of Economics and Management of Industrial Enterprises at the Polytechnic School of Engineering of the University of Turin, Italy. He has performed extensive research in Italy with the support of the National Research Council, as well as abroad in the area of economics and management of industrial enterprises. He is the author of thirty publications, many of which are in English, and an editor of the Journal of Managerial Finance.

Marcel Dissel

Marcel Dissel is a researcher at the University Bw Munich, and a research member of the Centre for Technology and Innovation Management (CeTIM). He holds a M.Sc. from the Erasmus University Rotterdam. He gained professional experience as a project manager for Serco in Australia, a multinational specialist in outsourcing and support services. More recently he assisted in the founding of CeTIM, where he has been a project manager for various major research projects (e.g. EU-IST 5FW Genesis, ICE-2000 Siemens). Currently, he is reading for a Ph.D. on uncertainty management for high-tech venturing and is a visiting scholar at the University of Cambridge. His research interests focus on organizational capabilities and decision making for managing innovation in rapid-change environments.

Clare J.P. Farrukh

Clare Farrukh is a senior researcher at the Institute for Manufacturing, Cambridge University Engineering Department. She holds a B.Sc.B.Eng. in Chemical Engineering from the University of Nottingham and spent six years as a process engineer working on engineering projects and new product introduction before joining the University in 1995. Her research activities are concerned with the development of practical tools for supporting technology management in industry and have included a methodology for assessing technology management processes and a fast-start roadmapping technique for linking technology resources to company objectives. In addition she plays an active part in the co-ordination of a Technology Management Network for academics and industrialists.

Marta Araújo Tavares Ferreira

Dr. Marta Araújo Tavares Ferreira is Professor of Knowledge Management and Innovation at the School of Information Science of Universidade Federal de Minas Gerais (UFMG), Belo Horizonte, Brazil. She holds a doctoral degree from Ecole Centrale des Arts et Manufactures de Paris, France. As an engineer, she worked in Strategic Planning for Comissão Nacional de Energia Nuclear, in Rio de Janeiro. More recently, she was a Visiting Fellow at Ecole de Bibliothéconomie et des Sciences de l'Information of Montreal University, Canada. She joined UFMG in 1993 to teach innovation, information and knowledge management in regular graduate and undergraduate programs, as well as executive education programs. She has published two book chapters and several papers in scientific journals and congress proceedings and directed several master and doctoral researches.

Edi M. Fracasso

Dr. Edi Madalena Fracasso is a full professor at the Federal University of Rio Grande do Sul. School of Administration, Porto Alegre/Brazil. She teaches courses in Management of Science and Technology and Research Methods for master's and doctor's degree programs. She also teaches an undergraduate course in Project Elaboration. In 1991 she created and since then she had been coordinating the Nucleus of Management of Technological Innovation – NITEC – whose research is concerned with the processes of generation, transference, diffusion and impacts of technological innovation in universities, public organizations, enterprises, industries and regions. She holds a Doctor's Degree from Harvard School of Education and a Master's Degree is Public Administration from the University of Southern California. Her undergraduate degree in Education is from the Federal University of Rio Grande do Sul. Dr. Fracasso's more recent research and publications focus on: university-enterprise interaction and impacts of science and technology investments.

Lourdes Terezinha T. Francisco

M.Sc. Lourdes T. Francisco is a collaborate research at NITEC – Nucleus of Management of the Technological Innovation, based at the Management School of the Federal University of Rio Grande do Sul. (UFRGS). She holds a graduate degree in Chemical Engineering (1998) and a master's degree in Administration (2002) at UFRGS. Her master dissertation theme was about Indicators of Results' Evaluation for Public Supported Research Projects; especially those financed by the Research Support Foundation of the Rio Grande do Sul State – FAPERGS. In 2001, she works as a research assistant at the Management Science Faculty of the Mondragon University (Basque Country, Spain), in a project about the New Technologies of the Information and the Communications in Leader Regions and Basque Country. Now, she's working in the elaboration of a real System of Results' Evaluation for Research Projects Supported by FAPERGS, under the coordination of Dr. Edi M. Fracasso, Ph.D., NITEC's co-ordinator.

Oliver Gassmann

Dr. Oliver Gassmann is Professor at the University of St. Gallen and Director of the Institute for Technology Management. Between 1996 and 2002 he worked at Schindler Corporation, headquartered in Ebikon/Switzerland, where as Vice President Technology Management he was responsible for Corporate Research and Strategic Technology Management worldwide. He holds Masters and Ph.D. degrees in business administration and economics from University of Hohenheim-Stuttgart and St. Gallen. His work experience includes different functions at Daimler-Benz, Festo, Norma and Kolb in England, Ireland and Singapore. Between 1994 and 1996, he was a research associate at the Institute for Technology Management. He is member in several boards, such as the Board for Science and Research of Economiesuisse, the Committee Stratégique Euresearch, the Editorial Board of R&D Management. He is also teaching in several Executive MBA programs. His research focuses on international R&D and strategic innovation management. He has published five books and over 40 publications in the area of technology and innovation management.

Georges Haour (Editor)

Dr. G. Haour is Professor at IMD, where he teaches Technology Management and directs executive programmes for managers coming from technology companies worldwide. He also works at Generics, in Cambridge, UK, in the area of technology ventures and startups. Dr. Haour is an advisor to companies in Europe, North America, Japan, and Singapore, in the area of technology ventures and R&D/Innovation management. Born in Lyon, France, he obtained a degree in Chemical Engineering from the Ecole Nationale Supérieure de Chimie de Paris. He has undergraduate training in Law and Economics (Paris). He has a Master of Sciences (New

York) and a Ph.D. in Chemistry and Materials Science, from the University of Toronto, Canada.

Prior to joining IMD, Dr. Haour was manager at Battelle, in Geneva, where, for nine years, he led a business unit carrying out innovation projects on behalf of companies in Europe, Japan and the USA. Several of his innovations have been licensed to firms, resulting, on several occasions, in substantial new business for the client-companies. Earlier, he was a researcher at ATT's Bell Laboratories, in Murray Hill, New Jersey. He also worked with Marshall McLuhan at his Centre for Culture, Society and Technology, in Toronto. Dr. Haour has more than 70 publications, as well as eight granted patents. He is currently doing research on Creating Value through Technological Innovation.

Jussi Heikkilä

Dr. Jussi Heikkilä is Professor (acting) of Industrial Management at Helsinki University of Technology, Finland. He holds a DSc (Tech) degree from Helsinki University of Technology and MBA degree from Webster University. As an engineer and manager he worked for several years in building and building materials industries in the Middle East, Asia and Western Europe. More recently, he worked as research associate at IMD International, Lausanne, Switzerland, and as research director at TAI Research Centre of Helsinki University of Technology. He has twice been recipient of the European Foundation for Management Development case writing award. His present research focuses on operations strategy, demand/supply chain management and project management. He is the author or co-author of several conference papers and research articles. His articles have been published among others in Production and Operations Management, International Journal of Logistics: Research and Applications, International Journal of Project Management, International Journal of Technology Management, Journal of Strategic Change, and Journal of Operations Management.

James E. Henderson

James Henderson is an Assistant Professor of Strategic Management at Babson College where he teaches undergraduate, graduate and executives industry and competitor analysis, national business systems and corporate level strategy. His research interests include industry and competitive analysis, corporate governance, learning and strategic decision making, and critical mass phenomena. Prior to joining Babson, Professor Henderson was a consultant at Mars & Co. devising business unit and corporate level strategies for clients in various industries including beverage cans, hotels, and automobiles. Professor Henderson received his Ph.D. in Strategic Management at INSEAD, focusing on the subject of capacity expansion decisions in the global petrochemical industry. He also received his Undergraduate in Economics and French and MBA from the University of Western Ontario, Canada.

Kate Hoye

Kate Hoye is a doctoral candidate in Systems Design Engineering at the University of Waterloo, Ontario, Canada. Her interest in university-industry technology transfer is rooted in personal experience. While concluding an undergraduate engineering degree (B.A.Sc. Systems Design) and starting her graduate studies at the University of Waterloo, Kate was a partner in a research and design spin-off company. The launch product was awarded first place in the Ontario and Canadian Engineering Competitions and the business concept was awarded first place in the Ontario Collegiate Entrepreneur competition.

Francis Hunt

Francis Hunt is a researcher at the Institute for Manufacturing, Cambridge University Engineering Department. He holds an M.A. in Mathematics from the University of Cambridge and a doctorate in informatics from the Ecole des Mines de Paris. He has worked as a software and mathematical consultant before to joining the University in 1999. His research activities are concerned with the development of practical tools for supporting technology management in industry, with particular focus on software. Current projects include researching tools for supporting embedded software sourcing decisions and investigating the opportunities and risks for companies engaging with open source software.

Juliana Hsuan Mikkola

Juliana is a Research Assistant at the Copenhagen Business School, Department of Operations Management. She received her B.Sc. degree in electrical engineering from University of Houston in 1987 and her M.B.A. from St. Mary's University in 1993. She also received a Licentiate of Science of Economics degree (in Logistics) from the Helsinki School of Economics and Business Administration in 1998. Professionally, she worked as a Design Engineer and Design Team Leader at Motorola's Automotive and Industrial Electronics Group. Later on she became an Executive Trainee of Motorola's Corporate International Operations Program dealing with the management of communications technology in Latin American. She has published in European Journal of Purchasing and Supply Management and Technovation, and has made contributions to a couple of books. Her research interests include modularization in NPD vis-à-vis supply chain management and industry structure, mathematical modelling, and portfolio management of R&D projects.

Chris Ivory

Chris Ivory is a lecturer in the University of Newcastle upon Tyne Business School. He has a Masters degree from the department of Policy Research into Engineering Science and Technology (PREST) in the University of Manchester and a B.Sc. from Brunel University in West London. He is presently completing a PhD with PREST. He has held research posts at UMIST in Manchester and in Newcastle University. Most recently, he was a Research Associate at the Centre for Urban and Regional Development Studies at Newcastle University.

Bernhard R. Katzy

Bernhard R. Katzy started his professional career with an apprenticeship as car mechanic and later studied and earned master degrees in electrical engineering and business management. He holds a PhD in industrial management from University of Technology (RWTH) Aachen in Germany and a second Ph.D. (habilitation) in general management from University of St. Gallen, Switzerland. He is lecturing MBA and Executive MBA courses at leading European business schools, e.g. St. Gallen University, Rotterdam School of Management, European Business School and ESADE Barcelona. He is professor at the University BW Munich and founder of CeTIM – Center for Technology and Innovation Management, which is located at University Bw Munich and Rotterdam School of Management. His research interest is about entrepreneurial management of fast growing high-tech firms and the emerging industrial structures for the information age.

Tarek M. Khalil (Editor)

Dr. Tarek M. Khalil is the Founder and current President of the International Association for Management of Technology (IAMOT). He is Professor of Industrial Engineering, former Chairman of the Department of Industrial Engineering, and former Dean of the Graduate School, University of Miami, Florida, USA. Dr. Khalil is author and editor of more than 10 books, 3 National Science Foundation sponsored workshop reports on Management of Technology and 300 publications in his areas of expertise. He is the recipient of many national and international awards in the field, including a Doctor Honoris Causa from the Institut National Polytechnique de Lorraine, France and the Technical Innovation Award from the Institurte of Industrial Engineers, USA for his "Significant and Innovative Technical Contributions to the Industrial Engineering Profession". He has conducted extensive educational and training programs in MOT for industry, government employees, international organizations and educational institutions worldwide.

Christian Koch

Christian Koch is Engineer, M.Sc. and Associate Professor of management of production at the Group for Construction Management, Department of Civil Engineering at the Technical University of Denmark. He has written intensively on information technology as change driver in organisations and as innovation, especially on Enterprise Resource Planning systems (ERP). Other interlinked interests are virtual organisations, virtualisation in manufacturing and participation of employees in technological change. He is currently co-managing EU-IST research on enterprise systems implementation. Present research interests include management innovation, new forms of management and organisation and innovation processes in construction. He has published in journals like Technology Analysis and Strategic Management, Organizational Change Management and International Journal of Innovation Management. A recent single authored book (in Danish, 2001) analyses experiences on ERP in Danish Manufacturing concerning change management, configuration of the technology and human resource issues.

Jouni Koivuniemi

Jouni Koivuniemi is working as a project manager and a researcher at the Department of Industrial Engineering and Management, and at Telecom Business Research Center at Lappeenranta University of Technology, located in Lappeenranta, Finland. He holds M.Sc. (Tech.) degree from Lappeenranta University of Technology. He is currently carrying out his doctoral thesis in Management of Technology on the subject of product innovation management in networked environments. His main research interests include innovation management systems and processes, front end of innovation and strategic evaluation and selection of R&D projects. As a researcher and project manager he has participated on several applied research projects with industrial partners. He has published several papers in international conferences, books and journals.

Masayuki Kondo

Dr. Masayuki KONDO is a Professor of Innovation Policy and Technology Management at Graduate School of Environment and Information Sciences, Yokohama National University. He received his Ph.D. in Management Engineering from Tokyo Institute of Technology. He has master's degrees in engineering from University of Washington, Tokyo Institute of Technology and Stanford University. He joined the Ministry of International Trade and Industry (MITI). During the service in MITI, he served as an R&D manager of the Micromachine Project and the Hypersonic Jet Engine Project, a Director of Office for Research and Statistics Planning and a Director of Technology Evaluation Division. He also served as an Associate Professor at Graduate School for Policy Science, Saitama University; worked as an Industrial Economist at the World Bank in Washington, D.C.; was a Visiting Fellow of the Royal Institute of International Affairs (Chatham House) in U.K.; and served as a Professor at Graduate School of Entrepreneur Engineering, Kochi University of Technology. He also taught at the French ENPC Graduate School of International Business in Tokyo concurrently.

Olli Kuivalainen

Mr. Olli Kuivalainen is researcher and doctoral student at Telecom Business Research Center, a multidisciplinary research institute of Lappeenranta University of Technology (LUT), Finland. He holds a M.Sc. (econ.) degree from Lappeenranta University of Technology. Before joining Telecom Business Research Center in January 2000, Mr. Kuivalainen has worked as a research associate at Department of Business Administration of LUT and in a consulting indus- try. His current research interests are in internationalisation of small and medium sized knowl- edge-intensive firms (especially information and communication technology firms), and in in- ternational strategic management/marketing. He has also published two articles in the edited books and he was a member of the research team that received best paper award from IAMOT 2001.

Kalevi Kyläheiko

Dr. Kalevi Kyläheiko is Professor of Economics, especially Technology Research at Lappeen- ranta University of Technology (LUT), Finland. He holds Ph.D. degree in economics from LUT and M.Sc. and B.Sc. degrees from Turku School of Economics. He is currently the Dean of the Department of Business Administration at LUT. He has been a research associate at the University of Göttingen (Germany) and University of Manchester (UK), and a Visiting Fellow at the University of Bremen (Germany). He teaches economics of information age and technol- ogy management and innovation strategy courses both in economics major and MBA and ex- ecutive education programs. He has published about 20 articles in refereed journals and books, five books and about 100 papers on technology management, transaction cost economics, lo- gistics, inventory management, and methodology of economics. He is also one of the recipients of the 2001 best paper award at the IAMOT Lausanne Conference with focus on internationali- zation of high tech SME's.

Julian E. Lange

Dr. Julian E. Lange is BabsonWebberMustard Term Chair in Entrepreneurship and Benson Distinguished Entrepreneurship Fellow at the Arthur M. Blank Center for Entrepreneurship at Babson College, where he teaches M.B.A., undergraduate, and executive education courses in new venture creation and venture growth strategies. Dr. Lange has previously served as assis- tant professor of finance at Harvard Business School. He is a Phi Beta Kappa, Magna Cum Laude graduate of Princeton University and holds an M.B.A. from the Harvard Business School, and an A.M. and Ph.D. in Economics from Harvard University. Dr. Lange is founder and president of Chatham Associates, a management consulting firm that assists businesses in building competitive advantage. He was president and CEO of Software Arts, Inc., creator of the first electronic spreadsheet (VisiCalc), and was a founding trustee of the Massachusetts Software Council.

Louis-A. Lefebvre (Editor)

Dr. Lefebvre, MBA is a full professor in the Mathematics and Industrial Engineering Depart- ment at the École Polytechnique de Montréal. He is director of ePoly, the École Polytech- nique's Center of Expertise in Electronic Commerce. This Center is dedicated to research and diffusion of new ways of conducting e-commerce and of simulating the technological platforms required to support supply chain environments and product life cycle management. Dr. Lefebvre is also the Canadian representative at the OCDE workshop on e-commerce and the knowledge-based economy and member of workgroup of the European committee on electronic commerce. Professor Lefebvre is past-president of the International Association for Management of Technology – IAMOT, which has more than 600 accredited members in 46 countries. Since fall 2000, Dr. Lefebvre is a council member of the SAP Global Institute for Innovation and knowledge development.

Benoît Leleux

Dr Leleux is the Stephan Schmidheiny Professor of Entrepreneurship and Finance at IMD - the International Institute for Management Development where he coordinates venture capital and entrepreneurship-related activities in both MBA and executive education programs. He was previously Visiting Professor of Entrepreneurship and Director of the 3i VentureLab at INSEAD and Associate Professor and Zubillaga Chair in Finance and Entrepreneurship at Babson College, Wellesley, MA (USA) from 1993 to 1999. He obtained his Ph.D. at INSEAD, specializing in Corporate Finance and Venture Capital. He holds an M.Sc. in Agricultural Engineering and an M.A. in Education from the Université Catholique de Louvain (Belgium), and an MBA from Virginia Polytechnic Institute and State University. He was a Fellow of both the Sasakawa Young Leaders Program in Japan and the College for Advanced Studies in Management (CIM) in Brussels.

William Leo

William Leo holds a Ph.D. in nuclear physics from Columbia University and is also a graduate of IMD's Executive Development Program. After a career in physics research, he turned to industry where he became involved in the development and promotion of optical memory cards. Joining CFG S.A. in 1996, a Swiss company specializing in microelectronics miniaturization for the industrial sector, Mr. Leo currently holds the post of Director of Marketing. In addition to handling the everyday marketing operations for CFG, he is responsible for managing the transfer of OLED technology from the EPFL to CFG.

Ian McLoughlin

Ian McLoughlin is Professor of Management and Head of the University of Newcastle upon Tyne Business School. His research interests are the management of transformational change in technology-based and technology-related projects and new organisational forms. He is currently Principal Investigator on a major EPSRC-funded programme examining organisational and information system architectures to deliver 'joined-up' public services in the UK. He is also a co-investigator on an Australian Research Council project exploring new patterns of normative control in a steel plant. He has held visiting positions in Europe and Australia and is currently a Professorial Research Fellow at the Centre for Change Management at the University of Wollongong. He has published widely in academic journals and books. His most recent publications include: 'Critical Perspectives on Technology, Organisations and Innovation' (edited with D Preece and P Dawson); the four volume Routledge 'Critical Perspectives on Business and Management' series (2000); and 'Creative Technological Change: The shaping of technology and organisation', Routledge, 1999.

Jean Micol
Jean Micol is co-director of the postgraduate program in Management of Technology (MoT), which is jointly organized by the Swiss Federal Institute of Technology (EPFL) and the Business School of the University of Lausanne. Born in 1949 in France, he graduated from the Swiss Federal Institute of Technology - Lausanne, (EPFL) and got a Master of Business Administration from Columbia University - New York in 1975.

He initially worked as industrial engineer at Brown Boveri AG in Baden. After his MBA, he joined Nestlé US operations as financial analyst and was later named division controller in Paris and subsequently evolved towards managerial positions in Sales and Marketing. In 1984, he was hired by Digital Equipment Corp. in Geneva as European Marketing Manager for Educational Services Business, generated substantial growth in revenues by pioneering new fields and later became in charge of the business development and drove the introduction of new technical support services on a world-wide basis. In 1994 he joined as scientific advisor the Center for Management of Technology at the Swiss Federal Institute of Technology – Lausanne (EPFL). His research interests include Management of R&D and Innovation as well as Entrepreneurship. He acts as an expert in Brussels for the Research and Technology Development program.

In parallel to his regular professional activities, he invented a new printing process and deposited a patent. He has also been directly involved with the creation of new start-up companies in Europe and the US. He is chairman of the board of a Swiss company.

Kamal Munir
Dr. Kamal Munir is Assistant Professor at the Judge Institute of Management, Cambridge University. He holds a Ph.D. degree from McGill University, Canada. Prior to joining the Judge, Dr. Munir worked as an engineer, management consultant and lecturer. He has published several papers on technology management and is currently studying instances of radical technological innovations in various industries. He is a member of the Academy of Management, Strategic Management Society, INFORMS and the International Association for Management of Technology.

Ville Ojanen

Ville Ojanen is working as a researcher at the Department of Industrial Engineering and Management, and Telecom Business Research Center at Lappeenranta University of Technology, located in Lappeenranta, Finland. He also teaches product and technology strategy, as well as R&D and innovation management at the university. He holds M.Sc. (Tech.) degree from Lappeenranta University of Technology. As a researcher, he has co-operated with several Finnish high-tech companies from different industries. His main research interests and the topic of his doctoral thesis are related to performance analysis and management of R&D. On this research area, he has several international publications.

Rob Phaal

Dr. Robert Phaal is a Senior Research Associate in the Engineering Department at the University of Cambridge. Robert joined the Centre for Technology Management in 1997, with research interests in the areas of the strategic management of technological knowledge, and associated decision support tools and processes. Recent activity has focused on the development of a method for rapid initiation of the technology roadmapping approach in organisations, linking technology resources to company objectives. Other interests include industrial sustainability and foresight, working with the UK Department of Trade and Industry to develop a technology roadmap for the Foresight Vehicle consortium. Robert has a background in general mechanical engineering, numerical modelling and software development, consulting and contract research.

Nelson Phillips

Nelson Phillips is Beckwith Professor of Strategy and Marketing at the Judge Institute of Management, University of Cambridge, UK. Prior to joining Cambridge, Nelson was an Associate Professor at the Faculty of Management, McGill University, Canada. Nelson is a member of the editorial boards of Journal of Management Inquiry; Strategy and Organization; and Tamara. He has published widely in journals such as Academy of Management Journal, Organization Science and Organization Studies. Nelson's research interests include interorganizational collaboration; management in cultural industries; discourse methods; institutional theory; innovation and technology management; and multinationals and international development.

Mette Praest Knudsen

Dr. Mette Praest Knudsen is Assistant Professor at Department of Marketing, University of Southern Denmark in Odense, which she joined in August 2001. She received her Ph.D. from the Aalborg University in Denmark, and M.Sc. in Economics from Odense University, Denmark. During her Masters work she has been working for the Fraunhofer Institute of Systems Research and Innovation, Karlsruhe, Germany. She is a member of the Danish Research Unit for Industrial Dynamics (DRUID) (www.druid.dk) and part of the LINK project (www.cbs.dk/link) headed by Professor Nicolai Foss. The LINK project is concerned with economic organization of learning, incentives, and knowledge. Her main areas of teaching cover strategic alliances, international market relations, e-business and international technology management.

Kaisu Puumalainen

Mrs. Kaisu Puumalainen is Professor of Marketing at the Lappeenranta University of Technology, Finland. She holds a Licenciate in Technology degree from the Lappeenranta University of Technology. Her previous publications are in the fields of Entrepreneurship, Export Market Orientation, Customer Need Assessment, Internationalisation, Knowledge Management, and Diffusion of Innovations. She has received two best paper awards in international conferences, and has published two articles in edited books. The journal publications are in International Journal of Research in Marketing, Australasian Marketing Journal, R&D Management and forthcoming articles in European Journal of Marketing and Journal of Business Research. Her current research interests are in the field of ICT industry marketing, especially the internationalisation and innovation diffusion issues.

Peter Roe

Dr. Peter Roe is a professor in the Systems Design Engineering department at the University of Waterloo, Ontario, Canada. He received his B.A.Sc. (Engineering Physics) from the University of Toronto, and his M.Sc. and his Ph.D. (Applied Mathematics and Electrical Engineering), from the University of Waterloo. He has been a visiting professor at a number of universities in Canada, U.S.A. and Europe, and is the author or co-author of about 100 technical publications, books, etc.

Karl Ruping

Karl Ruping, Esq. is a Fellow at the Advanced Studies Program of the Massachusetts Institute of Technology. He holds a Juris Doctorate degree from Boston University and is a leading intellectual property attorney specializing in computer science technologies. His academic career includes studies at Harvard University, London School of Economics, University of Vienna, and University of Tokyo. Mr. Ruping was an Adjunct Professor at Temple University and holds a visiting position at Hoseo University of South Korea while a member of the Board of Advisors to the Korean government's iPark venture business project.

Mr. Ruping is president and founder of incTANK, a technology incubator and early-stage VC fund. With its headquarters in Cambridge, MA, incTANK has established regional offices in Tokyo, Japan and Seoul, South Korea. Mr. Ruping manages a diverse management team and advises startups in developing Internet infrastructure, network security, and enterprise software technologies. More detailed background is at www.mit.edu/~ruping or www.inctank.com.

Sami Saarenketo

Mr. Sami Saarenketo is researcher and project manager at the Telecom Business Research Center, a multidisciplinary research institute of Lappeenranta university of Technology. He holds a M.Sc. (econ.) degree from the Lappeenranta University of Technology and is finalizing his Ph.D. at the same university. His current research interests are in the field of international marketing, especially the internationalization of Information and Communication Technology (ICT) companies. His dissertation will handle the internationalization strategies of SMEs in ICT industry. He was a member of the research team that received best paper award from IAMOT 2001, and has published two articles in edited books.

Anja Schulze

Anja Schulze holds a Masters degree of Business Administration from the University Erlangen-Nürnberg, Germany. Since 1999 she is a Doctoral Candidate at the Institute for Technology Management at the University of St. Gallen, Switzerland. In 2000, she was significantly involved in a European Benchmarking Project for "Knowledge Management" as a research associate. Hereafter, she conducted a workshop series regarding knowledge management in industrial innovation processes, where 10 well-known companies from Germany and Switzerland were involved. Comprising 20 European companies, she conducted a study to identify aspects of corporate culture that are essential preconditions for successful knowledge management, specifically for sharing and utilizing corporate knowledge successfully. The study was completed in spring 2002. She also developed the conceptual design for executive seminars, e.g. "Sm@rt Innovation: knowledge management as a key success factor in managing innovation processes". Moreover, she has been involved in several research and consulting projects, regarding knowledge management and innovation management.

Harm-Jan Steenhuis

Dr. Harm-Jan Steenhuis is Assistant Professor of Operations Management at Eastern Washington University, Spokane, USA. He holds Ph.D. and M.Sc. degrees in Industrial Engineering and Management from the University of Twente, Enschede, the Netherlands. His Ph.D. research focussed on the international transfer of aircraft production technology and included research in the Netherlands, USA, UK, Romania, India and Brazil. After completing his Ph.D. he worked as a post-doctoral researcher at North Carolina State University on technology transfer between university and industry. He joined Eastern Washington University in Summer 2002. He has presented numerous papers on international technology transfer as well as industry-university technology transfer at international conferences and has published papers in journals such as Technology Analysis & Strategic Management, Technology in Society and International Journal of Technology Transfer and Commercialization. His work has also appeared in books published by IAMOT.

Olli Suolanen
Olli Suolanen works as a Supply Chain Management Consultant at IBM Finland. He holds MSc Industrial Management degree from Helsinki University of Technology, Finland. Before joining IBM in fall 2001, he worked as a researcher at the TAI Research Centre. His research focused on the areas of supply chain management, ERP-systems and simulation. He has co-authored one book and several international conference papers of his research in these areas.

Bernard Surlemont
Dr Bernard Surlemont is Professor of entrepreneurship at the University of Lausanne (HEC) and Director of the Entrepreneurship Research Center of Liège University. He obtained his PhD in Management from INSEAD, where he also holds an MBA. His research focuses on entrepreneurship in high-tech businesses and university spin-offs. Dr Surlemont is a Board member of a number of start-ups and VCs, as well as a Board member of several liaison offices between universities and industries. He is an advisor to the European Commission and expert acting in the area of incubators for international institutions.

Alfred Thwaites
Alfred Thwaites graduated from the University of Durham with a Bachelors degree in Economics after a number of years of working in industry. He went on to complete a Masters Degree on the subject of Entrepreneurship in the Northern Region of England. From 1976 to 1978 he was the Sir Sadler Forster Fellow in Regional Development Studies at the University of Newcastle upon Tyne and went on to become a senior research associate, lecturer and senior lecturer in the Department of Geography, University of Newcastle upon Tyne. He was the Deputy Director of the Centre for Urban and Regional Development Studies (CURDS) from 1982 to 1994. He has conducted research for local authorities, departments of UK government, the EU and OECD as well as a number of Research Council funded projects.

Marko Torkkeli
Marko Torkkeli is currently Professor of Information and Communication Technology Business in the Department of Industrial Engineering and Management at Lappeenranta University of Technology. His research interests focus on strategic technology selection, group support systems and information systems in knowledge management. His studies have been published in the International Journal of Production Economics, and several conferences in the fields of technology management and information systems. He worked as a visiting researcher at the Wharton School of the University of Pennsylvania in 2001-2002.

Markku Tuominen

Markku Tuominen is professor and Dean of the Department of Industrial Engineering and Management at Lappeenranta University of Technology, Finland. Dr. Tuominen received the D.Sc. (Tech.) degree from the Helsinki University of Technology, Finland, in 1980. Since 2001 Dr. Tuominen has been a member of science and technology board at the Academy of Finland, an expert organisation in research funding and science policy. His current research interests include computer aided strategic analysis, technology management, and decision support in engineering management. He has published widely in international journals on these research areas.

Roger Vaughan

Dr Roger Vaughan is a senior researcher with the University of Newcastle upon Tyne Business School in the UK. Both his BSc in Naval Architecture and Shipbuilding and his PhD on computer based decision processes are from Newcastle. As a shipbuilding engineer he was a founder member of an international consultancy developing ship construction facilities in a number of countries. He joined British Shipbuilders as Director of Productivity with responsibility for the implementation of CAD/CAM technology and then became Chief Executive of Swan Hunter, the shipbuilding company, where he was responsible for a number of major civilian and defence projects. He became head of the School of Management at Newcastle University where he redesigned the MBA programmes, giving the part time programme an accent on the major project industries. He has joint-authored papers on major engineering projects, particularly those that are services led.

Cristina Rodrigues de Borba Vieira

M.Sc. Cristina Rodrigues de Borba Vieira is an adviser at Porto Alegre City Hall, Rio Grande do Sul, Brazil, and works as a researcher at the Nucleus of Management of Technology - NITEC. She holds M.Sc. degree from the Administration School at Federal University of Rio Grande do Sul and B.Sc. degree from Economic School at Federal University of Rio Grande do Sul. She works with technological innovation, technology transfer mechanisms, science and technology policy, lean production and supply chain.

IkuoYamada

Mr. Ikuo Yamada holds B.Eng. degree from Keio University, Tokyo, Japan. He joined Mitsubishi Electric Corporation, Tokyo, Japan in 1961. His career in the company is outlined as follows: 1989-1993, general manager of Engineering Management Headquarters (Tokyo, Japan); 1993-1994, dean of Corporate University (Hyogo, Japan); 1994-2000, managing director of Mitsubishi Research Institute, Inc. (MRI) (Tokyo, Japan). Now he holds the post of advisor to the Board of Directors of MRI and also executive director of the Engineering Academy of Japan. He has received the Prize of Progress from the Institute of Electrical Engineers of Japan (JIEE) for "Research on Security Monitoring System for Electric Power System" in 1975. He received the Best Chairman of the Year Award from the IEEE EMS in 1998. He was director of Information Processing Society of Japan in 1985-1986, vice chairman of the Institute of Electrical Engineers of Japan (JIEE) in 1992-1993, and vice chairman of the Operations Research Society of Japan in 1996-1997. He was chairman of the IEEE Japan Chapter of EMS in 1998-2000. He was a member of the Board of Directors of the Japan Society for Science Policy and Research Management (JSSPRM) and now councillor of JSSPRM.

Hiroyuki Yamasaki
Dr. Hiroyuki Yamasaki holds B.Eng., M.Eng., and Ph.D. degrees all from Shizuoka University, Hamamatsu, Japan. He is an admitted Chartered Engineer (C.Eng.) with the British Engineering Council. He joined Mitsubishi Electric Corporation, Tokyo, Japan in 1985. His career in the company is outlined as follows: 1985-1991, senior engineer of the LSI Laboratory (Hyogo, Japan), 1991-1995, assistant manager of Strategic R&D Planning Group of ULSI Laboratory (Hyogo, Japan); 1995, manager of R&D Planning Office, ULSI Laboratory. He presently holds the post of manager of the Strategic Planning Group, ULSI Development Center. From 2001, he is also an Advisor, Japan Productivity Center for Socio-Economic Development (Tokyo, Japan). He has received the Takayanagi Memorial Award for "Research on Novel Solid-state Imaging Devices with Inherent MNOS Memory" in 1986, and the Meritorious Person Award from Sanda City (Hyogo, Japan) in 1993. He lectured at the Graduate School of Engineering, Shizuoka University, in 1991, and was a visiting associate professor at the Center for Joint Research, Shizuoka University, in 1996. He is founding secretary of the IEEE Japan Chapter of EMS and correspondent of Japan of IAMOT. He was a member of the Board of Directors of the Japan Society for Science Policy and Research Management (JSSPRM) and now councillor of JSSPRM. He is cited in Who's Who in the World (16-19 Edition). His web site is www.DrYamasaki.com.

Paulo Antônio Zawislak
Paulo Antônio Zawislak is currently Associate Professor of Economics, Management and Technology in the School of Business Administration at the Federal University of Rio Grande do Sul (EA/UFRGS, Brazil). He began his education in Brazil and received his doctorate in Economics and Management at the Université de Paris VII in 1994. His principal research interests are in the fields of economics and innovation, and management of technology and operations. He is working on a research for the Brazilian government dealing with industrial cooperation and competitive strategy, where automotive industry, product development, lean manufacturing, and supply chain management are major related subjects.

Max von Zedtwitz (Editor, Contributor)
Dr. Maximilian von Zedtwitz is Professor of Technology Management at IMD-International, Lausanne, Switzerland. He holds Ph.D. and MBA/lic.oec. degrees from the University of St. Gallen, and M.Sc. and B.Sc. degrees from ETH Zurich. As an engineer and scientist, he worked in MIS development for Siemens in Florida, and in nucleon simulation research for ATR-International in Japan. More recently, he was a research associate at the Institute for Technology Management in Switzerland, and a Visiting Fellow at Harvard University in Cambridge, Massachusetts. He joined IMD in Summer 2000 to teach international innovation strategy, R&D management, and technology-based incubation in MBA and executive education programs. He has published two books and more than forty papers on international innovation management and R&D. He is the recipient of the 1998 RADMA prize for best paper with focus on practicality in the R&D Management Journal.

Libero Zuppiroli
Libero Zuppiroli graduated in Paris in 1969 as a telecommunications engineer and obtained his PhD in solid-state physics in 1976. He became an associate professor in physics at the Ecole Polytechnique in France in 1985, and has been a full professor at the Ecole Polytechnique Fédérale de Lausanne, Switzerland, since 1993. His main interest is in the field of electrical and optical properties of electroactive organic materials.

SECTION I

ENTREPRENEURSHIP AND VENTURE CREATION

Management of Technology
Copyright © 2003 by Elsevier Science Ltd.
All rights of reproduction in any form reserved.
ISBN: 0-08-044136-X

1

DYNAMIC CAPABILITIES FOR ENTREPRENEURIAL VENTURING - THE SIEMENS ICE CASE

Bernhard R. Katzy, CeTIM at University Bw Munich, Germany[†,]*
Marcel Dissel, CeTIM at University Bw Munich, Germany[**]
Franziska Blindow, University of St. Gallen, Switzerland[***]

INTRODUCTION

The telecommunication industry is faced with disruptive technology changes. New businesses are arising at such a pace that traditional organisations are hardly able to deal with them and risk taking is becoming more necessary to excel in this industry. To accommodate these changes requires a change from administrative management, stemming from the pre-deregulated business era, to entrepreneurial management techniques.

In this context, we are studying the dynamic capabilities of management and how these have evolved in an exploratory case study. The dynamic capability research has emerged from theoretical streams such as the resource-based-view of the firm. However to date little

---

[†] We wish to acknowledge the Enterprise Network Division of Siemens, for the access to the case material and in particularly Philippe Voirol for his initial insights through his academic work for the University of Fribourg.

[*] Dr. Bernhard Katzy is Professor of Technology and Innovation Management at the University Bw Munich, and director of the Centre for Technology and Innovation Management (CeTIM) at RSM Business School and University Bw Munich. Email: prof.katzy@cetim.org

[**] Marcel Dissel is a researcher at the University Bw Munich, a member of CeTIM, and a visiting scholar at Cambridge University, UK. Email: Marcel.Dissel@CeTIM.org.

[***] Dr. Franziska Blindow holds a PhD from St. Gallen University.

empirical research has been done and thus the observation of dynamic capabilities remains difficult.

The objective of this paper is to report a case study, on which we have grounded the conceptual establishment of the two dynamic capabilities: incubating and grafting new ventures. The process of entrepreneurial venturing shows two distinct phases. Firstly, the re-combination of technological and marketing knowledge in entrepreneurial initiatives, and secondly the continuous organisational innovation. These processes are supported by the distinctive capabilities, which we refer to as incubating and grafting. In the following sections these capabilities will be discussed with respect to the evidence provided by the case.

We are using a grounded approach (Eisenhardt, 1991), and report a longitudinal case study of the Enterprise Networks division (ICE) of Siemens Switzerland. The case follows an ongoing change project initiated at Siemens in order to address the problems outlined above. The department focuses on both data and voice solutions for enterprises.

To academia this research intends to contribute conceptual clarity (Dyer, 1991) on entrepreneurial dynamic capabilities. Although the concept has been developed by a longitudinal case study at one company, which implies that the degree of generalisation has yet to be discovered, it provides first concrete candidates of a dynamic capability concept for entrepreneurial venturing. The scope of this empirical research therefore contributes to the overall research agenda of dynamic capabilities in general, and specifically opens the discussion towards more concrete and applicable concepts of how dynamic capabilities work within specific environments.

Furthermore to management practice this research intends to contribute a concept that allows for a more systematic approach to enhance successful entrepreneurial venturing in highly competitive environments. The successfulness of the concept derived from our case is indicated by a number of changes supported by its members that resulted in a lean organization. These changes enabled the existing sales/marketing organizations and the innovation process to interface. The concept explains a process based on two venture phases that determines the absorption degree of new innovations in the exiting sales organization. The dynamic capabilities for entrepreneurial venturing allow for careful management of the new business development process. This concept helps managers and decision-makers to plan and organize their processes as to optimally benefit from new innovations.

The remainder of the paper is structured as follows: firstly, we will present a theoretical foundation of dynamic capabilities on entrepreneurial venturing. Secondly, we will briefly discuss the research methodology. Thirdly, followed by the presentation of the case study data we extract two distinct dynamic capabilities for the entrepreneurial venturing process. We close the paper with directions for further research.

THEORETICAL FOUNDATION AND RESEARCH METHODOLOGY

Entrepreneurial Venturing

This paper focuses on the process of entrepreneurial venturing in the telecommunication industry. For this paper we make a distinction between traditional administrative management practices and entrepreneurial venturing. The latter is based on risk taking, development of new opportunities and an orientation towards growth. *"Entrepreneurs realise opportunities by combining resources in new ways to create value and secure returns through new activity"* (Garnsey, 1998). We define entrepreneurial venturing as the process of incorporating entrepreneurship and new business models into an existing organisation. A key challenge in this process is to overcome the interface barrier between new product/solution development processes and the sales/marketing and logistics processes, otherwise known as the firm's productive base.

Entrepreneurial Venturing relates to a firm's ability to ensure that technology is adopted by the market (Rogers, 1962). Especially for high technology industries this adoption process is the most unsettled phase of the venturing process (Moore, 1998). High tech firms need to be able to introduce new innovation to the main market (early and late majority markets) in a rapid and routine manner (Moore, 1998), in order to create a profit stream out of the innovations and thus create a competitive advantage.

The entrepreneurial venturing process can be seen at a start-up level in small independent business units. However, the management competencies to integrate this process in a larger setting (large-scale commercialisation) can be found in larger organisations. Such organisations already have the capacity to carry out large-scale sales activities, which makes it possible to realise an opportunity. The existence of such activities is also referred to as the *productive base* of the company (Penrose, 1959). A firm requires a productive base to carry out a productive activity (Penrose, 1959). We have focused on ventures that reside in such larger organisations. Dynamic capabilities (Teece, 1995) are required by these organisations to systematically support the process of entrepreneurial venturing and realise opportunities.

Dynamic Capabilities

Technology-based industries encounter new technologies that can be disruptive in one or more aspects to their knowledge base. They often face these changes with limited ability to react due to financial or managerial commitments. In these situations firms should have capabilities to innovate (Nelson and Winter, 1982; Nelson 1991; Zollo and Winter, 1999; Teece *et al.* 1997). Simply having processes to produce a certain product or service will not be enough to sustain a competitive advantage. These capabilities require appropriate organisational and managerial routines to enable them to innovate and take economic advantage. These dynamic capabilities, from a Schumpeterian perspective, must enable the firm to innovate and make that innovation profitable over and over again (Nelson, 1991).

The emerging literature on dynamic capabilities draws on the resource-based view of the firm (e.g. Hayes *et al.*, 1988; Itami, 1987; Iansiti, 1994; Teece, 1994; Kogut and Zander, 1992; Nelson and Winter, 1982; Teece *et al.*, 1997) that states that the firm's resources are an essential structure for innovation.

The concept of dynamic capabilities is based on "*antecedent organisational and strategic routines by which managers alter their resource base*" (acquire and shed resources, integrate, and recombine them) (Eisenhardt and Martin, 2000) to generate new value-creating strategies (Grant, 1996; Pisano, 1994). In line with Teece, Pisano and Shuen, (1997) we define dynamic capabilities as:

"*Dynamic capabilities are what enable a firm to integrate, build, and reconfigure internal and external competencies to address rapidly changing environments (Teece et al., 1997). Dynamic capabilities are the firm's processes that use resources to match and even create market change. Dynamic capabilities thus are the organisational and strategic routines by which firms achieve new resource configurations as markets emerge, collide, split, evolve, and die*" (Teece *et al.*, 1997).[1]

Teece and Pisano (1994) identified three classes of factors that determine how a firm's dynamic capabilities evolve:

- Processes: managerial, technological and organisational routines
- Positions: current endowments of technology, customer bases, and suppliers
- Paths: available strategic alternatives.

Competitive advantages and competitive disadvantages (Moss Kanter, 1994) of firms rest on distinctive managerial and organisational processes (ways of co-ordinating and combining). These are shaped by the firm's specific asset positions (internal and market) and moulded by the evolutionary and co-evolutionary path(s) it has adopted or inherited (Teece *et al*, 1997). Managerial and organisational routines are referred to as a firm's routines or patterns of current practice and learning. Positions are being defined as current specific endowments of technology, intellectual property, complementary assets, customer base, and the external relations with suppliers and complementary partners. Paths relate to a firm's strategic options and the presence or absence of increasing returns therein. "Where a firm can go is a function of its current position and the paths ahead. Its current position is often shaped by the path it has travelled."(Teece *et al.* 1997). The firm's processes and positions collectively encompass its

---

[1]   "The term "dynamic" in this context is not used in the sense of multi-period analyses but refers to situations where there is rapid change in technology and market forces, and "feedback" effects on firms" (Teece *et al.*, 1997).

competencies and capabilities. The competitive advantage of the firm is seen to be sustainable at the firm level through repeatedly creating short-term business.

Drawing on this theoretical foundation the following section briefly describes the methodology for the longitudinal case study at Siemens ICE.

Methodology

We have used a grounded approach for the case study research (Eisenhardt, 1991; Glaser, 1967). Given the early stages of theory development on dynamic capabilities, we followed the logic of grounded theory by building our research on an exploratory case study. This method has already been successfully used in the emergent field of continuous innovation (e.g. Burgelman, 1991; Leonard-Barton, 1995; Brown, 1997), and it is consistent with the problems of theory development in the field of organisational capabilities (Verona, 1999). It can be hard to develop normative prescriptions on capabilities from cross-sectional studies (Henderson, 1990). Organisational capabilities are the result of complex processes comprising of the accumulation of small decisions and actions undertaken over many years in a situation of great uncertainty that can hardly be identified by quantitative research. In this sense, qualitative research is better suited to explore their nature.

Our longitudinal case study ran from 1999 to 2002 and encompasses in-depth semi-structured interviews with CEO, middle managers as well as all employees participating in the innovation diffusion process. Amongst these were the Director of the research centre, the Vice President responsible for Business Development and several managers directly involved in the projects leading to the development of VoIP and Security Systems. Also archival data based on financial statements, internal documents, industry publications and other written material were included. The interviews began with a brief description of the respondents' background and their organisational role. We then concentrated on the process of new business development, to detect the different dynamic capabilities used to stimulate and manage new business development. Interviewees were asked to describe the process and their role in it. Subsequently they were asked to explain possibilities for the improvement in new business development. We tried to leave the questions as open as possible, thus letting the results emerge from our respondents. We also never directly asked about «dynamic capabilities» or analogous concepts.

The analysis began with the identification of relevant capabilities as explicitly mentioned or indirectly implied by our informants. After having identified relevant capabilities, we tracked actions, decision and structural features that were considered to be at their basis. Five interviewers, including the three authors, conducted the analysis independently and integrated the findings with the results of the archival collection. Our aim was to build on and move beyond our informants' interpretations, in an attempt to interpret facts and narratives within an emerging theoretical framework.

THE CASE OF ICE AT SIEMENS SWITZERLAND

Background

Siemens is an electrical engineering and electronics multinational company employing over 440,000 employees in over 190 countries. Siemens qualifies as an innovative firm as 80 percent of their offerings are developed over the past five years. Furthermore the investments made in R&D exceed €5 billion and approximately 49,000 employees are engaged in research and development. The revenues stem from 6 business segments: energy, industry, healthcare, transportation, lightning and information & communications.

In our case study we will focus on the business segment of information & communications (I&C) in the Enterprise Network Division (ICE) in Switzerland. Traditionally the national subsidiaries of Siemens are sales outlets of Siemens Group. However, the I&C division in Switzerland is different in that it also strongly engages in R&D activities (R&D budget of 51 million Euro, of which 18 million Euro is allocated to the ICE division), especially in the voice over IP section.

Siemens Switzerland head office is located in Zürich and employs 3900 people. The annual turnover of Siemens Switzerland was €1.1 billion in 1999, with the Enterprise Networks department accounting for an annual turnover of €160 million. The turnover has risen 69% in the accounting period from Sept. 1998 to Sept. 1999. During this time, the Enterprise networks department employed approximately 500 people.

ICE operates in the Telecommunication Enterprise Network market. The customers are enterprises for which tailor made information and communication solutions are provided in 5 major areas: Voice networks, Data Networks, Application (Hardware and Software) Services, and recently Converged Networks (Voice over Data Networks).

The telecommunications services market is increasingly outperforming the telecommunications equipment market in volume. This development is driven by the trend in demand for comprehensive, customised solutions and new hardware / software functionality. The mixture of traditional and IP-based networks and the stronger penetration of applications increases complexity, which is visible in converged products where Voice is digitally routed over Data networks such as Internet Protocol (VoIP) and ATM.

The requirements for change (July 1999 – January 2000)

Within the ICE division competencies in the information business and in the communication business proved very competitive for the development of innovative VoIP systems. However inefficiencies emerged on the interface between the new product/solution development department and the sales and marketing organisation. The division's management board perceived the interfaces between the small entrepreneurial ventures (new businesses) and the large sales organisation as unsatisfactory (i.e. long lead times, inefficiencies, dissatisfaction of employees), which instigated the change efforts described in this case.

Using the product life cycle (Abernathy and Utterback, 1978) Siemens found a profound change in the pattern of innovation. Based on the 1995 figures, this curve shows a life cycle of 3 years, with investments of approx. 10 million Euro per product. This curve shows a positive cash flow during the maturation phase of the life cycle, and thus the existence of so-called cash-cow products is evident.

This representation of the business was valid until 1995. In the telecommunication industry a range of factors has been reported to cause drastic changes in the life cycle of the products.

Compared with the traditional curve, the market-life cycle has shortened to 9 months, and the required pre-investments have more than doubled. An example of the new life cycle is depicted below and shows a study of a Wireless device made by Siemens.

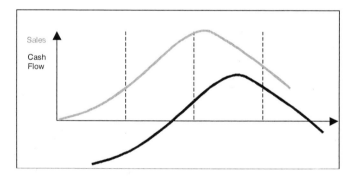

Fig. 1.1. The traditional life cycle.

Two initial conclusions can be drawn from this study. Firstly, the cash cows in the product portfolio disappear. Secondly, architectural innovation (Henderson and Clark, 1990) becomes a requirement, because the pre-investments and technologies have to be rapidly integrated.

This is particularly true for VoIP where voice technology and LAN technology come together for one product. IP Telephony and Voice over IP (VoIP) are key themes in the telecommunication industry. IP is an acronym for "Internet Protocol" - a network level data transfer protocol which is often used for networking PCs and accessing the Internet.

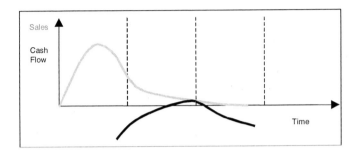

Fig. 1.2. The present life cycle on the telecommunications market (Source: Siemens 1999).

The benefits offered by IP telephony are to cut the cost and investments of communication between various business sites. The innovation came in the form of IP telephony gateways which no longer link individual terminals such as PCs via the Internet, but connect entire communication systems located at different sites. This ensures that the infrastructure familiar to the user (telephone, features, and dialling behaviour) remains intact. At the same time new possibilities can be offered, e.g. the call can be routed (transparently for the user) by the telecommunication system via an IP telephony gateway and the Internet by means of the Least Cost Routing functionality.

VoIP innovations are typical architectural innovations where the components do not change however the architecture between these components does (Henderson and Clark, 1990). Voice components such as the PBX (communication servers) and Data networks are integrated.

At the ICE division level it was evident that the incubation of such solution oriented competence centres were well supported. In the VoIP competence centre, the manager of the department was also an entrepreneur (previously owner of a company) and therefore created a small venture within the company. This venture brought together the backgrounds of both data and voice engineers, and focussed on solutions with own projects.

The processes of the independent centres were not adapted to the existing two sales organisation: Voice Networks (telephone); and Data Networks (computers, Local Area Networks).

It was found that the malfunctioning of the integration of the data and the voice side of the company was a result of two existing cultures. Siemens is a traditional telecom producer and has telephony competencies. In 1996 the need for data communication led to the decision to buy a data company (employing approx. 90 people). A separate data division, Siemens Nixdorf, initially bought the company. In 1998 this division (approx. 120 people) integrated with the ICE division. However, the different technology orientations implied a degree of culture conflict. The voice side, which used to work with over 95% of Siemens-made products, now had to collaborate with a data organisation, which used to work with more than 95% of products and components from external suppliers. In general, we have observed that the culture from the data side is flexible in nature due to co-operation with relatively young and flexible organisations, which are generally considered as having a more flexible and autonomous stance towards the innovation process.

Impact on operational and innovation processes

The ICE division ran two separate order management processes, which required over 23 transaction systems. The incompatibility of the two IT worlds (legacy systems) led to the need for increasing co-ordination efforts to be put in place when customers ordered data, voice and converged equipment and solutions.

The incompatibility stems from the division's history, in that it (the voice side) used to deal with fairly stabile customers, like the national phone operator. However due to the liberalisation, deregulation and privatisation trends the market has become more competitive. More customers came on the scene, and thus competitors. Previously the organisation received clear-cut orders (from the voice side of the business) from well-known customers with relative well-known products. However the environment changed to the provision of more complex innovations to a diversified market.

On a divisional level we found increasingly complex innovation problems due to a decentralised organisation. The technological knowledge of the new (converged) products could not be diffused in the regionally organised department. Switzerland has 3 dominant regions with their own language and culture (French, German and Italian). The regionalisation was considered to be appropriate from a customer relation perspective (one regional face to the customer). However from a technological perspective the knowledge of these complex businesses was not available in all parts of the country. In an interview, a presales consultant confirmed this

> *"... sometimes I have to spend up to 2 days to find the best supplier for a particular cable, even though I am almost certain that the same problem has already been solved somewhere else in the organization".*

Customers also perceived this lack of knowledge transfer in the sales process. A customer who ordered Swiss-wide PBX's and telephone-sets, came to the conclusion that the installation differed in Lugano (Italian region) from the one in Basel (German region). Due to the enhanced and more complex features of the products, his employees, who travelled frequently between the two sites, had to learn how to operate the same equipment twice, because the installation was not standardised.

The lack of knowledge transfer was not limited to the different regions within the same function (presales, technician), but equally occurred cross-functionally. Interviewees demonstrated that diverging sales strategies limited Siemens in optimising the sales of new products. For instance customers expressed their concern on several occasions where they were aware of new Siemens products before the sales-force were.

The lack of knowledge transfer was further limited by the organisational competencies and the motives of the sales-force to concentrate on old and familiar products instead of innovative solutions. A quote from a salesman:

> *"Why would I spend a day on trying to sell one VoIP system, whilst I can sell 3 PBX systems in the same time".*

Traditionally the sales-force specialised in selling products "sales of boxes" as a result of the traditional supplies to the national phone operator. But as a customer put it:

> *"I do not care what kind of PBX is in my cellar, I just want to make a phone-call"*

The above mentioned process implications were further embedded in the remuneration mechanisms. The remuneration scheme was sales oriented and depended on the individual sales volumes. Established products generate better sales than new products. Although new businesses have been explored using pilot projects and specialists and the use of so-called competence centres, there were no clear rewards for sales to invest in building the sales competence on new products. The product and solutions managers, who where responsible for the introduction of these new products, were organised as a support function (overhead). As a result the information flow of new product information was seen as unsatisfactory by the sales organisation.

Such interface problems between the product department and the sales department culminated when nation-wide big projects were to be realised. These projects required the co-operation of numerous employees from different departments and regions. This resulted in insufficient accessibility by phone, lingual barriers and lack of readiness to co-operate.

Rapid Product Switching in the Development and Sales Departments

In the course of this analysis it became clear that the ICE division needed new organisational competencies. During an interview session the following drawing was produced to show the competence had to quickly move from one innovation to the next, and thus has to switch from life cycle to life cycle as a routine. It shows that the organisation has to be able to quickly switch from innovation to innovation, rather than to rely on "cash cows". A separate business

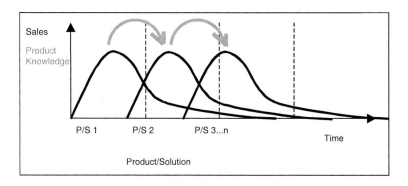

Fig. 1.3. Switching Business Opportunities.

strategy was required for the division, in addition to the corporate strategy, in order to deal with the flow of new business opportunities and sustain competitiveness.

The ICE 2000 project (Jan. 00 – June 00). The division's board decided to engage in an ongoing process change management initiative. ICE had previously undertaken three Business Process Re-engineering projects, which were all unsatisfactory. The last project resulted in a description of the processes within the ICE division, however the organisation was not able to implement recommendations for improvement of the processes. This led to the start of a new project (so-called ICE2000) in January 2000. This project aimed to check the current processes against the results of the last project (which ended in June 1999) and furthermore improve the processes.

The ICE 2000 project resulted in a new process concept. Figure 1.4 further below is a graphical representation of the new process concept.

Phase one represents the customer contact. The input for this phase focuses on informing and establishing potential customers. As a result of the increasing competitive markets, the former sales activities have been redefined. The former sales representatives mainly focused on maintaining the existing customer base. As the national operator, the biggest customer of the department faced more competitors, which affected the need for more active sales actions to be taken by the division. This led to the creation of a new process coined "Hotmaking" (making potential customers interested). The output is defined as a sales lead, which is the input for the phase two, Customer Relations Management.

Customer Relations Management is the second result from the redefinition of the old sales-force. Customer Relations Management receives the sales lead from Hotmakers, the call desk, or requests for proposals from existing customers. The task is to turn these sales-leads

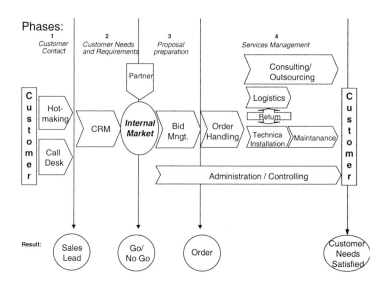

Fig. 1.4. New Process Concept ICE.

into clear business opportunities. This phase is characterised by a high customer focus, in which the customer requirements and needs are defined. The output is a clear business opportunity that will be presented to the internal market.

The previously described process implications and incompatibilities led to the common understanding of having an internal market structure within the order mechanism. Internal market is a metaphor for switching. The rules of the game were seen as a means to generate the dynamic capability of getting new products into the sales organisation.

Phases 3 and 4 are the actual bid management and the service management processes (including the distribution, installation, maintenance, and consulting). These processes are predominantly technology oriented. The internal market represents the negotiation between the sales pull and technology push activities.

Organizational Changes

In order to increase exploitation of the opportunities arising from new innovations, the organisation has been restructured to support an entrepreneurial spirit. With respect to the interface inefficiencies identified during the project between the product/solution development departments and the operational side of the business (e.g. marketing, sales, presales and installation and services) the division aimed to create better co-ordination between these two functions by allowing internal business ventures. The focus for this analysis is based upon the process for large innovative projects.

Firstly the division created the so-called Business House, in which new ventures are incubated as so-called venture groups. The Business House is a combination of the previous product management and solution management departments. Engineering specialists together with business experts develop new product/solution combinations in dedicated business venture groups. The venture leaders are responsible to produce a business plan in order to shift the focus from mere product development to business development. In addition to development activities the venture groups have the objective to start pilot projects with selected customers to test the commercialisation of the innovations. The Business House supports these venture groups. They serve as an incubator, providing the necessary funding and facilities to start-up business ventures.

Secondly the sales side of the operations is structured in customer areas instead of regional areas. The sales/customer relations management departments now cover specific customer groups such as Banking and Insurance companies, Hospitals, etc. Where previously this department's role was to produce a concrete sale, now the main output is a concrete customer requirement.

In addition the pre-sales teams, who bring in the specific innovation-related expertise, function as specialists on specific areas of expertise rather than on a region and will be led by a pool of project managers. When the customer relation managers have identified concrete requirements for a customer they co-ordinate the project jointly with the project management pool. The project management pool evaluates the opportunities and accordingly composes a virtual team of presales people (specialists) in order to compile a bid. When this results in a sale the project manager will co-ordinate the installation and the maintenance accordingly.

New capabilities

The division has introduced a new co-ordination mechanism in order to allow for more rational go/no-go decisions. This mechanism is based on network co-ordination, where the project manager is able to compose virtual teams by negotiating with the several specialist areas. The virtual team becomes a project oriented team build up out of pools (ventures) of specialist. Co-ordination is based on the internal market in which negotiations can take place within certain rules.

The interface between the Business House and the Operations department can be explained using a revolver metaphor. The Business House builds the bullets – the venture groups, which are successively inserted into the revolver – the operations department. The mechanism of a revolver exists of one barrel for several chambers of bullets. This is true for the operations department, which should portray a single source of competence in marketing and selling towards the customer. The co-ordination mechanism allocates each sales opportunity to the correct group of specialist (ventures).

When a start-up is successfully nurtured in the business house it will be integrated into the operational department. A team of specialists will then transfer their knowledge in their respective field of expertise (e.g. VoIP) to the operational department. The sales/customer relations department is then able to feed this internal venture with business opportunities, by exposing the tested solution to the extensive sales network. The mechanism of systematically placing new ventures into the operational department can therefore be identified as a new dynamic routine.

In summary, two distinct phases for the ventures can be identified when looking at the Siemens Division. Firstly, the incubation phase, where the new venture is nurtured to make a business out of an innovation. Secondly the venture is grafted into the existing operational processes, by systemically reconfiguring the organisation continuously. These two capabilities will be addressed in the subsequent chapter.

BUILDING OF DYNAMIC CAPABILITIES AT ICE

Dynamic Capabilities for the Entrepreneurial Venturing Process

In the case study, we have observed the entrepreneurial venturing process on a business venture level (so-called venture groups). New entrepreneurial ventures, in our case within an organisation, go through several phases. We have focused on the interface where the new venture is developed but has to be adapted into the productive base (sales/operations organisation).

The division is organised in two main groups: the business house and the sales/operations department. The business house is responsible for the product/solution development. The sales/operations department is responsible for the sales and customer relation management and the co-ordination of the technical installation, logistics and maintenance.

In the business house new ventures are created, which act like entrepreneurial "start-ups." This means that each venture is supported in business related issues, such as developing business models and innovation specific sales processes, in addition to the pure development of the new product or solution. The venture groups can test their business models using pilot projects. This phase of the venture is referred to as the incubation phase, where the business provides the necessary competencies, budget and support for these "start-ups."

When innovations are ready to be exposed to the sales network of the division, the ventures can be integrated into the productive base. This change is an organisational one, for the venture is no longer strictly dependent and supported by the business house, but interfaces with a different department. This is the second phase in the entrepreneurial venturing process, which we have termed grafting. Grafting means the successful installation of a venture into the sales/operations department. These two phases of the entrepreneurial venturing process, and the interface between these phases, require dynamic capabilities. Parallel to the two venture phases, we have observed two dynamic capabilities that are developed in the organisation to support the entrepreneurial venturing process.

Building of Dynamic Capabilities at ICE

We draw on the dynamic capability framework (Teece et. al., 1997) to trace the development of these two dynamic capabilities in the Siemens division. The framework suggests that paths shape the specific asset position of the firm, which in turn shape the processes. Subsequently these processes build the dynamic capabilities.

The Siemens ICE case confirms this theory for dynamic capabilities for entrepreneurial venturing, and by identifying the paths, positions and processes at Siemens ICE, we are able to extract how the above-mentioned capabilities are being built.

Paths. We have identified 2 major paths that ultimately shaped the capabilities build at the division.

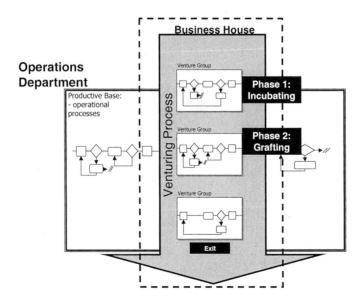

Fig. 1.5. Incubating and Grafting Capabilities.

- Firstly we identified the technological trend where the telecommunications industry integrated the data networks (local area networks). This trend extends to the current trend of the convergence of voice and data solutions.

- Secondly, the changing patterns of the product life cycle derived from the changes in the telecommunication market, the increasing R&D pre-investments required, and the decreasing life span can be identified. The new curve shows the need for a constant capability to switch and diffuse new architectural knowledge on the products and solutions throughout the venturing process.

Positions. In accordance with Teece, Pisano and Shuen (1997) our case shows how these changes contributed to the current specific asset position at ICE. Firstly, the technological position, as determined by the previous path of the architectural innovation, is interpreted as a lack of architectural knowledge diffusion of innovations, between the voice and data sides of the division. Although the technical inventions appeared to be successful, the diffusion of this knowledge did not reach the sales organisation.

Instead of benefiting from the complementary assets brought by the extensive sales network and the business house (e.g. award winning inventions), the two did not meet. They were opposing each other and the lack of co-ordination had a negative influence on the processes.

Processes. The lack of diffusion of the architectural knowledge of the VoIP innovations throughout the organisation resulted in inefficient process co-ordination. In our study we have found a range of examples that illustrated these inefficiencies. This was particularly visible at the interface between the „old" sales organisations (both voice and data side with independent order mechanisms), and the new product/solution developments and successful technology oriented competence centres.

The process change management project "ICE 2000" involved 25% of all employees working at the division. This allowed both sides to acknowledge these inefficiencies. The learning effect created a shared mental model throughout the division, resulting in a new process concept including a new co-ordination mechanism between the operational side and the R&D side of the division. In addition the organisation became aware of the necessity not only to re-engineer the processes to their current asset position, but also to systematically update its routines and the organisation as they move forward.

Incubation as a dynamic capability

The subsequent results of this (ongoing) learning process within the division led to the transformation of the organisational routines at the interface in question. The re-organisation

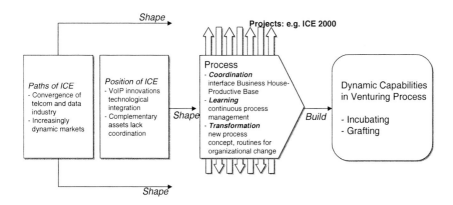

Fig. 1.6. Building of Dynamic Capabilities at ICE.

introduced a business perspective in the former product and solution houses (now termed Business House). This is where the inventions are put to the market to pilot test the business potential.

Grafting as a dynamic capability

Although previously, incubations on an ad-hoc basis proved successful, the systematic instalment of these business ventures into the productive base (sales organisation) had not been dealt with yet. The traditional processes of the sales organisation were difficult to influence and impossible to rationalise in terms of terminating or accepting a particular order throughout the critical phases of a (large) project.

The transformation of this particular process by implementing a so-called "internal market", allowed the sales pull and the technology push sides to negotiate. Subsequently the business ventures, arriving in this process after incubation, are able to function as bullets in a revolver, switching from venture to venture and consequently being exploited by the sales "gun." We have coined this integration process grafting, the "young tree" - incubated in the business house, can now be planted in the productive base.

CONCLUSIONS AND FURTHER RESEARCH

Contributions. Looking at Siemens from a dynamic capability perspective, the significance of the entrepreneurial venturing process stands out. The entrepreneurial venturing process at

Siemens created an interface between new product development and sales/operations and was divided into two phases, incubating and grafting. For both phases we identified two corresponding dynamic capabilities. Incubating and grafting play a fundamental role as a dynamic capability that allow rapid changing innovations to be exploited by the existing sales network.

Implications. The case study of Siemens is one telecommunications equipment manufacturer among many that faces transformation of its voice and data businesses. There are obvious limitations to what can be inferred from the analysis of a single case. Through in-depth case research the study tried to detect some dynamic capabilities in entrepreneurial venturing. Although methodologically consistent with the status of the theory and the prescriptions to select a sample, this paper represents a local theory of one case, which delivers two candidates of dynamic capabilities. These however do not claim to be generalised results.

Future Research. The evidence discussed in this exploratory case study provides a useful starting point for future research. Similar future studies should test the degree of generalisation and the concept developed in our case. Secondly, the interface studied in our case has a limited scope of analysis. Additional dynamic capabilities for the process of entrepreneurial venturing can be explored such as the phase out of old products and services. Following this direction, future research will strengthen the findings on entrepreneurial venturing, providing a framework for firms competing in turbulent environments.

BIBLIOGRAPHY

Abernathy, W. J. and J. M. Utterback (1978). Patterns of Industrial Restructuring. *Technology Review*, **80** (7), 1-9.

Brown, S. L. and K. M. Eisenhardt (1997). The art of continuous change: Linking complexity theory and time-paced evolution in relentlessly shifting organizations. *ASQ*, **42**(1), 1-34.

Burgelman, R. A. (1991). Intraorganizational ecology of strategy making and organizational adaptation: Theory and field research. *Organization Science*, **2**, 239-262.

Dyer, W. G., Jr., A. L. Wilkins and K. M. Eisenhardt (1991). Better Stories, Not Better Constructs, to Generate Better Theory: A Rejoinder to Eisenhardt. AMR, **16** (3), 613-619.

Eisenhardt, K. M. (1991). Better Stories and Better Constructs: The Case for Rigor and Comparative Logic. *AMR*, **16** (3), 620-627.

Eisenhardt, K. M. and J. A. Martin (2000). Dynamic Capabilities: What are they? SMJ, **21**, 1105-1121.

Garney, E. (1998). A Theory of the Early Growth of the Firm. Ind. and Corp. Change **3**, 523-560

Glaser, B. G. and A. L. Strauss (1967). The Discovery of Grounded Theory: Strategies for Qualitative Research. Weidenfeld and Nicholson, London.

Hayes, R. H., S. C. Wheelwright and K.B. Clark (1988). Dynamic Manufacturing - Creating the Learning Organization. The Free Press, New York.

Henderson, R. M. C. and K. B. Clark (1990). Architectural Innovation: The Reconfiguration of Existing Product Technologies and the Failure of Established Firms. *ASQ*, **35**, 9-31.

Iansiti, M. C. and B. Kim (1994). Integration and Dynamic Capability: Evidence from Product Development in Automobiles and Mainframe Computers. *Ind. and Corp. Change*, **3** (3), 557-605.

Itami, H. and T.W. Roehl (1987). Mobilizing Invisble Assets. Harvard University Press, Cambridge.

Kogut, B. and U. Zander (1992). Knowledge of the Firm, Combinative Capabilities, and the Replication of Technology. *Org. Studies*, **3**, 383-397.

Leonard-Barton, D. (1995). Wellsprings of Knowledge: Building and Sustaining the Sources of Innovation. Harvard Press, Boston (MA).

Moore, G. A. (1998). Crossing the Chasm. Capstone, Oxford.

Moss Kanter, R. (1994). Collaborative Advantage: The Art of Alliances. *HBR*, **72** (3), 33-43.

Nelson, R. R. and S. G. Winter (1982). An Evolutionary Theory of Economic Change. The Belknap Press of Harvard University Press, Cambridge (MA).

Nelson, R.R. (1991). Why do firms differ, and how does it matter? SMJ, **12**, 61-74.

Penrose, E. T. (1959). The Theory of the Growth of the Firm. Basil Blackwell, Oxford.

Pisano, G. (1994). Knowledge, integration, and the locus of learning: An empirical analysis of process development. *SMJ*, **15**, 85-100.

Rogers, E. M. (1962). The Diffusion of Innovation. The Free Press, New York

Teece, D. J. and G. Pisano (1994). The dynamic capabilities of firms: An introduction, *Ind. and Corp. Change*, **3** (3), 537-556.

Teece, D. J., G. P. Pisano and A. Shuen (1997). Dynamic Capabilities and Strategic Management. *SMJ*, **18** (7), 509-533.

Verona, G. (1999). A resource-based view of product development. AMR, **24** (1), 132-142.

Zollo, M. and S. G. Winter (1999). From organizational routines to dynamic capabilities. INSEAD Working paper series, 99/48/SM.

Management of Technology
Copyright © 2003 by Elsevier Science Ltd.
ISBN: 0-08-044136-X

2

AN IDEAL CORPORATE RESEARCH INSTITUTE STRUCTURE FOR THE 21ST CENTURY

Ikuo Yamada, Tokyo, Japan[*]
Hiroyuki Yamasaki, Hyogo, Japan[**]
Jun'ichi Baba, Tokyo, Japan[***]

INTRODUCTION

The environment surrounding Japanese companies has changed immensely in recent years as the result of various factors. Some commonly known matters include the extended downturn in the country's domestic economy in 1990s, the trend of attaching more importance to individualism with the advance of knowledge-based society, the advancement of IT, and expansion of the relative importance given to financial economics. The former two are domestic factors, while the latter two are global factors. It is our belief that the four following points are vital themes and measures that Japanese corporate research institutes must adopt for the 21st century, thus enabling them to adapt themselves to such environmental change.

1. Not only increase the competitiveness of the company through the development of products, but to develop business models which will provide additional benefits to the operations structure as well.
2. Analyze and understand the IT resources required for developing new business models.

---

[*] Mr. Ikuo Yamada is Advisor to the Board, Mitsubishi Research Institute, Inc. in Tokyo, Japan. Email: i-yamada@mri.co.jp.

[**] Dr. Hiroyuki Yamasaki is Manager, Strategic Planning Group, Mitsubishi Electric Corporation in Hyogo, Japan. Email: h.yamasaki@ieee.org.

[***] Dr. Jun'ichi Baba is Consultant to Mitsubishi Electric Corporation in Tokyo, Japan. Email: baba@tim-japan.org.

3. Establish fundamental IT resources and conduct educated analyses of such resources and the company's competitive environment.
4. Analyze the problems related to knowledge development and associated risk involved in the promotion of IT resource advancement.

It is of special importance that companies transform management from "product and process oriented development," "closed division-based development" and "old-fashioned estimation procedures" to "serious consideration of new business models," "open, joint development with external organizations" and "ability to change continuously with the times." Furthermore, it is also important to review the newly evolving "experience economy."

Generally, the attainment of success in the field of research and development (R&D) requires many certainties. Most of the value of a company's laboratories is dependent upon continuous successes; essentially, ensuring that the value of one's assets today continues to remain the same in the future). The general manager of a research institute must endeavor to ensure the perpetual success of expectations, which depends upon the mutual trust built between research engineers and a company's stakeholders (e.g., executives, customers, stockholders, and regional communities). Regarding financial market growth, the research institute must consider the expense for the aforementioned continual change, create the means of cash flow and bear the costs of R&D.

The fundamental fountainhead of knowledge is the individual, and the attainment of intellectual knowledge merchandise is achieved through teamwork. For this, proper personnel evaluations and mobility of personnel are necessary.

THE IMPORTANCE OF BUSINESS MODELS

"To date, Japanese industry has adhered to technological innovation and maintained a tendency to neglect the revolutionary movement to novel business models." (Itoh, 2000)

The fault of Japanese companies

We believe that the success of Japanese companies was firmly based on creating organizational structures that manufactured high-quality products at low cost through improvements in manufacturing processes and perpetual technological innovation in the past. Such technological strengths made Japanese enterprises more capable than their European and American rivals in the areas of production technology and product improvement in many fields. However, a matter of fact is that, in terms of profitability, Japanese companies lag far behind their European and American counterparts; and compared to them, estimated actual values of Japanese companies are very small.

The main reason for this is that Japanese companies have long neglected business model innovation. In the 1980s, Japanese companies gained profits applying the old-fashioned business model doctrine of "market share is supreme." The concept was to increase profits by increasing productivity and reducing overhead production cost per unit. However, in the 1990s, increasing market share did not always create a linear rise in profit, and ever-growing competition made it increasingly harder to obtain a high market share. The opinionating words of general trading firms and electric products companies quickly became obsolete.

Realizing that increasing market share does not always maintain an organization's profitability, American companies focused their interests and efforts on developing new, innovative business models in addition to technological innovation. Adopting a policy of "analyze and consolidate," US companies began withdrawing from unprofitable businesses and radically rethinking common business models, concentrating all energy on constructing new business models. As an example, Intel secured an overwhelming share of the memory market in the 1970s. But in the 1980s when Japanese companies challenged the market and price competition intensified, Andy Grove (COE) and Gordon Moore (president) simply decided to withdrawal from the memory market, and entered the business of designing and manufacturing microprocessors, a product with greater added-value. As a result, while Japanese semiconductor companies began reporting loses as they maintained a focus on gaining market share, Intel, who implemented a new business model focusing on microprocessors, was reporting a return on investment of 30%; a figure that holds strong even today.

Typical behavior pattern of Japanese companies

A comparison of the typical behavior patterns of Japanese and American companies reveals some interesting facts. When sales slowed down in the '90s, the first action introduced by Japanese companies was cost reduction. Of course, cost reduction activities for factories were developed; for example "at each post, an X% reduction is to be achieved." Consequently, the behavior of management to attempt to earn a profit by stressing continuous cost reduction activities in manufacturing processes made all persons aware of the inappropriate cost reduction policies and caused immeasurable damage to employee morale. Employees personally felt the damage as well, through cuts in salaries, leading many to feel that the current cost reduction policies would continue indefinitely, and employee cost reduction efforts eventually slackened. Furthermore, Japanese companies failed to implement innovative business models simultaneously with their cost reduction plans. There are numerous cases of commonplace business models where business profits simply disappeared. Still reminiscing of their successful experiences in the '80s, the thought of business model innovation was far from their minds, especially the idea of anything like Net business research.

On the contrary, US enterprises set out introducing thorough cost cutting plans devised to be carried out hand-in-hand with renovation of operations, essentially implementing new, innovative business models. Management decisions were made quickly giving careful consideration to technological innovation and cost reduction, two important factors of innovative business models. Special attention was given to the incorporation of information networks based on the Internet into most business models as well.

The management of corporate laboratories should always keep the following words in mind: " Corporate research has to create more than new products; it must build the prototype of the continuously innovating company." (Brown, 2000).

CREATING A BUSINESS MODEL

The most important fact in the construction of a business model is to fully understand the future direction of the economy; thus one must closely analyze the main flow of business today

The rise of the experience economy

One massive flow that requires our attention has been described by Jeremy Rifkin as "the rise of the experience economy" (Rifkin, 2000). In other words, the age of purchasing an item in the market and owning it will become old-fashioned. Products to be purchased will rather be cultural experiences and services such as traveling abroad, improving health, fashionable items, cuisine, sports and games, music, movies, television, cyberspace and so on. Here, the important thing is new experiences, and thus the name "experience economy." The following are viewed as reasons for this transformation to just-in-time application and experience.

1. In this extreme era of change (technology, consumer demand, etc.), the meaning of possession has been lost. (Use it, don't own it!)
2. The resounding voice of today's consumer, "Is there anything that I want that I have not yet had" (suggesting month-on-month sales are dropping continuously) and "I want to experience more that I have not yet experienced."

Conversion from possession to use

The ratios of property value and market value differ greatly when expressed in terms of possession or use (lease of actual assets and external business trust). Although the assets of IBM and Microsoft are 16.6 and 0.93 billion dollars, respectively, the corporate values placed on them are 70.7 and 85.5 billion dollars, respectively.

The US motion-picture industry is an early example of business model innovation. From the beginning of movie production and lasting into the early 1950s, movies were mass-produced and distribution closely controlled providing the movie experience. But then the US Supreme Court stepped in and set out dismantle the cinema chain as it was in violation of the Antimonopoly Law. As a result, risk related to the financial affairs of movie production increased and return on investment decreased. Here the major movie companies turned to independent production and became investment companies in their own right, offering in exchange for capital the distribution rights to theaters, television stations and video sales.

In the future, all knowledge-intensive industries will operate utilizing such independent partner networks. Hollywood actually started this nearly a half century ago: a major enterprise controlled finances and circulation, and forced the possession of the assets and control of the small enterprise.

Conversion to cultural capitalism

Daniel Bell classified modem civilization into three domains: economic, governmental and cultural (Bell, 1993). Participation is the important value in the governmental domain, and self-realization and improvement are important in the cultural domain. More than a century ago, the governmental and cultural domains combined to form a mercantile environment that makes the economic domain.

Capitalism, too, has advanced through stages, from commercial capitalism to industrial capitalism, and now to "cultural capitalism," where value is determined by access to cultural experiences. Possession is taken seriously, rights excluding other companies become a strong point, and one loses sight of "the rights not excluded from use" with industrial capitalism. However, "rights not excluded from use" can be restored; for example, following the attainment of citizenship, the introduction of women's rights and the environment movement, thus increasing power. The fear that regional cultures would be damaged appeared with the commercialization of cultural value. In a way, this is the same as the destruction of the natural environment through industrial capitalism. Here, one can sense a balance of culture and commerce taking on form as a matter of economic significance the 21st century. A precondition of a strong economy is a strong community, because a strong community fosters social trust and understanding. Trust and understanding are necessary characteristics for economic transactions in the future.

A new mission of education in the future will be to exploit the use of the global network economy and the area of cyberspace called "virtual reality" to experience vast cultures.

FUNDAMENTAL CORPORATE IT ASSETS

For the continued promotion of IT development, corporate Laboratories are obliged to adapt and support the "experience economy" trend and thoroughly promote the Internet. The fundamental mindset must be that of open management, refraining from hiding matters internally.

As for the use for IT, it is not merely a technical tool. Rather, it can be said to be an effective social (cultural) tool for corporate culture and unity. Of fundamentally high importance even though use is common in industry, each company applies IT in unique ways. Such applications create the fundamental IT properties distinct to each company. By developing these IT properties, contributions to the capabilities of a research institute are achieved. These include human, technological and relationship assets (Ross, Beath and Goodhe, 1996).

Human assets

The human asset is information specialists; those individuals capable of solving problems through the utilization of IT as well as handling and managing IT-related business opportunities. IT specialists have the "talent," "business understanding" and "problem-solving ability" for IT technologies. IT managers utilize the skills of their IT staff to integrate old-fashioned systems with the new. As for understanding the business, it is important that each member shares in the responsibility of developing solutions for problems related to IT working together with members of business groups.

Technological assets

Technological assets consist of the fundamental hardware and software environments (platforms) and databases for information technology. The two following points are important characteristics of technological assets.

1. A well-defined technology architecture (Regulated distribution of hardware, software and support. Data to be shared, data compilation method, server location, application method and technology support are all defined.)
2. Standardization (limiting expenses, maintaining high-quality support and simplifying system integration.)

Relationship assets

Relationship assets are the benefits that are born from the relationships held between the IT staff and business groups. They share the risk and responsibility for attaining the goals of the company. Mutual trust between parties, respect for each other, ability to communicate freely, adjustment flexibility and negotiation power are necessary for ascertaining true joint responsibility. Furthermore, top management must be involved in setting the order of priority for IT so that limited resources may be invested effectively. Many companies therefore establish an IT steering committee that is chaired by an upper-level manager. Relationship asset value is enhanced through IT planning, development and actual experience of application. Non-discriminative collaboration between the IT staff and members of the business group is of great importance. Figure 2.1 shows the relationship assets (Ross, Beath, and Goodhue, 1996).

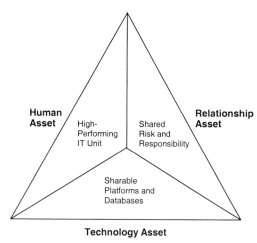

Technology Asset

Fig. 2.1. IT assets (Ross, Beath, and Goodhue, 1996).

IT assets and the corporate environment

The three IT assets are independent factors; however, each mutually and closely related to the others. For example, as a result of relationship assets, through mutual respect, members of business groups trust that IT staff are sufficiently skilled (human assets), while the capabilities of the IT staff are dependent upon the quality of present technologies and cost (technological assets).

The individual responsible for IT collaborates with the business group to evaluate the present conditions of the three IT assets and resolve weak points. Then he/she must develop a strategy that extends to and incorporates the strong points. Here, it is necessary to evaluate the competitive environment simultaneously with the evaluation of IT assets. An example of a combination of these two factors is shown in Table 2.1 (Ross, Beath, and Goodhue, 1996).

In this table, the present state of a company is described in relation to a ship set out on a voyage. Top management must lend a hand to the company if it shows a sign of beginning to sink (for example, a new individual responsible for information being brought in from outside). For a company that is adrift, it is necessary to devise a strategic order of priority for preparing IT solutions and handling related activities. It is best to first start from the relationship asset, although all three must be implemented in succession (e.g., steering committee with an upper-level manager as the chairperson). The company that turns its bow windward takes on new challenges and uses its experiences to further increase its strength. It devotes itself to systematic learning during the course of the voyage and hones its skills in preparation for the next confrontation.

Table 2.1. IT Assets and Corporate Environment (Ross, Beath, and Goodhue, 1996).

	The Competitive Environment	
State of Assets	Immediate Threat	No Immediate Crisis
Weak	**Sinking** Start bailling Rapid, risky change	**Drifting** Set a course Relationship building
Strong	**Luffing** Trim the sails Focused response	**Cruising** Go full speed ahead Adaptive learning

Effective IT management is one necessary and important skill for creating success out of strategic business processes. Communications and information are becoming increasingly vital as business tools, thus it is even more important to support the ability to quickly introduce excellent IT strategies that are cost efficient. Even though every company purchases the same software, uses individuals who are skillful in the same areas of specialty and entrusts its business to the same dealers, there are companies that will succeed in creating value and those which will not. There is difference in the technologies obtained by the companies, the skills required to use them or the ways of using them. What does make a difference is the capability to create and strengthen IT assets that other individuals or companies cannot imitate. Therefore, each IT investment should not be considered only in terms of direct cost and effect, but also in terms of influence on IT assets overall. The creation and strengthening of IT assets are the responsibility of the organization as a whole, and a persistent effort is necessary.

THE PROBLEM OF LOCATION AND RISK IN DEVELOPMENT OF KNOWLEDGE TO MAINTAIN IT COMPETITIVENESS

A major portion of the value of a research institute is its ability to maintain a "continuation of expectations" for results (Yamanouchi, 1998).

Amidst the flow of pushing the limit and systemization of each specialized technology is the request to the corporate research institute to quicken the pace of development. As a self-derived conclusion, it is difficult to possess all of the technologies required to maintain positive expectations for results on a continual basis. As a point of strengthening the organization, a company must realize or establish its core technological strengths and then collaborate with other companies in a strategic alliance or joint venture carefully matching technologies that create a synergistic effect in the market. Now is an important time to expand cooperative relations in the form of venture businesses, as can be witnessed by the effective funding of such companies by powerful and distinguished entities. Within this current, research institutes must search out partners efficiently.

Even to present day, many newly established US companies related to the Internet business have experienced problems of poor management, bankruptcy and massive layoffs. From the very beginning, the rise in the price of stock shares in such a company is not the result of substantial earnings being reported. On the contrary, the price is speculative as to how well the company might do in the future. If it maintains the business strategy, the speculative price may enable the company to expand into new areas of business. The chairman of AOL, Steve Case, did a splendid job of pushing up the value of the company's shares to 17 trillion yen, at which time he purchased Time Warner for 8 trillion yen

Since April 2000, American hi-tech stocks have not been performed as well as in the past, making capital turnover in the market difficult, and the prominent management strategy of giving priority to market share rather than profit broke down. As an undeveloped new market, it was believed that by holding a majority share of the market, it would be possible to control the industry from an early stage and then create profit. However, the strategists failed to implement the "industry's standard management strategy." Rather than being tolerant as previously believed, there was an anxious atmosphere regarding the circulation of capital in the market for Net businesses. From around 1998, competition intensified throughout the industry with a new movement, massive expenditures centering on IR, where money flowed like water into advertising and promotions pushing sales. But profits failed to be generated and investors abandoned ship.

Major corporations are quick to take action and adopt the Net business strategy, and are also active about reorganizing and business renewal. In the US, matters were not expected to improve. Still, it seemed like Net related businesses rushed in at the last minute to claim the survivors.

The primary factors of the money circulation crisis in the 20th century were deemed the hedge fund, speculative movements of international investment banks and so on. In the global market economy of the 21st century, it is believed that the money circulation crisis will repeat itself. Now the element of speculation enters the process of knowledge development. In this instance, the problem should be considered giving weight to the argument of profit margin and knowledge in capitalism. Our desire is to cultivate a better understanding of both.

Regarding profit margin

Under capitalism, profit margin is brought forth thorough the medium of difference (Iwai, 2000). Today, the thing that brings forth difference is knowledge. Difference creates the advantage over competition in the marketplace and brings forth the profit margin through manufactured goods, level of service, level of business model and level of corporate culture (meta-management: that which is behind ordinary management).

Regarding knowledge

According to Puraton, knowledge is defined as "true faith justified." Moreover knowledge is divided into that which is expressed by writing and drawing, and that which is tacit knowledge. It is important to cultivate this tacit knowledge, new differences (innovation), and establish useful locations to bring it forth (e.g., a location for exchanging information and understanding with customers). As a process of knowledge creation, the following five steps are mentioned (Nonaka and Takeuchi, 1995).

- Shared ownership of unknown knowledge
- Make general idea
- Justify general idea
- Make draft and original form
- Instruct group that requires the knowledge

Moreover, the development of something new requires risk (economic costs that happen directly or indirectly as a result). In deciding the degree of risk, there those who apply knowledge to determine whether they will obtain a particular convenience from an object (the customers) and those with the skill of knowledge sellers (the producers), whose talents are capable of gratifying the requirements of the aforementioned. First, we classify objects applicable to knowledge.

1. Special items sold to specified customers - e.g., a roller to be sold to an iron foundry.
2. General items sold to customers in a wide class - e.g., semiconductor memory, software, etc.
3. Items reflecting customers' systems - business model, etc.
4. Items reflecting customer value - Corporate culture, etc.

According to 1, customers and producers are both specialists, and their occupational morals as well as level of knowledge are high. Moreover, industrial facilities are expensive and entry barriers are high. In this case, the risk of knowledge development can be calculated. According to 2, customers are not always specialists and the level of knowledge as well as rate of completion of producer is not high. Through technological innovation, manufactured goods deemed impossible in the past have evolved (e.g., vacuum tube made possible with introduction of the semiconductor). For 3, all-round knowledge is necessary for both producers and customers. As a consequence, cooperative development is necessary for both. In comparison with 1 and 2, the object is complicated and the continuation of a trusting relationship between producers and customers is maintained at high cost (investment in management resources). Regarding 4, as corporate culture is brought forth from the vision or intentions of top management, it plays a part in deciding the fate of the company. Sometimes appraisal is resultant of a judgment of history.

Calculating the risk of knowledge development is difficult without 1 as it seems difficult to explain knowledge development from the point of economical rationality. It is thought that the promotion of knowledge development "guarantees company existence through R&D, so called continuation of expectations." This is taken to be the same as "money now will exist as money in the future."

The fact that money has an accepted value does not mean that it has the value of commodities. Unless set forth by common agreement, governmental order or national law, money has no designated value. (If considering an encoder developed by a private company or simply electronic money conveyed by electromagnetic waves, it is easy to understand.) Money being accepted as money, one expects others to accept it as money with value whenever and wherever it is used, and this expectation will continue in the future (Iwai, 2000). In the case of knowledge development and money, it is said that support of value is expected and forecast for the future. For these expectations and forecasts, problems occur depending on the relation of how knowledge and money are actually used.

Regarding location that fosters knowledge

The source of knowledge is individual people, and to create merchandise from knowledge requires teamwork. It is our belief that an appropriate metaphor for team is "location." C.I. Barnard once said that a team is a "structure" resembling "attractive location" or "magnetic location" as used in physics (Barnard, 1938). Nonaka used the general concept of "location" in his theory of knowledge management (Nonaka and Konno, 1998). In Japan, the general concept of "location" requires a philosophical explanation (Ueda, 1987).

Nonaka's "location" is required to attain corporate competency in the 21st century (Nonaka and Konno, 1998). Accordingly, it is said that the basis of corporate fulfillment is "location." Partner selection is based on "location." And since "location" is cultural, it is believed that "location" becomes a level of corporate competition, from products and services to business models and corporate culture. Until recently, Japanese corporate R&D has specialized in foundation and application, but it must now specialize in "location."

Today, the network era has sparked new construction work connecting the corporate head office and each business group. Within organizations, active exchange between small groups is nurturing new value (Wenger and Snyder, 2000). Head offices now offer locations and arrangements that promote interaction, and set a clear vision as an organization. In the office, it is important to create and grow practical associations and to make it a location for knowledge creation (Yamasaki and Baba, 1996; Yamasaki, Suzuki and Baba, 1998).

Through exchange between each business group and the head office, the general course of an organization can be regulated. Our belief is that organizations should created as if living organisms (Clippinger III, 1999). It is necessary for the creation and development of organizations to proceed as complex systems of science.

Controlling speculation and risk

Professional speculators participate in a market where they buy and sell seeking short-term profits. Rational speculators estimate that other players are expecting a shortage or surplus of materials in the future and concentrate on the omniscience and omnipotence of being the first to make the charge. When the professional speculators begin buying and selling amongst themselves, the price set is void of the actual conditions of shortage or surplus of materials. The fact is, the existing market price consequently becomes that expected by the speculators. At such times, there is nothing tangible supporting the price, and even trifling news or an unfounded rumor is sufficient to set off violent fluctuations. This causes a substantial disturbance in the economy and brings on instability. We believe that, in substance, speculation should be eliminated. Then again, it has been said, "Life itself is speculation."

In industry, there is a speculative element in all companies. But there is a solemn difference between inadmissible speculation and the thought of admissible business (Miyagawa, 1996). There is a vivid distinction between speculative dreaming of making a fortune instantaneously, speculation of an object that generates immense profits, a business that is based on detailed investigations and research, or a company that operates under scrupulous accounting practices.

For knowledge development, the one supporting factor is the value of "continuation of expectation." Consequently, if expectations become separated from other substantial items, there is possibility of speculative appearance occurring. For professional items, there is a vast difference of knowledge and ability among the persons concerned (e.g., imagine a management layer investing in a department to develop a highly advanced computer). In this case, the one thing that maintains a steady relationship between the people concerned is "confidence." If confidence were to be lost, the speculative phenomenon for knowledge development would reach a state of crisis, and the development process itself collapse.

The work ethics of the people concerned must be high to maintain confidence. As for future problems such as knowledge development, if a mistake in judgement should occur, one must openly admit it and ensure that lies are never told. Moreover, within the area of one's responsibility, it is important to be able to provide a simple, easy-to-understand explanation of technical items (specialist's accountability).

KNOWLEDGE CREATION POLICY OF MITSUBISHI ELECTRIC

Mitsubishi Electric's knowledge creation policy for the company's continued existence in the IT era is discussed in this section.

In-house venture program (Yamasaki and Yamada, 2000)

In April 2000, Mitsubishi Electric (MELCO) introduced an in-house venture program (MVP-MELCO) to create new business models (Fig. 2.2). The company also established an incubation center to support employees' activities to develop business opportunities. The center assists in the drafting of business plans and establishment of new companies, with the aim of fostering as many successful venture businesses as possible. It also operates as a secretariat to develop MVP-MELCO. Various measures have also been implemented by the Japanese government as part of its economic policy to introduce regulations and economic assistance that promote the development of venture business. Thus, environments where it is easier for venture businesses to be launched have been setup, and employees can now find assistance to take their ideas, integrate rapidly advancing IT, and develop successful products or businesses.

At present, it is difficult for general venture businesses in Japan to efficiently manage corporate accounting and legal affairs by themselves. In addition, the original creator of an idea often attempts to handle all of the administrative matters, from development to accounting, by themselves fearing that his/her ideas might be stolen. As a result, the business often fails due to poor management practices. We believe that our in-house venture system minimizes such risks,

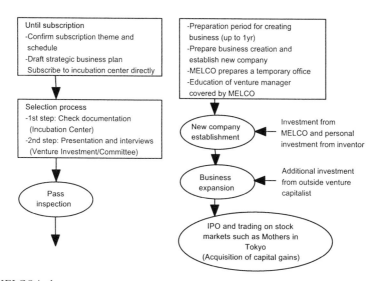

Fig. 2.2. MELCO in-house venture program.

and is the easiest and safest way for companies that only know how to operate in the traditional economy (T-economy) to start venture businesses.

Executive Chief Engineer system – The corporate watchdog

In April 2000, MELCO introduced the position of executive chief engineer one level of seniority above the existing position of chief engineer. Initially the responsibilities of the chief engineer included the studying and understanding of economic and technological trends, and then, based on their information, the planning and establishment of strategies for technological and operational development in individual business groups and laboratories. In particular, their principal duty was to attend the meetings and conferences of global business organizations and academic circles and collect information on behalf of the company.

The Executive Chief Engineer System, which now positions those chief engineers who have become well-known in business and academic circles as company directors, was launched to realize quick decision-making for technological and management strategies in the IT era. Another merit of this system is that it supports the need to develop a corporate climate where importance is attached to technology. Each executive chief engineer is responsible for making operational reports to the general managers of the R&D and production groups, and is expected to play the role of a high-level corporate watchdog, collecting all kinds of information.

Performance-based annual salary system

In March 1998, MELCO introduced and implemented an annual salary system based entirely on performance to its management-level staff. As a result, the conventional seniority system and practice of lifetime employment have been removed Each department is assessed in three ranks according to the overall business performance of the company, and annual salaries are then calculated by multiplying a basic fluctuating salary and a fixed rate. Under the conventional system where wages increased according to the number of years of service, high wages were often paid to employees regarded as not having done satisfactory work from a corporate viewpoint.

Non-managerial employees do not participate in the performance-based annual salary system. As methods to reward employees, consideration is paid not only to monetary remuneration, but also to the degree of freedom in work and assigned position.

Hedging R&D risk

The concept of the present value of expectation is defined as follows:

$$Present\ value\ of\ expectation = \frac{E_1}{1+p} + \frac{E_2}{(1+p)^2} + \frac{E_3}{(1+p)^3} + \ldots\ldots$$

where, E_1 is expectation in the first year, E_2 is expectation in the second year (in continuum) and p is interest rate. Here, we define the growth rate of expectation as α:

$$E_1 = E_0(1+\alpha)$$

$$E_2 = E_1(1+\alpha) = E_0(1+\alpha)^2$$

$$E_3 = \ldots\ldots$$

E_0 : Initial value of expectation

Therefore, the present value of expectation when R&D is initiated becomes:

$$\frac{E_0(1+\alpha)}{1+p} + \frac{E_0(1+\alpha)^2}{(1+p)^2} + \ldots\ldots = E_0\left\{\frac{1}{1+q} + \frac{1}{(1+q)^2} + \ldots\ldots\right\}$$

where,

$$q = \frac{p-\alpha}{1+\alpha}$$

Here, q is the effective rate of interest according to the succeeding expansion of expectation. If α is large, q becomes negative; in other words, the rate of interest is negative, meaning that a profit will be produced.

CONCLUSION

Anxious regarding the fact that Japan has fallen behind the USA in the IT revolution, many Japanese companies are now rapidly increasing their investments in IT. Our stance is that these companies should reconsider such hasty actions. The greatest difference between IT and conventional technologies is the speed of evolution. If a company makes a large investment to introduce the most advanced IT equipment and systems, there is a very high possibility that the equipment and systems will soon be outdated. In this sense, outsourcing becomes an important strategy; however this involves the risks that the technical level of the outsourcing party lags behind the times and the services provided are fixed by contract.

It is the business manager, not the IT specialist, that should assume the responsibility for designing business models, and corporate research institutes must play an important roles here as well. Designing a business model is completely different from designing operational procedures, and it must include strategic decision-making. What signals should be read from market trends, which data and analysis models should be used for reading such signals, what kinds of measures should be taken therein; all of these questions must be studied and resolved by corporate research institutes. The roles to be played by these facilities continue to grow in importance. If provided with the ability to learn using proper business models and techniques, the business scale of major corporations will produce decisive advantages over the competition.

BIBLIOGRAPHY

Barnard, C.I. (1938): *The Function of the Executive*, Harvard University Press.

Bell, D. (1993): *The Coming of Post-Industrial Society*, New York: Basic Books.

Brown, J.S. (2000): *IEEE Engineering Management Newsletter*, vol.50, Second Quarter 2000.

Clippinger III, J.H. (1999): *The Biology of Business*, Jossey Bass.

Itoh, K. (2000): *Corporate Brand Management*, Nikkei Shimbun, Tokyo.

Iwai, K. (2000): *The 21st Capitalism*, Chikuma Book, Tokyo.

Miyagawa, T. (1996): *Baron Koyata Iwasaki - Management Principal growing Mitsubishi Group* -, Chuo-Koron Book Press, Tokyo.

Nonaka, I. and Konno, N. (1998): The Concept of "Ba": Emerging Foundation of Knowledge Creation, *California Management Review*, vol.40, no.3, pp.40-54.

Nonaka, I. and Takeuchi, H. (1995): *The Knowledge Creating Company: How Japanese Companies Create the Dynamics of Innovation*, Oxford University Press, New York.

Rifkin, J. (2000): *The Age of Access*, Jeremy P. Tarcher/Putman.

Ross, J.W., Beath, C.M., and Goodhue, D.L. (1996): Develop Long-Term Competitiveness through IT Assets, *Sloan Management Review*, vol.38, no.1, pp.31-42.

Ueda, K. (1987): *The Philosophy of Dr. Kitaro Nishida*, *I*, Iwanami Book Press, Tokyo.

Wenger, E.C. and Snyder, W.M. (2000): Communities of Practice: The Organization Frontier, *HBR*, Jan.-Feb., pp.139-145.

Yamanouchi, A. (1998): The View Point of the Evaluation of R&D in the Firm, *Journal of Science Policy and Research Management*, vol.13, no.1/2, pp.42-47.

Yamasaki, H. and Baba, J. (1996): New Wave of Managing Innovation, *Proceedings of IEEE Engineering Management Society, International Conference on Engineering and Technology Management IEMC96*, pp.761-765.

Yamasaki, H., Suzuki, H. and Baba, J. (1998): Knowledge-Creating Organization in Japanese Corporations - Management and Characteristics Thereof -, *Management of Technology, Sustainable Development and Eco-Efficiency*, (Selected Papers from the Seventh International Conference on Management of Technology, Orlando, Florida, Feb. 16-20), pp.37-46, Elsevier, Amsterdam.

Yamasaki, H. and Yamada, I. (2000): Revolution of Knowledge Creating Companies in Japan, *Proceedings of 2000 IEEE Engineering Management Society EMS 2000*, pp.630-636.

Management of Technology
Copyright © 2003 by Elsevier Science Ltd.
All rights of reproduction in any form reserved.
ISBN: 0-08-044136-X

3

CORPORATE TRAJECTORIES AND THE STRATEGY AND STRUCTURE OF R&D

Jens Frøslev Christensen, Copenhagen Business School[†,*]

INTRODUCTION

After World War II and way into the 1980s the *central R&D lab* represented the dominant paradigm for managing R&D in large technology-intensive corporations (Whittingon, 1990). However, as large companies have increasingly become multi-divisional, multi-national, multi-business and multi-technology companies they have become increasingly difficult to assist from central labs (Christensen, 2002). As a result, R&D-intensive large companies have over the last nearly two decades experienced a general wave of downsizing, decentralization, outsourcing and internationalization of R&D (Boutellier et al., 2000; Coombs and Richards, 1993; Coombs, 1996; Floyd, 1997; Gerybadze and Reger, 1999; Howells, 1990; Iansiti, 1997; Kaufman et al, 1996; National Science Board, 1992; Rubenstein, 1989; Whittington, 1990). However, these tendencies have not been equally powerful in all industries and categories of companies, and rather than a new dominant paradigm of highly decentralized, internationalized and outsourced R&D structures we have witnessed ongoing experimentation and restructuring with different governance structures in which new more market-like and market oriented structures are combined with efforts to assure both long-term and coordinated R&D investments (Birkinshaw and Fey, 1999). Hence, the times of one dominant paradigm of organizing corporate R&D seems over.

[†] An earlier version of this article has been presented at the IAMOT 2001 Conference in Lausanne, Switzerland. Another version of the article will be published in a forthcoming issue of Research Policy.

[*] Jens Frøslev Christensen is Professor of Management of Technology at Department of Industrial Economics and Strategy, Copenhagen Business School. Email: jfc.ivs@cbs.dk.

What is the logic behind what seems an endlessly ongoing process of restructuring of the R&D organization in many technology-intensive manufacturing companies? This paper tries to combine a structural contingency perspective and an evolutionary perspective in analyzing this theme. It is argued that different kinds of organizational incongruities constitute critical sources of change in the organization of R&D. One such organizational incongruity may evolve between the overall changes in the structure and strategy of the company, and the existing mode of managing and organizing R&D. Most large companies are subject to long periods of relative inertia in terms of organizational and strategic development. They develop along what we shall term *corporate organizational trajectories*. Such trajectories are mostly hard to change, and much restructuring of the R&D organization reflects adaptations to such overall trajectories. Another type of organizational incongruity reflects tensions developing primarily within the R&D organization, either between emerging new strategic objectives in the R&D organization and the existing mode of managing R&D, or between emerging new R&D structures and the existing R&D-strategy.

Since it is difficult, if not impossible, to precisely measure efficiency and effectiveness in management of innovation and technology, changes in organizational and managerial practices related to R&D tend to be based on management's attempts to come up with organizational solutions to remedy inter-subjectively perceived deficiencies or accommodate new strategic objectives. Such perceived incongruities and deficiencies constitute ongoing sources of organizational modification and restructuring. However, while this contingency perspective seems to provide valid explanations of individual restructuring decisions, the evolutionary notion of corporate trajectories may explain the way the pattern of decisions over the longer term are locked into particular company-specific paths of development.

Hence, the paper proposes an analytical framework in which an evolutionary view of corporate trajectories is combined with a contingency perspective on the strategy and structure of R&D. This framework is used to interpret a comparative, longitudinal study of two Danish technology-intensive companies, one representing a decentralizing organizational trajectory (Danfoss), the other a centralizing and integrative trajectory (Grundfos). The question to be faced is, what are the determinants of the major or minor restructuring associated with the management of R&D, and what is the underlying logic behind the pattern of such decisions over a span of several decades?

The paper is structured as follows. First, a short account of the analytical framework is provided. Then the two case companies are presented. The historical trajectories of corporate organization and management of innovation and technology are outlined in a descriptive fashion. Finally, the case studies are analyzed and discussed according to the analytical framework.

ANALYTICAL FRAMEWORK

The inherent tensions between different and changing strategic objectives and between strategic ambitions and organizational solutions provide a continuous source of trade-off concerns and compromises in the evolutionary development of the company's strategy, organization and culture, and most large and growing companies have to deal with the never-ending issue of harmonizing these concerns in a context of bounded rationality and institutional constraints (Roberts and Greenwood, 1997).

This broad perspective underlies the present analysis of changing modes of managing R&D. Consistent with Chandler's notions of strategy and structure, management of R&D is here analytically differentiated into R&D strategy, that is, the explicit or implicit longer term direction of R&D investments, and the R&D structure, that is, the organizational mode of managing R&D. Furthermore management of R&D is divided into two sub-functional categories, management of innovation and management of technology. Management of innovation signifies the management and organization of *the individual innovation processes* with the objective to produce commercially successful product innovations while economizing on time and resources. Management of technology signifies the management and organization of *the company's technology base* (the portfolio of existing and prospective technological capabilities underlying product and process development).

This paper has three objectives. First to align a structural contingency perspective on strategy and structure with an evolutionary perspective on companies' long-term course of development. Second, to apply such a framework to the analysis of the dynamics of R&D management in large companies. Third, to interpret two longitudinal case studies within this framework and, thus, in an explorative way test the validity of the framework.

The contingency perspective used takes its point of departure in Chandler's (1962, 1977) theory of strategic and organizational dynamics implying that accumulating organizational tensions or incongruities give rise to organizational changes that seek to reestablish coherence between the strategy and the organizational structure of the firm. Extending this perspective into the area of management of R&D, the policy implications would be twofold in that the mode of managing R&D should correspond to both (i) the overall strategy-structure constellation and dynamics of the company, and (ii) the specific objectives of the company's innovation and technology strategy[1]. However, in the real and highly dynamic world of technology-based competition, perceived organizational incongruities and deficiencies constantly emerge and give rise to pressures for changes in the organization of

---

[1] The notion of strategy is here used in the sense of Mintzberg and Waters (1985) as "a pattern in a stream of decisions" encompassing the full spectrum between deliberate or planned strategy at the one end and emergent strategy at the other.

R&D. In other words, an optimal, one and for all, congruence or coherence will never be obtained.

Two categories of organizational incongruities are specifically pertinent in this particular context: incongruities induced by changes in corporate strategy and structure, and incongruities exclusively associated with the arena of R&D management. The former involves changes in the overall strategy-structure profile of the company that lead to requirements for adaptive changes in the mode of managing R&D, despite possible misalignment with existing priorities in innovation or technology strategy. The latter category of incongruities is associated with tensions internal to the domain of management of R&D. Such incongruities can, in the Chandlerian mode of analysis, be interpreted in terms of the interplay and tensions emerging between R&D strategy and structure: between emerging new strategic objectives in the R&D organization and the existing mode of managing R&D (in line with the conventional Chandlerian proposition that "structure follows strategy"), or between emerging new R&D structures and the existing R&D strategy (in line with the reverse dynamics, namely that "strategy follows structure"[2]. But this category of incongruities may also involve emerging tensions between the two sub-functions of management of R&D, management of innovation and management of technology. One illustration of this would be the way in which a change in the mode of managing *innovation* (for example a change towards decentralized responsibility for product innovation) contribute to undermine both the rationality of the existing mode of managing *technology* (for instance, an up-front technology strategy linked to a central research laboratory) and thereby establish a perceived incongruity between the mode of managing *innovation* and the mode of managing *technology*.

Even if the incongruities are reflected in tensions and organizational and strategic processes within the firm, the drivers of such incongruities may be external or internal to the firm, or both. In the first case, a company's strategy-structure constellation, which has proved effective in relation to one epoch's industrial, technological or institutional dynamics in its environment, may prove highly ineffective in a subsequent epoch characterized by new competitive or other external dynamics, even when the internal strategy-structure mode is highly coherent. Thus, for example the very coherent "strategic planning" style characterizing IBM's overall corporate strategy and structure as well as the specific mode of managing R&D was highly successful in establishing IBM as the dominant player in the global computer markets in the 1960s, 1970s and early 1980s, but it also contributed to lock IBM into a

---

[2]   Of course, the strategy and structure may also be so intimately co-evolving that it is not possible to identify the one part as driving the other.

trajectory - associated with its strong dependence on the mainframe markets - that increasingly was out of tune with the competition (Chandler, 1994)[3].

It is the proposition of this paper that such a contingency-based framework for understanding organizational change tends to be framed by long-term evolutionary firm-specific trajectories that are hard to change. Evolutionary perspectives on the firm argue that firm behavior is strongly influenced by the routines, capabilities and organizational structures of its previous history (Nelson and Winter, 1982, Teece et al., 1994). In the evolutionary literature the notion of paths or trajectories have primarily related to patterns of technology-specific change ("technological trajectories", cf. Dosi, 1982), to firm-specific or sector-specific patterns of technological change (the so-called Pavitt-taxonomy, cf. Pavitt, 1984), or to path-dependent dynamics of learning and organizational change (Teece et al., 1994, Lehrer, 2000). Here we shall use the notion of corporate organizational trajectories to signify path-dependent development patterns in the overall strategy-structure constellation. Especially we shall argue that companies with a long history of institutional continuity[4] are subject to long periods of relative inertia in terms of organizational and strategic development.

The two companies studied in this paper reflect different modes of governance: Grundfos represent a more hierarchical mode that is in accordance with the transaction costs arguments against outsourcing of technology and Schumpeterian arguments for in-house protection of radical ideas in their formative stages (Birkinshaw and Fey, 1999). Growth has been induced rather through a strategy of vertical integration than a strategy of business diversification. Danfoss represents an increasingly market-oriented mode that is in accordance with economic efficiency and incentive criteria associated with theories of the M-form company (Chandler, 1962; Williamson, 1975) and some more common trends during the last decades in the development of both the overall corporate organization and the specific R&D organization. None of the companies have been forced to dramatic turnarounds due to external threats from competitors as the case been with IBM and many other large incumbents (Chesbrough, 2002, Christensen, 1997, Lovas and Ghoshal, 2000). Figure 3.1 outlines the most distinctive similarities and differences in strategic emphasis in Danfoss and Grundfos.

---

[3]   As an illustration of this interpretation of IBM's lock-in, Mandel (2000) argues that this position remained even after IBM had launched its first and very successful PC: "IBM ... fell behind in the PC race because it kept trying to protect its profitable mainframe business. As a result, it introduced the laughable PCjr in 1984, with its chiclet-like keyboard, rather than following up the success of the original IBM PC. It's natural for large corporations to decide that protecting their existing profit streams is more important than taking a chance on an unproven product" (p.27).

[4]   E.g., companies with a long history without radical reconfiguration of the corporate identity due to mergers, wars, enforced demergers, etc. (Cantwell and Fai, 1999). This does not mean that such companies have been immune to strategic, organizational, technological and other kinds of changes. Most companies with a long history, including those with long institutional continuity, have experienced both incremental and radical changes in their strategies and structures.

The two basic questions of the paper is, (i) to what extent and how does the overall corporate trajectory impact on the mode of managing and organizing R&D, and (ii) what is the scope for distinct R&D trajectories, as based on the dynamics of co-evolving R&D strategy and structure, either in congruence or at odds with the corporate trajectory? We shall primarily focus on the 'internal' process side of the story.

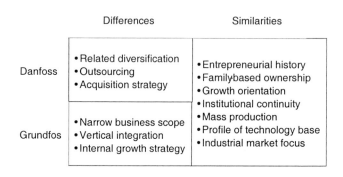

Fig. 3.1. *Differences and similarities between Danfoss and Grundfos.*

THE TRAJECTORIES OF CORPORATE ORGANIZATION AND MANAGEMENT OF R&D IN DANFOSS[5]

Trajectory of corporate organization: A case of decentralization and diversification

Since its establishment in 1933 Danfoss has developed from a one-person firm to a global corporation with an annual turnover of 14.8 billion DKK (2000) and about 17,000 employees, 95 sales companies abroad and 53 factories in 21 countries. The company today manufactures thousands of different products, particularly mechatronical products for a very diverse set of primarily industrial markets within refrigeration controls, motion controls, and heating and water controls.

Through its nearly 70 years of existence, a characteristic feature of Danfoss has been technology and market-related diversification. The founder of Danfoss, Mads Clausen, a

---

[5]   This section on Danfoss is based on a comprehensive case study by Iversen and Christensen (1999). The study has involved numerous interviews especially with R&D managers and several visits to Danfoss from 1995 to 1999.

paternalistic entrepreneur, played a decisive role in this development by excessively pushing forward the venturing into related product markets. During most of Danfoss' existence growth and diversification has primarily been generated through internal investments. However, during the last 20 years, and especially the 1990s, this pattern has changed in favor of acquisitions which have primarily been conducted with the objective to strengthen market positions and establish sales synergies by offering related products to existing customers and through Danfoss' existing distribution and sales network.

Danfoss has also undergone substantial technology diversification. Thus, from an initial mechanical engineering base, Danfoss' technology base has gradually come to include capabilities in mechatronics, hydraulics, electronics, software, and materials. Scale economies, effective and high-quality manufacturing and "design for manufacturability" are critical competitive advantages of Danfoss's most important products - certainly of the most successful of them all: the radiator thermostat.

As Danfoss has grown due to diversification and internationalization, the corporate organization has gone through several stages of change away from the original functional or unitarian (U-form) structure and towards an increasingly decentralized multidivisional (M-form) structure. The first steps were taken in 1971, a few years after the death of Mads Clausen, when three "product groups" (later to be termed divisions) were established with the assignment to take responsibility for their respective product lines and for building their own development, sales and accounting functions[6]. Much of the manufacturing and purchasing operations, however, remained centralized, just as the central R&D lab retained responsibility for the longer term R&D efforts.

By the mid and late 1980s it became increasingly clear for top management that the corporate organization was stuck halfway between a centralized, functional organization which represented the residual parts of the 'old' Danfoss, and a divisionalized and decentralized organization representing the expansion of the divisions and their request for further autonomy. In 1988 subsidizing internal sourcing ended, and the divisions assumed organizational and financial responsibility over parts of the hitherto central purchasing of components and other inputs.

To enhance collaboration between divisions a number of cross-divisional committees were set up covering such areas as standardization, marketing, production technology, product development and information technology. During the 1990s Danfoss also promoted inter-divisional efforts in nurturing key technologies of importance for more than one division (see below).

---

[6]   The three groups were termed 'Compressors Group', 'Automation Group' and 'Hydraulic and Burner Components Group'.

The number of divisions has grown to 11 in 1999, and the powerful forces operating in favor of divisional autonomy have continued. Decision making responsibilities have extensively been delegated to divisional management, even the right to implement, for example, venture projects or acquisitions[7]. In 1996 the corporate R&D lab was closed in order to strengthen the divisions' responsibility for their own R&D. The following year divisions assumed responsibility over the corporate-level manufacturing plants. Furthermore, to promote inter-divisional coordination the divisions were grouped into three divisional groups, Refrigeration Controls, Motion Controls, and Heating and Water Controls according to criteria of similarity and common interest.

Up until the 1970s Headquarters and most of the productive activities were still located near the small town Nordborg where Danfoss was founded. Since then Danfoss has increasingly become a globally distributed company, and in 1997 the number of employees working abroad exceeded the number working in Denmark.

Roughly Danfoss has undergone the classical Chandlerian organizational trajectory implying a change from the early entrepreneurial organization in which the founder was in full control, to first a functionally differentiated and more professionalized organization, and then - since around 1970 - an increasingly full-fledged M-form structure within which organizational restructurings more or less regularly have taken place.

Towards a decentralized mode of managing innovation and technology

In the 1960s Danfoss was a quickly growing company with a conventional R&D lab, Corporate Technology and Research (CTR) responsible for both the management of innovation and technology development. However, up through the 1970s the newly established and expanding product divisions gradually developed their own capacity for managing innovation. Moreover, they gained growing control over resource allocation decisions and project formulations in CTR. This resulted in increasing numbers of small projects without much coherence and overall guidance. In the 1980s CTR regained significant autonomy by focusing on a more limited number of strategic R&D projects (technology development) and venturing projects (radical innovation outside the existing range of Danfoss businesses). However, this simultaneously resulted in a decoupling of the linkages to the divisions.

As the product divisions increasingly became capable of managing their own innovation processes within their respective business domains, CTR gradually changed from being a general R&D lab to becoming a center for corporate management of technology and related services. While most of R&D in Danfoss was carried out in CTR in the 1960s and early 70s, the CTR-based R&D in the early and mid 1990s only covered about 20% of total

---

[7]   Moreover, the responsibility for the product lines has increasingly been delegated to the individual product line units within the divisions.

corporate R&D[8]. By then around one fourth of total costs in CTR was directly financed by the divisions.

Thus, other activities than R&D-projects successively came to play an increasing role within CTR: technical extension services to the divisions, management of patents, standardization and certification, quality systems, and management of technology across the corporation. The latter set of activities were initiated in 1989 when the director of CTR and some divisional R&D managers began to explore the opportunities for promoting cross-divisional sharing of technologies. These efforts were prompted by the executive committee's concern about the possible negative effect of the increasing decentralization of R&D for the overall coherence of the corporation.

A new tool called the Technology Pyramid was developed with the objective to contribute to the creation and diffusion of technological capabilities. The Technology Pyramid contains a selection of technologies in which Danfoss can (or wants to) claim world-class expertise, and which have significant value for more than one division[9]. In other words, the Technology Pyramid is not a total directory of the corporate technology base (the complete portfolio of technological capabilities). It is a continuous reflection of the strategic prospects and priorities for the corporate technology base. At the same time it is a tool to promote inter-divisional coordination and build integrated technological competencies across different parts of the corporate organization. A number of cross-divisional committees reviews the status of the key technologies in the corporation, and a technical advisory group is responsible for the practical work and decisions concerning the Technology Pyramid. One to five gatekeepers are responsible for the actual development and monitoring of each of the key technologies, and inter-divisional experience groups implement specific improvement and development activities. A data base is continuously being developed with the aim of storing all relevant information concerning the key technologies for easy access by the users of the Technology Pyramid. The corporate technology management activities also include the development of tools for analyzing technologies and the maintenance of a directory listing the technological expertise of all Danfoss employees assigned to technology development.

As part of the major decentralization and reorganization measures in 1996 it was decided to close CTR that by then had 150 employees. This was done to spur divisional management to take full responsibility for R&D and to more thoroughly integrate technology and business strategies. Top management felt that the existence of CTR tended to become an excuse for not building sufficient technological capabilities at divisional levels. However, the management of technology activities were maintained at Headquarters. In 1999 it was decided

---

[8]   Divisional R&D expenditure as a percentage of divisional turnover varied from 2% to 10%.

[9]   For technologies that are only important to one division, the division in question is expected to take full responsibility.

to collect the various corporate venture and business development projects within a new corporate department that was exclusively to focus on venturing projects[10]. The strategic intent behind this decision was to revitalize the tradition in Danfoss for entrepreneurial business venturing[11]. Already the following year the corporate venture strategy took a new turn when a distinct venture company, fully owned by Danfoss, replaced the venture department. The purpose is to invest and participate in business development of entrepreneurs and entrepreneurial companies dealing with areas connected to or affiliated with Danfoss' core areas. A two-figure million DKK of venture capital is planned to be invested annually (www.innovation.danfoss.com).

The restructuring with respect to R&D - and especially the closure of CTR - have been implemented with the intention to stimulate a stronger bottom-up commitment to and responsibility for R&D . This is reflected in the implementation of a project sponsoring scheme to stimulate a bottom-up commitment to long-term coordinated R&D. According to this scheme the Headquarters can fund 50% of projects if the proposals a) are backed up by at least two divisions, b) have a long-term explorative perspective, and c) do not have a natural home base within one of the divisions. One current example is a program for upgrading the software development competence with participation of seven product lines. A small team from the corporate level coordinates a number of software development projects which, beside developing specific software components, aim at accumulating and sharing capabilities in software development.

Over the last 30 years the corporate R&D activities have gradually been spread throughout the corporation within each of the divisions and the many companies abroad[12]. In a dynamic context in which the product divisions have grown larger, increasingly autonomous, and have build their own R&D functions, there are no doubt that the technology management efforts, especially as linked to the Technology Pyramid and other inter-divisional networking activities, have exerted some overall "guiding" and co-ordination influence on the increasingly

---

[10] Examples of these ventures are water hydraulics and analytical sensors.

[11] This does not imply that all venturing activity will take place at corporate level. There continues to be some venture activities at divisional level as well.

[12] While product development activities increasingly take place in some of the foreign subsidiaries (for example development of compressors for refrigerators and freezers in Mexico and large frequency transformers in USA), most of the more fundamental R&D activities still takes place in Denmark. This pattern, however, seems to be changing due to the aggressive acquisition policy. Since an increasing number of acquired companies possesses strong R&D capabilities, it is likely that not only product and process development but also fundamental technology development will increasingly be conducted abroad.

dispersed technology base[13]. Not a top-down guidance, but a guidance based on interaction and consensus building. However, cross-divisional exchange of technological knowledge is generally limited perhaps because the measures have been voluntary and not supported by significant incentive mechanisms.

THE TRAJECTORIES OF CORPORATE ORGANIZATION AND MANAGEMENT OF R&D IN GRUNDFOS[14]

Trajectory of corporate organization: A case of centralization and integration

Grundfos was established in 1945 and has since then developed from a small artisan company to a global corporation with an annual turnover of 9 billion DKK (2000) and close to 11,000 employees, 60 companies outside Denmark, including 9 production companies, and sales companies in 36 countries. Today the company is the world's third largest producer of pumps and pump systems and the global leader within circulator pumps. More than 90% of the 8 million pumps produced annually are circulator pumps.

Through most of its nearly 60 years of existence a characteristic feature of Grundfos has been a narrow product market scope (a focus on different categories of pumps and pump systems) combined with a consistent policy of vertical integration. Thus, the company has in-house development and production of most of the components embodied in the pumps and the production equipment used in producing the pumps. The production subsidiaries abroad are obliged to buy components from within the Group, even if this policy has recently been somewhat relaxed in regard to the more simple manufacturing processes. Generally growth has been driven by vertical integration (for instance of electrical motors, other pump components including electronic control systems, and dedicated tools and machinery), inroads into new pump categories (circulator pumps, centrifugal pumps, submersible pumps), into new application areas (building services, industry, water supply, environmental applications), and into new national markets. Grundfos has predominantly pursued growth through internal investments rather than through acquisitions. The few acquisitions that Grundfos has conducted have been take-overs of smaller competitors.

---

[13] It is also likely that the increasing focus on job-rotation of managers as well as other cross-divisional committees and networks have played a similar role in promoting coherence - or at least – to some extent countervailing the inherent tendencies towards fragmentation that are associated with ongoing diversification, internationalization and divisionalization.

[14] This section on Grundfos is based on a comprehensive case study by Christensen et al. (2002). The study has involved numerous interviews especially with R&D managers and several visits to Grundfos from 1994 to 2001.

Underlying the trajectory in favor of vertical integration has been the consistent commitment to realize scale economies through mass production, and the founder of Grundfos, Poul Due Jensen was, until his death in 1977, a driving force in shaping this strategic focus.

While Grundfos has remained a pump company, the technology base has undergone substantial diversification. From the original mechanical engineering base, Grundfos has acquired distinctive technical capabilities within processing of stainless steel plates, hydraulics, new materials, and power and control electronics. However, it is a common judgment in Grundfos that the competitive advantage of Grundfos is rather based on the capacity for quickly and effectively combining several distinctive capabilities than on one particularly competitive capability. Especially, Grundfos is renowned for its unique ability to integrate product development, process development, and manufacturing operations, and moreover to integrate the motor, the electronic control system and the pump into an 'intelligent' system.

The overall Grundfos organization has remained a functional U-form organization, reflecting the fact that Grundfos has not undergone any substantial business diversification. However, the increasing product segmentation, market differentiation and diversity of the technology base has given rise to a more proliferated organization, in which for example the manufacturing function comprises increasingly specialized sections for specific pump types or components in Denmark as well as abroad, and the sales organization comprise both corporate-level functions, national sales companies, and increasingly strong regional units responsible for the coordination and control of the sales and marketing efforts in the transnational regions. Similarly, the R&D activities have been subject to continuous reorganization and proliferation (see below). Generally, however, the functional and unitary features have remained intact, and still most of the critical functions are situated close to Headquarters in the small town, Bjerringbro where Grundfos was founded.

Like Danfoss, Grundfos has gradually changed from being an expansive entrepreneurial firm to becoming a professionalized functional organization. However, unlike Danfoss, Grundfoss never embarked upon the divisionalization wagon, but remained a predominantly U-form organization. However, within this structure, Grundfos has internationalized parts of its manufacturing, sales and distribution activities.

Centralization and integration of management of innovation and technology

Within the pump industry Grundfos is perhaps the most high-profile in terms of innovation and R&D. In 2000, 380 million DKK were devoted to R&D, corresponding to over 4% of the turnover. R&D is devoted to product and process development and research in new materials. For both products and processes, emphasis is focused on improvements through the integration of new technology, including especially electronics, new materials and new manufacturing methods. Product development is targeted at making pumps smaller, increasing their performance, making them more user-friendly, making them consume less energy, and the developing of pumps for new applications.

Until the mid 1980s the product and process development activities were assembled in one central unit in Bjerringbro. This created a very integrative approach to product and process development, a unique feature of Grundfos. However, in 1985 Grundfos decided to transfer development activities to the individual factory sections dedicated to particular pump categories. This was done to create closer integration between development activities and manufacturing operations. However, even if this objective was obtained, some new problems emerged. Since development tasks were carried out by employees who had their normal work linked to operational tasks, the development projects tended to become excessively long and costly. Another problem was the lack of coordination between especially tool and machine construction across the individual factory sections, implying that several identical tools were constructed a year.

The recognition of these problems gradually contributed to create momentum in favor of centralizing R&D and establishing a project organization. In 1987 top management decided to join the different machine and tool construction sections, as well as the research department with its associated materials laboratory, within a new center to be termed the Technology Center (TC) close to Headquarters' main building. The decision process required considerable discussions especially with the sceptical factory sections.

The primary objective was to build a strong and concerted technological platform that would help maintain and expand the leading position in vital fields such as stainless steel, new materials (e.g., composite materials), surface treatment, and the development of process technologies. The center was inaugurated in 1990 - an investment of approximately 100 million DKK, the largest in the history of the corporation. TC employs around 350 R&D employees and is financed predominantly from the Group.

Product development activities, however, still remained distributed among the individual production factories. While TC was being build, the organization of product development was being discussed at a series of strategy meetings. The product development departments were perceived to have become too self-contained and reluctant to engage in close coordination which was considered necessary not only to obtain economies of scope in product design and component sourcing but also to accommodate the increasing requirements for inter-disciplinary coordination of the growing number of complex technologies used in product development. The discussions resulted in a decision to join all product development departments in one Development Center.

In 1993, product developers and product managers from the different sections were transferred to the newly-built Development Center (DC). A project-oriented form of organization crossing professional and organizational boundaries was set up according to a matrix principle. The interior design of DC, where an open work environment facilitates communication and exchange of knowledge, reflects this project orientation. The close juxtaposition of TC and DC has made direct communication among the altogether nearly 700 employees very easy.

Prior to the decisions to centralize R&D, top management had come to recognize that effect electronics, a field in which Grundfos like most of its competitors had no expertise, would very likely become a critical part of pumps in a not too distant future. Consistent with the general 'doing-it-yourself' philosophy, Grundfos decided in the mid 1980s to become a first-mover with respect to integrating electronics into pumps. The starting point was the ambition to develop a robust and low-price micro-frequency converter. This venture project was situated at a distinct location in Bjerringbro separate from the existing R&D activities. The electronics unit developed a strong entrepreneurial culture quite in contrast to that of the well-established mechanical engineering culture in the existing R&D organization. In cooperation with large foreign semiconductor companies Grundfos moved much deeper into both the development and the production side of ASICs (Application Specific Integrated Circuits) than its competitors, and Grundfos succeeded in becoming the first to develop a micro-frequency converter that makes possible the continuously variable control of speed in the pumps. Today approximately 450 people work in the electronics factory, and for Grundfos the electronics capabilities have come to constitute a corner stone which has contributed to create an in-depth theoretical understanding of motors, pumps and systems.

In 1995 a Business Process Reengineering analysis of the overall organization of R&D resulted in a decision to create a unitary R&D division with all R&D activities gathered in Bjerringbro. This implied an organizational coordination of TC and DC, and the closure of the marginal product development activities outside Bjerringbro. The main organizational principle of the R&D division has been to align a competence and a business or application perspective in a matrix structure. In an attempt to create a more market-oriented R&D organization product group managers were assigned superior responsibility for the commercial development of the respective application areas (building services, industry applications, water supply and water applications). One year after the R&D division was set up the electronics expertise in Grundfos was considered to be so mature that it would be feasible to separate development and production and integrate the former into the R&D division.

After the experiment with relative decentralization of R&D in the early 1980s[15], Grundfos has gradually centralized corporate R&D within the Technology Centre and the Development Centre and under the coordination of the R&D division. This development has created a strong commitment to a more profound and long-term technological development, to

---

[15] In retrospect this experiment is not by top management considered a failed one. Rather, it is considered a necessary learning process that accumulated important insights with respect to issues of coordination between operations and development.

cross-disciplinary integration of diverse technological expertise areas, and to tight alignment between product and process development. In such a centralized R&D organization the market dimensions in innovation processes tend to become neglected, and Grundfos has for many years tried to countervail this inherent tendency by actively seeking to integrate and strengthen the roles of product managers and product group managers. The most recent attempts in this direction were initiated in 1999 through a series of organizational changes with the objectives to focus product development within the three main product-market segments and to leverage market orientation in product development by involving the regional sales organizations directly into the development organization.

ANALYTICAL DISCUSSION

Comparing the corporate trajectories in Danfoss and Grundfos

The case studies demonstrate that both companies have been subject to consistent trajectories in their overall strategy-structure profiles. It seems as if the two companies already from their early years had been genetically coded for particular trajectories of corporate development, and this can to a large extent be explained by the imprints of their respective founders, Mads Clausen's energetic commitment to diversification through venturing in Danfoss, and Poul Due Jensen's equally energetic commitment to design automatic pumps for global markets through mass production in Grundfos. Both companies were initially subject to similar kind of trajectories involving the transformation of the small paternalistic, entrepreneurial firms into professional large functional firms. No doubt, the vigorous and ubiquitous founders did not always make that process very smooth. However, the trajectory was structurally less complicated in the Grundfos case than in the Danfoss case, because while the U-form was perfectly congruent with the focused business strategy in Grundfos, it was already early on quite at odds with the ongoing venturing and diversification strategy in Danfoss. During the 1950s and until Mads Clausen's death in 1966, the organizational coherence of Danfoss was only assured within the unitarian frame due to a mixture of Mads Clausen's personal controlling endeavors and an increasingly overloaded functional management team.

While Danfoss during the early 1970s embarked on a distinct new corporate trajectory the existing trajectory in Grundfos remained dominant although it had to adapt to new strategic challenges. In Danfoss the new trajectory implied the classical Chandler-story of organizational innovation from a U-form to an M-form structure in congruence with the sustained strategy of diversification (Chandler, 1962, 1977). More specifically, since the practiced pattern of diversification in Danfoss has been (and still is) of the related type (both market- and technology-related), the organizational trajectory towards the M-form, implying decentralization in the form of divisionalization, has at several occasions been counterbalanced by central procedures to pursue coordination (exploit the benefits from relatedness) across divisions, for instance the establishment of cross-divisional committees and a divisional group structure. In the Grundfos case, no distinct organizational discontinuity can be identified. Rather we see that the existing trajectory combining vertical integration, functional differentiation and a quite centralized governance structure has been consolidated while acknowledging the increasing proliferation and internationalization of the product markets served[16]. Especially during the 1970s and 80s the establishment of sales subsidiaries and production facilities in many different countries represented a challenge to the hitherto highly centralized and regionally concentrated sales and manufacturing functions.

The case studies also show that since Danfoss began to implement the M-form structure in the early 1970s, the two companies have pursued very different organizational modes of managing R&D. Below the R&D trajectories in the two companies will be analyzed in order to clarify the role of two kinds of triggers of organizational changes, those related to the overall organizational trajectory and those directly related to incongruities and strategic changes within the R&D organization.

The R&D trajectory of Danfoss

In Danfoss we have seen that over the last nearly 30 years most technological innovation activities (except for a few venturing projects) have become fully delegated to the product divisions. This development has been imposed by the general forces underlying the divisionalization process, namely the incentives for expanding the autonomy and financial accountability of the product divisions. Thus, the change in the development organization was not caused by specific changes in objectives of innovation strategy; rather the causal chain was the reverse, the divisionalization of technological innovation gradually contributed to a change in the de facto innovation strategies. Even if we do not have a full account of the specific styles of managing innovation in each of the 11 divisions, our general impression is that divisionalization of innovation has implied a stronger focus on ongoing product development and less focus on fundamental R&D required for building new distinctive technological capabilities. Moreover, divisionalization has implied increasing focus on inter-functional linkages (e.g. between product development and marketing) as related to the limited business scope of the individual divisions. Altogether this means that by far the most innovative efforts

---

[16]   The organizational discontinuity in Danfoss and continuity in Grundfos were also reflected in their different ways of handling the succession after the death of their respective founders and top managers. In Danfoss a new CEO was recruited from outside the founder's family. In Grundfos the founder's son, Niels Due Jensen, took over the top position. This not only represented continuity in terms of family bonds; Niels Due Jensen shares with his father a strong technical ingenuity and a vision of technological leadership.

have become dedicated to incremental and custom-specific product development[17]. Prior to Danfoss' embarkment on the divisionalization trajectory, the central R&D lab was responsible for most innovative activities in the corporation. The lab was congruent with the then functional corporate structure, and even if data concerning the objectives of innovation strategy of the lab in the 1960s and early 1970s is sparse, the long-term venture activities seemed to play a prominent role. During the era of divisionalization the central lab increasingly showed incongruity vis-à-vis both the overall tendency towards divisional autonomy and accountability, and the emerging, more incrementally oriented, divisional innovation strategies. This was reflected in increasing difficulties in aligning the long-term horizon of the central lab and the shorter-term commercial inclination of the divisional R&D units. A series of specific measures sought to deal with these problems: Increasing divisional control over the lab's activities, the implementation of a management tool for coordinating technology development in different divisions (the "technology pyramid"), and the increasing divisional funding of the lab projects.

However, the perceived incongruity between the corporate trajectory and the R&D structure did not disappear, and the closure of the central lab in 1996, a decision made by top management and not R&D management, represented a fundamental elimination of this incongruity. As this structural resolution was implemented, the agenda of managerial attention shifted. Even if the justification of the closure of the central lab was to induce divisional R&D to take a more offensive stance in technology strategy, non the less there was some concern that the closure of the lab would rather contribute to reinforce the already existing incrementalist bias in innovative efforts. In a prevailing regime of divisional short-termism, how would Danfoss be able to accumulate radically new technological capabilities and continue the business venture culture that had been the "trademark" of Danfoss throughout its early history? These considerations led to two initiatives for modifying or countervailing the divisions' natural inclination towards exploitation rather than exploration (Levinthal and March, 1993). One was the co-funding scheme according to which the Group may contribute to fund more radical and cross-divisional innovative investment projects. The other was an attempt to strengthen venture efforts by setting up a venture department close to Headquarters with the responsibility for nurturing a series of high-tech venture projects, and more recently the establishment of a distinct venture company. Moreover, the technology management procedures associated with the "technology pyramid" were continued at corporate level after the closure of the central lab.

---

[17] In contrast, some of the venturing projects, especially those organized in the corporate venture function, possess substantial elements of quite radical technical renewal. The impacts of the recently established venture company cannot yet be reviewed. However, it may reflect a tendency to strengthen the 'outsourcing' of venturing activities as compared to in-house venturing.

In sum, Danfoss has witnessed an overall trajectory towards divisionalization of R&D imposed by the overall divisionalization drivers of the corporation. This has lead to increasing market-focus and incrementalism in innovative efforts despite the various countervailing measures to promote explorative investments in innovation and business development and coordination across divisions.

The R&D trajectory of Grundfos

Grundfos has not experienced a similar break away from the functional structure, hence R&D has not been exposed to strong pressures for decentralization incurred by the overall strategy-structure development as the case has been in Danfoss. Only the increasing proliferation and internationalization of the manufacturing operations have given rise to considerations on how to coordinate product development, process development and manufacturing operations. The relative decentralization of R&D to the individual factories in the mid 1980s both reflected the emergence of new objectives in innovation strategy and some more corporate-wide dynamics. With respect to the former, a commitment to create tighter coordination of innovative and operational activities in order to obtain "design for manufacturability" gained support among R&D management. But also corporate-wide strategic reflections played a role in this decision. The growth dynamics of the late 1970s and early 1980s implied an increasing recognition of the need to internationalize different operational activities, not only the sales and distribution organization but also parts of the production system. In other words, during this phase in Grundfos' history it was increasingly acknowledged that some level of decentralization was necessary in order to realize the growth opportunities in international markets. Finally, the decision to co-locate R&D with the manufacturing sections also reflected the relatively strong political position of the manufacturing side within the corporation. This position can historically be attributed to the founder's strong dedication to quality-based mass production and the tradition of in-house development of the production tools and machinery. Thus, a large share of R&D has always been dedicated to the production side.

For the R&D organization this relative decentralization reflected a quite radical departure from the hitherto centralized structure, and this could potentially have initiated a new organizational trajectory leading to a much more distributed R&D profile in which, for instance, the production units abroad gradually would build up capacity for incremental, custom- and country-specific innovation. However, such a scenario never materialized. Instead, the R&D management increasingly became aware of inefficiencies in the new co-located R&D and manufacturing sections (increasing product development time and poor coordination of R&D among the sections). The emerging dissatisfaction with this R&D structure contributed to create momentum for what eventually, during the late 1980s, developed into a dramatic turnaround in innovation strategy - followed by structure - implying a commitment to become the technological and innovative frontrunner of the pump industry. This 'new momentum' underlies the re-centralization processes during the 1990s of all R&D within the Technology Center and the Development Center. Even if the centralized nature of technological innovation can be said to match the company's narrow product focus and functional organization, the more specific organizational set-up for innovative activities reflects well-digested objectives in the company's innovation strategy rather than specific imprints from the overall corporate dynamics. Grundfos has traditionally been a strongly production- and technology-driven company with a focus on the inter-functional interfaces between product development, process development and manufacturing operations. The substantial investments during the 1990s in fundamental technology development and increasing focus on inter-disciplinary linkages across technologies while maintaining tight relations between product and process development[18] demonstrates a concerted commitment to be a first-mover with respect to implementing quite radical technical renewal of (primarily) existing products and processes. This is furthermore underlined by the long-term investments in building radically new technological capabilities within control electronics.

The recentralization process, however, came stepwise and was not guided by a comprehensive masterplan. First, attention was directed at the process technology development activities which became integrated in the new Technology Center together with a research center in materials technologies. Secondly, focus shifted to the product development function that became collected and integrated into the new Development Center situated right next to the Technology Center. Thirdly, attention was directed, through a Business Process Re-engineering analysis, towards the issue of coordination between the two centers, and as a consequence the R&D division and a matrix-like structure was established in 1996 - an outcome that was not anticipated when the decision to build the Technology Center was taken nearly ten years earlier. Fourthly, the efforts by the late 1990s to organizationally and physically integrate the electronics development activities into the main R&D organization reflected the maturation of the electronics capabilities and the need to assure a more effective integration of this capability and the "old" mechanical engineering capabilities in ongoing innovation processes. Each of these decisions was taken separately, but they were sequentially related in the sense that they were mobilized as new organizational incongruities or deficiencies were perceived and recognized by management as unintended consequences of the implementation of previous decisions.

An implication of this centralization and integration trajectory characterizing the R&D organization is that Grundfos has chosen for a technological first-mover position and an organizational focus on coordination across technical disciplines and across product and

---

[18] However, the interface between product and process development, on the one hand, and manufacturing operations, on the other hand, is likely to have been weakened as a consequence the re-centralization of the innovation processes.

process development activities. The potential down-side of this organizational design is a weak commercial orientation and market coupling associated with product innovation. This problem has been subject to ongoing concern and various attempts to integrate a "market function" in the shape of product managers and product group managers into the R&D organization. The numerous changes in the tasks, roles and positions of the product managers and the recent attempts to integrate the regional sales units in the development organization, bear witness to the difficulties of creating a stronger market orientation in the midst of a highly technology-focused organization[19].

The sequences of these decisions constitute a distinct centralization and integration trajectory since the mid 1980s. Moreover, the massive increase in R&D investments during this period has contributed to regain the technological pioneer role that also characterized the early phases of Grundfos. Combined, the recentralization and the front-runner mobilization can be interpreted as a re-adaptation of the R&D trajectory to match the overall corporate trajectory. In this sense Grundfoss is an extremely coherent corporation (Christensen and Foss, 1997, Christensen 1998).

Comparing the R&D trajectories in the two companies

As earlier noted management of R&D can be analytically differentiated into two subcategories, management of innovation and management of technology. According to a Chandlerian perspective, the mode of managing innovation and technology should reflect the deliberate innovation and technology strategies of the company. However, often the reverse dynamics takes place, namely that the innovation and technology strategies are de facto reflections of an R&D organization primarily imposed by the overall corporate strategy and structure with little explicit considerations for R&D strategies. Below we shall briefly compare the drivers of change with respect to the two subcategories of R&D management.

Taking the last 15 years into account, the two companies have witnessed totally opposite trajectories in the organization of R&D.

Management of innovation, i.e. the management and organization of product and process innovations, has in Danfoss become the exclusive domain of the product divisions (and increasingly the product lines within the divisions), and the prime driver in this development has been the overall corporate trajectory towards a full-fledged M-form company. The divisionalization of management of innovation has induced increasing incrementalist and

---

[19]   To some extent this problem may be less precarious than in many other industries, since most circulator and other pumps that Grundfos sell on the world market are fairly standardized products in which the all-dominant competitive product features are easily internalized in the mental maps of developing engineers (making pumps smaller, increasing their performance, and making them consume less energy).

market oriented focus in product innovation. In Grundfos the centralization of management of innovation into the Development Center in close association with the Technology Center has been driven rather by the offensive innovation and technology strategy mobilized from the end of the 1980s and onwards, than by pressures to adapt to the overall corporate trajectory[20]. This has induced a commitment in favor of more radical technological innovation.

By delegating management of innovation to divisional level Danfoss has created a "structural" market orientation in innovative activities and, potentially, a weak technology position. In contrast, Grundfos has created a "structural" inclination for a strong technology orientation and a weaker market orientation, the latter of which has been sought modified by the integration of a "market function" (product managers and product group managers and recently the directors of the regional sales units) in the central R&D organization.

Managing technology deals with the management and organization of the corporate technology base with respect to three types of objectives: technology diversification, technology integration, and management control of technology investments.

Re. Technology diversification. Both companies have expanded their portfolio of technological capabilities, and even if the process of technology diversification has followed similar paths (for instance to build expertise in electronics, software and materials technologies), the specific proliferations have differed. Danfoss has a more diverse technology base when specified at a disaggregate level due both to Danfoss' larger size and to its more diverse product range. On the other hand, Grundfos probably has developed more in-depth knowledge within some of its high-priority areas. While technology diversification in Danfoss takes place within the 11 divisions without any significant overall guidance, technology diversification in Grundfos is or can be subject to concerted action and long-term corporate commitment in terms of funding and guidance. Even if most R&D is of an applied nature, the substantial long-term investments in materials research and electronics have provided Grundfos with an in-depth know-how in new distinctive technologies that are gradually becoming integrated in the various pump products.

Re. Technology integration. Technology integration, involving cross-disciplinary learning, is in Danfoss subject to substantial barriers to the extent this learning involves cross-divisional dialogue and exchange[21]. Especially, the decentralization of corporate R&D has contributed to

---

[20] The fact that this re-centralization has also implied a re-adaptation of the R&D organization to the overall corporate trajectory is here considered a side effect.

[21] One exception is that one of the divisional groups, Refrigeration Controls comprising three divisions, has set up a common R&D unit to deal with cross-divisional R&D-projects.

this development. Even if corporate measures such as the cross-divisional committees (including the Technology Pyramid) and sponsoring projects to some extent promotes such learning, the measures are voluntary by nature and are not assisted by any incentive mechanisms and therefore rarely lead to distinct cross-divisional projects. In Grundfos cross-disciplinary learning is systematically dealt with in the matrix-like organizational set-up of the R&D division in which professional and functional boundaries are sought eliminated.

Re. Management control of technology investments. The corporate management control of the divisions in Danfoss primarily focuses on financial performance and this is reflected in the divisional approach to managing innovation and technology, namely a strong concern for relatively short-term commercialization and amortization of R&D investments. This is an effect of the general system of corporate control and not of a specific system for controlling R&D. In other words, economic incentives drive divisions away from explorative, high-risk and long-term orientation in R&D projects towards incremental low-risk projects. In contrast, Grundfos has shown a strong commitment to explorative investments of substantial size in relatively high-risk projects with a long time horizon. These investments are funded by the corporation and not - to the same degree as R&D investments in Danfoss - subject to management control of their commercial pay-off. As a diversified company with strong financial performance incentives, Danfoss has better opportunities for amortizing R&D investments across different product lines and venturing activities than Grundfos where much of the R&D investments have been guided more by managerial judgement of long-term options than by the prospects for short-term commercial pay-off.

This comparative analysis not only shows that the R&D trajectories of the two companies have systematically been moving in opposite directions over the last more than 15 years. The analysis also shows that the primary drivers of the general mode of managing R&D seems to have differed between the two companies. While in the Danfoss case the mode of managing R&D has been subject to strong corporate forces to adapt to and become congruent with the corporate organizational trajectory, the mode of managing R&D in Grundfos has to a larger extent been driven by deliberate or emergent innovation and technology strategies at the corporate level. The case studies also show that the build-up of organizational tensions and incongruities is a constantly ongoing phenomena and that creating coherence vis-à-vis one set of interfaces may give rise to new evolving incongruities and deficiencies vis-à-vis another set of interfaces (Pavitt, 1998).

CONCLUSION

This paper has proposed an analytical framework for understanding what may sometimes seem to be a freefloating or fashion-induced experimental dynamics in the organization of R&D in large industrial corporations. The framework tries to link a structural contingency and coherence argument with an evolutionary trajectory argument.

The contingency argument suggests that different kinds of organizational incongruities constitute critical sources of change in the organization of R&D in large technology-intensive companies. One such organizational incongruity may evolve between the overall changes in the structure and strategy of the company, and the existing mode of managing and organizing R&D. Another type of incongruity relates to internal tensions between emerging new R&D strategies and the existing mode of managing R&D, or between newly changed R&D structures and the existing R&D-strategy. The two case studies show that such a contingency framework can explain individual sequences of decisions of structural changes in the R&D organization. This perspective, however, has a static bias and is not able to explain the dynamic inter-sequential and inter-temporal changes taking place.

The evolutionary argument can provide this dynamic perspective. The notion of firm-specific organizational trajectories suggest that firms, as they mature, develop along paths that are based on imprints from strategies and structures implemented quite early on in the history of the firm. Such trajectories are generally highly difficult to change unless they inherently accumulate organizational incongruities that lead to severe deficiencies (as in the typical change from the U-form to the M-form structure), or they lead to misalignment with industrial and technological dynamics of the external competition (as in the case of IBM's turnaround from the 1980s and into the 1990s).

The two case studies have shown that the overall strategy-structure trajectories of the corporations are important co-determinants of the long-term development of the R&D organization. While Danfoss has undergone the "classical" change from a U-form to an M-form trajectory, Grundfos has not yet experienced a dramatic change in its corporate trajectory. Neither of the two companies have so far experienced changes in the external competitive or technological environment of a scope justifying or enforcing strategic and organizational turnarounds.

Moreover, the studies have shown that we may identify a firm-specific R&D trajectory reflecting the dynamics of the evolving constellations of R&D strategy (possibly differentiated into innovation and technology strategy) and mode of managing and organizing R&D (possibly differentiated into management of innovation and management of technology). In accordance with a ressource-based and evolutionary view companies to a large extent pursue their own routes of development based on their own idiosyncratic learning experiences. This is not to deny the fact that every epoch seems to have its own more generic management fashions (e.g.

in favor of downsizing, outsourcing, decentralizing, etc.) that are sought diffused through especially the large management consulting firms. Finally, the studies have shown that even if there seems to be an inherent tendency to pursue corporate coherence (Christensen, 1998, Christensen and Foss, 1997) between the overall organization and the R&D organization, the dynamics of and interplay between the corporate trajectory and the R&D trajectory constantly creates the basis for new incongruities that require managerial response. Thus, the urge for corporate coherence and organizational clarity simultaneously tends to give rise to structurally defined weaknesses that are often later sought remedied by measures which again increase the organizational complexity. The combined contingency and evolutionary perspective seems to provide a promising analytical framework for dealing with such organizational dynamics in companies showing institutional continuity with respect to corporate identity and ownership.

BIBLIOGRAPHY

Birkinshaw, J. and C.F. Fey, (1999): Organizing for Innovation in Large Firms, *Working Paper*, London Business School.

Boutellier, R., O. Gassmann, and M. von Zedtwitz (2000): *Managing Global Innovation*, Berlin, Springer.

Cantwell, J. and F. Fai (1999): Firms as the source of innovation and growth: the evolution of technological competence, *Journal of Evolutionary Economics*, Vol. 9: 331-366.

Chandler, A.D. (1962), *Strategy and Structure. Chapters in the History of the Industrial Enterprise*, Cambridge MA, The M.I.T. Press.

Chandler, A.D. (1977): *The Visible Hand: The Managerial Revolution in American Business*, Harvard, Cambridge, Belknap.

Chandler, A.D. (1994): The Functions of the HQ Unit in the Multibusiness Firm, In: R.P Rumelt, D.E. Schendel and D.J. Teece (Eds.): *Fundamental Issues in Strategy. A Research Agenda*, Boston, Mass., Harvard Business School Press.

Chesbrough, H. (2002), Assembling the Elephant: A Review of Empirical Studies on the Impacts of Technical Change upon Incumbent Firms, *Comparative Studies of Technological Evolution* Vol. 7: 1-35.

Christensen, Clayton M. (1997): *The Innovator's Dilemma*, Boston, Mass, Harvard Business School Press.

Christensen, J.F. (1998): Management of technology in multiproduct firms, In: R. Coombs et al. (Eds.): *Technological Change and Organization*, Cheltenham, Edward Elgar.

Christensen, J.F. (2002), Corporate strategy and the management of innovation and technology, *Industrial and Corporate Change*, Vol. 11: 263-288.

Christensen, J.F. and N.J. Foss (1997): Dynamic Corporate Coherence and Competence-Based Competition: Theoretical Foundations and Practical Implications, In: A. Heene and R. Sanchez

(Eds.): *Competence-Based Strategic Management*, Chichester and New York: John Wiley and Sons.

Christensen, J. F., M. Overgaard and M. Iversen (2002): *Grundfos – Strategy, Structure and Management of Technology*, Department of Industrial Economics and Strategy, Copenhagen Business School.

Coombs, R. (1996): Core competencies and the strategic management of R&D, *R&D Management*, Vol. 26: 345-355.

Coombs, R. and A. Richards (1993): Strategic Control of Technology in Diversified Companies with Decentralized R&D. *Technology Analysis an Strategic Management*, Vol. 5: 385-396.

Dosi, G. (1982): Technological paradigms and technological trajectories, *Research Policy*, Vol. 11: 147-162.

Floyd, C. (1997): *Managing Technology for Corporate Success*, Aldershot, Gower.

Gerybadze, Alexander and Guido Reger (1999): Globalization of R&D: recent changes in the management of innovation in transnational corporations, *Research Policy*, Vol. 28: 251-274.

Howells, J. (1990): The location and organisation of research and development: New horizons, *Research Policy*, Vol 19: 133-146.

Iansiti, M. (1997): *Technology Integration: Making Critical Choices in a Dynamic World*. Boston MA., Harvard Business School Press.

Iversen, M. and J. F. Christensen (1999), *Danfoss – Corporate Strategy, Economic Organization and Management of Technology*, Department of Industrial Economics and Strategy, Copenhagen Business School.

Kaufman, A., M. Merenda and C. Wood (1996): Corporate Downsizing and the Rise of "Problem-solving Suppliers": the case of Hadco Corporation, *Industrial and Corporate Change*, Vol. 5: 723-760.

Lehrer, M. (2000): The Organizational Choice Between Evolutionary and Revolutionary Capability Regimes: Theory and Evidence from European Air Transport, *Industrial and Corporate Change*, Vol. 9: 489-520.

Levinthal, D. and J. March (1993): The Myopia of Learning, *Strategic Management Journal*, Vol. 14: 95-112.

Lovas, B. and S. Ghoshal (2000): Strategy as Guided Evolution, *Strategic Management Journal*, Vol. 21: 875-896.

Mandel, M.J. (2000): *The Coming Internet Depression*, New York: Basic Books.

Mintzberg and Waters (1985): Of Strategies, Deliberate and Emergent, *Strategic Management Journal*, Vol. 6: 257-272.

National Science Board (1992): *The Competitive Strength of U.S. Industrial Science and Technology: Strategic Issues*. Committee on Industrial Support for R&D.

Nelson, R. and S. Winter (1982): *An Evolutionary Theory of Economic Change*. Cambridge, MA., Belknap Press.

Pavitt, K. (1984): Sectoral patterns of technical change: Towards a taxonomy and a theory, *Research Policy*, Vol 13: 343-373.

Pavitt, K. (1998): Technologies, Products and Organization in the Innovating Firm: What Adam Smith tells us and Joseph Schumpeter Doesn't, *Industrial and Corporate Change*, Vol. 7: 433-449.

Roberts, P.W. and R.Greenwood (1997): Integrating Transaction Cost and Institutional Theories: Toward a Constrained-Efficiency Framework for Understanding Organizational Design Adoption, *Academy of Management Review* Vol. 22: 346-373.

Rubenstein, A. (1989): *Managing technology in the decentralized firm.* New York, Wiley.

Teece, D.J., R. Rumelt, G. Dosi and S. Winter (1994): Understanding Corporate Coherence. Theory and Evidence, *Journal of Economic Behavior and Organization*, Vol. 23: 1-30.

Whittington, R. (1990): The Changing Structures of R&D: From Centralization to Fragmentation, In: R. Loveridge and M. Pitt (Eds.): *The Strategic Management of Technological Innovation,* Chichester UK, John Wiley & Sons.

Williamson, O. E. (1975): Markets and Hierarchies: Analysis and Anti-Trust Implications, New York, The Free Press.

Management of Technology
Copyright © 2003 by Elsevier Science Ltd.
All rights of reproduction in any form reserved.
ISBN: 0-08-044136-X

4

RISK-MANAGEMENT IN INCUBATORS

Karl Ruping, incTANK, Cambridge, MA[*]
Maximilian von Zedtwitz, IMD-International, Lausanne, Switzerland[**]

INTRODUCTION

With the rise and fall of New Economy companies, there has been a sharp increase in the number of incubators followed by a recent correction in the market for this new form of venture capital investment. While in 1980 less than 10 incubators existed world-wide, they numbered over 1,100 by mid-2000 with nearly half located in the United States. In the first half of 2000, six new incubators were established every week (Economist, 2000). The growth was driven by the rapid increase of new ventures and startup companies of all flavors, many of them founded by student entrepreneurs and company defectors.

However, after the crash in the Internet-startup market-the mainstay of new business plans that were attracted to the incubator mode- several incubator IPOs have been cancelled and some of the leaders, such as CMGI and Softbank, were trading at near 10 to 20% of their earlier highs. While incubation may no longer be the 'flavor of the month' among investors, there is still a need for this business facilitation, possibly on a smaller scale and more specific areas of technology than what emerged in the heady days of 1999/2000. Indeed, the chances that a high-tech business idea is formalized into a successful public company are 6 in a million (Nesheim, 2000: 1).

---

[*]   Dr. Karl Ruping is Principle of incTANK, an incubator in Cambridge, Massachusetts, and a Fellow of the Advanced Studies Program at MIT, Cambridge. Email: ruping@mit.edu.
[**] Dr. Max von Zedtwitz is Professor of Technology Management at IMD-International, a business school located in Lausanne, Switzerland. Email: zedtwitz.imd.ch.

This paper looks to the incubator business model in general, not to justify their popularity among investors, but to outline how risk is managed and how other technology facilitation models, such as traditional R&D departments, can benefit from the lessons of incubation. Our research is based on personal experience in incubator management as well as the study of technology incubators in the Boston area and in Switzerland. We consider the various risks involved in incubating fledging technology startups in an environment of uncertain opportunities, changing technologies, and shifting investor interest. The reoccurring and fundamental theme is that incubation risk is bifurcated into one part that can be lessened before engaging into a venture, and a second part that can be managed internally during the period of incubation. While these risks cannot be eliminated completely, there are management strategies that can minimize the overall level of risk across the incubator portfolio and across a strategic distribution of incubation resources.

We begin with a definition of risk, a comparison of the venture supervisor with the R&D project supervisor, and an introduction to the various forms of venture business investment. Section two focuses on the incubator model and the two forms of risk inherent to incubation. Next we discuss the different risk management approaches available across the incubation process. We conclude with a brief comparison of risk strategies between the incubator supervisor and the corporate R&D project advisor.

DEFINITIONS: RISK, TYPES OF VENTURE INVESTORS, AND INCUBATORS

In the context of venture business investment, risk is the finite probability of failure, across a spectrum of possibilities from underperformance to outright bankruptcy, weighted with a factor indicating the significance of the occurring event. A similar definition applies to risk in the context of the traditional corporate R&D department across a spectrum of possibilities from the unsatisfactory pace of development progress to the complete failure to reach a proof of concept.

The venture supervisor is the active investor who, like the traditional R&D project advisor, oversees the performance of the startup team and the development of the new technology. This can be an angel, a professional VC, or a strategic corporate investor. In contrast, the entrepreneur acts like an empowered project manager: both are in charge of developing a business opportunity based on a list of specifications (business plan), a project team (startup team), and a project budget (limited venture capital). Like internal corporate high-risk projects, an entrepreneur faces the pressure to succeed in time and on budget, operates under financial and technological uncertainty, and is subject to the emotional and social stress from employees, corporate peers, and even family members. Differences do exist across this analogy, but these are largely a difference of degree. For example, failure by the project manager may lead to a lost promotion or dismissal, whereas an entrepreneur's failure leads to unemployment as well as financial loss in terms of foregone salary in the form of worthless stock options.

The traditional R&D project and the venture startup both face funding uncertainties. High-risk corporate research projects typically have a singular funding source with a secure short-term and medium-term budgeting, competing for a limited budget with other R&D projects. Projects are terminated for a number of mostly company-internal reasons, such as reprioritization of corporate research objectives. The entrepreneur's funding sources are typically more varied and subject to greater risk. Capital is obtained from an open market where general economic conditions determine capital flows, changing financial market sentiment impacts startup valuations, and the flavor-of-the-week business plan leads investor interest. And this funding is not free. Capital investment buys ownership rights as well as some form of management control by which the capital provider seeks to minimize investment risks.

There are generally four categories of venture investors. First, the *corporate investor* is the mature company seeking investments in startups that have some strategic importance to its industry, market or technology. Generally these funds invest in mezzanine startups or mature companies that have a complete business plan, a defined product, and a secure management team. Among the largest is Intel Capital, which boasts $7.5 billion in valuation across 450 invested companies. A new chip factory costs Intel up to $6 billion, but with the newly intensified competition it is far from certain whether this chip will actually pay back the investment. Hence, Intel may be well advised to invest a few billion dollars on a number of competing startups. Each has a high rate of failure but only one has to succeed to justify Intel's strategy.

Second is the traditional *venture capital fund* that invests across industries, technologies, and markets. Professional VCs select their investment candidates after a rigorous evaluation process that considers growth opportunities, business plans, industry and market factors, as well as the strength of the technology and team. These experienced investors usually secure board positions and certain management participation rights, serving as advisors and mentors to the startup team.

Third, *angel investors* are affluent individuals or industry professionals who provide high-risk capital at the early stage. Typically this investment is not based on exhaustive industry or venture team/technology evaluation; rather, angel investors act on an intuitive understanding of the business opportunity or area of technology; often they are motivated by the achievement of higher goals or a certain self-imposed mission. Similar to angel investors are the Three F's: friends, family, and fools. These emotional participants are available in the establishment stage. While their investment may be high risk and with equity ownership, the Three F's tend to have little involvement or professional role in the business itself (unless they are part of the founding startup team).

A relatively new from of venture support—but at the center of this paper—is *incubation*. A cross between professional angel investors and established VCs, incubators provide high-risk seed money and early stage advice. Their investment decisions are based on a professional due diligence review, but the depth of this review is limited by the early nature of startup team and the uncertain (or yet to be conceived) business plan. Incubators are actively involved in the establishment and initial management of the new company. Indeed, some business plans come from internal brainstorming of the incubator staff. Such is the case of one of the most successful incubators, IdeaLab.

The incubator model is itself in development, with subcategories emerging. A traditional (or "real") incubator offers physical office space along with resident support staff and local professional services. A "virtual incubator" offers no dedicated office, but does provide direct managerial support and seed funding to get the startup up and running. A further appellation is the "accelerator", an incubator that supplements the startup team and brushes up the business plan to a level sufficient to attract a VC or strategic corporate investor.

OPERATION/INTERNAL RISK VS. ENVIRONMENTAL/INCOMING RISK

Identifying the nature of investment risks is the first step in adopting a mitigation strategy for the incubator or the R&D manager. In recent years, risk has been moved from a task delegated to actuarial specialists or lower-level managers to the top of a CEO's agenda. Particularly in competitive industries, risk is not considered a disadvantage but an opportunity to maximize commercial returns under a strategy of dynamic strategic planning (see e.g. de Neufville, 1990). As such, risk has been dissected in multiple ways. Since the main value-added of incubators is their direct involvement in running and leading a venture at the early stage of its development, we choose to distinguish between operational and environmental risk:

1. *Operational or Internal Risk*: Operational risk is internal to the investment promotion process where the choice of activities determines the likelihood of success. In short, these are activities under the investor's control. Operational risk can be managed by the apportionment of resources, quality of management assistance, and distribution of investment funds across the stable of startup clients. Poor technology, incompetent management, and unqualified employees all increase the risk of internal failure of the venture, and ultimately the performance of the investor's portfolio.

2. *Environmental or Incoming Risk*: Environmental risk is risk inherent to early stage investment that is beyond the control of the investor. For example, unforeseeable shifts in an industry, the introduction of superior technology by a competitor, sectoral stock market fluctuations, or natural disasters may negatively affect the viability of a new venture.

Business angels, venture capitalists and incubators are all exposed to these two types of risk. Each category of investor, however, is affected differently by operational and environmental risk:

- Business Angels are exposed to both types of risk without much ability to control the occurrence of detrimental events of either type, or to manage the impact of these events on their risk portfolio;
- Venture Capitalists and Corporate Investors may hedge against environmental risk by building cross-industry or multinational investment portfolios, but remain exposed to internal risk as their influence on day-to-day startup management is limited;
- Incubators are vulnerable to external risk as they must focus on a particular technology or a geographic region, but they attempt to control internal risk by actively participating in the management of the startup.

In this contribution we focus exclusively on real incubators: venture capitalists that provide office space and on-site management support for budding startups. We address two major issues for these incubators:

1. How to lower external or environmental risk.
2. How to manage internal or operational risk.

We expect these findings to be valuable for internal and independent entrepreneurs as well as venture capitalists and other high-risk project supervisors.

HOW TO PROACTIVELY MINIMIZE ENVIRONMENTAL OR EXTERNAL RISK

There are three stakeholder groups in the incubation process: investors of the incubator fund, incubator management, and entrepreneurs being incubated. The investor provides capital resources to the incubator much like in a traditional VC fund. The incubator then invests these funds into a small number of early-stage startup ventures. An incubator also invests resources in the form of managerial support, professional assistance, and suitable office space. The incubator assumes the risk of individual startups, while the investors of the incubator fund are exposed to the pooled risk of these investments. In this respect, incubators act not only as capital brokers but also as risk brokers between startups and senior investors (see Fig. 4.1).

The nature of risk between investor and incubator is different from the risk between incubator and startup. On the one hand, investors seek to keep their risk at a minimum by adopting portfolio-based strategies that determine their capital investments across a menu of incubators, venture capital funds, and other investment vehicles. On the other hand, the startup entrepreneur faces a single risk matrix that cannot be managed over a portfolio strategy. Indeed, incubators attract startups with inexperienced management and immature technology

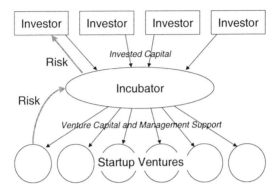

Fig. 4.1. Risk and capital flows: Incubators as risk brokers.

through a crude form of adverse selection. This is because a more experienced or self-dependent startup would not need the incubation support, and would more likely be financed by a pure venture capitalist. Also, dependency on a geographical or industrial area (economic risks) will determine the risk level of the individual startup. In this chapter we focus on the risks of *selecting* new startups and managing those startups once they are funded by the incubator or VC investor.

Entrepreneurship is a business in which risk-taking and failure are two related fundamental elements. A startup may falter due to unpredictable changes in the particular industry, technology or market sector. Operating in an environment of inevitable uncertainty, an incubator cannot completely avoid this environmental risk. The challenge is to minimize environmental risk by engaging in portfolio-based investment strategies. Every startup is associated with a unique risk matrix based on its particular characteristics, such as management team experience, level of technological advancement, and competitive status. When investing in several startups, the joint risk level may be a function of its parts if these risk matrixes are complementary. The incubator can hedge, to a certain extent, against environmental risk by investing in a diversified portfolio of startup clients with differing risk matrixes.

Portfolio diversity for environmental risk can be realized across various startup characteristics. The most significant diversification criteria are:

1. Industry, technology, or market sector;
2. Geographical markets;
3. Development stage of portfolio startups; or
4. Investment size of fund across portfolio startups.

Focus in industry/technology/market sectors

Part of an individual startup's risk is dependent on the particular industry, technology, or product/service market in which it operates. Despite the efforts of the startup team or professional advisors, an early stage investment is exposed to unforeseen technological change or the emergence of new competition in a particular sector. Investors may therefore aim at distributing risk across different, sometimes competing technologies. An example comes from the battle between JVC and Sony over video format. Despite the fundamental strengths of an investment in the technically superior Betamax video format, the success of the competing VHS model rendered a genre of products unprofitable in the early 1980s. VHS won and Betamax lost; JVC reaped substantial revenues and Sony faced a setback in terms of R&D investment as well as—more importantly—time. Within the market for video players, a diverse investment strategy across different technologies would have resulted in a less risky portfolio for the consumer electronics manufacturer.

The venture capital investor enjoys an advantage over the corporate R&D project supervisor in that the high exposure of one technology or market can be partly offset by investing in a different sector through an unrelated company. A weakening in B2B dot-com companies, for example, may be offset by strong interest in biotechnology startups. Extending this further, the rational investor should seek a portfolio across multiple industrial, technological, and market sectors with divergent environmental characteristics and, thus, risk matrixes. The environmental risks of any one startup cannot be eliminated, but the aggregate risks of an investment portfolio can be reduced by strategic diversification.

Despite the benefits of a diversified investment strategy, the incubator has limited flexibility in minimizing its exposure across different sectors. Rather, an incubator's "investment charter" is limited to a particular set of industries, technology areas or markets. This investment charter is generally a contractual limitation on the scope of investment that the incubator management can pursue. Usually there is a range of investments with some logical relationship, such as investments in information technology and Internet e-Commerce. A more tenuous charter would feature disparate technologies such as biotechnology and new media entertainment.

Why do incubators have a defined investment charter that limits their investment strategy? There are two reasons: upward signaling to investors (external limitation), and institutional competence or synergy (internal limitation). Both external and internal limitations are core elements of the incubator's risk management strategy.

To begin with, investors are an external limitation on the scope of an incubator's investment charter. The senior investor is engaged in it's own risk management strategy of ensuring a diversified portfolio across defined sectors. An incubator is just one investment in a portfolio that may include competing VC funds and structured capital investments. To maintain such a portfolio, senior investors prefer to invest in incubators with a clear sector focus.

An internal limitation on portfolio scope is the incubator's area of professional competence. Management skills, professional experience, and networking exposure tend toward one sector a set of related sectors. When departing beyond the incubator's "scope of competence", risk of failure increases. Moreover, internal diversification reduces the potential synergy that may arise from small ventures of similar sectors being incubated under the same roof. Part of why a startup team chooses to approach a particular incubator is the expected synergy generated from cooperating with complementary startups already present in the incubator or more mature companies that have graduated from the incubator.

Portfolio scope results in two conflicting dynamics in terms of environmental risk management: a broad range of investments in diverse sectors vs. a limited range of investments in one's sector of competence. In one respect, risk is reduced with a larger portfolio of investments across sectors with counterbalancing risk matrixes (see Fig. 4.2, lack of diversification). With a given management skill set, however, risk increases as the number of investments extends beyond the sector or sectors in which the incubator is competent to operate (see Fig. 4.2, lack of competence). The horizontal axis lists individual startup investment opportunities classified in sectors and ranked according to competence attractiveness. This is a dynamic list, revised with every new start-up candidate or the adoption of new business sectors. It is a challenging and critically important responsibility of the incubator to prioritize new start-up opportunities based on his objective assessment of several ambivalent factors. Due to the discretization by individual startups, both risk curves will look rugged rather than smooth as depicted. On any single startup increment to an existing portfolio, incubator management seek to balance the benefit of portfolio risk dilution relative to increased risk of investing beyond the scope of competence.

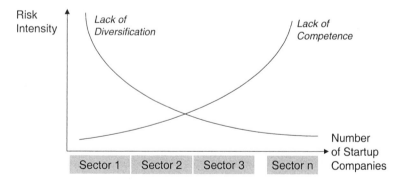

Fig. 4.2. Competence focus versus portfolio diversification

In practice, there is some flexibility in an incubator's focus. Investors may approve the decision of an incubator to accept a particularly attractive venture opportunity even if it lies outside the incubator's original charter. For some larger or more established incubators, a strong track record and the breadth of experience may justify a broader investment scope. Leading incubators and VCs such as CMGI or Softbank enjoy more flexibility in establishing a diversified stable of startups. But even if investors can be convinced of this deviation, the effectiveness of a multi-segmented incubator is not certain.

Focus on Geographical Location

Investment risk has a geographical element beyond the industry, technology, or product/service area in which the startup operates. Fluctuations in regional market demand, changes in local or national politics, and unexpected natural disasters are truly environmental risk factors. The individual startup has limited control over these geographical risks. The incubator's exposure to such risks can be minimized across in a geographically diversified investment portfolio.

In today's global financial market the VC's money is portable, but the incubator's physical plant is not. Immobile office space and other physical assets are at the center of traditional incubation, and are the major attraction for the startup client. Further, professional service networks are often in close proximity to the office: in-house counsel, accountants, human resource consultants, and professional secretaries are not fungible assets that can be easily mobilized beyond commuting distances, much less time zones.

Incubators attract a local population of potential entrepreneurs. The desire of a diverse portfolio and the demands of remaining within one's area of competence must be satisfied within constraints that are far more narrow than that faced by a traditional VC. For an incubator to function efficiently, this local population must supply a sufficient number of technologically sophisticated personnel that need the expertise of experienced incubator managers. Thus this risk element depends on both the supply of business plans and the supply of other incubators.

The importance of geographical limitation is easily overlooked. Particularly in the Internet economy and the biotech sector, startups think and act global from the very beginning. The point here is not the client's access to distant markets, but the incubator's operation in a particular location, and its attractiveness to a local supply of potential startup clients.

Focus on Development Stage

An investment portfolio comprising different stages of corporate maturity is a possible tool to reduce the impact of environmental risk. Venture companies are from across the spectrum of pre-establishment, early stage, mezzanine and mature/pre-IPO. The underlying assumption is that the longer a venture survives and the further along a technology is in development, the lower the risk of failure. A corollary is that the more advanced the company, the closer the produce or service is to market and the sooner the exit opportunity. Simply put, risk decreases with time.

Similarly to R&D budget allocation in large organizations, venture capital funding can be spread across initial, early, mezzanine and mature stages of investment to secure the optimal portfolio. By contrast, the incubators' choice of investment is restricted to pre-establishment and early-stage startups. Why? An incubator attracts inexperienced management teams by the turn-key operations and professional management.

There are advantages to focusing on early stage ventures. The opportunity for the experienced investor/entrepreneur to control the establishment of a new venture, for example, will reduce the likelihood of damaging mistakes made by inexperienced teams acting alone. Further, the return on a successful venture investment is greatest for those who secured an early equity position. Many of these advantages are realized much later, after a startup has 'graduated' from the incubator and a portfolio of mature equity investments has been developed, or at the exit event.

There are competing pressures between investing in mature companies with marketable products or technology and lower risk, and early startups having higher potential rates of return and more opportunity for control but with higher risk in terms of reaching maturity and eventual exit. The incubator's selection is limited to the set of early stage startup clients, a population of venture companies with high potential returns but also the highest rate of attrition.

Investment Volume

A final portfolio strategy is investment volume. Generally, a conservative investor should distribute funds across a large number companies to ensure a market rate of return. Even an aggressive VC investor will want to avoid a portfolio focused a small number of volatile ventures. Similar to projects in pharmaceutical drug development pipelines, the higher the number of individual projects, the lower is the variance of average success of survival, hence the better are the predictions of average return on investment. Here again, the incubator model has limited flexibility in engaging in a well-diversified portfolio strategy.

The pursuit of a high number of individual projects/ventures would be outside the scope and possibility of an incubator. Even most industrial R&D organizations make use of rules-of-thumb when assessing the investment values of current R&D projects.

An incubator does not have the opportunity to distribute risk across a comfortable number of individual clients, as one would advise in an uncertain environment. The incubator's value proposition is providing a fertile environment within which the startup client can develop a business plan, build a functioning team/technology, and secure sufficient VC funding before it becomes independent. These activities require physical resources – in the form of office space and infrastructure. The incubator must find the optimal size given the volume of startup "traffic" and the demands of the particular industry/technology/market genre. Virtual incubators and VC funds do not have this strict physical plant limitation.

The incubator is further limited in engaging in high-volume investing by personnel bandwidth. The greater the volume of investments, the more the incubator operations will be constrained by overhead limitations, management inefficiencies and information costs. This model is not easily scalable. Business plans are drafted, teams supplemented, technology developed, and market strategy researched with the assistance of incubator staff at a critical stage in the startup lifecycle.

In this chapter we have focused on the environmental or external risk of real incubators. We have seen that an incubator is more limited in the choice of startup ventures; at the same time the incubator attracts a different clientele of entrepreneurs. In conclusion, the total incoming risk is on average higher for incubators than for venture capitalists. Incubators accept this disadvantage because unlike more distant capital providers, they can actively lower the attrition of prospective entrepreneurs by becoming involved in managing their startup operations. This is the topic of the next section: internal risk management.

HOW TO MANAGE OPERATIONAL OR INTERNAL RISK

Portfolio techniques cannot eliminate all risks. As we have seen in the previous section, for instance, the incubator has limited flexibility in reducing the environmental risks inherent to technology innovation. In this chapter we focus on how—relative to alternative forms of technology investment—an incubator is more effective and efficient in *managing* operational risks, otherwise known as internal risks.

Incubators actively participate in the conception, inception and internal management of new startups. A "real" incubator provides a physical office and the infrastructure needed to get a startup established and operational in a short period of time. In addition the incubator supplies professional services and human resources that an inexperienced team may not be able to attract or afford. In short, the startup is under the incubator's roof and immersed in the incubator's staff. For this menu of services and the investment in high-risk early startups, the incubator demands an equity premium that a mezzanine or mature team is not willing to pay. It is this community of early startups that incubators attract as clients. It is also the population of venture companies that is the most distant from an inventor's payoff: the exit event.

There are two results of this near-symbiotic relationship between incubator and client: information flow (a prerequisite for risk evaluation) and management control (i.e. risk management). First, the incubator model allows for a direct, daily flow of information between the neophyte startup and the experienced incubator staff. From the incubator manager's perspective, this allows for direct monitoring of the startup's performance and, thus, risk scenario. With incubator staff actively involved in the day-to-day operations, the internal problems of a startup are rapidly brought to the incubator's attention. Issues that may otherwise take a period of time to percolate up to the VC are immediately visible and readily addressed by the incubator. From the perspective of the new entrepreneur, this on-site guidance provides real-time assistance and direct advice. Further, an inexperienced team is exposed to the professional environment of the incubator staff and can also learn from more mature startups associated with the incubator.

Second, the incubator generally enjoys, and exercises, greater managerial control over a startup during its period of incubation. This is defined formally in the incubation contract, and develops further with the close proximity and daily involvement of startup management with incubator staff. This control translates to operational risk management—an incubator's involvement in decision-making matters will ensure that certain growth strategies or corporate policies are firmly in place. This does not ensure success, but it does provide the more experienced incubator manager a direct role in affecting necessary change. And this is not necessarily adverse to the startup. Indeed, an outside investor may feel more comfortable with a startup that has emerged from a competent incubator.

In contrast, the traditional VC monitors an investment externally from the boardroom or through periodic management meetings. Upper-level staffing and professional outsourcing services may be referred by the VC, but even drastic measures to steer a startup back on track are usually motioned through the startup management team. The VC exercises control and engages in communication as does the incubator, but the VC's have a more distant and a narrower per-startup bandwidth. The startup team has a tendency to filter out negative operational news such as internal team conflict, technical glitches, negative market feedback, etc. Thus, the VC faces certain operational risks internal to the investment startup even when playing an active, but still distant, managerial role.

How does operational risk strategy actually function? The role of the incubator manager is critical. This individual is assigned to a particular startup, interfaces with the new team and directs the specific incubation process. Generally he or she mentors the startup management team with strategic advice and personal resources. While staff members and professionals may be assisting the startup, it is ultimately the incubator manager who commissions the human resources. The incubation manager rarely oversees more than two startups at a time, acting like a parent to fledgling children: Protection while they are in their infancy, strict oversight during development, and gradual introduction to the world of business. The faster this process takes place, the better for both parties.

CONCLUSION

Venture business investors face the risk of unproven technology, changing markets, emerging competition, and uncertain funding. In this paper we have looked to the nature of risk management among incubators. While a traditional venture capital fund can diversify relatively effortlessly across sectors, an incubator's investment strategy is restricted in scope by the demands of senior investors, the realities of professional competence, the narrow segment of early stage startup clients, and the support needs of these clients. The fundamental dilemma for the incubator remains the scope of competence versus scope of investment portfolio, i.e. the incubator's investment charter versus the senior investor's own interest in portfolio diversification.

Incubation is an investment niche with a great deal of inherent risks. To minimize exposure, the incubator should differentiate between external and internal risk and adopt the appropriate risk strategies for each. External or environmental risk may be lowered by a diversified portfolio across market sectors, geographical locations, development stages, and investment volume. This form of risk can also be reduced by attracting startups that fit the incubator's internal competence profile. Internal or operational risk depends on the mix of financial and human resources employed across the portfolio companies during the incubation process. With these investment strategies, direct monitoring of early progress, and active management control are interdependent factors that the intermediary risk broker - the incubator – can efficiently manage on behalf of the senior investors.

The incubator and the corporate R&D manager face similar challenges in high-risk projects: they have limited flexibility in reducing environmental risks. They are able, and expected, to reduce residual risk by playing an integral role in the development of a venture or a project. They differ in that the incubator operates under harsh market conditions, competing for capital inflow from various sources and vying for entrepreneurs who have a number of incubation options. The corporate R&D supervisor, on the other hand, is relatively insulated with greater job security, more secure financing, and an established internal labor pool. These characteristics may in part account for the poor reputation corporate R&D labs have for managing high-risk projects.

Corporations can look to incubators as both a model and as a tool. Internal incubators may be a means of stimulating technological innovation, a process that generally occurs outside of the corporate lab. The R&D manager can look outside of the corporation to venture startups as a source of newly emerging technologies. A startup that has been nurtured in an incubator has also been exposed to risk minimization strategies that should appeal to the more conservative corporate partner or suitor. Indeed, corporations have become senior investors in leading technology incubators to both enjoy high investment returns and to secure access to promising new technologies that would not otherwise thrive in their R&D labs.

A new alternative model is to create internal incubators, much like some companies have established internal VC funds. The path to internal incubation, however, may require significant changes in the internal corporate bureaucracy, managerial mindset, and R&D culture that developed over the lifetime of the established corporation. Traditional industrial R&D and new venture incubation are approaches not in conflict but rather in competition. We are confident both will be able to co-exist and benefit from each other.

As the venture investment community continues to evolve in an environment of uncertainty, a new breed of sophisticated incubators will emerge. These successful technology and business facilitators will be successful in their ability to initially select investments such to minimize environmental risks and in their ability to manage their portfolio companies such to minimize operational risks. The result will be a larger probability of success among the incubated venture startups and higher returns for senior investors. It is these incubators that will offer a model both for corporate R&D departments to emulate and for business scholars to study.

BIBLIOGRAPHY

Economist (2000): Hatching a new plan. August 10, 2000.
Nesheim, J. (2000): *High Tech Startup*. New York, The Free Press.
de Neufville, R. (1990): *Applied Systems Analysis*. New York, McGraw-Hill.

Management of Technology
Copyright © 2003 by Elsevier Science Ltd.
ISBN: 0-08-044136-X

5

THE CHINESE MODEL TO CREATE HIGH-TECH START-UPS FROM UNIVERSITIES AND RESEARCH INSTITUTES

Masayuki Kondo, Yokohama National University, Yokohama, Japan[†,*]

ABSTRACT

China vigorously creates a large number of high-tech start-ups from universities and research institutes recently. This strategy is fairly successful especially in software industry. □This success is explained by four kinds of factors: supply factors, driving factors, demand/market factors, and enabling factors.

INTRODUCTION

China is now successfully creating high-tech start-ups from universities and research institutes. These high-tech start-ups are especially visible in Beijing. Although China had not utilized a high science and technology potential well as a planned economy for economic development until recently, the government is now eager to utilize it for economic development by all means. The pendulum swung from one extreme, where science and technology was remote from industry, to another extreme, where commercializing science and technology was flourishing.

[†] This article is based on Kondo (2001a, 2001b).

[*] Dr. Masayuki Kondo is Professor of Technology Management Course at Graduate School of Environment and Information Sciences, Yokohama National University, in Yokohama, Japan. Email: mkondo@ynu.ac.jp.

The aim of this chapter is to analyze the Chinese mechanism to create high-tech start-ups from universities and research institutes successfully and to draw lessons from Chinese experiences for economies in transition and developed countries with a special focus on Japan. The economies in transition possess high potential of science and technology that used to be separated from industry as China does but they are not successful in making use of their potential for economic development. The developed countries are trying to redefine the role of universities in the context of a national innovation system to utilize universities and research institutes for economic development[1].

The analytic framework of this Chapter is similar to the framework of Porter (1990) for national competitive advantage. Supply factors and demand factors are analyzed as Porter analyzes factor conditions and demand conditions. Then, strategies and supports of the government and mother organizations of spin-off companies are analyzed, instead of analyzing firm strategy, structure, and rivalry and related and supporting industries as Porter does.

Based on the framework above, the author conducted interviews with high-tech spin-offs from universities and research institutes as well as the survey of existing literatures[2]. The interviewed spin-offs were those in CAD (computer-aided design) software industry from Tsinghua University, Beijing Aerospace University and the Chinese Academy of Science (CAS) in Beijing in July 2000.

This Chapter first describes the situation of high-tech start-up creation from universities and research institutes in the Beijing Region, where many high-tech start-ups from universities and research institutes are concentrated. It further describes the situations of Tsinghua University, the best science and technology university in China, and some software institutes of the Chinese Academy of Science, the most prestigious research organization in China, in detail. Then, it analyzes the factors that make universities and research institutes and their researchers to create start-ups in China. The analysis deals four factors: supply factors, driving factors, demand/market factors, and enabling factors. Finally, some implications of this Chinese Model for Japan are presented before the conclusion.

FLOURISHING HIGH-TECH START-UPS FROM UNIVERSITIES AND RESEARCH INSTITUTES

In China, many high tech start-ups are found in Beijing where many universities and research institutes are located. This section examines the situation of high-tech start-ups in Beijing,

---

[1]   See Brett *et al.* (1991) for the discussion of university spin-off companies in developed countries and see Etzkowitz *et al.* (2000) for the discussion of the role of universities.

[2]   The author's interviews were conducted with Prof. Kobayashi of Tsukuba University; and useful information was gained from Tohoku Bureau of MITI (1999).

especially in Zhongguancun, and the situations of two representative organizations, Tsinghua University and the Chinese Academy of Science.

Beijing High-Tech Zone

Zhongguancun, which means "Zhongguan Village," in Beijing is famous as a region where high-tech start-ups are clustered and is called the China's Silicon Valley in China (see Hashida, 2000).

This region has only a twenty-year history. The first high-tech private enterprise "Advanced Technology Development Service" was established in this region in 1980 by Dr. Chen Chun-Xian of the Chinese Academy of Science. He decided to establish such a company after he visited Silicon Valley and Route 128 in the United States in 1978 and 1980.

In 1983, the Chinese Academy of Science (CAS) and the local government of this Haidian District established "Science and Technology Development Center" to commercialize the research results of CAS. Facilitated by this organization, high-tech start-ups were established. The number of start-ups increased to 8 in 1983, 40 in 1984 and 148 in 1987. In 1988, the Beijing Municipal government officially designated a 100 square kilometer region including Zhongguancun as an official Beijing High-Tech Zone by law. After 1988, this Zone developed smoothly (Figure 5.1). It housed nearly 6,000 enterprises in 1998. While many of them had some relations with universities or research institutes, it was estimated around 1,000 enterprises were university spin-offs.

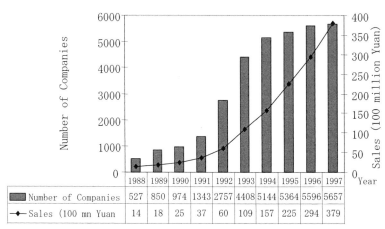

	1988	1989	1990	1991	1992	1993	1994	1995	1996	1997
Number of Companies	527	850	974	1343	2757	4408	5144	5364	5596	5657
Sales (100 mn Yuan)	14	18	25	37	60	109	157	225	294	379

Source: Tohoku Bureau of MITI, Report on the Promotion of Technology Transfer from Universities in Tohoku Region (in Japanese), March 1999.

Fig. 5.1. Development of Beijing High-Tech Zone.

This Beijing High-Tech Zone possesses a high research potential and service facilities. The Zone contains 73 universities, 232 research institutes and more than 378,000 science and technology researchers[3]. The Zone also has various kinds of service facilities for start-ups. Many incubation centers have been established. Further, custom offices, tax offices, bank branches, law firms, accounting firms and consulting firms have been established to assist start-ups. In November 1997, the management committee of the region was established to improve the business environment by introducing public investment. The roads were still under construction in July 2000.

Tsinghua University

Tsinghua University is the best university in China in the field of science and technology, from which also Prime Minister Zhu Ronji graduated. It possesses 3,600 faculty members and 17,000 students[4]. It participates in national high-tech projects, such as 863 Program and Torch Program, and receives the largest amount of R&D budget as a university. It received 350 million Yuan in 1997.

The university was the R&D base in the fields of nuclear energy, microelectronics and high-speed information network. Tsinghua University has been active in transferring technology to industry. It established "Science and Technology Development Department" as an internal Technology Licensing Organization (TLO) in 1991. This TLO has the staff of 39 employees, of which 6 employees hold doctoral degrees. The majority of the staff, 25 employees, were recruited from outside. This TLO established "Science and Technology Network" covering 96 domestic and overseas companies to promote cooperation with the industry. The university also established 39 research centers together with local governments and enterprises.

Regarding spin-off companies, the university established the first company to produce software for export in the 1980s. In 1995, it established Tsinghua University Enterprise Group as a holding company and accelerated the activity of spinning off companies. The profit of the Group increased rapidly since then (Figure 5.2). The Group has the whole shares of 18 companies and major shares of other 18 companies. The spin-off companies are located on campus or in Tsinghua Science Park built by the university. In the early days, all staff of spin-off companies were recruited from the university; these days 10 percent of the staff are still recruited from the university but 90 percent are recruited from outside.

In addition to the own venture capital, the university has established the cooperative relations with several provincial governments and a Hong Kong company to provide capital to

---

[3]   This data is supplied by Dr. Su Jing of National Institute of Science and Technology Policy (NISTEP).
[4]   The same as above.

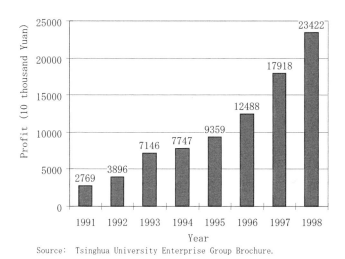

Source: Tsinghua University Enterprise Group Brochure.

Fig. 5.2. Profit of Tsinghua University Enterprise Group.

start-ups. Other than the university headquarter, individual departments also spin off companies by themselves or cooperating with the headquarter.

The reasons to spin off companies are as follows:

1. to commercialize advanced university research results that are not commercialized by domestic enterprises,
2. to make profits to finance university research and employees' welfare, and
3. to provide internship opportunities to students.

The accumulated impact of university spin-offs is enormous[5]. Regarding income from university technologies, spinning off companies is better than licensing according to Bray et al. (2000).

Chinese Academy of Science

The Chinese Academy of Science (CAS) is a prestigious research organization commonly seen in a planned economy. It has 123 research institutes, 13 branch institutes and 3 universities. The number of staff amounts to more than 60,000, of which 16,000 are advanced science and technology personnel.

The Academy created a TLO named "Department of High-Tech Promotion and Enterprises" to transfer technology to the industry. This Department, together with the local government, established "Science and Technology Development Center" to commercialize the research results of CAS as mentioned in the section of Beijing High-Tech Zone. It also established a venture capital named "China Science and Technology Promotion and Economic Investment Company." This Company invests 10 percent of its fund as seed capital, 20 to 30 percent as start-up capital and the rest as growth capital.

The reasons to spin off companies are as follows.

1. It is difficult to find partners to commercialize research results. Large enterprises are too busy to restructure themselves; and Town and Village Enterprises (TVEs) do not have technological capabilities.
2. The research results of CAS are not ready for immediate commercialization.
3. CAS needs to acquire funds.

In addition, CAS restructuring policy is a strong driving force to spin off companies. CAS is trying to decrease the size of its organization to a half. CAS has a staff reduction policy as follows:

1. to make one third of researchers engage in advanced research,
2. to make another third to start up companies, and
3. to make the rest to find jobs in the market.

In the case of Institute of Computing Technology (ICT) that has about 1,000 researchers, 60 researchers were selected as pure researchers in 1998. Later, 30 researchers were added. Around 200 researchers chose early retirement and another 100 went to Legend Group, the largest spin-off company from CAS. The rest are engaged in starting up companies.

Legend Group. Though CAS span off more than 900 companies, Legend Group is the most successful one. Its history went back to 1984. CAS-ICT New Technology Development Company was created by 11 CAS researchers with the investment from CAS. The purpose was to commercialize CAS research results and to finance CAS. This was the beginning of Legend Group. In 1985, the first product, a Chinese character card, went to market.

The Group grew smoothly as a personal computer (PC) maker since 1990 when it developed the first Chinese 486-type PC. It sold 1,470 thousand PCs in 1999 and held the largest PC share, 21 percent, in China (see Nikkei Newspaper, 2000). The success is due to a) low price, b) pre-installed Chinese character software and c) good customer support service with 2,000 repair stations.

The Group still has a strong tie with CAS. It donated a research institute to China Science and Technology University managed by CAS to reeducate its staff and to recruit new staff. CAS keeps 65 percent share of the Group.

---

[5]   In the case of Massachusetts Institute of Technology, see Bank Boston (1997).

FACTORS TO CREATE HIGH-TECH START-UPS FROM UNIVERSITIES AND RESEARCH INSTITUTES

This section analyses the success factors in China to spin off high-tech start-ups from universities and research institutes. The analysis finds four kinds of factors: supply factors, driving factors, demand/market factors, and enabling factors (Figure 5.3).

Supply Factors

Regarding high-tech start-ups, universities and research institutes are the only supply sources of high-tech in China except from overseas. As commonly seen in a planned economy, Chinese large enterprises used to be basically production units[6]. They do not possess high-tech research units, such as central corporate laboratories, though they possess development and design units. Small-and-medium-size enterprises, such as TVEs, are not able to conduct high-tech research.

This source of high-tech is not small. In China, there are 130 thousand scientists and engineers in universities and 157 thousand of them in research institutes (Table 5.1). Moreover, there are nearly 70,000 graduate students (Table 5.2).

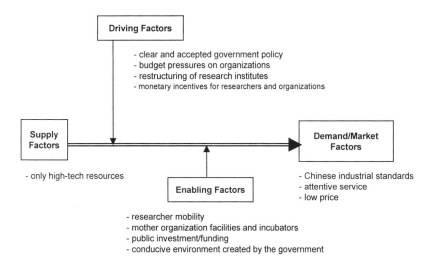

Fig. 5.3. Chinese Model to Create High-Tech Start-ups from Universities and Research Institutes.

---

[6]   See Kondo (1997a) for the separation of research function and production function in China.

Table 5.1. R&D Personnel in 1994 (unit: thousand persons).

	Universities	Research Institutes
R&D Personnel	139.1	207.9
Scientists and Engineers	129.9	156.8

Source: Ministry of Science and Technology, China Science and Technology Statistics 1995.

For commercialization, it is difficult for universities and research institutes to find partners. Large enterprises are busy restructuring themselves to survive; and small enterprises, such as TVEs, do not possess technological potentials to jointly commercialize the research results of universities and research institutes.

Table 5.2. Graduate students in 1994.

	Total	Natural Science	Engineering
Master Course	56,627	15,393	41,234
Doctoral Course	12,487	4,332	8,155

Source: National Research Center for S&T for Development, Ministry of Science and Technology.

Driving Factors

The application of research results for economic development became a national policy since 1985 in China. In 1985 "the Decision of the Central Committee of the Communist Party on Science and Technology System Reform" was made. Its concept was that science and technology was one of production powers. Since then, various policy measures were taken.

The Chinese government, on one hand, took severe measures to compel universities and research institutes to find revenue sources other than the government. These measures were:

1. abolishing equal government funding to any university or research institute,
2. obliging universities and research institutes to make research results public and commercialize them, and
3. restructuring universities and research institutes and their employees.

Since each university or research institute itself is a small society to provide education, medical services and so on, it must be financially solid and has to find new revenue sources. To acquire outside funding, technology trade became very active as pointed out by Kondo (1997b).

The restructuring of research institutes is fairly drastic. All 242 research institutes under the 10 state bureaus administered by the State Economics and Trade Commission were corporatized. Other research institutes under the central government and local governments are to be corporatized with some exceptions. These research institutes will be companies themselves or to become a part of a large enterprise.

As for CAS, it will reduce the number of research institutes by half. As described in the section of Chinese Academy of Science, CAS will cut its staff size to one third and is making one third of its staff to start up companies with the assistance of CAS. Thus, many companies are being founded by the CAS staff now.

The government, on the other hand, provides a favorable environment for universities and research institutes to spin off companies. "Decision on Accelerating Science and Technology Made by the Central Committee of the Communist Party and the State Council" in 1995 encourages universities and research institutes to spin off companies[7]. In the same year, the government bestowed independent legal status on national universities (see Endo, 2000). The government admits a great flexibility to use public property to create and foster high-tech start-ups and has increased individual incentives for professors and researchers to do business. The government also provides various tax incentives for high-tech start-ups.

The incentives for individual researcher have been enhanced. The Decision made by the Ministry of Science and Technology, the Ministry of Finance and the other three Ministries in March 1993 states that applied technology should be valued more than 20 percent of an initial capital when a company is established using technology developed by a university or a research institute and that more than half of that technology value belongs to a chief researcher of the technology. Furthermore, Law to Promote Commercialization of Science and Technology Results enforced in 1996 states that 20 percent of profits of a technology-based start-ups from a university or a research institute should be paid to the researcher or researchers that have developed its technology.

Demand/Market Factors

In the Chinese market, there are no existing domestic competitors for high-tech products. However, competitors come from overseas. Some factors in the market are found to provide competitive advantages to Chinese spin-off companies from universities and research institutes, especially in CAD software market.

---

[7]   The encouragement from top is important. See Chrisman (1995) in the case of University of Calgary.

Chinese CAD software market requires customization including Chinese characters. Moreover, China has a well-established national system of industrial standards which used tobe compulsory. Customized CAD software to comply with this national standards system is much more appropriate to use to design mechanical systems than internationally-used general-purpose CAD software, because components easily available in China are based on the Chinese industrial standards.

Among others, it is fortunate that Chinese large-scale customers, state-owned enterprises, exist in key industries and infrastructure industries. Chinese CAD software companies are in a better position to provide attentive services because they know various internal behaviors of these customers. It is also convenient for customers that service engineers of the Chinese CAD software companies are stationed in nearby places.

Price is also an important factor. In addition to the price of CAD software itself, Chinese enterprises prefer smaller software to be installed in a low-price PC with a usual display to international general-purpose large software that requires an expensive workstation with a graphic display. They do not prefer complicated software that requires an expensive workstation with a large graphic display yet. Since Chinese CAD software start-ups know minimum functions required by Chinese customers, they can develop small software to eliminate unessential functions that general purpose software has and can provide smaller and cheaper software catered for Chinese customers.

Enabling Factors

This section analyzes factors to enable universities and research institutes to spin off companies in three aspects: a) human resources, b) facilities and c) funding.

For human resources, high-tech companies can hire high-tech engineers easily despite the low people mobility policy. In general, it is extremely hard to change the place where one lives in China. However, high-tech engineers can get the permit to reside in a new place in a few months and can officially change the place of registration in three years.

Moreover, the spin-off companies from universities and research institutes have a close contact with their former institutions and their researchers supervise graduate students in many cases. Thus, these companies have opportunities to select and hire qualified students. For the founders of spin-off companies from universities, they can keep their positions in their universities. Surely, their salaries decrease according to the decrease of their working load at their universities.

For facilities, a spin-off company can rent a space in the buildings of its mother organization. It can use equipment and software of its mother organization free of charge provided that 50 percent or more of its share is held by the mother organization. A spin-off company can also stay in a university related research park or a high-tech zone. There exist about 40 university-related research parks and 53 national high-tech zones[8]. In high-tech zones, there are about 100 incubators, which are called "New and High-Tech Innovation Centers," to assist start-ups.

For funding, universities and research institutes themselves have some funds to invest in their spin-off companies, as seen in the cases of Tsinghua University and CAS. Local governments and state owned enterprises as well as foreign companies also invest in spin-off companies from universities and research institutes.

The government also provides R&D grants to develop high-tech products and to commercialize those products. Many of spin-off companies receive R&D grants before or after they are founded from 863 Program or Torch Program that aims at developing high-tech and high-tech products. These research grants support spin-off companies to keep operation.

In addition, preferential value-added tax rates for software and integrated circuit products are helpful for start-ups producing these products (see Shang, 2000). A usual value-added tax rate of 17 percent is reduced to 3 percent for software and 6 percent for integrated circuit products.

Other than the three aspects discussed above, the central and local governments, universities and research institutes are making all-out efforts in spinning off companies from universities and research institutes to create high-tech companies as a national goal, as stated in the mission of Torch Program[9]. In a region where supporting infrastructure for start-ups is not well developed, high-level of supports are needed[10].

IMPLICATIONS FOR JAPAN

The Japanese government announced a plan in 2001 to create 1,000 university spin-off companies in three years from FY 2002[11]. The government intends to mobilize science and technology potential of universities to revive the Japanese economy.

For high tech start-ups from public research institutes, the Japanese government already gave an independent status to former national research institutes in 2001 and bestowed some autonomy on them. The government encourages those institutes to transfer technologies to industry. Some of them have started creating spin-off companies.

Regarding supply factors, Japan has a large number of researchers. In the university departments, there are 123 thousand regular researchers and 45 thousand doctoral course students in 2000. These numbers are comparable to those of China. In public research institutes

---

[8]   See Shang (2000) for the Chinese regional science and technology policy.

[9]   According to Steffensen *et al.* (1999), an important factor in the success of a spin-off company is the degree of support from its parent organization.

[10] Roberts *et al.* (1996) at the same time point out the importance of high selectivity.

[11] See Kondo (2001c) for the situation of university spin-off companies in Japan.

in the fields of natural science and engineering, there are 29 thousand regular researchers. This is number is small compared to that of China.

Regarding driving and enabling factors, Japan could learn some lessons from the experiences of China in creating university spin-off companies. First, government policy to make use of science and technology potential of universities and research institutes for economic development is clear and well accepted in China. In Japan, government policy on this issue is becoming clear but it is not necessarily accepted by all parties concerned yet. Some programs to develop positive attitudes towards start-ups from public research organizations and to create national role models are desired in Japan.

Second, the government puts pressures, such as budget cut and staff reduction, on universities and research institutes in China. In Japan, science and technology budget is increased to strengthen science and technology potential. Portfolio management among pure basic research and fundamental but industry-oriented R&D is needed to allocate science and technology budget. At the same time, some considerations are required on how to provide research grants to encourage industry-related R&D. Creating start-ups could be conditions for a certain R&D grant.

Third, a large incentive is given to mother organizations and researchers when a spin-off company is established regarding equity structure in China. In Japan, an attractive incentive scheme is needed for both management of mother organizations and researchers. For example, when technology is transferred to a start-up company, it should be possible for a mother public organization to receive some portion of the equity of that company instead of initial royalty payment in cash.

Forth, researcher mobility is enhanced in China. In Japan, some measures, such as fixed-term employment without renewal for young researchers and a national portable pension system, might be needed to attract young researchers to new start-up companies in addition to incentives such as stock option.

Fifth, various forms of assistance to start-ups are provided by mother organizations and both central and local governments in a flexible way in China. In Japan, such kind of assistance need to be provided in a speedy manner without cumbersome procedures and thick documents. A policy should be evaluated by outputs and outcomes not by inputs and procedures.

CONCLUSION

China is fairly successful in creating high-tech companies from universities and research institutes as well as from other sources. Though China has little entrepreneur education at universities and few private venture capital firms, the strong determination, all-out efforts and flexible arrangement of the government make high-tech start-ups flourish in China.

This fact in China provides rather optimistic views about high-tech start-ups from universities and research institutes in Japan and economies in transition. Japan could create high-tech start-ups from universities and research institutes with proper driving and enabling forces since it possesses high-tech researchers at universities and research institutes and has favorable conditions for start-ups, such as the existence of venture capitals and university-level entrepreneur education. Economies in transition also have the potential to create spin-off companies from universities and research institutes since they have qualified researchers at universities and research institutes.

REFERENCES

Bank Boston (1997). *MIT: The Impact of Innovation.*

Bray, M. J., and J. N. Lee (2000). University revenues from technology transfer: Licensing fees vs. equity positions, *Journal of Business Venturing* **15**, 385-392.

Brett, A. M., D. V. Gibson and R. W. Smilor (eds.) (1991). *University Spin-off Companies*, Rowman & Littlefield Publishers, USA.

Chrisman, J. J., T. Hynes and S. Fraser (1995). Faculty entrepreneurship and economic development: the case of the university of Calgary, *Journal of Business Venturing* **10**, 267-281.

Endo, H. (2000). *World Strategy of China's Education Revolution* (in Japanese), Koyu Shuppan, Tokyo.

Etzkowitz, H., A. Webster, C. Gebhardt and B. R. C. Tera (2000). The future of university and the university of the future: evolution of ivory tower to entrepreneurial paradigm, *Research Policy* **29**, 313-330.

Hashida, T. (2000). *Silicon Valley in Beijing* (in Japanese), Hakuto-Shobo, Tokyo, Japan.

Kondo, M. (1997a). Technology Strategy In A Transitional Economy --The Case Of China's Machine Tool Industry--, *Development Engineering*, **3**, 81-96, Tokyo.

Kondo, M. (1997b). China: Technology Policy in a Transitional Economy – Engineering Research Centers to Bridge Research Units and Enterprises –, *J of Science Policy and Research Management,* **12**, No.3/4, 169-192, Tokyo.

Kondo, M. (2001a). Chinese Model to Create High-Tech Start-Ups from Universities and Research Institutes, *Proceedings of IAMOT 2001, The Tenth International Conference on Management of Technology*, Lausanne, March 19-22, 2001.

Kondo, M. (2001b). China's Mechanism to Create University Spin-off Venture Businesses (in Japanese), *Development Engineering* **7**, 17-26.

Kondo, M. (2001c). National systems to create university spin-off venture businesses in Japan and Germany. In: Dundar F. Kocaoglu and Timothy R. Anderson (Editors): *Technology Management in the Knowledge Era*, pp.463-467, PICMET, Portland, USA.

NIKKEI Newspaper (2000). Legend Group: A Rapid Growth to be an IT Company (in Japanese), August 28, 2000.

Porter, M. E. (1990). *The competitive advantage of nations,* The Free Press, New York.

Roberts, E. B., and D. E. Malone (1996). Policies and structures for spinning off new companies from research and development organizations, *R&D Management* **26**, 1, 17-48.

Shang, Y. (2000). Regional Innovation System and Science & Technology Development in China, *Proceedings of RESTPOL2000*, Kashikojima, Japan, September 5-7, 2000.

Steffensen, M., E. M. Rogers and K. Speakman (1999). Spin-offs from research centers at a research university, *Journal of Business Venturing* **15**, 93-111.

Tohoku Bureau of MITI (1999). *Report on the Promotion of Technology Transfer from Universities in Tohoku Region* (in Japanese), March 1999.

Management of Technology
Copyright © 2003 by Elsevier Science Ltd.
All rights of reproduction in any form reserved.
ISBN: 0-08-044136-X

6

INNOVATION MANAGEMENT UNDER UNCERTAINTY: A SYSTEM DYNAMICS MODEL OF R&D INVESTMENTS IN BIOTECHNOLOGY[#]

L. Martin Cloutier, University of Quebec, Montreal, Canada[*]
Michael D. Boehlje, Purdue University, West Lafayette, Indiana, USA[**]

INTRODUCTION

Whether in agriculture, pharmaceutical, or manufacturing industries, biotechnology-related firms are engaged in a wide range of research, development, regulatory approval, manufacturing, and commercialization activities in support of new product innovation. Maier (1998) has described the diffusion of innovation as a complex system of reinforcing and balancing feedback loops with significant time delays and timing decisions. The sequence of activities from the R&D to commercialization also involves technology choices subject to substantial uncertainty. For example, one of the decision problems for a genetics company developing new kinds of seeds is R&D investment allocation between (1) a biotechnology-based event research program, and (2) the natural breeding research program. With the advent of gene marker technology that will enhance the speed and precision of natural breeding undertakings, more complex decision situations will arise in the future. For example, decisions

---

[#] This article was previously published in Systems Perspectives on Resources, Capabilities, and Management Processes (J. Morecroft, R. Sanchez and A. Heene, ed.), pp.57-68. Pergamon, Oxford.

[*] L. Martin Cloutier, Ph.D. is a professor in the Department of Management and Technology at the University of Quebec at Montreal. Email: cloutier.martin@uqam.ca.

[**] Michael D. Boehlje, Ph.D. is a professor of Agribusiness Management in the Department of Agricultural Economics, Center for Agricultural Business, at Purdue University. Email: boehlje@agecon.purdue.edu.

could involve understanding contemporaneous complementary, synergetic, investment trade-offs over time between and within platforms.

The essential problem for any firm investing in R&D and new technology is whether streams of expected profits earned through innovation will create sufficient economic value to justify investments that must be made not just in R&D, but also throughout the value chain. The specific objectives of this chapter are to present a conceptual framework illustrating the decision problem in developing, for example, new corn genetics from R&D investment to commercialization, and to use a system dynamics model to explore decision trade-offs regarding alternative investment decisions and the patterns of value capture, taking into account time delays.

RELEVANT LITERATURE AND CONCEPTS

Economic research into innovation in the agricultural sector has resulted in explanations of the aggregate rates of return on investment (Huffman 1998), highlighted the economic incentives for various types of technological change (Biswanger 1974; Hayami and Ruttan 1985), and clarified the structural implications of various types of technology transfer and R&D investments (Sunding and Zilberman 2000). Other researchers (particularly sociologists) have looked at the innovation adoption process and the characteristics of various adopters of new innovations (Rogers 1957). Thus far, however, studies have not focused on the management issues and decision problems involved in choosing a technology or technology platform and the commercialization of the results of the R&D activity.

Barney and Lee (1998) have argued that economic uncertainty breeds tensions between the transactions cost concepts of minimizing opportunism and the strategic options concepts of maximizing flexibility. These tensions are further exacerbated by the need for firms to establish coordination mechanisms that secure property rights from endogenous learning activities. It has been posited by Sanchez (1995: 138) that "the concept of strategic flexibility (that is, strategic options) in product competition represents a fundamental approach to the management of uncertainty." The term strategic options refers to a firm's ability to alter decisions about resource access as well as interfirm relationships over time to achieve economic returns in dynamic product competition.

At the foundation of the systems approach are positive feedback (represented by a reinforcing loop) and negative feedback (represented by a balancing loop). Positive feedback creates a reinforcing behavior and the negative feedback stirs the system towards an equilibrium position. The identification of positive and negative feedback structures in economic and management systems are key to modeling and gaining insight into accelerating speed, the development of new innovation, and the emergence of standards (Shapiro and Varian 1999; Steman 2000). From a management of technology perspective, Sanchez has suggested that the dynamic product competition problem can be conceptualized using the reinforcing loop among technologies, product strategies, interfirm coordination mechanisms, and the business environment (see Figure 6.1). In biotechnology, the reinforcing loop could be substituted by a balancing loop if any of the changes identified in the reinforcing loop of Figure 6.1 were to oppose one of the changes at a given point in time. For example, changes in conducts and competitive environments could oppose changes in technology. This is represented by the minus sign in the feedback loop in Figure 6.1.The impact of this would be to slow down or impair the potential adoption of a biotechnology innovation. However, the long time delays between the many strategic decisions that drive the positive feedback loop of Figure 6.1 forward require empirical inquiry and modeling to better understand how both economic uncertainty and time delays may affect strategic decisions. In this discussion, we provide a systems model for such an exploration.

A DECISION MODEL

The R&D choice between natural breeding programs or biotechnology as a technology platform for bringing new crops to market (or the optimal portfolio of these two platforms) can be best framed as a dynamic multi-stage decision problem. We represent this problem as an investment decision in which the economic payoff of investing in a technology platform is the result of 1) the market penetration as measured by acres of a particular variety of crop grown from the new seed to be developed, and 2) the margin on sales after all production costs (that

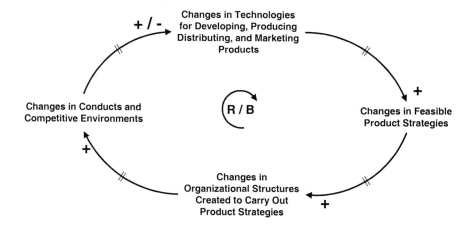

Fig. 6.1. Systemic relationships and positive feedback among technologies, product strategies, organization structures, and competitive environments (adapted from Sanchez 1995).

is, the net revenue that can be allocated as a return to the R&D investment). Both market penetration and margins follow time paths that depend on market acceptance and competition, as we detail later. The decision criteria used in making the technology platform choice is to choose the most valuable real option—the natural breeding technology platform or the gene-splicing biotech platform (or some combination or mixed strategy)—expected to result from sequential R&D investments.

Figure 6.2 provides an overview of the key components/stages and drivers of our decision problem. This conceptualization identifies three key stages in the decision problem: R&D, multiplication (technology transfer) and ramp-up, and market introduction and commercialization. R&D involves the identification and development of seeds that includes a

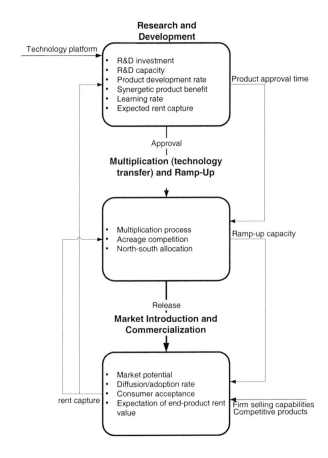

Fig. 6.2. The process of transforming technology from R&D to Commercialization.

trait or attribute "event" such as yield, drought resistance, pest resistance, protein content, etc. This stage also involves obtaining whatever regulatory approvals are necessary to proceed to the next stage of multiplication and ramp-up.

In the multiplication and ramp-up stage, the volume of product obtained from the R&D stage is expanded and multiplied to obtain sufficient volume for commercial sales. In natural breeding programs, the biological growth process imposes on the ramp-up stage both time delays and uncertainties resulting from the natural laws of biology. With genetic modification technology, opportunities for gene-splicing may alter these time delays and reduce the uncertainty of growth processes. Once ramp-up provides adequate volumes for commercial sales, the new product is released to the third stage of market introduction and commercialization.

In the commercialization stage, the new variety is made available to the marketing/sales force, and it is adopted by producers depending upon a number of factors, including availability of competitive products and producers' expectations of the net benefits of the new seed's attributes or variety.

Each stage in this process can be impacted by various drivers or influences that affect the rate of development, as well as the cost and effectiveness of performing other functions or activities at each stage. In the R&D stage, a major determinant of performance will be the technology platform selected for development. Natural breeding programs have fairly well understood cost, efficiency, and effectiveness parameters, as well as typical rates of improvement in identifying and isolating specific traits or attributes. Biotechnology platforms generally complement this advancement, but frequently do so only at a higher cost. The R&D in biotechnology depends on the success in generating an "event" (for example, insect or herbicide resistance, or some nutritional characteristic) and in successfully inserting this event into a plant species. Expected benefit streams combined with the availability of R&D funding will also impact the rate of investment in R&D activities. Finally, any regulatory requirements and the speed with which any regulatory approvals can be obtained are usually major determinants of R&D activity. In general, regulatory processes will be much more significant in driving R&D when using a biotechnology platform compared to a natural breeding program.

Although the multiplication and ramp-up stage can be much more complicated than that depicted in Figure 6.2, the two major drivers of the speed, effectiveness, and efficiency of this stage are the multiplication process and the capacity to multiply. The multiplication process is the biological and/or biotechnology determined procedure for taking germplasm from the R&D stage and increasing the volume to a level adequate for market introduction. This process is driven by the biological growth process of plants in the case of natural breeding programs, but with the biotechnology platform, it is accelerated through gene splicing and other technologies. The second determinant, capacity to multiply, depends on two major decisions: 1) how much acreage is available for seed stock production, given development of competitive products that also are demanding multiplication and ramp-up acreage, and 2) whether the seed stock production activity will take place only in the northern hemisphere, only in the southern hemisphere, or in both hemispheres (which would double or even triple annual multiplication and ramp-up capacity).

Once a product is released to the marketing and sales organization for introduction and commercialization, its acceptance by producers will depend significantly on their understanding of customers' (or end-users') net benefit expectations. The behavior of technology adoption is typically represented using an adoption/diffusion pattern summarized by a cumulative logistics (or S-shaped) growth curve (see for exemple Day and Schoemaker 2000; Sterman 2000). But the shape and characteristics of adoption will also depend on the performance of competitive products; if an effective competitor has been introduced into the market, the level and rate of adoption can be substantially reduced. Furthermore, the capability and capacity of the marketing program and the sales force will impact the purchasing behavior of producers and their level and rate of adoption of the new product. Adoption levels and rates and commercialization may also be a function of consumer (or end-user) acceptance of the biotechnological platform and its transgenic products. And equally important is the concept of value decay for products that have enhanced attributes, such as increased protein content. If producers think that this enhanced value will be retained over a number of years, then more producers may be willing to adopt seeds based on a new technology. If the value is expected to decay rapidly because of commoditization, substitution, mitigation or downstream buyers, than the adoption level and rate will be lower.

A DYNAMIC MODEL REPRESENTATION

We now examine dynamic product competition in the agricultural biotechnology market using a dynamic systems simulation model. System dynamics modeling and simulation can be used in scenario analysis to understand the influence of uncertainty and time delays in the sequential decisions of firms developing new seed products and technology in general (Coyle 1998; Morecroft and Sterman 1994). The simulation results explore and contrast the consequences of adopting seeds developed using natural breeding methods versus the ones complemented by a biotechnology event. The simulation explores the impacts of time delays, and differences in adoption, diffusion, and producer acceptance related to both technologies. The natural breeding technology has a longer time-to-market than the biotechnology method. Producer acceptance, however, is represented as having a higher degree of uncertainty for biotechnology-based products. In reality, a mixed strategy scenario combining the natural breeding and biotechnology platform is not likely to create the most value. By simulating alternative illustrative scenarios, the model helps to develop a deeper understanding of the underlying economic dynamics and the impacts of timing of decisions on economic value creation and decay.

The influence diagram of Figure 6.3 elaborates the innovation process summarized in

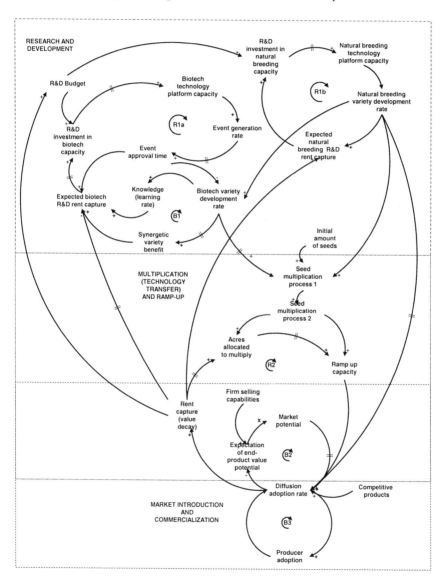

Fig. 6.3. Influence diagram: From R&D to Commercialization.

Figure 6.1 and captures the dynamics of the three innovation process stages depicted in Figure 6.2. The influence diagram is a means to represent the process "microstructure" underlying the dynamic and nonlinear "macrobehavior" of the system of interacting processes – processes that might be carried out by one firm, or in separate firms coordinated by different governance structure including joint ventures, strategic alliances, etc. The three stages of Figure 6.2 are depicted within the dotted-line boxes in Figure 6.3 and include the main reinforcing and balancing feedback loops within the innovation process.

The R&D stage includes two reinforcing loops (R1a,b) and one balancing loop (B1). The reinforcing loops (R1a) and (R1b) illustrate the R&D capacity expansion trade-offs between the natural breeding and biotechnology platforms. The development of the biotechnology platform emphasizes investment in R&D infrastructure toward generating a particular "event". This biotechnology event could eventually be commercialized in the seed of any compatible naturally bred crop species. Investments in the biotechnology R&D platform can be commercialized across many crops, while the natural breeding program emphasizes the incremental selection of traits within a crop species. Thus, the nature of these R&D investments programs has the interesting characteristic of being complementary in output, while inducing competition for budget and land inputs over time. Seeds are complex inputs into production agriculture and include a large number of characteristics sought by producers. Thus, genetics companies while pursuing the biotechnology R&D event research program must maintain the natural breeding technology platforms across a number of crops.

Note that there is a key time delay between the expected capture of profits and any increase in R&D capacity through making investments in R&D capacity.[1] The overall R&D capacity is also constrained by the trade-offs between the technology platforms. The R&D capacity in the natural breeding and biotechnology programs influences the respective discovery/invention rate and ultimately influences expected R&D rents. Added R&D capacity translates into increased discovery/invention rates for both platforms. The balancing loop (B1) shows the effect of the event approval time delays on synergetic benefits of the natural breeding and biotechnology platforms that moderates the potential for rapidly expanding profits through R&D exploitation.

The success in inserting the R&D biotechnology event within the seed of a crop influences the dynamics within the multiplication and ramp-up stage. For both platforms, there is a parallel two stage seed multiplication and ramp-up process. The objective of the first seed multiplication process is to secure enough seeds to reach to the seed production stage. This depends on the initial quantity of seeds available. The genetics company must then, in a second stage, combine acreage allocation decisions with the number of seeds available. An acreage allocation decision must be made between growing seeds that contain the biotechnology event

---

[1] In a fully developed system dynamics model, time delays would be quantified explicitly.

and the ones that are identical in all respects but for the event. The reinforcing loop (R2) shows the acres allocated to planting with the seed that may contain the biotechnology event which influences the ramp-up capacity, which in turn then influences the adoption/diffusion rate. Finally, the adoption/diffusion rate influences profits captured and acres allocated.

The market introduction and commercialization stage is premised on the behavior of a cumulative logistics (or S-shaped) growth curve (see Figure 6.4). This stage contains two balancing feedback loops (B2 and B3) and one reinforcing loop (R3) within its own internal microstructure. The latter also influences the behavior of the multiplication and ramp-up and the R&D stages. The balancing feedback loop (B2) shows the microstructure of the diffusion/adoption process. Expectations of end-product value, influenced by sales force capabilities and the new product adoption rate by producers, influences the size of the potential market. The market potential influences the diffusion/adoption rate, with a time delay. As the diffusion/adoption rate increases, the adoption process eventually slows down because the market potential is being fully addressed. The diffusion/adoption rate is reflected in the growing number of product users, hence in market acceptance (also with a time delay), as seen in the balancing loop (B3). The diagram also includes the influence of exogenous competitive products that limit the rate of diffusion/adoption. Finally, the rate of adoption influences the profits captured, and profit capture increases R&D investments (with a time delay). The profits obtained are part of the feedback loop that influences R&D budget, the future allocation of that budget, and further allocations between the biotechnology and the natural breeding programs (R3).

ILLUSTRATIVE RESULTS

We next present the results of simulations of a numerical simplification of the influence diagram presented in Figure 6.3. The results illustrate the market introduction and commercialization stage of the technology transformation process introduced in Figures 6.2 and 6.3, as well as the most critical influences from the R&D and multiplication and ramp-up stages. These results suggest the importance of the dynamic and non-linear behavior of the underlying microstructure of the model.

Three simulations presented below illustrate some of the adoption tradeoffs between a natural breeding program and a biotechnology event-based program. The first results are presented in Figure 6.4 and are based on the assumption that the limit of adoption of products based on natural breeding or that include a biotechnology event will be identical. The evident difference between the two technology platform choices is the greater profit that results from the biotechnology-based platform and the resulting larger number of producers and higher rate of adoption.

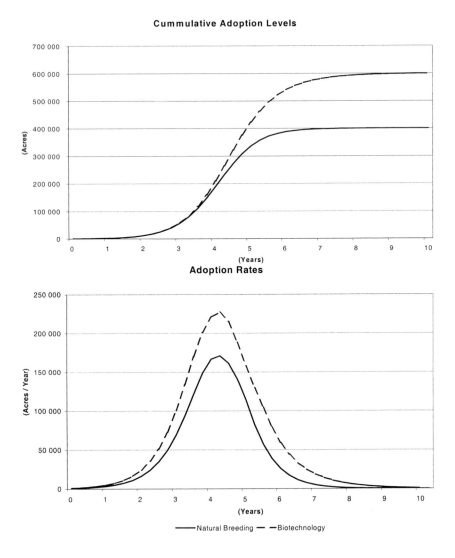

Fig. 6.4. Assumes same adoption time delay but longer value decay for biotechnology than for natural breeding.

The next results, shown in Figure 6.5, show what would happen if the expected profits were the same for both natural breeding and biotechnology products, but adding the condition that the adoption time delay of biotechnology-based product was slower. In that case, the model shows that the product based on natural breeding achieves a higher adoption level.

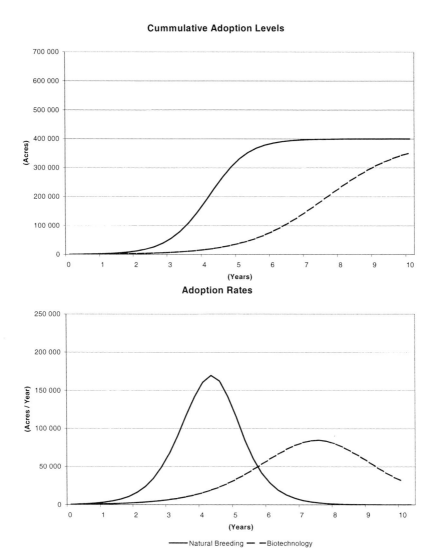

Fig. 6.5. Assumes faster adoption for natural breeding than biotechnology, and same time delay for value decay.

The third simulation results, shown in Figure 6.6, show what happens when products of natural breeding methods are assumed to have a speedier time of adoption than biotechnology-based products, and when the products of the biotechnology platform are assumed to have a greater profit potential because the platform can support further improvements over a longer period or can be distributed over a large number of plant species. These results show that the path of adoption is actually slower at first for the seed that contains the biotechnology event, but eventually the biotechnology-based product creates a larger market in spite of its initial slower adoption rate.

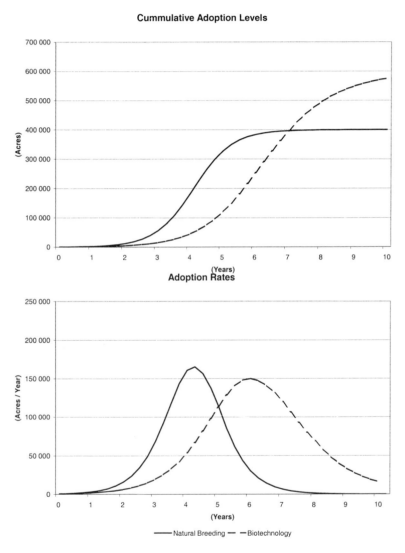

Fig. 6.6. Assumes faster adoption and value decay for natural breeding than for biotechnology breeding.

CONCLUSION

We have illustrated the application of system dynamics modeling in the investigation of technology adoption and diffusion processes in genetic improvement using biotechnology and natural breeding platforms. The results presented here establish the importance of time delays and feedback loop interactions (reinforcing and balancing) in building up R&D capacity, market acceptance, and profit streams. Developing insights into the impacts of various time delays is essential to improving our understanding of the dynamic and non-linear behavior of such systems. Systems modeling could also facilitate the analysis of a portfolio that would combine the synergetic components of natural breeding and biotechnology platforms. The introduction of the gene marker technology in interaction with the biotechnology platform would be an example where the use of a system dynamics model would inform the joint interaction of these two platforms over time. The results presented in this discussion suggest how systems modeling can be employed by decision-makers to achieve greater understanding of such issues before committing large amounts of resources.

LITERATURE CITED

Barney, J. B. and W. Lee (1998). "Governance under uncertainty: Transactions costs, real options, learning, and property rights," Reference No. 124140, Fisher College of Business, Ohio State University.

Binswanger, H.P. (1974). "A microeconomic approach to induced innovation," Economic Journal, 84, pp. 940-958.

Coyle, G. (1998). "The practice of system dynamics: milestones, lessons and ideas from 30 years of experience," System Dynamics Review, 14, pp. 343-365.

Day, G.S. and P.J.H. Schoemaker (2000). "A different game," in Schoemaker, P.J.H., Day, G.S., P.J.H. Schoemaker and R.E.Gunther (eds.) Wharton on Managing Emerging Technologies. Wiley & Sons, pp. 1-23.

Hayami, Y. and V. M. Ruttan (1985). Agricultural Development: An International Perspective. Baltimore, MD: Johns Hopkins University Press.

Huffman, W. E. (1998). "Finance, organization and impacts of U.S. agricultural research: Future prospects," paper prepared for conference Knowledge Generation and Transfer: Implications for Agriculture in the 21st Century, University of California, Berkeley, June 18-19, 1998.

Maier, F.H. (1998). "New product diffusion models in innovation management – A system dynamics perspective," System Dynamics Review, 14, pp. 285-308.

Morecroft, J.D.W. and J.D. Sterman (eds.) (1994). Modeling for Learning Organizations. Portland, OR: Productivity Press.

Rogers, E. (1957). Diffusion of Innovations, Iowa State Agricultural Experiment Station, Special Report no. 18. Ames, IA: Iowa State University.

Sanchez, R. (1995). "Strategic flexibility in product competition," Strategic Management Journal, 16, pp.135-159.

Shapiro, C. and H.R. Varian (1999). Information Rules: A Strategic Guide to the Network Economy. Boston, MA: Harvard Business School Press.

Sterman, J.D. (2000). Business Dynamics: Systems Thinking and Modeling for a Complex World. Boston, MA: Irwin-McGraw-Hill.

Sunding, D. and D. Zilberman (2000). "The agricultural innovation process: Research and technology adoption in a changing agricultural sector," Handbook of Agricultural Economics.

Management of Technology
Copyright © 2003 by Elsevier Science Ltd.
ISBN: 0-08-044136-X

7

THE ROLE OF THE SMALL DEDICATED FIRMS IN THE STARTING PHASE OF THE BIOTECHNOGENETIC REVOLUTION

Nicola Dellepiane, Politecnico di Torino, Torino, Italy [*]

ABSTRACT

This paper presents an analysis of the public and private industrial strategies that had great influence in shaping the scenarios in the start-up phases of the two main technological revolutions of the second half of the last century (the first electronic revolution started in the late 40s and the biotechnogenetic revolution started in the 70s). The paper analyses in particular the role of small dedicated firms and highlights the main differences between their strategic positions, in the start-up phases of the two revolutions. With reference to the still in progress start-up phase of the biotechnogenetic revolution, the paper discusses how certain changes in public strategies and policies could bring about a more rapid and fruitful increase of the speed of this phase. This could take place mainly as the result of securing peer competitive conditions between large companies and small dedicated companies, operating the former in part and the latter in full in this area. A thorough understanding of the scenarios, in which the biotechnogenetic revolution is developing and of the dynamics of the interactions between non-peer competing players in this arena, should be gained by dedicated entrepreneurs who intend to enter it successfully. This can contribute to orientating the small fully dedicated entrants in better shaping their own strategies and to sharpening their decision-making methodologies.

[*]   Prof. Dr. Nicola Dellepiane, Professor of Economics and Management of Industrial Enterprises, Corso Duca degli Abruzzi 24, Polytechnic School of Engineering University of Turin, Italy. Tel.: 0039 011 5647228.

INTRODUCTION

When techno-scientific breakthroughs take place (such as the first electronic revolution started in the late 40s), public strategies and policies shape the scenario within which large companies and small specialized newcomers will work out their own industrial strategies of participation in the competition for exploiting the fruits of such breakthroughs. All together these strategies will have a fundamental impact on the rate of progress of the industrial applications of such breakthroughs. (Rosenberg, 1985; Landau and Rosenberg, 1986).

This paper analyses the main issues that shaped the formulation of the public and private industrial strategies in the start-up phases of the two main revolutions of the second half of the last century (the first electronic revolution started in the late 40s and the biotechnogenetic revolution started in the 70s). Their comparison shows basic differences, but also the potential of appropriately utilizing certain similarities. With reference to the still in progress start-up phase of the biotechnogenetic revolution, certain changes in public strategies and policies could bring about a more rapid and fruitful increase of the speed of this phase and also contribute to maintaining the US leadership position. This could take place mainly by making possible peer competitive conditions between large companies and small dedicated companies operating the former in part and the latter in full in this area. Gaining a deeper insight, into the potentials and the obstacles present in the industrial applications of the biotechnogenetic revolution, should contribute to orientating, especially the small dedicated entrants who want to play a winning role in it, in better shaping company strategy in this risky scenario and also contribute to sharpening decision-making methodologies.

THE START-UP PHASE OF THE ELECTRONIC REVOLUTION

The electronic revolution (Weiner, 1973; Linville and Hogan, 1977), whose industrial effects have been gigantic, started in 1947 with the invention of semiconductor devices at Bell Labs a part of the American Telephone and Telegraph.

The transistor substituted the vacuum tube for amplification of electric currents, with the advantage of smaller size, greater reliability, generation of less heat and lower costs. The integrated circuit was developed in the early 60s. It is a single component (chip) that performs functions that had previously required groups of components wired together. By the end of the 60s, medium-scale integration had been achieved. Large-scale integration was achieved in the mid-70s, a time when the start-up phase of the electronic revolution can be considered completed. Such a revolution has been continuing with very large-scale integration and is being continued with the progressive trend towards nanoelectronics.

Market pull for an alternative to the vacuum tube triggered the electronic revolution and the consequent birth of the semiconductor industry (Nelson, 1982) that was able to meet the needs of military and aerospace, which urgently required smaller and more reliable devices generating less heat. The parallel relevance of the transistor to computer and commercial applications emerged spontaneously.

The key invention that started the electronic revolution, the transistor, arose from fundamental R and D in an industrial laboratory (Bell Labs) which was an arm of a major corporation, ATT, that also would be a significant user of the new technology.

Public strategy that speeded up the electronic revolution

The accelerated development of the start-up phase of the electronic revolution was the result of the strong technological starting base outlined above as well as of the very skilful role of the US Government and of the contribution of the small dedicated electronic firms.

The basic strategic move, that triggered the speedy and successful development of the electronic revolution, was the consent decree (U.S. vs. Western Electric Company, 1956 Trade Case), which ended an antitrust suit against ATT. The decree required ATT to license its patents to US firms without royalty and to establish moderate rates for licences under future patents. ATT was restricted to its existing markets of telecommunications, government defense and aerospace and prohibited from entering into highly lucrative markets such as commercial electronic computers. However, semiconductor R and D in the telecommunication, military and aerospace markets was not separable from R and D applicable to areas such as commercial computers from which ATT was prohibited. So Bell Labs continued to be the main national laboratory for semiconductor R and D and to diffuse without discrimination the results of their research. The consent decree rules also encouraged personnel mobility from Bell Labs and Western Electric (ATT's manufacturing arm) to new employment in firms exploiting the results of Bell's research, without fear of legal suits for theft of trade secrets. This caused an impressive free transfer of know-how.

The potential strength of this scenario was enhanced by a well finalized use of Federal funds made available from the US Government, its Department of Defense (DoD) and the National Aeronautics and Space Administration (NASA), all craving for the miniaturization and reliability that the electronic revolution could make available. Market pull was therefore a fundamental characteristic of this scenario.

The provision of Federal funding to many research laboratories, besides Bell, also had a leveraging effect on the private funding of R and D. Federal funding was also addressed to demonstration projects using semiconductor technology such as, for example, the building of a small digital computer at Texas Instruments (Asher and Strom, 1977) and to the development of semiconductor production capability of large corporations such as General Electric, RCA and Raytheon. These companies were thereby helped to speed up the obsolescence of the vacuum tube technology in which they had very large investments (Linville and Hogan, 1977). On the other hand, substantial Federal funds were also given for R and D, and in the form of well-secured contracts, to those newly born, small dedicated firms that could show how quickly they were able to respond to requirements for miniaturization and reliability.

The role of small dedicated start-up companies

The major contributions, of small dedicated start-up firms, to the development of the electronic revolution in the US, were to diffuse semiconductor technology and to stimulate competition. Diffusion of semiconductor technology occurred because the small firms exploited new markets. They quickly and successfully took new technology from the laboratory and adapted it for large-scale production (Tilton, 1971). The small firms also stimulated competition. They acted as flexible and independent sources of advanced semiconductor technology and introduced a dynamic component into the industry. They were a potential danger for the large companies pre-existing the electronic revolution and still heavily relying on vacuum-tube technology. Not only were these companies forced to speed up their entry into semiconductor technology, but they were competitively stimulated in the R and D area, in production techniques and in promptness and flexibility to satisfy a demand which was largely programmed by government needs and was financially well supported by contracts.

Many of the new small firms were formed to market definite products and, because of the availability of well-finalized Federal contracts, an entrepreneur needed relatively little capital to enter the market and its risk was modest.

One can then state that all the most relevant factors that could accelerate the implementation of the electronic revolution were synergically combined. This brought about an unequalled success. Wide and relatively secure industrial spaces for a large number of companies of different sizes and missions were made available. Competition became more a stimulant of the progress of this whole industrial area than a cutthroat struggle to prevail over others. This type of struggle may become a negative factor especially if those which prevail can do so because they operate in power positions which have scanty interest in the rapid economic exploitation of technological breakthroughs.

The electronic revolution developed quickly and profitably for all the actors, because an industrial environment was created where competitors had real peer opportunities (consent decree and its consequences) and the Government acted as a stimulator and risk reducer for all who could meet criteria of efficiency and reliability. Outstanding results were achieved. They took place first in the US domestic market; whereas internationalization took place later on, as an offshoot of the US start-up phase.

THE START-UP PHASE OF THE BIOTECHNOGENETIC REVOLUTION

The start-up phase of the biotechnogenetic revolution has been science-pushed (U.S.Congress, O.T.A., 1984). Basic biomedical research in the American universities, supported by Federal funds, has produced results which have opened the way to a wide set of potentially highly innovative industrial applications in pharmaceuticals, diagnostics, animal and plant agriculture, specialty chemicals, commodity chemicals, food additives and substitutes and environmental control.

The two basic technologies with which the biotechnogenetic revolution started were the recombinant and monoclonal antibodies (MABs). Then, other technologies have been and are being developed: variant approaches to MABs, more sophisticated recombinant technologies and technologies connected with the manufacturing of oligonucleotides, oligopeptides and oligosaccharides. More recently the genetic technologies, named genomics, pharmacogenomics, proteomics, glycomics, gene shuffling and others have been emerging. The technologies of small-molecule mimetic compounds, on the other hand, are emerging as non-biotech, with a highly competitive capacity vis a vis those of biotech. One can also remark that the market potential of such successive waves of breakthroughs is only partially exploited before other waves come onto the scene. In addition there has been a progressive involvement, in the biotech area, of micromechanics, microelectronics, micromechatronics and other advanced technologies to be used as an increasingly necessary support in designing and manufacturing biotechnogenetic products.

Market needs, for biotechnogenetic products that more effectively substitute existing non-biotech ones or for products that cater for unfilled needs, are wide. But much wider is and will be the kaleidoscope of biogenetic technologies, because of their derivation from the complexities of the mechanisms of nature.

Financial hurdles

The biotech revolution is inevitably developing on too many technologies chasing a much lower and limited number of applications through competing technological pathways, often aiming at the same or similar results. Too many technologies are therefore chasing too few financial resources. Important strategic issues arise from this technological-financial characteristic of the biotech revolution.

Many small dedicated biotech firms (SDBFs) were set up, starting in the mid 70s, mainly by university professors, to try to commercially exploit research results for which they had obtained some form of property rights and protection (Kenney, 1986). These firms were very weak financially (Borgman, 1983), since initially they could only count on the financial resources conferred by the founders and by speculative venture capital.

Small dedicated electronic firms were set up to produce and market definite products, very often under Federal contract, and this required relatively little capital to enter the market. Small dedicated biotech firms have been and are started, without any form of public support, as research laboratories, with the objective of determining how to make products often completely new and of uncertain market potential. This implies uncertainty about success in product and process development and uncertainty as to the marketability and end-uses of the products. In fact both the technological pathways to make biotech products and the potential uses of such products are often manifold and sometimes hardly foreseeable. Complex, high-risk decisions result with the need for much higher amounts of financial resources.

Venture capital has often supplemented the modest financial resources initially brought in by the researchers-starters. Venture capital funds and private venture investors, having no obligation or constraint to stay in a venture, often tended and tend to cash in, by means of an initial public offering (IPO), the high profits deriving from their early entry. Lack of stability in the sources of financing results; this particularly affects risky entrepreneurial initiatives in forefront technologies. In fact, these initiatives need long times to reach their goals and are craving for stability to maintain control over their own endeavours. That is probably the reason why Alex Zaffaroni, also known as the Jim Clark in biotech, has often stated: "Avoid venture capitalists if you can" (Forbes, May 2000). If small biotech start-ups are not protected from impatient venture capitalists, they will be battered by unforgiving stock markets (The Economist, June 1999), and, let me add, by overwhelmingly powerful large corporations.

Venture capital, as is usually practiced, is too shaky a financial support for small biotech ventures. It has certainly given an important push to the start-up phase of the biotech revolution. Its prevalent effect, though, has been to promote proliferation of start-ups, leveraging on the proliferation of biogenetic technologies, rather than their growth as independent companies, from R and D to production and market. With its speculative ins and outs, venture capital may compel small dedicated biotech companies to resort, often untimely and with poor success, to stock offerings and to begging funds from large corporations. SDBFs can obtain funds from large corporations, interested in having a bridgehead in the biotech area, by selling them equity of the company, by setting up joint ventures with them and by selling or licensing research results to them. However, it is important to remark that in the US a particular source of venture capital is available which, if its original rules were restored, could have favourable effects on both strategies of biotech start-ups and progress of the biotech revolution. It is the limited partnership (LP).

Limited partnership: a powerful propeller that was very unwisely choked

Limited partnerships are a source of venture capital (Michaud, 1982; U.S. Congress O.T.A., 1984, 1990; Meeks, 1986; Merrifield, 1986) that can remarkably help to uncouple the financial needs, for single R and D projects and possibly for the commercial exploitation of their results, from the utilization of the company's financial resources, thereby avoiding negative effects on its financial structure. As a consequence, LPs greatly reduce the need for the small company to resort to the wavering stock markets and to large corporations, which are in a position to get the giant's share from relationships with small start-ups. Each LP is established to carry out a well-defined project with well-defined objectives. The company runs the partnership as principal partner. The limited partners bring capital, but have no authority on how to run the partnership. They have to stay in the partnership till the project is over (either successful or not) or be replaced by other limited partners who accept the same commitment. The limited partners have the great advantage of deducting, from their usually very high personal income, the heavy losses which the LP always incurs in the development of the project. Furthermore, limited partners can deduct from their taxable income, immediately after the LP is formed, as much as 85 to 95 percent of their initial investment. They also have the fiscal advantage of having any income from sales of the results of the project treated at the reduced rate of capital gains (U.S. Congress, O.T.A., 1984).

The operational mechanism of the LP is the following. The LP orders the company to carry out the research and development project and sometimes industrial production and commercialization and pays the company for this task. So, the company can avoid procuring financial resources for the project in ways that can negatively affect its financial structure and its future prospects (for example issuing debt or selling stocks or part of its technology to large corporations). In fact, the cost of the project becomes a revenue for the company. The company may even show a profit, as long as the LP goes on, even if it still has no product to sell, or no other type of revenue. The company can also take advantage of an income statement in the black to collect other financial resources at favourable conditions. The other great operational advantage of LPs is that the small firm can decide whether and when to use financial resources to buy the results of the partnership's work, or let the partnership sell them to third parties, knowing fairly well what it buys or allows to be sold (U.S. Congress, O.T.A., 1984; Chemical and Engineering News, 1986).

Unfortunately the main rules, that were making LPs such a favourable financial tool for the small dedicated biotech firms, were cancelled in 1986. A form of partnership, the stock warrant off-balance sheet R and D financing (SWORD), remains available, but its rules restrict the interest of potential partners to partnerships set up with the larger and more successful biotech firms.

All this caused a progressively considerable drop in the use of LPs.

While DoD and NASA, in the start-up phase of the electronic revolution, generously funded industry to produce the products needed in military and aerospace applications, no particular public financial support was made available to sustain the start-up of the biotech revolution, except for the favourable rules governing LPs. Their repeal has increased the financing problems of the SDBFs. So, SDBFs had and have to get by with speculative venture capital, stock offerings and funds obtained from large corporations, which require very difficult strategic decisions.

Stock offerings and funds obtained from large corporations pose important strategic problems to biotech start-ups

Initial public offerings of SDBFs, before the stock market crash of October 1987, were successful on average (sometimes exceedingly so, like that of Genentech), because the public had not yet realized that the fruits of R and D might be more distant than anticipated. Second and third round offerings were, in general, implemented with less successful results.

This pattern seems to have been repeated, on average, during the 90s for IPOs and successive offerings of the newly formed start-ups created to exploit progressively advanced technological patterns.

Venture capital would often take the opportunity of the initial public stock offering, or sometimes of a subsequent offering, to release equity and make high and quick profit. When the IPO is not due to the decision of a dominating presence of venture capital eager to cash big surpluses as soon as this is feasible, deciding whether to launch an IPO has been a crux for many small biotech companies. In fact it implies the company finding itself in a rough ocean where the satisfactory continuation of this form of financing is subject either to producing earnings (an event almost unlikely in the 80s and still infrequent for start-ups with a few years of life) or attaining at least potentially fruitful intermediate results in the company R and D program.

As to the financial resources that SDBFs have obtained from large corporations ("collaborative ventures"), a minor part has come from their acquiring participation in the equity of SDBFs, a sort of "corporate venturing". Resorting to this form of financing increases the risk of the small company being taken over by a large one. The largest part of financial resources has come and is still coming from research, development and licensing contracts and sometimes also from manufacturing and marketing contracts with large corporations interested in exploring the biotech area. Small firms often find it difficult to obtain contract clauses which protect them adequately. How to deter opportunism within a relational biotech contract has been discussed in the literature (Deeds and Hill, 1998). The case of the Searle (then Monsanto)-Genex dispute, with its really disastrous consequences for Genex, is emblematic. In general, contracts have been tightly written, making it difficult for small biotech firms to pursue and develop other research findings which might occur in the course of the contracted work.

The R and D contracts cause the small firm to receive fees, in proportion of the progress results delivered. The licensing contracts cause the firm to receive royalties if and when the large corporation decides to bring or succeeds in bringing to the market the objects of the licensing deal. The ifs and whens of this process are regulated by the strategy of the large corporation, which definitely aims at controlling the speed of development of the biotech revolution.

For example, large corporations producing vaccines, with conventional approaches, are trying to gain control of potentially competing new vaccine technologies not yet operational, developed by small start-ups, through licences or stake in the equity of the small start-ups that are developing them. Another example is that of recombinant insulin for which Eli Lilly acquired the licence from Genentech in order to modulate the presence on the market of its animal insulin. In another case, when the biogenetic technology for recombinant hemoglobin, which was being developed by small start-up Somatogen, was believed, by large corporation Baxter, to be a threat to its more conventional product derived from human blood, Baxter acquired Somatogen at $9 per share. This happened in a moment when Somatogen's stock price was low compared to the $18 of its IPO. The statements of Baxter about the utilization of Somatogen's technology do not seem to indicate a quick commitment to bring to the market products based on Somatogen's technology. They only indicate the intention to 'capitalize' on it to develop next-generation products. In other cases drug design technologies are at stake. For example, the large corporation Glaxo is investing internally in the non-biotech approach of small-molecule mimetic drug design. At the same time, it is trying to maintain control of Maxygen, one of Zaffaroni's biotech start-ups. Maxygen is experimenting advanced technologies of gene shuffling to design drugs, a pathway entirely different from small-molecule (Genetic Engineering, January 2000).

Small firms have also to take into account that contract revenues are likely to decrease as a source of financing. In fact there is a strong economic incentive for large companies to bring the development work in house, especially when it approaches its final stages.

Large companies have suffered no disadvantages in these contracts with small biotech firms except a possible loss of the money paid to the small firms, should they not bring to a successful end their research. As the only potential buyers of innovative technologies and owners of sufficient financial resources to commercialize them, large companies are exerting a great deal of control over the rate at which the start-up phase of the biotech revolution evolves. They are in a position to condition the existence and development of many financially weak, small firms operating in the biotech area.

The strategic decision, of which know-how and technology to make available, in exchange for financial resources, to large corporations, has been crucial for the survival and eventual development of small firms. This decision is to be taken in a way not to dangerously curtail proprietary know-how and at the same time provide the financial resources, to be added to those obtained from stock offerings, sufficient to fuel proprietary projects and at the very least secure independent survival. The evaluation of the "give and take" of these contracts is becoming progressively more difficult as the start-up phase of the biotech revolution progresses. In fact, the number of new technological pathways, beyond the initial technologies of monoclonal antibodies and recombinant DNA, has been increasing very much.

The relative low margins from licensing technology are to be compared with the potential contribution that this transfer of technology can give to the progressive strengthening of the competitive advantage of large corporations. This strengthening, in the long run, would dramatically act against an independent growth of small firms.

A difficult decision for the small firm is the relative contribution, of stock issues and of sales of know-how and technology, to collecting financial resources. This decision has to be matched with the selection of the scientific-technological areas in which the firm would operate and of the projects to be developed in these areas. The requirements of financial resources are quite different according to the type of technology and its industrial applications (Borgman, 1983).

The scenario emerging from the decision gamble in the biotech arena

The positive contribution given by American SDBFs to the start up phase of the biotechnogenetic revolution is certain. Had the research on, and the utilization of, biogenetic technologies been entirely left to large corporations operating in the areas where such technologies have potential applications, the rate of progress of the start-up phase would have been slower. In fact, the techno-scientific achievements of SDBFs, often only provisional and prospective, stimulated the attention of potential large users of such technologies and caused them to devote financial resources to the biotech area.

However, the small firms were and are not yet in a position to have a wide choice in deciding which of their scientific know-how to sell to large corporations, in exchange for financial resources to feed the proprietary part of their techno-scientific endeavours. Having given away usually the most near-term promising part of their know-how, SDBFs have often been forced to more advanced technological frontiers and to perpetuate their role of providers of advanced learning curves.

The fact that SDBFs are pushed to progressively advanced technological frontiers tends to consolidate their role in stimulating the progress of the biotech revolution, but also the fact that the actual rhythm of its implementation will remain governed by large corporations.

Examining the technological and financial decisions of small biotech firms, one can observe that, in most cases, they were such as not to lead these firms to bring successfully and independently to the market important new products as final results of their techno-scientific endeavours. The majority of the SDBFs have been confined to research laboratories (or boutiques as it is often said) that sell or license the results of their research as they approach commercial exploitation and that are pushed to explore more advanced frontiers of biotechnogenetics. Hence, they have often acted as cavies to explore the potential of such frontiers, while nearer-term results and their fruitful applications have been progressively exploited mainly by large corporations interested in exploring the biotech area. These are not only American, but also large European and Japanese companies motivated by the need to get the new technologies from the most qualified suppliers. On the other hand, US small biotech firms have been particularly incentivated to set up licensing contracts with foreign companies, because these companies often allow them to keep market rights for the US (which is often not the case when dealing with large American corporations) and sometimes even to share some market rights in foreign countries. All together these are better conditions than those that could be obtained from large American corporations. This fact accentuated the international characteristics of the start-up of the biotech revolution, as opposed to the start-up of the electronic revolution which remained for a while within the US, also because the small firms were not pushed to sell technology abroad to collect financial resources for survival. From the standpoint of the US competitive position in biotechnology, however, this transfer of technology out of the country has contributed to strengthening potential competition from large non-American companies.

The interactions between SDBFs and large corporations have certainly provided a push to the start-up phase of the biotech revolution in the US, which were able to quickly gain a leading position.

This, however, is often an overemphasized point, which only evidences a (supposed) synergic, complementary nature of these two types of actors. Indeed, in certain cases there are synergies, but frequently there are also compulsory one-way symbioses, from the small to the large, to ensure oxygen to the small as long as the large think that this is profitable for them.

The big competitive game to share, in the long-run, economic fruits of the biotech revolution has been played, from the beginning of the start-up phase, with a progressive advantage of large corporations, American but also European and Japanese. These corporations are progressively becoming the masters of the rate of development of the biotech revolution and also its prime beneficiaries. Often they become the arbiters of the survival of many small biotech firms and of the technological patterns these firms pursue. In fact, the content of the research contracts with large corporations and of licences to them may be easily imposed on small biotech firms, which need financial resources in order to carry on an independent activity capable of securing at least company survival and possibly a sort of autonomous development. Being so constrained regarding the part of their present R and D they can retain to develop for themselves, small firms may be pushed to explore more advanced new technological pathways, thereby increasing their risk profile.

Very few of the early start-ups, among which Amgen and Genzyme, have managed to select and implement the right combination of financial, technological and product choices that have allowed them to grow so successfully as to bring some of their own more remunerative products to the final market. They have been able to internally generate financial resources which, together with carefully selected contributions from contracting and licensing, have boosted their stock value and avoided them becoming the object of takeovers.

One can find in many sources, including company prospectuses, letters to shareholders in annual reports and interviews with CEOs, that the original intent of many of the early SDBFs was to grow as "integrated firms" from R and D to production and market, though in limited segments and niches. Indeed these companies are the best suited to do so, because of their full involvement in this novel techno-scientific area as their unique mission. Supposed better capabilities of large corporations do not seem justified as the reason why SDBFs leave to large corporations approval procedures and manufacturing and marketing of biotech products. This happens because small start-ups are not financially strong enough to further develop and exploit their great potential capabilities in these areas. They are indeed progressively constrained to resort either to forms of financing such as selling know-how to large corporations, which works against their unique mission, or to successive stock offerings that often do not give an adequate contribution.

A 1990 survey (Ernst and Young, 1990) shows how the persistence of the above mentioned negative financial biases caused a high percentage of companies to completely change their early expectations of an independent and possibly vertical (from R and D to manufacturing and marketing) development. Of a very large sample of companies surveyed, 39% indicated as the most likely expectation within five years' time that of selling themselves to a large corporation and 32% that of trying a merger with another SDBF to increase the possibility of survival at least as a research company.

Decision making in SDBFs

An examination of the main decisions taken and pathways followed by SDBFs may help to explain the reasons for the results obtained.

From what has appeared in the literature, the analysis of the decision-making process in SDBFs seems a neglected area, probably because it is very difficult to interpret the information that can be gleaned from start-up companies. The contributions, in the scientific literature, appear mainly devoted to particular decisions, looked at in isolation and analysed in terms of how decisions have been taken on particular matters, with reference to historical data. However, there seems to be no attempt to analyse in perspective these particular types of decision and even less to insert them into company decision-making systems. Some examples are the following.

The decisions about location taken by the new small biotech firms and the consequent formation of industrial clusters have been analysed (Prevezer, 1997).

The rate of new product development by SDBFs has been examined as a function of their strategic alliances (Deeds and Hill, 1996). The study considers the number of products, that the firms have on trial, as new products on the market. It is well known that, especially in the biopharmaceutical area, a high percentage of products on trial fails to reach the market.

Hence products on trial are not meaningful in identifying the impact of the number of alliances on successful product development.

A study, (Deeds and Hill, 1998), examines "opportunistic action within research alliances in the biotechnology industry" [1] and a study (Zahara, 1996) presents indications of the different technological factors (such as using more internal or external R and D sources) mainly exploited by independent and by corporate sponsored biotechnology ventures.

Instead, an analysis of the motives for the decisions taken by SDBFs in their alliances, joint ventures, contracts and licences would certainly be a more useful contribution than studies of the type described above.

For both the early SDBFs and those born more recently to try to exploit new technological paths, sharpening their decision-making approach could strengthen their competitive standing in an arena where operational conditions are not particularly favourable to them. Resorting to systematic collection of subjective probabilities of the events, with which the technological and financial decisions of the firm have to be confronted, should be of great help in constructing the company's decision tree. This would allow managers to estimate the expected values of the results the company would attain according to the decisions they take, among those indicated on the tree. The high complexity and high degree of uncertainty of the decision-making process of such firms makes it advisable that experimental work be done to sharpen their decision-making approaches.

Outlines of public strategies that could enhance the performance of the start-up phase of the biotech revolution

A Government strategy capable of ensuring real peer competition to all the actors in the US biotech arena has been missing in the, still in progress, long start-up phase of the biotech revolution.

The consent decree was the pillar of the US Government strategy that gave a fundamental contribution to securing real peer competition in the start-up phase of the electronic revolution.

Though the scenario of the biotechnogenetic revolution presents different characteristics from that of the electronic revolution, one should observe that any form of antitrust rules can have favourable effects on the standing of small biotech start-ups and on their evaluation by the market. A very recent example has been that of OSI Pharmaceuticals, a small biotech company that researches drugs to treat cancer and diabetes. OSI was developing anti-cancer drug OSI-774 jointly with Pfizer. The drug was in an advanced state of development and, typically, would have finished under Pfizer's control. When Pfizer acquired

---

[1] It has often been observed that there is no biotechnology industry, but industries in which biotechnology and in particular biotechnogenetic methods are used.

Warner-Lambert, further increasing its gigantic standing, the Federal Trade Commission ordered Pfizer to divest itself of the drug as a condition for its acquisition of Warner-Lambert and OSI was awarded exclusive rights to the 774 drug. OSI's shares skyrocketed from about $10 to $80.

Though potential anti-trust actions may not be frequent in the biotech arena and hence their contribution to generating more peer competitive conditions between large and small actors may be modest, there are other potential moves that could contribute remarkably to restoring peer competitive conditions in the biotech arena, in the same way as the consent decree greatly helped to establish them in the start-up phase of the electronic revolution.

Restoring and increasing the very attractive characteristics of LPs could still be the very pillar of an equivalently winning strategy in the start-up phase of the biotech revolution. This would greatly reduce the risk component of company development plans. Being able to amply resort to this form of financing would cause a more profitable exploitation of the R and D results of SDBFs and increase the possibilities of their independent development. Moreover, if SDBFs enjoyed a more peer competitive position vis a vis large corporations, the latter would be obliged to consider SDBFs as potential competitors instead of bright pioneers of new learning curves that the large corporations have the power to exploit when and how they want, in the framework of their overall strategy. Hence, also cooperation deals between large corporations and SDBFs could be built in a way that would bring enhanced synergic results, avoiding compulsory symbiotic conditions. The give away of biogenetic technologies to foreign corporations, to which so many US SDBFs have to resort, could be greatly reduced. In this framework, mergers between SDBFs would be made much easier and fruitful. They would further strengthen SDBFs' standing vis a vis large corporations and be an important propeller of a quicker development of the biotech revolution.

As a matter of fact OTA (U.S. Congress O.T.A., 1984 p.302 and p.539) warns that "LPs are probably critical to the survival and growth of SDBFs" and states that "if SDBFs can surmount the financial hurdles to commercial production, the pace of technological advance and market development likely will be accelerated significantly and the competitiveness of the US firms using biotechnology probably will be increased".

Also recalling the incentives fed into the start-up phase of the electronic revolution, other pillaring points of a winning strategy could be the following.

A winning move would be to shift, to the development of industrial processes and production scale up, a part of the huge financial resources devoted by the US Government to basic biological research. In fact, industrial development and scale-up have proved, in the biotechnogenetic area, more lengthy, difficult, uncertain and expensive than in other new technological areas.

One can remark that Japan, taking advantage of the cheaply accessible heap of results of the American basic research, amply financed by the US Government, has been allocating much of its subsidies to applied research, especially in scaling up production processes. In addition it has obtained, often cheaply, technology from US SDBFs. This strategy has helped Japan to reduce its competitive disadvantage with respect to the United States.

Another important stimulus would be rapid depreciation of the capital assets required for pilot plants and for production scale-up, which was one of the positive stimuli that helped the electronic revolution. Considering the foreseeable persistent red bottom line for SDBFs, unless they can widely resort to LPs, a form of refund should be envisaged in each year for the tax credit from rapid depreciation that these companies could obtain if they had earnings.

Other important stimuli could be easily implemented by improving patent legislation rules and export rules for biological products (Gibbs, 1987) in a way that would reduce otherwise insurmountable obstacles for SDBFs. Prohibiting the export of drugs and especially of biologics unapproved in the US penalized in particular SDBFs, besides damaging the economy of the US biotech area. Also due to Genentech's complaints, this rule was amended in 1986 (Genentech, 1983).

In the start-up phase of the electronic revolution, demand was very much increased by orders from government institutions or their affiliates and this facilitated a low-risk profitable development of many small companies and a rapid progress of the electronic revolution. Except for the Orphan Drug Act (1983), which gives substantial financial incentives to companies manufacturing products for rare diseases, incentives to initially push demand of approved biotech products have been non-existent. They might have had a certain relevance in the case of biotech products with higher prices but with potential advantages in end-uses with respect to existing ones, and also in the case of absolutely new biotech products, especially diagnostic and therapeutic ones, and might have helped more SDBFs to advance from R and D to manufacturing and on to the market.

The role of SDBFs could have been more incisive, in fostering the start-up phase of the biotech revolution and the US leadership, if public strategies had contributed to put them in a peer competitive position. Since this phase is in progress (and still rather slow), implementing at least the most relevant of these strategies could become a winning move for the US.

The international scenario

The relevance of the contribution of SDBFs, to the progressive and successful start-up of the biotech revolution and to the entry of large corporations into the biotech area, was well perceived by the governments of the main industrialized countries.

In the absence of a spontaneous generation of such small dedicated firms within the industrial tissue of their countries, some of these governments thought that a public thrust to create small firms of this type would be a propeller for the biotech revolution also in their countries. This objective has only been very limitedly reached.

In England, particular care was taken to integrate the public push to create SDBFs, such as Celltech, with private support, resources and freedom of action.

In France, the few SDBFs created in the 80s were mainly the fruit of public financing, hence a sort of public research laboratories that had to operate within the boundaries of a public mobilizing plan, whose ambitious objective to recover the French delay in the biotech area was not reached. A few of these small French companies were born by joint public financing and that of large corporations. This means in practice public aid to large corporations to set up their own biotech research laboratory in the form of a controlled company. This is certainly not the way to create those dynamic competitive interactions between large corporations and small dedicated firms which has contributed to the more advanced position of the US with respect to other industrialized countries.

The German Government, instead, disregarded, in the early start-up phase of the biotech revolution, any type of sponsoring of SDBFs, because they "are not in line with the German mentality" (Bio/Technology, 1983).

Recently, signs of important European strategic changes in fostering the biotech revolution, by promoting private entrepreneurship in this area, have become evident. This improvement will probably stop widening the gap between Europe and the US.

As to the Japanese Government, it did not bother to help the promotion of the biotech revolution through SDBFs. This promotion has been obtained by coordinating and integrating the initiatives of many large corporations potentially interested in experimenting biogenetic technologies in a part of the manufacturing processes of the industrial sectors in which they operate. The Japanese biotech area got remarkable help from American SDBFs, which have increasingly resorted to licensing to large Japanese corporations most of their advanced technologies in exchange for financial resources and for keeping the rights to exploit these technologies in the US.

In this scenario, large European and Japanese corporations, well aware of the potential contributions that could be obtained from independently developed SDBFs, have been moving either to acquire American SDBFs, because of the technology they wanted to get hold of, or to contract the purchase of this technology from them. These deals have been numerous; the most outstanding of them was the acquisition of Genentech, one of the leading American SDBFs, carried out by the Swiss company Roche. A collateral move of a few large non-American corporations has been the transfer of their biotech research centers to the US, in order to more quickly capture brainware and know-how where they had reached their highest potential. The most clamorous example was the transfer of Hoechst's biotech research to the Harvard Medical School. These moves somewhat decreased the competitive standing of the US in the biotech area and also contributed to a rapid internationalization of the biotechnogenetic revolution. All in all, the relevance of large American and foreign corporations in controlling the rhythm of the development of the biotech revolution has been increasing and the American SDBFs have found themselves in a progressively non-peer competitive position.

CONCLUSIONS

The types of interventions outlined in this paper can still be implemented. They will make it possible for the US SDBFs to attain a more peer competitive position in the biotech arena, thereby generating positive effects on the rhythm of development of the biotech revolution and on the reinforcement of the US leadership.

A thorough understanding of the scenarios, in which the biotech revolution is developing and of the dynamics of the interactions between non-peer competing players in this arena, should be gained especially by entrepreneurs who intend to enter it successfully. More appropriate and wide-framed decision-making approaches should also be worked out by small dedicated firms operating at the frontiers of technology.

REFERENCES

Asher, N. and L. Strom (1977). *The Role of the Department of Defense in the Development of Integrated Circuits.* Arlington, Va.: Institute for Defense Analysis.

Bio/Technology (1983). New trends in financing biotechnology. September, p. 556.

Borgman, L.W. and Co. (1983). Financial issues in biotechnology. *Contract Report prepared for the O.T.A., U.S. Congress,* March.

Chemical and Engineering News (1986). Genentech to buy out two research partnerships. 64: 5.

Deeds, D.L. and C.W.L. Hill (1996). Strategic alliances and the rate of new product development: an empirical study of entrepreneurial biotechnology firms. *Journal of Business Venturing,* 11, 41-55.

Deeds, D.L. and C.W.L. Hill (1998). An examination of opportunistic action within research alliances: evidence from the biotechnology industry. *Journal of Business Venturing,* 14, 141-163.

Ernst and Young (1990). Biotech 91: a changing environment. *Ernst and Young,* San Francisco, Ca.

Forbes (May 1 2000). Test-tube sex.

Genentech Inc. (1983). Supplemental comments by Genentech, Inc. on proposed new drug and antibiotic regulations. *US Food and Drug Administration Docket No. 82N-0293,* January.

Genetic Engineering (January 1 2000). Maxygen uses DNA shuffling as core technology.

Gibbs, J.N. (1987). Exporting biotechnology products: a look at the issues. *Bio/Technology,* 5:46, January

Kenney, M. (1986). *Biotechnology: The University-Industry Complex.* Yale University Press, New York, NY.

Landau, R. and N. Rosemberg (eds.) (1986). *The Positive-Sum Strategy: Harnessing Technology for Economic Growth.* National Academy Press, Washington, D.C.

Linville, J.G. and L.C. Hogan (1977). Intellectual and economic fuel for the electronic revolution.

Science, 195: 1107.

Meeks, B.N. (1986). RDLPs soon to become financial dinosaurs. *Genetic Engineering News,* 6 (8), September.

Merrifield, D.B. (1986). R and D limited partnerships are starting to bridge the invention-translation gap. *Research Management,* 3: 9-12.

Michaud, S. (1982). The dark side of R and D shelters. *Venture,* November, p.28

Nelson, R.R., ed. (1982). *Government and Technical Progress: A Cross-Industry Analysis.* Pergamon Press, New York.

Prevezer, M. (1997). The dynamics of industrial clustering in biotechnology. *Small Business Economics,* 9: 255-271.

Rosemberg, N. (1985). *Perspectives on Technology.* Armor and N.Y.: M.E. Sharpe, Inc.

The Economist (June 26,1999). Biotech's father William.

Tilton, J. (1971). *International Diffusion of Technology: The Case of Semiconductors.* Brookings Institution, Washington, D.C.

U.S. Congress O.T.A. (1984). *Commercial Biotechnology: An International Analysis.* Elmsford, N.Y.: Pergamon Press Inc.

U.S. Congress O.T.A. (1990). Financial issues affecting biotechnology: at home and abroad. *Transcript of a Workshop,* September.

U.S. vs. Western Electric Company, 1956 Trade Case (CCH 68,246 (D.N.J.,1956).

Weiner, C. (1973). How the transistor emerged. *I.E.E.E. Spectrum,* January, 24-33.

Zahara, S.A. (1996). Technology strategy and new venture performance: a study of corporate–sponsored and independent biotechnology ventures. *Journal of Business Venturing,* 11, 289-321.

Management of Technology
ISBN: 0-08-044136-X

8

RISK ANGEL NETWORKS FOR THE 21ST CENTURY: A REVIEW OF BEST PRACTICES IN EUROPE AND THE USA[1]

Karl Julian E. Lange, Babson College, Wellesley (MA), USA[*]

Benoît F. Leleux, IMD - International Institute for Management Development, Lausanne, Switzerland[**]

Bernard Surlemont, HEC - Université de Lausanne, Lausanne, Switzerland[***]

ABSTRACT

Developments in web technology are creating new opportunities for entrepreneurs and venture investors alike and facilitate the emergence of new breeds of introduction services connecting these parties more efficiently. The paper relies on clinical analyses of over 40 identified "best practice" angel networks in the US and Europe to provide a systematic study of the newest and most innovative practices in angel networks, focusing in particular on the use of information technology to facilitate the flow of ideas and capital to startups and early-stage companies and

---

[1]   A revised version of the paper is forthcoming as "Angel Networks for the 21st Century: Best Practices in Europe and the US", Chapter 4 in D. Cetindamar (Editor): *The Growth of Venture Capital: A Cross-Cultural Comparison*, Greenwood Publishing Group, Quorum Press, 2002.

[*]   Dr. Julian E. Lange is BabsonWebberMustard Term Chair in Entrepreneurship and Benson Distinguished Entrepreneurship Fellow at the Arthur M. Blank Center for Entrepreneurship at Babson College.

[**]   Benoit Leleux, Stephan Schmidheiny Professor of Entrepreneurship and Finance, IMD - International Institute for Management Development, 23 Chemin de Bellerive, P.O. Box 915, CH-1001 Lausanne (Switzerland); (T) 41/21/618.03.35; (F) 41/21/618.07.07. Email: leleux@imd.ch.

[***] Dr Bernard Surlemont is Professor of entrepreneurship at the University of Lausanne (HEC) and Director of the Entrepreneurship Research Center of Liège University.

its implications for tomorrow's private equity markets and the financing of high potential ventures.

INTRODUCTION

Informal venture capital represents a pool of high-risk growth equity estimated conservatively at 10 times the size of formal venture capital, a significant force in the financing of startup firms and hence of critical importance to economic development. Angel networks are taking full advantage of the new information technologies to become more efficient in generating deals and distributing information about private equity activities, significantly reducing the informational and search costs associated with the old "atomistic" format of angel investing. Yet little is understood about the key success factors of angel networks for the 21st Century. This paper provides a survey and typology of best practices in angel networks in two major geographic areas, Europe and the US, focusing in particular on the use of information technologies such as the Internet to facilitate the flow of ideas and capital to startups and early-stage companies and its implications for tomorrow's private equity markets and the financing of high potential ventures.

ANGEL INVESTORS AND NEW VENTURE FUNDING

Informal venture capital, also referred to as angel capital, represents a pool of risk equity fundamental to the startup and initial growth phases of high-potential ventures. The term "angel" originated in the early 1900's and referred to investors on Broadway who made risky investments to support theatrical productions (Utterbach et al., 1999). Today, the term refers mainly to high net worth individuals who invest in and support start-up companies in their early stages of growth[2]. In addition to providing financing, angels typically support the company by providing guidance and assistance with recruiting, management, networks, distribution connections, etc. Also referred to as informal or independent investors, they are said to represent the largest pool of equity capital in the US, many times larger than formal venture capital (Wetzel, 1986a, 1986b).

The willingness of many angels to invest (1) in first-time entrepreneurs, (2) at the search or seed levels of development, and (3) to get involved at reasonably small amounts of capital (less than $100,000) makes invaluable contributions to the pre-formal venture capital development of many technology ventures. An early study by Freear and Wetzel in 1987 on the financing of 284 New England high-tech firms founded between 1975 and 1986 found that, out of the 62% that had to rely on external equity for their growth, individual angel investors were

---

[2] In the US, the term "angel" is often associated with "accredited investors" defined under SEC Rule 501 as an individual with a net worth of at least $1 million or earnings in excess of $200,000 per year (Levin, 1994).

Table 8.1. Angels and venture capitalists contributions to new venture fundings.

Financing Round ($k)	Number of Individual Angels Investing	Distribution of Angels Investing (%)	Number of Venture Capitalists Investing	Distribution of VCs Investing (%)
<250	102	58	8	5
250–500	43	24	14	8
500–1,000	15	8	31	18
>1,000	17	10	120	69
Total	**177**	**100**	**173**	**100**

Source: Freear and Wetzel (1987)

the most common source of funds providing 177 rounds of equity financing for 124 firms. Ninety firms raised equity from venture capital funds in 173 rounds. Table 8.1 below summarizes how individual angel investors and venture capitalists invested in the rounds of financing.

A more recent study by Benjamin and Margulis (1996) similarly finds that more than 61% of the 480 startup firms in their sample were financed through business angels (Fig. 8.1).

In recent years, angel investing has seen rapid growth and increased systemization. Evidence of increased activity and systemization can be found in the increase in angel group enrollment and activity. From 1995 to 1998, the number of members in the Band of Angels

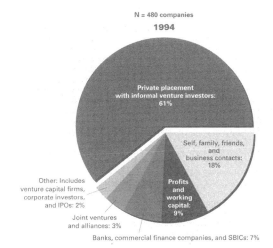

N = 480 companies
1994

Private placement with informal venture investors: 61%

Self, family, friends, and business contacts: 18%

Other: Includes venture capital firms, corporate investors, and IPOs: 2%

Profits and working capital: 9%

Joint ventures and alliances: 3%

Banks, commercial finance companies, and SBICs: 7%

Source: Benjamin and Margulis (1996).

Figure 8.1. Preferred sources of financing for US startups (1996, N=480).

organization, a Silicon Valley angel group, grew from 12 to 110 (McLaughlin, 1998). The Band of Angels invested in 19 deals in 1995 and 23 deals in 1997. The average investment per company increased from $290,000 to $535,000. The growth in activity and systemization is occurring not only in Silicon Valley, but also across the U.S., in Europe and in other countries. For example, in the last five years, the Boston/Route 128 area has seen the emergence and growth of at least a dozen new and different angel groups (Utterbach et al., 1999). In Europe, starting from a few confidential entrepreneurs' clubs in 1995, angel networks and other new venture support groups now number in the hundreds.

ANGEL NETWORKS AND VENTURE SUPPORT SERVICES

The market for informal venture capital is said to suffer from two related crippling inefficiencies: the extreme discretion of most business angels and the high search costs of angels for businesses and businesses for angels (Riding, 1997; Wetzel, 1986a). These inefficiencies are often invoked to support the existence of a "funding gap" preventing valuable opportunities from being materialized.

As a response to these perceived shortcomings, a number of organizations have been created, referred to alternatively as match-making services, angel networks, venture support bureaus or business referral services (Harrison and Mason, 1996). A forerunner in the effort was the Venture Capital Network (VCN) established in 1984 in New Hampshire, now called the Technology Capital Network operated by the MIT Enterprise Forum. From these pioneering days, angel networks have mushroomed and taken on more and more different shapes and modus operandi to cover more varied business realities.

The development in the 1990's of the "network economy", capitalizing on the new opportunities created by the Internet, has also affected the angel network community. From mostly limited access subscription services, venture support networks have developed new means of serving the needs of both investors and entrepreneurs: from matchmaking events to internet cocktail parties à-la-First Tuesday, from incubators to specialized publicly-listed early-stage funds, new means of closing the perceived funding gap have been hatched. This study investigates innovative best practices in the angel networking field across a number of countries in an attempt to understand the key drivers of "performance" in this vital field of endeavor.

RESEARCH METHODOLOGY

Any major effort to understand best practices in the global networked economy needs to take a global perspective. This research effort surveys 40 leading angel networks across 8 European countries (UK, France, Belgium, Spain, Switzerland, Finland, the Netherlands, Germany) and the US. Open-ended interviews of business angel network managers were conducted by phone or through face-to-face meetings. The interviews, taped or recorded, covered a number of different aspects of the networks' operational histories as well as underlying motivations and rationales. The aspects covered included the history of the network, from inception to its current form, its sponsors, financing and mode of operation, rules for admission and continued participation, services provided to members, screening rules, etc. Table 8.2 below lists the name of angel networks in the sample, as well as their country of origination. Some of these

Table 8.2. Sample of angel networks.

Angel Network Name (founding year)	Country
First Tuesday - London (1998)	UK
British Venture Capital Association (1983)	UK
Natwest Angels Service (1995)	UK
National Business Angels Network (1997 as NBAN; LINC before)	UK
European Technology Forum (1998)	UK
Great Eastern Investment Forum (1994)	UK
Venture Capital Report Ltd (1978)	UK
Xenos (1997)	UK
Cambridge Network (1998)	UK
E-Start (1999)	UK
OION - Oxfordshire Investment Opportunity Network - Oxford	UK
Group Professional Networks (1994)	France
IPEN - International Private Equity Network (1996)	France
BusinessAngels.com (1998)	France
International Venture Capital Forum (1997)	France
Planet Start-Up (1999)	France
Capital-IT (1999)	France
Defi Start-Up (1998)	France
Leonardo Finance (1995)	France
Invest'Essor	France
ICEVED - Intl Center for Venture Development (1999)	Spain
Sitra (1996)	Finland
Smart Capital (1999)	Switzerland
Vlerick Business Angel Network - Gent	Belgium
WABAN – Mons	Belgium
SOCRAN – Liege	Belgium
BAMS - Business Angels Matching Services - Louvain La Neuve	Belgium
BeBAN – Brussels	Belgium
NEBIB	Netherlands
BAND	Germany
Business Angels Club Berlin	Germany
UniversityAngels (1999)	USA
Wellspring Angel Fund (1998)	USA
Walnut Venture Associates	USA
128 Venture Capital Group (1983)	USA
Angeltips.com, Inc. (1999)	USA
CommonAngels.com (1998)	USA
The Enterprise Corporation	USA
Technology Capital Network (1984)	USA
Colorado Capital Alliance – Boulder (1996)	USA
PEAK – Boulder	USA

networks operate across boundaries, such as UniversityAngels.com, taking full advantage of the networking capabilities and scalability of the web.

A TYPOLOGY OF VENTURE SUPPORT SERVICES

This study does not focus on characteristics of business angels per se but investigates the innovative operating models of venture support services, or business angel *networks*. The Bank and Finance Commission in Belgium (CBF) defines a Business Angel Network (BAN) as a "structured network which offers business angels the possibility to access projects in need of financing". As such, the typical roles undertaken by BAN include part or all of the following: (1) Identify investors and entrepreneurs; (2) Organize some channels through which the two parties can meet; (3) Coach and mentor entrepreneurs and their projects; (4) Provide feedback mechanisms for entrepreneurs to build on investor comments and suggestions; (5) Facilitate later rounds of financing by providing connections to banks and venture capitalists; and (6) Guarantee the confidentiality of all parties involved. The business angel network literature typically distinguishes four fundamental types of networks (Coveney and Moore, 1998; Mason and Harrison, 1997) but the survey conducted here supports the need for a finer typology.

Table 8.3. Typological dimensions of venture support services.

Typological Criteria	⇐	⇒
Financing Mode	Private	Public
Profit Orientation	For Profit	Not For Profit
Preferred Financing Stage	Early Stage Preferred	All Stages
Investment Sectors	Specialist	Generalist
Screening and Support	Active	Passive
Geographical Reach	Regional or Local	National or Pan-National
Type of Services Offered	Introduction Services Only	Broad Offering (coaching, mentoring, incubating, team building, funding, etc.)

Financing Mode

Where most of the early players on the European scene were publicly funded and supported, a number of new actors are set up and operated on purely private grounds. Examples include BAMS, BusinessAngels.com, First Tuesday, etc. Independent of their public or private nature, most networks rely heavily on sponsoring and subscription revenues to operate. A EU commission report estimates that, on average; a BAN can only breakeven after 5 years of existence (EBAN, 1998). In the U.S., most angel groups have been have been suppliers of private capital funded by high net worth individuals.

Profit Orientation

Profit orientation can often be related to the financing mode, with public BANs often operating relatively simple forums for introduction on a non-profit basis, whereas private BANs tend to offer enlarge service offerings and clearly intend to generate revenues from the activities. In the U.S. most angel groups are driven by an underlying profit motive on the part of their participants, but are non-profits themselves, generating revenues to cover costs, but leaving the profit orientation to the investors who fund particular deals (for example: Walnut Venture Associates, CommonAngels.com, Technology Capital Network). Recently, some BANs have emerged with a distinct profit-making approach, taking compensation in the form of fees for introductions and equity or warrants in companies that are funded through their network (e.g. Angeltips.com). Hybrids do exist, such as NBAN in the UK, financed both by the Department of Trade and Industry (DTI) and private sponsors such as Barclays and Lloyds.

Preferred Financing Stage

By definition BANs were mostly created to bridge the early stage funding gap. This is particularly true in the U.S., where there is a well developed and funded venture capital community. However, some BANs do not hesitate to invest in all stages of a company development. For example, PEAK (Colorado), OION and NBAN have little restrictions in terms of stage of financing.

Investment Sectors

Many angel groups concentrate on particular sectors, with many emphasizing "high tech" investments in telecomm, information technology, and the Internet. For example, in the U.S., Walnut focuses on information technology companies in rapidly growing markets. OION defines itself as high tech oriented. An extreme case of specialization in the UK is First Tuesday's Internet "cocktail party" and matchmaking events. Other BANs seem to have followed the latest fashion into "new media" projects: the International Venture Capital Forum of Sophia Antipolis has struggled in 1999 to maintain a decent representation of biotechnology projects in its annual lineup simply because of a lack of projects presented.

Screening and Coaching

Some intermediation services take very active roles in screening projects to be presented to investors and coaching them to ensure consistent quality and satisfactory presentation.

CommonAngels.com selects potential investments through an initial screening questionnaire and submission of an accompanying executive summary submitted by entrepreneurs concerning their businesses. Firms that pass through that initial screen must then make a presentation to a small group of network members, and if successful, are then permitted to present to a breakfast meeting of the entire membership (approximately 50 investors). Another example is the International Venture Capital Forum in Sophia Antipolis, which actively screens projects submitted for presentation at the annual matchmaking event (keeping less than 25% of the all projects submitted) and requires attendance and participation at presentation coaching sessions organized by a major sponsor, Deloitte and Touche. Still other angel groups provide a more classic caveat emptor approach.

Geographical Reach

In the UK, networks such as OION (Oxford) or LINC (Scotland) act primarily on a local basis, whereas NBAN offers a nationwide coverage. Similarly in Germany, the Business Angel Club Berlin has a regional focus, where BAND claims a national reach. In France, Invest'Essor focuses on the Paris area, where BusinessAngels.com has a national audience, as does NEBIB in the Netherlands. Most groups in the U.S. have had a regional focus (e.g. Walnut, 128 Venture Capital Group); recently, however, groups with a national focus are beginning to emerge (e.g. Angeltips.com, garage.com).

Three interesting outliers with a pan-national dimension are worth mentioning. First, BAMS operates across Belgium, Luxembourg and Northern France. Second, and most notably, First Tuesday operates a network of local chapters now represented in some 65 cities across Europe. The First Tuesday model is described in more detail below. Finally, UniversityAngels.com uses Alumni affiliation as a channel to link up entrepreneurs and startup financiers across boundaries.

Types of Services Offered

From the traditional matchmaking role, BANs have developed a broad range of service offerings for entrepreneurs and investors alike. Even in matchmaking, a number of models have evolved. The simplest introduction format is the non-threatening networking event organized by First Tuesday: screening is minimal and anyone with an interest in the Internet economy is welcome to join the fray. At the other end of the spectrum are pay-for-service matchmaking groups which actively match investors and projects for a fee (e.g. Angeltips.com). Beyond matchmaking, BANs are also offering business plan coaching, directly or indirectly (the International Venture Capital Forum for example partners with Deloitte and Touche for the active coaching of selected projects before presentation at the annual investment conference), active financing support, team building and management recruitment services, incubation support (logistics, shared offices, etc.), and even direct investment into the projects.

COCKTAIL PARTIES AND VIRAL NETWORKING: FIRST TUESDAY'S FIREBALL

First Tuesday's debut was nothing short of astounding. Modeled along the lines of the *Churchill Club* or the *DrinksExchange* in San Francisco, in what is referred to as the Silicon Valley format, First Tuesday offers an informal cocktail-party style forum for anyone interested in the new economy and new media, i.e., the Web. The gatherings appeal to both actual and would-be entrepreneurs, investors and professionals alike, anyone with an interest in keeping abreast of the latest developments in the field. No gimmicks, no beauty contest[3], just a friendly, casual atmosphere and a chance to mingle with like-minded individuals who share a common interest in the cause of the Internet, and the opportunity to hear speeches from highly visible flag bearers of the new economy.

By late 1999, a short year after the first gathering in a crowded and noisy London pub, First Tuesday had been launched across Europe and the rest of the world, in 17 cities, creating venues where anybody with a bright idea could come to start building a new media business. By March 2000, First Tuesday had operating chapters in 38 cities over four continents: London, Amsterdam, Budapest, Tel Aviv, Geneva, Hamburg, Sydney, Moscow, Frankfurt, Paris, etc. with more opening every month. Over 40,000 people had requested announcements and information from all over the world. More than 10,000 people were attending First Tuesday events worldwide every month, and more than 60 cities were on the waiting list to get onto the First Tuesday bandwagon.

The First Tuesday business model relies on at least five different revenue streams: (1) Matchmaking, physical and on-line; (2) On-line job databases; (3) Special conferences and events, mostly financed through sponsors and subscriptions; (4) Website revenues for advertising services provided to a very targeted clientele; and (5) Brand licensing through partnerships with international service providers. Beyond the traditional BAN support functions, First Tuesday is also adding to the mix the ability to actually invest directly or indirectly in projects, to leverage the resources of its extensive chapter base, and to tap the large intellectual bandwidth of its members and partners.

---

[3] "Beauty Contest" is the colloquial name for the more classic angel network presentation model, where entrepreneurs are given the opportunity to present their projects to a select audience of potential investors, hopefully to arouse their interest and ultimately entice them to part with their money.

INTERNET AND BUSINESS ANGEL NETWORKS

A common theme encountered across all surveys is the tremendous impact the Internet economy is having on venture support services. Not only is the new economy putting a reinforced urgency on the need to network but the new information technologies on which the economy is built are also changing the very channels through which these networks can be established.

Disintermediation is already taking place according to many angel networks surveyed: it is becoming more and more difficult for many classic matchmaking services to charge for their basic introduction services since entrepreneurs find it relatively easier to access the financing sources without their help. More refined billing systems are taking shape, for example with introduction services taking direct equity stakes in their pupils or charging only on a success fee basis.

At the same time that some of the classic foundations of startup intermediation are being attacked, opportunities are also being created all around. Active and continuing venture support services in the form, for example, of incubators and hatcheries, are emerging everywhere. The strict financial focus is giving way to a broader definition of "resourcing" the firm, to include help in structuring the management team, recruiting key players for growth, or establishing solid boards of directors and advisors. The reduction in search costs also means entrepreneurs have a better ability to shop their deals around, increasing the likelihood of funding and a better match with investors. Increasingly, projects can be found on multiple network services at the same time.

Angel groups are generally taking advantage of the Internet to keep in touch with their dispersed membership, with some groups highlighting their "virtual" characteristics (e.g. CommonAngels.com describes itself as a virtual organization). Most of the information exchange takes place through email and attachments of backup data or presentations, with face-to-face meetings being reserved for due diligence activities and presentations by entrepreneurs to the full membership of the angel group.

NEW ACTORS EMERGING IN THE BUSINESS OF BAN

Most BANs operate on the basis of match-making. Their major purpose remains the provision of services and opportunities for matching supply and demand for finance of start-ups and early stage businesses. From a financial point of view, many of these actors are playing the game of economies of scale and try to quickly gain a critical mass to finance their activities through membership fees and consulting services. Consequently, most BANs try to build volume and keep an equilibrium between business angels and entrepreneurs in an attempt to remain neutral. It is interesting however to notice that many business angels complain about the services provided by some BANs and in particular about the lack of selectivity and the poor quality of projects they provide. For instance, a common angel complaint is that only second hand projects go through organized networks[4].

Consequently, there are pressures on BANs, as there are on any intermediaries, to add value to their services. As far as the services for angels, this means being able to develop credibility and confidence in the projects that are proposed to them. This requires the ability to organize very careful selection among the business investment opportunities and to insure that selection criteria agreed to by the angel network membership will be closely followed.[5] During our interviews, we observed emerging initiatives that are going in the direction of helping entrepreneurs to structure their businesses, hire professional management, develop strong business plans, manage intellectual property rights, etc. These activities are often supported by business angels and are mostly originate in the private sector. Some are developed by individuals acting as a network of "professional" business angels like Innode in Belgium. Others group professional partners coming from complementary horizons like the Vlerick Venture Coaching backed by a legal firm (one of the big five), a major bank, and the University of Gent. Still others are purely spin-offs of major players like the recent Arthur Andersen initiative to develop business incubators or are groups of ex-consultants backed by business angels like Peak Business Development Co. in Denver, Colorado.

Our expectation is that BANs will evolve toward such a new profile: moving toward a role of investment recommendations and business coaching, exerting a very high selectivity on projects, financing their activities through participation in the projects (stock or options) and with a much smaller base of business angels that trust and rely on the network they back. Concurrently, high traffic / low selectivity marketplaces will continue to develop, such as UniversityAngels.com, NVST.com or FindYourAngel.com, providing raw intermediation with little value-added services, relying on advertising-based revenue streams to sustain themselves. These "internet turbo-charged" angel networks very much still follow the traditional model but taking advantage of the web scalability. These emerging models are described in Table 8.4.

NEW VENTURE SUPPORT SYSTEMS: 21ˢᵗ CENTURY CHALLENGES AND OPPORTUNITIES

With the 21ˢᵗ Century at our doorstep, it was interesting to hear from established and new players in the business angel network community about their fears and expectations, reviewing some new modes of operations and challenging older ways of doing things. The survey

---

[4] It is actually interesting to note that very few BANs track or provide records of successful investments. From our fieldwork, we have reason to suspect that a one reason for this might be their very poor performance.

[5] Although, in some countries (i.e. Belgium and UK), legislation forbids BAN to formulate investment recommendations.

Table 8.4. Contrast between traditional and emerging BAN.

	Traditional BAN	Emerging BAN
Core business	• Matchmaking • Education/services	• Investments recommendations • Project structuring • Business incubation
Projects selectivity	Low to moderate	Very high
Mode of financing	• Membership fees • Consulting fees • Service fees	• Combination of consulting fees and shares
Size (#of BA)	Large	Small

conducted here highlights the very dynamic nature of the industry, which has been riding on the coattails of the Internet revolution and its networking focus. New angel networks are emerging every day, and new models are being created every other week. In particular, the new information technologies are helping bridge the decades old problem of connecting early stage projects and risk investors.

Where a clear trend towards disintermediation is already visible, challenging existing fee-for-service introduction services, the increasing resource needs of startups open up a new world of opportunities for venture support services. Equity-for-service models are being adopted rapidly, leading to more dynamic realignment of risk and returns between parties involved with launching new ventures. The attention is also shifting away from pure financial intermediation services to a more global resourcing approach, where finance is just one piece of a very complex puzzle. Increased attention is being placed on team building, management recruitment, the assembling of world-class advisory boards and the provision of highly visible and competent directors. The creation of macro-networks (networks of networks) is also seen as a natural extension of services to a global audience.

Defining what constitutes performance for venture support systems is an issue that deserves further discussion. In many instances, the creation of active venture networks is sufficient performance. Clearly, being able to provide evidence of actual startup funding and resourcing, and consequent value creation in the economy, would be even better. Quantifying such value contribution would of course challenge many systems' abilities and would be open to bias charges of one sort or another.

REFERENCES

Benjamin, G. A. & J. Margulis, (1996). *Finding Your Wings: How to Locate Private Investors to Fund Your Venture*. New York: John Wiley & Sons, Inc.

Coveney P. & K. Moore, (1998). *Business Angels Securing Start Up Finance*. New York: John Wiley & Sons.

EBAN and EURADA (February 1998). "European Business Angels Network: Dissemination report on the Potential for Business Angels Investment and Networks in Europe."

Freear, J J. & W. Wetzel, (1990) "Who bankrolls high-tech entrepreneurs?" *Journal of Business Venturing* 5, 77-89.

Harrison, Richard T. and Colin Mason, (1996). *Informal Venture Capital: Evaluating the Impact of Business Introduction Services* Hemel Hempstead: Woodhead-Faulkner Publishers Limited.

Levin, Jack (1994). "Structuring Venture Capital, Private Equity, and Entrepreneurial Transactions". Chicago: CCH, Inc.

Mason C. & R. Harrison, (1997). "Business Angels Networks and the Development of the Informal Venture Capital Market in the UK: Is There still a Role for the Public Sector?," *Small Business Economics* 9, 111-123.

McLaughlin, G., (1998). "Angel Investing: Silicon Valley", presentation in Chicago. Reported in Utterbach et al. (1999). "Venture Support Systems Project: Angel Investors." Cambridge: MIT Entrepreneurship Center, MIT Entrepreneurship Center.

Riding, A, L. Duxbury, & G. Haines. Jr., (August, 1997). "Financing Enterprise Development: Decision-Making by Canadian Angels," *Conference Proceedings for the Entrepreneurship Division of the Association of Management and International Association of Management*, pp. 17-22.

Utterbach, Matthew, Kenneth Morse, Howard Stevenson and Michael Roberts, (1999). "Venture Support Systems Project: Angel Investors." Cambridge: MIT Entrepreneurship Center, MIT Entrepreneurship Center.

Wetzel, William E Jr., (1986a). "Entrepreneurs, Angels, and Economic Renaissance", in R.D. Hisrich (ed.), *Entrepreneurship, Intrapreneurship and Venture Capital*. Lexington, MA: Lexington Books, pp.119-139.

Wetzel, William E Jr, (1986b). "Informal Risk Capital: Knowns and Unknowns", in D.L. Sexton and R.W. Smilor (eds.), *The Art and Science of Entrepreneurship*. Cambridge, MA: Ballinger, pp.85-108.

Management of Technology
Copyright © 2003 by Elsevier Science Ltd.
All rights of reproduction in any form reserved.
ISBN: 0-08-044136-X

9

THE IMPACT OF VENTURE CAPITAL IN DENMARK

Claus E. Christensen, Ministry of Economics and Business Affairs, Copenhagen, Denmark[*]
Jesper L. Christensen, Aalborg University, Aalborg, Denmark[**]

INTRODUCTION

Governments around the world have been eager to stimulate the development of a national venture capital industry. These efforts share a common rationale: that venture capital has a positive impact on the growth of small and innovative firms and consequently on performance variables such as economic growth, innovation, productivity and employment. This is clear in both academic papers, in as much as these are normative, and in policy-oriented reports (European Commission, 1995, 2001a, 2001b; OECD, 1998).

The purported positive relation between venture capital and performance variables has to some extend been confirmed in empirical studies, but it seems to be correct to conclude in line with Wright and Robbie (1998), that empirical analyses of the outcome of venture capital funding has not yet been systematically scrutinised. Wright and Robbie claim that research has only begun expanding within the past 15 years and emphasise the lack of studies on the *performance* of venture capital. They point to one potential method of pursuing this task, which is illustrated by the following passage:

> *"A relatively neglected data source concerns the possibility in some environments to analyze differences in performance between enterprises which*

[*] Claus E. Christensen, Danish Ministry of Economic and Business Affairs, Slotsholmsgade 10-12, 1216 Copenhagen K, Denmark. E-mail cec@oem.dk.
[**] Jesper Lindgaard Christensen, Department of Business Studies, Aalborg University, Fibigerstræde 4, 9220 Aalborg Ø, Denmark. E-mail jlc@business.auc.dk.

have been supported by venture capitalists and those which have not." (Wright and Robbie, 1998, p.562).

The present paper follows the implicit advice of Wright by dealing with effects of venture capital on factors such as growth in employment and revenue, and financial performance. These variables are compared for a group of venture-backed firms and a control sample of firms, who we know have not received venture capital, but otherwise share the same characteristics (size and industry). In addition, it is discussed what is it exactly that venture capital firms add to a company except pure capital.

Venture capital is defined as being investments in unquoted firms usually associated with high risk and in its original sense primarily directed towards young, often technology-based firms with a high growth potential.[1] Because of the high risk associated with venture investments a high failure rate may be expected, and the return on the investments must therefore be harvested in the form of a capital gain. The financing instruments are consequently equity or otherwise financing by instruments either convertible to shares or rendering a return, which is related to the profits of the firm. In addition to capital the venture investors add advice and management assistance to the firm. Often the venture firm takes a place on a firm's board.

Innovative and high technological firms are often considered to be the main force behind the future growth of any economy and venture capital is seen as essential to the financing of the innovative process (see for instance OECD,1998; and European Commission, 1995). Venture capitalists are needed to support high-risk investments in small technology based firms because traditional financial institutions are reluctant to finance such firms. Phenomena such as moral hazard and adverse selection are often mentioned as reasons for lack of finance sources for new innovative firms (Himmelberg and Petersen, 1994; Myers and Majluf, 1984).

Despite the increasing interest in venture capital as finance source for small and innovative firms in the Western economies, there exist very few empirical studies focusing on the economic impact of venture capital. The main reason may be the lack of appropriate data sources and thereby less sophisticated analytical approaches to the problem. A by-product of the four-decade long American tradition for venture capital is that most analytical work in the field is based on American experiences.[2]

This chapter is structured as follows: Section 2 contains a short overview of existing empirical work focusing on economic impact of venture capital. To provide the framework of

---

[1]   Even in official statistics there are different views on venture capital definitions. For example, in the US the MBO/later stage equity financing is not included in the definition of venture capital as it is in Europe.

[2]   Mason and Harrison (1999) review the development of research in the venture capital area. Among others they conclude that the research issue has only become popular within the past decade, but it is a fast growing branch.

the subsequent growth analysis and the period we are investigating, a short description of the Danish venture capital market is given in section 3, while section 4 describes our data set including construction and methodological problems. Section 5 deals with qualitative effects of venture capital as seen by the portfolio firm. In section 6 we focus on quantitative impacts of venture capital on the variables growth in revenue, employment growth and financial performance of the venture-backed firms relative to other similar firms. Finally, section 7 contains concluding remarks.

ECONOMIC EFFECTS OF VENTURE CAPITAL - EMPIRICAL FINDINGS

Whereas the majority of existing academic studies focusing on the impact of venture capital builds on American experiences, our paper focuses on the impact of venture capital in a European country where the venture capital market is less developed and less matured and where the financial system is more bank-oriented than in the US. To our knowledge there are only a few European studies on the impact of venture capital financing. Three such studies should be mentioned. Firstly, EVCA/Bannock Consulting did an impact study on "Pan-European Study of Performance of Venture Capital" (European Commission, 1997). Secondly, a study of effects of venture capital was made for the British Venture Capital Association (BVCA, 1999). Thirdly, a study was done in Sweden on the performance of venture-backed firms compared to the performance of a group of listed firms (Isaksson, 1999). The former EVCA/EC-study is relatively weak in its statistical coverage with respect to Denmark and several other European countries except France and the UK. We shall therefore throughout our discussion of effects of venture capital in Denmark refer to the studies from the UK and Sweden. These studies resemble our study and have indeed inspired it on some points.

The remaining parts of this section include a short summary of different academic studies focusing on economic impact of venture capital. We focus on the impact of venture capital on economic factors such as employment, sales and profitability. But as a start we discuss earlier work focusing on whether venture capital is actually primary invested in young and innovative firms as proposed by the theoretical arguments for the beneficial of venture capital.

Gompers (1995) finds that US venture capitalists mainly invest in early stages of the firm's development and in technology-intensive and innovative branches. Furthermore, Gompers finds that venture capital to a greater extent is invested in firms with a high market to book value, which can be interpreted that the valuation of firms is based on intangible assets.

Hellman and Puri (1998) find results that are in lines with Gompers (1995) by categorising firms by either innovators or imitators depending on their announced business strategy. They find that a firm with an innovation market strategy has a higher probability of being financed by venture capital and that venture capital is invested earlier in the development stage for firms with an innovator strategy compared to firms with an imitator strategy.

European studies confirm to some extent the American studies. Murray and Marriott (1998) contend that not only has American venture capital been traditionally more oriented towards early stage, technology-based firms, the development has also showed a widening gap in this respect in comparison to European counterparts. A Swedish report (Isaksson, 1999) finds that venture capital in Sweden is primarily invested in technology-intensive industries such as ICT, technical R&D, electronics and telecommunication, in new established and young firms (less than 5 years old), and in smaller firms (less than 50 employees). A study made for the British Venture Capital Association (BVCA, 1999) finds the same pattern for venture investments in the UK.

Even if the impact on revenue and employment intuitively should be straightforward to analyse, then the number of existing studies is rather limited. The main reason for this is most likely the lack of appropriate data sources. Isaksson (1999) finds that venture-backed firms have significantly higher employment and revenue growth rates than other similar firms do in the years after the venture investment. Similar BVCA (1999) finds that venture-backed firms have much higher growth rates than firms in the FTSE-250 at the London Stock Exchange.[3] Bruno and Tyebjee (1985) and Manigart and Struyf (1997) find that venture capital has a positive influence on firms' sale growth rates. Furthermore, Manigart and Struyf (1997) note that higher sales rates among venture-backed firms were at the expense of lower profitability in the following years.

In addition to the economic impact of venture capital referred to above, Hellman and Puri (1998) investigate the impact of venture capital on "time to market" for new products. They find that venture capital reduces time to market for new products produced by firms with an innovator strategy, while there was no influence on "time to market" for new products produced by firms with an imitator strategy.[4] Another example is Brav and Gompers (1997) who investigate impact of venture capital on the performance of publicly listed firms in the period after an IPO. They find that venture capital improve the performance of the firms in a five years period after an IPO. The authors interpret this finding as an indication of that venture-backed firms are better prepared for the cultural changes and higher requirements for information following an IPO. Lerner (1998) investigates the impact of public subsidies to small technology-intensive firms under the SBIR program in the US during the period 1983-97. Firm's revenue and employment growth are positively affected by public subsidies but only

---

[3]   A comparison with FTSE-250 firms seems inappropriate because of the different characteristics of the two firm types. In general it is very important that a control sample match the venture-backed firms in any aspects besides the involvement of venture capital.

[4]   Definitions of innovator and imitator strategy are the same as above.

in areas with a high concentration of venture capitalists. A SBIR grant can therefore be seen as a certificate that may attract private venture capital and boost firms' growth performance while pure public grants are inappropriate for boosting firms' growth performance.

THE DANISH VENTURE CAPITAL MARKET

The venture capital industry in Denmark is relatively young compared to other European countries. Most venture capital companies were established in 1983 to 1985, and the industry developed rapidly shortly after the take-off. But only a few years later the industry declined rapidly to a negligible size due to negative business conditions in the economy. In 1990 a new deficit record for the Danish venture capital firms was set, the number of venture capital companies declined from a top level of 26 in the end of the 1980s to 12 of which only 4-5 were active investors, and both new corporate investments and capital supply to the venture capital industry became stagnant. Moreover, in line with the development in European venture firms, the investment profile of the industry, changed in the first half of 1990s towards risk averse investment strategies, with the majority of investments occurring in the later stages of the firms development (Christensen, 1997).

After the collapse in the beginning of the 1990s the venture capital industry in the mid-1990s followed the general upturn of the economy in Denmark and throughout Europe. Not only did funds raised increase, and the number of venture capital firms increased, also the actual pace of investment began slowly to regain momentum.

In the past few years the venture capital industry has literally boomed as well as increased its focus on early stage investments, as shown in Figure 9.1. The government has generally been active in stimulating the market with a combination of direct participation and arms-length inducements to help market forces work. In addition, there has been great political awareness on the needs for a more developed venture capital market, which in it self has created even more focus upon this financing source. Furthermore, complementary financing sources have developed hand in hand with the development of venture capital, notably corporate venture capital and to some extent business angel financing.

The number of venture capital firms has increased steadily from 1994 onwards reaching an all time high of 35 today. It should be added that these 35 venture capital firms is considered as a very conservative figure, as the definition of venture capital used here is rather narrow.

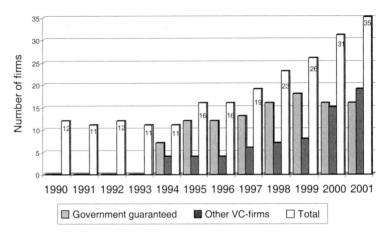

Source: Own survey and The Danish Growth Fund (2001).

Fig. 9.1. Numbers of Venture Funds in Denmark, 1990-2001.

Table 9.1 shows a substantial amount of capital available as well as rapid growth rates. The total size of the market can be estimated to approximately 900 million Euro in 2000. This may even be a conservative estimate as some of the important actors have made successful trade sales and are planning to channel substantial amounts of these revenues to venture activities.

Table 9.1. Capital available in venture funds in Denmark, selected years in million Euro.

	Capital available in 1994	Capital available in 1998	Capital available in 1999	Estimated capital available in 2000
All venture capital firms	278	423	484	757
Other venture funds				134
Total				891

Note: The information is derived from a survey we did in beginning of 2000 among all the Danish venture capital firms. In addition, in order to verify the information provided by the venture capital firm's annual reports and homepages from these venture capital firms have also been investigated focusing upon total equity capital and liquid funds (including securities) for each firm.

The often-used EVCA-figures include also later stage funds, whereas these funds are excluded from the estimate above. Even so, it is clear that the present investigation of the size of the market render considerably higher magnitudes compared to what has hitherto been thought from EVCA-statistics.

Similar conclusions can be derived from investigations on investments made in table 2. Again, compared to EVCA accounts, and even using a much more narrow definition of venture capital, the actual Danish figures are substantially higher than EVCA estimates. Thus, EVCA estimate investments in Denmark to approximately 22 million Euro in 1997, and approximately 40 million Euro in 1998. The present account show an estimate of 95 million in 1998 or more than double the EVCA estimates.

Table 9.2. Venture capital investments in still existing firms in Denmark, selected years in million Euro.

	Capital invested in 1994	Capital invested in 1998	Capital invested in 1999	Estimated Capital invested in 2000	Cumulative Investments by February 2000
All funds	28,5	95,2	139,8	184,3	420,7

Note: The numbers presented include foreign investments in Denmark.
Source: Own survey (see note at table 1), annual reports, homepages and business press.

Much of the rapid development has taken place after 1998 and this increase is expected to continue. The changes have not only been quantitatively, both structural and behavioural changes have taken place. One such structural change is the development on the medium-/large firm market where a number of equity funds have become active. Although these funds are not necessarily targeting their investments towards the same firms as venture capital firms, then the markets are interrelated, and an increase in the demand for shares in one part of the market may have spill-over effects on the prices at other parts of the market.[5]

THE DATA

Data for our analysis has been collected by the following procedure. First we identified all venture capital investors in Denmark by using different sources such as the European Venture

---

[5] It is clear that the crash of NASDAQ stock exchange in March 2000 had an impact on especially the ICT-related segments of the venture capital industry, but also it had a hampering effect on the market as a whole.

Capital Association (EVCA), business press, The Danish Growth Fund and WEB pages etc.[6] Next we collected information about portfolio firms among the venture capital firms from 1990 onwards for 10 years. The venture capital firms were asked to provide information on existing venture-backed firms from earlier investments. In case of merger or acquisition the continuing firm is included in the sample. We therefore concentrate on successfully venture-backed investments while no attention is paid to venture-backed firms that for different reasons have been closed down. With this approach, and after cleaning the data, we identified approximately 300 existing venture-backed firms in Denmark. We consider the sample to be a very good indicator for the total number of venture-backed firms in Denmark at the beginning of year 2000.[7] Thus, we believe to have close to all the venture-backed firms in Denmark in our sample, which is rather unusual. In fact, to our knowledge there is no other census surveys on the effects of venture capital.

Using the identified venture-backed firms we collected some financial data from a commercial business register for the period 1994 - 1998. It was possible to get (partly) financial data for the period 1994-1998 for approximately 250 of the venture-backed firms. Some of the recent portfolio investments are too new to have published annual reports. At the same time we made a qualitative data set based on telephone interviews among the portfolio firms. A realised sample of 121 firms (41%) was interviewed by telephone in April-June 2000 to get information about the venture capital investment.[8]

Next we constructed a control sample of firms matching the survey of venture-backed sample by number of employees and industry characteristic in 1999. A sample of 371 firms was selected matching the size and industry characteristics of the venture-backed firms.[9] In total 224 firms were selected for participation in the qualitative interview and contacted by the interviewers. Of these 165 (74%) agreed to participate. The data on the control sample of firms includes both financial and quantitative data for a 5 years period.[10]

Several methodological difficulties arise when trying to separate the impact of venture capital from other factors determining the growth or other performance variables of a firm. One problem is the usual "everything else being equal" problem, that is, it is hard to know what

---

[6]   The Danish Growth Fund (VækstFonden) is a public owned fund with the aim of strengthening the growth potential of Danish trade and industry through financing small and medium-sized enterprises.

[7]   Manigart *et al.* (2002) create a sample of 565 venture-backed firms in Belgium for the period 1987-1997. They estimate to cover 57% of venture investments in Belgium in their sample. As we focus upon a relative narrow definition of venture capital (e.g. excluding MBO funds) and for a smaller country in a shorter period, it seems fair to conclude that the number of venture capital-backed firms we found in Denmark is realistic.

[8]   In total the interviewers contacted 175 venture-backed firms rendering a response rate of 71%.

[9]   The venture-backed firms were divided into 39 subgroups (13 branches and 3 size classes). A proportional number of firms in each subclass were selected to the control sample.

[10] Further details on the data and the survey can be found in Christensen (2000).

would have happened were venture capital not available. Moreover, venture capital is rarely the only financing source and advisor for firms. Therefore, it is often difficult to separate out the net effects of a single financing source. We address these problems in two ways. Firstly, we use quantitative data from different sources and compare the performance of venture-backed firms relative to similar firms without venture financing. Secondly, we analyse the qualitative effects of venture capital by interviewing venture-backed firms to separate the effects of the venture capitalist.

Another methodological problem is defining in what period we are to measure the effects of venture capital. For instance, there may be effects from the involvement of venture capitalists even after the exit of the venture capitalist, e.g. a general upgrading of competencies of the management. We focus on the performance of the venture-backed firms in the years after the first venture capital investment, where the venture capitalist is still involved in the investment. Due to a limited time period for venture capital in Denmark we do not consider the performance of the firms after the venture capitalist has exited the investment.

One major methodological problem that we do not consider in this paper is the doubled-sided causality when comparing the performance of venture-backed firms relative to non venture-backed firms. For example, a higher than average growth of venture-backed firms may be caused by the involvement of the venture capital firms ex post of the investment. However, it may also be caused by an ex ante ability to select firms who are potentially fast growing. Analysing this problem requires knowledge on the information set of venture capitalists at the time of investment. To our knowledge studies dealing with this issue do not exist.

THE INVOLVEMENT AND BENEFITS OF VENTURE CAPITAL

One of the characteristics of the venture capital is that the venture capitalist besides financial strength also contributes with additional managerial competencies and mentoring of the investee firm. The *organisation* of how venture capitalists are tutoring investee firms may differ from case to case. In most cases the venture capital firm take a seat in the board of the firm. In fact, this is so in 79% of the firms in our sample of venture-backed firms.

A somewhat different issue is the *degree* of involvement. Investments may be made quite differently with respect to the involvement of an investor. An investor may be only passively providing capital, or he may be heavily influencing the development of the firm. According to the firms in our survey an assessment of this aspect varies from not at all active (10%) varying to extremely active (19%), as shown in Table 9.3. A majority of the firms consider the involvement of the venture fund to be "to some degree" or more. It is to be expected cf. the definition of venture capital, that at least some involvement would be reflected in the responses. It is, however, uncertain what level one should expect.

Table 9.3. The degree of involvement of the venture capital firm, %.

Not at all	To a small extent	To some degree	A lot	Very much	Do not know	No. of obs.
10	16	21	29	19	4	112

Question: "How involved do you think the venture capital firm is in your company?"
Source: Own survey.

There are no differences between firms of different size and innovation intensity, which could be said to be somewhat surprising. One should perhaps expect small firms to need more guidance, hence requiring more involvement from the venture capital firm.

A Swedish survey (Isaksson, 1999) asked a similar question but used a 6-point scale. Although this complicate direct comparisons the results indicate that Swedish venture capital firms are a bit more involved in the portfolio firm.

Table 9.4. Contributions of venture capital, high scores/shares.

Contribution	Denmark[a]	Sweden	UK
Relations to other financing sources	50		
Strategy	39	19	29[b]
Sounding board for new ideas	38	21	60
Financial advice	35	37	36
Contacts and networks	32	23	
Increase the R&D activities of the firm	17		
Increase the general level of competence within the firm	17		
Increase the ability to develop new products	12	3	
Increase knowledge on the market	10	6	23[c]
Recruitment	9	8	13
Increases abilities of the firm to manage innovation projects	6		
Increase the technical know-how of the firm	4		
Other contributions (share who list one or more)	21		0
Challenging status quo			47

Notes:
[a] In the Danish survey high scores are calculated in the usual manner: Share of respondents answering Very large effect + large effect compared to all responding. In the Swedish survey high scores are the two top levels of a 6-grade scale. In the British survey the numbers just denote the share of firms in non-MBO's who ticked the contribution.
[b] "Corporate strategy/direction + marketing strategy".
[c] "Contacts or market information".
Source: Own survey, Isaksson (1999) and BVCA (1999).

Moreover, there is apparently no uniform opinion of whether the involvement of the venture capital firm is seen as something positive or the opposite. Statements from firms during the interviews provide documentation of a variety of opinions on this point.

A related issue is the content of involvement, or other words, what is it venture capital provides in addition to capital? On this point surveys in Sweden and the UK are to some extent comparable. In Table 9.4 the main results from these surveys are included together with results from our own survey. Minor differences in the formulation of the questions and in the scale used for assessment make direct comparison a bit difficult, but still possible.[11]

The results indicate that Danish firms primarily see the contribution of venture capital as a link to other financing sources. Second, "Strategy", and the somewhat related categories "Sounding board for new ideas", "Financial advice" and "Contacts and networks" are important. It is evident from the results that "Technical know-how" is not seen as a major contribution from the venture capitalist. From a management of technology perspective this witnesses a complementarity between the more soft areas of management like networking and harder issues like technologies.

As should be expected the percentages from the Swedish survey are below the Danish (as a 6-point scale was used). There is nevertheless agreement on the importance of "Strategy", "Sounding board for new ideas", "Financial advice", "Contacts and networks" as opposed to another group "Increase the ability to develop new products", "Increase knowledge on the market" and "Recruitment". The British survey is less comparable but emphasises more the innovative contribution from venture capitalists – "Challenging status quo" and "Sounding board for new ideas" came out as top-priority contributions. These UK findings may be worth to consider for the Nordic venture capital industry.[12]

THE IMPACT OF VENTURE CAPITAL

Impact of venture capital as viewed by the firm

The previous section gave some indications regarding the content of the contribution of venture capital. In this section we shall go a bit deeper in trying to quantify the impact of venture capital. This approach is both based on the subjective statements from the firms and based on

---

[11] One complication is that the British survey lists the percentage of firms who see each sub-issue as a contribution from venture capital, whereas the firms are asked to assess each sub-issue on a scale 1-5 in Denmark and 1-6 in Sweden. Nevertheless, the ranking of the issues provides useful information on what are the primary non-economic effects from venture capital.

[12] Interestingly, many Danish firms see even more contributions from the venture capital firm. Respondents were asked to specify such additional contributions. Reviewing those statements rendered two dominating categories: the ability of the venture capital firm to improve the functioning of the board, and a positive image effect from the financing. The latter is interesting and came rather surprising.

more objective data on the development of the investee firm. In the latter approach we use information on the firms in our control sample.

The subjective assessments on the effect of the venture capital firm reveal rather clear results. Firms were asked a hypothetical question "Without the involvement of the venture capital firm would the firm then either be closed down, developed slower, had the same development, developed faster (see Table 9.5). On this point the British survey is directly comparable, and is thus included in the table.

Table 9.5. Impact of involvement by the venture capital firm, %.

	Closed down	Developed slower	No change	Developed faster	Do not know	No. of obs
The UK	55	43	1	0	1	87
Denmark	24	40	21	4	11	112

Source: Own survey and BVCA (1999).

About two thirds of the Danish firms state that they would either not have existed or would have developed in a slower pace without venture capital financing. One out of five firms believe they would have had an unchanged development, while only 4% believe they could have managed better without venture capital. The perception concerning the impact of venture capital in the UK seems to be higher compared to Danish venture capital.

Asking additionally about the effects of venture capital also indicate positive answers. As displayed in Table 9.6, 87% of the firms attach either some, great or very large impact to the venture capital financing, while only 10% think the impact has been small or none/negative.[13]

Table 9.6. Impact by the venture capital firm involvement – Denmark, %.

None/ Negative	Small positive	Some positive	Large	Very large	Do not know	No. of obs
2	8	45	28	14	4	112

Question: "How much do you think the involvement of the venture capital firm influenced the development of your company?" (Source: Own survey.)

---

[13] One would presume that the effect might be related to the involvement of the venture capital firm, in other words, it should be expected that a greater involvement would help the portfolio firm to grow faster. Indeed, when checking the growth pattern of firms (growth in employment 1994-1998) vis-à-vis the degree of involvement by the venture capital firm, a statistically significant, positive relation was found.

The Swedish survey is to some extent comparable on this point, although a different scale was used. Table 9.7 shows that 83% of the firms rate the importance of the venture capital firm in the 3-6 range on the 6-point scale.[14]

Table 9.7. The impact from the involvement of the venture capital firm - Sweden, %.

No impact					Very large impact
4	13	17	24	19	23

Question: "How much do you think the involvement of the venture capital firm influenced the development of your company?"
Source: Isaksson (1999).

The British survey also used a slightly different scale, but showed very large effects of venture capital, as is evident from Table 9.8.

Table 9.8. The impact from the involvement of the venture capital firm – the UK, %.

None	Small	Important	Crucial	Do not know	No. of obs
2	3	40	54	0	87

Question: "How much do you think the involvement of the venture capital firm influenced the development of your company?"
Source: BVCA (1999).

The respondents were then asked to make a rather difficult, hypothetical guess about the quantitative effects of venture capital and specify these effects on impact on revenue and employment (presented in Table 9.9). With this question it was a precondition that the firm was established before 1999, as it would not make sense to ask about effects in a period when there was no history. Consequently the number of respondents were reduced from 112 to 67. In addition, a large share (25-36%) did not dare this guess. Therefore, the results here should be interpreted with caution.

Although a clear positive effect may be detected, on the other hand, a large share of the respondents who chose to respond thought the development of turn-over would have remained the same without the venture financing. Presumably, this reflects that not all venture capital

---

[14]   In the Swedish survey it was not specified whether a positive effect was asked for. So, a firm that felt its development restricted by the venture capital firm would probably assess the impact of the venture capital firm to be rather high, although this should not be interpreted in a positive manner. It is, however, likely that this bias has some minor importance.

Table 9.9. Anticipated development without venture capitalist involvement, %.

	Larger	Less	No change	Do not know	No. of obs.
Turn-over	1	28	34	36	67
Employment	0	39	33	28	67

Source: Own survey.

firms are active owners. In the cases where the venture capital firm just provide financing the effect is likely to remain zero or negligible.

The quantitative impact of venture capital

Our analyses of financial data are based on the period 1994-1998 where we calculate average growth rates from the year of investment and up to 1998 for revenue and employment growth rates for venture-backed firms and firms in the control samples, respectively. Table 9.10 present mean and median annual growth rates for the two samples.

Table 9.10. Annual growth rates for revenue and employment.

	Venture-backed			Control sample			z-value
	Mean	Median	N	Mean	Median	N	
Revenue	36.6	7.7	96	15.7	9.9	52	1.64[*]
Employment	23.2	8.2	162	5.9	2.7	137	3.53[**]

Note: "*", "**" and "***" mean the result is significant at 10%, 5% and 1% level respectively.
Sample sizes are in general lower than the total numbers of firms identified in section 4, due to missing information on relevant variables.
Source: Købmandstandens OplysningsBureau, annual accounting data for various years.

The annual employment growth rate for venture-backed firms from the year of the investment to 1998 is 23.2%, while it is 5.9% for the firms in the control group. The result suggests a strong link between venture capital and the firm's employment growth rate. The result is statistically significant, as the z-statistics reject the null hypothesis for equal means at a 5% level. The z-value is 3.53, while the critical level is 1.65.

The mean revenue growth rate is also significantly higher for venture-backed firms. The mean annual revenue growth is 36.6% for the venture-backed firms compared to 15.7% for the non venture-backed firms. The higher revenue growth is significant at a 6% significance level. On the other hand, the median growth in revenue is higher among the firms in the control sample (9.9% vs. 7.7%).

The large difference between the averages and median values indicate a large dispersion of results. This is to be expected in any sample of small and medium-sized firms concentrated in innovative industries, and particularly with high-risk venture-backed firms where the stars of the portfolio account for a disproportionate element in the growth in portfolio values. In statistical terms the distribution of the sample is right skewed. This reflects an informal rule in venture investments claiming that about one of ten investments are characterised as a star investment with very high returns, while four out of ten investments yield moderate positive returns and the rest of the investment result in negative returns.

Higher annual employment growth rates among venture-backed firms are confirmed by OLS regressions (presented in Table 9.11). Using employment growth as the dependent

Table 9.11. OLS regressions of annual employment and revenue growth rate.

Dependent variable:	Employment growth		Revenue growth	
Independent variables	Basic regression	Size and Industry dummies	Basic regression	Size and Industry dummies
Intercept	19.18***	41.73**	44.46**	1.70
	(3.73)	(2.51)	(2.34)	(0.03)
Venture Capital	11.45**	10.8**	13.34	0.87
	(2.45)	(2.15)	(0.77)	(0.05)
Age	-0.56***	-0.50***	-1.27*	-0.96
	(-3.38)	(-2.76)	(-1.93)	(-1.52)
R^2	0.071	0.095	0.045	0.198
Adj. R^2	0.064	0.063	0.024	0.137
F-value	11.11	2.99	2.19	3.28
Number of observations	296	296	144	144

Note: "*","**"and "***"mean the coefficient is significant at 10 %, 5 % and 1 % level respectively.

Two different dependent growth variables are presented: employment and revenue. Venture capital is a dummy variable taking value 1 if the firm has received venture capital in the period and 0 elsewhere. The variable Age is firm age, controlling for that younger firms tend to grow faster than more mature firms do. Column 2 and 4 include dummies for size and industry characteristics. These dummies are in general insignificant (results not shown) as expected, due do the selection criteria in the construction of the control sample.

Source: Købmandstandens OplysningsBureau, annual accounting data for various years.

variable the regression shows that venture-backed firms have over 10% higher growth rates than non venture-backed firms. The regression also shows that younger firms tend to grow faster than older firms. Similar regressions on growth in revenue do not confirm a positive influence of venture capital on revenue growth rates after controlling for firm age. This is in accordance with the weaker statistical power of the simple z-test in Table 9.10.

Our results strongly indicate that venture capital may help firms to grow faster than other similar firms. The higher growth rates are motivated by two factors. First, a venture capital investment, and the following nurturing from the venture investor in the form of management assistance, supervising etc., may have a positive influence on the firm's growth rates. Second, the higher growth rates may be caused by the venture capital investor's ability to select the best potential investments among the portfolio companies. If this is the case then there may be a bias towards high growth companies in the portfolio of venture capital firms. In empirical work it is not possible to identify the causality between potential growth expectations and positive impact of venture capital after the investment is made. An obvious conclusion is that both factors affect the result. Venture capitalists have undoubtedly skills and experience in their investment fields to identify investment opportunities with high growth potentials. On the other hand it make sense that the continuing nurturing of the portfolio firms, in the form of carrying through business plans, introduction to network and access to alternative financial sources etc., all have a positive influence on the growth of venture-backed firms.

A comparison of venture-backed and non venture-backed firms for different firm size show that the employment growth rate is significantly higher for smaller venture-backed firms, while there is no differences between venture-backed and control group firms for larger firms. Revenue growth shows a similar pattern, but the results have less statistical power than employment growth. The results are in line with that venture capital has the most positive influence in small firms, while the advantage decreases as firms becomes bigger and maturer. One reason may be that the value-added to the firms from the venture capitalist in form of experience and knowledge in combination with risk capital decreases, as the firm becomes bigger. The result may therefore also explain why venture capital investors are specialised in young firms, often in highly innovative and technological intensive industries.

We subsequently analyse financial performance of the venture-backed firms relative to other firms in the years after the venture capital investment (return on equity and return on total capital with results presented in Table 9.12).

Levels for return on total capital and return on equity for the venture-backed firms are negative in both the investment year and 1998 while the corresponding numbers are positive for the non venture-backed firms in the control sample. Further, there is no clear indication of improvement in financial performance from the investment year and up to 1998, return on capital seems to be unchanged in the period while return on equity has worsened during the period.

Return on total capital seems to be significantly higher in the control sample of non venture-backed firms. One explanation could be that the higher growth rates among venture-backed firms are at the expense of lower financial performance. In unreported calculations we test whether high growth rates in performance variables such as employment and revenue are at the expense of lower returns on financial performance variables. Our hypothesis is that there is

Table 9.12. Return on capital in venture-backed firms.

	Venture-backed				Control sample			
	Mean	Median	No. of obs.	Share >0	Mean	Median	No. of obs.	Share >0
Return on total capital								
Year of invest-ment or 1994	-8.0	1.0	182	45	10.6	9.6	129	91
1998	-15.7	-1.6	237	43	7.6	7.7	127	81
Change in return on total capital %-point								
From year of investment/1994 and until 1998	-0.02	0.5	174	47	-0.8	-0.8	129	38
	Mean	Median	No. of obs.	Share >0	Mean	Median	No. of obs.	Share >0
Return on equity								
Year of investment or 1994	-16.3	1.3	152	53	19.7	14.0	123	89
1998	-22.0	-1.1	196	49	22.4	16.0	132	110
CHANGE IN RETURN ON EQUITY %-POINT								
From year of investment/1994 and until 1998	-7.3	-3.6	173	62	-1.5	0.34	121	55

Note: Samples are calculated without extreme observations by excluding observations distributed more than two standard deviations away from the mean value in the full sample. Two standard deviations are approximately equal to a 95% confidence interval.

Calculations of returns on equity exclude firms with negative equity in the year of consideration.

Number of observations is not consistent with the level values of the accounting figures in the investment year and 1998 due to different number of observations and outliers in the samples.

Source: Købmandstandens OplysningsBureau, annual accounting data for various years.

a negative relation between financial performance in the sample of venture-backed firms and a positive relation between non venture-backed firms. We use growth in earnings before interests and taxes (EBIT) as the dependent variables and growth variables such as revenue and employment as explanatory variables. The results are ambiguous, but in general there is a significant and positive relation between firm growth and financial performance among firms in the control sample, while there is no relation or negative relation between firm growth and financial performance in the sample of venture-backed firms. We interpret these results as an indication of our hypothesis that the high growth of venture-backed firms is at the expense of financial performance. This interpretation is in line with the nature of venture capital, which is to stimulate growth in order to increase the market value of the investee firm, rather than expecting income from dividends. It is also in line with the results of Manigart and Struyf (1997).

CONCLUDING REMARKS

The purpose of this paper was to analyse the economic effects of venture capital in Denmark using two different approaches. First we made a qualitative evaluation based on interviews among venture-backed firms in Denmark. Next, using accounting data we evaluated the quantitative impact of venture capital on factors such as employment and revenue growth. Our results are obtained on a unique data set, which contains all existing venture-backed firms in Denmark in the period 1994-99.

The general conclusion is that venture capital seems to have a substantial positive impact upon the development of firms. Both subjective statements from venture-backed firms and objective data for the development of portfolio firms compared to a control sample of firms render clear positive effects. For example, 24% of the respondents claim that their company would have been closed down had venture capital not been available, and another 40% claims that the company would have developed in a slower pace. These statements are backed by our growth analysis where venture-backed firms have significantly higher employment and revenue growth rates.

Venture capital firms are often involved in the firm, although there is a big diversity both on whether this is the case and whether it is positive or negative. When the venture capitalist is heavily involved it first and foremost help the firm with relations to other financing sources. Secondly, with roughly equal weight, it may help with strategy development, financial advice, networking, and sounding board for new ideas. The venture capitalist is generally not involved in the technical side of the investee firm. Although it is not possible to ascribe exactly how much of the development of a firm is due to the contribution by venture capital firms, then the results clearly indicate that the assistance seems to render positive, indirect effects on the growth of firms.

The quantitative analysis shows that employment and revenue growth in the years after the first investment is significantly higher for venture-backed firms than among non venture-backed firms. Analysing profitability shows that non venture-firms seems more profitable than venture-backed firms in the year after the investment. A possible explanation may be that higher growth rates are at the expense of a lower financial performance and venture-backed firms are more focused upon growth potentials and market value of the firm rather than upon short run profitability. Finally the dispersion of the results indicates that venture capital indeed is highly risky relying on a few extremely fast growing portfolio firms. Thus, venture capital firms manage risk in relation to a portfolio rather than on the basis of assessment of individual investee firms. This is in line with the nature of venture financing to rely on a few successful firms in the portfolio, whereas this may produce above-average mortality among the investee firms.[15]

From a policy perspective our analyses on the impact of venture capital seems to support the implicit rationale behind initiatives to boost the venture capital industry currently seen in most Western European countries: that this way of financing mechanism is stimulating growth in the economy. This has been more of a presumption than an empirical fact. Despite the methodological problems, in our results there are strong indications of the benefits of venture capital in financing small and innovative firms and our study suggest that the benefits are not restricted to the US firms, as has been studied previously.

REFERENCES

Brav, A. and P. Gompers (1997). "Myth or Reality"? The Long-Run Under Performance of Initial Public Offerings: Evidence from Venture Capital and Non-Venture Capital-backed Companies. *Journal of Finance* **52**, 1791-1822.

Bruno, A. V. and T. T. Tyebjee (1985). The Entrepreneurs Search for Capital. *Journal of Business Venturing,* **1**, 61-74.

British Venture Capital Association - BVCA (1999). *The Economic Impact of Venture Capital in the UK.* Bannock Consulting, London.

Christensen, J. L. (1997). *Financing Innovation.* Report made for the European Commission, TSER programme.

Christensen, J. L. (2000). *Effects of Venture Capital on Innovation and Growth.* Report made for the Danish Ministry of Trade and Industry, Copenhagen.

The Danish Growth Fund (2001). *Det danske marked for venture capital og private equity.* Vækstfonden, København.

European Commission (1995). *Green Paper on Innovation.* The European Commission, Brussels.

---

[15]   This was also found in Manigart *et al.* (2002) although it was clear in their study that the type of financier was important, as government backed venture funds had more survivors in their portfolios.

European Commission (1997). *Pan European study of Performance of Venture Capital.* The European Commission and Bannock Consulting.

European Commission (2001a). *Innovation, Technology and Risk Capital.* Enterprise Papers No. 5. The European Commission, Brussels.

European Commission (2001b). *Enterprises' Access to Finance.* European Commission Staff Working Paper (2001) **1667**. The European Commission, Brussels.

Gompers, P. (1995). Optimal Investments, Monitoring, and the Staging of Venture Capital. *Journal of Finance*, **50**, 1461-1489.

Hellman, T. and M. Puri (1998). *The Interaction between Product Market and Financing Strategy: The Role of Venture Capital.* Mimeo. Stanford University.

Himmelberg, C. and B. Petersen (1994). R&D and Internal Finance: A Panel Study of Small Firms in High-Tech Industries. *Review of Economic Studies* **38**, 38-51.

Isaksson, A. (1999). Effekter av venture capital i Sverige. NUTEK, Stockholm.

Kortum, S. and J. Lerner (2000). Assessing the contribution of venture capital on innovation. *Rand Journal of Economics*, **31**, 674-692.

Lerner, J. (1998). The Government as Venture Capitalist: The Long Run Impact of the SBIR Program. *Journal of Business*, **72**, 285-318.

Manigart, S. and C. Struyf (1997). Financing High Technology Start-ups in Belgium: An Explorative Study. *Small Business Economics*, **9**, 125-135.

Manigart, S., K. Baeyens and W. van Hyfte (2002). The Survival of venture capital backed companies, *Venture Capital,* Vol. 4, no. 2, 103-124.

Mason, C. and R. Harrison (1999). Venture capital: rationale, aims and scope. In: *Venture Capital* (Mason, C. and R. Harrison, eds.), Vol.1, No. 1, 1-46.

Murray, G. C. and R. Marriott (1998). Why has the Investment Performance of Technology-Specialist in the European Venture Capital Funds been so Poor? *Research Policy* **27**, 947-976.

Myers, S. and N. Majluf (1984). Corporate Financing and Investment Decisions when Firms have Information that Investors Do Not. *Journal of Financial Economics,* **13**, 187-221.

OECD (1998). *OECD Jobs Strategy: Technology, Productivity and Job Creation.* OECD, Paris.

Wright, M. and Robbie, K (1998). Venture Capital and Private Equity: A Review and Synthesis. *Journal of Business Finance & Accounting*, **25**, 521-570.

Management of Technology
ISBN: 0-08-044136-X

10

UNTANGLING SERVICE-FOR-EQUITY ARRANGEMENTS[1]

James Henderson, Babson College, Wellesley (MA), USA[*]

Benoit Leleux, IMD - International Institute for Management Development, Lausanne, Switzerland[**]

ABSTRACT

Consulting firms historically serviced clients for a cash fee, with profitability viewed as a function of their staff's perceived value-added and the type of clients taken on. The rapid emergence of a more entrepreneurial environment, fueled by the tremendous increases in equity value, generous stock option plans and more-than-receptive IPO markets, and the consequent loss of human talent to startup businesses, have forced these firms to reconsider their classic modus operandi (fee-for-service) and adopt, sometimes reluctantly and experimentally, equity-for-service arrangements. The conversion to an equity-incentivized model is both a defensive move (to retain human capital and prevent or slow down the defections to startup companies) and an offensive one (to generate new business from cash-poor, prospect-rich companies and leverage the firm's core competencies). This paper addresses strategic, financial, and organizational issues to investigate the potential impacts of

---

[1] A related version of the paper, entitled "Service-for-Equity Arrangements: Entrepreneurialism or Greed?" with James Henderson (Babson College), is forthcoming in Subir Chowdhury, editor, *Financial Times Prentice Hall Next Generation Business Series*, London: Pearson Education Limited, 2002.

[*] James Henderson is an Assistant Professor of Strategic Management at Babson College.

[**] Benoit Leleux, Stephan Schmidheiny Professor of Entrepreneurship and Finance, IMD - International Institute for Management Development, 23 Chemin de Bellerive, P.O. Box 915, CH-1001 Lausanne (Switzerland); (T) 41/21/618.03.35; (F) 41/21/618.07.07. Email: leleux@imd.ch.

such equity-enabled arrangements, and to gain a better understanding of the underlying risks and benefits of such innovative service models.

INTRODUCTION

Historically, consulting firms serviced clients for a fee, typically a per-diem rate based on the number of consultants employed on each project and their ranks. Thus, profitability was seen as a function of their staff's perceived value-added and the type of clients taken on. This model limited the ability of these professional service firms to grow much faster than the rate at which new staff could be hired and trained. Approximately 7% of consulting engagements, though, have been "equity-for-service," "value based pricing," and "performance based compensation" arrangements (Consulting News, 1999.) Indeed, equity-for-service contracts are not new. For example, Anderson Consulting took equity stakes in defense contractors it helped restructure in the 1980s (Economist, 2000.) What is new is the interest and growth in this method of pricing. With the rapid emergence of a more entrepreneurial environment, fueled by the tremendous increases in equity value, generous stock option plans and more-than-receptive IPO markets, and the consequent loss of human talent to startup businesses, have forced professional service firms to reconsider their classic modus operandi (fee-for-service) and adopt, sometimes reluctantly and experimentally, equity-for-service arrangements.

The conversion to an equity-incentivized model is both a defensive move (to retain human capital and prevent or slow down the defections to startup companies) and an offensive one (to generate new business from cash-poor, prospect-rich companies and leverage the firm's core competencies). For example, McKinsey recently established eight "business accelerators", part of @McKinsey, which has already taken stakes in more than 50 clients this year alone, BainLab fulfills the same functions at Bain & Co., while Internet consulting firms that took equity based compensation in 1999 plan to double the number of arrangements in 2000 (EDP Weekly's IT Monitor, 2000.)

These arrangements represent a fundamental shift in all aspects of a consulting firm's operations, including strategy/marketing (e.g. risk profile, and client relationships), financial management (accounting, portfolio management, conflict of interest) and organizational behavior (retention, compensation, morale hazard, etc.) However, since this model is such a new phenomenon, we, as researchers and consultants, know very little about potential unintended negative or positive consequences on a consulting firm's performance.

The objective of this paper, therefore, is to untangle the potential positive and negative consequences (whether intended or not) of equity-for-service arrangements on a consulting firm's performance. The expected contribution of the paper is to offer the $55 billion consulting industry a better understanding of the underlying risks and benefits associated with such service arrangements. The study draws on six months of in depth fieldwork on four pairs of similar service providers: strategy consultants, advertising agencies, product development and executive search firms. The paper first provides an initial background and perspectives on the topic. The second section will describe the sample of consulting firms in the study, their activities with respect to service-for-equity arrangements and their experience. Based on this study, the third section then provides the areas of concern, and potential positive and negative feedback loops regarding service-for-equity arrangements. The final section discusses the limitations and implications of the study.

BACKGROUND

Since service-for-equity arrangements are such a new phenomenon, no identifiable research has been found in the area. However, identifying closely related phenomena such as corporate venture capital and incubators may be useful. Indeed a typology of corporate equity investments can be developed using the percentage of investment income/total income on one axis and investment horizon on another, as in Figure 10.1.

Corporate Venture Capital

Corporate venture capital or strategic investing occurs when companies take minority stakes in typically start-up ventures either related or unrelated to their existing business. Recently, these funds have increased rapidly partly to take advantage of the rapid changes in new technology, to establish a stake in the Internet economy, and to participate in the attractive returns made by

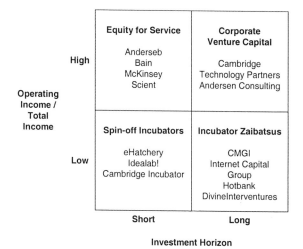

Fig. 10.1. Taxonomy of Organized Equity Investors.

the independent venture capital funds. Indeed, corporate investors accounted for 30% of the commitments to independent funds in 1997 up from about 5% in the 1990-1992 period (Gompers and Lerner, 1998). However, the returns of existing businesses still often outweigh those of new ventures. Researchers have found that only one company in seven yields an ROI greater in their corporate venturing activity than in their existing businesses within a six-year period (Block and MacMillan, 1995). Furthermore, more than 50% of ventures fail. Typically, out of 10 ventures, one is particularly successful, 2-3 ventures are mildly successful and the rest are failures in that they do not reach their cost of capital. Finally, investments made be corporate venture capital funds are in general not as successful as those made by independent venture capital fund (Gompers and Lerner, 1998). As a result, these programs have often been short-lived.

Researchers in the last two cycles of corporate venture capital programs (e.g. the seventies and eighties) have provided numerous reasons why corporate venture capital programs have not been fully effective. A well-defined mission for the corporate venture capital activity may not be provided (Fast, 1978; Siegel, Siegel and MacMillan, 1988). Top management may seek to accomplish multiple potentially incompatible objectives such as gaining access to emerging technologies and, at the same time, generating attractive financial returns. Furthermore, commitment to the corporate venturing may be insufficient (Hardymon, DiNino and Salter, 1983; Rind, 1982; Sykes, 1990). Middle managers may resist efforts in providing venture capital as they would prefer funds to be allocated to internal programs. In addition, unlike venture capitalist, corporate venture capitalist may hold onto their losing investments longer as there is a greater "strategic" interest in it. Finally, top management has been reluctant to remunerate their venture managers through profit sharing, fearing the potentially large payments if the investments were successful (Block and Ornati, 1987). Overall, the two waves of corporate venture capital have been harrowing experiences for the companies involved. However, learning from direct experience or from the experiences of others may help the longevity of the next corporate venture capital cycle.

Incubators

Responding to disadvantages of pure venture capital investors, incubators, accelerators and Internet keiretsus have become a new way to nurture start-ups in the new economy. Early stage venture capital backed start-ups found that they spent more than forty percent of their first six months on non-value added administrative issues (Hansen et al, 2000). Thus, incubators, in return for an equity stake, provide fledgling companies a number of time saving services not provided by venture capital outfits such as office space, funding, recruiting, accounting, legal counsel, public relations, insurance, employee benefits, and in some cases preferential access to important companies and busy executives. While incubators are thus providing "services in exchange for equity" their business is entirely reliant on their equity stakes in the start-ups. As a result, some incubators such as idealab!, eHatchery, and Cambridge Incubator, try to unload their stakes in the start-ups as quickly as possible to venture capital firms. However, some of the incubators including CMGI, Internet Capital Group and divineInterventures hold onto their stakes for a longer period with the intention of creating a modern form zaibatsu.

While over a hundred of these for-profit "incubators" have emerged over the past few years, there is growing agreement that only a few will survive. Those that only offer a generic place and basic services for entrepreneurs would unlikely be providing much value. As the high risk capital industry enters into another cyclical downturn, few of these companies would be able to sustain operations without a return on their investments. However, the 26% that do provide value added networking and preferential access to important executives/venture capital firms are more likely to survive (Hansen et al, 2000). Yet, even these incubators including CMGI, Internet Capital Group and divineInterventures have seen their shares plummet over the last six months as worries over the sustainability of their business models have increased.

Service-for-equity arrangements, which are part of a large fee for service consulting firm, combine the corporate venture capital and incubator models. Typically they represent a small portion of the consulting companies' total revenue base but are a way for them to earn significantly more than the traditional fee-for-service model. The background of corporate venture capital funds and incubators leads us to pose the following questions for service-for-equity arrangements. First, how do consulting firms deal with the increased risk associated with taking on service-for-equity arrangements? Second, what are the implications for client relationships? Third, how to consulting firms account for these arrangements and manage the portfolio of investments as more are taken on? Fourth, how do consulting firms disperse the proceeds from a liquidation event? Fifth, what are the organizational implications? Finally, are service-for-equity arrangements a temporary phenomenon created out of the dot com fever or are they truly a way for consulting firms to add value for their clients? The lack of research on the topic coupled with these numerous unanswered questions led us to an inductive research approach described in this paper.

RESEARCH METHODOLOGIES

Because of the novelty of this topic, we resorted to using a multiple case design where each case served to confirm or disconfirm the conclusions drawn from the others (Yin, 1984). Personal, telephone and email interviews were conducted with eight participating organizations, which range in size from under $50m to excess of $2bn in annual revenues. They include pairs of similar service providers: strategy consultants, advertising agencies, product development and executive search firms. This was consciously done to explore the implications across firms of different sizes and functions served. Refer to Table 10.1 that describes the eight professional services firms studied.

Table 10.1. Description of consulting firms.

Pseudonym	Industry	1999 Sales	No. of Equity Positions Opened/Liquidated	% of Clients Paying in Equity
Company A	Strategy Consulting	50m-100m	57/17	30%
Company B	Strategy Consulting	1b+	5%-20% clients	
Company C	Advertising Agency	50m-100m	2/0	N/A
Company D	Advertising Agency	50m-100m	4/1	11%
Company E	Product Design	Under 50m	10/3	25%
Company F	Product Design	Under 50m	9/0	21%
Company G	Executive Search	100m-500m	35/0	5%
Company H	Executive Search	N/A	20/0	3%

There were three data sources included in the study. First, in-depth semi-structured interviews were conducted lasting approximately 2 hours with senior managers of each of the eight participating organizations. Interviewees were all senior managers and included President, CEO, CFO, Director of Business Development and Managing Partner. Follow up questions were submitted to participants several weeks later. The interviews began by asking these managers to describe why they have adopted service-for-equity arrangements before examining intricacies and consequences of taking that decision. Refer to Table 10.2 for a list of the questions asked.

Secondly, interviews were conducted with experts in the areas of accounting, corporate finance and corporate law in order to become more familiar with more particular issues associated with taking equity in clients in return for services provided. Finally, secondary sources were used via new retrieval databases (Lexis-Nexis, Dow Jones, etc), industry publications and financial analyst reports. This information was used to identify prospective interviewees and to learn about the phenomena in the first place.

POSSIBLE CONSEQUENCES OF SERVICE-FOR-EQUITY ARRANGEMENTS

The data from this research indicate that whether professional service firms take on service-for-equity engagements opportunistically or through a top down process, several aspects of a consulting firms operations will be affected including strategy, financial management, and organizational behaviour and, hence, will need to be reconsidered. Based partly on the interviews but also through deductive reasoning we developed a list of potential

Table 10.2. List of interview questions.

Introduction
- Why did you take on service-for-equity arrangements?
- How many equity positions do you currently hold?
- What percentage of client fees is taken in equity?
- How do you determine the percentage of client fees to take in equity?

Risk Profile
- How do you determine the length of equity ownership?
- How would you structure the equity compensation?
- What are your strategies to mitigate the potential downside effects?

Client Relationships
- How widely is this practice used? What types of clients have you done this with?
- How does word of mouth impact the client base?

Portfolio Management
- How is the value of the equity determined?
- How are the investments managed?

Accounting
- How are the equity positions recorded for 1) accounting purposes and 2) tax purposes?
- How is success measured?
- What is the legal structure of the organization that retains the equities?

Conflict of Interest
- How are potential conflicts of interest reconciled?
- Has the nature of the arrangement altered the way these projects are conducted?

Retention and compensation
- What relevant human resource issues must be addressed?
- How is project staffing relative to equity participation structured?

complementary and contradictory effects on behaviour and performance by taking on service-for-equity arrangements.

Strategy/Marketing

The research showed that the two biggest areas of why consulting firms entered into services-for-equity arrangements was to leverage their services through potentially greater rewards than through the traditional fee-for-service model and to gain access to a new client base. However, these also had ramifications on the management of the client development process.

Risk Profile: Equity stakes clearly provide a significant <u>upside potential</u>, in excess of what the company could ever charge on a fee-for-service arrangement. Thus it unleashes the consulting firm from the dictatorship of the profits-as-a-function-of-number-of-consultants model. However, the capital industry is inherently cyclical, following the bulls and bears of the stock market. As the consulting industry enters service-for-equity arrangements, it also takes on a significant exposure to market risk. "If in some future year when the economy suffers a downturn and your normal consulting profits contract, at the same time you can find that your portfolio gets devalued as well, so you get a double whammy. But in the good years, you'll have more profit from normal operations and the value of your portfolio will also go up. So it tends to amplify the business cycle impact on a consulting firm", states Steven Sprinkle of Deloitte Consulting. We refer to this effect as the modified risk profile, which suggests that professional services firms might build in a risk premium for equity-compensated clients. Assuming full cash payment from clients is equated to a 0% risk premium, consulting firms may be able to determine an appropriate expected rate of return based on an understanding of the client, market conditions and other factors.

Given these two potential effects, consulting firms would likely spend some effort addressing the size of their exposure and ways to mitigate it prior to taking equity. First, the majority of profiled institutions made reference to the risk of foregoing fees on break-even levels and "hard" costs. As such, the percentage of service-for-equity engagements to the total number of engagements was low ranging from 3% (typically for the opportunistic players) and 30% (for the top down players).

Second, before executing a service-for-equity arrangement, all profiled firms also conducted some type of due diligence effort. This ranged from Company A validating market size and potential to Company E's technical due diligence and Company D's reliance on its professional services partners (legal and venture capital firm) to screen deals.

Third, within each service-for-equity arrangement, only the top down firms had taken 100% equity in a company. For the rest of the companies interviewed, they would typically charge their fixed costs in fees and take the rest in equity. Strangely, only Company B, (a top down player) demanded an additional risk premium when taking equity. In summary, consulting firms mitigated their exposure to downside risk primarily by taking on limited number of equity for service engagements, which would still incorporate fees to cover the fixed costs such as salaries and administration.

Client Relationships: In many instances, service-for-equity arrangements allows professional service firms to attract an entirely new class of clients, which otherwise would not have qualified, i.e. the cash-poor, opportunity-rich companies. As a professional services firm grows this segment, a positive new pool of client effect, based on word of mouth could generate over time. Indeed, the majority of the companies stated that the primary objective in taking on service-for-equity engagements was to gain access to the prospect-rich cash-poor clients and the vast majority of the engagements were for privately held high technology start-ups.

Furthermore, a willingness to work for a client on a service-for-equity basis could in and of itself, signal to the market the positive outlook for the firm as perceived by the consulting group. Indeed, the greater the reputation of the consulting firm in its existing market, the greater the strength of the signal, leading to potentially higher liquidation valuations of the clients that they have invested in. This could lead to a further segmentation of the consulting population on the basis of the perceived quality of the <u>certification effect</u> provided. In other words, potential clients may shop for the highest certification-effect consultant that would have them as a client. The stock of reputation built by the professional services firm would be the result of past equity-for service successes and potential spillovers from the fee-for-service side. Indeed, adopting service-for-equity arrangements did result in some positive word-of-mouth effects especially for the larger players. In particular, Company B, a large strategy consultant firm stated once that they announced their intention in providing service in return for equity, they saw a significant increase in interest from cash-poor clients. "It has clearly opened the floodgate of dot-com companies."

Yet, this positive word of mouth effect could have additional unintended consequences. First, as the floodgates open with cash starved clients asking for professional services, the queue for potential engagements increases dramatically. This queue could potentially result in too much business development time spent on reviewing and sifting through uneconomic projects, which would have been spent on preparing and bidding on traditional fee-for-services engagements. We call this the <u>backlog effect</u>. The majority companies stated that this was a big problem. "If we considered every proposal it would be very time consuming," stated Company B. "You get all the crazies now knocking on your door. It takes time to sift through these. It takes time to sift through. You must be disciplined and know where to add value. We look at about 10-20 pursuable deals a month," declared Company E. "It (service-for-equity) has had a strong marketing impact, generating some good opportunities. More than we would have liked," affirmed Company F. Furthermore, no firm could verify whether there was indeed an incremental increase in business overall.

Existing fee-paying clients or new clients that would normally accept fee-for-service arrangements may be more enticed to pay in equity rather than in cash, potentially to the detriment of the consulting firm's cash flow. Clearly, when a consulting firm enters into service-for-equity arrangements, it is sending a signal that it is willing to "put its money where its mouth is." "Consulting for equity is a more compelling way for strategy consultants to say that they are really in the business of creating value," states W. Achtemeyer, president and CEO of the Parthenon Group (Consulting News, 1999). Because of this increase in buyer choice, bargaining power could rather shift towards the clients. We refer to this negative externality as the <u>altered client incentives</u>. While this potential effect could be present, none of the companies profiled could verify that it actually had occurred.

Financial Management

Providing a service-for-equity offering not only has contradictory strategic and risk implications for client development but also ambiguous effects after a service-for-equity project has been completed. Several issues arise in accounting, portfolio management and governance.

Accounting: Accounting for the equity-for-service portion of the consultant's business may be more than they bargained for. Can the increased equity value be recognized as straight capital gains or are those the actual value perceived for services provided over the years, i.e. ordinary income? The annual increase in the equity stake value could actually be interpreted as the actual payment for services provided by the consulting firm to the client during that fiscal year, i.e. ordinary income for the business, creating a tax liability even without the actual realization of the equity investment. Issues of taxation are further complicated as it is difficult, if not impossible, to compute fair market values for these privately held equities and options. We refer to this as the tax mismatch effect. Only one company (Company A) out of the eight had significant experience in liquidity events and they refused to answer this question. The rest of the consulting firms profiled stated that they were struggling over this issue. Some were not recording the equity positions at all whereas others were recording them at the equivalent value of services provided. "We do not consider anything to be revenue until it is marketable. We have our own expected values recorded internally to keep track of the ventures," stated Company B. "According to our CFO, you cannot put a value on it. To us, it's basically worth nothing. So he would never put it on our balance sheet as an asset," affirmed Company C. "The CFO is close to putting them away in a drawer as there is a problem in establishing value," admitted Company D.

Furthermore, the majority of the profiled firms struggled with appropriate values for equity positions. Several profiled firms relied on the term sheet for venture-backed clients or conducted their own valuation. Others, such as Company C and D utilized an outside venture capital firm to determine company values. Company A sometimes utilized an option-pricing model to determine values, although they acknowledged that this was also complicated with non-public firms.

Consultants face the same issues as venture capitalists when it comes to liquidating private equity investments. Such equity stakes are subject to extensive restrictions, in particular if the stake grows over time to being considered significant, i.e. over 5%. Liquidity of such stakes is often minimal, and likely to remain so. Unlike venture capitalists that would simply distribute the stakes to their limited partners, consulting firms may face interesting problems distributing these private equity stakes to their partners or associates. The liquidity problem is likely to be most apparent for the firms in which they invested more aggressively, i.e. those they probably identified initially as having the greatest potential. While some consulting firms (often the opportunistic ones) were still grappling with this issue, a few (primarily the top down) had established a partnerships or LLCs, which would "house" the investments until they were liquidated. "During the course of the year, we would fund this partnership with all the equities that we took in. A consultant would get unit participation in that fund. If the fund were partially liquidated, the consultant would get a piece of it. Consider the funds as closed end mutual funds for each year," explained Company A.

Portfolio Management: Along with the liquidity problem is the availability of liquidity events. "When we get a green light from the client that they think it's time for us to sell, we will sell and not try to hold on for any further gain. We don't believe we are in the Peter Lynch business of figuring out should we hold or should we sell", states William Achtemeyer, president and CEO of the Parthenon Group (Consulting News, 1999). Yet, there may not be very many opportunities for the firm to sell its investment. In that case, as the percentage of total cash flow from investment activity increases, the firm may no longer maintain a client-service focus as its prime offering. We call this the portfolio management issue, an area that consulting firms do not traditionally have much expertise. Furthermore, these portfolios will most likely be unbalanced (e.g. too much weighting in one sector) presenting significant downside risk if there were a downturn in the sector. As David Shpilberg of Ernst and Young states, "Service-for-equity is a trend whose time has come, but the portfolio management of the resulting investments needs to be handled by professional investment managers or venture capitalists" (Consulting News, 1999)

As all of the profiled firms had taken a handful of equity positions for a substantial period of time, with only 15% of them having been liquidated, this portfolio management issue had become very real. Since no formalized "portfolio manager" or "fund manager" positions had been created in any of the companies profiled, little management of portfolio risk had been assumed. Even in the top down firms where special funds were established to "house" the investments, there was no one overseeing the portfolio. Rather the partner in charge of his account was typically responsible for overseeing his investment. For example, Company A (top down) stated that the partners sometimes sat on the boards of their clients so that they could at least monitor their investments. Company B denied that there really was a problem whereas others admitted something needed to be done in the future. "Our holdings are not that significant to do that. There are not any decisions as such because there is nothing the portfolio manager could do. Some of the partners look at their holdings but not much can be done," argued Company B. "We are trying to get more serious about this. We need somebody to help question assumptions, and assess all of the deals," admitted Company G.

Furthermore, because partners for the most part take on the responsibility of overseeing their investments, the potential for return may not be viewed in the same way. Indeed, no standard method to measure success emerged from the interviews of the consulting firms. They ranged from being able to feed a separately established venture fund (e.g. screening mechanism), to getting two home runs out of ten investments (e.g. portfolio success), to revenues per employee (e.g. traditional measure), to a return on investment figure (e.g. for each investment), to just being able to liquidate them. This conflict in objectives and success is certainly reminiscent of the problems of corporate venture capital funds.

Governance: Potential <u>conflicts of interest</u> can emerge. Outside of tax and audit practice areas, no regulations or guidelines exist for professional services firms. Indeed, this issue is one of the reasons why six of the largest audit/consulting firms have decided to split. Refer to Table 10.3. By breaking apart, they can circumvent the SEC auditor independence rules allowing the consulting practices to provide service-for-equity positions or to make direct investments in clients. This conflict of interest issue is not new. Indeed, before the growth in service-for-equity arrangements, only a few consulting firms such as Bain and Co. clearly state that they only work for one client per industry whereas the vast majority conducted projects for a number of companies in the same industry often simultaneously. However, holding equity stakes could make it potentially much larger. Many established consulting firms have long stated that companies, in which they have an equity stake, may receive preferential treatment over their rivals despite the supposed firewall of silence around competing projects. Thus, any potential new client may be more reluctant to trust a consulting firm offering service-for-equity arrangements to its rivals, potentially decreasing total revenue streams.

There were varying opinions around the conflict of interest issue amongst the profiled firms. Both Company A and B argued that the clients interests whether equity was taken or not were always taken into consideration. However, the other companies did mention that it was a

Table 10.3. Consulting audit separations.

Parent Company	Spin Off	Details
BDO Seidman	Consulting Unit	Expected 6/2000
Ernst & Young	E&Y Consulting	Acquired by Cap Gemini 2/00
KPMG	KPMG Consulting	S-1 Filed 4/00
Andersen Worldwide	Andersen Consulting	Separated in 1989, IPO under discussion
Deloitte & Touche	Deloitte Consulting	Spin off/separation under discussion
Grant Thornton	Consulting Practice	Intention to go public announced 2/2000

serious issue. For example, Company E admitted that many of the roles and responsibilities were gray and need to be made more explicit, yet nothing had been done to achieve these ends. Company F stated that a separate venture capital entity would soon become a necessity, so that it would provide a deliberate focus and help to maintain a distinction across the consulting firm and venture group.

While there may be greater conflicts of interest with respect taking on several companies within the same industry, adopting service-for-equity does allow the consulting firms to "work more closely with clients", and to generate business from them over the long-term. "Consulting for equity … offers something that is more tangible, a sense of partnership and alignment of the consultants' interests with those of the clients'", stated Orit Gadiesh of Bain & Co. However, these partnerships can be used to generate increased emotional capital, or buyer switching costs, thus, increasing the relative bargaining power of the consulting firm. Going forward, professional service firms could hold their clients hostage using the implicit threat of "selling out", as a way to ensure additional business with them.

Yet, this behaviour could also backfire on the consulting firms. If serious operational problems did appear, a venture capitalist would consider a rapid culling of the project, but a consulting firm may see an opportunity to provide additional services. The consultants' commitment to a venture may, however, go beyond financial rationality in order to justify their original decision to take equity. This escalation of commitment can clearly lead to less-than-optimal decisions.

Most of the profiled companies responded with the positive aspects (i.e. greater attention, higher commitment) of taking on service-for-equity. "Some clients might feel they will get more attention, but we make no distinction (between equity or fees for services rendered.) There is likely more excitement from the consultant's perspective, but it is purely psychological," stated Company B. Yet, since only 15% of the 137 investments had been liquidated, these issues, while not mentioned, could indeed still arise.

Organizational

Providing a service-for-equity offering not only has contradictory strategic and risk implications for client development and ambiguous effects after a service-for-equity project has been completed, but also organizational ramifications.

The willingness on the part of the consulting firm to enter into service-for-equity arrangements is a way for them to stem the tide of departing consultants. "It is a way for Parthenon's consultants to get a piece of the e-action without having to switch careers," W. Achtemeyer, president and CEO of the Parthenon Group (Consulting News, 1999). Yet, engaging in service-for-equity may only increase the exodus of qualified consultants by providing an implicit endorsement of the higher rewards to be obtained this way. The consultant actually providing the services to the client firm may be more willing to "jump ship" because of the higher equity stakes he/she is likely to obtain working directly for the client company instead of contributing to the consulting "equity pool." Thus rather than stem the tide of parting consultants with an additional compensation kicker, this implicit endorsement may, in fact, add to consultant departures. While the profiled institutions could not prove that the employee turnover had decreased because of taking on service-for-equity arrangements, all of them argued that equity participation could only help rather than hinder employee attrition.

Service-for-equity arrangements could also create a caste problem, or the existence of "citizens of different rank" within the consulting organization, especially if the consultants on the engagement were the only ones benefiting from the equity gains. Many of corporate venture capital programs were disbanded or redesigned for this very problem. Venture managers were making more money than the president of the company. In consulting firms, those who are not benefiting from the significant upside potential of these equity stakes may be very frustrated. Yet, there are only so many projects that can be conducted on an equity basis. Clearly, this divergence in remuneration could hinder cooperation within the firm and have an impact on exodus.

Furthermore, as more projects are taken on a service-for-equity basis, more consultants may be interested in selling "service-for-equity" projects to otherwise fee-paying clients in order to gain personally, potentially at the detriment of the firm as a whole. This moral hazard problem is akin to internal cannibalization of the cash revenue source.

Company A, D, E, and F all provided equity-based compensation to staff, regardless of participation on specific projects. These firms tie equity-based compensation to periodic employee appraisals, a tactic, which negated the caste and moral hazard problem. For example, Company A used incorporated partnerships to which employee phantom equity was contributed by calendar year; distributions were then made in accordance with an employee's tenure with the firm. Companies G and H, in the executive search area, typically distributed the gains by project teams. Company G admitted that the caste problem was an issue since members of their private equity and e-business practices were, on the whole, the ones who received equity, whereas other practice areas did not.

In total, numerous effects on performance (whether intended or not) may occur with the introduction of service-for-equity arrangements. Some of these consequences are more positive in nature whereas others are more negative overall leading to an uncertain result on company performance. Indeed, among interviewed firms, only 15% of the 137 equity-based engagements have reached a liquidation event. After removing one firm with significant experience, Company A, this percentage falls to 0.5%. Thus, the upside potential has yet to be realized. The jury is still out on service-for-equity arrangements.

DISCUSSION AND IMPLICATIONS

In this paper, we sought to untangle the intended and unintended consequences of adopting a service for equity model. The conversion to a service-for-equity model is both a defensive move, to retain prevent or slow down the defections to startup companies, and an offensive one, to generate new business from cash-poor, prospect-rich companies. Yet since service for equity is so new, we, first, researched other similar types of equity investments such as corporate venture capital funds and incubators and secondly, conducted clinical fieldwork on eight consulting firms active in offering this model.

Corporate venture capital is a way for companies to emulate the large financial gains of venture capitalists and to open a window onto new technologies and business models. However, they have historically suffered from lower returns than their existing businesses, incompatible objectives, insufficient commitment, and remuneration problems. Incubators have become a new way to nurture start-ups by providing essential services, i.e. office space, recruiting, accounting etc., in return for an equity stake. Thus, their businesses are entirely reliant on the success of the startup companies. Some try to unload their equity investments as quickly as possible to venture capital firms, whereas others have tried to build the equivalent of a modern form keiretsu by taking majority stakes in the companies. Both are reliant on the economy, availability of venture capital and the attractiveness of the IPO market. As a result, both corporate venture capital funds and incubators tend to be phenomena that appear when the economy is performing well and disappear when the economy is performing poorly.

Based on our interviews with these eight companies, our conclusions are similar to those found for corporate venture capital funds and incubators. Service-for-equity models will likely be a temporary phenomenon. Refer to Figure 10.2, which summarizes the consequences of offering service-for-equity and their effects on company performance.

We start the model with what we believe is the major driver of the longevity of providing service-for-equity contracts, the growth in the capital markets. If the capital markets start to slow and decline, due to a recession, we would expect the venture capital financing to dry up, the availability of IPO's to decline. This effect would in turn decrease the number of liquidation events for a consulting firm with a portfolio of equity investments. Hence, the

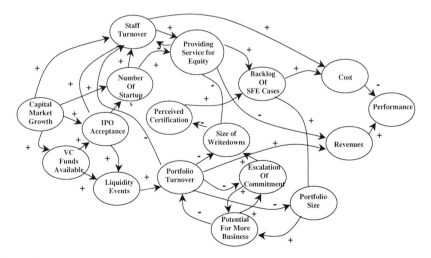

Figure 10.2. Model for Service-for-Equity arrangements.

number of equity positions would start to grow, perhaps to levels that would make the firm uncomfortable. In order to justify their equity positions, they make seek additional business, thereby increasing their commitment to these companies. This could lead to a dangerous vicious circle as sooner or later write-downs would have to be made, thus lowering the firms overall reputation. This experience would likely lead the company to reverse its decision to provide service for equity contracts. In addition, there may be a self-correcting mechanism as the number of start up companies decline due to the lack of risk capital. Staff turnover would likely slow down as the financial attractiveness of joining a startup wanes. Furthermore, as the number of start-ups decline so may a consulting company's need to serve them.

Thus, similar to corporate venture capital funds and more recently incubators, service for equity arrangements will likely be a short-term phenomenon, appearing in growth periods but again disappearing during recessions.

REFERENCES

"The case for consulting for equity," Consulting News, August 1999, p. 7-8.
"CN Exclusive on consulting for equity," Consulting News, December 1999, p. 6.
"Investment fund lets Monitor do more for clients, staff," Consulting News, September 1999, p.5.
"Consultancies seek piece of the action through VC deals," Consulting News, October 1999, p.7.
"Investing flourishes as 'take-a-stake' fever hits consulting," Consulting News, November 1999, p.8-9.
Hansen, M., H. Chesborough, N Nohria, and D Sull, (2000). "Networked Incubators: Hothouses of the New Economy." Harvard Business Review, p. 75-83.
Leonhardt, D. (2000). "Consultants are putting a new price on advice," New York Times, January 16, p. A23.
Yin, R., (1984). Case Study Research: Design and Methods. Beverly Hills: Sage Publishers.

Management of Technology
Copyright © 2003 by Elsevier Science Ltd.
ISBN: 0-08-044136-X

11

VALUATION PROCESS OF NEW TECHNOLOGY VENTURES: PERCEPTIONS OF THE VARIOUS PEOPLE INVOLVED IN THIS PROCESS

Jean Micol, École Polytechnique Fédérale de Lausanne (EPFL), Management of Technology[*]
Laia Bertran Rabassa, Universidad Politecnica de Cataluña (UPC)[**]

INTRODUCTION

The emergence and rapid diffusion of new technologies are reshaping the economies and societies around the world. These new technologies are not only creating new products, processes and services, but are also changing the characteristics and performance of organizations. The ways in which organizations interact in an economy have been affected with networking, co-operation and the fluid flow of knowledge within and across national borders. Globalization is, at present time, a reality. In this changing environment, innovation plays an essential role. Technological innovations have provided dramatic advance in performance and service to the society. There are nowadays critical for the success/survival of firms and hence, for the growth of economy.

Start-up enterprises are important sources of new idea and innovations, because of that, they may have an advantage over traditional firms in emerging industries where demand patterns are unclear, risks are large and the technology has yet to be worked out. If enterprises are one of the engines of the economy, the entrepreneurs are the enterprises' fuel. New

---

[*] Jean Micol is co-director of the postgraduate program in Management of Technology (MoT) which is jointly organized by EPFL and the Business School of the University of Lausanne. E-mail jean.micol@epfl.ch.
[**] Laia Bertran Rabassa is a graduate in Industrial Engineering from UPC.

technology ventures need entrepreneurs hungry of new challenges ready to face this new technological world and their ability to innovate is essential to the new economy.

The role of science in the innovation process has strengthened collaboration between industry and university, and has occasionally resulted in spin-offs from university laboratories. As a matter of fact, universities are most often the technological source of innovations developed in/transferred to start-up enterprises.

Once having the appropriate technology to develop products, start-ups require financial resources. Among the existing capital sources during seed stage are Family, Friends, State and Business Angels. However, start-up enterprises in new technology require both financial and management support. The last two sources mentioned and Venture capitalists can provide these supports to entrepreneurs.

To better understand the perception of key players in the innovation and entrepreneurial process, a research study on the three types of people involved in the Valuation Process of New Technology Ventures has been undertaken with the survey of innovators, entrepreneurs and investors.

METHODOLOGY

In order to achieve the purpose of the research study, three questionnaires, one for innovators, one for entrepreneurs and one for the investors, were developed. They are made up of three parts and whenever feasible their questions are similar in order to facilitate comparison.

Please, rank from 1 (highest) to 6 (lowest), for each group below, the items in terms of:
- IMPORTANCE : Items' importance in a new venture valuation process (1ˢᵗ column)
- PERFORMANCE: Your perception about how the enterprises you invest in are performing (2ⁿᵈ column)

TECHNOLOGY	IMPORTANCE	PERFORMANCE
The potential applications and products that can be derived from the technology considered		
Who specifically will be interested in the technology considered		
The strengths and weaknesses of the technology versus other alternative/competing technologies		
The technological risks associated with products/service offering		
The protection of Intellectual Property		
Other technological considerations, specify:		

MARKET	IMPORTANCE	PERFORMANCE
Very understanding knowledge of the market, its size and growth, etc...		
Prime customer target and the expected market share		
The competitors		
The entry barriers faced to penetrate the market		
Market risks for the technology, products or services considered		
Other market considerations, specify:		

HUMAN RESOURCES	IMPORTANCE	PERFORMANCE
A management team that shares an appealing vision		
A balanced and committed management team		
A management team with strong leadership		
A well qualified working team		
A management board with high personality/visibility/competent profiles		
Other human resources considerations, specify:		

Globally, what percentage weight would you give to each group in the Valuation Process? Technology......%; Market......%; Human Resources......%

Fig. 11.1. Common part in the three questionnaires.

1. First Part: The questions of the first part identify common characteristics among the members of each group of people interviewed.
2. Second Part: The second part aims to find out the perceptions and the opinions of the interviewed people about the tools used to value an innovation or a company, the process of negotiation between the entrepreneur and the investor, and some other aspects around this process.
3. Third Part: The third part is identical for the 3 targeted questionnaires developed. Arrived to this point, a ranking valuation has to be given to several items concerning technology, market and human resources, both from the perspective of the importance these items have in the Valuation Process of New Technology Ventures, and from the perspective of performance.

SURVEYING AND COLLECTING DATA

Breakdown of the samples

As can be observed in Table 11.1, a total of 89 potential respondents to the questionnaires were identified and contacted. The most numerous group was the entrepreneurs and the smaller group was the innovators. However, as the table shows, innovators were the most receptive group when being asked to participate in this study, with a 79% participation rate. For entrepreneurs, the percentage of respondents is low compared to innovators, with 31%. On the other hand, 28% of responses from investors is a substantial percentage when considering that the contact established with them was through electronic mail only. Globally, from a total of 89 contacted people, 33 have participated in this study, that is 37%.

Table 11.1. Breakdown of the sample sources.

	CENSUS OF POPULATION	% FROM THE TOTAL OF THE CENSUS	RESPONSES	% FROM THE TOTAL OF THE RESPONSES	%OF RESPONSES
INNOVATORS	14	16%	11	33%	79%
ENTREPRENEURS	39	44%	12	36%	31%
INVESTORS	36	40%	10	30%	28%
TOTAL	89	100%	33	100%	37%

Sample sources

- *Identification of innovators*: Through the articles published in several editions of the magazine "Le Dialogue - s'informer pour innover"[1], an EPFL publication focused on

---

[1] Magazine published by CAST- Centre d'Appui Scientifique et Technologique

innovations, it was possible to find the latest innovations of different laboratories from the school.

- *Identification of the entrepreneurs*: The proximity of a scientific park -PSE- next to the EPFL and the links between both institutions, were the key to an easy identification of entrepreneurs of high-tech ventures. The goal was to interview all of them, or at least as much as possible.

- *Identification of investors*: The way chosen to identify investors was to search them through the SECA (Swiss Private Equity & Corporate Finance Association, www.seca.ch) member directory published in Internet. Only those who invest in new technology ventures and start-ups, mainly in Switzerland, were selected to be potential respondents.

ANALYSIS OF COLLECTED DATA: INNOVATORS

Attributes of an ideal receptor of the innovation

What is the ideal profile of the persons or organizations that are going to receive a transferred, licensed or sold innovation?

To get this information, interviewed innovators were asked to describe by three characteristics what they think the ideal receptor of their innovations should be. It is remarkable here that although the question was formulated in an open way, there were many coincidences in innovators' opinions. The result to this question is a ranking of the 3 most mentioned attributes (Fig. 11.2).

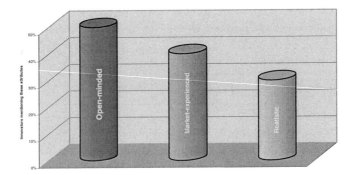

Fig. 11.2. Top 3 attributes of a receptor of innovations.

Attributes of an ideal innovator

It was aimed to know what is the profile of an ideal innovator, so interviewed innovators were asked to give 3 attributes to describe it.

Next figure shows the most mentioned adjectives, they can be considered the "top five attributes of an ideal innovator" (Fig. 11.3).

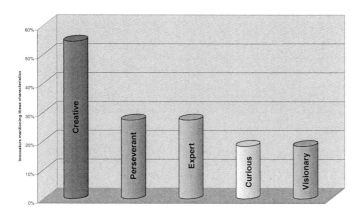

Fig. 11.3. Top 5 attributes of an innovator.

ANALYSIS OF COLLECTED DATA: ENTREPRENEURS

"Entrepreneurs are the fuel, engine, and throttle for the economic engine of a country" (Timmons, 1994: 5).

The common characteristic of the members of this sample is that all surveyed entrepreneurs have their enterprises located in the scientific park PSE. All the enterprises studied have been founded between years 1997 and 2000, 42% of them were founded in this last year.

Attributes of an ideal entrepreneur

One of the most important foundations of a new enterprise that determines whether it succeeds or not is the entrepreneur himself (Roberts, 1991: 245-246).

Many studies have been based in knowing the profile of the entrepreneur, but this study has aimed to know the own perceptions of entrepreneurs about themselves, and what it is needed from their point of view to be an "ideal" entrepreneur.

Entrepreneurs were asked to define three attributes that, in their opinion, an ideal entrepreneur should have. It is interesting to see that there are four characteristics that were

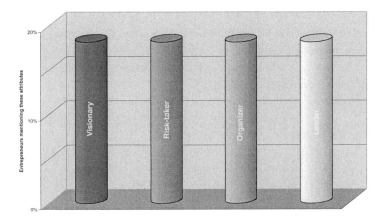

Fig. 11.4. Top 4 attributes of an entrepreneur, from entrepreneur point of view.

mentioned more than once and have been considered as the "top 4 attributes of an entrepreneur". Apart from these most mentioned adjectives, entrepreneurs have given a wide list of attributes that they consider to be essential in order to become a better entrepreneur, this list can be found after the figure of top attributes.

Herein there is the list of all the attributes mentioned by surveyed entrepreneurs (in bold the most mentioned attributes, Table 11.2).

Table 11.2. Characteristics of an ideal entrepreneur.

Characteristics of an ideal entrepreneur

Visionary	Independent	Team player
Risk-taker	Enthusiasm	Flexible
Organizer	Self confidence	Manage people
Leader	Courageous	Convincing
Innovator	Will	Communication skills
Original	Persistent	Ability to learn
Proactive	Tenacity	Market feeling
Dynamic	Hard working	Brilliant
Optimist	Experienced	Rich
Ambition	Market knowledge	

Attributes of an ideal investor, in entrepreneurs opinion

How entrepreneurs would like their potential investors to be, what are the attributes that they most value in investors? In order to find it out, entrepreneurs were asked to describe an ideal investor.

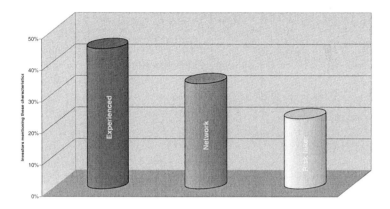

Fig. 11.5. Top 3 attributes of an investor, from entrepreneurs point of view.

It is worth noting that 40% of entrepreneurs think that experience is the first attribute than an investor should have. Entrepreneurs like experienced investors bringing experience in the investment world, international experience, experience in new technology ventures investments and with established records of success when investing. In second place, entrepreneurs appreciate the possible networks of investors. Strong network in the appropriate

Table 11.3. Characteristics of an ideal investor.

Characteristics of an ideal investor

Experienced	Flexible	Non-intrusive
Network	Straight	Honest
Risk taker	Top-notch investment team	Good portfolio of companies
Money	Know the core business	Aggressive
Fast decision	Commitment	Long term thinking
Analytical minded	Track record	Positive spirit
Unlimited funds	Disregarding forms	Constructive thinking
Understanding	Visionary	
Present	Management abilities	

field, and thus, good connections are elements that entrepreneurs look for in investors. Entrepreneurs also think that the ideal investor should be risk taker, an important attribute when talking about new technology ventures.

Surveyed entrepreneurs described the ideal entrepreneur in many ways (Table 11.3, in bold the most mentioned attributes).

ANALYSIS OF COLLECTED DATA: INVESTORS

All the investors of this sample are venture capitalists (none of them defined himself/herself as business angels or private investor when answering the questionnaire).

Among other kind of companies, the members of the sample invest in new technology enterprises, and the majority of them, 80% of cases, has invested in enterprises belonging to a scientific park, at least once.

Attributes of an ideal investor

When analyzing data collected, the first two attributes of an ideal investor according to entrepreneurs, are identical to those identified by investors themselves.

40% of surveyed capitalists think that experience and network are essential characteristics to be a good investor, and more than 20% mention that an investor needs to be a deal maker.

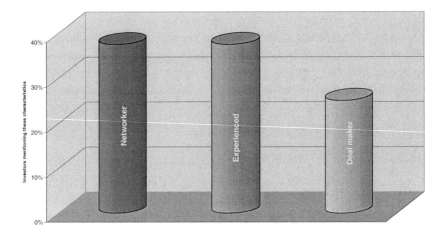

Fig. 11.6. Top 3 attributes of an investor, from investor's point of view.

Below are all the mentioned attributes of an ideal investor (in bold the most mentioned ones).

Table 11.4. Characteristics of an ideal investor.

Characteristics of an ideal investor

Networker	Sector focus	Character
Deal maker	Strategic and financial input	Global exposure
Experienced	Energetic	Mix of people with different
Charismatic	Bringing sales	backgrounds
Entrepreneurship	Coach with strong strategic	Money for further financing rounds
Honest	and conceptual capabilities	Fairness

Attributes of an ideal entrepreneur, in investors opinion

What are the attributes than investors most value in entrepreneurs, how should an ideal entrepreneur be from investors' viewpoint?

Many characteristics were given by venture capitalists, but it is remarkable that more than half of the surveyed investors coincide in saying that the ideal entrepreneurs should have experience in entrepreneurship. To demand such attribute is "natural" but the supply is somewhat scarce. As the reader will remember: entrepreneurs look for experienced investors, which in turn look for experienced entrepreneurs! Innovative and market-oriented are also mentioned by investors.

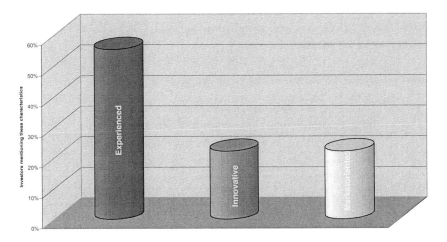

Fig. 11.7. Top 3 attributes of an entrepreneur, from investors' point of view.

Apart from the top three attributes (in bold), below are the other mentioned characteristics that an ideal entrepreneur should have.

Table 11.5. Characteristics of an ideal entrepreneur.

Characteristics of an ideal entrepreneur

Experienced	Strong communication skills	Leader
Innovative	Networker	Extensive network
Market oriented	Ready to work in team	Focused and matured personality
Visionary	Ambitious	Honest
Stamina	Realistic vision	Driven
Former success story	Well-rounded	Over 10 years experienced
Strong staying	Industry know-how	Coachable
Willpower	Creative	Hungry

VALUATION

It is appropriate to give some attention to the softer, human side of valuation. Value is, after all, very much like beauty- it is framed in the eye of the beholder. And every beholder is different. Because of their experiences, education, prejudices and goals, people see the world in many different ways (Boer, 1999: 1).

Methods to value

This study also aimed at identifying what methods people involved in new technology use when valuing enterprises and innovations. For this reason a list of 10 methods that are commonly used for valuation, were given to surveyed people (Table 11.6) and they marked the ones they use for valuing purpose.

Table 11.6. Methods commonly used to value a company.

Methods commonly used to value a company	
NPV - Net Present Value	**IRR** - Internal Rate of Return
DCF - Discounted Cash flow	**BV** - Book Value
PE - Price to Earnings	**OM** - Option Model
SM - Sales Multiple	**EV** - Exit Value
PP - Payback Period	**MC** - Market Comparable

Giving value to enterprises

The frequency of citation of each method used by entrepreneurs and investors is represented below in Fig. 11.8.

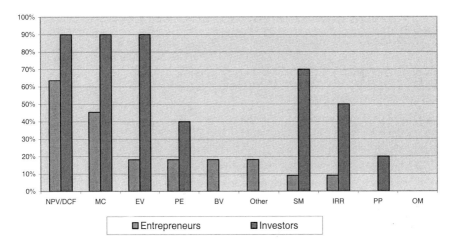

Fig. 11.8. Frequency of citations: Entrepreneurs and investors.

Entrepreneurs most used methods are Discounted Cash Flow with 63% and Market Comparable with 45%. Venture capitalists use mostly Discounted Cash Flow, Market Comparable and Exit Value, all for 90%. Entrepreneurs and Venture Capitalists coincide for the most used methods. Venture capitalists did not mention any other method used except for Ebitda.

Giving value to innovations

An important part of the innovators sample, (36%) does not answer the question as they say they are not interested in the economic value of their innovations. An answer received from one of these innovators summarizes this idea: "We are researches and we stop when we transfer the technology. It is not the role of a researcher to know the value applying financial methods. However, a researcher really knows when an innovation is really valuable".

All the innovators that use any method to value their innovations use the Market Comparable method! One conclusion that can be derived from this is that Market Comparable is a fairly easy and objective way to probe beyond what innovators currently understand about their competitiveness in target markets. Market Comparable or benchmarking is a process

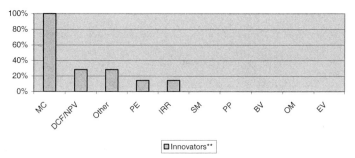

Figure 11.9. Used methods by innovators.

through which an innovation can be compared with other similar products found elsewhere. As one innovator mentioned: "It is useful to have an idea of the industry prices".

After having analyzed what methods innovators, entrepreneurs, and venture capitalists use to value innovations and enterprises, it can be said that the application of different valuation methods provides a framework within which a range of possible values can be established. Each of these approaches provides a different perspective in the overall valuation process. The results derived from any specific method may or may not be representative of a innovation or company's earnings capabilities over several future periods due to events that are unforeseeable.

The role of technology, market and human resources in the Valuation Process of New Technology Ventures

Valuation for newly-formed emerging growth companies is far more speculative than setting the value of more established, mature companies. Unlike newly-formed companies, established companies that are about to go public can more easily be compared to similar companies that are already trading on the public markets[2].

It has been attempted here to identify the importance of the technology, the market and the human resources as essential factors in the Valuation Process of New Technology Ventures. With this purpose, five items belonging to each of the 3 domains (technology, market and human resources) had to be ranked by surveyed people. The five items of each group had to be ranked from 1 to 6, being 1 the highest and 6 the lowest. It has to be mentioned that apart from the 5 identified items in each domain, respondents could add another item that they considered important. The 3 X 5 items initially presented were derived from experience and literature.

---

[2] Cameron, M., *The valuation of newly-formed technology companies.* http://www.whiteandlee.com

Importance of each item for innovators, entrepreneurs, investors

Before seeing the results obtained from collected data, it is appropriate to look at the percentages of answering.

Table 11.7. Response rates.

Technology	Imp.	Market	Imp.	Human Resources	Imp.
Innovators	100%	Innovators	36%	Innovators	64%
Entrepreneurs	100%	Entrepreneurs	100%	Entrepreneurs	100%
Investors	100%	Investors	100%	Investors	100%

As it can be seen, innovators are the group that showed more difficulties when ranking. Although all of them ranked technology items, only 36% felt in a position to rank market

Table 11.8. Average values of essential in terms of importance, given by the three groups of surveyed people.

TECHNOLOGY	Innovators	Entrepreneurs	Investors
Potential applications and products derived	1.6	2.6	2.1
Who will be interested	3.1	2.4	2.7
Strenghts and weaknesses of the technology	1.7	3.1	2.3
The technological risks	3.2	3.7	3.0
The protection of Intellectual Property	2.3	2.5	3.3

1 means highest and 6 lowest

MARKET	Innovators	Entrepreneurs	Investors
Understanding knowledge of the market	2.0	2.3	1.6
Customer target and market share	2.3	2.4	1.9
The competitors	2.0	2.9	2.2
The entry barriers	4.0	3.0	2.5
Market risks	4.5	3.2	3.0

1 means highest and 6 lowest

HUMAN RESOURCES	Innovators	Entrepreneurs	Investors
Management team with appealing vision	2.0	2.8	2.7
Balanced management team	2.5	2.3	2.3
Management team with leaderhip	2.5	2.9	2.7
Well qualified working team	1.7	2.5	2.4
Highly competent management board	3.2	3.1	3.1

1 means highest and 6 lowest

items. The percentage increased up to a 64% when ranking human resources aspects. Both entrepreneurs and investors ranked the proposed items in 100%.

After collecting and appropriately treating data, Table 11.8 shows the average ranking values of each item in terms of importance in a new venture valuation process, obtained from surveyed innovators, entrepreneurs and venture capitalists.

It has to be reminded that the range ranking values is from 1 to 6, with 1 for the highest value of importance and 6 for the lowest importance.

It must be noted that for some category of respondents, the total numbers of items selected is below 5 (or 6) and therefore the average rating provided by these respondents is lower than in other category. This is for example the case for the investors ranking the market domain and for the innovators ranking the human resources domain.

In order to appreciate in more detail the different perceptions and opinions, in terms of importance, given to each item by the various people, figures of next subsections show in a graphically way the mean values of each item obtained after treating the data collected from the survey.

Importance of technological items

As can be seen from Fig. 11.10, all the proposed items have a high importance under the viewpoint of innovators, entrepreneurs, and investors. It can be observed that no item has a mean value beyond 3,7. Considering the ranking range from 1 (highest importance) to 6 (lowest importance), this confirms that the items proposed are relevant.

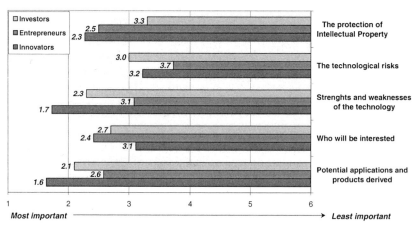

Fig. 11.10. Valuation indices for surveyed people in accordance with how important technological aspects are in a new venture valuation process.

In a general view, "potential applications and products derived from a technology considered" is the most important aspect for both innovators and investors, while for entrepreneurs, the most important aspect is "who will be interested in the technology considered".

On the other hand, innovators and entrepreneurs coincide in ranking "the technological risks" as the less important item, while for investors it is "the protection of Intellectual Property". This is somewhat surprising and could be due to the fact that for investors, a patent is in any case a prerequisite. This remains somewhat an enigma as one would think that such protection would provide them an "assurance" of the true novelty of the innovation considered.

Importance of market items

It can be observed in Fig. 11.11 that what it is considered the most important aspect when valuing the market for the three groups of surveyed people, is "understanding knowledge of the market".

On the other hand, the least important item for the three groups is "market risks", being under innovators opinion, not very important as the mean value is 4,5.

Innovators give more importance to the item "competitors" than investors and entrepreneurs do.

Importance of human resources aspects

Fig. 11.12 shows the mean values in terms of importance given by surveyed people. Comparing this figure with the technology and market ones, it can be seen that in human

Fig. 11.11. Valuation indices for surveyed people in accordance with how important market aspects are in a new venture valuation process.

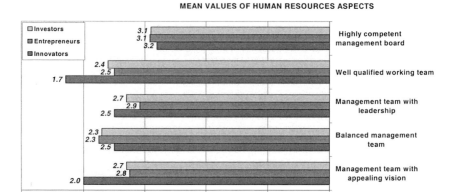

Fig. 11.12. Valuation indices for surveyed people in accordance with how important human resources aspects are in a new venture valuation process

resources aspects, the opinions of three respondents groups, are more similar than they were in technology and market items. This may be due to less distinct items here.

Innovators, entrepreneurs and investors agree to rank as the least important item the "highly competent management board". On the other hand, the most important item, from entrepreneurs and investors point of view, is a "balanced management team", while for innovators the most important is a "well qualified working team". This is probably due to the fact that strategic issues and organization deployment less concern innovators.

Comparative rankings of importance

Table 11.9 summarizes all the information that has been previously pointed out, giving the final ranking position of each identified item, under the point of view of surveyed people.

Other essential items under the technology, market, human resources domains

Apart from the 15 identified essential items asked to be ranked, surveyed people mentioned some others which they think are also important when giving value to new ventures.

Other technological considerations:
  ➢ Innovators viewpoint:
    • Fundamental science aspects
    • To develop the technology faster than competitors do
  ➢ Entrepreneurs viewpoint:
    • Feasibility of the technology architecture

Table 11.9. Final ranking positions.

	RANKING POSITION		
TECHNOLOGY	Innovators	Entrepreneurs	Investors
Potential applications and products derived	1	3	1
Who will be interested	4	1	3
Strenghts and weaknesses of the technology	2	4	2
The technological risks	5	5	4
The protection of Intellectual Property	3	2	5
MARKET	Innovators	Entrepreneurs	Investors
Understanding knowledge of the market	1	1	1
Customer target and market share	3	2	2
The competitors	1	3	3
The entry barriers	4	4	4
Market risks	5	5	5
HUMAN RESOURCES	Innovators	Entrepreneurs	Investors
Management team with appealing vision	2	3	3
Balanced management team	3	1	1
Management team with leaderhip	3	4	3
Well qualified working team	1	2	2
Highly competent management board	5	5	5

> Investors viewpoint:
  - Technological environment
  - Uniqueness of the technology

Other market considerations
> Innovators viewpoint:
  - To be first in market
  - To have customer references
> Investors viewpoint:
  - High visibility of customers

Other human resources considerations
> Innovators viewpoint:
  - Competent leaders
  - Management team with expertise and talent
  - Management team with creativity
  - Candidates which work 80 hours/week
> Entrepreneurs viewpoint:
  - Participation of the management team in the stock options plan

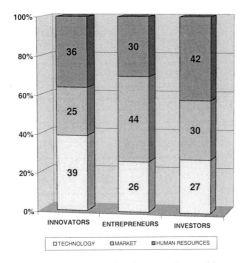

Fig. 11.13. Percentage weights of technology, market and human resources.

> Investors viewpoint:
  • Tough persons who keep control
  • Management team well disposed to be coached

Global percentage weights of technology, market and human resources in the Valuation Process of New Technology Ventures

Once having ranked the identified essential items in terms of importance and performance, innovators, entrepreneurs and investors were asked to give a global percentage weight to technology, market and human resources in the Valuation Process of New Technology Ventures. It was aimed to know their opinions about the global importance of these when valuing either innovations or enterprises.

Fig 11.3 shows a comparison of percentage weights given by innovators, entrepreneurs and investors, to the three elements considered.

CONCLUSIONS

This study underlines that innovators, entrepreneurs and investors bring different outlooks and expectations to the Valuation Process of New Technology Ventures. They do not think alike and have diverse backgrounds and motivations.

High-tech industries are fundamentally different from other industries, so it is not surprising that high technology ventures need to approach valuation process differently not just with hard data. In fact, many intangible aspects concerning Technology, Market and Human Resources are critical when valuing New Technology Ventures.

This research study exposes that while innovators give more importance to Technology in the valuation process, new-tech entrepreneurs think that Market aspects are the most valuable, and finally, investors think that Human Resources aspects are the most important ones to take into account when valuing a new technology enterprise.

They provide subjective evaluation inputs of major importance and the various mathematical methods are used as sanity checks to make sure the relative values seem to fall within reasonable ranges.

Finally, the Valuation Process of New Technology Ventures cannot be considered as a strict chain of tasks to be followed. As it takes place between persons, human aspects and emotional responses are determinant in the process, because, at the end, it simply becomes a negotiation between two parties.

BIBLIOGRAPHY

Boer, F. P. (1999), The valuation of technology. Wiley & Sons Inc, Business and financial issues in R & D. John Wiley & Sons.

Broadview white paper (September 1999), Charting a course through turbulence: IPOs, M&A and the pursuit of shareholder value.

Ettlie, J. E. (2000), Managing technological innovation. John Wiley & Sons.

Javeau, C. (1992), L'enquête par questionnaire. Editions de l'Université de Bruxelles

Jolly, V. K. (1997), Commercializing new technologies, getting from mind to market. Boston: Harvard Business School Press.

McKinsey & Company Inc., Planning for growth. Business planning for a successful venture.

Moore, G. A. (1995), Inside the tornado. Marketing strategies from Silicon valley's cutting edge. Harper Business,.

Rivette, K. G. (2000), D. Kline, Rembrandts in the attic, unlocking the hidden value of patents. Boston: Harvard Business School Press.

Roberts, E. B. (1991), Entrepreneurs in high technology. Lesson from MIT and beyond. Oxford University Press

Rogers, E. M. (1995), Difussion of innovations. Free Press, 4th edition,.

Thiétart, R.-A. et coll. (1999), Méthodes de recherche en management. Paris: Dunod.

Timmons, J. A. (1994), New venture creation. Entrepreneurship for the 21st century. Irwin McGraw Hill, revised 4th edition.

SECTION II

KNOWLEDGE MANAGEMENT

Management of Technology
Copyright © 2003 by Elsevier Science Ltd.
All rights of reproduction in any form reserved.
ISBN: 0-08-044136-X

12

TECHNOLOGICAL COMPETENCE AND ECONOMIC PERFORMANCE: WHO PERFORM BETTER IN TURBULENT ENVIRONMENTS?

Mette Praest Knudsen, University of Southern Denmark, Odense, Denmark[#,]*

INTRODUCTION

The relationship between the ability to produce products, market them and earn profits is well-established in stable markets. But, in a dynamic and uncertain environment, firms strive to survive by continuously building new competencies and adapting these to the existing portfolio of competencies in the organisation. Thus the relationship between technological competencies and economic performance becomes anything but straight-forward. In dynamic and turbulent markets, like e.g. telecommunications, competition is based on new technologies and technological artefacts and to a lesser extent the product itself, and thus the distinguishing factor becomes the underlying technological competencies. The question arises, whether it is better to build competencies on a continuous basis, to break away from time to time to consolidate, or to stick to the well-known knitting of well-proven patterns? Or, to state this

---

[#] The data used for this research were supplied by Fraunhofer (ISI) in Germany (http://www.fraunhofer.de/german/profile/isi.html) and Idate in France (www.idate.fr).

[*] Dr. Mette Praest Knudsen is Assistant Professor at University of Southern Denmark, Department of Marketing. Email: mpk@sam.sdu.dk. http://www.samnet5.sdu.dk/scripts/infoweb.dll/info?lang=dk&grp=mar&id=MPK.

differently, if a competence group encompasses those firms that pursue the same pattern of competence change, then:

> *What pattern of behaviour lead to better performance, i.e. which competence groups perform better over time?*

The article starts by setting the theoretical scene and introduces the notion of competence groups. These are viewed as research tools leading to the formulation of expectations regarding the relationship between different competence groups and economic performance. Following the data and method section a descriptive analysis of key economic ratios is carried out. Finally, the main conclusions are drawn up and recommendations for management of technology are provided.

COMPETENCE GROUPS AND PERFORMANCE

Both the theoretical (Dierickx and Cool (1989), Nelson (1991), Dosi and Marengo (1993)) and the empirical relationship (Malerba and Marengo (1995), Schmoch (1995), Patel and Pavitt (1998)) between technology, R&D and performance have been at the centre of attention in numerous strategic management studies. Over time, the theoretical arguments have shifted in focus, from early arguments favouring a linear relationship between R&D and performance (e.g. Kamien & Schwartz (1975)) to recent efforts emphasising the cumulative effects of R&D investments on profitability (e.g. Nelson and Winter (1982)). According to the latter process-based perspective numerous firm-specific learning effects associated with competence accumulation complicate the relation between R&D and performance. Recent studies often view such complications as multiple history-dependent firm-specific processes that frustrate attempts of uncovering any simple empirical relation between R&D expenditures and financial performance (David (1994), Levinthal (1996), Dosi (1988)). If we accept this recent process-based argument, both the indirect effect of competence accumulation, as well as the direct effect of R&D will influence performance.

The notion of competence groups[1]

Sanchez and Thomas first introduced the notion of competence groups and defined them as: *groupings of firms that engage in similar competence building or leveraging activities at a given point in time* (1996: 86). In a previous study Praest (1998: chapter 6) identified three groups of competence accumulating behaviour based on combinations of competence building, leveraging and erosion in a selection of technological fields. Obviously, a further option exists

---

[1]   A thorough development of the competence group notion can be found in Praest (1998 and 1999) including definitions of competence dynamics and the actual development of the competence groups.

where the firm may deliberately or through the competitive interactions not have any competencies in a particular field of technology. The derived competence groups draw on the notion of exploitation and exploration by March (1991). Exploitation represents the reproduction of existing knowledge sources within the domain of the firm. Exploration, on the other hand, represents the production of new knowledge based on search in the external environment. Applying these notions to the changing patterns of behaviour, exploitation equals stable development drawing on existing competencies, whereas exploration represents abrupt explorative patterns of behaviour with rapidly changing profiles. Exploitation then comes to reflect the firms that engage in similar competence profiles over time, defined as combinations of competence building, leveraging and erosion. In a similar fashion, exploration reflects those firms that are involved in abrupt changes over time shifting between e.g. competence erosion and competence building, thus initiating turbulence.

Expectations to Competence Groups and Performance

Firms in the exploitation group develop their competence base through stable development paths leading to diversification of the competence portfolio. These firms are expected to experience low growth, but sustained levels of performance, partly because they are positioned behind the technological frontier. The survival of these firms resides in the ability to exploit existing opportunities through adaptation to the competence base thereby ensuring lower risk.

The exploration group is characterised by radical changes in the competence base through abrupt and continuous changes. The aim is to shape the technological frontier in the technological fields of specialisation, primarily, through exploration of new and upcoming technological opportunities. Thus, the firms invest heavily in creation of new technological competencies through processes of trial and error in R&D. As a result of the massive R&D investments these firms will experience difficulties in becoming high performers (which is not to say that they are not competitive). Moreover, large differences within the group may appear as a consequence of the fundamental uncertainty about the results and outcome of R&D. This indicates that the exploration group will experience an expected lower performance overall than the exploitation group, whereas within the primary area of competence the exploration group will perform better. Moreover the R&D investments will be highest in the exploration group.

Two possible reasons for adopting a mixture of exploitation and exploration exist, first, firms may aim at sustaining their competitive position through mixed processes of knowledge creation, adaptation and consolidation. These firms are expected to perform very well as they induce continuous processes of competence updating. Second, the firms may stand under pressure from market dynamics, which forces more expensive and rapid reactions. The latter type of behaviour is based on fluctuations, that are not necessarily controlled, and may lead to performance fluctuations. For the mixed competence group, the expectation is that the firms will perform well, if they belong to the former group, but, if they belong to the latter, low performance and decreasing sales are expected to be the result.

The second involuntary reason for ending up with a mixed strategy arises from the effects of uncontrolled external influences, which causes an extensive financial pressure especially within telecommunications. As performance is expected to be constrained the R&D expenditures are expected to follow performance and decrease. On consolidated[2] level, the figures are not expected to give such a negative picture of the group, since the dynamics within telecom are more extensive, than in the average industry and exactly therefore is the potential for survival high. If the firms have a solid financial base, a period of pressure can be resisted, until the firm has consolidated its competence base and over time start to earn profits.

The stability of the competence group notion

The competence group notion, as applied here, is based on similarities in technological focus and in behavioural patterns, extracted from the competence accumulating activities. Industrial competence groups are expected to be similar on at least one dimension within the group, but to be dissimilar from other firms outside the group.

Changes in the competence group may affect the performance of the firm, but does also affect the industry as such. This sub-section addresses, what may cause a change in group. The first inducement to change lies in the external environment. According to Gorman, Thomas and Sanchez (1996: 92), dynamic environments shift the emphasis towards competence building and therefore also towards a destabilising path. Thus, changes in the environment, either through external chocks or competitor actions can induce the firm either to act by changing its own competence base, or to change its behaviour and move to a different group. When the degree of change in the industry increases the need for constant competence building and leveraging can lead to a change in group and thereby to a redefinition of the close technological competitors. The second inducement to change is barriers to competence building or leveraging, which will make the firm more exposed to external pressure. One way to address these barriers is through diversification into related areas see e.g. Markides and Williamson (1994: 155) on 5 types of related diversification.

Provided the continuous need for competence building and leveraging we should indeed expect changes but these will not result in changes in the competence groups as these are part of the behavioural pattern, only when the patterns are changed may we expect changes in the competence group structure. Hence, the assumption is therefore that once a firm is assigned to

---

[2]   We operate with two levels of performance. First, consolidated level which corresponds with all activities of the firm and thus includes all business areas, whereas telecom refers to the a sub-business area being a sub-group of the consolidated level. In a highly diversified company the telecom area will account for only a very small fraction of the overall strategy, and thus the turbulence have a smaller overall effect.

a group then it will remain there throughout the analyses. The stability of the competence group notion and as they are used in this paper has been analysed at length in Knudsen (2000).

DATA

The competence groups are identified in 3 steps: first, the level of specialisation is calculated[3], then the type of competence change (competence building, leveraging or erosion) is determined and based on the combinations of these are the firms grouped into either of the groups. Furthermore, the paper operates with discretionary variables to measure change. Three time points (1989, 1992, 1995) are applied for the economic data and are related to the competence groups for the changes in periods 1980-82; 1983-85; 1986-88; 1989-91;1992-94.

A firm is part of the <u>exploitation</u> group when the changes in specialisation in 1980-82 to 1983-85 resembles the changes from 1989-91 to 1992-94. If abrupt changes in the profiles over the years are seen both inward and outward then the firm is part of the <u>exploration</u> group, and finally a firm is assigned to the <u>mixture</u> group when shifts inwards are rapidly substituted by outward moves. In this paper, the exploitation group consists of Alcatel, AT&T, GEC, IBM, Siemens and Fujitsu; the exploration group contains Ericsson, Nokia, NEC, Toshiba and Sony; and the mixed group includes Matsushita, Hitachi, Motorola, Philips and Bosch, all of which are telecom hardware equipment manufacturers.

The paper uses two types of measures, single characteristics (e.g. R&D expenditure) and key ratios (e.g. R&D/turnover). The key ratios are used to evaluate, whether the firm uses a relative large amount of resources to build the technological competencies, whereas the key characteristics show the relationship between the competence groups.

In the following we explore the data in more detail. Patent data are used as an indicator of technological competence. This does not mean, that patents measure all technological competencies in a firm, but only, that within telecommunication, this is an instrument, which is assumed to be used to the same degree by all firms and therefore can assess the relative differences in competence accumulating behaviour. The advantages from using patents are, first, that they can be assigned directly to the firm, second, the data point is objective and third, the IPC classification allows for assignment of the technology to the exact technological field, e.g. mobile communication. These advantages makes the indicator accurate and easy to control.

---

[3]   The specialisation indicator RPA is a measure of the share of the firms activity to all the firms activities in a given technological field to the share of all technological fields to the total of all patents (Soete and Wyatt 1983). This means that a firm with an above average specialisation is, relatively seen, performing better, from a technological perspective, than other firms within the particular technological field. This measure determines that a firm e.g. builds competencies if the level of specialisation is below 0 (below average) and the change in RPA is above 10, which means that the level of specialisation increases from a below average level.

The data are selected based on a five step process, first, the technological field of telecommunications is defined using International Patent Classification (IPC)[4]. In this paper, an aggregate for the core of telecommunications as compared to a broader definition. This means that technologies with a peripheral connection to telecom has been excluded. Second, the patent applications are searched in World Patent Index (WPIL) for the time period 1980-94. These data are pooled in five intervals: 1980-82, 1983-85, 1986-88, 1989-91, and 1992-94[5]. Third, the 16 largest firms (on average over the period) in terms of numbers of patent applications are identified. Fourth, specialisation indices (RPA)[6] are calculated to enable the identification of the behavioural patterns. The reason for choosing RPA is that it enables analysis of the interdependencies between the single firm and the industry (see footnote 3). Finally, based on the specialisation indices the firms are assigned to a competence group. For the method and the background please consult Praest (1999).

To make the economic data compatible across currencies and to adjust for differences in firm sizes two calculations are carried out. First, the number of employees is used as weights to adjust for differences in firm size and the purchasing power parity (PPP)[7] converts all data into US $. The data cover R&D expenditures, turnover and net income at both consolidated level and within telecommunications. As these data are not entirely complete an estimation procedure has been applied in case of missing data; for further details about the procedure and the reliability assumptions consult appendix A. The financial data along with the key economic ratios are presented in Appendix B (tables B1 and B2).

The use of lag structures in estimations of relationship between input and output has been discussed among others by Grupp and Maital (1996: 12), who used a 4 year lag. In a turbulent industry like telecom, which is characterised by shorter technology lifecycles a lag structure of 2 years seems relevant. In the present analysis, a lag of 2 years indicates that a comparison between R&D and patents is based on patent applications filed in 1986-88 and R&D invested in 1985.

---

[4]   The exact definitions can be obtained from the author.

[5]   The application of intervals is required because of limitations in the data set. Only a small number of patents (especially in the first years) are available for the single firm in each year. To get statistical valid calculations the data are pooled in intervals throughout the paper.

[6]   Due to space limitations we refer to some introductory texts for the definitions and methods of calculation. See e.g. Grupp (1998) for a general introduction into indicators, among others specialisation index and patent share; Soete and Wyatt (1983) on the definition of the specialisation measure, and finally Pavitt (1988) on the use and abuse of patent data.

[7]   A different method to unify currencies is to use exchange rates, but these tend to be easily influenced by general economic instabilities e.g. changes in oil prices. One problem with the use of the PPP is the clear advantage of the American firms to all other nationalities, but this advantage tends to be smaller than the bias obtained by using exchange rates.

WHO PERFORMS BETTER IN TURBULENT ENVIRONMENTS?

Several measures can be used to interpret the strategic importance of telecommunications as compared to other technological fields. In the following section we attempt to compare the groups to identify whether there are significant differences in the core descriptive measures. Remember that the groups of firms are formed based on the technological competencies measured by the patent data and therefore are no patent results presented in the following section[8].

R&D Expenditures

Table 12.1 presents the R&D expenditures for the competence groups outlining a shift in the competence group with the highest investments in R&D from the exploitation group (at the consolidated level) to the exploration group in telecom. An increase in R&D adjusted by employees means that the firm is distributing more funds to the single employee or the number of R&D personnel is increasing more than the staff in the remaining functions to an unchanged R&D budget. An increase can therefore be seen as a signal of increased focus on R&D in telecom.

Despite increases in investments by the exploitation group in telecom the exploration group remains ahead. The expectation outlined above is therefore supported as the exploration group does invest more in R&D than the exploitation group in telecom even though the difference between the two groups is diminishing. The mixed group spends less on R&D than the other two groups, which does not necessarily imply 'bad performance', but simply is a statement of a different behavioural pattern.

Table 12.1. The R&D Profile of the groups (average of groups members in Mio $ PPP per 1000 employees).

		1989	1992	1995
	Exploitation	12.2	13.2	16.2
Consolidate	**Exploration**	10.4	10.3	12.0
	Mixture	6.9	8.8	9.3
	Exploitation	2.8	2.9	4.5
Telecom.	**Exploration**	5.7	4.8	5.5
	Mixture	2.1	1.8	2.1

---

[8]   Table 12.B1 has however one patent measure namely share of patents in telecom to total.

The smaller distance between the groups is caused by an increase by the exploitation group from 2.8 to 4.5 Mio. $ PPP/1000 empl. from 1989 to 1995. Within the groups large differences can be seen (see appendix B). Four firms have relatively larger expenditures than the remaining twelve firms, where Ericsson ranks first, AT&T ranks second, Nokia ranks third and Motorola ranks fourth. Especially, for Ericsson and Nokia the increases from 1989 to 1995 are remarkable. Above it was expected that the exploration group will invest heavily to finance the extensive search behaviour in telecommunications. Finally, the level of R&D is high, increasing and only in a few cases decreasing from 1989 to 1995. This was also expected to ensure continuous renewal of the resource base and the technological competencies, which requires high levels of R&D and effective protection of the competence base to maintain the competitive position.

Performance indicators

Tables 12.2 and 12.3 presents both the unweighted and weighted calculations on turnover. Turnover is used as a performance indicator to account for the direct ability of the firms to convert competencies into financial outcomes. Although the exploration group experiences a boost in 1992, the group is still well-behind the exploitation group and even the mixed group has a higher average turnover than the exploration group. In telecom, the differences between exploration and mixture is much smaller, which is an indication that the exploration group earns a relatively larger share in telecom than the mixed group. Once turnover is weighted by the number of employees then the results are reversed (see table 12.3) in favour of the expressed expectations above.

On consolidated basis the results are unchanged where the exploitive group performs better, whereas in telecommunications the explorative group is the better performer. These results now correspond with the expectation raised above. The adjustment for firm size indicates that the exploitation group represents the larger firms in the sample. Thus, the unweighted results account for the absolute performance of the groups. The results therefore

Table 12.2. The level of turnover of the groups (average of groups members in Mio $ PPP).

		1989	1992	1995
	Exploitation	29749.2	37976.1	32657.0
Consolidate	**Exploration**	9000.3	20199.9	17399.3
	Mixture	20223.4	27663.6	31521.0
	Exploitation	5401.3	6878.5	8276.3
Telecom.	**Exploration**	3078.4	3696.8	4277.9
	Mixture	2405.4	3239.4	4558.7

Table 12.3. The Level of Turnover of the groups (average of groups members in Mio $ PPP per 1000 employees).

		1989	1992	1995
Consolidate	Exploitation	119.7	148.8	173.9
	Exploration	117.9	131.3	151.6
	Mixture	104.3	124.4	138.9
Telecom.	Exploitation	22.0	28.5	49.5
	Exploration	33.4	50.2	54.5
	Mixture	17.6	23.3	29.1

also indicate that the exploitation groups has the stronger financial basis for survival in periods of trouble and the better foundation for boosting the R&D departments.

Finally, with net income the results are becoming blurred (see table 12.4). The consolidated data reveals that the exploitation group is a better performer than the other groups both in 1989 and 1992, whereas the mixed group catches up and takes the position as best performer even quite substantially (4.5 as compared to respectively 1.6 and 1.1 Mio. $ PPP/1000 empl.). In both 1989 and 1995, the explorative group has the highest level of net income in telecom, whereas in 1992, the exploitive group is the best performer.

The performance of the exploration group in 1992 is negatively influenced by NEC's poor performance, and thus the performance set-back is not a general decline, but a temporary phenomenon. In general, however, the results on net income are not quite as clear as in the case of turnover. This may though be caused by country-specific influences on the firms and by the nature of the concept. In the following analyses we will therefore disregard this measure.

Table 12.4. The level of net income of the groups (average of groups members in Mio $ PPP per 1000 employees).

		1989	1992	1995
Consolidate	Exploitation	5.7	2.0	1.1
	Exploration	3.2	0.8	1.6
	Mixture	3.5	1.8	4.5
Telecom.	Exploitation	1.0	1.1	-1.8
	Exploration	1.3	-0.2	2.8
	Mixture	0.7	0.6	1.6

R&D to turnover in telecom and consolidated

This sub-section focuses on a comparison of the shares of R&D to turnover. A well-known distinction that is often used is between high tech and low tech industries and companies. In the literature telecommunications has been labelled a high tech industry. Following the conventions, a share of above 7-8% of turnover is considered high tech. In the following we investigate, first whether the share for consolidated level is in fact lower than for telecommunications, which would be expected as many diverse industries are subsumed under this heading. Second, the levels of the single firms are investigated. A high share of R&D to turnover can be viewed as a strategic investment resulting in competence building and maintenance leading to higher payoffs at later points in time. An increase over time can be attributed to a strategic change that is expected to result in competence building.

On the consolidated level (table 12.5 columns 1-3), exploitation spends a higher share on R&D than exploration and the mixed behavioural type. Especially, out of the top five firms the four are from the exploitation group. NEC ranks first in 1989 of all firms with 15.8%, but the share decreases to approximately half the level in 1995. Other firms initiate the same decreases in the considered time period (e.g. IBM, Sony, and Philips). One exception is Ericsson, which raises the ratio of R&D to turnover from 8.9% to 15.3% and moves from rank

Table 12.5. Comparison of R&D to turnover in telecom and on consolidated level.

	R&D/turnover consolidated (%)			R&D/turnover telecommunications (%)		
	1989	1992	1995	1989	1992	1995
EXPLOITATION	**9.4**	**9.3**	**9.5**	**14.5**	**10.2**	**9.3**
Alcatel	7.5	9.4	10.1	N/A	6.7	8.5
AT&T	6.1	4.5	11.1	13.4	9.7	7.8
Fujitsu	10.3	11.4	9.9	10.0	15.8	9.4
GEC	10.1	9.9	9.2	23.3	8.4	9.9
IBM	10.9	10.1	8.4	N/A	42.2	18.3
Siemens	11.3	10.7	8.2	11.8	6.8	6.6
EXPLORATION	**8.5**	**8.6**	**8.4**	**11.9**	**7.4**	**10.7**
Ericsson	8.9	15.7	15.3	7.9	10.9	11.2
NEC	15.8	8.0	7.1	27.4	9.2	9.2
Nokia	5.1	6.1	6.9	5.9	7.4	6.8
Sony	6.6	6.3	6.0	N/A	N/A	29.6
Toshiba	6.1	6.7	6.5	N/A	N/A	17.9
MIXTURE	**6.7**	**7.1**	**6.6**	**10.8**	**8.8**	**8.3**
Bosch	5.9	6.7	6.9	4.9	2.7	5.8
Hitachi	5.8	6.7	6.5	16.7	21.7	21.6
Matsushita	5.8	5.6	5.4	N/A	20.1	17.9
Motorola	8.2	10.4	8.1	15.9	7.7	5.7
Philips	8.0	6.3	6.0	N/A	13.8	24.1

six to rank one. On average, though, the three competence groups keep the share at consolidated level approximately unchanged.

From table 12.5 (columns 4-6) the estimated share of R&D to turnover in telecom shows larger variations. Exploitation invests the highest share in 1989, but this decreases to the level of the consolidated basis in 1995 (app. by one third of the level in 1989).

Both exploration and exploitation have slightly decreasing shares, but these remain above the consolidated level. Within the competence groups large variations are seen. Only Hitachi remains in top five with rank three. The largest decreases are seen for NEC, Motorola and AT&T, on the other hand the largest increases are seen for Sony and Philips.

The fact that the share of R&D to turnover in telecom lies above the share at consolidated level supports the characteristics of the industry as being turbulent requiring above average investments in R&D. Although the firms in the sample to some extent are also engaged in other high-tech industries like e.g. semiconductors (e.g. Motorola and Philips) the investments into telecommunications remain high. From the above findings it cannot, in general, be supported that R&D in telecom has been given a much clearer focus although it must be characterised as high tech. This can be explained with the fact that even before 1989 telecommunications was a large and important technological field with large potential for revenue, but clearly, for some firms telecommunications has become much more important.

Relative importance of R&D and Turnover

In this sub-section we turn to compare the strategic importance of telecom within each of the groups and for the firms. A high share of R&D in telecom compared to consolidated level indicates a high strategic importance of telecom and may give higher variance in turnover. The reason is that telecom as a high tech and high velocity industry may lay serious constraints on the firms ability to survive through environmental distortions. A comparison of the share of R&D to the same share in turnover may highlight whether the firms are able to convert investments into turnover and ultimately performance (compare columns 1-3 with 4-6 in Table 12.6).

The relative importance of R&D measured as the share of R&D expenditures in telecom to consolidated highlights the exploration group as the most focused of the groups, where on average 40% of R&D is spend on telecom (1995). However large variations can be seen within the groups; Ericsson spends from 87% to 69% in 1995 on telecom, whereas Hitachi spends around 6%. Remember that Hitachi was investing more than the other firms in R&D to turnover, which combined highlights the highly diversified nature of Hitachi's competence profile. Nokia increases from rank 7 to rank 1; more than tripling its investments in telecom. The overall levels remain rather constant around 25%. This figure shows that for this sample of firms telecom accounts for a quarter of all R&D expenditures. The exploitation and mixture groups are fairly similar in terms of shares and at either stable or slightly decreasing levels. For

Table 12.6. Comparison of relative importance of R&D and Turnover.

	R&D in telecom to R&D consolidated (%)			Turnover in telecom to Turnover consol. (%)		
	1989	1992	1995	1989	1992	1995
EXPLOITATION	28	22	27	29,7	31,7	39,3
Alcatel	42	25	35	n.a.	47	50
AT&T	55	41	54	25	19	78
Fujitsu	15	18	14	16	13	15
GEC	20	18	21	9	21	19
IBM	17	14	18	n.a.	3	8
Siemens	22	15	17	21	24	21
EXPLORATION	37	33	40	47,7	62,9	44,9[a]
Ericsson	87	68	69	98	98	95
NEC	48	31	36	28	27	27
Nokia	20	46	71	17	38	72
Sony	18	12	16	n.a.	n.a.	3
Toshiba	13	8	11	n.a.	n.a.	4
MIXTURE	24	18	19	19,7	25,7	23,5
Bosch	19	10	13	23	24	15
Hitachi	6	6	7	2	2	2
Matsushita	11	11	11	n.a.	3	3
Motorola	67	46	43	34	63	61
Philips	16	15	20	n.a.	7	5
All	27	20	25	*21*	*17*	*21*

the turnover measure the level is unchanged for the exploration group, but the share would have increased had it not been for the low numbers of Sony and Toshiba.

Notice especially the low ability to convert R&D investments into turnover with shares of R&D around 15 and shares of turnover around 3 for both Sony and Toshiba. These results are not a characteristic of these two firms alone, but can also be seen for Matsushita, Hitachi and Philips. These are members of the mixture group and may account for some of the bad results of the group and even be seen as a sign of the effects of external turbulence that was discussed previously. Another significant result is the level of turnover by Ericsson in all three years, where a significant share of turnover comes from telecom. As noticed above a very high share may increase the vulnerability of the firm towards environmental turbulence. This is exactly what has been seen for Ericsson in the beginning of year 2000 with large rounds of layoffs and problems with profitability. With the large increase of the share for Nokia this might be an indication that Nokia could run into the same difficulties as Ericsson are in. However, presently Nokia seems to be staying clear of such problems. The exploitation group seems to be utilising their competencies very well as the share of turnover is higher than the share of R&D. This could indicate a superior ability to rely on exploitation of existing knowledge areas in new ways. However, continuous knowledge exploitation may lead to competence traps see e.g. Dosi and Malerba (1996); Levinthal and Myatt (1994) and Levitt (1988). Thus, even so the group seems to be performing well, further development along these lines may jeopardise future survival.

CONCLUSION

The results indicate that, within telecommunications, <u>exploration</u> is the best performing group characterised by a lower consolidated R&D budget than the exploitation group but a higher budget in telecommunications. Table 12.5 revealed a catch-up in the share of R&D to turnover in telecom to be the largest relative investor in 1995. Thus, both absolute and relatively seen is the exploration group the largest investor in telecommunications. But compared to the theoretical expectations a larger difference between the exploration group and the other groups was expected, although a smaller difference can be explained by the high growth in turnover. Hence, the growth in R&D is not enough to cause an effect on the share of R&D to turnover, which again is related to the substantial increases in turnover. The group has with its aggressive pattern of competence accumulation remained successful in turning R&D into new competencies and further into financial performance.

But the results also reveals extensive fluctuations in net income, which can be caused by trial and error processes in R&D. Other explanations may also be of relevance; Leiponen (2000) investigated and found some support that combinatory characteristics are one source of performance differences, i.e. competencies are more valuable in some combinations than others. Obviously, such explanations should be investigated further in the future.

At the consolidated level, the <u>exploitation</u> group is the best performer. The group has the highest performance in terms of both turnover and net income (besides net income in 1995), and in terms of R&D to turnover with a ratio of around 9.4%. With the higher shares of R&D to turnover also in telecommunications it may appear as the exploitation group is attempting to forego the problems of competence traps by moving into new competence groups. To investigate such a trend further a dynamic modelling approach taking into account not just competence changes but also group changes should be initiated. However, as highlighted by this dataset the group looses its first rank when we turn to telecommunications, and even slides down on a third place measured on net income. This is a clear sign that the increased investments have not yet paid off for the firms.

Finally, the <u>mixed</u> group faces a number of problems. The good news are that the group seemingly faces a high potential through the success of Motorola. Another positive point is the catch up in net income, in 1995, at consolidated level. The bad news are found in the pressure from the other groups as seen by the almost consistent third ranking. The behaviour of these firms seem, at a first glance, to change often, but the changes are really effects of changes in the external environment. Thus, the highly focused activities of the competitors set the existing competencies of the mixed group under pressure. This was seen in the lack of ability to convert the R&D investments into performance. The group performs better than the explorative group at consolidated level, but the group is lagging behind in telecommunications, which is a sign that specifically in telecom is management of change and turbulence necessary skills.

Some methodological problems have influenced the analysis in a negative way. First, apparent problems in the financial data require more disaggregated data for further analysis. These data should be related directly to the business area in order to rule out estimation problems. Moreover, market shares of the firms at best in telecommunication sub-fields (e.g., mobile phones) would enable very direct comparisons of competence activities and performance. Finally, the analysis would have gained exploratory power by introducing a dynamic method, which include and exclude firms based on changes in the industry, which would enable changes in the competence groups.

However, for management of technology some indications are clear. Based on the results of the mixed group the firms should take into account the competence accumulating activities of the competitors. The pressure set from the other groups demand very high investments to catch-up with the competence gaps. As the evolution has been extensive, these changes are obviously very costly and time-consuming. On the other hand, the recent experiences of Ericsson can, based on the available data, point to the problems of getting to specialised in telecommunications alone. Today, Ericsson struggles with immense problems. Without going into detail the figures for Ericsson were rather drastic with shares of turnover in telecom to consolidated level above 95% causing immediate problems as a reaction to the environmental turbulence starting in the late 1990'ies. Thus, apparently the better performing firms are those that dare to bet on extensive search patterns causing many failures but also immediate success (for some!). The larger conglomerate firms in the exploitation group performs well, but is lagging behind compared to the exploration group, even with Sony and Toshiba in the group to take down the overall result for the group. The problems for Sony has so far been the very strong capabilities in imaging, consumer electronics and design and with weaker technological competencies that could lead ahead. The rather clear trends of the empirical results point to the importance of positioning and technology monitoring.

The conclusion is that much has to be done in verifying, how firms gain competitive advantages and how they sustain them. The results indicate that the importance of turbulence caused in the external environment increased over the period, thus urging the firms to actively take into account the activities of the competitors in strategic decision making. The suggestion is therefore to advance research, which incorporates the external environment and to stress that internal knowledge creation without attention to the external reality is a dangerous path to take.

REFERENCES

David, P. A. (1994). Why are Insitutions the 'Carriers of History'?: Path Dependence and the Evolution of Conventions, Organizations and Institutions. In: *Structural Change and Economic Dynamics*, **5**(2): 205-220.

Dierickx, I. and K. Cool (1989). Asset Stock Accumulation and Sustainability of Competitive Advantage. In: *Management Science*, **35**: 1504-1514.

Dosi, G. (1988). The Nature of the Innovative Process. Technical Change and Economic Theory. G. Dosi, C. Freeman, R. Nelson, G. Silverberg and L. Soete. London, Pinter Publishers: 221-238.

Dosi, G. and F. Malerba (1996). Organizational Learning and Institutional Embeddedness. Organization and Strategy in the Evolution of the Enterprise. G. Dosi and F. Malerba. London, MacMillan Press: 1-24.

Dosi, G. and L. Marengo (1993). Some Elements of an Evolutionary Theory of Organizational Competencies. Evolutionary Concepts in Contemporary Economics. R. W. England. Ann Arbor MI, University of Michigan Press: 157-178.

Gorman, P., H. Thomas, et al. (1996). Industry Dynamics in Competence-based Competition. Dynamics of Competence-based Competition: Theory and Practice in the New Strategic Management. R. Sanchez, A. Heene and H. Thomas. Oxford, Pergamon: 85-98.

Grupp, H. (1998). Foundations of the Economics of Innovation. Edward Elgar,

Grupp, H. and S. Maital (1996). Innovation Benchmarking in the Telecom Industry. In: *Sloan School of Management, MIT*, **WP# 153-96**.

Kamien, M. I. and N. L. Schwartz (1975). Market Structure and Innovation: A Survey. In: *Journal of Economic Literature*, **13**(1): 1-37.

Knudsen, M. P. (2000). Demarcation of Technological Competence Groups: Methods, Problems and Future Opportunities. Research in Competence-based Management. R. Sanchez and A. Heene. Stamford, JAI Press Inc. **6C**: 255-285.

Leiponen, A. (2000). Collaboration, Innovation and Firm Performance: Increasing Returns from Knowledge Complementarities. Helsinki, The Research Institute of the Finnish Economy (ETLA).

Levitt, B. and J. G. March (1988). Organizational Learning. In: *Annual Review of Sociology*, **14**: 319-340.

Levinthal, D. (1996). Learning and Schumpeterian Dynamics. Organization and Strategy in the Evolution of the Enterprise. G. Dosi and F. Malerba. London, MacMillan Press: 27-41.

Levinthal, D. and J. Myatt (1994). Co-Evolution of Capabilities and Industry: The Evolution of Mutual Fund Processing. In: *Strategic Management Journal*, **15**: 45-62.

Malerba, F. and L. Marengo (1995). Competence, Innovative Activities and Economic Performance in Italian High-Technology Firms. In: *International Journal of Technology Management*, **10**(4/5/6): 461-477.

March, J. G. (1991). Exploration and Exploitation in Organizational Learning. In: *Organization Science*, **2**(1 (Feb)): 71-87.

Markides, C. C. and P. J. Williamson (1994). Related Diversification, Core Competences and Corporate Performance. In: *Strategic Management Journal*, **15**: 149-165.

Nelson, R. R. (1991). Why Do Firms Differ, and How Does It Matter? In: *Strategic Management Journal*, **12**: 61-74.

Nelson, R. R. and S. G. Winter (1982). An Evolutionary Theory of Economic Change. The Belknap Press of Harvard University Press, Cambridge Massachusetts.

Patel, P. and K. Pavitt (1998). The Wide (and Increasing) Spread of Technological Competencies in the World's largest Firms: A Challenge to Conventional Wisdom. The Dynamic Firm: The Role of Technology, Strategy, Organization, and Regimes. A. D. Chandler, P. Hagstöm and Ö. Sölvell. Oxford, Oxford University Press: 192-213.

Pavitt, K. (1988). Uses and Abuses of Patent Statistics. Handbook of Quantitative Studies of Science and Technology. A. v. Raan. Amsterdam, North Holland.

Praest, M. (1998). Changing Technological Capabilities in Hith-tech Firms: A Study of the Telecommunications Industry. In: *The Journal of High Technology Management Research*, **9**(2): 175-194.

Praest, M. (1999). Evolutionary Patterns of Technological Competence Accumulation: A Measurement Proposition. Mobilizing Knowledge in Technology Management, Copenhagen.

Sanchez, R. and H. Thomas (1996). Strategic Goals. Dynamics of Competence-Based Competition: Theory and Practice in the New Strategic Management. R. Sanchez, A. Heene and H. Thomas. Oxford, Pergamon: 63-84.

Schmoch, U. (1995). Evaluation of Technological Strategies of Companies by Means of MDS-Maps. In: *International Journal of Technology Management*, **10**: 426-440.

Soete, L. G. and S. M. E. Wyatt (1983). The Use of Foreign Patenting as an Internationally Comparable Science and Technology Output Indicator. In: *Scientometrics*, **5**(1): 31-54.

APPENDIX A: ESTIMATION OF R&D BUDGET AND NET INCOME

The data set covers net income, turnover and R&D at consolidated firm level, as well as turnover at telecom sub-level. Thus, R&D and net income at the sub-level telecom are lacking. This section develops an estimation procedure to calculate these.

The problem in using consolidated data instead of data at the telecommunications level can be illustrated as follows. If one would compare competencies in telecommunications and let these explain consolidated performance, one of two situations would occur; the firms would have to compete in telecommunications alone or any identified relationship would be based on pure luck. Therefore some indicator of performance at the telecom sub-level is needed.

The estimation procedure rests on three assumptions:

Assumption 1: Within all technological fields is the propensity to patent equal.

Assumption 2: The firms distribute the same share of R&D expenditures to achieve the same level of technological activity; i.e. the relationship between R&D and patents across the sample firms is the same.

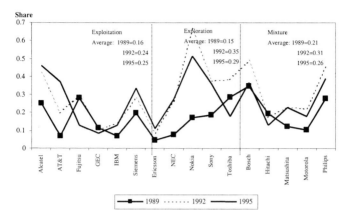

Fig. 12.A. Share of patents to R&D on consolidated basis (1989, 1992, 1995).

As long as the research object is the relationship between the competence groups, then is merely the second assumption necessary. But for the analysis of the second research question (c.f. section 7) the application of assumption 1 is required.

A 'loose' test of assumption 2 is carried out graphically, based on data from Table 12.B1 and presented in Fig. 12.A. If the curve of each year was horizontal then the assumption would be true. For the comparison between the groups the curve structures in each of the three parts of the figure should be fairly alike.

The first section of Fig. 12.A presents the results for the exploitation group, the second the exploration group and finally the mixture group. A decrease in share over time means that the firm either applies for fewer patents to an unchanged level of R&D or increases R&D investments to an unchanged rate of patent applications (see e.g. GEC or Hitachi).

Notice should furthermore be taken of Nokia, which both in 1992 and 1995 experience a steep rise in the share. Thus, the results of Nokia may influence the results of the exploration group as such. This possible outlier can impact the analyses in the following manner; a rise in the share, as a result of a decrease in R&D, will make the regression curve start closer to origo, and potentially increase the discrepancy within the competence group (for a discussion see section 5).

In general, the 1992 curve seems to lie above the curves of the two other years. Thus, in 1992 the propensity to patent was higher overall or R&D was lower than in the years to compare with. This can impact the results in section 6 by making the regression curve, of that particular year, shorter. Across the groups only small differences are seen, which leads to the conclusion that assumption 2 seems realistic.

Assumption 3: The profitability of all fields is the same.

The profitability of the technological fields is clearly varying, but because of the lack of data at the telecom level this assumption must be introduced in order to estimate net income. The relationship is estimated using between turnover in telecommunications to total turnover to get net income in telecom.

The estimation procedure is split into two steps:

1. Calculate the share of core telecommunication applications to all patent applications.
2. To estimate R&D in telecom, multiply R&D expenditures on consolidated level with the result of step one.

The equation for the estimation of R&D expenditures in telecommunications is then:

$$R\&D(tele) = R\&D(cons.) * \frac{Pat.(tele)}{Pat.(tot.)}$$

Formula 1: Estimation of R&D expenditures in telecommunications

Following the same procedure, but instead inserting turnover in telecom and total turnover yields:

$$NI(tele) = NI(tot.) * \frac{Turn(tele)}{Turn(tot.)}$$

Formula 2: Estimation of net income in telecommunications

Thus, net income in telecommunications is equal to the share of turnover in telecommunications to total turnover, multiplied by net income at consolidated level.

Table 12.3 presents the financial figures for each of the 16 firms and for the three competence groups, and Table 12.4 presents the results of the estimations. Throughout the paper these groupings will be used as unit of analysis. The importance of firm size has been touched upon earlier and thus most of the analyses are carried out with an adjustment by size. The adjustment is calculated based on the number of employees. Finally, firms with missing data will be excluded in the particular time period, but be included, when data are available. This is particularly a problem in the analyses including telecommunications turnover and net income in telecommunications.

APPENDIX B

Table 12.B1: Key Figures of 16 Telecommunications Firms (1989, 1992, 1995).

	Net income (Mio. $ PPP)			Turnover (Mio. $ PPP)			Turnover in tele (Mio. $ PPP)			R&D (Mio. $ PPP)			Share of Patents in Telecom. to total		
	1989	1992	1995	1989	1992	1995	1989	1992	1995	1989	1992	1995	86-88	89-91	92-94
EXPLOITATION	**1529.8**	**327.6**	**260.6**	**29749.2**	**37976.1**	**32657.0**	**5401.3**	**6878.5**	**8276.3**	**1726.1**	**3268.8**	**2959.3**			
Alcatel	739.1	1096.9	-3864.5	21541.5	25144.2	24232.0	N/A	11918.3	12225.3	1624.3	2351.5	2447.3	29.88	34.09	42.59
AT&T	2697.0	3807.0	-853.0	50976.0	64904.0	21413.0	12782	12198.0	16603.0	3098.0	2924.0	2385.0	38.23	40.59	54.39
Fujitsu	351.7	65.0	254.7	11994.6	18330.4	18430.1	1886.4	2369.4	2832.5	1240.5	2087.1	1832.4	10.15	17.95	14.47
GEC	885.4	1017.3	841.8	11294.9	17028.2	17046.3	964.4	3625.0	3256.7	1135.6	1677.4	1567.2	13.72	18.23	20.66
IBM	3758.0	-4965.0	4178.0	62710.0	64523.0	71940.0	N/A	2200.0	5900.0	6827.0	6522.0	6010.0	11.74	14.22	17.99
Siemens	747.4	944.4	1006.8	28970.5	37927.1	42880.7	5972.5	8960.4	8840.6	3258.3	4050.7	3514.0	13.97	14.94	16.55
EXPLORATION	**303.8**	**173.3**	**-58.0**	**9000.3**	**20199.9**	**17399.3**	**3078.4**	**3696.8**	**4277.9**	**978.2**	**1102.5**	**1234.5**			
Ericsson	206.2	48.8	545.5	4423.8	4793.1	9907.7	4331.8	4679.4	9403.3	394.7	752.0	1513.8	49.45	67.55	69.35
NEC	324.0	81.5	199.8	15488.3	20098.3	21324.7	4281.6	5334.2	5810.7	2441.7	1608.4	1504.9	31.28	30.51	35.57
Nokia	24.8	-113.7	371.4	3624.0	2856.6	6124.8	621.9	1076.7	4391.5	183.1	175.0	421.1	15.70	45.56	70.79
Sony	364.1	639.6	-1659.6	10778.4	20352.6	22535.9	N/A	N/A	738.9	713.8	1283.5	1353.0	11.54	12.11	16.16
Toshiba	599.9	210.4	252.8	19096.0	25149.9	27103.2	N/A	N/A	1045.5	1157.6	1693.6	1759.4	8.22	8.06	10.60
MIXTURE	**684.9**	**193.3**	**882.7**	**20223.4**	**27663.6**	**31521.0**	**2405.4**	**3239.4**	**4558.7**	**1438.4**	**1840.2**	**2032.6**			
Bosch	296.7	247.2	265.7	14496.5	16633.7	17315.9	3263.0	3947.8	2614.7	854.5	1112.1	1195.2	13.34	9.73	12.65
Hitachi	932.5	679.6	644.4	32161.4	41356.5	42952.4	643.2	827.1	859.0	1879.0	2766.7	2780.5	3.68	6.49	6.67
Matsushita	1072.6	707.2	512.0	27654.2	39675.7	39308.4	N/A	1188.2	1359.2	1603.2	2226.1	2138.8	6.95	10.74	11.38
Motorola	498.0	453.0	1781.0	9620.0	13303.0	27037.0	3310.0	8374.0	16422.0	784.0	1386	2197.0	45.53	46.43	42.63
Philips	624.5	-420.6	1210.6	26010.9	27349.1	30991.4	N/A	1859.8	1538.5	2071.4	1710.3	1851.4	10.73	15.03	20.03

Source: Idate (France) www.idate.fr

Table 12.B2: Estimated R&D budget and Net income (1989, 1992, 1995).

	Share of R&D in tele to R&D cons. (%)			Est. R&D in telecom. (Mio. $ PPP)			R&D/1000 employees in telecom. (Mio. $ PPP/emp.)			Est. net income in telecom. (Mio. $ PPP)			Net Income/1000 emp. in Telecom. (Mio. $ PPP/emp)		
	1989	1992	1995	1989	1992	1995	1989	1992	1995	1989	1992	1995	1989	1992	1995
EXPLOITATION	**2.2**	**4.7**	**3.9**	**785.5**	**700.3**	**765.2**	**2.83**	**2.86**	**4.54**	**240.3**	**252.4**	**-310.2**	**0.96**	**1.11**	**-1.82**
Alcatel	2.3	2.9	2.4	721.6	801.7	1042.2	3.43	3.95	5.43	N/A.	519.9	-1949.7	N/A.	2.56	-10.17
AT&T	1.8	2.5	1.8	1710.8	1186.8	1297.1	6.03	3.80	9.90	676.3	715.5	-661.4	2.39	2.29	-5.05
Fujitsu	6.6	5.6	6.9	187.7	374.7	265.1	1.80	2.41	1.61	55.3	8.4	39.1	0.53	0.05	0.24
GEC	5.1	5.5	4.8	224.8	305.8	323.7	1.54	2.47	3.94	75.6	216.6	160.8	0.52	1.75	1.96
IBM	5.9	7.0	5.6	1161.8	927.7	1081.4	3.03	3.08	4.80	N/A.	-169.3	342.6	N/A.	-0.56	1.52
Siemens	4.6	6.7	6.0	706.5	605.3	581.7	1.94	1.47	1.56	154.1	223.1	207.6	0.42	0.54	0.56
EXPLORATION	**2.7**	**4.0**	**2.7**	**365.1**	**274.1**	**457.7**	**5.71**	**4.82**	**5.49**	**98.6**	**8.8**	**158.8**	**1.29**	**-0.24**	**2.81**
Ericsson	1.2	1.5	1.4	341.6	508.0	1049.9	4.93	7.67	12.4	201.9	47.7	517.8	2.92	0.72	6.13
NEC	2.1	3.3	2.8	1175.0	490.7	535.2	11.30	3.82	3.54	89.6	21.6	54.4	0.86	0.17	0.36
Nokia	5.0	2.2	1.4	36.6	79.7	298.1	0.89	2.98	8.82	4.3	-42.8	266.3	0.10	-1.60	7.88
Sony	5.7	8.3	6.2	126.4	155.4	218.7	1.60	1.31	1.58	N/A.	N/A.	-54.4	N/A.	N/A.	-0.39
Toshiba	7.9	12.4	9.4	146.0	136.4	186.6	1.17	0.81	1.07	N/A.	N/A.	9.8	N/A.	N/A.	0.06
MIXTURE	**5.6**	**6.5**	**5.4**	**259.0**	**285.5**	**377.5**	**2.12**	**1.84**	**2.09**	**85.6**	**70.0**	**242.5**	**0.70**	**0.61**	**1.64**
Bosch	5.3	10.3	7.9	160.9	108.2	151.2	0.92	0.64	0.95	66.8	58.7	40.1	0.38	0.35	0.25
Hitachi	17.5	15.4	15.0	107.3	179.5	185.4	0.39	0.55	0.56	18.6	13.6	12.9	0.07	0.04	0.04
Matsushita	9.4	9.3	8.8	171.4	239.2	243.5	0.89	0.99	0.92	N/A.	21.2	17.7	N/A.	0.09	0.07
Motorola	1.5	2.2	2.4	525.9	643.6	936.5	5.06	6.01	6.60	171.3	285.2	1081.8	1.65	2.67	7.62
Philips	6.3	6.7	5.0	329.5	257.0	370.8	1.08	1.02	1.40	N/A.	-28.6	60.1	N/A.	-0.11	0.23

13

THE CONCEPT OF INDUSTRY AND THE CASE OF RADICAL TECHNOLOGICAL CHANGE

Kamal A. Munir, Judge Institute of Management Studies, University of Cambridge, UK[†,*]
Nelson Phillips, Judge Institute of Management Studies, University of Cambridge, UK[**]

ABSTRACT

In the strategic management literature, the concept of 'industry,' usually defined with reference to products or services that are close substitutes, is widely deployed as an aid in competitive analysis. While this concept serves managers well in relatively stable periods, in this paper we argue that the same concept is of little use during times of significant technological change. Following a radical technological discontinuity, industries suddenly lose the central product, technology or design around which they are organized. Since the idea of an industry is firmly rooted in a central product (e.g., the "VCR industry" or the "PC industry"), a firm's competitive environment cannot be characterized as an 'industry' until a new dominant design emerges and it is again possible to discern what constitutes close substitutes. Therefore, while making sense of a firm's competitive environment in terms of 'industry' may be useful during periods of stability, it can be dangerously misleading for researchers and managers in the face

---

[†] A revised and updated version of this paper was published in Journal of High Technology Management Research, 13 (2), Kamal A. Munir and Nelson Philips, "The concept of industry and the case of radical technological change." 2002 (c) Elsevier Science Inc.

[*] Judge Institute of Management Studies, University of Cambridge, Trumpington Street, Cambridge CB2 1AG. Email: k.munir@jims.cam.ac.uk.

[**] Nelson Phillips is Beckwith Professor of Strategy and Marketing at the Judge Institute of Management, University of Cambridge, UK.

of radical technological change. We go on to argue that for firms engulfed in technological change the concept of 'activity network' – a broad group of firms struggling to shape or influence the perceived value, nature and technique for carrying out a particular activity – should be substituted for 'industry'. We illustrate our argument using the case of the photographic industry, which is currently experiencing a profound technological shock that is rapidly eroding traditional industry boundaries.

INTRODUCTION

This paper deals with an increasingly important question: to what extent is the concept of industry useful for managerial decision-making and conducting research in the face of radical technological change? While the concept of industry, traditionally defined as a group of firms producing close substitutes (e.g., the VCR industry, or the Semiconductor industry) (Bain, 1956; Porter, 1980), has proven useful as an aid to analysis during periods of stability, we argue against a reliance on the concept when firms are experiencing major technological change. We illustrate our argument with the help of the contemporary case of digital imaging technology, which is revolutionizing what was until a few years ago, the photographic 'industry.' As digital technology threatens to replace the chemical based imaging technology around which the photographic industry has been based for several decades, competition for incumbents is coming from several sources well beyond the traditional boundaries defined by 'the photographic industry.' In such situations, managers who use the traditional concept of 'industry' to make sense of the reality that faces them may end up with erroneous and potentially disastrous understandings of the competitive threats they face and of the competitive dynamics that are redefining their business.

But our argument here is not just that we need to do away with the concept of industry in times of technological uncertainty. Since episodes of drastic technological change are throwing industries into a state of flux more and more frequently, it is essential that we come up with an alternative concept to ground competitive analysis during these times of technological flux. Indeed, several researchers have called for subjecting the age-old concept of industry to renewed scrutiny and have suggested that firms be grouped around competencies or the critical information that they share (Bettis and Hitt, 1995; Sampler, 1998; Bettis, 1998). The analysis of the technological change in photography, however, suggests that while these alternative conceptualizations may work well during periods of relative stability, when great uncertainty clouds the future of an established industry, a more dynamic concept is needed to comprehend competition. Accordingly, we develop a theoretical concept – 'activity network' – that we define as the group of firms struggling to shape or influence the perceived value, nature and technique for carrying out a particular activity. Activity networks are composed of a number of subgroups, each formed around different technological trajectories and competing standards. We argue that this conceptualization characterizes a firm's competitive environment much more accurately during times of radical technological change.

We present our argument in several steps. First, we describe the current conceptualization of the industry concept, outline the main criticisms of the concept, and link it to the idea of a dominant design. We then discuss the process through which a dominant design emerges after the occurrence of a radical technological change, outlining some of the wider changes caused in the competitive landscape. We go on to describe the case of the photographic industry, where a dominant design has not yet emerged, and discuss how competition during this period is fundamentally different from that which we see in stable industries characterized by a dominant design. Based on the experience of the photographic industry, we propose activity network as an alternative to the present industry concept and discuss conclusions and implications for strategy practice and research.

OPENING THE INDUSTRY BLACK BOX

'Industry' is a central concept in numerous academic fields including economics, industrial organization economics, competitive strategy, technology management, and public policy. Within management, the idea of an industry is at the heart of several theoretical perspectives including the resource-based (Wernerfelt, 1984; Barney, 1986; 1991; Hamel and Prahalad, 1994; Barney, 2001) and positioning (Porter, 1980; 1985) views that dominate the literature. Most of this research subscribes to a notion of industry derived from industrial organization economics according to which an industry denotes a group of firms that produce close substitutes. This notion also forms the basis for the well-known Standard Industrial Classification (SIC) system developed by the US Bureau of the Census. This four-level system classifies all units providing goods and services into ten broad functional divisions (e.g., mining, manufacturing, services), next into groups within divisions (e.g., health services, legal services, educational services), then into individual industries within groups (e.g., offices of physicians, nursing and personal care facilities, and hospitals), and finally into providers of more specific products or services (e.g., within hospitals there are general medical and surgical hospitals, psychiatric hospitals, and so on)[1]. The SIC codes are based on the assumption that since a group of firms is engaged in the manufacturing or selling of products that are close substitutes, their performance can be compared by comparing their market share and profitability. This conceptualization of industry boundaries forms the basis for much research and practice in strategy. Entry/exit ratios, competition coefficients, and intensity of rivalry are all calculated using it. Thus, we commonly come across statements such as "a total of n firms

---

[1]   This system was developed by the federal government in the U.S. as a way of classifying industrial activity
    for purposes of data collection and dissemination.

entered the television industry between 19xx and 19yy." This drawing of boundaries is seldom questioned and implications are drawn from such analyses for competitive dynamics within all 'industries.' It is clear that the creation of such boundaries does carry several benefits. In order to be able to compare performance of one firm to another, researchers and managers need to delineate a group of firms. Thus, by drawing boundaries on the basis of close substitutes, managers are able to benchmark themselves against other firms within their industry and researchers are able to link success and failure to the position of a firm within that industry.

A number of researchers have consequently emphasized the importance of industry boundaries for both managerial decision-making and research (Levitt, 1960; Porac, Thomas, Wilson, Paton and Kanfer, 1995; Sampler, 1998; Bettis, 1998). For managers, where they draw the boundaries of their industry shapes their perception of the competitive arena and determines their actions towards other actors in the competitive field. For researchers, "where we draw the boundary of an industry determines what questions we ask and how we ask them. It suggests what might be interesting to study. It tells us what our results mean and where our prescriptions are applicable" (Bettis, 1998: 359). Sampler concurs: "one of the most fundamental questions for industry structure and IO economics is how industry boundaries are defined, because this influences industry concentration, the role of substitutes and many other factors" (Sampler, 1998: 348). But as Bettis points out, while the current conceptualization of industry has a "pervasive influence in organizing our agenda", it is seldom questioned (Bettis, 1998: 358).

In an attempt to fill this gap, Sampler (1998), Bettis (1998), and others have questioned the validity of the criterion that we use to draw industry boundaries. For example, Sampler (1998) has suggested that instead of treating a product or service as a point of reference, we should define an industry according to the critical information possessed by firms about the same group of customers. Sampler argues that the arrival of the 'information age' has fundamentally challenged the traditional boundaries of competition for firms. Information is therefore a critical resource that is increasing in importance everyday. It forms the basis for competition among an increasing number of firms that could be members of widely different 'industries' according to the traditional definition of the concept. For example, AT&T may have more customer information about a particular set of customers than the bank where these people have been carrying out their financial transactions. Based on this information, AT&T, a firm from a completely different and unrelated *industry*, may enter the financial services business and successfully challenge the incumbents.

On the other hand, in line with the resource-based view, Bettis (1998) argues that firms should be clustered together on the basis of the competencies that they share or wish to develop. He suggests that strategic management must not only be understood in terms of individual business units competing within a particular product or service market, but that it should be conceptualized in terms of the dynamically changing groups of firms that compete against other groups of firms in the provision of a good or service. Indeed, he maintains that competition is no longer between single firms, but is now driven by 'webs' of firms supporting particular technological standards or platforms. Within these webs or networks, firms compete against each other to capture firm rents while firms outside compete for access to web membership. Thus, the relevant environmental entity is no longer 'industry' but a cluster of firms with similar competencies.

The arguments for grouping firms around critical information (Sampler, 1998) or competencies (Bettis, 1998) seek to attack the supposedly misplaced criterion that is used to draw industry boundaries. According to these authors, understanding one's industry in terms of close substitute products may have enormous negative repercussions for firms, including hiding potential competitors from view or leading to a misunderstanding of the basis of competition in their business. But while these criticisms, and the corresponding solutions, are interesting and useful during periods of technological stability, during times of radical technological change grouping firms according to competencies or critical information is not very helpful as the nature of the product or service itself is uncertain. Firms with completely different competencies, and information about entirely different markets, may become competitors depending on the direction of technological development that takes place.

Similarly, analyses based on the popular and rather liberally used classification 'emerging' industries (see e.g., Porter, 1980) do not offer much help since these are generally based on traditional notions of 'industry' and fail to grasp the uncertainty produced by radical technological change where boundaries between suppliers and competitors are blurred, new competencies brought to the fore and new evolutionary paths chalked out. Instead, studies of 'emerging industries' assume a much more stable structure (Porter, 1980; Aldrich and Fiol, 1994). Thus, Porter states, "every industry begins with an initial structure -- the entry barriers, buyer and supplier power, and so on which exist when the industry comes into existence" (1980: 162). Porter (1980) is clearly not directly concerned with the case of firms engulfed in radical technological change. In Porter's work, firms are considered as new entrants staking out domains in an unexplored territory. However, the case that we encounter much more frequently is that of mature industries renewing themselves through fundamental technological changes. Such industries undergo a complete transformation that includes a period where no central product or design exists to unify firms in that competitive arena. Instead firms congregate around an activity (say photography) with competing claims about the best way to carry it out. While firms are supposedly driven by the mission to meet changing customer needs and expectations, they have an equal, if not greater interest in preserving their existing competencies.

As a central product or service is defined through competition and collaboration among firms, the inter-organizational ties and products or services that defined the industry so far evaporate, giving way to new relationships and products or designs. From the time when a radical technological discontinuity occurs to the point when a dominant design emerges, the group of firms that previously constituted an industry has completely renewed itself. A new group generally emerges often with many completely new constituents and around a new product (think of the typewriter giving way to the word processor or vacuum tubes giving way to transistors). After such radical technological changes, a new 'industry' co-evolves with dominant designs. By implication, utilization of the industry concept during eras of ferment can paint a distorted picture of reality for researchers and managers.

Our question here, then, is how to understand what occurs when traditional industries come apart due to technological flux. How should researchers and managers conceptualize the competitive arena under these conditions? We will begin by reviewing the literature on technological discontinuities and then use the case of the photographic industry to develop a conceptualization of the competitive arena that is more applicable to this increasingly frequent situation.

TECHNOLOGICAL DISCONTINUITIES AND DOMINANT DESIGNS

Our existing understanding of technological evolution is framed by the idea of technology cycles, a concept borrowed from ecological theory (Tushman and Murmann, 1998). Technology cycles are composed of technological discontinuities that trigger periods of technological and competitive ferment (Fig. 13.1). These turbulent innovation periods end with

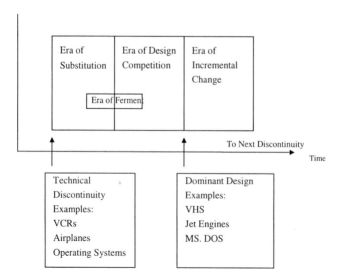

Fig. 13.1. Adapted from Anderson and Tushman (1997).

the emergence of an industry standard or dominant design (Abernathy & Utterback, 1978; Tushman and Anderson, 1986; Utterback, 1994). The dominant design is assumed to be 'selected' in the sense that it is the only design that is able to survive the competition for resources. The emergence of a dominant design ushers in a period of incremental as well as architectural technological change (Henderson & Clark, 1990) that, at some point, is broken by the next substitute design. This subsequent technological discontinuity then triggers the next wave of technological variation, selection, and retention (Tushman et al, 1997).

The significance of a technological discontinuity is enormous. These advancements in technology often destroy prevailing incremental innovation patterns and threaten to render existing capabilities useless. Tushman and Anderson (1986) label such discontinuities as 'competence-destroying,' to distinguish them from 'competence-enhancing' technological changes of a more incremental type. After competence-destroying discontinuities, which we will henceforth refer to as simply discontinuities, innovators struggle to develop applications based entirely on the new technology. These applications generally employ widely different architectures, configurations, features and standards (Tushman et al, 1997). As a result, various trajectories are opened up along which technological evolution in the industry can take place. These include innovations based on existing technologies, various designs based on the new technologies, and, quite often, hybrid technologies which promise to marry the strengths of an entrenched technology to the promised benefits of a new technology.

Technological discontinuities that lead to a dominant design are usually unpredictable advancements in technology that destroy existing incremental innovation patterns and threaten to render existing capabilities useless. Thus, the emergence of a dominant design in a product class means adaptation or extinction for competitors. If a firm has all its resources committed to the existing technology, and does not possess the absorptive capacity (Cohen and Levinthal, 1990) to develop the required capabilities in the new technology, it may find itself locked-out of the market (Schilling, 1998). Thus, when Eastman Kodak's roll-holder camera became the dominant design in the photographic industry, most firms specializing in dry-plate cameras went out of business (Jenkins, 1975). On the other hand, when the VHS standard emerged as the dominant design in the VCR industry, firms engaged in the production of Betamax VCRs were able to adapt, although at significant cost (Cusumano, Mylonadis & Rosenbloom, 1992). Often, however, even after competitors decide to adapt their designs to the dominant design, they are not able to manufacture products based on the new design efficiently enough, and thus cannot sustain themselves for long. Studies at the population level have shown (e.g., Baum, Korn & Kotha, 1995) that many firms disappear from the competitive arena when a new design emerges.

At a more general level of discussion, the centrality of technological change in industry evolution is finally being recognized. The battle cry for a re-evaluation of strategic management concepts around the changing technological landscape has been getting louder and louder. The co-evolution of technology and 'industry' deserves far more attention than it has received in the past. In the following sections, we describe a situation where technology is still evolving and discuss how it first dissolves an existing industry and then reconstitutes it under a different guise and with different constituents.

TECHNOLOGICAL CHANGE IN THE PHOTOGRAPHIC INDUSTRY

The photographic industry provides an excellent study in how a radical discontinuity can reconfigure the competitive landscape. Until 1980, the industry was firmly established around chemical-based imaging technology. Indeed, photography was defined in the dictionary as the formation of an image when light fell on a chemically coated surface. The evolution of this technology was accompanied by the birth of firms that specialized in manufacturing cameras, film and other related equipment, as well as those which made developing and printing film their business. The consumption chain was well set. The user bought film, took photos and dropped the film at the photofinisher who developed and printed the film for the user. The advent of digital imaging technology[2] in the early 1980s, however, has threatened to completely disrupt this arrangement. The chemical-based technology provides the bread and butter for millions in this industry who are involved in producing 35mm film, the various cameras that utilize the film, or photo processing. The bulk of the profits for the largest companies in the industry, Kodak and Fuji Film, come from sales of 35mm film. Now 35mm film has suddenly become a product that could be useless in a few years, leading to the gradual bankruptcy of several hundred thousand photofinishers along with many equipment manufacturers.

At the same time, a host of firms such as Sony, Toshiba, Epson and Hewlett-Packard have entered the photographic industry, each fiercely challenging the incumbents. These firms are joined by a number of software companies such as Adobe and Microsoft, hardware companies such as Intel and IBM, and printer and scanner manufacturers to redefine how photography is carried out. Predictably, in order to prolong the life of existing technology and thus preserve their core competence, almost all the major players, led by Kodak, joined together to introduce a new technology – "Advanced Photo System" (APS[3]) – that utilized chemical based imaging technology. This technology is labeled the. At the same time, Kodak

---

[2]   While chemical-based imaging involves the use of light to form an image on a chemical surface, digital imaging technology utilizes a sensor that scans the subject and stores that information in 1s and 0s. This information is then compressed and stored in whatever storage device the camera uses.

[3]   APS allows users to get pictures in various sizes. The APS film is also smaller allowing for smaller cameras. Finally, it offers drop-in loading. The quality is comparable to 35mm cameras.

led a coalition of incumbents to introduce a hybrid technology in the form of 'Picture CD'[4], which allows customers to digitize their images while continuing to use their existing film-based cameras. This has led to the availability of several completely different technological designs in the market including those based on traditional 35mm, APS, PictureCD, and purely digital technology. Within digital technology, various designs utilizing completely different component technologies (for sensors or storage media, for example) are in competition with each other as well as with the other technologies. The four different trajectories along which the 'industry' may evolve, arguably all equally plausible, are discussed briefly below.

Silver-halide based 35mm Format

35mm silver-halide film represents the core of the current photographic system through which most people capture images. Most cameras that we see around us are designed for this format. Innovations in emulsion technology have led to extremely high picture quality while innovations in production technology have meant declining prices for cameras and much better quality point and shoot (automatic) models (almost rivaling SLR quality). The design has become extremely well-entrenched in the market: it offers the best quality, most convenience, and the 35mm film is processed cheaply and widely. Consequently, the 35mm film and camera system has a genuine claim to being the most 'feasible' technology out there.

Advanced Photo System (APS)

Despite its advantages, the 35mm film is very easy to incorrectly load into the camera. Also, processed negatives and prints have to be kept together, and finding the correct negative when you want to make reprints or enlargements can be troublesome. APS was introduced by the five largest companies in the photographic industry as the solution to such problems and boost sagging interest in photography. APS film is smaller (24mm) than 35mm (thus allowing for the construction of smaller cameras), but because of advances in emulsion engineering, the quality is equally good. The new system adds a magnetic layer coating to the film that is used to record specific camera data to help the photofinisher make better pictures. The user can take images in three different sizes and the film is designed for foolproof loading (drops in like a battery cell). Finally, you cannot open the camera if the film is not rewound fully inside the cassette, thereby eliminating the possibility of opening the camera by mistake. APS film is slightly more expensive than 35mm and its processing more costly. As yet, several photofinishers still do not have the equipment to process APS films, although the number is increasing. APS is

---

[4]   In order to defuse the threat that an entirely digital future poses to its existing competencies, Kodak has launched an enormous campaign for digitization of existing images. That is, the customers continue using films but receive their images on a CD rather than (or along with) on paper.

incompatible with 35mm format (cameras or finishing equipment) but its proponents claim it to be the photographic system of choice in the future.

Picture CD[5]

Despite insisting for several years that 35mm silver halide photography was the best alternative available to consumers, by 1992 Kodak was trying to cement a marriage of chemistry and electronics with a photographic compact disk (CD) and developing purely digital cameras. With the Picture CD, the customer is able to get photographs on CD (along with prints). Now that most computers have CD drives, anyone with a CD-ROM drive can put in the disc and view the pictures. Picture CDs are more expensive than either 35mm or APS, but offer the advantage of digitization: users can email or enhance them on their computers. Proponents of Picture CD technology claim it to be the future of photography, an ideal blend of silver-halide imaging technology and digital technology.

Digital Imaging

Several firms whose primary business has always been electronics have a strong interest in seeing digital imaging succeed. They are, however, hampered by several limitations. Currently, for example, most digital cameras in the amateur segment of the market do not match the image quality of silver halide technology. Also, digital cameras are expensive to produce and require high quality color printers if the user wishes to have his/her images on paper as well. Also, a computer is needed where the images can be downloaded, enhanced and e-mailed. Moreover, unlike the other technologies, a dominant design still has not evolved in digital imaging. Specifically, it still remains to be decided what kind of memory device, sensor and file compression format a standard digital camera will include. However, because digital cameras offer substantially more advanced features[6], proponents claim it to be vastly superior to all other alternatives.

According to many in the industry, before the digital imaging discontinuity that prompted APS and Picture CD, silver-halide represented not a claim but a fact. It was unquestioningly accepted as the best method of capturing images. The parameters of performance were explicitly defined and established and the technology was taken for granted. Routines were firmly established around its use and users knew exactly what to do and how to do it. The technology, in other words, was fully integrated into everyday life. There were no

---

[5]   Kodak first introduced a more expensive version called Photo CD. It then introduced Picture CD. Photo CD was targeted at the Professional segment, while Picture CD aimed at the much larger amateur market.

[6]   Several models of digital cameras now boast features such as deleting unwanted photos, enhancing the image in several ways, several formats (color, b&w or Sepia), voice recording with each image, separable lenses, and even email facility directly from the camera.

controversies concerning its utility and feasibility. However, all this changed as APS was introduced, the option of digital imaging gradually became more feasible in terms of price, and Picture CD appeared on the horizon. The parameters of performance started to change and, the black box (Latour, 1987) of silver-halide photography has been opened exposing this deeply entrenched technology to scrutiny. As the dominance of silver-halide imaging technology is being challenged, various technologies are vying to replace it, each claiming to be the most feasible solution.

DISCUSSION

The photographic industry provides an excellent example of the uncertainty faced by firms as they wait for a new dominant design to emerge following a radical technological shock. Suddenly, which resources will be critical in the future, or what products will be at the center of the reconstituted industry, comes to depend on the trajectory along which the technology evolves. Investing in the development of new competencies requires substantial investments which firms are reluctant to make when great uncertainty clouds the future. The not so old example of video cameras is fresh in collective memories: When first introduced, video cameras were expected to wipe out still cameras. With video cameras providing pictures, voice, as well as motion, who in his/her right mind would buy a still camera again, industry analysts figured. However, despite drastically reduced prices, video cameras ended up as a niche product while the still camera market continued to grow.

Despite their clout or competencies, no one firm is in a position to control the direction of the process of evolution and certainly not in any position to prevent new entrants from entering and drastically changing the existing relationships that define the metamorphizing group. In this situation, the competitive arena exhibits four critical characteristics: the rapid transformation of the competitive arena; the absence of a dominant design; the shifting basis of competition; and the changing objective of competition. Table 13.1 summarizes these four aspects and distinguishes between the dynamics characterized by periods of stability and rapid change.

With the advent of digital imaging technology, the competition for Kodak is no longer only other film manufacturers but a plethora of firms including digital camera manufacturers, memory storage manufacturers, software developers, printer/scanner manufacturers, PC manufacturers and so on. The competition is driven by the struggle to define how photography is best carried out: through traditional means, by using APS cameras and film, Picture CDs or entirely through digital technology. As Christensen (1997) argues, when industries are faced with radical technological changes, decision-making cannot be based on existing understandings of customer needs and expectations. Indeed, as technology rapidly advances, new techniques evolve for carrying out photography. These new technologies instantly

Table 13.1. Summary of key competitive dynamics that characterize periods of relative stability and rapid technological change.

Key Dynamics	Era of Stability or Incremental Change	Era of Rapid Technological Change or 'Ferment'
What is the appropriate arena of competition?	Industry	Activity network
What defines competition?	Dominant Design (silver-halide based imaging technique)	Competing designs and trajectories (Silver-halide; APS; Picture CD; Digital (within digital: designs of memory storage device, sensors, file-format etc).)
What is the basis of competition?	Similar competencies (chemical-imaging)	Different competencies (firms competing on the basis of their competencies in chemical-imaging, digital technology, software/hardware development and so on)
What is the objective of competition?	Market share	Establishment of standards; consolidation of trajectories

introduce the user to new possibilities, forming the foundation for future expectations. Moreover, as the technologies underlying previously distinct products converge, various activities are amalgamated leading to spill-overs across traditionally drawn boundaries between businesses or industries.

At this stage, the boundaries marking traditional territories and strongholds dissolve, exposing firms and their competencies to new competitive pressures whose direction and magnitude is still uncertain. For example, in the photographic industry, managers are no longer struggling to merely increase market share in existing product categories, but have an overarching worry: defining how photography will be conducted in the future while preserving existing competencies. The battle is for the definition of a future in which respective competencies will be preserved. During this era of ferment (Tushman & Anderson, 1986), the competition is not for market share, but to create the path along which the industry will evolve. What role each firm will play later on is still undecided. Kodak's future is being shaped by Fuji as well as Adobe (which makes the software to enhance images on a PC); by Nikon as well as Sony; by Polaroid as well as Intel; by Canon as well as Hewlett-Packard (which makes printers, digital cameras, computers and scanners). Obviously, focusing on one product or service is a strategy Kodak can hardly afford. It would be foolish to focus on its 'industry' as defined by close substitutes to its current products. It is too early to treat software companies as potential suppliers, or digital cameras as a 'substitute' product. A dominant design has yet to emerge in this industry, and in its absence, identifying the competitors, suppliers, substitutes, critical information and competencies is impossible. Kodak or Fuji are no longer competing for market share in a well-defined market. Instead, they are competing to shape the future of photography, the central activity. We can express this argument as a proposition:

> *Proposition 1: During times of technological ferment, competition for market share and profitability between traditional competitors will be replaced by competition to define the new dominant design for the product or service.*

The battle to define the future of photography revolves around defining the key problem that must be solved through technology (quality, convenience, compatibility, user-friendliness, price and so on) and establishing standards on that particular trajectory. For example, Kodak would like to establish Picture CD as the dominant technology in the industry, whereby users take pictures using Kodak's existing films and cameras and then have them digitized on CDs (thus preserving and perpetuating Kodak's core competencies). For this reason Kodak, and all those who share its interests, promote quality of image (where digital technology still lags behind) as the key criterion on which performance should be judged. From their perspective, photographs are not simply functional artefacts. Memories, it is argued, are more important than the dishes in one's cabinet. "These are the things people grab first when their house catches fire. And obviously, we need silver-halide technology to take really good quality images"[7]. Similarly, it is forecast that for a large majority of the existing customer base, silver halide will be the system of choice. It is argued that since "a typical customer is a mother with two full-time jobs (professional and household), she cannot conceivably cope with all the equipment and instructions, and spend the time to produce her own prints, when she can buy the complete service conveniently and cheaply at any corner of any street or by mail"[8].

Along with the struggle to consolidate particular trajectories, within digital imaging a battle is being waged between various firms to establish standards for file formats and storage media. Sony, for example, is pressing ahead with its own digital cameras that utilize a memory storage device called a 'memory stick,' while Kodak and various other manufacturers are using "Compactflash" or "Smartmedia" cards. At the same time, standards for file format (JPEG or TIFF etc) and sensors (CCD or CMOS) are being fought over. The competition is no longer only those firms that make close substitutes, but all those who are working to influence, shape or determine how photography will be carried out. Thus, Kodak's competitors include not only Fuji, Agfa and a handful of other film manufacturers but, as we argued above, Sony, Adobe, Intel, Cannon, Lexar Media and a host of other companies that support alternative standards or

---

[7]   Interview with Jeff Vanscoyk, Vice President of digital products at Minolta.

[8]   Johanne Mussche, President of Photo Marketing Association International. *Photo Marketing Magazine*, February, 1999.

whose interests lie in consolidating alternative technological trajectories. We refer to this group of firms as an 'activity network' since it represents a flux of business activity around a central activity where firms are constantly working to shape and influence how this activity is carried out. Restated as a proposition:

> *Proposition 2: During times of technological ferment, activity networks will form as new and previously unknown competitors enter the competition to redefine the dominant design.*

Conceptualizing an Activity Network

We define an activity network as a group of actors who are directly or indirectly involved in shaping or carrying out a particular activity. For example, Fuji, Kodak, Canon, Sony or Toshiba along with photofinishers (directly involved in providing the equipment that makes the activity of photography possible), paper, chemical or lens manufacturers (indirectly responsible for making photography possible), America Online, Adobe, PC manufacturers (interested in promoting enhancement and sharing of digitized photos) and scanner/ printer manufacturers (interested in promoting digitization and printing photos at home) are all members of the photography activity network. Such firms are easily recognizable since they are connected in one way or another to the design, manufacture, delivery, or use of various artifacts that are competing to become the 'best' way to carry out the central activity. They are, in a sense, self-identified by their interest in influencing the way people carry out the activity in question. Through collective, though not necessarily collaborative, action these firms determine how an activity is perceived, valued and carried out in society. Notice the fundamental difference from the industry concept here: while industry is defined with respect to a product, function, critical information or even competencies, an activity network is distinguished by the central activity, thus connecting us directly to the end user. From such a perspective, Sony, Adobe, Kodak, Intel and all photofinishers are all part of the photography activity network and hence competitors. While all members of an activity network may represent individual interests, there is always some common ground among them where collaborations can be built. Kodak, chemical companies and photofinishers, for instance, are all vying to perpetuate chemical-based imaging. On the other hand, Sony is trying to bypass this traditional channel that represents Kodak's strength. Finally, within digital cameras, several hardware and software firms are competing to establish the next standard within this product category. Thus, activity networks are composed of 'webs' or 'networks' formed around different technological trajectories and competing standards. This is in line with Bettis' description of evolving industries, where webs are formed around competencies, and competing standards during eras of ferment. Existing competencies determine which trajectory a firm chooses to promote, which in turn influences the standards that are supported by it.

Proposition 3: Activity networks will be composed of various competing coalitions supporting alternative and competing technologies or standards.

Thus, members of an activity network do not only vie for market share or profitability, but also to determine how an activity comes to be defined. This process of definition has been discussed separately by institutional theorists (DiMaggio and Powell, 1991; Tolbert and Zucker, 1996), path dependency theorists (Arthur, 1989; Van de Ven and Garud, 1994), evolutionary theorists (Nelson and Winter, 1982; Baum, Korn and Kotha, 1995) and sociologists studying the evolution of technology (Callon, 1986; Latour, 1987). All these theorists are concerned with the process through which chaotic processes of change settle down into discernable patterns, resulting in the apparent choice of one technological trajectory over another and the establishment of standards. This process involves the determination of what resources are critical, what defines success and what positions in the field are pivotal (Leblebici, Salancik, Copay and King, 1991). While a detailed analysis of these dynamics is beyond the scope of this paper, we suggest that competition revolves around the institutional definition of the central activity while preserving respective competencies. How an activity is valued (e.g., is photography an integral part of all social occasions? Should people have a camera with them at all times?), perceived (e.g., cameras used to be status symbols, but have now become 'fun' things; does photography constitute an invasion of privacy? Is it art? What objects are worth photographing), and technologically carried out (35mm vs. APS vs. Picture CD vs. Digital Cameras) is determined as a result of negotiations among firms, consumers and other institutional actors. All these actors, of course, may not be in the same industry or the same SIC code (Appendix I contains a partial list of the SIC codes which comprise the photographic industry). Thus, the relationship that proves to be crucial to how an industry evolves and domains are staked out is between the activity and its institutional definition.

It is also important to recognize the fundamentally different nature of competition in times of radical technological change. During an era of incremental change, or of relative stability, only those firms that try to wrest market share away from the focal firm are deemed competitors. In contrast, competition during an era of ferment revolves around the consolidation of trajectories and establishment of standards. Competitors include not only the firms that make the same product, deliver the same service, possess critical information about one's customers, or share the same competencies but also those who, while in arguably different industries, refuse to support the focal firm's standards or recognize the latter's technology as the most 'feasible' solution to the problem at hand. As trajectories consolidates and universal standards emerge, activity networks devolve into technological communities

(Wade, 1995) and finally crystallize into one or several 'industries' formed around the various products and services which make carrying out the activity possible (e.g., camera, film or software industries) (this discussion is summarized in Table 13.1). We can express this idea in the form of a propostion:

> *Proposition 4: Once one coalition succeeds in establishing a new dominant design, an industry will reform and conventional competition for market share and profitability among firms producing close substitutes will be re-established.*

CONCLUSIONS & IMPLICATIONS

Industries co-evolve with dominant designs (Van de Ven and Garud, 1994; Aldrich and Fiol, 1994). Variation, selection and retention (Tushman and Murmann, 1998) are not discrete events, but consist of several interacting processes that 'coproduce' each other (as shown by Van de Ven and Garud, 1994). The very technical advancements and institutional rules that are initially created to facilitate industry emergence subsequently become inertial forces that hinder subsequent technical developments (Van de Ven and Garud, 1994: 442). Immediately after a radical technological discontinuity, the existing structure of an industry begins a process of metamorphosis in which technological, social and political events interact to define the future path, and consequently the constitution of the industry. While this process is underway, *an "industry" does not exist.* The industry disappears with the central product or function. While some members of the industry might be able to transcend the radical discontinuity, they would no longer follow the rules of the old industry. Out of several possible permutations and combinations, some are selected in, and the foundation for an industry is laid.

In this era of ferment, competition is driven neither by critical information about customers (Sampler, 1998), nor defined by similar competencies (Bettis, 1998). While information about existing customers and their purchasing behavior etc. may be a valuable resource, it is of limited value when radically new markets are evolving since the identity of the new market is still being defined (Christensen, 1997). Similarly, defining an industry according to competencies (Bettis, 1998) is futile in times of change or upheaval. While Kodak and Fuji share critical competencies, Sony has completely different competencies in a technological sense. Similarly, Adobe or Intel again have different competencies, and would not therefore be classified as members of a single industry. Of course, in due time, when the market settles down, a dominant design emerges and the basis for competition shifts from radical innovations to efficient production, direct competitors will come to share competencies and particular information will be sought after. However, until that happens, choosing which critical competencies to develop, and identifying competitors, remains a task full of uncertainty and risks.

This phenomenon is not, of course, limited to the photographic industry, but characterizes all industries that are subject to technological innovation. And, as the rate of technological change accelerates, is more true of more industries. Consider the television industry, where once easily identifiable boundaries have changed dramatically with the advent of cable systems, telecommunications and interactive computer networks. As Bettis and Hitt (1995) argue, in the near future, all forms of communication will likely be carried into a facility (home, business or other organization) by one cable, which may be owned by the electric utility company, the telephone company, the cable television company, the satellite television company, the facility owner, or some combination. It is also likely that one piece of equipment, albeit complex, at the customer site will be used for traditional purposes such as watching movies, and nontraditional uses such as banking. The result is a jumbling of the communications, computer, software, television, and other industries. In anticipation of this eventual environment, there have been a large number of mergers and strategic alliances between communications, computer, cable, and movie firms in recent years. In the face of radical technological change, competition cannot be defined by close substitutes or similar competencies. Indeed, as illustrated by events in the television industry, in future years, the competitors of CBS may include not only firms like NBC, ABC, HBO and CNN but also AT&T, the baby bells, Microsoft, Apple and Sony (Bettis and Hitt, 1995: 13).

Similarly, as Bettis (1998) has pointed out, while by considering only PC manufacturers as their competition, firms in the personal computer industry would not be wrong by traditional industry definition, the non-competitor status thus awarded to firms such as Intel or Microsoft could cost them dearly. Indeed, Apple paid dearly for considering only IBM as its competitor, while Intel and Microsoft captured most of the profits in the industry by making software compatibility (instead of hardware capability) the key criterion for users. In the near future, technological developments in fuel cells, or mobile telephony among several others are set to seriously challenge established industries and notions of competition. Managers relying on traditional concepts to understand the reality of competition may be the first casualties.

The case of radical technological change poses serious questions for traditional concepts in strategic management research. It is apparent that a large gap exists between the dominant theories of organizational competition and the social reality of rivalry in most organizational fields. In a world that is increasingly driven by technology, it is important to recognize that after radical discontinuities firms compete for the future not the present. This requires discarding the static notion of industry and strategizing within an activity network. Organizations begin as members of competing webs or networks within an activity network, and only when the dust settles down, and a central design emerges, become members of an industry. At those junctures, organizations are not competing to maximize market share in existing markets or meet currently understood and perceived customer needs. Instead they are competing to redefine the central activity, market and eventually the industry. Moreover, they are not competing against traditional competitors (producers of close substitutes) or new entrants making the same product, but against all firms that are acting to shape the perception, value or technique through which the central activity is carried out.

We hope that our discussion will provoke future researchers into taking a more critical view of the industry concept. How we define an industry holds major implications for the formulation of competitive strategy. As argued by Porac et al (1995), rivalry in the competitive arena is driven by two strategic questions, "who are our rivals? And "how do we compete?" The "how" question has attracted most of the empirical research. The "who" question is typically answered anecdotally by defining rivals as those organizations that are "most similar" to each other, with similarity being considered an objective property of interorganizational space (Porac et al, 1995). We have argued in this paper that the "how" and "who" questions merit different answers depending upon whether a firm is in an era of ferment or incremental change. While during periods of stability, everyday competitors may be those selling similar products or delivering similar services (thus constituting an industry), the competitive dynamics in the era of ferment are substantially different. Industry is in an evolutionary stage, and suppliers, competitors or barriers to entry are still unidentified. In such a case, if managers conceptualize their competition in terms of 'industry' it would only serve to put blinders on their vision.

Aldrich and Fiol (1994), among many others have stressed the importance of paying more theoretical attention to the period during which a new industry emerges. In this paper, we have argued for the need to examine the process through which an existing industry dissolves and then re-congregates. Technology is one of the candidates that can trigger this process. In fact, in view of the rapid acceleration in technological change, firms are forced to reckon with radical discontinuities more frequently than ever (Bettis, 1998). It is of paramount importance that they recognize the limits of the industry concept, which often acts as a key framework within which managers make decisions.

In this paper, we have drawn our arguments from both the empirical case of the photographic 'industry' and existing understandings of competition and technology management. Photography is a particularly illustrative case study for several reasons. First, it is illustrative since this 'industry', and the change that it is presently undergoing, reflect the characteristics of many other industries and their experiences: it is a relatively stable and well-understood competitive arena that has been rocked by a dramatic technological innovation which has undermined the dominant design to a point that was unthinkable for incumbents a few years ago. Almost any industry can experience this sort of event and many industries will over even a relatively short term.

Second, the photographic industry was particularly sensitive to changes in techonology due to the highly integrated and complex nature of the underlying dominant design. The 35 mm camera depends on highly advanced chemistry, electrical and electronic engineering, optics, and a range of other fields. A complex web of specialized firms had grown up to support the dominant design and firms had developed very specialized competencies that are only valuable as long as the existing dominant design stays dominant. Any significant challenge threatens to destroy a broad coalition of firms who will therefore fight back fiercely to protect their businesses. The photographic industry is therefore a particularly good example through which to explore the connection between dominant designs and industries, and the politics of technological change in established industries.

The photographic industry is also illustrative because of the obvious ties between the social and technological aspects of photography. Thus, as digital imaging has gained ground, the social meaning of photography (Who should take photos? When should photos be taken? etc.) has been gradually transformed. One of the things that made the photographic industry seem so stable – the way in which it was embedded in everyday practice – is also what made changes in the everyday practice of photography so dramatic in their effects. Similar changes are occurring in mobile telephony and fuel cells, for instance, and the example of the photographic industry is illustrative in understanding the effects of these changes.

REFERENCES

Abernathy,W. & Utterback, J. (1978). Patterns of industrial innovation. Technology Review, 80: 40-47.

Aldrich, H. & Fiol, M. (1994). Fools Rush In? The Institutional Context of Industry Creation. Academy of Management Review, 19(4), 645-670.

Anderson, P. & Tushman, M. (1997). Managing Through Cycles of Technological Change, in M. Tushman, & P. Anderson (Eds.), Managing Strategic Innovation and Change: A Collection of Readings, 45-53. Oxford University Press: New York.

Arthur, B. (1989). Competing Technologies, Increasing Returns, and Lock-in by Historical Events. The Economic Journal, 99, 116-31.

Bain, J.S. (1956). Barriers to new competition. Harvard University Press, Cambridge, MA.

Barney, J. (1986). Strategic Factor Markets: Expectations, Luck, and Business Strategy. Management Science, 32, 1231-1241.

Barney, J. (1991). Firm Resources and Sustained Competitive Advantage. Journal of Management, 17, 99-120.

Barney, J. (2001). Is the Resource-Based "View" a Useful Perspective for Strategic Management Research? Yes. Academy of Management Review, 26, 41-56.

Baum, J., Korn, H. & S. Kotha. (1995). Dominant Designs and Population Dynamics in Telecommunication Services: Founding and Failure of Facsimile Transmission Service Organizations, 1965-1992. Social Science Research, 24, 97-135.

Bettis, R. (1998). Commentary on 'Redefining Industry Structure for the Information Age' by J.L. Sampler. Strategic Management Journal, 19, 357-361.

Bettis, R. & M. Hitt (1995). The New Competitive Landscape. Strategic Management Journal, Summer Special Issue, 16, 7-19.

Callon, M. (1986). Some Elements of a Sociology of Translation: Domestication of the Scallops and the Fishermen of St. Brieuc Bay. In J. Law (Ed.) Power, action and belief: A new sociology of knowledge? Pp 196-233. Routledge and Kegan Paul: London.

Christensen, C. (1997). The Innovator's Dilemma: When New Technologies Cause Great Firms to Fail. Boston, MA: Harvard Business School Press.

Cohen, M. & Levinthal, D. (1990). Absorptive Capacity: A New Perspective on Learning and Innovation, Administrative Science Quarterly, 35, 128-52.

Cusumano, M., Mylonadis, Y. & Rosenbloom, R. (1992). Strategic Maneuvering and Mass Market Dynamics: The Triumph of VHS over Beta. Business History Review (Fall), 51-93.

DiMaggio, P. & Powell, W. (1991). The Iron Cage Revisited: Institutional Isomorphism and Collective Rationality in Organizational Fields, in W. Powell & P. DiMaggio (Eds.) The New Institutionalism in Organizational Analysis. Chicago: The University of Chicago Press.

Hamel, G. & Prahalad, C.K. (1994). Competing for the Future. Harvard Business School Press, Boston, MA.

Henderson, R. & Clark, K. (1990). Architectural innovation: The Reconfiguration of Existing Product Technologies and the Failure of Established Firms. Administrative Science Quarterly, 35, 9-31.

Jenkins, R. (1975). Images and enterprise. Baltimore: John Hopkins Press.

Latour, B. (1987). Science in Action: How to Follow Scientists and Engineers through Society, Cambridge MA: Harvard University Press.

Leblebici, H., Salancik, G., Copay, A. & King, T. (1991). Institutional Change and the Transformation of Interorganizational Fields: An Organizational History of the U.S. Radio Broadcasting Industry. Administrative Science Quarterly, 36, 333-363.

Levitt, T. (1960). Marketing Myopia, Harvard Business Review, July-August, 45-56.

Nelson, R. & S. Winter. (1982). An Evolutionary Theory of Economic Change. Cambridge, MA.: Harvard University Press.

Porac, J., Thomas, H., Wilson, F., Paton, D., & Kanfer, A. (1995). Rivalry and the Industry Model of Scottish Knitwear Producers, Administrative Science Quarterly, 40, 203-227.

Porter, M. (1980). Competitive Strategy. Free Press. New York.

Porter, M. (1985). Competitive Advantage. Free Press. New York.

Sampler, J. (1998). Redefining Industry Structure for the Information Age, Strategic Management Journal, 19, 343-355.

Schilling, M. (1988). Technological Lockout: An Integrative Model of Economic and Strategic Factors Driving Technology Success and Failure, Academy of Management Review, 23 (2), 267-284.

Tolbert, P. & Zucker, L. (1996). The Institutionalization of Institutional Theory, in Clegg, S., Hardy, C., and W. Nord, (Eds.) Handbook of Organizational Studies. Thousand Oaks, CA: Sage Publications.

Tushman, M. & Anderson, P. (1986). Technological Discontinuiteis and Dominant Designs: A Cyclical Model of Technological Change, Administrative Science Quarterly, 35, 604-633.

Tushman, M., Anderson, P. & C. O'Reilly. (1997). Technology Cycles, Innovation Streams and Ambidextrous Organizations: Organizational Renewal through Innovation Streams and Strategic Change, in M. Tushman, & P. Anderson (Eds.), Managing Strategic Innovation and Change: A Collection of Readings. Oxford University Press: New York.

Tushman, M. & Murmann, J. (1998). Dominant Designs, Technology Cycles, and Organizational Outcomes, Research in Organizational Behavior, 20, 231-266.

Utterback, J. 1994. Mastering the Dynamics of Innovation. Boston: Harvard University Press.

Van de Ven, A. & Garud, R. (1994). The Co-evolution of Technical and Institutional Events in the Development of an Innovation, in Baum, J. & Singh, J. (Eds.) Evolutionary Dynamics of Organizations. 425-443. New York: Oxford University Press.

Wade, J. (1995). Dynamics of Organizational Communities and Technological Bandwagons: An Empirical Investigation of Community Evolution in the Microprocessor Market. Strategic Management Journal, 16, 111-133.

Wernerfelt, B. (1984). A Resource-Based View of the Firm, Strategic Management Journal, 5 (2), 171-180.

APPENDIX I

A Partial List of SIC codes covering the Photographic Industry.

Code	Business
3663	Photo transmission equipment-mfg.
7384	Photo finishing laboratories, except for the motion picture industry
3641	Photoflash and photoflood lamp bulbs and tubes
3861	Photoflash equipment, except lamp bulbs-mfg.
2675	Photograph folders, mats and mounts-mfpm-mfg.
2499	Photographic frames, wood or metal-mfg.
4822	Photograph transmission services
7221	Photographers, portrait; still or video.
5043	Photographic cameras, projectors, equipment and supplies - wholesale
7384	Photographic labs
3827	Photographic lenses
7335	Photographic studios, commercial.
7221	Photographic studios, portrait.
5946	Photographic supply stores
3081	Photographic sheets, film and plastics
3229	Photomask blanks
3826	Photometers, except photographic exposure meters

Management of Technology
ISBN: 0-08-044136-X

14

KNOWLEDGE-BASED VIEW ON INTERNATIONALIZATION: FINNISH TELECOM SOFTWARE SUPPLIERS AS AN EXAMPLE

Olli Kuivalainen, Lappeenranta University of Technology, Finland[*]
Kalevi Kyläheiko, Lappeenranta University of Technology, Finland[**]
Kaisu Puumalainen, Lappeenranta University of Technology, Finland[***]
Sami Saarenketo, Lappeenranta University of Technology, Finland[****]

ABSTRACT

The internationalization pattern of small and specialized software suppliers is often different from that of more mature service or manufacturing industries. The small information technology and communications (ICT) companies are often characterized as born globals, showing very fast and extensive international growth enabled by the use of external resources such as partners and networks. The purpose of this study is to identify knowledge-related

[*] Telecom Business Research Center, Lappeenranta University of Technology, P.O.Box 20, FIN-53851 Lappeenranta. E-mail: Olli.Kuivalainen@lut.fi.
[**] Dept. of Business Administration, Lappeenranta University of Technology, P.O.Box 20, FIN-53851 Lappeenranta. E-mail: Kalevi.Kylaheiko@lut.fi.
[***] Telecom Business Research Center, Lappeenranta University of Technology, P.O.Box 20, FIN-53851 Lappeenranta. E-mail: Kaisu.Puumalainen@lut.fi.
[****] Telecom Business Research Center, Lappeenranta University of Technology, P.O.Box 20, FIN-53851 Lappeenranta. E-mail: Sami.Saarenketo@lut.fi.

factors that may contribute to the speed and extensiveness of internationalization. We will launch an evolutionary knowledge-based model that makes it possible to derive the basic determinants of the company's ability to benefit from their current knowledge base and capabilities. The basic determinants of our internationalization model are appropriability (tacitness and patent protection), threat of opportunism, economies of scale, economies of scope / synergies, path dependency, asset specificity and the monopoly power of complementary assets providers. The next step is to derive empirical hypotheses based on our main knowledge-related determinants and their effect on the scale and speed of internationalization. The hypotheses are tested empirically with a survey of 171 small and medium-sized software and content providers in Finnish ICT sector. The results show that most of the proposed knowledge-related determinants really have significant effects on the pattern of internationalization.

INTRODUCTION

This paper explores the *internationalization* process of high-tech firms from the *knowledge-based* perspective. In our view, the competitiveness of the modern firm and hence the basic motives for its internationalization are primarily based on their intellectual organizational resources and capabilities. We agree with Teece (1998: 289) who proposes that "firm level competitive advantage in open economies flows fundamentally from difficult to replicate knowledge assets". However, the problem with this idea is that the very concept of knowledge is often used vaguely in most theories of internationalization (one of the best reviews is Dunning 2000). In order to make the discussion more analytical we suggest a *knowledge-based* theory of the firm as a point of departure for a modern intrnationalization theory. On this basis we also claim that one of the core issues in the explanation of the internationalization process is how to organize the governance structure of the firm i.e. where and for what cost the knowledge is developed, created, received, and transferred.

In the following we will clarify the tricky knowledge concept by setting it into the context of a well-known resource-based view of the firm (e.g. Wernerfelt 1984; Barney 1986; Foss 2000). This fundamentally static view emphasizes the so-called VRIN attributes (valuable, rare, inimitable, and nonsubstitutable) of physical, human and organizational resources as main sources of the firm's competitive advantage. Next we will extend and re-organize it in terms of evolutionary economics-related concepts (e.g. Nelson and Winter 1982; Kyläheiko 1998). In this endeavor the knowledge-related elements behind value creating potential of resources are emphasized. This extension makes it possible to focus on knowledge-related processes, such as replication of existing knowledge base, learning induced partial replication as well as knowledge creating, knowledge integrating and knowledge transferring mechanisms. They all are of great importance when trying to make sense of the issue of knowledge-inspired internationalization processes at the firm's decision-making level. This dynamic process view, known as the knowledge-based view in this paper (cf. Teece and Pisano 1994; Eisenhardt and Martin 2000; Foss 2000; Metcalfe 2000), is of great relevance since technological discontinuities and ability to manage knowledge acquisition in turbulent markets affect the choice of the internationalization entry mode and timing strategies. To be able to analyze crucial value added-creating aspects of internationalization our basic knowledge-based model will be completed by taking into account also the main determinants of the boundary of the firm choices i.e. static and dynamic determinants of transaction and management costs are analyzed as well (cf. Blomqvist et.al. 2001).

ON KNOWLEDGE-BASED VIEW OF THE FIRM

Some preliminaries

The proponents of the dynamic capability or knowledge-based tradition Teece and Pisano (1994: 537) interpret firms as generators of *dynamic capabilities,* which help "in appropriately adapting, integrating, and re-configuring internal and external organizational skills, resources and functional competences toward changing environment." According to this view the competitive advantage of firms lies basically in their dynamic capabilities "rooted in high performance routines operating inside the firm, embedded in the firm's processes, and conditioned by its history." The last part of this sentence refers to the issue of *path-dependency* that is important when trying to understand firms´ internationalization decisions. The opportunity window of the firm is always constrained by its existing routines and capabilities. Hence, the firm cannot change its development paths ("firm trajectories") quickly and flexibly as, for instance, traditional neoclassical microeconomic models assume. The more there exist the *economies of scale*, the more the firms have to specialize in their path-dependent capabilities and the more vulnerable they become in turbulent markets. On the other hand, the more there exist *complementarities* between dynamic resources and capabilities the more the firm's potential to sustain competitive advantage is enhanced. In our view, international partnerships and other ways of internationalizing can effectively be used as useful complementary sources of (external) capabilities to promote flexibility.

On basic knowledge categories

First we introduce the basic knowledge categories and the main knowledge-related mechanisms in our evolutionary framework (cf. Blomqvist and Kyläheiko 2000). In our view, knowledge bases of the firms consist of three basic knowledge categories:

Tacit knowledge ("know-how") is assumed to be embedded either in the firm organization as a whole (which makes it very easy to protect against the imitation attempts of

242 Management of Technology

rivals) or in teams. Tacit knowledge gives rise to cumulative learning-based internalities which enable a firm to exploit economies of scale and utilize better the opportunities offered in terms of outsourcing or networking strategies. There are two types of basic mechanisms that make Marshallian internalities possible; replication and partial replication. These localized learning effects make path-dependent firm-specific trajectories possible and enable the crucial differences between firms even within the same industry. On the other hand, tacitness makes it also hard to transfer knowledge between the firms thus sometimes forcing the firms to use foreign direct investments (FDI's) as their strategic tools.

Fully articulated codified information ("know-that") in turn makes it possible to exploit the externalities generated through external knowledge bases created by other firms and research institutions. They are sources of network externalities and the most important mechanisms related to them are knowledge transferring and knowledge creation through integrating.

Generic knowledge incorporates both aspects of above mentioned knowledge categories.

According to our approach the firm can be seen as a *repository of knowledge*. Firms that are internationally able to create and manage knowledge, that is valuable, rare and hard to substitute to others, are able to increase their value and to strengthen their competitive advantage. Hence, knowledge becomes a main source of competitiveness and potentially a tradable (if protectable) asset. In brief, the knowledge-based firms choose a strategy, where *the combination of tacit and generic knowledge forms the core competitive asset and core competence of the firm.*

There are several partly hidden aspects in our knowledge notion. Knowledge is often *complex* demanding special education and experience to be utilized and refined further. *Absorptive capacity* is badly needed. Even then the human beings are often only *boundedly rational*, which means that their ability to utilize information for rational decision making is limited. It is not possible to articulate and codify all of the knowledge. Because of the *tacitness* of the knowledge that transfer of knowledge becomes a special problem. Knowledge is also needed in production on a *continuous basis*, but often it cannot be traded on the market place due to severe *market failures* (Kyläheiko 1998). Thus the intangibles and competencies of the firm may also crucially limit the growth and internationalization of the firm (Metcalfe 2000). Since new knowledge always has to be connected with the existing one, it is more efficient that firms focus on their core capabilities and trade these idiosyncratic capabilities with other organizations focused on complementary capabilities. If this is not possible due to tacitness the only possibility is to use FDI's or to network.

In addition, knowledge is often *firm-specific*. Organization stores its knowledge in its operational routines, which can be seen as an attempt to gain organizational knowledge to manage in the complex and uncertain environment. It is these intangible *organizational routines and capabilities* that basically differentiate one organization from another. Moreover, knowledge is often also *asymmetric* i.e. unevenly distributed, which raises the fear for potential opportunism (Williamson 1975; Kyläheiko and Miettinen 1995). Since codified knowledge is *imitable,* the *ownership* and *intellectual property* issues are critical in order to make knowledge more appropriable and, consequently, more valuable.

INTERNATIONALIZATION THEORIES AND THE CONCEPT OF BORN GLOBAL

Rapid internationalization processes of SMEs have gained a lot of interest among scholars recently. At this particular context, the emerging phenomenon of *born global firms* is acknowledged (Rennie, 1993; Madsen & Servais 1997; Knight 1997). By definition born global firms aim at international markets right from their initiation (or soon thereafter). In order to comprehend the phenomenon, we will briefly review the existing theories on internationalization and the concept of born global on the following. The principal theories are usually divided into (i) *behavioral theories* (*stages theory and network approach*) and (ii) theories that use concepts in the field of *economics*.

The stages theory of internationalization was an attempt to formulate a longitudinal theory of international expansion. In this theory, internationalization is being seen as an orderly process progressing incrementally from purely domestic operations, via exports and foreign direct investments, into full-fledged multinational business. The stages pattern of internationalization has been identified by e.g. Luostarinen (1979). An early prominent formulation of this approach was offered by Swedish researchers in the form of Uppsala model (Johanson & Wiedersheim-Paul 1975; Johanson & Vahlne 1977, 1990), according to which a company gradually increases its commitment both in terms of operational modes, the variety of modes used and the range of markets penetrated in foreign markets. Andersen (1997: 31) notes that the Uppsala model actually builds on the resource-based theory of the firm: Increased market knowledge is supposed to lead to increased market commitment and vice versa. It has been argued that the U-model is weak, because it uses only one explanatory variable (experiental knowledge) and hence, is not likely to provide a sufficient explanation for a firm's internationalization. Instead, it ends up being a description of a most typical sequence of internationalization. (E.g. Johanson and Vahlne 1990) Furthermore, as Autio et al. (2000: 909) point out, this approach stresses the inertial and reactive character of business organizations, neglecting the entrepreneurial strategic choice. However, inertial behavior can be understood from the path-dependency perspective.

Newer approaches to internationalization incorporate the concept of networks. This perspective focuses on non-hierarchical systems where companies invest to build up and monitor their position in international networks (Johanson and Mattson 1988). Particularly interesting studies have been conducted by e.g. Coviello and Munro (1997) and Bell (1995), since the focus on these studies is in the network relationships and internationalization of small software firms.

Economics-based explanations include e.g. monopolistic advantage theory (Hymer, 1976), FDI theories and internalization/transaction cost theory (Buckley and Casson, 1976). Transaction cost theory has been used in internationalization especially to explain the choice of entry mode (Anderson and Gatignon, 1986; Erramilli, 1990; Erramilli and Rao, 1993). Most of these approaches are extensions of the theory of the firm. Firm-specific advantages overcome the disadvantages of operating in distant markets and shape the international operation modes.

Lately, a number of studies have described the phenomenon where some companies take a "fast-track" route in their internationalization process. The traditional, risk-averse and incremental pattern to international markets is no longer followed. On the contrary, these companies are "born global" - having international focus right from their founding. Most of the traditional internationalization theories and transaction cost approach are based on the assumption that the FDI or total control over operations is the most preferred entry mode. This notion has been recently challenged by network and born global approaches, which point out the importance of the external resources in the internationalization of the firm. Several terms have been used in the studies to describe the fast-internationalizing companies. Oviatt and McDougall use the term International New Ventures (1994) and Global Start-ups (1995), Rennie (1993) and Madsen & Servais (1997) have adopted the term, Born Global, applied also in this study. The central notion is that some entrepreneurs possess a set of skills and knowledge that enable the firm to internationalize more rapidly. For example, experience from earlier international jobs makes it possible to exploit windows of opportunity seen in foreign markets. This is consistent with the knowledge-based view, as both emphasize continuous learning.

Due to the global nature of the industry like ICT early internationalization is becoming virtually a necessity for all firms within, regardless of size and age. This may, however, be facilitated since the barriers to enter global marketplace are collapsing. Markets are deregulated, new communication technologies advance, new ways of trading, e.g. e- and m-commerce emerge, and transportation becomes more inexpensive and faster.

Knowledge-based economy is a reality (e.g. Dunning 2000). Thus, the main issue for the firms and individuals is the possession of knowledge; i.e. the wealth creating activities have become knowledge intensive. The organizations need capabilities to access and organize knowledge intensive assets globally, to integrate them with their competitive advantage and with their partners' value adding activities (Dunning 2000; Kogut and Zander 1993). In this context, evolutionary theory utilized in our chapter focuses on the firm's long-term strategy towards asset accumulation and organizational learning capabilities. Organizational advantages have an effect on entry mode choice in internationalization, because the firm chooses the mode, which enables it to sustain the competitive advantage. We claim that our knowledge-based evolutionary framework can capture most of the relevant features of more or less descriptive born global analyses in a way which makes it possible to utilize analytical devices of modern theories of the firm (cf. Foss 2000).

TOWARDS EVOLUTIONARILY INSPIRED KNOWLEDGE-BASED VIEW ABOUT INTERNATIONALIZATION

Our knowledge-based endeavor starts from some basic findings of evolutionary economics (cf. Nelson and Winter 1982; Metcalfe 1989). We interpret *evolution* as historical transformation of a system through *endogenously* generated change and apply the cultural evolutionary *"Blind Variation-Selection-Retention"-triad* as a starting point. In order to better understand the dynamics of strategy formation concerning internationalization we connect this scheme with the evolution of knowledge i.e. with the *knowledge creating, transferring and integrating processes.*

The main role of *alert entrepreneurs* is to trigger off *variation*-generating new combinations (technical artifacts, new routines, new management methods, new organization types, etc.) on which selection works. However, *selection* always needs time to operate and to pick up fitter new combinations. This, in turn, depends upon the *organizational inertia.* Hence, in the evolutionary theory of the firm, organizations have a double role: they are the sources of "new combinations" (*variation*) and they provide a stable hierarchic network of path-dependent routines and capabilities which are continuously replicated (*retention or replication*). *Partial replication* makes it possible to adapt through modifying existing routines. Now we can touch upon the heart of evolutionary explanation of *the internationally sustainable competitive advantage.* The partly tacit and collective nature of firm-specific capabilities may result in sustainable profits, if the firm can combine and replicate its static and dynamic organizational routines, core competencies and more or less idiosyncratic resources in a way which is precarious to imitate and costly to replicate by rivals.

Hence, the explanation of sustainable rents does not mainly rest on Ricardian rents which are due to scarce idiosyncratic resources (as is the case with the static resource based theory), but on the more extensive explanation where rents profited from innovations can be viewed as the sum of *Ricardian + monopoly + Schumpeterian (entrepreneurial) rents.* The latter type of rent refers to the case where the innovating firm is quick enough to maintain its competitive advantage through effective replication of static organizational routines and through establishing new competencies by means of dynamic capabilities (cf. Winter 1995; Eisenhardt and Martin 2000).

Fig. 14.1 summarizes the basic structure of our *evolutionarily inspired knowledge-based theory of the firm.* The emphasis is no longer on resources per se, but on dynamically evolving internationally acquired routines and capabilities through which a web of

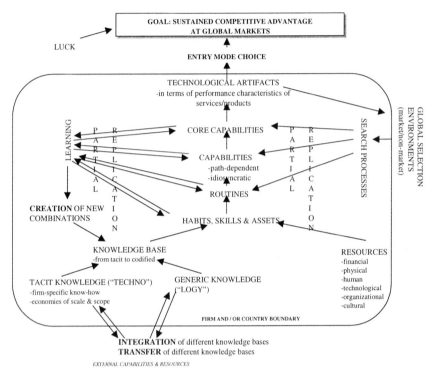

Fig. 14.1. Knowledge-based view of the firm in the internationalization framework (cf. Blomqvis and Kyläheiko et al. 2000).

coordinating relationships connecting firm-specific resources are replicated. According to this interpretation, the resource and knowledge bases of the firm determine its routines and is subject to learning and variety through the path-dependent *search mechanisms* that the firm uses. The emphasis is "on the challenge of leveraging the existing resource position into a more favorable future position" (Winter 1995: 151). This can be done only in terms of not-yet-existing, *"would-be" dynamic capabilities.* They can be defined as "the capacity of a firm to renew, augment, and adapt its core competencies over time." (Teece, Pisano and Shue 1997). Dynamic capabilities generate new organizational and technological competencies by combining (i) joint contributions of tacit internal learning, (ii) R&D search routines, (iii) complementary capabilities, and (iv) generic knowledge. Consequently, *dynamic routines* and *capabilities* reflect and actualize the firm's latent competencies, which opens new business opportunities and make Schumpeterian rents possible.

ON RELEVANT TRANSACTION AND MANAGEMENT COSTS WHEN DETERMINING INTERNATIONALIZATION CHOICES

Our knowledge-based view regards the firm as an organization, which globally combines partly tacit and cumulative know-how ("techno") with generic and more or less codified information ("logy"). The firm's competitive advantage is mainly defined in terms of resources and static and dynamic routines and capabilities, which yield rents to firms only if they are (i) *valuable*, (ii) *rare* and *hard to imitate*, (iii) *non-substitutable (firm-specific)*, and (iv) subject to *imperfect competition*. Focusing upon the heterogeneity of capabilities implies that the *boundaries of the firm* have to be interpreted as critical strategic devices also when outlining a firm's internationalization strategy. It is a question of how to generate more value and how to strengthen the firm's international competitive position by utilizing internally produced and/or externally acquired knowledge-related capabilities and resources in the most efficient way in the international playground.

The concept of *transaction cost* has proved to be fruitful when explaining the range of the activities in which the firm engages. The focal point is to analyze those factors which give rise to static and dynamic *transaction costs* as well as static and dynamic *management costs* (more about them Williamson 1975; Blomqvist et. al. 2001). The former are related to the use of market mechanisms, whereas the latter are related to the running of the firm.

The firms realize different transactions using its routines/capabilities. Some internal and external capabilities already exist (static ones), whereas some have to be developed or created through partial replication or knowledge integration (dynamic ones). Outsourcing costs i.e. the costs of using external capabilities are called *transaction costs* (relating to search, planning, negotiating, monitoring, and enforcement) and the insourcing costs of using the internal capabilities are called *management costs* (relating to administration, control and monitoring as well as the costs of using low-powered bureaucratic incentives). The costs that are related to already existing routines/capabilities are called *static*, whereas those related to not yet existing potential capabilities are called *dynamic*.

The main TCE-related internationalization issue is to find out such an international *governance structure* i.e. a combination of outsourced, networked and insourced (through FDI's) transactions that minimize the sum of static and dynamic transaction and management costs. Of course, also the direct production and transportation costs have to be included into the calculations.

Williamson (1975) explicated the following determinants that give rise to (static) transaction costs: (i) bounded rationality, (ii) uncertainty, (iii) opportunism, (iv) information impactedness, (v) frequency of transactions, and (vi) asset (site, physical, brand name or human asset) specificity. In our empirical part we will focus on determinants (ii), (iii), (vi) which together constitute the archetype of the Williansonian argument, the so-called *hold up problem*.

In contrast to Williamson who stresses the ex post *hold-up* problems, Teece (1986; 1988) emphasizes innovation opportunities in terms of *tacit knowledge* embedded in rare, hard-to-imitate collective core capabilities. The competitive advantages can be sustained through cumulative learning, which is related to causal ambiguity and idiosyncrasy of new knowledge. In our Fig. (1) these processes are characterized in terms of partial replication loops.

Teece's key knowledge-related concepts are (vii) *complementary capabilities* and the *(viii) appropriability regime*. The former consists of the external capabilities that are needed to complete a firm's own internal capabilities. The strategically most important external capabilities affect the bargaining situation the more, the more inefficient are their markets. This implies higher transaction costs and, consequently, more insourced solutions i.e. more FDI's in the international context.

The *appropriability criterion* refers to the question of how easily a firm can protect its ideas from imitation. The appropriability does not only depend on legal protection (patents, trademarks, etc.), but the nature of knowledge is perhaps even more important. The more tacit knowledge is or the higher the economies of scale are, the more appropriate is knowledge. The idea of *replication* of organizational routines is relevant from this perspective, since it makes it possible to build up isolative mechanisms, thus promoting appropriability even in the case where resources are not idiosyncratic per se. The tighter the appropriability regime, the lower are the transaction costs, and the more preferred is a market or a network solution in international markets and vice versa.

When the firm utilizes mainly its own resources/routines and capabilities it can build on cumulative learning and exploit the (ix) *economies of scale and scope* i.e. it can utilize the advantages of tacit internalities through replication. We call them *governance benefits or ways to minimize dynamic transaction costs. In our internationalization set-up economies of scale and scope make it possible to be more international (i.e. to launch more international operations from company's total turnover) and to operate in more target countries than firms which cannot exploit economies of scale and scope..*

The governance structure presented in the framework does not directly include the international market entry modes. However, there is an analogy between the entry modes and markets, networks and vertical integration (insourcing) options. We relate vertical integration to FDIs, networks correspond with cooperative entry modes and market solution with different export options. Most problematic issues in ICT sector are digital products and the emergence of the e-business. These products can be transferred without the local presence through Internet. Hence, in e-business all the governance structures are possible. Therefore, we have included Internet into the frameworks as the fourth mode. The following *knowledge-related internationalization lessons* can now be formulated. The *integration or tight networking option i.e. the use of FDI's* is the best option when

- Uncertainty, the danger of opportunism and complexity are high,
- There are only few providers of complementary capabilities,
- Innovation requires large specific investments,
- Appropriability regime is loose,
- The markets of complementary capabilities are inefficient, and
- Trust between partners is lacking.

The market-based *outsourcing solution or some form of loose networking* is preferred in the opposite situation. Perhaps the most interesting *cooperative network options* (Williamson's hybrid governance structures) can be found when there exist simultaneously both pro-market and pro-integration fostering tendencies, which can be glued together through *trust* between international partners.

MAIN HYPOTHESES FOR EMPIRICAL ANALYSIS

These hypotheses are all based on the knowledge-based view of the firm presented earlier. Most of them can easily be interpreted in terms of our main transaction cost determinants introduced in Ch. 5 as well. H1, H2, and H3 are related to the Williamsonian hold-up problem. Hypothesis H4 tests the Teecean complementarity asset idea, whereas H5, H6, and H7 are related to the Teecean appropriability idea. H8, H9, and H10 deal with the issue of dynamic transaction costs. Hypothesis H11 relates to the evolutionary path dependency ideas. The basic assumptions related to the focal ICT industry are: market is global by nature, technological discontinuities exist and there is lack of global dominant designs in telecommunications technologies.

> *H 1:* *The higher the degree of uncertainty, the more the foreign direct investment modes are used in internationalization.*
>
> *H 2:* *The higher the risk of opportunistic behavior, the more the foreign direct investment modes are used in internationalization.*
>
> *H 3:* *The more specific the relevant assets are, the more the foreign direct investment modes are used in internationalization.*
>
> *H 4:* *The stronger the complementary providers are, the more international is the company.*
>
> *H 5:* *The more tacit new knowledge is, the more cooperative modes are applied.*
>
> *H 6:* *The more tacit new knowledge is, the more rapid is the internationalization.*
>
> *H 7:* *The better the company is able to patent its product, the more cooperative modes it uses in internationalization.*

H 8: The more there are possibilities to gain economies of scale, the greater is the number of target countries.

H 9: The more there are possibilities to gain economies of scale, the larger is the share of international operations from company's total turnover.

H 10: The more there are economies of scope, the larger is the share of international operations from company's total turnover.

H 11: The higher the path dependency is, the smaller is the share of international revenues.

EMPIRICAL STUDY AMONG FINNISH ICT COMPANIES

We conducted a test of our model with the highly knowledge-intensive ICT industry. The determinants of our knowledge-based model of internationalization were included in the hypotheses. There are also other resources and capabilities, domestic, global and target market conditions that influence internationalization process and the choice of foreign market entry mode. In the empirical study these attributes are included in the form of motives. Motives were identified and their effect was removed. The following Fig 14.2 presents the basic ideas behind the test assumptions.

Data collection

The population of interest was defined as small and medium-sized Finnish companies providing value added services in the information and communications technology (ICT) sector. These include content providers and software providers for service platform and management systems. Hardware manufacturers and companies providing mainly educational or consultancy services were not included in the study.

Since the companies of interest were operating in the ICT sector, an Internet- based questionnaire was used for data collection. The questionnaire was extensive consisting of 15 pages divided into three parts: the first part included the basic information of the firm, its products, technologies, employees, customers and competitors. The second part focused on the competitive advantages, position in the value chain and partnership issues. The final part included questions about internationalization and the future of the company. The questionnaire was pretested in five companies, and the time needed for completing the questionnaire was found to be approximately 45 minutes. In order to elicit responses, the respondents were offered a report of the results of the study, and a small personal gift.

Due to the rapid development of the ICT sector and the unsuitability of standard industry classification codes, there was no single up-to-date sampling frame available for the purposes of the study. Therefore, the names and contact information of the companies were searched from multiple sources, e.g. Kompass Finland Database, The Statistical Bureau of

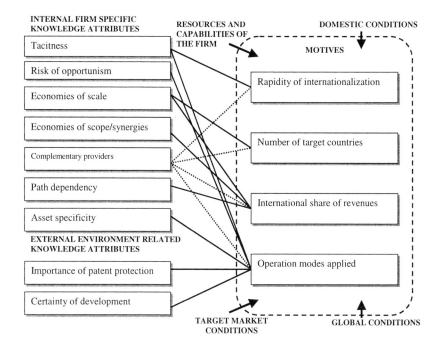

Fig.14.2. Tested hypotheses and complementary variables in empirical study.

Finland database of Finnish companies, IT magazines, and Internet sites of the companies themselves, universities, cities, science parks, incubators, venture capitalists, and industry organizations.

Altogether 405 companies were identified, and contacted by telephone between November 1999 and February 2000. In this phase, 17 companies were found ineligible, and 22 companies refused to participate in the study. Those 366 companies who agreed to participate on the telephone, received on the following day an e-mail message containing instructions for answering the web-based questionnaire. A reminder message was sent to those who had not returned their answer within two weeks.

171 companies returned their answers, resulting in effective response rate of 47% (171/366). In light of the response rate, and the comparison of early and late respondents, non-response bias did not become a problem. Thus the point of departure is the small – and medium-sized Finnish company active in telecommunications. In our empirical study we have their opinions.

Measures and descriptive information

The knowledge attributes were measured on 30 Likert- scaled items. Principal axis factor analysis was first performed on the items in order to uncover underlying dimensions. Nine factors emerged, explaining in total 62% of the variance. The Varimax-rotated factor loadings are shown in Appendix 1. The factor structure conforms very well to the hypothesized knowledge attribute variables; only synergies and autonomous versus systemic nature of the products seems to converge into one factor.

The final scales for the knowledge attribute variables were formed by averaging the items belonging to each factor. The reliability of the final scales was assessed by computing Cronbach's α, which is satisfactory for the scales measuring risk of opportunism, importance of patent protection, strength of complementary providers, and path dependency, whereas tacitness of knowledge and certainty of development seem to suffer from poor reliability.
The descriptive statistics and reliability coefficients for the scales are shown in Appendix 3, Table A. The companies' competitive advantage is typically based on substantial synergies, and tacitness of knowledge is high. The companies do not consider patents or threats by asset specificity or opportunism as important.

The dependent variables, i.e. internationalization variables include (1) speed of internationalization, which was measured as the number of years from the startup of the company to the start of its international operations (2) number of countries where the company is involved (3) international share of revenues (%) in years 2000 and 2002 (4) operation modes, which include four variables: Internet, export, cooperative modes and foreign direct investment. These variables were coded as dichotomies with value 1 assigned if the company uses the operation mode and 0 if the company uses some other operation mode(s).

The motives to internationalize were computed from 24 items by principal components factor analysis. The original items were measured on a scale ranging from −2 (inhibited internationalization to a great extent) to +2 (enhanced internationalization to a great extent). The analysis yielded seven factors together explaining 62.7 % of the variance. The factor structure is presented in Appendix 2. For the descriptive analysis additive scales of the motives were also formed by averaging the items that had the highest loading on each of the seven factors, see Appendix 3, Table 14.B.

Hypothesis testing and results

The hypotheses were tested using Spearman's rank order correlations for ratio scaled internationalization variables, and Mann-Whitney's independent samples test of medians for the operation mode variables. The correlations between knowledge variables and ratio scaled internationalization variables are shown in Table 14.1. The speed of internationalization is not associated with any of the knowledge attributes. Tacitness of knowledge has an almost significant negative correlation with the number of countries, indicating that the more tacit the company's knowledge is, the more the company's international operations are concentrated on only a few countries. On the contrary, strength of complementary providers is associated with large number of target countries. The current international share of revenues is negatively associated with tacitness and asset specificity, whereas intended future share of revenues correlates positively with the level of technological knowledge, importance of patents, synergies, and strength of complementary providers.

Table 14.1. Knowledge and internationalization.

Spearman correlations:knowledge and internationalization				
	Speed	# of countries	share 2000	share 2002
Tacitness	.03	-,19*	-,20*	-.05
Risk of opportunism	.14	-.02	.01	.08
Importance of patent protection	.06	.04	.06	,18**
Economies of scale	.14	.05	.14	,16*
Synergies	-.19	.00	.03	,30**
Strength of compl. Providers	-.12	,20*	.14	,18**
Path dependency	.05	.03	-.15	-,17*
Certainty of development	-.07	-.04	.10	.09
Asset specificity	.00	.01	-,22**	-.15
*significant at .10 level, **sig at .05				

The correlations between internationalization motives and speed, scope and share are shown in Table 14.2. As is the case with knowledge variables, motives seem to have no impact on the speed of internationalization. The presence of strong strategic motives enhances both the width and share of revenues. Also employee-related motives and following a foreign customer or partner contribute to a larger share of revenues from international operations.

The associations between knowledge attributes and internationalization, when the effects of motives were removed, are shown in Table 14.3. Some new effects of knowledge variables on the number of countries emerged. Companies with high path dependency and customer-specific assets have more target countries than less dependent companies. On the other hand, the effects of tacitness, patent protection and strength of complementary providers on the international share of revenues diminished, when the effects of motives were taken into account.

Table 14.2. Motives and internationalization.

Spearman correlations:motives and internationalization				
	speed	# of countries	share 2000	share 2002
Strategic motives	.01	,30**	,54**	,70**
Employees motives	-.16	.08	,35**	,28**
External enablers	.12	-.08	.04	.12
Foreign follow	.03	.14	,23**	,27**
Competitive env.	-.05	-.12	.10	,23**
Domestic follow	.00	.08	-.05	.07
Domestic competition	.10	.18	-.10	.06
*significant at .10 level, **sig at .05				

The effects of knowledge attributes on international operation modes are presented in Table 14.4. Companies using foreign direct investment modes have significantly lower tacitness and asset specificity than companies using other operation modes. Patent protection is more important for companies using cooperative internationalization modes.

Table 14.3. Knowledge and international controlling for motives.

Partial correlations: knowledge and intern. controlling for motives				
	speed	# of countries	share 2000	share 2002
Tacitness	,12	-,18	-,03	,09
Risk of opportunism	.19	.19	-,09	.05
Importance of patent protection	.02	-,01	.03	.13
Economies of scale	.09	.10	-,02	.05
Synergies	-,19	-,23*	,03	,27**
Strength of compl. Providers	-,05	,24*	,05	,08
Path dependency	-,02	,24*	-,05	-,15
Certainty of development	-,03	,01	-,01	,11
Asset specificity	-,02	,26**	-,14	-,09
*significant at .10 level, **sig at .05				

Table 14.4. Knowledge and operation modes.

Means of knowledge variables by internationalization mode

	Internet		Export		Cooper.		FDI	
	no (N=53)	yes (N=21)	no (N=22)	yes (N=52)	no (N=27)	yes (N=47)	no (N=59)	yes (N=15)
Tacitness	3.32	3.38	3.55	3.25	3.22	3.40	3,43**	2,97**
Risk of opportunism	2.33	2.42	2.32	2.37	2.29	2.39	2.40	2.18
Importance of patent protection	2.29	2.29	2.44	2.22	1,97**	2,47**	2.28	2.32
Economies of scale	3.23	3.19	3.10	3.26	3.12	3.27	3.21	3.25
Synergies	4.06	4.14	4.23	4.02	4.01	4.12	4.08	4.07
Strength of compl. Providers	2.80	3.00	2.77	2.88	2.93	2.80	2.92	2.53
Path dependency	2,25*	2,60*	2.18	2.42	2.35	2.35	2.37	2.24
Certainty of development	3.27	2.95	3.34	3.11	2,98*	3,30*	3.21	3.07
Asset specificity	2.23	2.04	2.13	2.19	2.39	2.05	2,30**	1,70**
*mean difference is significant at .10 level, **sig at .05 level								

Exporting companies are more driven by employee-related motives than companies using other operation modes, see Table 14.5.

Table 14.5. Motives and operation modes.

Means of motives by internationalization mode

	Internet		Export		Cooper.		FDI	
	no (N=53)	yes (N=21)	no (N=22)	yes (N=52)	no (N=27)	yes (N=47)	no (N=59)	yes (N=15)
Strategic motives	0.76	0.78	0.80	0.75	0.73	0.79	0.72	0.96
Employees motives	0.16	0.33	-0,19**	0,38**	0.20	0.21	0.14	0.46
External enablers	-0.21	-0.08	-0.09	-0.20	-0.16	-0.17	-0.22	0.04
Foreign follow	0.15	-0.10	-0.11	0.16	-0.21	0.25	0.01	0.39
Competitive env.	-0,12*	0,19*	0.02	-0.05	-0.07	-0.01	-0.09	0.18
Domestic follow	0.46	0.10	0.27	0.39	0.20	0.45	0.31	0.53
Domestic competition	-0.01	-0.26	0.07	-0.14	0.00	-0.13	-0.04	-0.23
*mean difference is significant at .10 level, **sig at .05 level								

SUMMARY AND DISCUSSION OF THE HYPOTHESES

This section summarizes our main findings concerning the knowledge-based hypotheses derived before.

H 1: The higher the degree of uncertainty, the more the foreign direct investment modes are used in internationalization.

Partly supported. The companies using cooperative operation modes in their internationalization feel that technological and market uncertainties are lower than companies using Internet, exporting or investment modes (FDIs). However, our cross-sectional analysis cannot reveal the direction of causality; on one hand it is possible that companies who cooperate feel less uncertainty; on the other hand companies feeling very uncertain about the future may be more inclined to operate alone. Furthermore, our measurement items may have been too vague and they need to be developed further.

H 2: The higher the risk of opportunistic behavior, the more the foreign direct investment modes are used in internationalization.

Not supported. Contradictory to our expectations, it seems that our sample companies do not perceive significant risk of opportunistic behavior. This is due to the fact that the smaller firms are more prone to avoid e.g. the risks related to financial matters. That makes the usage of the other, more inexpensive modes (i.e. contractual) applicable. However, we believe that in general, if the threat of opportunism is high, the operations are internalized in order to safeguard and sustain the competitive advantage. This assumption is based on TCE.

H 3: The more specific the relevant assets are, the more the foreign direct investment modes are used in internationalization.

Supported, almost significant effect. If the company is not dependent on one or few customers, it can use it assets in a more generic way. The investments are less risky as they are more applicable in many situations and for several customers. Thus, we believed that such companies use more investment modes and this proved to be significant. However, it is important to notice that the asset specificity may also have contradictory effects if the firm's assets are highly specific (e.g. idiosyncratic) and not easy to transfer.

H 4: The stronger the complementary providers are, the more international is the company.

Partly supported. The strength of complementary providers has almost significant effect on the number of target countries. As Teece (1998) points out, if the firm's internal capabilities are tied up with the complementary external capability, there's a need for more integration and this makes sense also in the international operations. Thus, if the customer (i.e. complementary provider) has the bargaining power and is international, it can be expected that the vendor is more international as well. Assuming that the value networks in the ICT sector are international, we consider that the more dependent the company is on other companies the more international it is. Strong complementary providers like e.g. Nokia operate in international networks, and require international presence from their partners. The strength of complementary providers, however, did not have any effect on share of international revenues, rapidity of internationalization and operation modes applied.

H 5: The more tacit new knowledge is, the more cooperative modes are applied.

No significant effect on dependent variables, but right directions. This can be related partly to the fact that the sample firms were young and small. Many of them were not focused, thus the difference between tacit and codified knowledge is difficult to draw and it may not be used as a clear antecedent of the operation modes yet. The tacit nature of the knowledge makes it also hard to transfer and in some cases, it may make the FDI only feasible option for the firm. We believe that the knowledge capabilities are essential factors when the strategic vision of the firm has become clear.

H 6: The more tacit new knowledge is, the more rapid is the internationalization.

Not supported. As tacit knowledge is easy to protect and difficult to imitate, we expected that in internationalization it is a better source for competitive advantage and enables the firm to overcome entry barriers. Due to the tacit nature of knowledge, the firm is able to use cooperative modes to pursue international competitive advantage, if the knowledge is transferable (i.e. the product or service is not idiosyncratic). In addition, the usage of the cooperative operation modes needs fewer investments and smaller firms could use them quicker than FDIs. However, our hypotheses failed probably because the tacitness is difficult to define and as stated in the previous hypotheses its role is not clear for the sample firms. A survey is always a "snapshot" and our measure has not been able to capture the concept in a valid and reliable way.

H 7: The better the company is able to patent its product, the more cooperative modes it uses in internationalization.

Supported. This hypothesis supported TCE completely. When the company is able to protect its knowledge, it is able to use the external resources/markets more effectively in its internationalization.

H 8: The more there are possibilities to gain economies of scale, the greater is the number of target countries.

Not supported. We believe that the basic hypothesis is correct in this sector (high-tech niche). Economies of scale are hard to achieve within limited home markets and, therefore, market expansion is a feasible option for growth. Our measurement items may not have been able to capture the issue well enough. The basic thinking behind the hypothesis was that in this sector the "first copy costs" are commonly very high. To amortize these costs, the small domestic markets are too small and therefore, there is a need to expand to several foreign markets very early.

H 9: The more there are possibilities to gain economies of scale, the larger is the share of international operations from company's total turnover.

Right directions and almost significant effect. However, it disappears when the effect of motives is eliminated. We assumed that if the economies of scale exist, the larger share of firm's turnover could be derived from international operations. Analyzing the result, related to the failed H 4 this may indicate that the economies of scale can be achieved from certain large target markets and thus, amount of countries is not as important as the market size.

H 10: The more there are economies of scope, the larger is the share of international operations from company's total turnover.

No effect in year 2000, supported in year 2002. Although the telecommunications business is global by its nature there are always certain aspects that need to be adapted/localized. The firms that can use their knowledge base for several products and services should be able to create more global products and thus, sell more internationally. While this is not clear at the moment, it is expected to have an effect in 2002. We believe that the participating firms will find a better focus in their operations in the longer term.

H 11: The higher the path dependency is, the smaller is the share of international revenues.

No effect in year 2000, almost significant effect in year 2002. However, it disappears when the effect of motives is eliminated. It was hypothesized that the previous technology choices of the firm will limit its possibilities to internationalize. This obviously is dependent on how tied the firm's knowledge is to certain technology and how large investments are required to change the path.

CONCLUDING REMARKS

We strongly believe that in highly knowledge-intensive sectors such as ICT, the more dynamic model is needed to describe and predict the internationalization patterns of the firm. Aspects like previous experience of the management, learning, intangible assets (e.g. tacit knowledge) are important attributes that should be included into the comprehensive studies. Knowledge-based view tries to tackle these issues, although it is seldom used in the studies of internationalization. Lately, evolutionary theory has been integrated into the modern OLI-paradigm (Dunning, 2000). However, more practical frameworks are needed. The emergence of born global firms is one of the issues that emphasize this need.

In this paper we have presented the knowledge-based view on internationalization. The determinants in our model are appropriability (tacitness and patent protection), threat of opportunism, economies of scale and scope (synergies), path dependency, asset specificity and strength of complementary providers. These are complementary to the traditional explanatory factors on internationalization.

Although we believe that our model captures some of the previously neglected aspects in internationalization, we have to admit that its explanatory power in our empirical study was not very strong. The hypotheses based on the knowledge-based view and TCE were only partly supported. This may be due to the difficulties in our survey, e.g. some of the measurement items did not take into account all the dimensions of the constructs. Furthermore, our study was cross-sectional and because most of the firms were young and small, their business strategies or capabilities were not clearly focused. We assume that this will change in the future and longitudinal studies would be even more supportive towards our model.

REFERENCES

Anderson, E. and H. Gatignon, 1986, 'Modes of Foreing Entry: A Transaction Cost Analysis and Propositions', Journal of International Business Studies **17** (Fall), 1-26.

Andersen, O., 1997, 'Internationalization and Market Entry Mode: A Review of Theories and Conceptual Frameworks', *Management International Review* (Special Issue 2), 27-42.

Andersen, O., 1993, 'On the internationalization process of firms: A critical analysis', *Journal of International Business Studies* **24** (2), 209-231.

Autio, E., H.J Sapienza and J.G. Almeida, 2000, 'Effects of Age at Entry, Knowledge Intensity, and Imitability on International Growth', *Academy of Management Journal* **43**, 909-924.

Barney, J.B., 1986, 'Types of Competition and the Theory of Strategy: Toward an Integrative Framework', *Academy of Management Review* (11), 791-800.

Bell, J., 1995, 'The internationalization of small computer software firms – A further challenge to "stage" theories', *European Journal of Marketing* **29** (8), 60-75.

Blomqvist, K. and K. Kyläheiko, 2000, 'Main Challenges of Knowledge Management: Telecommunications Sector as an Example', in the CD-ROM Proceedings of the 8th International Conference on Management of Technology, Miami, USA, 21-25.2. 2000.

Blomqvist, K., K. Kyläheiko and V-M Virolainen, 2001, 'Filling the Gap in Traditional Transaction Cost Economics: Towards Transaction Benefits-based Analysis using Finnish Telecommunications as an Illustration', will be published in International Journal of Production Economics.

Buckley, P.J. and M.C. Casson, 1976, The Future of Multinational Enterprises, New York: Holmes and Meier Publishers.

Coviello, N. and H. Munro, 1997, 'Network Relationships and the Internationalization Process of Small Software Firms', *International Business Review* **6**, 361-386.

Dunning, J. H., 2000, 'The Eclectic Paradigm as an Envelope for Economic and Business Theories of MNE Activity', *International Business Review* **9**, 163-190.

Eisenhardt, K.M. and J.A. Martin, 2000, 'Dynamic Capabilities: What are they? *Strategic Management Journal'* **21**, 1105-1121.

Erramilli, M.K., (1990): Entry Mode Choice in Service Industries, *International Marketing Review* **7** (5), 50-62.

Erramilli, M.K. and C.P. Rao, 1993, 'Service Firms' Entry Mode Choice: a Modified Transaction-Cost Analysis Approach', *Journal of Marketing* **57** (3), 19-38.

Foss, N. J., 2000, 'Equilibrium vs. Evolution in the resource-based perspective: the Conflicting Legacies of Demsetz and Penrose', in Foss, N. J. and P.L. Robertson (eds.), *Resources, Technology and Strategy: Explorations in the Resource-based Perspective*, London: Routledge, 11-30.

Hymer, S.H., 1976, 'The International Operations of National Firms: A Study of Direct Foreign Investment', Cambridge: MIT Press.

Johanson, J. and L.-G. Mattsson, 1988, 'Internationalisation in Industrial Systems – a Network Approach', in Hood, N. and J-E. Vahlne (eds.), *Strategies in Global Competition*, London: Croom Helm, 287-314.

Johanson, J. and J-E. Vahlne, 1990, 'The Mechanism of Internationalization', *International Marketing Review* **7** (4), 11-24.

Johanson, J. and J-E. Vahlne, 1977, 'The Internationalization Process of the Firm: a Model of Knowledge Development and Increasing Foreign Market Commitments', *Journal of International Business Studies* **8** (1), 23-32.

Johanson, J. and F. Wiedersheim-Paul, 1975, 'The Internationalization of the Firm: Four Swedish Cases', *Journal of Management Studies* (October), 305-322.

Knight, G., 1997, Emerging Paradigm for International Marketing: The Born Global Firm, Dissertation, Department of Marketing and Supply Chain Management, Michigan State University.

Kogut, B. and U. Zander, 1993, 'Knowledge of the Firm and the Evolutionary Theory of the Multinational Corporation', *Journal of International Business Studies* (4th quarter), 625-643.

Kyläheiko, K., 1995, Coping with Technology: A Study on Economic Methodology and Strategic Management of Technology, Lappeenranta University of Technology, Research Papers 48.

Kyläheiko, K., 1998, 'Making Sense of Technology: Towards Synthesis between Neoclassical and Evolutionary Approaches', *International Journal of Production Economics* **56-57**, 319-332.

Kyläheiko, K. and A. Miettinen, 1995, 'Technology Management and Entrepreneurship: A Critical View', in Birley, S. and MacMillan, I. (eds.). *International Entrepreneurship*. London: Routledge, 39-58.

Luostarinen, R., 1979, Internationalization of the Firm. An Empirical Study of the Internationalization of Firms with Small and Open Domestic Markets with Special Emphasis of Lateral Rigidity as a Behavioral Characteristic in Strategic Decision Making, Helsinki: Acta Academiae oeconomiae Helsigiensis, Series A: 30.

Madsen, T.K. and P. Servais, 1997, 'The Internationalization of Born Globals: an Evolutionary Process?', *International Business Review* **6** (6), 561-583.

Metcalfe, S., 1989, 'Evolution and Economic Change', in Silberstain, A. (ed.), Technology and Economic Progress, London: MacMillan, 54-85.

Metcalfe, J.S. and A. James, 2000, 'Knowledge and Capabilities: A New View of the Firm' in Foss, N. J. and P.L. Robertson (eds.), *Resources, Technology and Strategy: Explorations in the Resource-based Perspective*, London: Routledge, 31-52.

Nelson, R.R. and S. Winter, 1982, An Evolutionary Theory of Economic Change, Cambridge: Harvard U.P.

Oviatt, B.M. and P.P. McDougall, 1995, 'Global start-ups: Entrepreneurs on a worldwide stage', *Academy of Management Executive* **9** (2), 30-43.

Oviatt, B.M. and P.P. McDougall, 1994, 'Toward a Theory of International New Ventures', *Journal of International Business Studies* **25** (1), 45-64.

Rennie, M.W., 1993, 'Global Competitiveness: Born Global', *The McKinsey Quarterly* (4), 45-52.

Teece, D.J., 1986, 'Profiting from Technological Innovation: Implications for Integration, Collaboration, Licensing and Public Policy', *Research Policy* **15**, 285-305.

Teece, D.J., 1988, 'Technological Change and the Nature of the Firm', in Dosi. G. et al. (eds.), *Technical Change and Economic Theory*. London: Pinter Publishers, 256-281.

Teece, D. J., 1998, 'Research Directions for Knowledge Management', *California Management Review* **40**, 289-292.

Teece, D. and G. Pisano, 1994, 'The Dynamic Capabilities of Firms: An Introduction', *Industrial and Corporate Change* **3**, 537-556.

Teece, D., G. Pisano, and A. Shuen, 1997, 'Dynamic Capabilities and Strategic Management', *Strategic Management Journal* 18, 509-533.

Wernerfelt, B., 1984, 'A Resource-Based View of the Firm', *Strategic Management Journal* **5**, 171-180.

Williamson, O.E., 1975, Markets and Hierarchies: Analysis and Antitrust Implications, New York: Free Press.

Williamson, O.E., 1999, 'Strategy research: Governance and Competence Perspectives', *Strategic Management Journal* **20**, 1087-1108.

Winter, S.G., 1995, 'Four R's of Profitability: Rents, Resources, Routines, and Replication', in Montgomery, C.A. (ed.), *Resource-Based and Evolutionary Theories of the Firm: Towards a Synthesis,* USA: Harvard Business School, 147-178.

APPENDIX

Appendix 1. Varimax-rotated factor structure of knowledge attribute items

Item	Fac1	Fac2	Fac3	Fac4	Fac5	Fac6	Fac7	Fac8	Fac9
Patents act as references of our competence	.79								
Patents effectively prevent our competitors from stealing our ideas	.75								
Patents can help to shape the development of the industry, e.g. standards	.73								
The competitors are able to break our patent	.60		.35						
We cannot exploit our competitors' ideas, because their patent protection strengthens	.54								-.42
Importance of patents for sustaining your competitive advantage	.51		.35						
Risk of opportunism by strategically important partners		.82							
Risk of opportunism by large buyers		.79							
Risk of opportunism by subcontractors		.72							
Risk of partners breaking our contract		.71							
Extent of scale economies in distribution			.73						
Extent of scale economies in marketing			.65						
Extent of scale economies in production			.61						
Extent of scale economies in financing			.51				-.31	.48	
How can you adjust your key competencies to new technologies				.70					
Extent of synergies in using your key competencies for different purposes				.68					
Importance of quick absorption/application of new knowledge for sustaining your competitive advantage				.55					
Our products/services can be sold autonomously				-.53				-.40	
Our key competencies are in technologies that will be substituted by others				-.46	.44				
We are very dependent on other companies operating in the value chain					.84				
Commercialization of our key competencies is heavily dependent on other companies operating in the value chain					.84				
Our previous technology choices dictate the development of our key competencies						.84			
Our previous technology choices make us vulnerable to radical changes in tehcnological development						.77			
Degree of uncertainty about market development							.77		
Degree of uncertainty about technological development							.66		
Patents are important for sustaining competitive positions in our industry	.39						.41		
A large buyer forces us to make heavy investments, increasing our dependency on them		.41						.62	
Our bargaining power weakens, when there are few potential buyers								.53	
Importance of tacit knowledge for sustaining your competitive advantage									.80
Because of our tacit knowledge, we do not have to worry about our ideas leaking to others									.69

Appendix 2. Factor structure of internationalization motives

Motive to internationalize	Stategic	Employee	Enabler	Follow for.	Comp. env.	Follow dom.	Dom. comp.	Communality
Role in company strategy	.77							.68
Demand in intnl markets	.76							.66
Small home markets	.68							.56
Economies of scale in production	.61				.33			.57
Employees' willingness	.61	.39						.59
Employees' language skills	.42	.41						.46
Employees' knowledge of target markets		.83						.77
Employees' marketing knowledge		.70						.58
Employees' intnl experience		.67						.55
Employees' product/service knowledge		.60						.53
Availability of financing			.83					.71
Availability of expertise			.81					.70
Short product life cycles		-.33	.47					.50
Foreign customer	.34			.78				.77
Foreign supplier/partner				.74				.64
Risks of intnl business				.67				.64
Need of beachhead position					.72			.58
Lower price than competitors'					.69			.53
Legal issues/regulations				.45	.58			.58
Internationalization of competitors		.34			.51		.42	.60
Internationalization of domestic customer						.86		.78
Internationalization of domestic supplier/partner						.83		.70
Domestic competitive situation							.76	.66
Entry of foreign competitors into Finland		.42					.70	.74
Eigenvalues	4.55	3	1.89	1.65	1.51	1.25	1.21	
% of variance	18.9	12.5	7.9	6.9	6.3	5.2	5	62.7

Appendix 3. Descriptive statistics

Table 14.A. Descriptive statistics of the knowledge variables

Variables	Min	Max	Mean	Std.dev.	# of items	Reliability
Tacitness	1,5	5,00	3,35	0,84	2	,47
Risk of opportunism	1,00	4,00	2,28	0,77	4	,79
Importance of patent	1,00	4,29	2,25	0,72	7	,76
Economies of scale	1,00	5,00	3,06	0,75	4	,56
Economies of scope	2,00	5,00	4,00	0,60	3	,56
Strength of compl. providers	1,00	5,00	2,65	1,10	2	,82
Path dependency	1,00	4,67	2,35	0,79	3	,64
Certainty	1,00	5,00	3,17	0,81	2	,52
Asset specificity	1,00	4,50	2,14	0,86	2	,58

Table 14.B: Descriptive statistics of the internationalization variables

Variable	Min	Max	Mean	Std.dev.	# of items	Cronbach α
Speed	0	24	3.80	5.41	1	N/A
Number of countries	1	50	5.01	7.97	1	N/A
Share of revenues	1	80	21.21	20.48	1	N/A
Share of revenues	2	100	35.74	28.48	1	N/A
Internet mode	0	1	0.28	0.45	1	N/A
Export mode	0	1	0.70	0.46	1	N/A
Cooperative mode	0	1	0.64	0.49	1	N/A
FDI mode	0	1	0.20	0.40	1	N/A
Strategic motive	-2.00	+2.00	0.50	0.76	6	.78
Employee motive	-2.00	+1.75	-0.02	0.80	4	.73
Enabler motive	-2.00	+1.67	-0.12	0.62	3	.67
Follow for. motive	-2.00	+2.00	-0.11	0.84	3	.69
Comp. Env. motive	-2.00	+2.00	-0.09	0.55	4	.63
Follow dom. motive	-2.00	+2.00	+0.30	0.91	2	.70
Domestic comp.	-2.00	+2.00	-0.05	0.70	2	.50

15

KNOWLEDGE MANAGEMENT IN INNOVATION PROCESSES

*Anja Schulze, University of St. Gallen, Switzerland**

> *"For DuPont, accelerating innovation is the main objective*
> *of their Knowledge Management program."*
> (Extreme Innovation Inc., 1999)

INTRODUCTION

Currently, most companies are conscious of the constant need to innovate. Company operations must change to be in tune with a new economic landscape (Quinn et al., 1997: 20). Education increases, e.g. professional corps of engineers and scientists are constantly growing (von Krogh, Nonaka, 2000: 3). Information and Communication Technology – think only of the increasing computer capacity, the internet, or the seemingly endless emerging wireless networks – is triggering growing networks, which increase the exchange of information and the amount of knowledge one has access to. Subsequently, the importance of knowledge and its management has grown significantly and the task of every company is to build an organization that will meet the demands of the postindustrial knowledge economy.

One trigger of introducing Knowledge Management to Innovation Processes is the increasing complexity of products and services, in whichever more different technologies are combined and embedded. Therefore, the essentially different competencies must be available and used efficiently and effectively (Quinn et al., 1997: 13). This requires the Innovation Process to encompass the combination and integration of large numbers of participants, stakeholders, and their knowledge. The necessity of implementing knowledge management, with

---

* Anja Schulze is a Ph.D. student at the Institute for Technology Management, University of St. Gallen, Switzerland. Email: Anja.Schulze@unisg.ch

regard to innovation, is clarified further by Nonaka and Takeuchi (1995: 5) who argue that to-day's knowledge management is needed to create continuous innovation to gain competitive advantages. Yet, effective Knowledge Management will have different profiles in different business processes, depending on knowledge intensity and process complexity.

The emerging consensus on the importance of knowledge in organizations has fuelled much of the exploding interest in Knowledge Management practice and theory (Scarbrough and Swan, 2001: especially 6). However, much of this work fails to consider the purpose for which knowledge is 'being managed'. In this study, purpose is considered in terms of encour-aging innovation. Taking an interest in what companies expect from Knowledge Management as well as what they have been doing so far, several studies were analyzed. In a survey con-ducted by Knowledge Bridge Consulting, (2000), companies were asked what they expected from the efficient management of knowledge. The expectation to 'Strengthen their capability to innovate' was named most, along with 'Shorten time to respond to market needs'. Even though most companies are convinced, that the role which effective Knowledge Management can play in achieving best results with respect to product innovation is very significant and even though R&D was named third in answering the question who initiated Knowledge Management pro-jects KPMG Consulting (2000), the knowledge that has been managed is mainly to find in other areas respective departments, such as Sales and Marketing. The Knowledge Management discipline within R&D is still at an early stage (Armbrecht Jr. et al., 2001).

PRIOR RESEARCH AND RELATED LITERATURE

A considerable amount of research has been conducted regarding the role of knowledge man-agement in innovation processes (Carneiro, 2000; Johannessen et al., 1999; and Leonard-Barton, 1992). However, innovation is foremost depending on knowledge creation (Madhavan and Grover 1998: 1). An analysis of knowledge creation in innovation processes from a theo-retical perspective was done by Pitt and Clarke (1999). Madhavan and Grover (1998) studied cognitive team processes as one factor influencing knowledge creation in new product devel-opment teams. The research done by Swan, Newell, Scarbrough et al. (1999) focuses on net-works and networking as two aspects affecting knowledge creation and therewith interactive innovation. Research has been done investigating the transfer and re-combination of existing knowledge as one option for knowledge creation and innovation (Galunic and Rodan, 1998; Kogut and Zander, 1992; Dougherty, 1992). Corti and Lo Storto (2000) investigated knowl-edge generation during technical problem solving as one task during product innovation.

With the exception of this conceptual and qualitative research, there has been no em-pirical study where organizational knowledge creation in innovation processes has been ana-lyzed systematically. The goal of the study by Nonaka, Byosiere, Borucki et al. (1994) was to formalize and test a generic model of dynamic organizational knowledge creation. The study does not involve a relation of the model to innovation processes. Nonaka and Takeuchi (1995) use the innovation process to illustrate their model, yet they did not test the interrelation empirically. This is also true for von Krogh, Ichijo and Nonaka (2000a) where the new product development (NPD) process is used as an example for the knowledge creation process.

Knowledge intensive processes are defined as business processes that have a lower knowledge half-life than others; they require a long learning time before they can be mastered. Moreover, knowledge intensive processes rely heavily on the experiences and the know-how of the people involved. Complex processes are characterized by the involvement of a larger number of people, requiring a more complex coordination process, and a higher number of process steps. In addition, complex processes are more dynamic, because they are not organized the same way at iteration (Eppler et al., 2000). Since product innovation processes can be classified as knowledge intense as well as fairly complex, it is to find in the upper right section of Fig. 15.1:

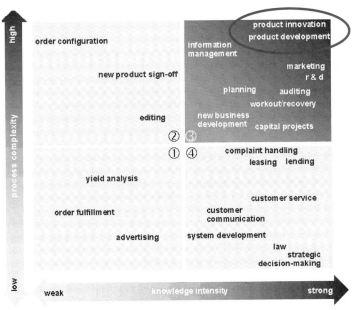

(Source: Eppler et al., 2000)

Fig. 15.1. Classification of business processes in regard to process complexity and knowledge intensity.

While the efficiency of business processes like order fulfillment or customer service relies mainly on the exploitation of existing knowledge or the dissemination of new knowledge, innovation has to focus on the process of efficiently creating new knowledge. Based on a model of von Krogh et al. (2000a), the 'company development in knowledge creation' follows three steps (see Fig. 15.2). (1) Firms begin their knowledge initiatives by trying to locate and capture valuable company knowledge. (2) The second step is characterized by the objective to make the company knowledge easily accessible to the organization and to find new applications for existing knowledge. (3) In order to be able to take the third step – enabling knowledge creation - the first two have to be inherited respective performed in an organization's business process. Since the first and second step stress the exploitation of existing knowledge or the dissemination of new knowledge, innovation has to focus on the process of efficiently creating new knowledge.

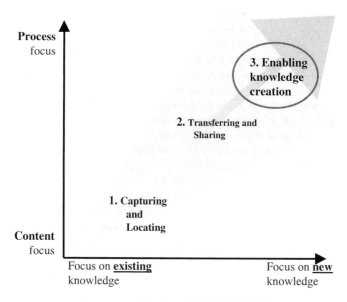

Source: von Krogh et al. (2000b: 259ff.)

Fig. 15.2. Evolution of knowledge management initiatives.

This paper is guided by an analysis of the knowledge creation process, the innovation process, and their interrelationship. Given that innovation is an episodic process, where the phases differ significantly in their characteristics, it appears unlikely that a single set of tools and methodologies for managing knowledge would be appropriate across all phases. Rather, it is proposed that the 'type' of knowledge creation changes during the process. Hence, this paper focuses on a thorough analysis of different types of knowledge creation in the phases of product innovation. Further, it investigates which approaches of knowledge management will be provided which support the different knowledge creation types and new insights regarding untapped potential enhancing the product innovation processes. The results of that analysis will serve as a base for further examinations of the implications of knowledge management on innovation management, answering questions like: To what extent can knowledge management support and improve a company's ability to innovate? What measures have to be taken to enhance innovating? It is important to note, that the paper was written taking the perspective of product innovations, specifically technological products. A transfer of the findings to process innovations, organizational or social innovations might be possible but that requires the dedication of further thoughts to it.

KNOWLEDGE, THE KNOWLEDGE CREATION PROCESS, AND MANAGING KNOWLEDGE CREATION

> *"[...] a company changes its knowledge through innovation [...]"*
> (Vicari, 1998: 211)

Knowledge

Researchers have introduced several definitions of the term *knowledge* over the years. Purists consider knowledge to be what is within and between the minds of individuals and is tacitly possessed, others determine knowledge as an asset based on data and information. Data, which refers to interpretable symbols (e.g., letters forming words and sentences), becomes information when it is given a structure. Further, information evolves to knowledge when it has meaning for the receiver. For example, organizational knowledge sets and routines may be seen as shared knowledge among those organizational members who have a contextual understanding of the organizational situation. To outsiders, these codified knowledge sets are mere information that may or may not have significance for them (Johnson, 2000: 9).

The reason for that great variability of these definitions is well explained by von Krogh et al. (2000a: 5): „Knowledge is one of those concepts that is extremely meaningful, positive, promising, and hard to pin down." (von Krogh et al., 2000a: 5). For this paper the knowledge definition of Probst et al. (1999) is adopted, which describes knowledge as the whole body of cognitions and skills which individuals and organizations use to solve problems. Moreover, knowledge includes both theories and practical, everyday rules and instructions for action Probst et al. (1999: 24). Further, knowledge does appear in different forms, whereas the most prevalent distinction is between *explicit* and *tacit* knowledge forms.

Explicit or codified knowledge refers to knowledge that is transmittable in formal, systematic language. It can be shared in the form of data, scientific formulae, specifications, manuals, etc.

and can be processed, transmitted and stored relatively easily. Explicit knowledge is captured in records of the past such as libraries, archives and databases (Nonaka and Takeuchi, 1995: 59).

Tacit knowledge is deeply rooted in action, commitment, and involvement in a specific context. It has a personalized quality, is almost intuitive, difficult to articulate and therefore formalize and transfer. (Polanyi, 1966) first proposed the tacit dimension of knowledge using the dictum that 'we can know more than we can tell'. Tacit knowledge involves both cognitive and technical elements (Nonaka et al., 1994: 338f.).

- Cognitive elements include schemata, paradigms, beliefs and viewpoints that provide perspectives that help individuals to perceive and define their world.

- The technical element covers concrete know-how, crafts, and skills that apply to specific contexts and refers to an individual's images of reality and visions for the future.

The Knowledge Creation Process

Knowledge creation fuels innovation, knowledge per se does not. Hence, the process by which new knowledge is created within the organization – in the form of new products, services, or systems – becomes the cornerstone of innovative activities (Nonaka and Takeuchi, 1995: 235). According to Nonaka (1994), the process of creating organizational knowledge is dynamic, interactive, and based on two different kinds of knowledge spirals: one at the epistemological and one at the ontological dimension.

The spiral at the epistemological dimension is anchored to the assumption, that human knowledge is created and expanded through social interaction between tacit knowledge and explicit knowledge. Nonaka calls this interaction 'knowledge conversion'. It should be noted that this conversion is a social process between individuals, not confined within an individual since an individual is never isolated from social interaction when he or she perceives things. Nonaka and Takeuchi, 1995: 61) Thus, through this 'social conversion' process, tacit and explicit knowledge expand over time in terms of both quality and quantity. The assumption that knowledge is created though the conversion between tacit and explicit knowledge allows us to postulate four different 'modes' of knowledge conversion: Socialization, Externalization, Combination and Internalization (see Fig. 15.3):

(1) **Socialization: from tacit to tacit knowledge:** The Exchange of tacit knowledge creates common mental models and abilities (Nonaka and Takeuchi, 1995: 91) define shared mental models as knowledge structures held by members of a team that enable them to form accurate explanations and expectations for the task, and in turn, to coordinate their actions and adapt their behavior to demands of the task and other team members. In order to exchange tacit knowledge, people do not necessarily need to use language. For instance abilities like crafts-

work can be shared and learned by observation, imitation, and praxis. The key is experience. In socialization, a 'field' of interaction is built.

(2) **Externalization: from tacit to explicit knowledge:** This phase includes the process of articulating tacit knowledge. The tacit knowledge will be transformed to models, pictures, and so on. Externalization is induced by dialog and collective reflection.

(3) **Combination: from explicit to explicit knowledge:** Combination is a process of connecting different areas of explicit knowledge. The exchange of knowledge is done with media like documents, meetings, phone, or computer networks. Sorting, adding, or combining develops the new combination of existing information. The classification of explicit knowledge can lead to new knowledge.

(4) **Internalization: from explicit to tacit knowledge:** Embodying explicit knowledge into tacit knowledge is determined as internalization and is closely related to learning-by-doing. When experiences through socialization, externalization, and combination are internalized into individuals' tacit knowledge bases in the form of shared mental models or technical know-how, they become valuable assets.

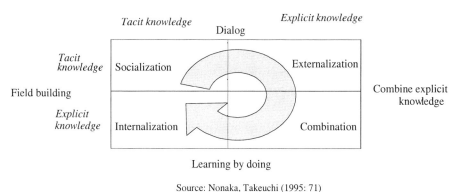

Source: Nonaka, Takeuchi (1995: 71)

Fig. 15.3. Knowledge creation through social interaction.

The other spiral takes place at the ontological dimension. The interactions between tacit and explicit knowledge will tend to become larger in scale and faster in speed as more actors in and around the organization become involved. Thus, organizational knowledge creation can be viewed as an upward spiral process, starting at the individual level moving up to the collective (group) level, and then to the organizational level, sometimes reaching out to the interorganizational level, and finally leading back to the individual level (Nonaka, 1994: 18ff.). Although each dimension produces a dynamic spiral, the truly dynamic nature can be depicted as the interaction of the two knowledge spirals over time. It is that dynamic process that fuels innovation. (Nonaka and Takeuchi, 1995: 235f.).

Managing Knowledge Creation

Managing knowledge is not literally possible.
(Armbrecht Jr. et al., 2001: 29)

As Nonaka (1994) states: "Organizational knowledge creation, as distinct from individual knowledge creation, takes place when all four modes of knowledge creation are 'organization-ally' managed to form a continual cycle." (Nonaka, 1994: 20) According to von Krogh et al. (2000a: vii) the term management implies control of processes that may be inherently uncontrollable or, at least, stifled by heavy-handed direction. From the perspective of the authors, managers need to support knowledge creation rather than to control it. That overall set of organizational activities that positively affects knowledge creation, is called knowledge enablers. The most important enablers that have been identified by von Krogh et al. (2000a) are (1) instill a knowledge vision, (2) manage conversations, (3) mobilize knowledge activists, (4) create the right context, and (5) globalize local knowledge (von Krogh et al., 2000a: 8). However, enabling knowledge creation means to provide the right context, which again requires managerial actions, whereas management is far more than control (Shenhar and Renier, 1996). Moreover, visions and goals without control are useless. Hence, the overall set of organizational activities and knowledge management approaches that positively affect knowledge creation will be named Management of Knowledge Creation hereafter, whereas knowledge management overall will be understood as applied systematic approaches to find, understand, and use knowledge to create value. The creation of value can be: enhance customer value, enable superior performance, create new capabilities, and encourage innovation (Liebowitz, 1999: 1-6). Examples for knowledge management approaches are Best Practice Catalogues, Communities of Practice, Debriefings, Knowledge Broker, Knowledge Maps, Yellow Pages. For descriptions of these examples and for more examples see Probst et al. (1999) or Liebowitz, (1999).

INNOVATION, THE INNOVATION PROCESS, AND INNOVATION MANAGEMENT

Innovation

At the origin of the technological innovation process are inventions or discoveries. As Webster points out, "We discover what before existed, though to us unknown; we invent what did not before exist." (Burgelman et al., 2001: 3) Invention or discovery involves the initial observation of a new phenomenon (discovery) or provides the initial verification, that a problem can be solved (invention) (Quinn et al., 1997: 3). Once the phenomenon or problem solution is incorporated in a product and once that product is introduced to the market, the term innovation applies. Further, a successful innovation is one that returns the original investment in its development plus some additional returns.

Among many typologies of innovation, technical and administrative innovation has widely been distinguished. Technical innovations are novel combinations of art, science, or craft employed to create the goods or services used by society. Administrative innovations involve organizational structure and administrative processes (Quinn et al., 1997: 3; Damanpour and Gopalakrishnan, 1999: 59). In addition to that, innovations can be differentiated in incremental and radical ones. Incremental innovations involve the adaptation, refinement, and enhancement of existing products. Radical innovations involve entirely new product categories.

This paper focuses on technical product innovations, and – since radical innovations will rarely be developed in organized innovation processes- incremental innovations.

The Innovation Process

The innovation process can be defined as the combined activities leading to new, marketable products (Burgelman et al., 2001: 4). Innovation processes can be found in a broad variety throughout the literature (e.g. Cooper, 2000; Thamhain, 1996: 9.4f.). The processes differ significantly in different industries and companies. Yet, all of them have certain characteristic phases in common. This allows the determination of a 'Generic Innovation Process'. The process starts with the generation of an idea, which will be developed further to become or to significantly improve a product. Next, the new or improved product is introduced to the market. Experiences gathered in all of these three phases serve as a rich base for new impulses, which again feed the generation of ideas. These steps are visualized in Fig. 15.4 and are briefly explained thereafter.

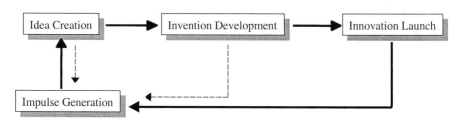

Fig. 15.4. The Generic Innovation Process.

Although describing the innovation process in that way is a convenient schematic there needs to be a caveat. Which is that these phases do not represent discrete stages. The limitations of stage models of innovation are well known. Rather, these different aspects of innovation are iterative, overlapping, and ultimately conflated. Hence the term episodes is used as opposed to stages (Swan and Clark, 1992)

(1) Create an idea: The creation of an idea is triggered by one or more impulses, which is a creative spark or the awareness of a problem or a new perspective on a topic, etc. Usually an informal network of people from inside and also outside the company is involved. These can be customers, suppliers, interns etc. Brainstorming, discussing their thoughts, thinking about cause and effect, experimenting they merge their impulses and develop ideas. Hence, idea creation is strongly dependent on individuals communicating face to face (Boutellier et al., 2000: 165). An idea in this context is a constructive alternative with the objective to apply to a certain technical question. The phase of idea creation can often be low-key, simmering for years, without well-defined structures.

(2) Develop an invention: Since there are no unlimited resources for pursuing ideas, they have to be evaluated and selected. Evaluations and selections can be performed in cross-functional teams, thus involving many parts of the organization. Subsequently resources are dedicated e.g. to technical development, and building prototypes. In successful cases, the following trial and error procedures will result in an invention. Here, an invention is understood as a technical solution. With experiments or simulations it can be shown, if the solution is functioning. The general objective is to create a tangible manifestation of the idea. At this point, however there is no certainty of a commercial application.

(3) Launch an innovation: After relating the invention to market studies and aligning potential product strategies with the company strategy, a systemized production concept will be worked out involving suppliers and sales channels. The new process/product has to be sourced for supplies. Marketing and sales channels have to be ramped up which foster demand. In the end, the customer's acceptance (sales) will decide, whether or not it is a viable product innovation.

(4) Generate impulses: The experience built up during the innovation process grows the intellectual property of the organization and its partners. Specifically, the involved individuals do learn and enrich their basis for deriving creative sparks, identifying problems, determining new perspectives, and therewith create impulses for new ideas.

Innovation Management

Innovation management has the objective to launch new technical solutions systematically and constructively. Aiming at that objective it can be characterized by the following tasks (Hauschildt, 1993: 23):

- Define innovation strategies (e.g. choose between the first or follower strategy)

- Set targets ("By the end of the year x % of products must not be older than x years.")

- Make decisions ("Shall the expensive development of a chemical process with unknown outcome be pursued further or not?")

KNOWLEDGE CREATION IN INNOVATION PROCESSES

> *„All innovation is a learning process*
> *through which people create the relevant new tacit and explicit knowledge*
> *that will enable them to coax ideas to maturity. "*
> (Miller and Morris, 1998: 90)

Purpose of the following chapter is to investigate the interrelation the knowledge creation processes with the generic innovation process. Each innovation phases involves knowledge creation (and also knowledge sharing, application, storing etc. as prerequisites of knowledge creation). However, each episode has a somewhat different focus in this respect. Idea creation, for example is more concerned with socialization, whereas concept creation and selection are more concerned with externalizing knowledge. It is likely then, that these episodes pose somewhat different challenges for Knowledge Management.

(1) Create an idea: Independent of the type of impulse, people will discuss it with others. This is necessary due to today's knowledge explosion. Individuals are very specialized and a single person can barely develop new product ideas anymore (Quinn et al., 1997: 13). Depending on the field of innovation, there might be discussions, simulations or even experiments to develop a creative spark to an idea. Now, even though there were several persons involved, the knowledge, the shared and developed, is not explicit yet. Employees who are interacting in that phase have common experiences, shared mental models and similar mind sets. Since mainly tacit knowledge is exchanged and acquired, socialization is the dominating knowledge mode here. Key aspects are trust and informal networking.

(2) Develop an invention: In order to be able to decide which idea should be pursued further, other employees e.g. a technology management board needs to understand the principles and solution that an idea claims to provide. Therefore members of that informal created group or personal network will have to articulate their (hidden) tacit knowledge. Otherwise it could not be communicated to people outside that personal network, who have a different mind set and speak a different 'language'. In other words, the ideas need to be externalized into concepts. These concepts might be written descriptions, prototypes, pilot projects etc. In doing so, the idea will be brought further, will be sharpened and finally refined to an invention. In Nonaka and Takeuchi's terms conceptualized knowledge has been created.

(3) Launch an innovation: The commercialization of a new product has to be carefully prepared. Involved are suppliers, distributors, advertising etc. In order to be successful, a holistic approach is necessary. The existing company knowledge and the knowledge of partners needs to be combined. A combination of existing explicit knowledge takes place and systemic knowledge is created.

(4) Generate innovative impulses: What generates innovative impulses? The awareness of certain problems or creative sparks is built on existing knowledge and experiences.
Hence, the process of internalization has to have happened sometime before. Based on that,
knowledge pieces are more or less consciously inter-linked. At certain, unpredictable moments
knowledge and information components fit like a jigsaw and make sense, all of a sudden. This
will be experienced more likely by someone with a large knowledge base than by someone
with a smaller knowledge base (Maier et al., 2001) In addition to that, creativity theory applies.
A creative individual is able to combine knowledge pieces in unconventional ways. He or she
is able to think out of the box instead of repeatedly using proven patterns and screens. However, creativity itself is not given to every individual. Therefore internalization of explicit (organizational) knowledge is key. Moreover, "Experienced-based operational knowledge often
triggers a new cycle of innovation." (Nonaka and Takeuchi, 1995: 72)

Findings from the previous paragraphs are visualized in the following Table 15.1:

Table 15.1: Knowledge conversion modes occurring in the phases of the Innovation Process.

	Socialization	Externalization	Combination	Internalization
Idea creation	**XXX**	X	X	X
Invention development	X	**XXX**	X	X
Innovation launch	X	X	**XXX**	X
Impulse generation	X	X	X	**XXX**

In this table, XXX is indicating that the specific knowledge mode dominates the other
modes in the according phase of the innovation process, while X is indicating that the knowledge mode plays a secondary role in the according phase of the innovation process. Furthermore, three propositions can be formulated:

(I)   One knowledge mode is dominating the others in the different episodes of a
       successful innovation process.

(II)   Yet, a knowledge mode does not occur exclusively.

(III) Therefore, the different episodes of the innovation process do require differ-
       ent knowledge management activities in order to be efficient.

MANAGERIAL IMPLICATIONS

Once the dominating knowledge modes in each step of the innovation process have been identified, management actions that support the development of innovations specifically can be applied. It is also important to note, Knowledge Management actions, which are useful in one phase of the innovation process, might be useless or even harmful in other phases of the process. Possible managerial implications will be discussed subsequently.

(1) Create promising ideas: Understanding that the effective creation of promising ideas takes place where socialization is supported, specifically where people trust each other, where they have common mental models, paradigms, and beliefs, knowledge management has to apply the according means and to build the according structures. Trust can be increased if sanctions of supervisors are limited, not only individual but also teamwork is rewarded. Moreover, it would be effective to support informal networking by encouraging frequent face-to-face meetings.

An example is Celemi's "Friday Night Club" which is an informal gathering on a local level; the employees meet up once per week in a restaurant in town. Also, Andersen's KSS (knowledge sharing session), which are held once per month from 12:00h - 13:30h support informal networking. Over lunch, anybody or any team can give a report on any subject and initiate a discussion. The lunch packages are paid for by the company for this purpose. The topic may or may not be related to the business. An important criterion for practical networks is that they are voluntary, contrary to project groups.

(2) Develop powerful inventions: Employees do not always have the time or skill for externalizing the ideas they have in mind. Different technical languages as well as different spoken languages (in transnational firms) are barriers in the knowledge explication process. One measure here is to employ experts that support the expression of ideas and thoughts. In addition to experts, formal structures, methods or tools could be implemented to support externalization of tacit knowledge.

At Celemi they strive to visualize as much as possible in order to exchange knowledge and experiences directly and easy. Hence, documentation is done written in text as well as in graphics and pictures, whereas the latter one is supported by the design center. The Design Center supports the development of graphs. Knowledge managers at Andersen are employees who support the process of information preparation. They act as facilitators. A knowledge manager must be very communicative and ideally master different languages. Apart from these, Andersen has content experts responsible for the correctness of the contents. There is a central organisation, called knowledge enterprise, which supports the publishing process (e.g. classification of content, editing) of knowledge assets on the global corporate intranet.

(3) Launch successful innovations: An effective combination of knowledge is essential in order to combine the knowledge leading to a victorious launch of a new product. Not just single employees, but people throughout the whole organization should be assured of the fastest access to the broadest variety of necessary knowledge, going through the fewest steps (Nonaka and Takeuchi, 1995: 82).

Formal networks and structured knowledge flows are the means to promote that. Since knowledge has to be combined which comes from outside the organization, namely knowledge of suppliers, distributors etc., the introduction of software tools, intranet and internet solutions are management means which could provide the required fast and easy access to the named knowledge.

(4) Generate innovative impulses: In order to enhance the process of learning, knowledge could be disseminated well directed. An information and knowledge overflow will hinder the enlargement of people's knowledge base by internalizing the experience of previous innovation processes and other experiences. In order to do so, the processes of learning have to be understood and incorporated into according organizational structures and concepts.

Managerial questions to answer are: How much time shall employees use to actively provide their knowledge to learn and internalize organizational experience? Is there dedicated time for that at all? If so, is it communicated to them? Would incentives for doing so support that process? Which incentives would have the best effect? In order to generate innovative impulses there needs to be creative chaos to some extent. Only in that way can the creation of impulses be stimulated.

CONCLUDING REMARKS

> *"[...] organizational knowledge creation is the key to [...] innovate."*
> (Nonaka and Takeuchi, 1995: 3)

The purpose of this paper was to analyze organizational Knowledge Creation Processes in various episodes of The Innovation Processes. The analysis can serve as a base to select appropriate Knowledge Management approaches that will effectively support The Innovation Processes. However, Knowledge Management approaches do not need to be developed specifically for The Innovation Process. Rather the appropriate application of established approaches is paramount.

Implications for future research comprehend an empirical test of the presented propositions. Since theorists and practitioners are still discussing the determination of knowledge creation processes, empirical results will also contribute to the comprehension of how knowledge is created.

Findings of the paper might as well be transferred: Other business processes consist - like the innovation processes - of a series of steps. The (research) question to answer is: are knowledge management methods to be used equally in all these steps or does management has to differentiate these depending on the process phase in order to have efficient knowledge management for that specific business process in place.

BIBLIOGRAPHY

Armbrecht Jr., F. M. R., Chapas, R. B., Chappelow, C. C., Farris, G. F., Friga, P. N., Hartz, C. A., McIlvaine, M. E., Postle, S. R. and Whitwell, G. E. (2001): *Knowledge Management in Research and Development* in: Research Technology Management, Vol. 44, Issue 4, pp. 28-59.

Boutellier, R., Gassmann, O. and Zedtwitz, M. v. (2000): *Managing Global Innovation* - Uncovering the Secrets of Future Competitiveness, Berlin, 2nd ed.

Burgelman, R. A., Maidique, M. A. and Wheelwright, S. C. (2001): *Strategic Management of Technology and Innovation,* New York, 3rd ed.

Carneiro, A. (2000): *How does Knowledge Management influence innovation and competitiveness* in: Journal of Knowledge Management, Vol. 4, No. 2, 2000, pp. 87-98.

Cooper, R. G. (2000): *Product Leadership: Creating and Launching Superior New Products* Cambridge, Mass.

Corti, E. and Lo Storto, C. (2000): *Knowledge Creation in Small Manufacturing Firms during Product Innovation: An Empirical Analysis of Cause-effect Relationships Among its Determinants* in: Enterprise and Innovation Management Studies, Vol. 1, No. 3, pp. 245-263.

Damanpour, F. and Gopalakrishnan, S. (1999): *Organizational adaption and innovation: The dynamics of adopting innovation types* in: The Dynamics of Innovation by Brockhoff, K. et al., 1999, Berlin.

Dougherty, D. (1992): *A Practice-centered model of organizational renewal through product innovation* in: Strategic Management Journal, Vol. 13, pp. 77-92.

Eppler, M., Seifried, P. M. and Röpnack, A. (2000): *Improving Knowledge Intensive Processes through an Enterprise Knowledge Medium* in: Proceedings of the 1999 ACM SIGCPR Conference.

Extreme Innovation Inc. (1999): *White Paper,* http://extremeinnovation.com/papers.htm

Galunic, C. and Rodan, S. (1998): *Resource Recombination in the Firm: Knowledge Structures and the Potential for Schumpeterian Innovation* in: Strategic Management Journal, Vol. 19, pp. 1193.

Hauschildt, J. (1993): *Innovationsmanagement,* München.

Johannessen, J.-A., Olaisen, J. and Olsen, B. (1999): *Managing and organizing innovation in the knowledge economy* in: European Journal of Innovation Management, Vol. 2, No. 3, 116-128.

Johnson, W. (2000): *Technological Knowledge Creation: A study of the enabling conditions and processes of knowledge creation in collaborative R&D projects,* Dissertation at the Schulich School of Business, York University, Toronto, Ontario, Canada.

Knowledge Bridge Consulting (2000): *Report,* http://www.knowledgebridge.ch/en/topic-e.htm

Kogut, B. and Zander, U. (1992): *Knowledge of the firm, combinative capabilities, and the replication of technology* in: Organization Science, Vol. 3, No. 3, August 1992, pp. 383-397.

KPMG Consulting (2000). *Report*
http://www.kmadvantage.com/docs/KM/KPMG_KM_Research_Report_2000.pdf.

Leonard-Barton, D. (1992): *Core Capabilities and Core Rigidities: A Paradox in managing New Product Development* in: Strategic Management Journal, Vol. 13, pp. 111-125.

Liebowitz, J. (1999): *Knowledge Management Handbook,* London.

Madhavan, R. and Grover, R. (1998): *From Embedded Knowledge to Embodied Knowledge: New Product Development as Knowledge Management* in: Journal of Marketing, Vol. 62, October 1998, pp. 1-12.

Maier, G. W., Prange, C. and Rosenstiel, L. v. (2001): *Psychological Perspectives of Organizational Learning* in: Handbook of Organizational Learning and Knowledge by Dierkes, M. et al., 2001, Oxford.

Miller, W. L. and Morris, L. (1998): *4th Generation R&D: Managing Knowledge, Technology and Innovation,* New York etc.

Nonaka, I. (1994): *A Dynamic Theory of Organizational Knowledge Creation* in: Organization Science, Vol. 5, No. 1, February 1994, pp. 14-37.

Nonaka, I., Byosiere, P., Borucki, C. C. and Konno, N. (1994): *Organizational Knowledge Creation Theory* - A First Comprehensive Test, in: International Business Review, Vol. 3, No. 4, 337-351.

Nonaka, I. and Takeuchi, H. (1995): *The Knowledge-Creating Company* - How Japanese Companies Create the Dynamics of Innovation, New York

Pitt, M. and Clarke, K. (1999): *Competing on competence: A Knowledge Perspective on the Management of Strategic Innovation* in: Technology Analysis & Strategic Management, 11, 3, 301.

Polanyi, M. (1966): *The Tacit Dimension,* London.

Probst, G., Raub, S., Romhardt, K. and Doughty, H. A. (1999): *Managing Knowledge: Building Blocks for Success.*

Quinn, J. B., Baruch, J. J. and Zien, K. A. (1997): *Innovation Explosion* - Using Intellect and Software to Revolutionize Growth Strategies, New York.

Scarbrough, H. and Swan, J. (2001): *Explaining the Diffusion of Knowledge Management: The Role of Fashion* in: British Journal of Management, Vol. 12, pp. 3-12.

Shenhar, A. J. and Renier, J. J. (1996): *How to define management: a modular approach.* in: Management Development Review, Vol. 9, No. 1.

Swan, J. A. and Clark, P. (1992): *Organizational Decision-making in the Appropriation of Technological Innovation: Cognitive and Political Dimensions* in: European Work & Organizational Psychologist, Vol. 2, pp. 103-128.

Swan, J., Newell, S., Scarbrough, H. and Hislop, D. (1999): *Knowledge management and innovation: - networks and networking* in: Journal of Knowledge Management, Vol. 3, No. 4, pp. 262-275.

Thamhain, H. J. (1996): *Managing Technology-Based Innovation* in: Handbook of Technology Management, by Dierkes et al., 2001.

Vicari, S. Troilo, G.: *Errors and Learning in Organizations* in: Knowing in firms by: von Krogh, G. and Kleine, D., 1998, London.

von Krogh, G., Ichijo, K. and Nonaka, I. (2000a): *Enabling knowledge creation* - How to unlock the mystery of tacit knowledge and release the power of innovation, New York.

von Krogh, G., Nonaka, I. and Nishiguchi, T. (2000b): *Knowledge Creation* New York.

Management of Technology
Copyright © 2003 by Elsevier Science Ltd.
All rights of reproduction in any form reserved.
ISBN: 0-08-044136-X

16

A TAXONOMY FOR KNOWLEDGE MANAGEMENT TOOLS

Rodrigo Baroni de Carvalho, BDMG / FUMEC, Belo Horizonte, MG, Brazil[*]
Marta Araújo Tavares Ferreira, Information Science School - UFMG, Belo Horizonte, MG[**]

INTRODUCTION

Concern of the role of knowledge in organizational survival is continuously contributing to the development of new ways to manage this precious resource. Knowledge Management (KM) is intended to be a discipline that will provide instruments to transform knowledge into a competitive advantage. In Davenport and Prusak (1998), knowledge is presented as the only source of a sustainable competitive advantage.

The pressure of innovation and speed of global markets have reduced product life cycle. Stewart (1998) states that the organizational market value is more influenced by the intellectual capital than by the financial capital. The creativity of knowledge workers has become the fuel of organizational growing. In the new knowledge society, we are supposed to be students and teachers at the same time. We need to have a student skill to learn fast the new knowledge of a changing world. On the other side, we need to be teachers in order to organize and distribute our knowledge.

KM is a complex combination of people, process and technology. Although technology is not the main component of KM, it would be a naive attitude to try to implement KM without any technological support. This paper intends to describe the Information Technology (IT) contribution to KM organizational programs. The main objective of this paper is to propose

[*] Rodrigo Baroni de Carvalho is Professor of Computer Science at FUMEC University Centre and a system analyst at BDMG, a development bank. Email: baroni@bdmg.mg.gov.br.
[**] Dr. Marta Araújo Tavares Ferreira is Professor at School of Information Science at the Federal University of Minas Gerais (UFMG), Brazil. Email: maraujo@eci.ufmg.br.

taxonomy for KM software. Eight KM software categories will be presented. Each software category presents different technological features emphasizing different KM aspects. This study concludes by presenting some trends to KM software and suggesting guidelines to those who want to apply it into KM programs.

INFORMATION TECHNOLOGY AND KNOWLEDGE MANAGEMENT

In Davenport and Prusak (1998), KM is described as the set of activities related to the generation, codification and transfer of knowledge. The main role of Information Technology (IT) in KM is to accelerate the speed of knowledge transfer. The KM tools are intended to help the process of collecting and structuring the knowledge of groups of individuals in order to make this knowledge available in a base shared between the whole organization. KM software can optimize the knowledge flow through network communities, transforming technology into a channel and knowledge into a message.

According to Stewart (1998), intellectual capital has 3 dimensions: human capital, structural capital and client capital. Structural capital is defined as the organizational skill to store and transfer knowledge and it includes the quality and extent of information systems, databases, patents, written procedures and business documents. So, KM software is better positioned in the structural capital dimension.

However, in Senge (1998), it is emphasized that a person can receive more information due to technological facilities, but it will not make any difference if the person does not have the appropriate skills to apply this information in a useful manner. This paper assumes that IT has a supporting role, not the main role, in a KM program. In other words, people are the real essence of KM. From this perspective, KM seems to be a convergence of IT approach with Human Resource approach. The KM ultimate challenge is to increase the chances of innovation that happen when the speed of technology and the creativity of human beings are brought together.

RESEARCH METHODOLOGY

The objective of this article is to present guidelines that will contribute to organizations that are planning to evaluate and acquire KM software. Due to the largeness of the concept of knowledge, the software market for KM seems to be quite confusing. Technology vendors are developing different implementations of the KM concept in their software products. Because of the variety and quantity of KM tools available on the market, the taxonomy will be a valuable support for an organization that is looking for the right tool for its specific needs. Throughout this paper, a KM software is considered to be a kind of software that supports any of the three basic KM processes described in Davenport and Prusak (1998): generation, codification and transfer.

First, it was necessary to analyze the software market in order to classify KM tools. The major difficulty of this work was the establishment of limits in a growing market. Because of the speed of change of software market, statistical techniques were not applied to build a representative sample of KM software. This research was developed in a more exploratory way. The sample of KM software was constructed by collecting KM related sites selected in Nascimento and Neves (1999), advertisement list of KM magazines (KM World, KM Magazine and DM Review) and digital libraries (brint.com).

The exploratory research resulted in a list of 27 software vendors. It was possible to contact 22 of these vendors who sent folders, technical briefings and demo versions of their software. After the evaluation of the different software, it was possible to identify some common features between them. The final taxonomy contains ten of the following categories:

- Intranet-based tools;
- Electronic Document Management (EDM);
- Groupware;
- Workflow;
- Knowledge based systems;
- Business Intelligence (BI);
- Knowledge map systems;
- Innovation support tools;
- Competitive intelligence (CI) tools;
- Knowledge portals.

INTRANET BASED TOOLS

Intranet is the ideal environment for sharing dynamical and linked information. The hypertext structure of intranets eases the navigation between knowledge chunks. Intranets are private networks that emphasize the organizational internal information. Intranets are becoming an important vehicle between the organization and their employees. This communication is usually passive because the user has to pull the information. This "pull style" is an alternative to the information overload generated by e-mails. The philosophy of intranet is to create a virtual place where information is classified and available. Intranets give more support to the codification and transfer of knowledge.

Intranet-based tools benefit from the increasing development of Web-based technologies. Besides that, the low cost of Web technologies is an appealing factor to many organizations. Intranet is evolving to the concept of enterprise portal (the tenth category).

Intranets are incorporating Boolean search feature of Web search engines, content categories and newsgroup services. Microsoft Internet Information Server is an example of software that can be used for intranet applications.

ELECTRONIC DOCUMENT MANAGEMENT (EDM)

EDM systems are repositories of important corporate documents. In Davenport and Prusak (1998), EDM systems are presented as explicit knowledge stores. In some organizations, document management can be the initial step to further KM.

EDM systems contribute to the organization of the vast amount of documents generated by office activities. Paperwork is still a reality and each document is a source of non-structured information that could be lost if not well organized. According to Bennet (1997), EDM systems provide a more efficient retrieval, better security and version control of documents. When intellectual workers find quickly and easily the useful documents, they are capable of investing their time in effective working instead of losing time in the search of the right information. EDM systems have many features, like cataloging and indexing, which were inherited from the traditional information retrieval systems which are studied in the field of Information Science.

Content Management Tools is another name for EDM systems. Content Management is interested in the management of the content in no matter what media the document is available: fax, e-mails, HTML forms, computer reports, paper, video, audio or spreadsheets).

Bad document management causes loss of documents, non-updated documents and sending of documents in wrong directions. This results in higher costs, bad decisions, fines in cases of loss of legal documents and misunderstandings between employees. The value of a document can be estimated by:

- Amount of time and effort spent on the creation of the document content;
- Quantity of times the document is used in business process;
- Importance of information provided by the document.

Excalibur RetrievalWare and File Net are examples of EDM systems.

GROUPWARE

The hierarchical organizational structure is not well suited to the speed of decision-making demanded by a competitive market. Organizations are searching flexible structures that can easily adapt to a changing environment. The need of cooperation between geographically dispersed workgroups is a critical issue to global organizations. The best specialists to solve a problem do not usually work on the same floor. Instead of reinventing the wheel, the enterprise must use groupware technology to overcome distances.

In Bock and Marca (1995), groupware is described as the type of software that is designed to help groups of persons that are not at the same place but need to work together. CSCW (Computer Supported Cooperative Work) is the new branch of Computer Science dedicated to the study of groupware technologies. CSCW involves not only technical aspects, but also social and organizational issues.

Groupware uses a push style where information is sent to the user. An informal communication style predominates in a groupware environment. People feel free to exchange opinions and collaborate. These features let groupware cover the three processes of KM. Microsoft Exchange and Lotus Notes belong to this KM software category.

WORKFLOW

Workflow is a system that supports standardized business processes. These processes regulate the information flow from person to person, from place to place, from task to task. Workflow applies to a business process that requires ordered and structured information.

The objective of workflow is to establish the process flow, following its steps and tracking each activity that composes the process. Workflow makes explicit the knowledge that is embedded in the process. The main difference between groupware and workflow is that groupware suggests an informal communication style and generates new knowledge. On the other hand, workflow is the formal codification of knowledge that already exists.

Cruz (1998) defines the 3 basic elements of workflow, also called 3 R's model:

- Roles: set of skills to execute a specific task;
- Rules: features that define how the data should be processed;
- Routes: logical paths for the knowledge flow through the process.

Aris Toolset from IDS Scheer is an example of a workflow system.

KNOWLEDGE-BASED SYSTEMS

Artificial Intelligence (AI) is the Computer Science field that has produced the first studies relating information to knowledge. Although most AI works failed to produce what was expected, some secondary results have contributed to the development of Computer Science. Nowadays, it is wise to realize that the initial proposal of AI during the 80's was quite ambitious.

Expert systems, CBR (Case Based Reasoning) systems and neural networks are some types of systems that use IA techniques. According to Galliers and Baets (1998), an expert system contains a limited domain knowledge base, an inference mechanism to manipulate this base and an interface to permit the input of new data and user dialog. An expert system is built on the observation of a specialist at work and on the mapping of part of this knowledge into derivation rules.

In Davenport and Prusak (1998), CBR systems are the kind of systems that involve the knowledge extraction from a set of narratives or cases related to a problem. When a user finds a problem, it can be checked against the case base in order to realize if there is or not some correlation with an old problem. CBR systems have been successfully used in help-desk and call-center applications.

Neural networks are more sophisticated systems that use statistical instruments to process cause-effect examples and learn the relationships involved in the solution. Neural networks are very flexible and intelligent systems because each new input results in an automatic reprogramming and consequent learning of new lessons about the environment. Computer Associates Neugents (neural agents) is an example of a neural network.

BUSINESS INTELLIGENCE (BI)

BI is a set of tools used to manipulate a mass of operational data and to find essential business information. BI involves 2 parts:

- Front-end systems: DSS (Decision Support Systems), EIS (Executive Information Systems) and OLAP (On-Line Analytical Processing) tools;
- Back-end systems: data warehouse, data mart and data mining.

Data Base Management Systems (DBMS) are the building blocks of a BI solution. First, the operational data generated by business transactions is extracted from the DBMS, filtered by some criteria and then migrated to the data warehouse. The frequency and schedule of updating between the operational and BI environment should be defined. IBM (2000) suggests that these environments should be separated for performance and security reasons.

After the BI back-end loading step, the front-end tools are able to identify hidden patterns inside the data and the user is free to build his own queries and strategic reports. The focus of BI is decision-making. Some BI systems are specializing on information related to clients, making an interface with CRM (Customer Relationship Management) systems and enhancing database marketing policies. At this point, there is a link between KM and client capital described in Stewart (1998). Business Objects is an example of a BI solution.

KNOWLEDGE MAP SYSTEMS

This category contains software that was specifically designed for KM. The categories presented before described software that are non-KM specific, but that could be used in a KM program. Knowledge maps work like yellow pages that contain a "who knows what" list. A knowledge map does not store knowledge. The map just points to people, creating opportunities for tacit knowledge exchange.

A standard knowledge map is fed with the profile of competencies of the members of an organization. The knowledge map provides an expert locator feature that helps users to find the experts best suited to work on a specific problem or project. A knowledge map categorizes an organization's expertise into searchable catalogs. Using a knowledge map, it is easier to identify people in terms of who they know, what they know and how proficient they are at a given task. Lotus Discovery Server and Trivium Gingo are examples of such systems.

According to Trivium (2000), Gingo allows the construction of knowledge trees that represent the organization's human resources potential and give a dynamic vision of available competences. A knowledge tree is a visual representation of a knowledge map and can be a quite useful tool to measure the human capital, as described in Stewart (1998). Human resources specialists use knowledge trees to match existing competences with strategic targets and to identify what kinds of know-how, essential for growth, are currently available. Trivium (2000) advises the use of knowledge trees to constitute project groups and manage individual mobility within the company. Knowledge maps also collaborate with training programs by detecting the competency zones where training forces are over deployed and poorly targeted zones where training initiatives are insufficient. A knowledge map can be represented as a matrix showing relations between what the organization needs to know and what the employees really know.

In Nonaka and Takeuchi (1995), socialization is described as a process where experiences are shared and common mental models and abilities created. A knowledge map is a way of using technology to approximate people with common interests. It offers opportunities to put complementary expertises in touch, more experienced people in contact with beginners. According to Terra (2000), knowledge maps facilitate tacit knowledge exchange because they provide a faster expert search and increase the chance of personal meetings. This approximation can probably result in face-to-face contacts that promote shared experiences and learning by observation, imitation and praxis (socialization), as well as by the combination of explicit knowledge.

INNOVATION SUPPORT TOOLS

Amidon (2000) defines innovation as the application of new ideas into products or services. Innovation Support Tools is software that contributes to knowledge generation along the product design process. These tools intend to create a virtual environment that stimulates the proliferation of insights.

Innovation support tools are especially used in R&D (Research and Development) departments and they intend to increase the productivity of communities of practice. The result of innovation can be measured by the number of new patents, design modifications of the existing products and development of new products. Tech Optimizer, software made by Invention Machine, is an example of an innovation support tool.

An innovation support tool may include different features:

- Technical database where patents, articles and research projects are recorded. Providing information suited to feed the explicit knowledge combination is frequently the starting point of innovation. By using this kind of tool, an R&D professional tries to acquire existing knowledge in order to apply it to a new context (combination). For example, a new type of plastic used in the aircraft industry can be adapted or adopted for medical use. This category may include digital specialized libraries;
- Graphic simulation features, which can facilitate internalization. Internalization (Nonaka and Takeuchi, 1995) is the process that enriches explicit knowledge, adding to it tacit knowledge, most frequently through usage and experience, but also through simulation;
- Combinatory tools, which help to consider unusual possibilities in the design of innovations, supporting the creativity process.

COMPETITIVE INTELLIGENCE TOOLS

Competitive intelligence (CI) aims at systematically feeding the organizational decision process with information about the organizational environment in order to make possible to learn about it and to take better decisions in consequence. In contrast to Business Intelligence (BI), CI depends heavily on the collection and analysis of qualitative information.

Fuld (2000) describes the CI cycle in five steps:

- Planning and direction: this step is related to the identification of questions and decisions that will drive the information-gathering phase.
- Published information collection: search of a wide range of sources, from government fillings to journal articles, vendor brochures and advertisements.

- Primary source collection: this step is related to the importance of gathering information from people rather than from published sources.
- Analysis and production: transformation of the collected data into meaningful assessment.
- Report and inform: delivery of critical intelligence in a coherent and convincing manner to corporate decision makers.

Fuld (2000) has evaluated the CI software offered on the market and has concluded that they offer better support to the second and fifth steps of the CI cycle. The other steps are very human-based and are only slightly benefited by technology.

On the second step, software agents perform the automatic collection of timely information from news feeds and search the Internet and corporate intranets for information from Web sites and internal documents. These agents are also called crawlers because they constantly scan the Internet and intranet for any new information about competitors, alerting the user when new data is found. On the fifth step, CI tools accelerate the dissemination of reports by sending e-mail reports according to users' preferences.

CI tools concentrate on the combination process of the knowledge conversion spiral. They act like a probe on information sources: the information that is obtained is filtered and classified before dissemination, so it is disseminated in an adequate format to facilitate combination.

VigiPro, software developed by CRIQ (Centre de Recherche Industrielle du Québec) and commercialized by CGI, and Knowledge Works, from Cipher Systems, are examples of this class of software.

KNOWLEDGE PORTALS

In an attempt to consolidate the various departmental intranets, organizations are constructing corporate intranets or portals that function as home pages to departmental intranet sites and external Internet resources (Choo *et al.*, 2000). A great contribution of portals is to integrate heterogeneous information sources, providing a standard interface to the users.

According to the authors, a portal's primary function is to provide a transparent directory of information already available elsewhere, not act as a separate source of information itself. Common elements contained in corporate portals design include an enterprise taxonomy or classification of information categories that help easy retrieval, a search engine and links to internal and external web sites and information sources.

But portals are evolving into more complex and interactive gateways, so that they may integrate in a single solution many knowledge management tool features presented before. They are becoming single points of entry through which end-users and communities can perform their business tasks and evolving into virtual places where people can get in touch with other people who share common interests. So, they may support the transfer of tacit knowledge, while standard intranets are more suited for the exchange of explicit knowledge. Besides, traditional intranet systems emphasize organization's own knowledge while portals go beyond organizational boundaries.

Personalization is a critical issue for knowledge portals. The knowledge workers may select their intranet, extranet and Internet favorite information sources, creating a customizable and personal workspace. This solution enables end-users to organize their work by community, interest, task or job focus. According to Lotus and IBM (2001), Lotus k-station presents a multi-page interface known as personal place, which is unique to each user. Besides providing personal access to knowledge, portals help users in the job of building community places. On-line awareness and real-chat capabilities are available throughout the portal. Therefore, the user can see who is online, connect with them instantly and get immediate answers.

Microsoft Digital Dashboard, Lotus k-station and Sopheon are examples of portals.

KNOWLEDGE MANAGEMENT SOFTWARE TAXONOMY SUMMARY TABLE

The following table 16.1 contains a summary of the categories presented before and their characteristics.

Table 16.1: Categories of Knowledge Management Software Summary Table.

Category	Origin of concepts	Example
Intranet-Based Systems	Computer Networks (Web technology)	Microsoft Internet Information Server
Electronic Document Management	Information Science	Excalibur RetrievalWare and File Net
Groupware	CSCW (Computer Supported Cooperative Work)	Notes (Lotus) and Exchange (Microsoft)
Workflow	Organization & Methods	ARIS Toolset (IDS Scheer)
Knowledge Base Systems	Artificial Intelligence	Neugents (Computer Associates)
Business Intelligence	Data Base Management	Business Objects
Knowledge Map	Information Science and Human Resources Management	Gingo (Trivium) and Lotus Discovery Server
Innovation Support Tools	Innovation and Technology Management	Invention Machine
Competitive Intelligence Tools	Strategic Management and Information Science	Knowledge. Works (Cipher Systems) and Vigipro (CRIQ/CGI)
Knowledge Portals	Computer Networks and Information Science	Digital Dashboard (Microsoft), Lotus k-station and Sopheon

CONCLUSION

There is a strong concentration on knowledge codification and transfer process among the KM tools analyzed by this research. In addition, it was observed that KM software supports better explicit and tacit knowledge. In other words, IT (Information Technology) needs to improve support to knowledge generation and tacit knowledge exchange.

There is a also a trend of functional convergence on the KM software market. Preserving initial features, vendors are incorporating extra features from others categories described on the taxonomy presented in this work. They intend to make their products more competitive by transforming them into KM integrated suites. For instance, Business Intelligence software could start to offer a knowledge map feature in a new version. So, there is not always a one-to-one relationship between the KM software and the taxonomy category. KM software can be classified in more than one category depending on its features. The taxonomy can be alternatively seen as an array of KM features that can be associated with software.

It is interesting to notice the differences between KM software and ERP systems like SAP, Baan, Peoplesoft and others. ERPs are usually implemented in a top-down style where the organization should adjust its processes to the system in a short period of time. It is impossible to do the same with KM software. Commitment and motivation of people is crucial to any KM program. The better KM software will not convince anybody to share knowledge. KM requires a long-term strategy to involve people and break paradigms.

The emphasis of IT lies on preservation of organizational memory. Many organizations only focus the conversion of human capital into structural capital in their KM programs. These organizations use KM as a discipline to extract part of the knowledge of their employees and then store it in a base. This approach is quite limited due to dynamic characteristic of knowledge. KM should be used to stimulate the creativity and innovation process. Like stagnant water looses its purity, organizational knowledge must be renewed.

The use of KM software requires a complementary organizational action in human policies. It should be clear that the organization gives more value to the distribution and more the possession of knowledge. KM needs to be integrated with organizational culture and values. The employees that contributed more to knowledge base should be rewarded.

As reported in literature and as we have ourselves learned from the study of two Brazilian organizations systems (Carvalho, 2000), their potential is most frequently under-evaluated and explored. In fact, their actual utilization stresses mainly their support to information access and retrieval, while their communication and collaboration dimensions are yet to be discovered.

The implementation of KM software is a complex process. The KM software needs not only to be integrated into the existing IT (Information Technology) infrastructure, but to the organizational culture, procedures and HR (Human Resources) policy as well.

KM brings a historical opportunity of coincidence between the needs of employees and employers. In a knowledge society, organizations need innovation and creativity to survive in a competitive market. Organizations are trying to create this environment by offering more flexible work schedules, less hierarchy, more autonomy and more life quality to their employees. Creative people supported by the right software will certainly be the most useful resource to organizations in the knowledge era.

BIBLIOGRAPHY

Amidon, D. (2000). *Knowledge Innovation.* Web site http://www.entovation.com

Bennet, G. (1997). *Intranets: Como Implantar com Sucesso na sua Empresa.* Campus, Rio de Janeiro.

Bock, G. and Marca, D. (1995). *Designing Groupware.* McGraw-Hill, New York.

Carvalho, R.B. (2000). *Aplicações de Softwares de Gestão do Conhecimento: Tipologia e Usos* (MSc dissertation). Programa de Pós-Graduação em Ciência da Informação da UFMG, Belo Horizonte.

Choo, C.W., Detlor, B. and Turnbull, D. (2000). *Web Work: Information Seeking and Knowledge Work on the World Wide Web.* Kluwer Academic Publishers, Dordrecht.

Cruz, T. (1998). *Workflow: A Tecnologia que vai Revolucionar Processos.* Atlas, São Paulo.

Davenport, T. and Prusak, L. (1998). *Working Knowledge: how organizations manage what they know.* HBS Press, Boston.

FULD & Company Inc. (2000). *Intelligence software report.* Web site http://www.fuld.com

Galliers, R.D. and Baets, W.R.J.(1998). *Information Technology and Organizational Transformation.* John Wiley & Sons Ltd., London.

IBM (2000). *The road to business intelligence.* Web site http://www-4.ibm.com/software/data/busn-intel/road2bi/step1.html

Lotus and IBM (2001). *Lotus and IBM knowledge management strategy.* Web site http://www.lotus.com

Nascimento, N. and Neves, J.T.R. (1999). A gestão do do conhecimento na World Wide Web: reflexões sobre a pesquisa de informações na rede. In: *Perspectivas em Ciência da Informação*, Vol. 4, pp.29-48. Academic press, Belo Horizonte.

Nonaka, I. and Takeuchi, H.(1995) *The Knowledge-Creating Company.* New York: Oxford Press.

Stewart, T. (1998). *Capital Intelectual.* Campus, Rio de Janeiro.

Senge, P. (1998). The fifth discipline. *HSM Management*, 9, 35-47.

Terra, J.C.C (2000). *Gestão do Conhecimento: o grande desafio empresarial.* Negócio Editora, São Paulo.

Trivium (2000). *Gingo: software for management solutions.* Web site http://www.trivium.fr/new/gingo/managem.htm

Management of Technology
ISBN: 0-08-044136-X

17

TACIT KNOWLEDGE MANAGEMENT IN A SME ENVIRONMENT: BUILDING THE KNOW-HOW REPOSITORY - A CASE STUDY

José Albors G, Universidad Politécnica de Valencia, Spain[*]

ABSTRACT

This paper intends to contribute to the understanding of knowledge management in the SME environment. It will attempt first to develop a literature review state of the art of KM and the SME environment, its relation to organisational learning and the description of the reference framework. It will describe the case of a group of medium size manufacturing and engineering SMEs in its effort to rationalise their production technology procedures with a computer based interactive information system. The paper outlines how the emphasis in explicit knowledge had to shift towards tacit knowledge and the relevance of the communication patterns between the different teams. It also describes the evolution from individual to organisational knowledge and how the ambiguity of the initial phase of the project opened a strong creative process.

> *"The essential is invisible to the eye"*
> The Little Prince, A. de Saint-Exupèry

---

[*]   Dr. José Albors is Professor of Project Management and Organizational Behaviour at Universidad Politecnica de Valencia (UPV), Spain.

INTRODUCTION: STATE OF THE ART

Knowledge management and the SME

The academic literature on knowledge management, although extensive, is scarce in relation to the SME environment. Most of the published material come from the United Kingdom where the Government has supported a number of initiatives in order to *"identify the knowledge management needs of smaller business"* (HMSO, 1998). Scase and Goffee (1987) explored the values of the small firm owner and its preference of internal development versus external advice. Some authors such as Scarborough (1996), Lightfoot (1996), Charston (1999), Kailer et al (1999), Frank (1993), Storey and Westhead (1998) have followed this line by outlining how the SMES relate with external consultants. Storey (1995) analysed the problems associated with training in SMEs, Perren et al (1999) pointed out the specific context needs of SME advice and Bryson (1997) has related growth and knowledge management. Other authors (Gibb, 1993; Kailer, 1999). have analysed public policies support of SME development. Finally, a number of articles analysing knowledge management activities in SMEs have been recently published: Sparrow (2001), Zetie (1998), Kailer (1999), Belotti and Tunalv (1999) Shelton (2000), Groom and David (2001), etc.

   Some of their conclusions of the study cases cited above will be applicable to our case such as: the owner manager involvement and relevant role in the learning and training area, his decision style, vision, values, mental models, market view, the SME need for just in time knowledge, the predominance of informal learning, the motivation factors, the change resistance, etc. Sparrow (2000) outlines that the SME is reactive to knowledge projects, which are generally driven by external pressure of customers rather than by technological push, as it's the case of large firms. The same author addresses the holistic aspects of knowledge management and the *sensemaking* role of knowledge in the SME context in the line pointed out by Weick (1995).

   Finally, the use of software for organisational learning has been reported by various authors (Houdek1998, Landes, 1999, Fischer, 1992 etc.).

The SME context: Organizational learning

In the traditional SME, learning had a special connotation in which the secrets (the *tacit* craft knowledge) of the company were transmitted traditionally from parents to their sons and the role of the apprentices was fundamental. In some cases these would become independent starting their own venture, giving birth to the *spin offs* of those times. Let us keep in mind that in our cities the occupations spread to settle down in the same neighbourhoods (tanneries, jewellers, cabinet makers, upholsterers, ceramists, glass makers, etc.) constituting primitive clusters. The employer unions constituted associations of arts and occupations that gave place to professional schools. Today in fact, with the breakdown of these Associations and the consequent loss of the apprentices, the SMES need new models to manage their knowledge. This is especially true in those more traditionally learning-dependent industries such as furniture, printing, textile, ceramics, etc., especially in times when technology is changing their crafts very quickly.

It is in this sense that organisational learning, as a discipline related to the collective capture, storage and reuse of the firm experience, has dealt with the organisation learning and subsequent change. That is the reason of its relevance to the SME experience since it will provide an alternative context to the situation described in the previous paragraph.

Organisational learning has been traditionally associated to action and decision-making (Cyert and March, 1963; Bateson, 1972; March and Olsen, 1975). Argyris (1977) defines organisational learning as the "*process of detection and correction of errors*". In his view organisations learn through individuals acting as their agents. This is closely related to the SME, which provides the learning context "*the individual learning activities, in turn, are facilitated or inhibited, by an ecological system of factors that may be called an organisational learning system*" (p.117). Furthermore, Huber (1991) points out "*an entity only learns if, through its processing of information the range of its potential behaviours is changed*".

At this stage we should point out that academics and practitioners distinguish between two models of learning, both associated to organisational change. Argyris (1977b) refers to them as single loop and double loop learning. The scheme shown in Fig. 17.1 resumes the learning process and both models. Learning is defined by the reaction to match or mismatch between intentions and outcomes in the organisation. The governing variables are defined in the Argyris model as those, which drive and guide the actions of the individuals (the organisation-acting agents). Single loop learning occurs either when matches are obtained or

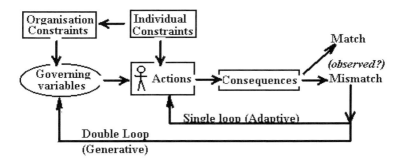

Fig. 17.1. Learning schemes and theories (adapted from Argyris, 1992).

mismatches are corrected by changing the actions. Double loop learning occurs when mismatches are corrected due to a process analysis, which alters the governing variables before the action takes place. Learning includes the whole process until a solution to a problem (mismatch) has been produced.

Other authors classify organisational learning following a similar pattern. *"Lower level versus higher level learning"* (Fiol and Lyles, 1985), *"Adaptive versus generative learning"*, (Senge, 1990), *"tactical versus strategic learning"* (Dogson, 1991).

The individual will be submitted to certain constraints or learning barriers which will produce breaks in the learning loops. These may be individual, organisational or cultural. They have been pointed out by March and Olsen (1975), Kim (1993) and Senge (1990) which refers to them as learning disabilities. Sparrow (1998) has summarised them from the SME point of view with a case study analysis. It has to be pointed out that with this model learning disabilities may be derived from the difficulties of appreciating the mismatch in the consequences of the organisation actions. One of the most evident for the small firm is maladaptation to gradual building threats, defined by Senge (1990b) as the parable of the boiling frog.

The organisational learning school so formed at MIT evolved towards the concept of the learning organisation. Senge (1990b) sets up its five components for the learning organisation of which team learning and mental models are core elements to the SME. Garvin (1993) introduces the concept of knowledge management in the learning organisation defining it as that which is "*skilled at creating, acquiring and transferring knowledge and at modifying its behaviour to reflect knowledge and insights*", pinpointing that learning implies a potential change in the organisation as Argyris (1977) had outlined in his double loop model. Ang & Damien (1996) point out that organisational learning is the process and the learning organisation the structure supporting it. In this sense Fahey and Prusak (1998) quote that "*a deadly sin in knowledge management would be failing to create a shared context for it*". It is clear then that, as we will conclude in or case, the SME will need a changed context if a continuous learning process has to be developed.

In this direction learning will be rewarded and supported through a culture of risk assumption, experimentation and cooperation (Watkins and Marsick, 1995). But the current firm organisational cultures may be unable to support the kind of learning required for the transformation of the firm into a learning organisation. Schein (1996) follows also the two learning models described above. Two types of learning are involved in changing the actual learning culture. The first type, adaptive learning, focuses on closing the gap between where we are and where we want to be. The second, generative learning (addressed by Schein as transformative learning), focuses on learning how to learn. The learners have discovered that the gap is contingent on learning new ways of thinking and need to review their cultural assumptions. This aspect is critical to many SMEs where the owners are culture generators.

In many cases, the SME does not work alone; it is in collaboration with other firms that the end product is delivered to a customer. Hence the joint learning of a group of interrelated SME's is important. The efficiency of the learning groups as cross community organisations, formal groups, informal networks, etc. have also been discussed as *"Communities of practice"* (Brown, 1991, Lave, 1993, Wenger, 1999), *"Virtual corporations"* (Davidow, 1992, Hale, 1997, Chesbrough, 1996), *"Networking firms"* (Miles, 1995, Bessant, 1999), etc. Clarke & Cooper (2000) support the idea of knowledge management as a collaborative activity in order to create this mentioned *"shared context"*. Cluster's theory makes use, amongst other factors, of this knowledge transfer to explain the competitive strengths of geographic concentrations of industry-specialized small firms. Examples have been proposed of Italy, Spain, the United Kingdom and the U.S.A. (Porter, 1998, Advani, 1997, Audretsch, 1993, Becattini, 1987, Harrison, 1998, Albors, 2002, etc.). Again this cooperative context provides an alternative to the traditional SME as the case described below will reflect.

THE PROJECT: OBJECTIVES AND CONTEXT

This paper will discuss the efforts of a group of small firms in order to develop an expert software model, which would optimise and manage a complicated printing process. This effort has been carried out through a R&D co-operative project (*Autogravure*) financed under the European Commission IV Frame Work program. Under this scheme a number of firms (in this case mostly SMEs) from various European countries sign a contract with the European Commission in order to carry out a common cooperative R&D project. The Commission finances up to 50 % of the project budget and the project partners are contractually bound to prove and demonstrate the project progress and results. The project lasted two and half years and had a preliminary budget of 1,1 Mill. Euros.

The printing industry for packaging materials represents a *"business system"* (Schon, 1973) in that the development of a successful product requires careful integration of the activities of the printing firm and its suppliers of ink, paper, technology or plastic support materials, and printing machinery. For example, without this integration, an ink supplier who develops new ink may find printers rejecting it because it does not work well with their printing presses or because it does not adhere to the material that is in use (see Fig. 17.2).

A rotogravure-printing firm from Spain led the project and five other *SMEs* participated in it. The firms belonged to different industries working all of them in the rotogravure sector. Some were equipment manufacturers (three Italian firms) from complementary sectors (not competitors), a plastic material supplier (a Greek firm), a printing ink producer from Spain, and a technology user (a manufacturer of sweets from Germany). A research institute from Spain from the Software developing field was also involved. There were a mixture of industries and cultures involved in the project (Albors, 2.000).

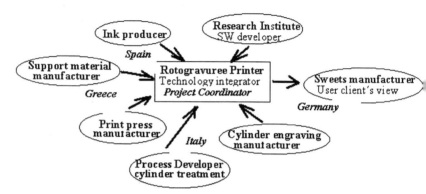

Fig. 17.2. The Rotogravure business system and the Autogravure project.

The project pursued several objectives, which could be simplified by describing it as the development of a QFD model[1] for the business system. This QFD model aimed at reaching a friendly software package which could support the daily operations. As it will be outlined later the existing processes in the rotogravure printing industry resemble a kitchen factory, where the cook's skills are determinant for the final results. Furthermore, in this case there were a number of different *cooks* speaking different languages and possessing different cultures such as artists (marketing publishers), mechanical engineers, production engineers, chemical engineers involved in the ink production, software analysts, managers, etc. The consequence of the combination of so many cooking skills was that repeating a client order with the same quality level was a very difficult task. This was closely linked also to the training level of the employees. The production manager of the leading printing firm pointed out that "*training a machine operator was a two three year task*" and that "*learning opportunities were scarce today due to the disappearance of the apprenticeship*". Then the project was also aimed at building a learning tool, which could facilitate learning, *by doing.*

If anything could characterise this project it was chaos and uncertainty. The reason was that from the very beginning it was designed and planned without a clear idea of which were the processes governing variables. Considered as a *system* the processes involved and their interrelation wasn't either clear at all. These cooking aspects implied that the engineers

---

[1]   Quality Function Deployment has been defined as a "structured process for identifying and transferring the voice of the client and convert it in product requirements through the steps of product or service development with the participation of all the functions intervening in it". It involves changes in the product development and production process in order to achieved the quality desired by the final client.

involved lacked a clear understanding or view of the system. As a consequence, the initial hypothesis appeared later to be misleading, which resulted in a project planning with an inadequate work breakdown schedule and with quite an inadequate time planning.

Due to the above reasons, until half through the project life the project objectives didn't seem to be feasible. And this after holding numerous meetings, discussions and controversies between the participants of the project partners and after a complete reorganisation of the project plans was carried out.

Towards the project completion it became apparent that it had become a knowledge management project. After analysing its development and difficulties the author (who acted as project co-ordinator) became interested in studying it from a KM point of view. This approach proved to be very useful to analyse the project outcome. This paper it's a reflection of the author experience after maintaining various discussions and interviews with the different actors involved in the project.

PROCESS WORKFLOW

As it has been mentioned, the project objective was to develop a model and an expert system, which could allow the maintenance of a high, predictable and sustainable quality level that would satisfy the client's requirements thus following the QFD objectives (see previous note).

Figure 17.3 shows the process-simplified *workflow*. In a first instance, the customer (in this case, the sweet manufacturer) discusses his requirements, which have been based on some drawings or sketches by their creative publishing firm or specialist, with the press supplier-marketing department. After some extensive discussions, an agreement is reached in relation to price, delivery, quality and scope of work.

Once an order is produced the sketches are sent to the prepress department of the supplier, which will develop the adequate interface[2] files, which can be processed in the printing process. Extensive work is required in this adaptation process since the client's requirements in the form of sketches; electronic drawings, etc. have to be transformed into electronic files, which are compatible with the subsequent processes.

The rotogravure process utilises coppered cylinders (equivalent to the plate support in offset), one per colour, in which cells are dented in order to collect the different colour inks and deposit it later into the material support surface, which has to be printed. These cylinders have to be prepared previously (and surface treated) depending on the conditions of the printing process in a complex galvano-technical independent process.

---

[2] This department, as others in the printing industry linked with the creative side, works in a Mackintosh environment while the rest of the firm's departments work in a Windows environment.

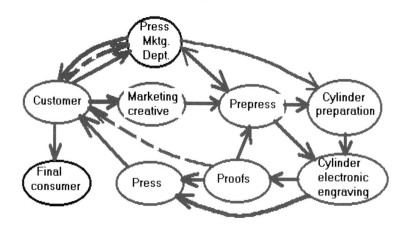

Fig. 17.3. Process simplified work flow.

The cylinder-engraving phase is also a complicated process, subject recently of a relevant technological evolution. Modern digitised processes with laser beams are substituting electronic and electromechanical technologies. This technology evolution is common to similar craft origin industries such as textile, paper print, ceramics decoration, etc. The project advantage was that its partners were technology leaders in their field.

The results of the engraving processes are checked with a proof press, before entering the production process, in order to control whether the quality levels have been reached. Again this phase will be made redundant by modern technologies. In the mean time the printing inks are formulated in accordance with the work requirements.

Once, the cylinders are checked and conform to the work specifications, the final printing press production phase begins. The rotary press has to be regulated and its main variables (such as press speed, band width, ink formula, band tension, etc.) set and managed in order to achieve the speed and quality required. The process finalises when the printed rolls have been cut and packaged.

Rotogravure printing has its origin in artisan work. Although technology has tended to substitute typical tacit knowledge (*cooking* know how) with more elaborate standards and norms, still the quality of most press shops, and especially in the SMES environment [3] depends on the skills of the machinists, engravers, operators, pre-press artists, etc. Due to this situation, and the fact that engraved cylinders are normally reutilised due to its high cost (each cylinder amounting approximately 1.500 €uros, and since each order utilises four or six depending on

---

[3]   Modern presses are fully automated but are only found in the premises of large firms.

the number of colours used, it means that storing 100 orders could mean an inventory of 750.000 €uros) it becomes a difficult task to repeat a certain level of quality, the exact colour tonality, etc. when a certain order has to be processed again. The skills of all the process operators play a relevant role in the process and its control. This was emphasised during the interviews held by the author with managers in various firms in the industry. Quality requirements have exerted a strong demand on codifying tacit knowledge, as it will be discussed later.

WORKING WITH KNOWLEDGE

Davenport (1998) distinguishes between data (a set of discrete objective facts), information (a message) and knowledge (a fluid mix of framed experience, values, contextual information and expert insight that provides a frame work for evaluating and incorporating new experiences and information). We shall discuss how these concepts could be applied and analysed in relation to this experience.

The project was confronted with a work process composed of a number of phases (the workflow previously discussed), which the technical literature only covered partially and from a partitioned (nor organised or classified) point of view.[4] On one side there was a number of historical data, which was collected through the process development for each order and with the objective of setting operating standards, etc. Except for some computerised operations (basically in the engraving process) most of the data was collected manually. Information, understood as contextualized and categorised data, was also collected and interchanged between the process operators and it was also managed in order to obtain certain desired results.

Knowledge, as a mix of experience, contextual information, and expert discernment was brought to the project by specialists from the participant firms, process operators, and workers, who seemed to be a relevant asset, as carriers of valuable tacit knowledge. Knowledge could also be found in the process routines, in every day practices, and in norms prepared by suppliers. Considering the process work flow as a value chain where the initial idea and wishes of the customer were completed until a whole packaging product was produced, knowledge could be considered moving down the chain and returning information and data through the chain. The model to be developed had to make common sense out of this flow. Figure 17.4 resumes this value chain idea.

---

[4] An extensive search of the technical literature showed how heavily the industry *know how* was based in dispersed knowledge. A visit to the Drupa fair in Dusseldorf (the largest world wide fair in the industry) and a number of conversations with specialists and suppliers confirmed this.

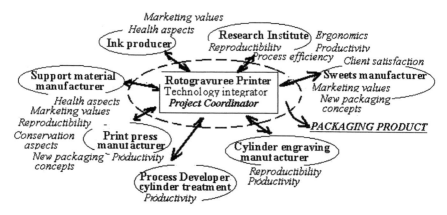

Fig. 17.4. Partner value contribution to the project.

Experience provided a relevant source of dynamic knowledge acquired through a formal and informal learning process by operating the production process, learning from suppliers, technical fairs, symposiums, etc. Rules of thumb were developed between participants through learning and observations. It was thought that the model to be built would incorporate a number of these. It should be then an intuition-based model compatible with a SME environment where this type of compressed expertise (Weick, 1995, p.35) is widely utilised.

The spiral model shown in Fig. 17.5, could illustrate the learning model that had helped to build knowledge in the participant organisations.

Fig. 17.5. Knowledge generating spiral.

The knowledge handled could be classified according to Polanyi (1966, p.27) as bi-dimensional: tacit and explicit knowledge. Tacit knowledge, specific to context, personal and hard to formalise and communicate predominated in those layers of the organisations closer to the operating environment and further away from automated areas. Explicit, codified knowledge, easier to communicate predominated in management layers and in those areas more prone to formalisation and automation.

Tacit knowledge, which was also more elusive to grasp, proved to be more critical and relevant to the process control, however, in spite of the initial lack of emphasis in it from the specialists' side. According to Johnson Laird (1983, p.54), tacit knowledge includes cognitive elements, mental models (e.g., Senge, 1990) that help the individual to define their environment and technical elements such as crafts, skills and know how. The former elements were found to predominate in the management layers while the latter prevailed in the operator's layers and were more difficult to formalise. Nevertheless it has to be outlined that tacit knowledge had a strong contribution to the process knowledge and challenged a number of theoretical assumptions which were part of the initial hypothesis.

Finally, and in order to summarise the discussion, the model proposed by Novins (1999, p.48) will be useful to categorise knowledge. Here knowledge is classified in two basic dimensions. The first refers to its broad or narrow range of application, local versus global. In the former case, it would be applicable and would be dependent on a given set of conditions, it could be considered detailed knowledge (i.e. applicable to a certain process phase). At the other extreme, the knowledge would be global in nature, applying widely across the processes, the industry, and the technical and cultural borders (i.e. the case of colour standards).

The second dimension of knowledge would refer to its level of transferability. Explicit knowledge, rule-based, which can be stated simply and in definite terms could be considered easily transferable. At the opposite extreme, transferability would be low when knowledge had a high tacit content, it was judgement based and with high sensitivity to the context (i.e. $x = a+b$, if... or $x = c+d$, when,...etc.). Therefore, according to its transferability the knowledge could be programmable or unique.

Figure 17.6 shows a matrix where knowledge has been classified according to those two dimensions.

Four basic types of knowledge can be categorized according to this matrix. *Quick access knowledge*, was easily managed by detail databases in the system utilised by the various specialist departments (i.e. ink or cylinders standards, customers files). *Broad based knowledge*, utilised by all the organisation was packaged in the software itself (i.e. general existing rotogravure standards). The most difficult areas were those related to the unique dimension of knowledge and have been pointed out by a shadowed area. *Specialised and infrequent knowledge* represented tacit knowledge utilised in some local areas, which contained a relevant set of skills difficult to transfer (i.e. the variables related to the various

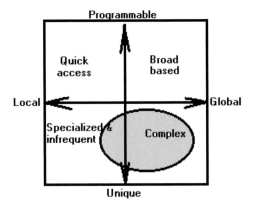

Fig. 17.6. Categories of managed knowledge (Novins, 1999, modified by the author).

types of ink utilised). This had to be managed separately depending on its importance in the process output. *Complex knowledge* was broadly used and difficult to transfer. It meant knowledge arduous to communicate and based in general recognised artisan skills. Here the approach was to develop general specifications and standards to handle it.[5] A large amount of time and effort was required here and the process was based on trial and error procedures.

THE PROCESS OF KNOWLEDGE CREATION AND MANAGEMENT

The project development could be classified in four distinct and characteristic phases. These do not include the project definition phase, which had led to the initial proposal, presented to the EC for funding.

During phase I the model was conceived. It required an analysis of the workflow process. A *"systems thinking"* approach[6] was required to fully understand the process. Meetings were held with all participants in order to identify the critical elements and the interrelation between the different process phases. Here a strong interchange of tacit knowledge took place. It has to be outlined that only the integrator could bring a wide systems approach since most participants had a partial view of the process (i.e. although support material interacts with the ink the supplier couldn't grasp many of the associated problems to this interface). Concepts and experience were the drivers of the discussions between the experts

---

[5] This was the case of the colour management standard and software package, which was the object of special treatment. This was difficult to transfer due tot its low standardisation.

[6] In the sense attributed by Senge (1990)

taking part. Part of the team components (the equipment suppliers) contributed their skills approach to the understanding of the process. During these meetings their mutual practical experience was interchanged. In this occasion some of the technical myths, which had been supported until then by the technical managers, were abandoned. This was the case of the influence of ambient temperature in the ink performance, which was held by plant engineers. In this particular case the ink manufacturer contributed to a better understanding of the product behaviour. As it has been mentioned tacit knowledge emerged as a critical element, especially due to the fact that all participants were SMEs. Most of the equipment manufacturers did rely more on tacit than on explicit knowledge and therefore complete technical manuals were not available. In many cases they argued that it was worthless to spent time preparing them when the press operators relied more on their own experience. The knowledge was generated through discussions, meetings and correspondence between project partners.

Phase II was related to the selection of what it was thought (at that time) were the critical process variables. These were independent or dependent from the client order requirements (i.e. final quality variables). Brainstorming meetings took place with the assistance of engineers and operators. During this phase, and as a consequence of the effort made, part of the accumulated tacit knowledge became explicit in the form of concepts, rules of thumb, etc. Its formalisation became a difficult task and led to the model structure. A special effort was required to select the quality parameters, which could define an acceptable set of standards of work quality and measurable quality levels. These quality parameters defined by experts in tacit terms (i.e. the picture sharpness or the colour homogeneity) had to be converted to quantifiable concepts or variables. This stage involved a certain level of chaos and often the team didn't see the light (in the industry quality terms its usually defined as whether the packaging looks good or not). At this stage the software experts started their work in the project.

During Phase III the efforts were concentrated in the build up of the model knowledge system and in its formalisation. The set of relevant variables was refined and additional brainstorming meetings took place. As a result a new set of explicit knowledge appeared which was more manageable. This phase lasted a shorter period and developed more smoothly. It seemed easier to manage explicit rather than tacit knowledge.

The tasks involved in Phase IV were related to the trial tests of the software model and its learning by the project team, plant operators and middle managers. The explicit knowledge created in the previous phase, in the form of a software model had to be translated somehow to the plant operators' language. It had to become again tacit knowledge, in order to be assimilated by the intuitive manufacturing environment. Here learning of the built up knowledge took place. Special effort was required to motivate participating personnel. This phase lasted longer and motivation to learn was critical as the following section will discuss.

The development and the timeline of the project are shown in Fig. 17.7. As it has been described, it can be explained by the knowledge spiral model proposed by Nonaka (1995, p.71) as shown in Fig. 17.7.

The elaboration of the model, actually in the testing phase, involved a great level of complexity, especially in relation to the understanding of the system. Certain decisions took some time to be taken. Mainly those related to the quality levels and standards such as when and how judge if a piece of work was acceptable, which was its quality level, etc. and specially how to standardise it if the decisions were to be made into rules of thumb.

Actually the project has finalised the construction of the model. Its situation could be defined, according to the Nonaka model (1995, p.84), as the cross levelling phase of knowledge generation with the model (a tangible software package) as the built archetype. It is expected that it will constitute also a learning tool since it has for that purpose an algorithm building and input tool, and it will allow new rules to be incorporated to it.

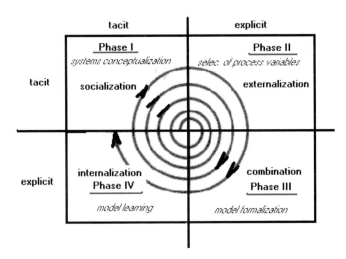

Phases/ Years	1	2	3	
I. Socialization				
II. Externalization				
III. Combination				
IV. Internalization				

Fig. 17.7. Project timeline and knowledge spiral model.

BARRIERS AND ENABLERS FOR ORGANISATIONAL KNOWLEDGE CREATION

The interviews with the actors and the experience of the project life showed that certain elements or conditions acted as enablers and others as barriers in the knowledge creation process at the organisation level. The project took place at group level but had effects at individual level.

It has to be taken into account that this project took place in an organisation network context, firms from various countries and possessing varied organizational cultures cooperated in the project. As an example, the culture of the final user was very practical and consumer oriented while that of some of the equipment manufacturers was more technically oriented. This meant that communication between forms and departments was sometimes difficult (i.e. the final user would be interested in how the packaging attracted the consumer attention but not at all in the technicalities of the achieved solution) It has to be taken into account that the individuals were taking part in an inter-firm project and the results were to be applied in one of the firms.

The process of organisational learning consisted partly in experiencing, capturing, storing and reusing experiences and knowledge, which were finally fed to computer design software. The process system rationality developed in phase I of the project (Moran, 1996), and the organisational memory or group *know-how* (Terveen, 1993) was an important asset in the program development. Fischer (1994) proposes that in the learning cycle a virtuous circle has to be closed whereas each participant needs to feel a personal benefit in order to be motivated to contribute. But benefits were not obvious immediately and therefore motivation was hard to implement in a day-to-day basis. This is the case of the final users marketing specialists, and the designers who believed things were already correct and had no patience to wait for results of a process that would take at least a year to reach him. On the contrary equipment manufacturers were more used to see the benefits of engineering and were more eager to innovate.

The following Fig. 17.8 illustrates this circle which is based in the users perceived utility. Thus this utility could be expressed as the following coefficient: benefit / expended effort. Logically the organisational memory will not be activated if previous projects produced scarce benefits. Here the management of the project had also a relevant influence communicating the project vision.

As a consequence, motivation appeared in first place as an enabler, or a barrier when absent. When participation and communication were enhanced from the management side it resulted in acceptance and will to participate in the project actively. This was in direct relation with the ability (and available time) of the management to link the project to the company's

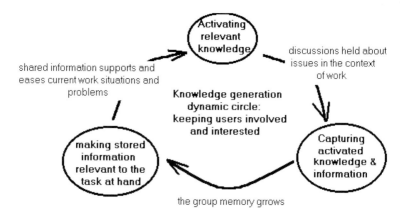

Fig. 17.8. The virtuous circle of knowledge generation (based on Fischer, 1994).

strategy and communicate it effectively. Nonaka (1995, p. 74) defines it as the organisational intention and Senge (1990b, p.9) includes it in the building of a vision (see below page 12). As it has been mentioned before, the SME manager-owner plays a critical role in KM projects but usually doesn't have enough time to cope with every day project tasks, which require a continuous care. Then and depending on the manager time availability the project performance would improve. Inter-firm and interdepartmental views of the project outcome had a relevant influence on their motivation. Their different time horizons, participation in the product life cycles, and their level of formal authority or influence proved to be critical in their project support.

Resistance to change was a barrier to the process. In some cases knowledge sharing meant a problem since knowledge was utilised in some areas as a defence wall and as a status keeper (Leonard-Barton, 1995)[7]. This was evident with the computing department, which opposed the project since its manager thought it would interfere with their responsibilities (it had to do with the general management decision of assigning the project management to other department). This required extra efforts from the management side to overcome it (some times with authority, others with more subtle approaches) and caused a number of delays in the project. Again, effective communication was a key factor. In the same direction, but in opposite sense, acted the need for information and knowledge. In some departments such as marketing where data and information were lacking for bidding purposes their members

---

[7]   Dorothy Leonard Barton (p. 54) writes about skills to which people bound up their competence. They may see a new knowledge generation tool as challenging them and will resist innovation in that direction. This was the case of the computers area. The author has often observed this situation.

expressed strong demand for more information, which could help them to improve their work and reduce the uncertainty of various tasks.

The new system made more evident the real levels of quality attained (which were not as high as expected) and this caused some restlessness in some areas, which were trying to justify their problems. The system would make quality information more evident and available. Transparency was a result of the new system since information about performance was more freely available.

Organisational culture was, as it has been mentioned, a critical element. Apart from the three levels of management culture pointed out by Schein (1996b): operator, engineering, and executive, other cultures such as marketing cultures or national cultures (this was an international project) interfered in project communication. Knowledge sharing became difficult by cultural mismatch (Allen, 1990, p.5). This was the case of prepress operators and publicity designers and printing specialists. The former having a technical approach while the latter had an artistic approach to the problems. In the same direction, production engineers had a more practical approach which collided with the creativity approach of the researchers from the research Institute collaborating in the project. The production engineer complained about "*the excess of creativity of the software developers, they have forgotten what we need and look more in the direction of what they think is fancy as this java language*"

In some occasions an excess of bureaucratic culture, placing emphasis on written memoranda rather than discussions and meetings (the influence of the general manager formalisation intentions), reduced the level of knowledge transfer (Davenport, 1998, p.102). It has to be taken into account that in some SME environments meetings are not well accepted due to cultural reasons, either due to an authoritarian culture where employees opinion was not accepted or due to the belief that the inter exchange of views was a waste of time. In this sense if learning had to become *double looped* in the Argyris sense (1977b) the organisation would finally had to be changed with the same learning dynamism. Otherwise learning would not be achieved without a cultural and a subsequent organizational change. For example, the general manager could be quoted complaining "*the difficulties lay in the fact that employees were busy with every day chores and they didn't have the vision of the project*". This implied that he didn't realize it was him who had to transfer this vision to his team and to convey the message of innovation and continuous improvement. The same question was posed by certain lack of team spirit in the organization that hampered team learning. Here the lack of coherence became a problem. If it was meant that a change was required while the organizational culture was conservative, management would have to be coherent and lead the organizational change. When this process didn't occur frustration (on the employee side) would be the final outcome.

When the project made evident the need for training, it became an enabler element, providing a motivation drive by moving the virtuous circle and increasing the absorptive capacity of knowledge recipients (Davenport, 1998, p.101).

Informal communication lines between individuals acted as strong links for knowledge transfer when they were available (Webber, 1993, p.27). In many instances informal conversations and discussions over a cup of coffee or in an airport lobby brought relevant light to many clues difficult to solve otherwise.

The knowledge spiral was also promoted by the openness of the project. The fact that experts from other disciplines, countries and firms interchanged periodic visits and discussions with the project team had a positive punctual effect in its development. These contacts also provided redundant information, which granted extra room for discussion. Nonaka (1995, p.81) has reported both elements as enablers for the knowledge creation process. This openness gave the partners the opportunity to observe other firms with different cultures and compare.

The role of middle management as a hinge for the knowledge generating process in the project and as a transfer line between the knowledge and the operating layer has to be outlined. As Nonaka (1995, p125) points out, top management creates the vision, the dream, while middle management develops the concrete concepts that operators can understand and implement. This was especially evident during phases II and IV when their basic task was to solve the contradiction between *what is* (the reality of operations) and *what ought to be.* (the wish of the management, the theory). Middle management had a critical role in managing and translating tacit knowledge (balancing its mental and skills content) and later leading the internalisation phase. This role is more evident in a SME environment where top management may be a single manager or owner with firm ideas and without pressure to change from above. Fig. 17.9 below shows schematically this relationship.

As this drawing shows, middle management communicates the knowledge management with the external environment and with the operating layer, a bottom up source and test bed of knowledge. Its role becomes fundamental in keeping the knowledge movement active by

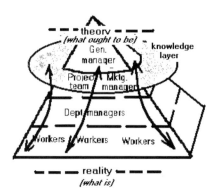

Fig. 17.9. Knowledge action layers.

questioning the official knowledge and contributing with tacit technical knowledge to the system.

CONCLUSIONS

As it has been outlined the tacit dimension plays a significant role when knowledge creation is concerned and especially in the SME environment. Contextualization of this knowledge is difficult due to the disproportionate weights of cognitive (mental models) and technical (skills) in the management and operating layers.

Knowledge creation and management is closely linked to the concept of a learning organisation, especially in a SME environment. The enablers of the learning organisation will allow a smoother process of knowledge generation. In the case described above systems thinking was fundamental to grasp the view of the process flow and its interrelations. Mental models allowed the transfer and handling of tacit knowledge and team learning was a basic tool for the development of the knowledge-generating tool. Finally, the building of the shared vision will support the leadership capacity that can keep the learning dynamism going in the future.

Human resources management plays a fundamental role in the whole process. In an entrepreneurial SME environment the individual, the task (knowledge generation) and the organisational context are closely linked. As Kao (1991, p.15) points out the three dimensions of the organisation: the individual, the task and the organisational context, will interact inside the external environment of the organisation. The environment will influence its strategy in the way the firm reacts to it (as pointed out in a reactive way), and in this case had a relevant effect on the knowledge interactions. The human resource management of the firm will drive the other two dimensions: the individual and the organisational context. Since the task (knowledge creation) has usually a creativity dimension it will present a management challenge on both the individual and the organisational context, which will have to be met with an adequate human resource management system.

ACKNOWLEDGEMENTS

The author is indebted with all *Autogravure* project partners and management who provided their insight and opinions on the development of the project. The European Commission financed it and it's placing a clear interest in the development of knowledge management projects in the European industry.

REFERENCES

Advani, A., (1997), *Industrial clusters, a support system for SMEs*. Report, 32. The World Bank.

Albors, J., Falco, A., (2000), The Autogravure Brite project, *Gravure,* Vol. 14, 2, pp. 62- 63, Rochester, N.Y.

Albors, J. (2002) Networking and technology transfer in the Spanish ceramic tile cluster. *Journal of Technology transfer,* **27**(3).

Allen, T., (1.990), *People and technology transfer,* The International Centre for Research on the Management of Technology, August, 5.

Ang, S., Damien, J., (1996), Organisational learning and. learning organisation, triggering events, structures and processes, *Academy of Management Meeting,* Cincinnatti, Ohio.

Argyris, C. (1977) Organisational Learning and Management Information Systems, *Accounting, Organisations and Society,* **2** (2), pp. 113-123.

Argyris, C., (1977b), Double loop learning in organisations, *Harvard Business Review,* no.77502.

Argyris, C., (1992), *On organisational learning,* Blackwell Publishers, Oxford., pp 67-70

Audretsch, D., Feldman, M., (1993), *Innovative clusters and the industry life cycle.* Centre for Economic Research Policy, London.

Bateson, G., (1972), *Steps to an ecology of mind,* New York, Ballantine Books.

Becattini, G.,(1987), ed. *Mercato e force locali: il distretto industriale,* Bologna, Il Mulino.

Belotti, C., Tunalv, C. (1999), Acquisition of Technological Knowledge in Small and Medium-Sized Manufacturing Companies in Sweden, *International Journal of Technology Management,* **18** (3/4), pp.353-371, Mar./ Apr.

Bessant, J., Francis, D., (1999), Implementing learning networks, *Technovation,* **19** (6/7), pp. 373-383.

Brown J.S., Duguid, P., (1991), Organisational learning and communities of practice, *Organisation Science,* **2**, pp. 40-57.

Bryson, J., (1997), Small and Medium sized enterprises, Business Link and the new knowledge workers, *Policy Studies,* Vol. 18, No. 1, pp. 67-80.

Charston, I, Badger, B, Sadler-Smith, E, (1999), Small Firm organisational learning; comparisons of the perception of need and style among UK support service advisors and small firm managers, *Journal of European Industrial Training,* Vol. 23, Issue 2, pp. 1-10.

Clarke, P, Cooper, M., (2000), *Knowledge Management and Collaboration,* Proc. 3d. Congress on practical aspects of knowledge management, Basel, Switzerland

Chesbrough, H.W., Teece, D.J., (1996), When is virtual virtuous?, *Harvard Business Review,* **1**, pp. 65-73.

Cyert, R.M., March, J.G., (1963); *A behavioral theory of the firm,* Englewood Cliffs, N.J., Prentice Hall.

Davenport, T.H., Prusak, L., (1998*), Working knowledge: How organisations manage what they know,* Harvard Business School Press, Boston.

Davidow, W.H., Malone, M.S., (1992), *The virtual corporation , structuring and revitalising the corporation for the 21st. Century,* Harper Collins, New York.

Dogson, M., (1991), Technology, learning, technology strategy and competitive pressures, *British Journal of Management*, **2/3**, pp. 132-149.

Fahey, L., Prusak, L., (1998), The eleven deadliest sins of knowledge management, *California Management Review* (**40**:3), pp 264-276.

Fiol, C.M., Lyles, M., (1985), Organizational learning, *Academy of Management Review*, **10**:4, pp. 803-813.

Fischer, G., Lindstaedt, S., Oschwald, J., Schneider, K., Smith, J., (1996), *Informing system design through organisational learning*, Proc. Int. Conference on Learning Sciences (ICL '96), pp 52-59.

Fischer, G., Nakakoji, K., (1992), Beyond the macho approach of artificial intelligence: empower human designers, *Knowledge based systems*, **5**, pp. 15-20.

Frank, H., (1993), Small business owners and consultants: an empirical analysis of their relationship, *Journal of Small business & Entrepreneurship*, Vol. 10 No. 4, July-Septem,ber, pp. 32-43.

Garvin, D.A., (1993), Building a learning organisation, *Harvard Business Review*, July-August, Mass.

Gibb, A., (1993), The enterprise culture and education. Understanding enterprise education and its links with Small Business entrepreneurship and wider educational goals, *International Small Business management Journal*, Vol. 11, No.3.

Groom, J.R., David, F.R., (2001), Competitive intelligence activity among small firms, *S.A.M. Advanced Mangement Journal*, Vol. 66, 1, pp. 12-20, Cincinatti.

Hale, R., William, R., (1997), *Towards virtual organisations*, Mc Graw Hill, London.

HMSO (1998), *Our competitive Future: Building the knowledge driven economy*, London.

Harrison, B., Kelley, M., Gant, J., (1996), Innovative firm behaviour and local milieu; exploring the intersection of agglomeration, firm effects, industrial organisation and technological change, *Economic Geography*, **72**, 3, pp. 233-258.

Houdek, F., Schneider, K., Wieser, E. (1998), *Establishing experience factories at Daimler Benz*, Proc. 20th. Int. Conference on Software engineering, ICSE, pp. 443-447.

Huber, G.P. (1991), Organisational Learning: The Contributing Processes and the Literatures, *Organisation Science*, **2** (1), February, 1991, pp. 88-115

Johnson-Laird, P.N., (1983), *Mental models*, Cambridge University Press, Cambridge.

Kailer, N., (1999), Deficits in the consulting of small and medium sized enterprises: empirical evidence from Austria, Germany and Switzerland and suggestions for improvement, *Journal of Entrepreneurship & Regional Development*.

Kailer, N., Scheff, J., (1999), Knowledge management as a service: co-operation between small and medium sized enterprises and training, consulting and research institutions, *Journal of European Industrial training*, Bradford.

Kao, J. J., (1991), *Managing creativity*, Prentice Hall. N.J.

Kim, (1993), The link between individual and organizational learning, *Sloan Mangement Review*. pp. 37-50, Fall.

Landes, L., Schneider, K., Houdek, F., (1999), *Organisational learning and experience documentation in industrial software projects*, Proceedings of the Workshop KRR5 at IJCAI'99, Stockholm.

Lave, J., Wenger, E.C., (1993*), Situated learning: legitimate peripheral participation*, Cambridge University Press, N.Y.

Leonard Barton, D., (1995), *Wellsprings of Knowledge: Building and sustaining the sources of innovation*, Harvard Business School Press, Boston.

Lightfoot, G., 1996, *Management, knowldege and control in small firms: The problems with professional advice.* Proceedings, 19th. ISBA national small firms Policy and research conference, 628-641.

March, J.G., Olsen, J.P., 1975, Uncertainty of the past: Organisational learning under ambiguity . *European Journal of Political Research, 3*, pp. 147-171.

Miles, R.E., Snow, C.C., (1995), The new network firm, *Organisational Dynamics*, pp. 5-17.

Moran, T., Carroll, J., (1996) *Design rationale: Concepts, Techniques and use*, Erlbaum, Mahwah, N.J.

Nonaka, I., Takeuchi, H., (1995*), The knowledge creating company*, Oxford University Press, Oxford.

Novins, P., Armstrong, R., (1999), *Choosing your spots in knowledge management: a blueprint for change*, The Ernst & Young Centre for Business innovation, New York, May.

Perren, L., Berry, A., Partridge, M., (1999), The evolution of management information, control and decision-making processes in small growth oriented service scetor businesses: exploratory lessons from four cases of success, *Journal of Small Business & Enterprise Development*, (6) 1.

Polany, M., (1966*), The tacit dimension, Knowledge in Organisations*, Butterworth, Boston.

Porter, M.E., (1998), *Clusters and competition*, Harvard Business School Press.

Scarborough, H., 1996, *Information systems for knowledge management*, in Scarborough, H. (ed) Macmillan Business: Basingstokw, Chapter 7, 177-189.In The management of expertise.

Scase, R., Goffee, R., (1987), 2nd ed. *The real world of the small business owner*, Beckenham, Croom Helm.

Schein, E., (1996), Can learning cultures evolve?, *The systems thinker*, **7**, (6), August, pp. 1-5.

Schein, E., (1996b), Three cultures of management: the key to organisational learning, *Sloan Mangement Review*, **38** (1), pp. 9-15.

Schon, Donald A. (1973), *Beyond the Stable State*, Norton, New York.

Senge, P.M., (1990), The leaders New York: Building learning organisations, *Sloan Management Review*, Fall 7-23.

Senge, P.M., (1990b), *The fifth discipline*, Century Business, London.

Shelton, R., (2000), *Techniplas: A short case study of knowledge management in a small firm*, Birmingham, UCE, Knowledge Management, Centre.

Sparrow, J., (2000), *Knowledge features of small firms*, Operations Research Society KMAC Conference, University of Aston, July.

Sparrow, J., (1998), *Organizational learning in small firms. Implications for Business support.* 21st. National Small Firms Policy and research Conference, Durham University Business Conference, November.

Sparrow, J. (2001), Knowledge management in small firms, *Knowledge and process Management*, Vol 8 (1), pp. 3-16.

Storey, D., Westhead, P., (1995), *Management training in small firms. A case of market failure*, Warwick Business School, Centre for SMEs (Ed.), Working Paper No. 29, Warwick.

Storey, D., (1998), *Six steps to heaven,* Warwick Business School, Centre for SMEs (ed.) Working paper, No. 59, Warwick.

Terveen, L.G., Selfridge, P.G., Long, M.D., (1993), *From folklore to living design memory. Human factors in computing systems,* Proc. INTERCHI'93, pp 15-22.

Watkins, K., Marsick, V., 1995, *The case for learning,* Academy of HRD 1995 Conference Proceedings.

Webber, A.M., (1993), What's so new about the new economy?, *Harvard Business Review* (Jan-Feb.), 28

Weick, K.E., (1995), *Sense making in organisations,* Sage Publications, California.

Wenger, E.C., Snyder, W.M., (1999), Communities of practice the organisational frontier, *Harvard Business Review,*

Zetie, S., (1998), *Knowledge management initiatives in manufacturing SMEs.* A report to City of Birmingham Economic Development Department. University of Central England Business School, Birmingham.

Management of Technology
Copyright © 2003 by Elsevier Science Ltd.
All rights of reproduction in any form reserved.
ISBN: 0-08-044136-X

18

TECHNOLOGY RE-USE: DEVELOPING A PRACTICAL APPROACH TO MAKING THE MOST OF YOUR TECHNOLOGICAL ASSETS[†]

Francis Hunt, Institute for Manufacturing, Cambridge University, UK[*]
Clare Farrukh, Institute for Manufacturing, Cambridge University, UK[*]
Rob Phaal, Institute for Manufacturing, Cambridge University, UK[*]

INTRODUCTION

Given the range of activities that could be considered to be re-use, it is useful to define what we mean by re-use:

> Engineering re-use is the business strategy of using existing technological assets that a company controls in the creation of new assets.

'Technological assets' are what Whipp (1991) terms technologies: '…products, processes and people. Here, people is a shorthand way of referring to the management methods, knowledge bases and modes of thought and action which underpin given products and processes'. Our definition of engineering re-use is extensive but does exclude the buying of assets controlled by other companies, and also makes clear that *engineering re-use is not a goal in itself*, but a means of realising business objectives. It is successful when the resources used to obtain an acceptable result are less than those that would have otherwise been required to create the new

[†] This article has been presented at the IAMOT 2001 Conference in Lausanne, Switzerland. The research was funded by the EPSRC Grant: GR/L56695/01.
[*] Francis Hunt, Clare Farrukh and Rob Phaal are researchers at the Centre for Technology Management within the Institute for Manufacturing at Cambridge. Emails: {fhh10, cjp2, rp108}@eng.cam.ac.uk.

asset. Clearly 'acceptable result' is a term defined with respect to the business strategy and may include such elements as customer satisfaction, employee satisfaction and long-term competitive position of the firm.

Re-use as a business strategy implies a trade-off between various factors such as performance, time, cost, risk and resource utilisation. The trade-off cuts across the organisation and may promote global interests at the expense of local ones; for instance a project deadline may be jeopardised by the requirement that the project generate components that can be re-used on other projects, and not merely ones that are sufficient for the task in hand. There may also be conflicts introduced between the desire of managers to reduce costs by re-use and the desire of designers to use their creative abilities.

A significant distinction is between development *with* re-use and development *for* re-use. The former is looking backward through time to locate what can be re-used and hence is largely about knowledge management, the latter is looking forward into the future to create assets that will be re-used and hence is largely about design. The two approaches naturally fit together, though development with re-use requires less up-front investment. However, evidence from the software world (Poulin 1999) suggests that high levels of re-use, as well as high levels of corresponding benefits, require systematic development *for* re-use.

Another useful distinction is between the *re-use potential* in a business situation and *re-use capability* of the organisation. Re-use potential is a measure of how much benefit would accrue from re-using assets in a particular situation, re-use capability is a measure of how fit an organisation is to conduct re-use activities. The re-use potential of a situation will be increased if the organisation has high re-use capability, with systems in place to enable re-use to be performed at minimal cost.

LITERATURE

In the words of Busby (1998) 're-use is an obvious but imprecise concept', and this is apparent in the fragmented nature of the relevant literature. Firstly there is work on general engineering re-use, looking at product platforms, mechanisms for transferring technology across projects, and re-usability matrices. Secondly there is much work in the area of software re-use. Thirdly, this all takes place against the general background of the knowledge management literature. We start by looking at general approaches to re-use in engineering.

Re-use is not a new idea in engineering and in many cases is just 'common sense'. Wheelwright and Clark (1992) note that long term success of a company is typically dependent on its evolving portfolio of products rather than on any single product and therefore aggregate product planning is essential. The tool they propose is a product development map (Wheelright and Sasser 1986) with which companies can map out the interrelations between core products and derivative variants. This links closely with the ideas of product platforms advocated by

Meyer and Lehnerd (1997) and Robertson and Ulrich (1998), amongst others, where, by creating a core of common technologies, a firm is able to efficiently develop derivative products that can be released serially or in 'waves'. Nobeoka and Cusumano (1995) focus on projects rather than products to assess the most effective ways, in terms of engineer hours, to transfer technology between them. They identify 'rapid design transfer', the transfer of design between two ongoing projects, as the most efficient method.

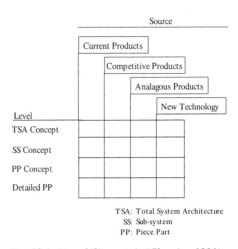

Fig. 18.1. Reusability matrix (Clausing 1991)

Re-use ideas have similarities with design for manufacture (Sanderson 1992) and robust design (Rothwell and Gardiner 1990). Design for manufacture emphasises, *inter alia*, minimising the total number of parts, developing a modular design, using standard components, designing for ease of fabrication and maximising compliance. Robust design instead focuses on using 'what-if' analysis to deliberately incorporate an element of 'stretch' in the design to allow for future derivative products. In re-use terms, there is a progression from design for manufacture, in which re-use ideas are employed to make the manufacturing processes more efficient; to robust design and product platforms, in which a more global re-use perspective is taken. The twin benefits of these approaches are the reduction of development times and costs, and the greater market coverage and flexibility.

Clausing (1991) proposes a 4×4 re-usability matrix (see Fig. 18.1) to investigate re-use relationships between products, plotting the architectural level of a part against its source. Different patterns across the matrix relate to the incremental, radical, modular and architectural types of innovation identified by Henderson and Clark (1990). Later work by Clausing's group integrates the use of the matrix more closely into new product development (Witter *et al.* 1994), extends the matrix to consider product families (Schnabel 1996) and considers the financial model behind re-use (Krinninger 1995; Yahia 1997).

The second broad area of re-use literature is that of software re-use. The idea of re-using software has become increasingly attractive as hardware costs have fallen dramatically in relation to software development costs. There are a number of books (Reifer 1997; Jacobson *et al.* 1997), survey articles (Poulin 1999; Yongbeom & Stohr 1998) and conferences (Frakes 2000) presenting an overview of work in this area, covering both the detail of the technical mechanisms enabling re-use and the wider business and social issues.

A number of key ideas are emphasised in software re-use. Firstly there is the distinction highlighted in the introduction, between design with re-use, and design for re-use. The latter contains an element of domain analysis (Prieto-Diaz 1990) which could be viewed as a type of 'robust design', moving beyond what is strictly necessary for the task in hand to what will be needed for the class of similar tasks. The concept of modularity is well developed in software development, originally as a way to control complexity and limit the unforeseen effect of changes, but it is also of key importance in enabling re-use.

The software re-use process is examined by a number of authors. Yongbeom and Stohr (1998) divide the activities into those producing re-usable assets and those consuming them. The former comprise identification and classification of assets and the latter retrieval, understanding, modification and integration of assets. Rada (1995) offers a more detailed breakdown under the three broad headings of asset creation, asset management and asset utilisation, and this three block structure is common to many of the re-use process descriptions surveyed by Lim (1997).

Before leaving the subject of software re-use it is useful to distinguish between software and other branches of engineering. One major difference is the virtual absence of a manufacturing stage in software engineering. The closest equivalent is compiling the source code, the 'blue print' for the software, into object code, but this consumes negligible resources and in effect, additional copies are free. In traditional engineering, making a part re-usable across a product line may increase the unit cost due to redundant functionality in any particular application, but reduce the machine set-up times and inventory costs through economies of scale. These considerations are not relevant to software. Similarly, the types of assets available for re-use in a manufacturing company will extend beyond those that have been considered in the software re-use literature. Thus although the software re-use literature provides useful input on engineering re-use issues, it cannot provide a complete picture.

Finally, we consider briefly some of the literature on knowledge management, which also impacts on re-use. Re-use can be considered as a concrete example of a knowledge management initiative, since knowledge is often the most crucial part of what is re-used. Classifying knowledge into different types is helpful, since it enables different procedures to be used to manage different types of knowledge. With particular respect to innovation studies, Fleck & Tierney (1991) distinguish between seven different types of knowledge (ranging from meta-knowledge, to informal and formal knowledge). Faulkner (1994) outlines fifteen different types as part of an attempt to build a composite typology. With respect to this, Coombs & Hull (1998) note that these types can also be grouped along another axis relating to five other distinct characteristics of knowledge, thus further complicating the task of classifying knowledge. Blacker (1995) offers a coarser grained classification separating knowledge into five distinct categories, and it can be seen that much of the existing literature on engineering re-use and software re-use focuses on what he terms *encoded* knowledge.

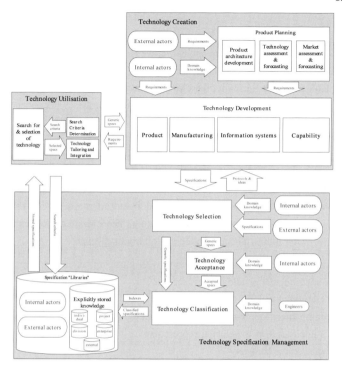

Fig. 18.2: Engineering re-use dataflow framework derived from Antelme et al. *(2000)*

Yeung & Holden (2000) go beyond this boundary and point out that successful re-use of *encoded* knowledge may itself rely heavily on re-use of *embrained* and *embodied* knowledge.

A framework built on work in engineering re-use, software re-use and knowledge management has been proposed (Antelme *et al.* 2000) and consists of two major elements. Firstly, a characterisation of asset types that specifies the 'what' of engineering re-use. The schema adopted by the framework is based on a definition of 'technology' put forward by Steele (1988) and the software characterisation dimensions of Karlsson (1995). Secondly, it includes a model of the re-use process that captures the data flows associated with re-use in an organisation, based on the work of Rada (1995), and shown in Fig. 18.2.

The model contains three high-level processes: technology creation, technology specification management, and technology utilisation. It highlights the agents, processes and data flows that support and facilitate engineering re-use. It is clear that re-use of even a seemingly unimportant asset has potentially broad implications across an organisation, from manufacturing processes and capabilities, through to organisational structure and data storage and access.

From this brief review of the literature, two major conclusions can be drawn. Firstly, the concept of exactly what is re-usable is unclear, however the framework of Antelme *et al.* (2000) is a useful first step forward, especially when combined with the concept of re-usable assets (Yeung & Holden 2000). Secondly, there is no clear guidance to industry on how to set about implementing re-use ideas in a company. This paper describes work to address this second gap.

RESEARCH METHODOLOGY

The aim was to develop re-use guidance in the form of a process methodology that could be applied within a company. Guidelines were developed based on a modified version of the framework above (Fig. 18.2) and the supporting literature. These draft guidelines were then taken into a phase of wider industrial consultation containing three stages:

1. A workshop to test draft guidelines, working with four companies from the aerospace, electronics, instrumentation and process sectors.
2. Structured interviews with ten companies to test revised guidelines, drawing in additional companies from the heavy electrical, automotive and optical sectors.
3. Complete guidelines sent to selected representatives in eleven companies, including a printing and a service company.

The next step is to test the guidelines further by observing their application in industry.

PROCESS DEVELOPMENT

It was recognised that organisations depend on a wide range of resources to support existing business activities, and also to support the development of new products and services. Such resources include both tangible assets, such as facilities and land, together with intangible assets, such as knowledge and relationships. The requirement for effective management of all types of organisational resources, particularly knowledge-based assets, is becoming more important as the pace of innovation and complexity of the business environment increase.

Due to this, the term 'asset' was chosen for the guide, where assets include the intellectual capital, physical resources and organisational capabilities that a company requires to achieve a sustained competitive position. This broad definition of assets includes both tangible and intangible types, such as parts, facilities, people, software, information, designs, systems, processes, knowledge, decisions, structures, relationships, brands and culture. Including this wide range of asset types is important for three reasons:

1. *Sources of value in the firm.* An organisation derives value from exploiting the resources (assets) that it controls, ranging from tangible assets such as land and facilities, to

intangible assets such as brands and business processes. Competitive advantage can be achieved if organisations exploit these resources to the full. Including the full range of areas where re-use might be beneficial ensures that the scope for potential re-use is not too narrowly defined.

2. *Assets do not usually exist in isolation.* For instance, while a focus on design re-use might be required, accommodating the linkages to other asset types can be critical for success (e.g. the related experience of the designers, and the tacit decisions embodied in the design).

3. *Company context.* The intention of the guide is to provide generic advice, supported by examples of specific re-use, to enable the application of the methods in a way that is suited to the particular circumstances that a firm faces. General principles of re-use can apply to any asset type, although the specific implementation depends on the particular type of resource, and the company context (i.e. the purpose to which re-use is being applied).

A strategy of systematic re-use is a way to improve the level to which available resources can be exploited by the firm. This is the process whereby the maximum value of the assets that the organisation controls is exploited, by designing, tailoring and integrating resources to create new innovative products, services and activities, while managing and replenishing the resource base of the firm. These concepts relate closely to key decision areas, including business, technology, product and manufacturing strategies.

Three key generic processes to be considered when developing a strategy and plan for re-use are elements of the re-use framework derived from Antelme *et al.* (2000). These are used to structure the implementation guidance:

i. *Asset creation:* the generation of new assets during the development of new products and services, together with the activities and systems that are required to support innovation. The new assets that are created in this process are likely to include combinations of existing (re-used) assets, and genuine innovations.

ii. *Asset management:* the storage and management of information and knowledge about current and new assets (including specifications and protocols), providing a 'library' that can support the asset creation process, and other activities in the business.

iii. *Asset integration:* the utilisation of existing assets by means of tailoring and integration to support the asset creation process.

The particular form that these processes take, and the systems required to support them, depend on the type of asset being re-used, and the particular company context, in terms of the business objectives, existing systems and pervading culture. It was found that, based on the framework, there are seven key issues that need to be considered if the benefits of re-use are to be attained:

Table 18.1. Key issues for re-use.

Re-use Processes	Key Issues
Asset management	• How to store, manage and retrieve knowledge about assets. • How to identify potentially re-usable assets. • How to classify and analyse re-usable assets.
Asset creation	• How to create new re-usable assets. • How to decide whether to re-use or not.
Asset integration	• How to integrate existing and new assets. • How to implement a re-use programme in the company, and how to assess success.

Based on the work above, it was realised that the guide needed to support both the development of a *strategy* for re-use which fits the company needs, and also the development of a *practical plan* for implementing re-use. A process to do this is outlined in the next section.

PROCESS DESCRIPTION

Building on the conceptual background and rich detail of the case study material, the initial process methodology for developing a re-use strategy and an implementation plan within a

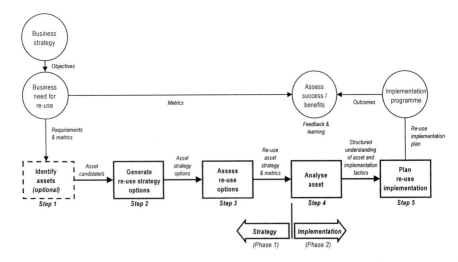

Fig. 18.3. Re-use support process.

firm was revised. The revised version is illustrated in Fig. 18.3. The re-use support process comprises the following elements:

Setting up the process:
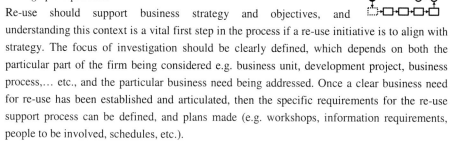
Re-use should support business strategy and objectives, and understanding this context is a vital first step in the process if a re-use initiative is to align with strategy. The focus of investigation should be clearly defined, which depends on both the particular part of the firm being considered e.g. business unit, development project, business process,... etc., and the particular business need being addressed. Once a clear business need for re-use has been established and articulated, then the specific requirements for the re-use support process can be defined, and plans made (e.g. workshops, information requirements, people to be involved, schedules, etc.).

Phase 1 - Strategy:
The first phase of the re-use process aims to develop a strategy for re-use, aligned with the business need identified above. This phase comprises three steps:

⇒ *Step 1 - Identify assets:*

    The overall purpose of re-use is to maximise the value of assets in the firm, and so this step is concerned with identifying the assets that are going to be considered for re-use, within the focus defined above. This step is optional, in that the asset to be considered for re-use may already be clear.

⇒ *Step 2 - Generate re-use strategy options:*

    A number of options may be available for re-use. For example, a range of assets may have been identified in Step 1, or for each asset a range of actions may be possible. The purpose of this step is to explore the possible options that would provide benefit in the context of re-use. These may range from fairly simple actions that provide immediate benefit, to significant initiatives that aim to produce large benefits.

⇒ *Step 3 - Assess the re-use options:*

    Once a range of options has been identified, they need to be assessed and compared, to establish the most appropriate strategy to pursue. A range of measures can be used to assess the various options identified, including the potential benefits, risks, effort and costs associated with re-use.

Phase 2 - Implementation:

The second phase of the re-use process aims to develop a practical plan for implementing the re-use strategy defined in Phase 1. This phase comprises two steps:

⇒ *Step 4 - Analyse asset:*

Once a particular asset (or assets) has been identified, and a re-use strategy has been defined, a detailed analysis of the asset is required in order for action plans to be developed. The purpose of this step is to explore the structure of the asset, in terms of the external relationships with other assets in the firm which may need to be considered when developing an action plan, and internal structure (sub-systems and their hierarchical relationships, together with types of associated knowledge).

⇒ *Step 5 - Plan re-use implementation:*

Once the nature of an asset has been analysed and understood, in terms of internal structure and external relationships, then detailed planning can proceed, to define concrete action plans that include relevant implementation factors, together with the business case for supporting the plan.

Follow-on actions:

The result of the above steps will be a re-use implementation plan, which will set out the requirements, milestones, deliverables and schedule for a re-use initiative or project. This initiative will need to be managed along the lines of other projects or initiatives in the firm. It is important that the performance and outcomes from any such initiative be assessed, with particular reference to the business need that stimulated the start of the process. Similarly it is important that lessons relevant to re-use processes in general are learnt, to enable the company to improve their re-use performance in future.

INDUSTRIAL CASE STUDIES

The re-use support process described above is intended to support a wide range of re-use aims, initiatives and decisions. Three generic examples of the re-use activities occurring in companies are given below. These are based on generalised data collected during the industrial consultation and illustrate the potential application of the process proposed.

1. A multinational company involved in the development, manufacture and distribution of chemical products for domestic and industrial use, identified a requirement to reduce the cost, time and effort associated with the design of a processing plant. Since similar modules are used in different applications it was possible to design these modules for re-use. Based on an analysis of current plant designs together with input from design and engineering experts, a high-quality database of processing modules was developed, incorporating detailed knowledge about the equipment. This database was integrated with other design support software, to enable engineers to incorporate the re-usable modules rapidly into

future designs. Improvements to the re-usable module designs can be added to the library as new systems are developed.

Key re-use issues include how to decide which modules should be included in the database, what information should be stored, how to structure and manage the information, and how to ensure that the knowledge can be integrated into future design processes.

2. Designers in a firm that develops scientific instrumentation are frequently faced with the decision as to whether a particular component or design from existing systems should be re-used in a new product. In each case a range of options are available, including developing a totally new design, re-using the existing design or component completely without modification, or a range of possible ways of re-using parts of the design or sub-components.

Key re-use issues include how to identify and compare the various design options in terms of benefits and risks. In this situation the design decisions that follow on from this can be addressed within the normal development process, although the possibility of future re-use should be considered if the 'totally new' option is selected.

3. A contract research and consulting organisation specialising in materials processing technology undertakes a wide range of multidisciplinary projects that require teams to be assembled quickly to tackle customers' problems. Being able to rapidly and efficiently locate technological knowledge, in terms of past projects and individual expertise, is a crucial issue if the firm is to exploit its intellectual capital fully. Many knowledge and information management systems could be used to support these objectives, ranging from complete enterprise resource planning solutions to the development and support of informal organisational networks. Based on an assessment of benefits and costs, two simple approaches were adopted, comprising a combination of a 'who knows' document, and a searchable electronic report archiving system. These systems were chosen because they delivered the desired benefits at a low cost, but also with little disruption or administrative burden to the project teams.

Key re-use issues include how to identify the knowledge in the organisation that has high value, and the technological and human factors that enable that value to be exploited.

CONCLUSIONS

From this work we can draw a number of conclusions:

- Re-use concepts from engineering and software can be applied to a wide range of types of technology and knowledge.
- Non-explicit assets are important if a firm is to realise the full value of their assets.

- The concepts of a re-use framework and the identification of re-usable assets have been developed into a practical re-use process.
- The proposed process fits well with the reality of re-use within a wide range of companies.

Additional tools can be integrated into the re-use process as appropriate, and the next steps for this research will involve further testing of the developed process guidelines under the framework of procedural action research (Maslen & Lewis 1994). Particular issues that require further consideration are:

- The role of specific tools and metrics to quantify the benefits in advance of implementing a re-use system.
- Further development of the implementation support.

REFERENCES

Antelme, R.G., Moultrie, J. and Probert, D.R. (2000), 'Engineering Reuse: a framework for improving performance', *Proceedings of the IEEE ICMET Conference*, Singapore, 12-17 November 2000.

Blacker, F (1995) "Knowledge, Knowledge Work and Organisations" *Organization Studies*, **16**(6), pp. 1029-1046

Busby, J.S. (1998), 'Causal explanations of the absence of reuse in engineering design organisation', *Engineering Design Conference '98: Design Reuse*, Ed. Sivaloganathan S. and Shahin T.M.M. pp 475-482.

Clausing D. (1991) 'Flexible Product Development', in *Proceedings of the Conference on Time-Based Competition: Speeding New Product Design and Development*, Vanderbilt University, Nashville, Tennessee 16-17 May 2000.

Coombs, R. and Hull, R. (1998), 'Knowledge management practices and path-dependency in innovation', *Research Policy*, July **27**(3) 237-253

Faulkner W. (1994), 'Conceptualizing knowledge used in innovation - a 2nd look at the science-technology distinction and industrial-innovation', Science, Technology and Human Val, **19**(4) 425-458

Fleck, J. and Tierney, M (1991), 'The management of expertise: knowledge, power and the economics of expert labour', Edinburgh PICT working paper 29, Research Centre for Social Science, University of Edinburgh.

Henderson R.M. and Clark K.B. (1990), 'Architectural Innovation: The Reconfiguration of Existing Product Technologies and the Failure of Established Firms', *Administrative Sciences Quarterly*, **35**(1), pp 9-30

Frakes W.B. (ed) (2000), *Proceedings of the sixth international conference on software reuse*, Vienna, June 27-29, 2000 Springer.

Jacobson, I.., Griss, M., Jonsson , P. (1997), *Software reuse: architecture process and organization for business success*, Addison Wesley Longman, New York.

Karlsson E-A. (ed) (1995), *Software reuse: a holistic approach*, Wiley, Chichester.

Krinninger A.U. (1995), A Financial Business Model for the Concept of Reusability in Strategic Product Development, unpublished MSc in Management dissertation, MIT.

Lim, W.C, *Managing software reuse*, Prentice Hall, Upper Saddle River, New Jersey 1998.

Maslen, R. and Lewis, M.A. (1994), Procedural action research, Working Paper for the Manufacturing and Management Division, Cambridge University Engineering Department, Cambridge University.

Meyer M.H. and Lehnerd A.P. (1997), *The power of product platforms: building value and cost leadership*, Free Press, New York.

Nobeoka, K. and Cusumano, M.A., (1995) 'Multiproject Strategy, Design Transfer, and Project Performance: A Survey of Automobile Development Projects in the US and Japan.', *IEEE Transactions on Engineering Management*, November, **42**(4), pp 397-409.

Poulin J.S. (1999), 'Reuse: Been There, Done That', *Communications of the ACM*, May, **42**(5). 98-100.

Prieto-Diaz, R. (1990), 'Domain analysis: an introduction', *Sigsoft Software Engineering Notes*, 15(2), April, pp.47-54

Rada R. (1995) *Software Reuse: principles, methodologies and practices*, Intellect, Oxford.

Robertson D. and Ulrich K. (1998), 'Planning for Product Platforms', *Sloan Management Review*, Summer 1998. pp 19-31.

Rothwell R. and Gardiner P. (1990), 'Robustness and Product Design Families' in *Design Management: A Handbook of Issues and Methods*, 1990, Oakley M (ed.), De Mozota B.B and Clipson C. (adv. ed.) pp 279-292

Reifer, D.J. (1997), *Practical software reuse: strategies for introducing re-use concepts in your organization*, Wiley Computer Publishing, Chichester

Sanderson, S.W. (1992), 'Design for Manufacturing in an Environment of Continuous Change', in *Integrating Design and Manufacturing for Competitive Advantage*, Susman, G.I. (ed.), Oxford, 1992. pp 36-55.

Schnabel, A., Leveraging reusability strategies in product development with product platforms and enhanced QFD, Working Paper for the Laboratory for Manufacturing and Productivity, MIT

Steele L.W. (1988), *Managing technology: the strategic view*, McGraw-Hill, London

Wheelwright S. and Clark K. (1992), 'Creating Product Plans to Focus Product Development', *Harvard Business Review*, March-April 1992. pp 70-82

Wheelwright S. and Sasser W. (1986) 'The New Product Development Map', *Harvard Business Review*, May-June 1986. pp 112-125.

Whipp R.,(1991), 'Managing technological changes: opportunities and pitfalls', International Journal of Vehicle Design, **12**,

Witter J.H., Clausing D.P. and Andrade R.S. (1994), Integration of Reusability and Interface Management into Enhanced Quality Function Deployment Methods, Working Paper for the Laboratory for Manufacturing and Productivity, MIT

Yahia, A. (1997), Strategic reusability planning and management in product development, unpublished MSc in mechanical engineering dissertation, MIT.

Yeung, C. and Holden, T. (2000), 'Knowledge Re-use as Engineering Re-use: extracting value from knowledge management', in *Proceeding of the 3rd International Conference on Practical Aspects of Knowledge Management*, Basel, Switzerland, 30-31 October 2000.

Yongbeom K., and Stohr E. (1988) 'Software Reuse: Survey and Research Directions', *Journal of Management Information Systems*, Spring, **14**(4), pp 133-147

19

TRAINS, CRANES AND DRAINS: CUSTOMER REQUIREMENTS IN LONG-TERM ENGINEERING PROJECTS AS A KNOWLEDGE MANAGEMENT PROBLEM

Neil Alderman, CURDS, University of Newcastle upon Tyne, UK[†,]*
Ian McLoughlin, University of Newcastle upon Tyne Business School, UK[**]
Chris Ivory, University of Newcastle upon Tyne Business School, UK[***]
Alfred Thwaites, CURDS, University of Newcastle upon Tyne, UK[****]
Roger Vaughan, University of Newcastle upon Tyne Business School, UK[*****]

[†] This research was funded by the joint UK research council Innovative Manufacturing Initiative Learning Across Business Sectors programme, through ESRC grant no. L700257003. We are particularly grateful to all participants in the project workshops and those who have spent time with the project team during the data collection process. Earlier versions of this paper were presented at the British Academy of Management Annual Conference, Edinburgh University, September, 2000 and the Tenth International Conference on Management of Technology, IAMOT, Lausanne, Switzerland, March, 2001.

[*] Dr. Neil Alderman is a Principal Researcher in the Centre for Urban and Regional Development Studies, University of Newcastle upon Tyne and a senior lecturer in the University of Newcastle upon Tyne Business School. Email: neil.alderman@ncl.ac.uk.
[**] Prof. Ian McLoughlin is Head of the University of Newcastle upon Tyne Business School. Email: i.p.mcloughlin@ncl.ac.uk.
[***] Chris Ivory is a lecturer in the University of Newcastle upon Tyne Business School. Email: c.j.ivory@ncl.ac.uk.
[****] Alfred Thwaites is a senior lecturer in the Centre for Urban and Regional Development Studies , University of Newcastle upon Tyne. Email: a.t.thwaites@ncl.ac.uk.
[*****] Roger Vaughan is a senior researcher in the University of Newcastle upon Tyne Business School. Email: roger.vaughan@ncl.ac.uk.

INTRODUCTION

It is evident that the relationship between customers for major engineering projects and their prime contractors is changing. Customers wish to take a diminishing share of the risk in a project by extending substantially the scope of supply to include the management, maintenance and updating of the operational phase of the project, and ultimately, perhaps, its decommissioning. This has created a shift in focus from the provision of a product to the delivery of a project composed of bundles of services, technologies and mechanisms of finance across the whole project life cycle, which in some cases may span several decades. Companies are building on existing project management experience to integrate a more complex range of activities in order to meet these new customer requirements. We have hypothesised elsewhere that this process represents a form of 'forced evolution' of traditional project management into what we have termed 'project integration' (McLoughlin *et al*, 2000).

This development, we suggest, will require radical changes in the capabilities of contractor organisations engaged in long-term engineering projects. This occurs not least through the need for contractors to procure new knowledge to cope with aspects of business and technology hitherto outside of their experience and expertise and thereafter to capture and embed the learning from the project in order to inform and benefit subsequent, and in practice parallel, activities. This creates a need for the development or acquisition of new knowledge in a variety of areas to deliver more complex customer requirements. Project integration involves project specifications that emerge from the development by the customer of a business proposition in a business plan that calls for a major engineering project. This proposition then has to be translated into a 'project scope' within which the project, its operation and its financing within the appropriate regulatory environment are broadly defined. Finally, the proposed project scope has to be decomposed into more detailed operational requirements for the design and assembly of the required project financing, project management, systems and technologies, operation and through-life support. This involves the development and application of strategies determining which aspects of the specification are sourced internally and which externally.

These challenges are illustrated in the context of three case studies of long-term engineering projects undertaken in the UK. The case studies are: firstly, a project to supply and maintain a fleet of high speed tilting trains for Virgin on the West Coast Main Line; secondly, the refurbishment, upgrading, operation and maintenance of wharf-side materials handling facilities for a steelworks in Argentina; and, thirdly, the design, construction and operation of a regional sludge treatment centre in the North East of England. The case studies are used to illustrate how new customer requirements create new challenges for knowledge management in a long-term project context.

THE CHANGING NATURE OF CUSTOMER REQUIREMENTS

Long-term engineering projects are typically encountered in the low volume or project-based industries. These projects are characterized by a customer organisation requesting a response from a contractor to a project specification (varying in detail from a detailed design through to a functional or cardinal point specification) and if successful with the bid, the delivery of the project to the satisfaction of the customer. In such industries projects are typically high cost, likely to be technologically complex, and each one is different. In such circumstances the project is arguably the most appropriate unit of analysis (Hobday, 1998) and project management skills can be seen as a generic competence (Winch, 2000). The outputs of such projects have been termed 'complex product systems' (CoPS) such as telephone exchanges, aircraft engines and so forth. Our cases of railway rolling stock, a sewage sludge treatment plant and wharf facilities for a steelworks also represent examples of this type.

However, it would be wrong to view the complexity of these projects purely in terms of their technical characteristics. For example, each complex long-term engineering project is likely to require new and substantially different intra- and inter-organisational relationships (alliances, supply chains, project teams etc.), technologies and financing, and to be carried out under different regulatory regimes. As Shapiro (1999) has noted, in such circumstances particular problems of knowledge management can be identified, especially in terms of learning from project to project and even between phases within the same project. At the same time, the mechanisms for learning that do exist are likely to be 'informal and haphazard' (Shapiro, 1999: 1). More generally, other research by the same research group has identified dependence upon suppliers and procurement difficulties; technical problems and uncertainties; organisation and project structure; and the management of requirements capture as key problem areas in developing complex product systems (Hansen and Rush, 1998). The latter issue represents a fundamental knowledge management issue for complex long-term projects.

In recent years there has been a shift in customer requirements in relation to many complex projects. Firstly, the customer now generally wishes to take a much-reduced share of the financial risk in the project. Secondly, the customer increasingly wishes the contractor to extend the scope of delivery to encompass responsibility for some or all of the management, maintenance and updating of the operational phase of the project, in part to maintain the residual value of the facility or equipment provided. Thirdly, they may wish the contractor to decommission and dispose of the project at the end of its life. The shift in customer requirements that is evident in projects such as the ones we are studying in this research may be caricatured in the following way:

> For the supplier, life used to be straightforward. The customer would send prospective suppliers a full specification. The supplier would bid, haggle on

terms and conditions, receive an order, subcontract what they could not do, deliver the product and walk away after the warranty period.

Today, the customer develops a business proposition to satisfy a market which the supplier has to understand as well as the customer. A response has to be constructed which involves the supplier in assembling innovative technologies, running an outsourced business on the customer's behalf, delivering the hardware and providing through life support with minimum risk and financial exposure to the customer.

These changes are being driven by, amongst other things, privatisation and associated new forms of regulation. Privatisation has removed from the market place many of the major 'public' clients (such as the National Coal Board, the Central Electricity Generating Board, or British Rail in the UK context) with the ability to finance large engineering projects. In their place has emerged a proliferation of private clients, many of which are entering the industry from very different backgrounds (witness again in the UK the takeover and merger activity amongst different utility companies, or the entry of bus operators into the rail market). Changed regulatory regimes have created new sources of competition as markets are opened up and have increased pressures for shorter delivery times, whilst at the same time increasing the complexity of the tendering process as contracts are placed for long-term concessions involving the supply, operation and maintenance of equipment.

Contractors may, therefore, find themselves integrating not simply the component systems of the project in order to deliver a complete 'product' (systems integration), but also a complex 'bundle' of products, services and systems (Gann and Salter, 2000) into an 'integrated solution' (Davies, 2001) in order to deliver the project through its entire life cycle. Critically, in such circumstances, the customer is concerned only with the output. This might be defined in terms of operational train miles over a certain time period in the case of railway rolling stock provision, or a specified tonnage of imported raw materials and exported finished product in case of the provision of handling facilities for a port. Typically, the provision of such a service will be contracted for a period of 10 years or more. The implication for the manufacturer is that more added value is perceived to lie in both the turnkey end of the business and in the through life support end, and revenues are increasingly found in the service component of such projects.

CUSTOMER REQUIREMENTS AS A KNOWLEDGE MANAGEMENT PROBLEM

Clearly, the sort of changes we have just outlined stand to move the traditional prime contractor into new areas of expertise and create new knowledge management issues for them. In such circumstances the 'project' becomes dominated by the need to understand the customer's own drivers, the necessary technologies and systems, the relevant suppliers, and knowledge about the commercial dimension to the project, particularly issues surrounding the financing of long-term concessions. Accordingly, for the provider of a complex long-term project, understanding the customer's requirements and identifying the most appropriate way of meeting those needs as perceived becomes a principal knowledge management task. This position is consistent with the concept from the marketing literature of market orientation, which refers to the behaviours required to create superior value for the customer (e.g. Narver and Slater, 1990; Kohli and Jaworski, 1990), one of which is a customer linking capability involving close communication and joint problem solving with the customer (Day, 1994). This literature, however, tends not to deal with this process as a knowledge management issue, nor does it focus on the particular context of the complex project, dealing instead primarily with repeat as opposed to one-off activities.

The satisfaction of changing customer requirements requires the acquisition and management of knowledge on an array of different fronts. These include: knowledge and understanding of what the customer wants and how those wants are changing (cf. Flint *et al*, 1997), of how to construct the package that will satisfy those wants, where and how to procure components of the package that can not be provided internally, and successful communication of this understanding within the organisation and to other project partners.

The conventional approach to knowledge management would conceptualise all of this as a problem of knowledge *capture* and of thence *transmitting* that knowledge through a more complex project structure. Solutions to such problems would focus on the development of procedures, tools, techniques and technological aids that facilitate capture and transmission. However, the problem for knowledge management research is that it is insufficient to regard knowledge as a 'given' commodity (Whitley, 2000) or 'asset' that can be acquired in the way that other material resources can and through similar means. As such, we prefer to see the issue here as one of the *production* and *consumption* of knowledge through a complex iterative process involving multiple actors and institutions whose relationships with each other are defined increasingly in terms of *networks* rather than markets or hierarchies. Project specifications are necessarily best developed in conjunction with the customer (Nellore *et al*, 1999). We therefore see 'knowledge' not as a 'given' but as continually negotiated and contested. Knowledge in this sense cannot be readily captured within a computer system and the problems that arise in attempting to achieve a match of expectations and understanding are largely people problems that have no easy technical fix.

For example, if knowledge concerning customer requirements were simply an artefact codified in the form of the customer's technical specification there would be a straightforward problem of knowledge transmission. However specifications, particularly, though by no means exclusively, those that deal with broad performance parameters rather than technical details, are not a foolproof guide to what the customer actually wants. Rather they are open to a high degree of interpretation, particularly when they are communicated from one context to another. Indeed, from this viewpoint, to occur at all, the transfer of knowledge of customer requirements across organisational boundaries *requires* acts of interpretation and re-interpretation. As Nonaka and Takeuchi (1995) argue, knowledge is created anew each time there is this exchange. However, contrary to Nonaka and Takeuchi (1995), we do not see knowledge as having somehow separable components of codified and tacit forms. Whilst some aspects of customer requirements are indeed codifiable in the form of specifications or project briefs, associated with this is always a tacit element that cannot be expressed in this way (Polanyi, 1966). The two components are intrinsically part of the same contextually dependent knowledge and understanding and cannot be separated in any meaningful way. The codified elements only constitute knowledge when interpreted within a particular context – knowledge is therefore contingent and there are serious limitations to the extent to which codification is possible (Marshall and Sapsed, 2000).

In the sorts of projects we are concerned with, this interpretation occurs within many different contexts such that there is no guarantee of any shared understanding between different organisations, actors and other agencies within the project network, nor indeed between different functions or actors within the same organisation (cf. Cohen and Levinthal, 1990). Knowledge is therefore something that resides within the individuals performing specific tasks: those preparing the specifications; those reviewing the bid; those drawing up the tender documentation and so forth. Knowledge is thus best conceptualised not as a commodity to be acquired or transferred, but as the context-specific outcome of a continual process (Blackler *et al*, 1998). Furthermore, as Blackler (1993) has argued, knowledge arises from 'the interplay of actions, language, technologies, social structures, implicit and explicit rules, history and institutions' (Blackler, 1993: 882). In this respect, it also has a 'local' character arising from the norms and conventions of conducting business in a specific national context, say, or sectoral, as a result of being embedded within a particular sector of industrial activity, such as the railway industry. The process of interpreting customer requirements will intrinsically reflect the 'local' character of knowledge in this way.

All of this indicates that there is a considerable potential for a mismatch – understood as different and potentially competing interpretations – between, for example, the customer's understanding of what they require and that of the contractor or their suppliers (Harland, 1996). We would suggest that organisations moving into long-term projects with the kind of characteristics we have discussed will quickly reach the limit of their internal competencies. Indeed, the paradox of 'core rigidities' means that it may be difficult for them to develop the necessary level of expertise in new areas of activity (Leonard-Barton, 1992). Such organisations and their collaborators will need to engage in a complex process of network building and maintenance in order to pull together the different capabilities needed (McLoughlin *et al*, 2001). For example, knowledge and understanding of what it is the project is trying to achieve will need to be shared between different network partners in order to ensure that the customer's requirements are understood and reflected in the product/service delivery at all levels of the network and supply chain throughout the project life cycle. The management of these network interfaces where knowledge production and consumption takes place becomes a critical task and activity of project management.

Something of what may be involved here is reflected in our recursive value model (Alderman *et al*, 1997). This attempts to represent the iterative process the contractor goes through in conjunction with the client, its suppliers and other agents, in interpreting the customer's requirements, Fig. 19.1. The recursive nature of this model emphasises the findings of Jenkins (1996), which suggest that it is the linkage between the customer and organisational actions that leads to performance outcomes as opposed to a 'customer focus;' *per se*. In this paper we focus on that part of the project activity that deals with the relationship between the manufacturer and the client, items [1] to [5] in Fig. 19.1.

The recursive nature of the model implies that this is a continual process where knowledge is a contextually defined outcome of interactions in the project network at any given point in the iterations which occur through the project life cycle.

We posit that the different knowledge requirements that arise during these iterations include the following:

- *Knowing who*? It is by no means obvious in long-term projects who 'the customer' is. The 'customer' often decomposes into a complex of different elements. A key distinction is between the 'client' – the organisation that places the order for the project – and other 'customers'. These may, for instance be end users or consumers (such as rail travellers), they may be intermediaries that the supplying organisation is contracted to, or they may be internal customers – the corporate board or another unit within the parent organisation. At the same time different actors, functions and organisations may give more or less priority to these definitions. Who the customer is at any point in time with regard to a particular part of the project may well be a contested issue in itself.

- *Knowing what*? The interpretation of customer requirements, particularly when they are subject to significant shifts or re-definition, requires a prior and parallel understanding on the part of the potential contractor of the dynamics of the customer's own business environment and their strategic response to it. Understanding the business imperatives underlying any project specification is a key element in coming to a view as to what the customer actually wants or needs. Again, such understandings are not easily acquired, especially where the changes concerned are generative of new market opportunities for contractors who are thereby seeking to understand rather different customer business contexts and responses from those they are conventionally used to.

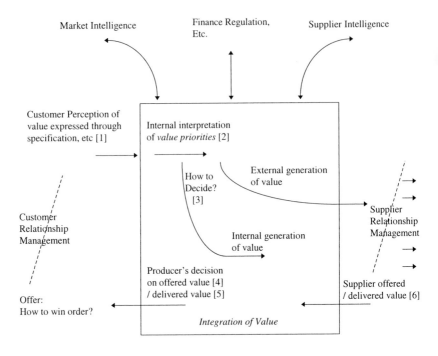

Fig 19.1. Recursive Value Model (Source: Alderman et al (1997)).

- *Knowing how?* Customer requirements for complex products delivered through long-term projects not surprisingly generate complex specifications. Decomposing these complex specifications, identifying where they may have gaps or be inarticulate in some aspect, are key interpretative processes. Similarly, defining and articulating the appropriate response, for example whether to 'make or buy', how to spread and share the risk of undertaking the project with key suppliers of systems, components, services or advice, again present points at which differing viewpoints and understandings may compete and require some resolution.

- *Knowing where and when?* To deliver value to the customer the contractor, and/or some other combination of partners within the project network, needs to successfully plot a trajectory and navigate through project space/time – what Winch (2000) terms 'riding the project wave'. It is here that some of the key 'within project' learning issues arise. Knowledge created has to be embedded in the planning and procurement processes as well as the processes of manufacturing, sub-contracting, operation and maintenance. In turn this knowledge will be consumed at subsequent points and in different contexts by those elements within the project network responsible for planning, procuring manufacturing, sub-contracting, operating, maintaining and disposing of the project. Again, the issues of interpretation, contestation and negotiation of customer requirements loom large.

- *Knowing why?* The networks required to deliver long-term projects to customers have to be built and maintained over-time. This is a multi-layered activity drawing in part upon well-established project management tools, techniques and so on. Such techniques enable – in principle at least – those engaged in project management to 'know' whether the project is meeting its plan, budget and operational performance and if not then the causation and the means by which its course can be corrected. However, arguably, effective management of long-term projects, like other forms of 'vulnerable project', requires an 'extended toolkit' for those involved (Boddy and Buchanan, 1993; also Buchanan and Badham, 1999). Here project mangers need to know less easily measured and tangible things. They need, for example, to know how to communicate and manage relationships with other network members and to be able to manage the diversity of interests and organisational cultures and sub-cultures which are necessarily brought together in long-term projects. Knowing how to manage with power and through politics, arguably become key elements of the 'extended tool kit' of long-term project management.

This latter knowledge management issue – a key activity of the 'project integrator' role identified above - is not considered here.

TRAINS, CRANES AND DRAINS: THE CASE STUDY PROJECTS

In this section we draw on some of the findings from the three case study projects. Our approach to exploring these issues constitutes a detailed analysis of what it is that the organisations, networks and the institutions, actors and technologies and other material resources that constitute them, actually do (Coombs and Hull, 1998). Shapiro's (1999) review of the literature on learning/knowledge management issues notes the paucity of research in the area of the capital goods projects in general. Our aim to is start to redress this problem by examining the specific case of long-term engineering projects. Accordingly, given the state of current understanding in this area, our methodology provides 'rich' or 'thick' descriptions of the knowledge management issues in this currently under researched and far from fully understood area where nevertheless significant practical and more conceptual insights might be gained.

The Northumbrian Water case study focused on a recently opened Regional Sludge Treatment Centre (RSTC) at Bran Sands on Teesside, a multi-million pound capital project involving the procurement and management of a range of technologies previously unfamiliar to the organisation. The project entailed the assemblage and management of a network of over 15 key contractors and other organisations, involving a mix of construction and manufacturing inputs. It also extends beyond this to involve the sources of raw material input to the treatment centre and the output of a final product in the form of an inert pelletised material for a range of potential users.

Clarke Chapman (at the time of the study, part of Rolls Royce Materials Handling) is a capital goods producer traditionally engaged in the manufacture and supply of mechanical handling equipment. It perceived its market opportunities to be growing in the area of 'build, operate, transfer' or 'refurbish, operate, transfer' projects involving a long-term facilities management contract with major port operators. The research investigated a project involving not just the supply of materials handling equipment, but also the financing, operation, maintenance and management of a complete wharf facility for a South American steelworks over a 12 year concession period. In order to acquire knowledge of port facility operation and management, Clarke Chapman entered into a joint venture with Portia, the consultancy arm of Mersey Docks and Harbour Company.

The long-term nature of contracts for ALSTOM Transport, our third company, reflects the fact that train operators are no longer seeking to purchase rolling stock alone from the manufacturer. They are looking to procure 'rail miles' or train availability over an extended period. For the train manufacturer a new capability requirement is the facility to carry out rolling stock maintenance and the knowledge that accompanies this. The study centred on the contract to design, manufacture and maintain high speed tilting trains for the West Coast Main Line, operated by Virgin Trains, a project incorporating high levels of risk and uncertainty and exacting performance targets.

The case studies were undertaken through in-depth interviews with senior managers and other staff engaged on the projects. Through these internal interviews, other key actors were identified and the research used a 'snowball' approach to build up a picture of the project network, through the supply chain, back to the ultimate customer and to other intermediaries that were involved in the project. The research also used the mechanism of inter-company workshops to explore key issues, one of which concerned the current topic of identifying and interpreting customer requirements. In the following section, a number of key knowledge management issues that have emerged as important in the context of long-term engineering projects are highlighted.

KNOWLEDGE MANAGEMENT ISSUES IN THE CASE STUDY PROJECTS

Knowing who is the customer?

Understanding who the customer actually is in complex long-term projects proved not to be a straightforward issue, as we intimated it might above. In the case of the projects we studied, which being long-term are still ongoing, the client for Clarke Chapman is SIDERAR, the Argentinean steel maker; for ALSTOM it is Virgin Trains; and in the case of the Regional Sludge Treatment Centre (RSTC) the client is Northumbrian Water itself. In all three cases there are other 'customers'. Clarke Chapman was contracted to the Joint Venture company SOM SA in Argentina for the supply of equipment. West Coast Traincare Ltd, which assumes responsibility for the maintenance of the Pendolino fleet, had an input into the design of the train. The leasing company (or ROSCO), Angel Train Contracts, which will own the trains, has a clear interest in the residual value of the rolling stock. For the capital investment team at Northumbrian Water Limited, the Board of Northumbrian Water is effectively their customer. In the RSTC project there are also customers in the form of industrial effluent producers whose effluent is processed by the Bran Sands Effluent Treatment Works (ETW) and resultant sludge by the RSTC. The latter two cases also provide instances where it is possible to regard the consumer as an ultimate customer. Rail users are the customers of the train operator and their views and requirements are reflected in the requirements of the client. In the water industry the consumer may be considered to be represented by the regulator, Ofwat. The regulator in this instance imposes considerable constraints and stipulations on the water company regarding water quality, return on investment and so forth, which have had to be taken into account in the RSTC project.

Each 'customer' has a different perspective and set of requirements that need to be managed and possibly reconciled. This can lead to problems, since different parts of the organisation (engineering, marketing, and procurement for instance) interact with different 'customers', or with different parts of the client organisation. Evidence was found of how the promises made by one group within the organisation were sometimes difficult to meet for another group. Because of this it is not always clear to everyone who the customer actually is. Moreover, the contract entered into by the supplier may not be with the ultimate client. Knowledge of who the customer is and who therefore has the ultimate say in relation to the acceptance or otherwise of the delivered 'product' is critical to the process of meeting those requirements to the client's satisfaction. These problems of alignment are often found to arise when some part of the contextual framework for understanding the customer's requirements is missing, as for example when a supplier with no prior experience of the industry is brought into the project network (Lamming, 1993; Nellore *et al*, 1999).

Knowing what: interpreting the client's 'vision'

One of the implications of the shift identified earlier is that the project specification contains much less technical detail than it would have in the past. This is a consequence of new entrants to an industry that do not possess the same technical capability as previous players. For example, train operating companies are interested in moving people, not in the engineering expertise required to design or maintain a train. Similarly, in the Argentinean steelworks case, the steel producer is not really interested in procuring and operating sophisticated materials handling equipment. Its core competence is steel production and steel products. In extreme cases what the client seems to be expressing is not so much a specification as a 'vision'. This vision may be encapsulated in a broad business plan. The job of the contractor is thus to interpret this vision and to come up with the detailed technical specification that best meets it. The nature of the interaction with the client is therefore rather different from the days when the tender negotiation involved engineers from both parties exchanging technical documents and verifying each other's calculations.

For the client, what matters is what the 'product' does, not how it does it. In terms of the design process, Virgin has interacted with ALSTOM through a document known as the 'Red Book'. This represents in essence an aspirational design, comprising, amongst other things, a series of visual images that capture what it is the client wants the train to look like and (just as importantly) what it should not look like. This approach is reminiscent of the way many architects interact with clients. The Red Book is thus an important mechanism for managing the process of conveying customer requirements.

Part of Clarke Chapman's approach to this issue of dealing with a vision or business plan from the client is to bring its detailed knowledge and expertise in materials handling to the project specification at the negotiation stage. When a potential client has no real expertise in port operations, but is merely concerned with achieving certain levels of throughput, the initial specification or requirement may be sub-optimal. The negotiation process involves Clarke Chapman in educating the client about what is possible and the most efficient way of achieving their business objectives. The company often offer improvements to the client's original specification with possible reductions in project cost. In this way the customer requirements are shaped by the contractor.

Given the long-term commitment of the contractor and the importance of future revenue streams from the operations and/or maintenance phase of the project, it has been recognised that customer expectations need to be managed carefully. There is a danger of creating too high a level of expectation. Moreover, visual impressions of the project offering, which may be created as part of the bidding process and become instilled in the client's mind, must be technically feasible if additional design and/or manufacturing cost is not to be built in.

Knowing how to deliver the customer's vision: the role of new technology

In our three projects much of this issue focused on how to procure the new technologies and associated 'know-how' required to deliver the projects. There are a number of factors affecting technological choices and creating demands for increasingly sophisticated technology. All three projects demonstrate this in some way. New regulatory demands led Northumbrian Water to commission a design competition amongst four prospective tenderers to identify the most appropriate technological solution for sludge treatment, given the directive to cease the dumping of sludge at sea and the unacceptability to the planning authorities of incineration as a disposal strategy. The resulting design of the RSTC is technologically sophisticated, but through the design competition the company has acquired considerable knowledge of sludge drying processes and the available technologies, enabling it to make a much more informed procurement decision than would otherwise have been the case.

For the upgrade of rolling stock for the West Coast Main Line, Virgin specified tilting train technology to enable it to achieve 140mph running and make substantial inroads into the journey times and train frequencies on that route. At the time of the bid ALSTOM did not possess a tilting technology of its own, so it entered into a joint venture with Fiat Ferroviaria in Italy to apply the tried and tested Pendolino tilting technology, although this technology still required considerable modification and adaptation to suit the rather different operating conditions of the WCML. ALSTOM has subsequently acquired a majority holding in Fiat Ferroviaria to give it effective control over this particular capability.

The long-term considerations of efficiency and maintainability also influence technological choices. Sophisticated control systems on the ship unloaders supplied by Clarke Chapman for the Argentinean steelworks are a crucial contributor to the improvement of port handling efficiencies. In this project the company decided to develop the control system technology in-house in order to build up its internal capability in this critical area. This decision reflected a trade-off between a possible over-reliance on external (and powerful) suppliers and the resources needed to complete the development within the project timeframe.

Knowing where and when: the role of intermediaries

The complexity of the long-term projects we are studying gives rise to a breadth and depth of knowledge requirements that neither the client, not the contractor, possess in their entirety. Consequently, we have found that intermediaries are an important source of knowledge and expertise in a whole variety of areas: financial, legal, commercial, technical, design and so forth. More importantly, intermediaries also act as arbiters in the interpretation of customer requirements, For example, on the West Coast Main Line project, Virgin used the designer Priestman Goode for the interior concept design, and ALSTOM subsequently contracted with Jones Garrard for detailed interior design work (Modern Railways, 2000).

Consultants also play an important role in interpreting regulations for the client, verifying technical specifications provided by the manufacturer and acting as the engineering interface. It is clear that our recursive value model is over simplistic in its portrayal of the interfaces between client and contractor. There are multiple interfaces at which information exchange occurs and when knowledge is created or transformed.

Finance forms a crucial part of the package in these projects, and financial intermediaries have been quick to recognise the opportunities for financial services provided by long-term engineering project. Financial knowledge is again something that has to be procured in some way and the involvement of these financial organisations adds to the contractual and network complexity of the project. The ability to offer a financial package is increasingly recognised as a source of competitive advantage in capital goods projects (Hutcheson *et al*, 1996) as the client either cannot or does not wish to use its own capital to finance the project.

Intermediaries can also be an invaluable mechanism for capturing the 'local' knowledge that is needed to operate projects in unfamiliar environments. Thus, Clarke Chapman relied on local consultants to advise and interpret the legal, tax and business culture regulations and norms in Argentina. Through having staff on-site in Argentina, much of the local custom of conducting business, together with an appreciation of the local regulatory environment, was effectively internalised and this comprised an important aspect of the learning on the project. It also enabled the company to recognise that procedures and principles that would be taken for granted in the British context were not known or understood by the local operatives and this fed through into issues such as the man-machine interface design.

DISCUSSION AND CONCLUSIONS

Long-term engineering projects involving complex products, shaped by changing customer and sometimes regulatory requirements, and delivered through collaborative networks involving many key interfaces, provide a fertile context in which to explore issues of knowledge management and organisational learning. This is particularly so in the kinds of project-based low volume capital-goods and construction industries which provide the focus of our three case studies. Customer requirements form a major source of dynamism in these projects and represent a critical knowledge management issue for the contracting organisation.

The case studies have furnished a rich picture of the conduct of complex long–term engineering projects. From our analysis thus far we offer the following tentative conclusions. First and foremost, we would question the conceptualisation of knowledge management as a process of knowledge capture and transmission. The case studies suggest that this is a partial and potentially misleading conceptualisation. There are also important issues of knowledge production and consumption. Customer requirements are not entirely clear to the customer let alone the contractor and other network actors. The process by which these are defined is not a one-off activity and there is a significant degree of interpretation, contestation and negotiation involved, which is amplified by the presence of intermediaries. In order to understand the implications of changing customer requirements it is necessary to understand the process of knowledge production and consumption through the iterative processes of the project life-cycle.

The case studies also raise questions concerning whether knowledge management should be regarded as a distinct discipline or just the latest management fashion (Scarbrough and Swan, 2001). Knowledge management in these complex long-term projects is embedded in day to day project routines. It does not appear useful at this stage to attempt to separate out knowledge management as a standalone discipline as it is draws attention away from the process of knowledge creation and use. Improvements in knowledge management on complex projects are unlikely to come about through dedicated knowledge management projects (Davenport *et al*, 1998), but as an integral part of more general improvements to the conduct and management of complex long-term projects. Ultimately, and this relates to the issue of 'knowing why' which we have not explored in this paper, the knowledge management problem is one of managing the frameworks within which individuals make sense of customer requirements that are codified in the form of specifications or other documents or media, so that a consistent interpretation is achieved. In long-term engineering projects this implies a change from the 'walk away at the end of the warranty period' mentality. We would suggest that such a shift in 'mind-set' requires the exercise by project managers and others of considerable political activity as network builders and maintainers.

In all cases, the networks of organisations that are involved in these projects are becoming more complex and more sophisticated. As more capabilities need to be acquired or outsourced, the issue of where in the network the critical knowledge resides becomes more pertinent. Integrators can no longer carry all the knowledge that they need in house. At the same time they must manage access to that knowledge. At a strategic level, decisions about knowledge procurement seem to be relatively straightforward. There are not too many options. It is interesting to note that in two of our case studies the knowledge management issue in terms of interpretation and understanding of new knowledge is effectively circumvented through the mechanism of the joint venture. This allows new knowledge and capability to be brought to the project without any immediate need for the contractor to assimilate that knowledge internally. Thus, joint staffing of the SOM SA joint venture company in Argentina allowed Clarke Chapman to concentrate on the refurbishment and installation of materials handling equipment and Portia to deal with the day to day operations and port management. Similarly, Fiat Ferroviaria has complete responsibility for the body shell, bogies and tilting technology on the Pendolino, which are delivered fully manufactured and ready for assembly at ALSTOM's Washwood Heath facility, and a specialist team from Italy has carried out testing of the tilt mechanism at Washwood Heath.

More pressing knowledge management problems seem to emerge in terms of the need to align different internal disciplines and external suppliers with the client's requirements. These difficulties stem from the different objectives that different functions or operational units within the organisation have and the different interpretative frameworks that each uses. Partly, it reflects on the variety of different customers that different parts of the organisation perceive themselves to be working for. Partly it reflects conflicting requirements that arise because of the division of long-term projects into a manufacture and supply side and an operate/maintain side. The latter requires attention to through life costs and design for maintainability, while first cost and subsequent spares business may drive the former. When the same organisation is responsible for both aspects of the project, which previously would not have been the case, these objectives are mutually incompatible.

Problems of alignment also arise for 'cultural' reasons. The change in the nature of the client and client requirements can change the nature of the relationship that disciplines such as engineering or procurement have to a project. New customer requirements require a change of thinking, a new approach to design or procurement problems, for example, and there is inevitably a transition period as individuals come to terms with changed circumstances and possibly a new *raison d'etre*. Ensuring that individuals learn and understand the requirements of new long-term engineering projects is perhaps the major knowledge management task facing organisations in this kind of business environment.

BIBLIOGRAPHY

Alderman, N., Maffin, D., Thwaites, A., Vaughan, R., Braiden, P. and Hills, W. (1997): Providing Customer Value: A Business Process Analysis Approach. In: *Managing Enterprises - Stakeholders, engineering, logistics and achievement* (D.T. Wright *et al* eds.), pp 203-209. London, Mechanical Engineering Publications Ltd.

Blackler, F. (1993): Knowledge and the theory of organisations: organisations as activity systems and the reframing of management. *Journal of Management Studies*, **30**, 863-884.

Blackler, F., Crump, N. and McDonald, S. (1998): Knowledge, organisations and competition. In: *Knowing in Firms: Understanding, managing and measuring knowledge* (G. von Krogh, J. Roos and D. Kleine eds.), pp 67-86. London, Sage.

Boddy, D. and Buchanan, D. (1992): *The Expertise of the Change Agent*. London, Prentice-Hall.

Buchanan, D. and Badham, R. (1999): *Power, Politics and Organisational Change: Winning the Turf War*. London, Sage.

Cohen, W.M. and Levinthal, D.A. (1990): Absorptive capacity: a new perspective on earning and innovation. *Administrative Science Quarterly*, **35**, 128-152.

Coombs, R. and Hull, R. (1998): Knowledge management practices and path dependency. *Research Policy*, **27**, 237 - 253.

Davenport, T.H., De Long, D.W. and Beers, M.C. (1998): Successful knowledge management projects. *Sloan Management Review,* **39**, 43-57.

Davies, A. (2001): *Integrated Solutions: the new economy between manufacturing and services.* Brighton, SPRU, University of Sussex.

Day, G.S. (1994): The capabilities of market-driven organisations. *Journal of Marketing,* **58**, (4) 35-52.

Flint, D.J., Woodruff, R.B. and Gardial, S.F. (1997): Customer value change in industrial marketing relationships: a call for new strategies and research. *Industrial Marketing Management,* **26**, 163-175.

Gann, D.M. and Salter, A.J. (2000): Innovation in project-based, service-enhanced firms: the construction of complex products and systems. *Research Policy,* **29**, 955-972.

Hansen, K.L. and Rush, H. (1998): Hotspots in complex product systems: emerging issues in innovation management. *Technovation,* **18** (8/9), 555-561.

Harland, C. (1996): Supply chain management: relationships, chains and networks. *British Journal of Management,* **7**, Special Issue, S63-S80.

Hobday, M. (1998): Product complexity, innovation and industrial organization. *Research Policy,* **26**, 689-710.

Hutcheson, P., Pearson, A.W. and Ball, D.F. (1996): Sources of technical innovation in the network of companies providing chemical process plant and equipment. *Research Policy,* **25**, 25-41.

Jenkins, M. (1996): Making sense of customers: an evaluation of the role of the customer in the subjective strategies of senior managers. *Journal of Strategic Marketing,* **4**, 95-115.

Kohli, A.K. and Jaworski, B.J. (1990): Market orientation: The construct, research propositions, and managerial implications. *Journal of Marketing,* **54** (2), 11-18.

Lamming, R. (1993): *Beyond partnership: strategies for innovation and lean supply.* London, Prentice Hall.

Leonard-Barton, D. (1992): Core capabilities and core rigidities: a paradox in managing new product development. *Strategic Management Journal,* **13**, 111-125.

McLoughlin, I.P., Koch, C. and Dickson, K. (2001): 'What's this "tosh"'?: Innovation networks and new product development as a political process. *International Journal of Innovation Management,* **5**, 275-298.

McLoughlin, I.P., Alderman, N., Ivory, C.J., Thwaites, A. and Vaughan, R. (2000): Knowledge Management in Long-term Engineering Projects. Paper presented at the Knowledge Management: Concepts and Controversies Conference, Warwick University, 10-11 February.

Marshall, N. and Sapsed, J. (2000): The limits of disembodied knowledge: challenges of inter-project learning in the production of complex products and systems. Paper presented at the Knowledge Management: Concepts and Controversies Conference, Warwick University, 10-11 February.

Modern Railways (2000): West Coast Route Modernisation. Modern Railways Special Report, June.

Narver, J.C. and Slater, S.F. (1990): The effect of a market orientation on business profitability. *Journal of Marketing,* **54** (4), 20-35.

Nellore, R., Soderquist, K., Siddall, G. and Motwani, J. (1999): Specifications - Do We Really Understand What They Mean? *Business Horizons,* November-December, 63-69.

Nonaka, I. and Takeuchi, H. (1995): *The Knowledge-Creating Company*. New York. Oxford University Press.

Polanyi, M. (1966): *The Tacit Dimension*. London, Routledge and Kegan Paul.

Scarbrough, H. and Swan, J. (2001): Explaining the diffusion of knowledge management: the role of fashion. *British Journal of Management*, **12**, 3-12.

Shapiro, G. (1999): Inter-project knowledge capture and transfer: an overview of definitions, tools and practices. CoPS Innovation Centre Working Paper No 62. Brighton.

Whitley, E. (2000): Tacit and explicit knowledge: conceptual confusion around the commodification of knowledge. Paper presented at the Knowledge Management: Concepts and Controversies Conference, Warwick University, 10-11 February.

Winch, G. (2000): The Management of Projects as a Generic Business Process. In: *Projects as Guiding Motives for Business* (A. Lundin, F. Hartman, and C. Navarre, eds.) pp 11-130. Dordrecht, Kluwer.

SECTION III

MULTI-ACTOR
INNOVATION

Management of Technology
Copyright © 2003 by Elsevier Science Ltd.
All rights of reproduction in any form reserved.
ISBN: 0-08-044136-X

20

INTELLECTUAL PROPERTY POLICIES AND UNIVERSITY-INDUSTRY LICENSING

Kate Hoye, University of Waterloo, Waterloo, Ontario, Canada[†,*]
Peter Roe, University of Waterloo, Waterloo, Ontario, Canada[**]

INTRODUCTION

University research has been identified as an important and sustainable source of a nation's economic growth (Gu and Whewell, 1999). It is particularly important in Canada where the universities are the second largest performers of research and development (Gu and Whewell, 1999). This realization has prompted a sharp increase in interest in university-industry technology transfer. An expert panel has recommended that the federal government institutes sweeping policy changes in order to promote the commercialization of university research (Expert Panel on the Commercialization of University Research, 1999) and these recommendations have fuelled an intense public debate.

Ideally, the actors in this critical debate would have access to copious research into university-industry technology transfer. Unfortunately, little appears to be known about several of the key relationships in this area. For example, many of the proposed federal policy changes would influence university intellectual property policies. These university policies were the target of the proposed changes because they are widely expected to be a significant predictor of

---

[†] This research was supported by an NSERC PGS-A scholarship. An earlier version of this research was presented at the ASAC 2001 conference in London, Ontario.

[*] Kate Hoye is a doctoral student in Systems Design Engineering at the University of Waterloo, located in Ontario, Canada. Email: kahoye@uwaterloo.ca.

[**] Dr. Peter Roe is a professor in Systems Design Engineering at the University of Waterloo, located in Ontario, Canada. Email: phoroe@uwaterloo.ca.

university researcher involvement with technology transfer activities and because they are one of the few aspects of the university environment which can be easily changed by administrators (Conceição *et al.*, 1998; Hairston *et al.*, 1998; Jaffe, 2000; Lee, 1996; McQueen and Wallmark, 1991; Petrick *et al.*, 1995/1996; Stevens and Bagby, 1999; Young-Kreeger, 2000). However, little work has been done in this area and prior investigations into this relationship have been inconclusive (Canadian University Intellectual Property Group, 1999; Jaffe, 2000). This investigation into the link between university intellectual property policies and university-industry technology licensing at Canadian universities is intended to begin to fill this gap.

CONTEXT

The Canadian University System

The Canadian university system is a good one in which to study the relationship between university intellectual property (IP) policy and university-industry technology licensing for three reasons. First, the vast majority of the post-secondary institutions are public universities that share the same mandate. Second, these institutions are maintained by relatively consistent funding systems. Third, they exhibit a wide diversity of IP policies.

In Canada, the term university refers to public, post-secondary, degree granting institutions. These universities vary from small liberal arts universities with less than three thousand students to large, multi-location institutions offering a wide range of undergraduate, graduate and professional degrees to over fifty thousand students. However, all Canadian universities are subject to the same three mandates: education, research, and community service. The public universities not only provide access to the majority of degree granting programs but also perform approximately one-quarter of the nation's research (CICIC, 2000).

These institutions are governed by and receive most of their operational funding through the provincial governments. The federal government provides funds for operating costs indirectly by providing transfer payments to the provinces and provides funds for research expenses directly, primarily through the three federal research granting councils (CICIC, 2000). The funding for the direct costs of university research is provided by the universities (35.7%), the federal government (28.8%), the provincial government (11.4%), industry (11.8%), private non-profit investors (11.1%) and foreign investors (1.3%) (Gu & Whewell, 1999). This structure implies that Canadian universities can be considered to receive comparable levels of operational funding and to compete for research funding on a relatively level playing field. This reduces the risk that an analysis of the levels of technology transfer activity across the universities will be contaminated by factors external to the universities.

In spite of sharing a mandate and being maintained by consistent funding systems, Canadian universities exhibit a wide variety of IP policies. In a recent Statistics Canada survey, university administrators were asked how the IP policies at their universities allocated ownership of the various kinds of IP. The university administrators reported that many schools allow researchers to own entirely or jointly the IP they created using university resources. This is in stark comparison with a number of other countries. For example, in the United States, all but three universities retain the rights to IP developed by their faculty using their resources (Bowers & Leon, 1994). Therefore, a Canadian investigation of the influence of IP policies on university-industry licensing is expected to be of international interest.

University Intellectual Property Policies

University policies are a component of the contract between the university and its faculty. They are legally binding documents that describe, among other things, both the type of technology transfer activities that university members can engage in and the distribution of the rewards from these activities. Some universities have a number of types of policy that govern technology transfer activities at the department or university level. However, this study was limited to IP policy, the most common type of university policy.

IP policies determine how the ownership of the patentable innovations arising from university research will be shared (Morrison and Wetzel, 1991) and may place restrictions upon the manner in which IP is obtained. Thus, they have significant potential to influence patenting and licensing of university innovations directly. Therefore, this study investigated the relationship between IP policies and the licensing of university technology.

Most university IP policies have a number of standard components. The policies typically acknowledge that the university has no legal claim to inventions that were developed by members of the university but without university support, such as use of university facilities, funds and personnel. Therefore, the innovations discussed in this study refer to innovations created with university support, unless it is noted otherwise. At the University of Waterloo, among many others, the university reserves the right to "royalty-free, non commercial use of developments, creations and data" resulting from university research (University of Waterloo, 2000).

Most IP policies state whether or not the institution claims ownership of university innovations or lets the ownership rest with the inventor. When the institution claims ownership of the innovation, inventors interested in commercialization of the device or process are required to make the innovation known to the appropriate university official(s). The university official or committee then determines whether or not the university is interested in pursuing commercialization possibilities. If the university does decide to pursue the technology transfer of the device or process it will typically keep the ownership of the IP, pay for the development of the IP, and arrange a revenue sharing contract with the inventor(s). The terms of the contract are either stipulated in the IP policy or negotiated on a case by case basis.

Most universities share any revenues resulting from the licensing of the IP once the direct costs of the IP development have been recovered. Six universities in Canada have introduced thresholds, above which, the inventor's share of the revenue decreases. For example, Memorial University has a three-level revenue sharing policy. When the university develops the IP, it receives all of the income from any associated licenses until the costs of developing the IP are covered. Beyond the repayment of the initial costs, the inventor will receive 50% of the next $200,000, 40% of the following $200,000 and 30% of the remaining revenues (Memorial University, 2000). One Canadian university employs the same revenue threshold concept, but beyond the threshold the university's share of the revenues diminishes. When Simon Fraser University is responsible for patenting and licensing university innovations, the university receives 50% of the revenues until the costs of developing the IP have been covered and 20% of any remaining revenues (Simon Fraser University, 2000). In all of the policies that specified a course of action, IP is granted to the inventor(s) in cases where the university official(s) decide that the university will not develop the IP.

When the institution allows the ownership of the innovation to rest with the inventor, the inventor can choose to ask the university to develop the IP if it offers this service. The process then duplicates the process when the university claims ownership of the IP. Inventor-owners can also choose to develop the IP independently or with the help of any third party. Most universities that allow inventor-ownership require that the inventor provide financial reports to the university. Some universities, including the University of Toronto, require that the inventor share the profits of independently developed IP with the university (University of Toronto, 2000).

Current university policies in Canada are very diverse. Some universities allow the inventor almost complete ownership over the innovation (Simon Fraser University, 2000; University of Waterloo, 2000). Other universities assume control of the commercialization process and claim the majority of the proceeds (Brock University, 2000; University of British Columbia, 2000; University of Victoria, 2000).

University Size, Type and Reputation

A university's ability to support technology transfer is naturally constrained by the degree to which the university's research produces patentable innovations. Larger universities have access to the research of more faculty members and thus are more likely to produce more patentable innovations. Universities that have more focus on research, as opposed to teaching, are more likely to produce patentable innovations. Finally, it is logical that universities with certain technologically intense programs like medicine, agriculture, engineering, computer sciences and the life sciences, are more likely to produce patentable innovations. Thus, when analyzing the relationship between university policies and university-industry technology transfer, the university size and type should be considered.

Technology transfer also depends on the support of a number of other organizations including the company or companies that commercialize the innovation, granting institutions, and venture capitalists. The university's reputation may influence the extent to which these organizations support technology transfer activities originating at that university.

University-Industry Technology Licensing

Technology transfer has been described as the formal process which moves the innovations resulting from university research into industry (AUTM, 2000). The licensing of IP is a well recognized form of technology transfer (AUTM, 1999; Boswell and Sauer, 1998; Gregory and Sheahen, 1991).

There are many different forms of technology related IP protection, including patents, industrial design registration, and material transfer agreements. All of the various forms of IP protection provide a successful applicant with legal rights to determine who can and cannot use the innovation for some fixed length of time. Patenting is the dominant form of university IP protection in Canada. It involves a lengthy and relatively expensive legal process that, if successful, provides the applicant with a protracted monopoly over the use of the technology in the country in which the patent is held (Statistics Canada, 2000). In 1999, Canadian universities reported holding 1,826 patents: 355 in Canada, 948 in the U.S. and the rest in other countries (Statistics Canada, 2000).

University licenses are contracts that allow the industry licensee to make use of university IP by using or selling some product or process. Unlike U.S. schools, Canadian universities have always had the right to grant exclusive licenses. An exclusive license guarantees that the same patent will not be licensed to any other entity thus ensuring that the licensee has acquired a legal monopoly on the right of use of the protected technology. This offers substantial incentive to adopt the new technology. In exchange for the license, the university and/or the researcher typically receive financial compensation (Boswell & Sauer, 1998).

Patenting and licensing is an important form of university-industry technology transfer because the temporary monopolies provided by patents allow researchers to provide licensees with a substantial incentive to adopt the innovation while simultaneously permitting the university researchers to publish their research (Conceição et al, 1998). Apart from being an important form of technology transfer in its own right, patenting and licensing are often incorporated in other forms of technology transfer. University technologies are sometimes patented by the university and licensed to spin-off companies. This approach allows the university to preserve the intellectual property in the event that the spin-off company fails. Patents are also used to transfer IP to organizations that commission contract research in a format that also allows the researcher can publish his or her results. In total, Canadian universities reported receiving $18.8 million in licensing revenues in 1999 (Statistics Canada, 2000).

Given that IP policies define the possible technology transfer activities and the rights and responsibilities of university members with respect to these activities, it is not surprising that university policies are a widely recognized factor in technology transfer (Conceição *et al.*, 1998; Hairston *et al.*, 1998; Jaffe, 2000; Lee, 1996; McQueen and Wallmark, 1991; Petrick *et al.*, 1995/1996; Stevens and Bagby, 1999; Young-Kreeger, 2000). In particular, the opportunity cost theory of technology transfer suggests that the extent to which researchers engage in an activity like technology licensing depends upon their evaluation of the merit of this activity relative to their academic, administrative and teaching activities (Bozeman, 2000). This is a significant point because, unlike employees in industry, researchers cannot be compelled to pursue projects that do not interest them (Canadian University Intellectual Property Group, 1999).

Media reports also appear to support the hypothesis that university policies influence the researcher's interest in engaging in technology transfer activities and thus alter the success of the institution as a whole. When the University of Toronto adopted a policy that granted more rights and rewards to the primary investigators, it seemed to revitalize that school's technology transfer (Piali, 1996). Interviews with researchers also supported this prediction by suggesting that researchers at inventor-owner institutions are deeply involved in technology transfer projects while researchers at institution-owner universities tend to be more peripherally involved (Piali, 1996).

In summary, preliminary evidence suggests that university IP policies do influence researcher support for technology licensing activities. However, the amount of licensing activity at a given university is also expected to be influenced by other university specific variables including university size, type and reputation.

DEVELOPING THE MODEL

A review of the Canadian universities' IP policies revealed that universities appear to offer their researchers two primary forms of incentives for patenting and licensing their inventions: sharing of licensing revenues and control of the commercialization process.

Many of these university IP policies have provisions for sharing licensing revenues with the university inventor(s). This financial incentive is generally received as personal income above and beyond regular salaries and research support. Licensing revenues for critical technologies are often in the millions of dollars; therefore, the financial gains of the researcher(s) may be quite significant. As a result, increased percentages of revenue sharing are expected to strongly increase the levels of technology licensing activity.

H1:   *Revenue sharing is positively related to the university's level of involvement in technology transfer activities.*

The literature indicates that researchers enjoy autonomy in the context of university-industry technology transfer (Daza Campbell and Slaughter, 1999). Therefore, policies that provide the researcher with more control over the technology transfer activities are expected to act as incentives. Some universities require researchers to provide the university with a 'right of first refusal'. If the university requires a right of first refusal, any researcher interested in commercializing an invention must describe the device to university administrators. If the university representative decides that the device or process seems promising, the university will develop the IP and attempt to commercialize the device. Other universities allow the researcher to choose between developing the IP independently and allowing the university to develop the IP. Since policies that do not reserve a right of first refusal increase the researcher's control over the technology transfer activity, they are expected to act as an incentive and thus result in higher levels of technology transfer activity.

H2:   *Researcher control is positively related to the university's level of involvement in technology transfer activities.*

University size, type and reputation are expected to influence the level of technology licensing activity supported by a university and thus are control variables in this study. The university's size and type tend to be highly correlated in Canada. Smaller institutions generally support fewer graduate programs or technologically intensive programs and thus can be expected to support even less technology licensing. Therefore, the university size and type will be collapsed into a single variable referred to as research intensity. The research intensity of the university is expected to change the availability of patentable technology and thus change the level of technology transfer activity.

H3:   *The research intensity of the university is positively related to the university's level of involvement in technology transfer activities.*

The university's reputation reflects its goodwill within the wider community. Therefore, a university's reputation is expected to influence the university's ability to interest potential licensees and the availability of other resources, including commercialization grants for prototyping activities or the availability of venture capital for university spin-off companies.

H4:   *The university's reputation is positively related to the university's level of involvement in technology transfer activities.*

Considered together, these hypotheses comprise a model of technology licensing. This model is summarized in the following figure.

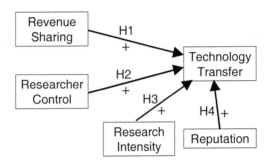

Fig. 20.1. The Relationship between IP Policy and University-Industry Licensing.

EVALUATING THE MODEL

Measures and Data Collection

In order to test this model, a cross-sectional study was conducted of the forty-eight degree-granting Canadian universities that are described by the Maclean's magazine annual university survey (Maclean's Magazine, 1999b). The study was limited to the universities that participate in the Maclean's survey because many of the other degree granting institutions are colleges or institutes that are affiliated with the major universities. These affiliates often rely on the larger institutions for a number of functions including technology transfer support services (Statistics Canada, 1999). Therefore, their inclusion would serve no purpose. Furthermore, limiting the study to those universities evaluated by Maclean's means that the magazine's ranking and categorization of the universities can be used to represent the two control variables: university reputation and university research intensity.

University research intensity: University research intensity was represented using the Maclean's categorization system for Canadian universities. This system represents universities as members of one of three groups. The Medical Doctoral group contains universities "with a broad range of Ph.D. programs and research, as well as medical schools" (Maclean's Magazine, 1999b). The Comprehensive category includes those universities that have "a significant amount of research activity and a wide range of programs at the undergraduate and graduate levels, including professional degrees" (Maclean's Magazine, 1999b). The Primarily Undergraduate universities are "largely focused on undergraduate education, with relatively few graduate programs" (Maclean's Magazine, 1999b). More specific measures of the research intensity of the top university in each category are detailed in the following table, to give the reader a general understanding of the universities represented by each category.

Table 20.1. Examples of the Different Levels of Research Intensity.

Category	University	Number of Full-time Faculty	Faculty with PhDs (%)	Social Sciences & Humanities Grants*	Science & Medicine Grants*
Medical-Doctoral	Toronto	6,200	97.3	$6,478	$63,438
Comprehensive	Guelph	620	96.7	$3,247	$45,352
Primarily Undergraduate	Mount Allison	140**	84.1	$1,658	$17,279

* From federal funding associations, per 100 eligible, full-time faculty members.
** Calculated using Association of Universities and Colleges of Canada information (2002).

As a qualitative variable with three possible states, research intensity was represented by two indicator variables. The first indicator variable represents Medical-Doctoral schools, and the second indicator variable represents Comprehensive schools. If both indicators are set to zero then the university is a Primarily Undergraduate university.

University reputation: The Maclean's reputational survey results were used to represent university reputation. In 1999, 5,467 participants were sent the survey, including CEOs, corporate recruiters, university officials, and high-school guidance counsellors, and approximately ten percent responded (Maclean's Magazine, 1999a). Participants were asked to rank universities in three categories: 'Highest Quality', 'Most Innovative', and 'Leaders of Tomorrow' and the results were combined to create an overall assessment of university reputation (Maclean's, 1999a).

University IP policies: Most Canadian universities post their policy statements on their web pages. These statements were collected and evaluated. When a university policy could not be located on a web site, an administrator with the research office at that university was contacted by email and requested either to provide the information or to indicate where the information was posted. Administrators at two universities confirmed that the universities do not have an IP policy at present. Administrators at eight university policies did not respond. A chi-squared test of a contingency table was used to check for a relationship between respondents and non-respondents and research intensity (Medical-Doctoral, Comprehensive, Primarily

Undergraduate). The test was not significant. Therefore there is no statistical evidence of non-response bias.

The university IP policy statements were used to assess the control and the financial incentives that each university offered its researchers. In order to assess the control that the policies provide to researchers, a variable was used to indicate whether or not the university reserves the right of first refusal. The percentage of the licensing revenues that is afforded to the researchers was recorded for both the case where the researcher develops the IP and the case where the university develops the IP. This assessment of the financial rewards offered to researchers was complicated by differences in how the universities administered the revenues. Some university policies do not list a percentage because the researcher's share is negotiated on a case by case basis. At other universities, the researcher's share changes as the licensing revenue increases. The existence of these 'revenue threshold's was also tracked.

Licensing: While there are no canonical measures for the success of technology transfer initiatives (Bozeman, 2000; CUIPG, 1999), simple counts of patents and licenses, ratios of these counts (Gregory and Sheahen, 1991) and revenues resulting from licensing have been used as indicators of technology licensing success (Brett *et al.*, 1991; CUIPG, 1999). In this study we are examining the relationship between IP policies and researcher support for technology transfer. Since, conceptually, both the independent and dependent variables are university conditions, we should use the measure that most closely reflects activities within the university. Patent counts are a more immediate indication of researcher support for licensing and they are less likely to be effected by external factors, such as trends in the economy, than licensing revenues. Furthermore, US patents account for the majority of the patents held by Canadian universities (Statistics Canada, 2000). Therefore, the number of U.S patents currently held by a Canadian university was used as the measure of technology licensing activity.

The patent counts were obtained through university-specific searches of an online searchable patent database (Delphion Intellectual Property Network, 2000). For each university a search was conducted for all U.S. patents with the university name listed as the assignee. Unfortunately, this search method will not identify patents that are independently developed by university faculty members. Therefore, there is a high probability that the patenting and licensing activities at inventor-owner institutions were underestimated.

Data Analysis

Of the 38 universities included in the study, 14 reserve the right of first refusal. With respect to the inventor's share of the revenues, assuming that the university develops the IP, 21 universities specified a percentage, ten negotiate percentages, and seven universities do not develop IP. Of the 21 universities that specified the researcher's share for the cases when the university develops the IP, 13 universities set the researchers share at 50%. In the cases where the university develops the IP, six universities have thresholds for total revenue above which the researcher's share of all future revenue drops. With respect to the inventor's share of the revenues, assuming that the researcher develops the IP, 32 universities specified a percentage, five negotiated percentages, and one university did not develop IP. Of the 32 universities that specified the researcher's share for the cases when the researcher develops the IP, 21 universities set the researcher's share at 100%.

The universities that did not specify the researcher's percentage share of revenues for both the cases where the university develops the IP and the cases where the researcher develops the IP were excluded from the evaluation of the model. A chi-squared test of a contingency table was done of the two groups of policy data, those that were included in the study and those that weren't, with respect to their research intensity. The test was not significant. Therefore, there is no statistical evidence that excluding the universities that did not specify the researcher's share biased the evaluation of the model.

Only a small minority of the remaining universities changed the researcher's percentage share of the revenues depending on one or more revenue thresholds. Furthermore, the existence of a revenue threshold was significantly positively correlated with the researcher's share of the revenues in cases where the university developed the IP. It is difficult to find significant results when very few data points fall into one of the two categories and multi-collinearity can obscure relationships between the independent and dependent variables. As a result, the threshold measure was removed from the overall model.

Table 20.2. Variable correlations and regression analysis.

	Correlations						Regression Analysis	
	1.	2.	3.	4.	5.	6.	β	p-value
1. Research Intensity (Medical-Doctoral)	1						3.41	0.018
2. Research Intensity (Comprehensive)	-0.567	1					-0.86	0.557
3. University Reputation	-0.387	-0.300	1				-0.45	0.001
4. Right of First Refusal	-0.056	0.151	0.023	1			1.46	0.061
5. Inventor Ownership if Univ. Develops IP	0.027	0.167	-0.008	0.125	1		-4.56	0.053
6. Inventor Ownership if Inventor Develops IP	-0.095	0.121	0.225	0.026	0.374	1	7.17	0.002

The required conditions for the multiple regression model were met and the indicators of the fit validated the model ($R^2=0.846$, $F=17.5$, p-value<0.005). Within the context of this model there was:

- Strong evidence of a positive relationship between the researcher's share of the revenues when the inventor develops the IP and technology licensing activity at that university

- Weak evidence of a negative relationship between the researcher's share of the revenues when the university develops the IP and technology licensing activity at that university
- Weak evidence that researcher control, as defined by whether or not the university reserves the right of first refusal, is related to university technology licensing activity
- Strong evidence that university reputation is related to technology licensing activity
- Mixed evidence regarding the relationship between research intensity and technology licensing activity

DISCUSSION

There is strong support for a positive relationship between the percentage of the profits awarded to the inventor in the cases where the inventor commercializes the IP and the number of patents held by the university. This relationship predicts that the universities offering the smallest percentage of profits (25%) to inventors will hold 38.6 fewer patents, on average, than the universities offering the largest share of the profits (100%) to investors. This partially confirms hypothesis one. Ideally, one could conclude that financial incentives promote technology licensing activities; however, causality can not be determined by cross-sectional studies. If causality is to be demonstrated, future research must include longitudinal studies of systems in change.

There is limited support for a negative relationship between the percentage of the profits awarded to the inventor in the cases where the university commercializes the IP and the number of patents held by the university. This may reflect the fact that many of the universities that award high initial percentages of the profits to their researchers also reduce the percentages awarded once a pre-determined threshold is reached. The negative relationship displayed in the study may demonstrate a negative reaction to this threshold-based system of profit sharing.

The study provided limited support for a positive relationship between the university reserving the right of first refusal and technology licensing activity. This relationship is likely to be relatively unimportant, even if it were more strongly supported, because the slope of the linear relationship is very small. It predicts that universities that require researchers to first offer their IP to the university have, on average, 2.1 more patents than university that do not reserve this right.

The positive relationship between right of first refusal and technology licensing activity contradicts hypothesis two. It is still possible that control is an important incentive for some researchers but that those researchers tend to develop IP independently. The technology transfer variable did not include any patents that were developed independently and thus would not have captured this relationship. A future evaluation of the relationship between policy and technology transfer should gather information about the independent activities of university faculty so that a more complete evaluation can be made.

In general, the relationships between the independent variables of interest and technology licensing activity were smaller than anticipated. This may be partly a consequence of the large number of universities with similar policy positions. Canadian universities currently hold a wide range of IP policies; however, the majority of the schools that specify the researcher's share of revenues assign the researcher half of the revenues after the repayment of IP development costs if the university develops the IP. An even larger majority assigns all of the revenues to the researcher if the researcher develops the IP independently. While this consistency may be desirable from the perspective of industry (Expert Panel on the Commercialization of University Research, 1999), it poses a research challenge by reducing the likelihood of obtaining significant results in multiple regression studies. Future studies of technology transfer might benefit from an alternate research design.

There is strong evidence that the university ranking has a negative relationship with the number of patents held by a university. The rankings are inversely related to university reputation; higher ranking numbers reflect worse reputations. Therefore, university reputation is positively related to the patents held by each university. An improvement of one in ranking reflects an increase of 0.20 patents, on average, and the predicted difference between patents held by the highest and the lowest ranked universities in a category is up to 4.2 patents. This supports hypothesis four.

Hypothesis three was partially confirmed by the study. There was evidence that Medical-Doctoral universities hold more patents than either Comprehensive or Primarily Undergraduate, but there was no evidence of a difference between Comprehensive and Primarily Undergraduate universities.

Both university research intensity and university reputation appear to be valuable control variables for technology transfer studies. They were both shown to have a statistically significant relationship with the dependent variable. Future research could investigate the relationship between the underlying factors with respect to the Maclean's rankings and categorizations and technology transfer activities at the various universities. A detailed understanding of the relevant environmental variables will be valuable in the design of future surveys.

CONCLUSIONS

This study has developed and partially validated a new model to resolve the relationship between university IP policy and the success of university to industry technology licensing activities. This is a first step towards providing the information and analyses that will allow university and governmental policy makers to develop policies that are sensitive to the university environment and thus encourage economic growth more effectively.

The evidence suggests that researchers value financial incentives and that the introduction of thresholds may act as a disincentive to researcher involvement in technology licensing. Both these points are quite significant for university policy makers because the decision to allocate funds to the university researcher is a balancing act between the provision of sufficient incentives for technology transfer, a highly desirable activity which contributes to a good public image, and the need for financial support for both university research and technology transfer support services.

While no evidence was found of a significant positive relationship between the researcher control provided by university policy and the amount of technology licensing activity at that university, this is quite likely to be an artefact of the measure of technology licensing that was employed. The technology licensing measure did not account for the independent patenting and licensing activities of the university faculty. We can recast this result by noting that, even excluding all independently developed patents, there is no evidence that universities that allow their researcher's control produce fewer patents. It follows, that, if all Canadian universities embraced the Expert Panel's recommendations and adopted a policy wherein universities reserve the right to first refusal (1999), there is a good chance that the system would become less effective but more measurable. Therefore, there is a real need for further evaluations of the relationship between policy and technology transfer, which include information about the independent activities of university researchers.

REFERENCES

Association of Universities and Colleges of Canada (AUCC) (2002) University Descriptions: Mount Allison [web page] http://www.aucc.ca/english/dcu/universities/mountall.html [Accessed June 10].

Association of University Technology Managers (AUTM). (2000) Surveys - Q and A about technology transfer [web page] http://www.autm.net/pubs/surveys/qa.html [Accessed June 15].

Association of University Technology Managers (AUTM). (1999) *AUTM Licensing Survey, Fiscal Year 1998*. AUTM, Norwalk.

Boswell, C. and Sauer, P. (1998) Maximizing yield in the technology harvest. *Chem. Mark. Rep.*, **254**, FR28-FR30.

Bowers, L.J. & Leon, V. (1994) Patent policies of 65 educational institutions: a comparison. *SRA J.*, **26**, 5-13.

Bozeman, B. (2000) Technology transfer and public policy: a review of research and theory. *Res. Policy*, **29**, 627-655.

Brett, A.M., Gibson, D.V. and Smilor, R.W. (1991) *University spin-off companies*. Rowman and Littlefield Publishers, Inc., Maryland.

Brock University (2000) Intellectual Property, [web page] http://www.brocku.ca/researchservices/integrit.html#ip [Accessed June 15].

Canadian University Intellectual Property Group (CUIPG) (1999) *Maximizing The Benefits.* Industry Canada, Ottawa.

Conceição, P., Heitor, M.V., and Oliviera, P. (1998) University-based technology licensing in the knowledge based economy. *Technovation*, **18**, 615-625.

Daza Campbell, T.I. and Slaughter, S. (1999) Faculty and adminstrator's attitudes toward potential conflicts of interest, commitment, and equity in university-industry relationships. *J. High. Educ.*, **70**, 307-352.

Delphion Intellectual Property Network (1999) *Advanced Text Patent Search* [web page] http://www.delphion.com/advquery [Accessed: June 15].

Expert Panel on the Commercialization of University Research (1999) *Public Investments in University Research: Reaping the Benefits.* Industry Canada, Ottawa.

Gregory, W.D. and Sheahen, T.P. (1991) Technology transfer by spin-off companies versus licensing. In: *University Spin-off Companies* (Brett, A.M., Gibson, D.V. and Smilor, R.W. eds.). pp. 133-151. Rowman and Littlefield Publishers, Maryland.

Gu, W. and Whewell, L. (1999) *University Research and the Commercialization of Intellectual Property in Canada.* Industry Canada, Ottawa.

Hairston, D., Crabb, C., Cooper, C. and Takeshi, K. (1998) Sticky issues for corporate-university R&D alliances. *Chem. Eng.*, **6**, 39.

Jaffe, A. (2000) The U.S. patent system in transition. *Res. Policy*, **29**, 531-557.

Lee, Y.S. (1996) 'Technology transfer' and the research university. *Res. Policy*, **25**, 843-863.

Maclean's Magazine (1999a) Reading the Rankings. *Maclean's Magazine*, **112**(46): pp. 70-83.

Maclean's Magazine (1999b) The Rankings. *Maclean's Magazine*, **112**(46): pp. 60-69.

McQueen, D.H. and Wallmark, J.T. (1991) "University technical innovations," In: *University Spin-off Companies* (Brett, A.M., Gibson, D.V. and Smilor, R.W. eds.). pp. 103-116. Rowman and Littlefield Publishers, Maryland.

Petrick, I.J. and Reischman, M.M. (1995/1996) Strategic development of engineering policies for patenting and licensing. *Society of Research Administrators (SRA) Journal*, **27**, 13-23.

Piali, R. (1996) My research, your development. *Can. Bus.*, **69**, 13.

Simon Fraser University (2000) *Simon Fraser University: Policies and procedures* [web page] http://www.sfu.ca/policies/research/r30-02.htm [Accessed: June 15].

Statistics Canada (2000) *The Survey of Intellectual Property Commercialization in the Higher Education Sector, 1998. Cat. No. 88F0006XIB No. 99-01* [web page] http://www.statcan.ca/english/research/88F0006XIB/99001.pdf [Accessed: September 4].

Statistics Canada (2000) *The Survey of Intellectual Property Commercialization in the Higher Education Sector, 1999. Cat. No. 88F0006XIB No. 01.* [web page] http://www.statisticscanada.ca/english/research/88F0006XIB/88F0006XIB00001.pdf [Accessed: December 20].

Stevens, J.M. and Bagby, J.W. (1999) Intellectual property transfer from universities to business. *Int. J. Technol. Manag.*, **18**, 688-704.

Trune, D.R. and Goslin, L.N. (1998) University technology transfer programs. *Technol. Forecast. Soc. Change*, **57**, 197-204.

University of British Columbia (2000) *UBC policies on research and technology transfer* [web page] http://www.uilo.ubc.ca/Collaborative%20Research/Policy.htm, [Accessed: June 15].

University of Victoria (2000) *Research Policy Guide*, [web page] http://castle.UVic.CA/uvic-policies/pol-1000/1200RPG.html, [Accessed: June 15].

University of Waterloo (2000) *Policy 73: Intellectual Property Rights*, [web page] http://www.adm.uwaterloo.ca/infosec/Policies/73a.html#Policy 73, [Accessed: June 15].

Young-Kreeger, K. (2000) Careers in technology transfer. *Scientist*, **14**, 32.

Management of Technology
ISBN: 0-08-044136-X

21

DEVELOPMENT OF OLED'S, A NEXT GENERATION FLAT PANEL DISPLAY TECHNOLOGY: EXPERIENCES FROM AN ON-GOING COLLABORATION BETWEEN INDUSTRY AND ACADEMIA

William R. Leo, CFG S.A., Morges, Switzerland[*]
Libero Zuppiroli, EPFL, Lausanne, Switzerland[**]

ABSTRACT

The flat panel industry is one of the fastest growing sectors today with an enormous potential market. Currently, the dominant technology is the liquid crystal display. However, new technologies such as plasma displays, field emission displays and organic electroluminescent devices (OLED's) are now emerging as challengers to this position. Unlike previous innovations, these new technologies are also pushing against the frontiers of science itself. This implies that achieving faster progress would require more active, focused scientific support as well as the technological and engineering development traditionally realized by the developing company. This seems to be born out by the current OLED industry wherein the current industry players are all closely associated with one or more academic laboratories. Lack of such support also seems to explain in part the slower development of earlier flat panel technologies such as the field emission display.

---

[*]   William R. Leo, CFG S.A., Avenue de Lonay 2, CH- 1110 Morges, Switzerland.
[**] Libero Zuppiroli, Laboratoire d'Optoélectronique des Matériaux Moléculaires, EPFL, CH-1015 Lausanne, Switzerland.

For management, this implies some new issues : the organization of a more intense working relation with an academic laboratory, the management of a science-technology interface and others.

We report on the experiences of a current technology transfer between *the Semi-Crystalline Solid State Physics Lab* (now *the Laboratoire d'Optoélectronique des Matériaux Molécul-aires*) at the Swiss Federal Institute of Technology at Lausanne (EPFL) and CFG SA, a private enterprise active in the flat panel display industry. The collaboration to develop and industrialize (OLED) technology has been on-going for more than two years and continues to this day. To ensure efficient transfer and development of the technology, a « strong coupling » scheme has been implemented between the two and has thus far produced excellent results.

INTRODUCTION

One of the important outgrowths of the information/microelectronics revolution has been the creation of the flat panel display (FPD) industry. Most prominently seen in notebook computers, palm-tops, mobile telephones, calculators, camcorders, digital cameras, watches, toys and other devices, flat panel displays today have a market value (1999) of $19.7 billion. Moreover, demand is such that *FPD*'s are expected to become even more ubiquitous in the coming years. Indeed, analysts are estimating market values ranging from a conservative $26 billion in 2004 to double and even triple this figure (Mentley, 2000 and Werner, 2000). This is to be contrasted with the standard cathode-ray-tube, (a device which celebrated its *100* [th] anniversary in 1998) which had a 1999 market value of $23.5 billion and is also predicted to have a $26 billion market in 2004. Whichever projection is used, however, it is clear that *FPD*'s constitute an enormous market which will become even larger.

Currently, the dominant FPD technology is the liquid crystal display (LCD) which commands over 90% market share. While the technology was invented in North America and Europe, it was the Japanese who invested heavily in its subsequent development and commercialization, in particular, the TFT active matrix technology used in full color displays. Today, Japanese, Korean and Taiwanese companies are the overwhelmingly dominant forces in the market. Nevertheless, the LCD is far from being the perfect display. Most notably it has a limited viewing angle, a slow response and lacks brightness. Manufacturing is complicated with low yields and is costly, requiring heavy capital investment. And while LCD technology has greatly improved in recent years, the market continues to demand better and cheaper flat displays. For this reason, new technologies are now emerging, for example, plasma display panels (PDP), field emission displays (FED) and organic light emitting displays (OLED) - all of which attempt to address some or all of these problems[1].

Organic light emitting device (OLED) technology is the youngest of these new technologies. Invented only about 17 years ago, it has made rapid progress and is today on the threshold of mass production. Over 50 companies are reported to be involved in OLED research or development along with many academic physics and chemistry laboratories. OLED technology makes use of carbon-based molecules which are deposited in extremely thin layers, on the order of a hundred nanometers thickness, between two appropriate electrodes. When an electric current is applied, bright light is emitted by the organic layers. Using the correct architecture and appropriate materials, low-voltage display devices, both monochrome and full color, can be made with this technology. OLED's offer many advantages over the current LCD. These include a much better brightness and 180° viewing angles due to the emissive nature of OLED's. They are thin and lightweight, have fast response times and are less power consuming than displays with equivalent brightness. Moreover, the use of organic molecules, as opposed to semiconductors, makes them easier to handle which should in principle lead to cheaper manufacturing. The almost monolithic structure of an OLED also makes it many times simpler than an LCD - or any of the newer technologies for that matter – further enhancing its advantages. Finally, new display devices such as flexible displays and transparent displays are possible or much easier to make with OLED technology thus enabling new applications. It is no wonder therefore that many in the industry find the OLED to be as close to the perfect display as one can hope.

Nevertheless, OLED technology faces many challenges. Indeed, making an OLED device will not only require further development of the organic materials and the device structure, but also new developments in many other technologies on which the making of a complete device will depend. For example, substrates with planarities on the nanometer scale, encapsulation materials with a high degree of impermeability to oxygen and humidity, electronics, patterning methods, manufacturing techniques and equipment and more. These issues are intimately linked and their roles are far from complete understanding even at the scientific level.

LESSONS FROM THE FLAT PANEL INDUSTRY

It becomes clear then that developing OLED technology also involves developing the science as well. This is probably true of many of today's newer technologies also. Indeed, the

---

[1] These are the three emerging electronic display technologies receiving the most attention, but they are by no means the only ones around. One interesting class of technologies is *electronic paper* which may turn out to be a true disruptive technology (see for example, The Economist Technology Quarterly, Dec. 9th-15th 2000).

development of the flat panel industry is probably illustrative of the high-tech sector as a whole. It is interesting therefore to look at the development histories of the dominant LCD and the two other principal emerging technologies : the *plasma display panel* (PDP) and the *field emission display* (FED). The development of each of these technologies contains lessons for technology management as a whole and illustrates how high-tech development strategies are now changing.

The Liquid Crystal Display

The history of LCD development is briefly summarized in Table 21.1 below. The development of this invention essentially follows the traditional scenario where there is a long time lapse between the discovery of the phenomena itself and the development of real devices. In this case, it was the application and development of the class of liquid crystals known as *twisted nematic* which ultimately led to viable display products in watches, games, telephones, appliances, etc. These are the monochrome, text displays which are found on many appliances today and go almost unnoticed by the average person.

Table 21.1. Brief History of LCD Development

1889 - Discovery of liquid crystal phase by Friedrich Reinitzer and Otto Lehmann
1963 - First demonstration of a liquid crystal display by R. Heilmeier at RCA Sarnoff Laboratories.
1971 - Twisted nematic (TN) liquid crystal display invented at Hoffman-La Roche
1973 - TFT Driver (thin film transistor) invented by Westinghouse
1983 - Super twisted nematic (STN) display demonstrated by BBC

It was the advent of the notebook computer and the need for flat, full color graphics displays, however, which drove the next wave of LCD technology development. Once again, the initial innovation was a North American idea: the *active matrix, thin film transistor* (TFT) driving technique. This is a complex semiconductor technology which requires making a panel with a matrix array of transistors, one for each color pixel on the display. For a simple VGA display with 640 x 480 display pixels (each display pixel consisting of three color pixels: red, blue and green), a calculation shows that close to one million transistors per panel are required. Not surprisingly, manufacturing yields were low because of the high probability of having one or more bad transistors on a given panel.

Unfortunately, management in American and European companies quickly rejected this technology as being too complex and expensive. This was not the case of the Asian companies, in particular the Japanese, who took a longer term view and continued to invest in active matrix technology well through the 1980's and up to this day. Development during these years was essentially technology oriented with advances made through pure engineering ingenuity. Very little scientific research was actually performed nor required. The development of active matrix technology again illustrates the traditional technology transfer scenario wherein the new technology is essentially developed by engineering ingenuity within the confines of the company.

Despite its complexity, active matrix technology has been quite successful, and is now in fact undergoing a second explosion driven by a second *killer app*: desktop monitors! The challenge here is to make still larger panels at lower prices. Although some Western critics have referred to the Asian investment in this technology as a "race to lose money", it would seem that today it has paid off. Indeed, active matrix LCD technology is by far the dominant flat panel technology today and almost entirely in the hands of Asian enterprises. In contrast, the number of American and European companies in the industry can be counted on the fingers of one hand and are all limited to niche markets such as military applications.

The Plasma Display Panel (PDP)

While the LCD is a general platform display suitable for many different applications it is still limited to relatively small sizes. The plasma display panel, in contrast, is basically aimed at one particular application: flat, large screen television.

At its simplest, a plasma panel consists of an array of miniature glass cells containing an inert gas, electrodes and a color phosphor. By applying a high voltage to the electrodes, an electric discharge is created which causes ultraviolet light to be emitted by the gas. The ultraviolet rays then strike the color phosphor which in turn emits colored light. Again the technology was invented in North America in the 1960's, while heavy investment was made mainly by Asian companies. Products are only now becoming available some 35 years later.

Plasma displays have excellent definition and color, are about 10% the thickness and 1/6 the weight of an equivalent CRT. They can thus be hung on the wall like a painting. Unfortunately, at prices between $12000 to $20000, they are about three to four times too expensive for the mass market. Indeed, whereas only a few years ago a total of 2 million units were projected to be shipped in the year 2000, today, that number is closer to 200000 at best (Jousse, 2000). For the moment, PDP's are thus limited to niche applications where cost is not a factor. Moreover, having been designed for large screen applications, smaller screens with high resolution are difficult to make with plasma technology so that other applications which are less price sensitive, for example, computer screens, are excluded.

Although the technology is intrinsically simpler than TFT technology, PDP's are plagued by the high cost of components and complex manufacturing steps. The electronic drivers and the glass panel alone account for 50% of the cost, for example. Indeed, development was along "traditional" lines, as we have noted, so that manufacturing issues for

PDP's were not addressed until the product was almost ready for production. The result is that today, sales of PDP's will be limited for at least another three years while alternative manufacturing materials and methods are investigated.

The basic lesson learned from this experience is that manufacturing issues in new technologies are an integral part of development and should be considered early on.

The Field Emission Display (FED)

Chronologically, the next new display technology to appear was the *field emission* display (FED). The FED essentially operates on the same principle as the cathode ray tube, i.e., electrons are made to impinge upon a phosphor screen which then emits light at the point of impact. However, in the FED the source of the electrons is different. In a CRT, this is an electron gun which emits a beam of electrons by thermionic emission. In a FED, an array of micro-points in the form of metallic cones, one for each color pixel, emits electrons under the application of a strong electric field only, without any heating of the material. This phenomena is known as the *field emission effect*, whence the name for the display. The use of a micro-point array thus allows the display to be very flat.

Table 21.2 briefly outlines the history of FED development. Although the application of the field emission effect to displays was already made in the 1960's, the FED was essentially launched by the development of micro-point technology some 20 years later. Thereafter, the time to market was considerably shorter than the LCD or the PDP.

Table 21.2. Brief History of the FED display.

> 1928 - Fowler-Nordheim Theory of field emission
> 1961 - Application of field emission to displays by K.R. Shoulders
> 1968 - Development of cathode matrix array using thin film technology by Carl Spindt at *SRI*
> 1986 - R. Meyer of *LETI* in France demonstrates feasibility of micro-point matrix cathode
> 1990 - *LETI* demonstrates 6-inch monochrome FED display
> 1991 - *LETI* demonstrates full-color FED display
> 1998 - First monochrome FED products appear

The FED is indeed a rugged, flat display which has drawn a particular interest from the aviation and military sectors where harsh environmental conditions are the norm. However, the FED is a very complex device and many fundamental manufacturing, engineering and materials problems remain to be solved. For this reason, the FED is currently limited to small sizes and monochrome devices. And despite the quick development time relative to the LCD or the PDP, the market perception is that the FED is "late", i.e., it is missing its window of opportunity.

This impression has been reinforced by the defection of a number of companies from the industry (most notably the *FED Corporation* which has taken up OLED technology instead and has renamed itself *eMagin*). Similarly, others players such as Sony and Candescent have called off their joint venture, while Motorola has abandoned development of micro-point technology because of the technical difficulties (Chinnock 2002). Indeed, a lack of cooperation in the industry and a lack of academic support for more technologically oriented problems have been cited as the reasons. This can be attributed perhaps to the "go it alone" attitude of the players - an attitude, which in retrospect, is inappropriate when given the complexity of the technology.

Thus, a lesson which can be taken from the FED experience is that technology is becoming so complex that industry cooperation is necessary in order to solve all the basic problems within an ever decreasing window of opportunity. In this context, academic research groups can play an important, indeed an essential role in the development as well.

The OLED

The discovery of electroluminescence in organic materials dates back to the 1960's when light emission from anthracene, a solid organic crystal, was first observed. At the time, however, the intensity was too weak to be useful. It was not until 1983 that researchers at Kodak discovered a strong light emitting organic compound known as Alq_3 with which they were able to produce a working, light emitting device. This was followed in 1989 by the discovery of light-emitting polymers at Cambridge in the UK. Although they are also organic compounds, the different physical properties of polymers open a different technological path to the production of light emitting devices. As we have mentioned, development has been rapid. In 1999, the first OLED product: a car radio with an OLED display by Pioneer, appeared on the world market and more recently in September 2000, a mobile telephone with OLED display by Motorola.

While the OLED industry is still forming, it is clear that the lessons from the PDP and FED experiences have been learned. Most notable are the industry alliances that have been formed and that are continuing to be formed; for example, Kodak and Sanyo who have teamed together to develop a full color active matrix OLED or Cambridge Display Technologies and Seiko who are collaborating to develop an ink-jet method for depositing polymer OLED's. In this same vein are the industry/academic alliances, for example, Cambridge Display Technologies with Cambridge University, Universal Display Corporation with Princeton & USC, Uniax with UCLA, Opsys with Oxford U., and not least CFG with EPFL. Moreover, manufacturing issues are taking on an early importance as new methods such as roll to roll processing are already being investigated by companies. Indeed, it is tempting to ask if these alliances are not the value chains of the future OLED industry in formation.

Thus, despite its complexity, the application of these lessons seems to have led to the rapid progress and success of OLED technology. The industry is, of course, still evolving and more changes are surely yet to come.

A "STRONG COUPLING" EXPERIENCE

It is in the context of OLED development that we present here our own experiences in the transfer of this technology from the Swiss Federal Institute of Technology at Lausanne (EPFL), a Swiss academic institution to CFG S.A., a microelectronics company with an offering in the custom design and assembly of complete LCD modules for the industrial sector. This collaboration is on-going at the time of this writing so that our experiences are less than conclusive. Nevertheless, we hope they will be of use to others entering into such ventures.

The collaboration was initiated in 1997 when CFG was first introduced to the work of one of us (LZ) in the area of organic electroluminescence. CFG, at the time, was looking for new opportunities to offset competition from forward integrating LCD manufacturers while the EPFL was also seeking industrial support for its developments. Recognizing the opportunity presented by this technology, CFG purchased exclusive licenses to the EPFL's patents while the EPFL transferred the basic know-how to CFG. The two parties also agreed to enter into a project to further develop the technology with partial funding from the Swiss Commission for Technology and Innovation (CTI).

Traditionally, transfer of technology agreements are limited to just that: a simple transfer of knowledge and information from the research institution to the industrial company after which it is up to the latter to develop the technology into commercial processes and products. The research organization then retains only a consulting role. This has also been a common process in larger companies where new technologies are passed from a research department to an independent development department with no more interaction than required. However, it became clear that this traditional "weak coupling" scheme could not work here. Indeed the complexity and novelty of the OLED technology were such that *active* scientific support would constantly be required to answer specific scientific questions as they arose in the course of development.

For this reason it was decided to enter into a "strong coupling" scheme in which a very close relationship between the two parties is maintained. To this end, a group was formed with members from both parties. The principal place of work was the EPFL. CFG also offered additional support through its mechanical design services, electronics laboratory and clean room facility. From CFG, a "resident" physicist was assigned to the EPFL first to learn the technology and then to actively participate in the development work. With support from the Swiss CTI, additional scientific and technical personnel were also hired to participate in the project. While officially under the responsibility of the EPFL, recruitment and hiring decisions were made after consultation with the other partner.

It should be noted that this technology team existed in parallel with the laboratory's scientific staff who continued to pursue their normal academic activities independently. Since the environment was relatively open, confidentiality issues had to be considered. The members of the working group were sensitized to the problem and asked to sign non-disclosure agreements. Requests for information from non-team members were also systematically referred to the group leader.

Weekly meetings were instituted with formal minutes being taken (Note that formal minutes of group meetings is not commonplace procedure in academic research!). In addition, CFG's project management (WL) was also invited to attend and participate in the information exchange.

The group was officially constituted in June of 1999 with the double goal of increasing the lifetime of the EPFL-CFG OLED and of developing a suitable encapsulation scheme for protecting the OLED from humidity and oxygen. A first milestone was set at achieving a lifetime of 1000 hours within one year. Note that OLED lifetimes in June 1999 were only on the order of 100 hours.

Current Status

As of this writing, 18 months have passed and rapid progress has indeed been made. The first milestone of 1000 hours lifetime was actually reached and surpassed in December 1999, a full six months ahead of schedule. Indeed, at the end of January 2000, device lifetimes were already measured at over 2000 hours and are currently at better than 5000 hours.

This achievement was made possible largely by a better understanding of the main degradation mechanisms, one of the more important outcomes of the project. As well, many other insights and discoveries were also made in the course of this work which although not directly related to the objectives, help nevertheless to advance understanding into making better OLED's.

As to the second goal: encapsulation, a new promising method has been developed for which a patent has been deposited. And as if to underscore the lesson, this method was invented through old fashion ingenuity without too much scientific support! Development on this method still continues however.

A Comparison

Given the results, there is no doubt that the "strong coupling" scheme has been very successful and produced the rapid advances being sought with this new complex technology. This is not to say that there have not been any problems; however, our overall experience has been very positive so far.

It would be interesting, of course, to compare this to what would have happened had another scheme, such as "weak coupling", been used. Sometime after the start of the collaboration, one of us (WL) had the opportunity to exchange experiences with a participant in another technology transfer project involving a similar organic molecular technology. Although the application domain was different, the technological challenges were very similar. This particular technology transfer actually took place 6 or 7 years earlier, but unlike the CFG license, non-exclusive licenses were sold to different companies in the same industry. Typically, a "weak coupling" technology development scheme was implemented. Because the technology turned out to be more complex than imagined, progress by the licensee companies was very slow. Moreover, collaborative development with the licensor, an academic institution, was also hampered because of the presence of other licensees, each a potential competitor. Information exchange and discussion was therefore difficult. The result was that six years later, the licensees still had not made much progress in developing marketable products. In fact, many, including our interlocutor, were considering abandoning the project altogether.

This very suggestive example would seem to validate our "strong coupling" hypothesis. One additional point which comes out of this case was the hampering effect of multiple licenses. A "strong coupling" scheme would certainly not have been possible had there been multiple licensees. Such a situation is advantageous for the licensor in the short run. However, if it impedes the ultimate development of the technology, neither licensee nor licensor wins.

Culture Differences

While our "strong coupling" collaboration has produced good results, there have nevertheless been moments of tension and stress making for less than optimal operation. Much of this can be explained by differences in professional culture between the members. In the group were physicists with a background in academic research, EPFL-trained engineers, technical-school trained engineers[2], technicians and the project manager from CFG (WL) who had both a marketing and scientific research background. From a normal management point of view this would be considered a homogeneous group with all members having the same cultural values. Under normal conditions this is true. However, under stress conditions, the existence of subcultures within the group may start to become apparent. Indeed, each subgroup has its own

---

[2]   In Switzerland, two types of engineering training exist. The Swiss Federal Institutes of Technology consisting of the EPFL and the ETHZ in Zurich offer a more theoretical based training leading to graduate level degrees. In addition, there are technical schools at the cantonal level which offer a rigorous, but more practical level of training.

professional values which the subgroup will emphasize or consider as higher priority under times of stress or conflict. Figure 21.1 summarizes these cultural values.

Fig. 21.1. Professional values of technical and scientific personnel.

For example, scientists will tend to favor the central ideas as more important than say the apparatus for demonstrating these ideas, whereas the engineers will consider the proper design and construction of the apparatus as primordial. Under a stress condition when delays become too long, some scientists will consider any additional work on the apparatus beyond its primary design capability as unnecessary attention to detail. The engineers in contrast will consider this as unprofessional "tinkering". Even among the engineers themselves there is a value difference between the EPFL-trained engineers and the technical-school engineers. The former will tend to value the design concept while the latter the process itself. Recognizing these differences is therefore an important task for management.

Similarly, there will also be many ideas which will be emitted in the course of development, all with merit and all exciting. This is inevitable and it becomes tempting for individual members to pursue these ideas. This, of course, has the potential of dispersing the group. Such problems emphasize the necessity of having a strong leader with recognized scientific authority. This person will set priorities in cases of conflict and refocus the group onto the work at hand.

SUMMARY AND CONCLUSIONS

Whereas technological innovation could proceed independently of science in previous years, the increasing complexity of new technologies are now pushing against the frontiers of science itself[3]. Given the rapidity with which these new technologies must be brought to market, the traditional separation between science and technology is becoming blurred. This seems to be

---

[3]   Indeed, it has been estimated that as much as one quarter of the US GNP is generated by quantum related technologies. See "Just Thanck Planck" (2000).

the case for the flat panel industry and in particular OLED's where academic research institutions are playing an important role in the overall development of the technology. For similar reasons, industry to industry collaborations are also becoming necessary.

For companies entering into high-tech technology transfers, it then becomes very important to judge the extent to which scientific support is an essential element. This may imply a different mode of collaboration between the academic and industrial partner. In the context of our own technology transfer this is the case so that we have opted for a "strongly coupled" mode of development, i.e., the formation of a unified project team consisting of members from both sides. The results thus far have been very encouraging. The milestones of the group have been reached well ahead of schedule and have already been surpassed by several fold. Another notable outcome has been the deposition of a new patent application. Moreover, comparison with a less successful but similar technology transfer case where a more traditional ("weak coupling") mode of transfer was used would seem to lend validity to this type of operation.

REFERENCES

Chinnock, Chris (2002), The Beginning of the End or the End of the Beginning?, *Displays Europe*, **3**, 17-18.

Jousse, Didier (2000). The Choice of a Glass Substrate and Some Other Challenges for the Manufacturing of Low Cost PDP, *Ecrans à Plasma*, Journée d'Etudes 16 mars 2000 edited by Le Club Visu, Society for Information Display - France.

"Just Thanck Planck"(2000), article in *The Economist*, Dec. 9th, 2000.

Mentley, Dave (2000). OLED Displays - Out of the Lab and into the Market, *Commercializing OLED's Conference,* San Diego, CA, USA, October 11-13, 2000. Intertech, Portland Maine USA

Werner, Ken (2000). The First IDMC and FPD Expo Korea Attract More Than 1000 People to Seoul, *Information Display*, **16**, 30-37.

Management of Technology
Copyright © 2003 by Elsevier Science Ltd.
ISBN: 0-08-044136-X

22

INDICATORS OF IMPACT OF JOINT PROJECTS FROM RESEARCH CENTERS AND ENTERPRISES

Lourdes Terezinha dos Santos Tomé Francisco, UFRGS, Brazil[*]
Edi Madalena Fracasso, UFRGS, Brazil[**]
Thaís de Azevedo, UFRGS, Brazil[***]

INTRODUCTION

Scientific developments and technological changes are happening fast, and countries, especially developing countries, face great limitations to investments in science and technology at the same time (S&T) (Shelton, 1997). Areas like sanitation, basic education and security take priority and get a bigger percentage of the resources. Even so, in the above mentioned countries the government is responsible for the most part of the national investment in S&T. 1% of the Brazilian Gross National Product (GNP) is invested in this area, being the government responsible for 80% of this sum (Brazilian Academy of Science, 1999).

Programs and projects of S&T in Brazil are financed by national and state institutions. In Rio Grande do Sul State, the Research Support Foundation of the Rio Grande do Sul State – FAPERGS, finances S&T projects from both public and private institutions using state government resources. Very often FAPERGS supports joint projects from research centers and enterprises aiming at stimulating their interaction, development of innovations and creating the conditions for the productive sector to increase its participation in S&T investments.

---

[*]   NITEC, Management School, UFRGS, Brazil. E-mail: loufranc@terra.com.br

[**]   Professor at NITEC, Management School, UFRGS, Brazil. E-mail: emfracasso@ea.ufrgs.br.

[***] Undergraduate student at NITEC, Management School, UFRGS, Brazil.

However, the importance of the research projects supported by institutions like FAPERGS is frequently unknown. According to Silva (1999) "people don't have the slightest idea of the institution investment in S&T", thus creating a barrier between the research groups and society. Besides, there is the question about which are the benefits of this investment for the society as a whole.

In this context, emerges concern about how to identify and evaluate the results of the public investment in S&T. According to MacLean et al (1999, p. 7) "evaluation aims first to ensure that limited money is well spent and second to demonstrate public accountability." That is, evaluation is a way to demonstrate to the society that resources have been used the best way as possible. Thus, the discussion related to the development of evaluation systems that considers both the selection and the impacts of S&T programs and projects is very relevant.

The FAPERGS has not yet used a system of result evaluation for its projects. However it has already exerted itself in defining an efficient system to evaluate its results. In 1998 a Commission was created to clear the returns of invested resources which outlined a set of quantitative and qualitative indicators and suggested case studies to demonstrate the non-quantifying results. The Brazilian research support foundations of São Paulo and Rio de Janeiro states (FAPESP and FAPERJ) can also reckon upon studies about the same issue (FAPESP, 1996; Ohayon, 1991; Campos, 1999).

As yet, there isn't any evidence that a system of results evaluation is really being used by any research support foundation (FAPs), in spite of all efforts. When indicators of results are used at all, normally they are indicators such as: total invested value, number of patents, number of scholars and courses supported and so on. Usually they limit themselves in presenting the destination of resources without indicating the consequent social-economic benefits.

It is a tough task formulating a system of this nature due to the intrinsic problems and difficulties in evaluating the results and impacts in S&T. The projects and programs have peculiar features, the organizations involved and the thematic areas too. In dealing with projects of Science and Technology, the impact of the results can just be perceived long-term, one more reason which makes the evaluation difficult. Besides evaluating the knowledge the main product developed in the project UEI is a rather complex task.

The remainder of this article presents a brief review and discussion on the problems involved in the setting of adequate indicators to evaluate the results and impact of S&T projects. The results of two university – enterprise interaction projects financed by FAPERGS in 1996 are then presented, using one set of proposed indicators to evaluate this type of project. An analysis is then made regarding the adequacy of these indicators for these cases.

PROJECT EVALUATION

Evaluation is a process aiming to determine in a systematic and objective way, the relevance, efficiency, effectiveness and the impact of activities in relation to specific goals (UNICEF, 1997).

The efficiency of a project is evaluated depending on the degree the defined goals are achieved. The effectiveness on the other hand, refers not only the degree the goals are achieved but also if they were achieved at an accepted cost - i.e., it's about the setting of a cost-benefit relation for the project. Not only cost of financed resources, but also of material and human resources.

The efficiency of a project is evaluated by measuring the degree of achievement of the defined goals. On the other hand, the effectiveness is measured by the relationship between goals` achievement and cost. Not only cost of financed resources, but also of material and human resources. Evaluation of project relevance is the result of the comparison of the importance of its goals in relation to other needs. As stated earlier, when dealing with insufficient resources, it is necessary that achieved results are part of the state-of-the-art in S&T, besides, having the potential to promote social return.

Evaluation of impacts is concerned with the effects of a project. These effects can be social, economic, technological, environmental or scientific. They may be felt in individuals, in the community or in the institution where the project is developed (UNICEF, 1997). Depending on the sphere or social group the perceived impact can have different classifications. One way to classify the impacts is by the span of time that is needed for the impacts to be felt: they can be long or short-term impacts. In the methodology of evaluation, it should be taken into account that "the further the impacts are located from the research, the more complicated are the links between the two" (Street & Barker, 1994: 171).

The project evaluations can have different purposes in relation to their goals. They can be useful in selecting the projects (ex-ante), follow and control the development (progressive) or evaluate the performance or success (ex-post) (Sbragia, 1984). Each has different criteria for its fulfillment, since they are used depending on defined goals. We are just interested in ex-post evaluation. Ex-ante evaluation of these projects is made when defining the projects to be financed.

The determination of an evaluation system relies on the establishment of appropriate indicators which will identify desired features of each project. The chosen set of indicators should summarize all the information needed to show the results and impacts due to the public resources invested. In addition, it should facilitate the planning and polices formulation process to the FAPS. Once the information is available in a systematic way, it is possible to proceed the evaluation and judgment of the project results.

INDICATORS OF PROJECT EVALUATION

Indicators of project evaluation are tools used to identify project results and impacts. In a classic definition, indicators stand for *"a series of defined data, that aim at answering questions about a phenomenon or a given system"* (OCDE, 1998a; p.79). They are variables whose function is to describe and measure certain features of a phenomenon or system, using quantitative or qualitative data, checking by means of analysis of the phenomenon or system itself.

There are problems and difficulties in defining these indicators. First, the fact that in the scientific system the main product is knowledge that is produced, transmitted and changed, with aggregation of new ideas. Since there are no direct ways to measure the knowledge, it is measured indirectly, through bibliometric indicators and patents (Velho, 1994). That is, there are no ways of quantifying the resultant knowledge, only ways of identifying its transference.

Another aspect to be considered is about the necessary features for a good set of indicators. Its main features should be validity, reliability, relevancy and feasibility of data collection. All evaluation is based on a principle of comparison: between the earlier and late state, between projects of the same group or different project groups. Thus it's necessary that the data be comparable between itself, that it can be collected the same way as in all cases.

According to Ohayon (1991), an efficient system of evaluating indicators should include questions divided into three areas:

- questions about the results of research (certified knowledge, training in research, transference to industry, etc) and its quality;
- questions about the effect of research, both on the dynamics of knowledge and the social economic or industrial sector;
- questions about the efficiency of management (product of quality, expected with no waste of resources).

In literature, there are various classifications and denominations for different set of indicators. Meanwhile, what define best classification or best set are the project features in evaluation and the purpose of the evaluation. It's necessary that we ask these questions: what are the potential results of these projects? What impact can they produce? Thus, we can have an idea of the kind of necessary indicator for the evaluation. About the university – enterprise interaction projects financed by FAPERGS, the evaluation criteria can be defined according to the goals established by the foundation for the group of selected projects.

According to Velho (1994), the indicators in S&T can be divided into four groups: Input, Product, Social Impact and Innovation. Input indicators demonstrate the resources used in S&T activities, both financial and human (for example: percentage of overall money spent on research, or number of people involved in scientific activities, etc). Product indicators determine the product developed through the use of input. For example: index of publicity, frequency of citation, number of produced patent, etc.

Social Impact indicators are of great value for strategic decision making, especially in developing countries where social problems are much more serious. Their aim is quantifying the impact of scientific activities in all societies, not only the economic impact, but also the creation of jobs and reduction of environmental pollution, for example.

Determining Innovation indicators has been the result of efforts of organizations like Economical Development Cooperation Organization (OCDE), from which Oslo's Manual came out in 1992. It outlines the guidelines for the setting of indicators to measure certain aspects of the innovation process in industry and the resources for innovation activity (OCDE, 1998a).

This classification is rather wide when it comes to weighing up in terms of projects, especially in relation to innovation indicators and the social impact. An UEI project has a relatively small purpose so that one can think of measuring its social impacts when considered solely. Another approach can be considered, identifying and evaluating the impacts of these projects only in the sphere of the company involved, where the results were applied. No doubt these impacts can also be considered social-economic, since all entrepreneurial activity has its impact on the society where the company is located (for example: new work post, taxes creation). Another sphere where we can identify the impacts of these projects is the University or Research Institution. In this case, the impacts can be considered more social than economical. The knowledge developed is transferred through people involved, contributing for competence formation, maintaining the scientific and technological flux. In addition, the projects make the purchase of materials and equipment easy; which can be used by students and in other projects.

According to the theoretical reference presented, also taken into account are the details of the kind of projects in discussion – university – enterprise interaction the following classification was proposed for a set of adequate indicators to evaluate its results (Fig. 22.1).

Input Indicators were divided according to their origin since both involved parts collaborate with resources for the project. Often the enterprise in addition to investing in research centers, invests also in its own installations or working hour. Product Indicators should consist of two kinds of products. Direct Product is all that results directly from research work, from scientific publication to new methodologies and patent, while Technology Innovation Indicators limit themselves to identifying and measuring improved or new products that have been marketed by the involved company, as well as the new or improved process and materials the company has been using, both resultant of project development.

About Impact Indicators, those regarding the impacts on the enterprise should include any changes and economical benefits caused by the use of the project result, like cost reduction and profitability increase. The social impact includes the effects the project provided on the

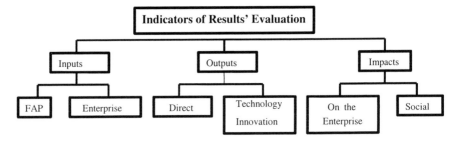

Fig. 22.1: Classification of proposed indicators.

society as a whole, like new jobs or jobs eliminated and increase on the taxation, as well the impacts on the University, like competence development, use of the case studies in graduation classes, creation of new research projects.

THE TWO CASES

To test a set of indicators for university – enterprise interaction project evaluation financed by FAPs, two projects were selected endowed with financial resources by FAPERGS in 1996. FAPERGS makes program announcements calling for grant proposals. The announcements define the goals to be achieved, as well as the amount of financial resources available and the criteria that will guide the judgment of the project proposals. The announcement for the program University – Enterprise Interaction aims at to promote the modernization of industry and to stimulate the introduction of new products and processes through joint research or technology transfer to the enterprises (FAPERGS, 1996). The projects chosen were the following:

Case 1: Reliability of Systems - this project aimed at improving the techniques of reliability of systems used by the company, searching for optimization of the quality of its product as well as competitive advantages. The company deals in the automotive components sector, being one of the biggest companies of its kind in Brazil, supplying several vehicle assemblers. In this project a methodology to analyze the reliability was developed, producing software for this purpose and its use in the process of quality control.

Case 2: Powdered Paint - the goal was a characterization of different resins used in producing powdered paint. With this, some significant improvement in the quality of a product whose market has been presenting significant increase was expected. The sector of the company involved in the project is responsible for the internal market of resins for many kinds of paint. A new technology for resin characterization and a new analysis technique was obtained. That allowed the development of two new resins and improvement in powdered paint quality.

Table 22.1 shows the result of these projects identified with the use of proposed indicators. The methodology used in identifying the results were interviews with people involved in the project, both in research center and enterprise. A questionnaire was used with questions concerning the consumed inputs, the developed product, the impacts and provided benefits. Before interviewing, analyses of the projects and the final report sent to FAPERGS by the researchers were made. Thus we could have an overall view of project considering different perceptions.

RESULTS ANALYSIS

Besides the indicators presented above others were proposed: new products developed, variation in the use of production factors, variation of work posts and employees, tax collection and patents. These results weren't presented in the studied cases not because they're unnecessary, but rather because some expected results (considered potential by the financing Institute) were not achieved in these projects.

As for the indicators of economic character whose function is evaluating this impact in the enterprise, no precise data were obtained. In two cases, people involved stated that there are difficulties when it comes to identifying these items, since none of the parts involved shows interest in collecting them. Thus there are no ways of filtering the portion of sales and profitability increase, for example, that was provided by the project results. There are also other factors that can cause these effects. Since the two are big companies, the project was considered small within its dynamics. The benefits are just perceived in the sector of the company involved in project development.

Considering what was said above, an analysis of project efficiency cannot be achieved. In order to establish the cost-benefit relation it is necessary that since the beginning of the project there is a control on costs and its impacts in the enterprise. This kind of control must also be used in the research centers where there is the largest diffusion of knowledge.

People interviewed said that the two projects achieved their goals. This information can also be found through the analysis of product indicators. So, the project efficiency can be checked through these data. The Competence Formation item shows that in the research center there is a greater number of people involved than in the enterprise. These indicators show the potential of progress that new knowledge can have, in addition to demonstrate the effective formation of human resources qualified scientifically and technologically.

Another fact that should be emphasized is the identification of intangible results. The importance of a character, not only quantitative, stands out during the evaluation process. The following results were obtained during the interviews (Table 22.2).

Table 22.1: Selected Results of University – Enterprise Interaction Projects.

		Project:	Reliability of Systems	Powdered Paints
INPUTS	FAP	Invested Value	R$ 10,060.00	R$ 50,000.00
		Scholarships granted:		
		scientific initiation		1
		new Master´s degree	1	
	ENTERPRISE	Invested Value on Research Center	R$ 1,000.00	R$ 6,000.00
		Invested Value in the Enterprise	R$ 25,000.00	R$ 6,000.00
		Invested Value as % of the revenue	0.0260%	0.0019%
OUTPUTS	DIRECTS	Articles Published:		
		national meetings	1	2
		international meetings	3	1
		Theses		1
		Masters Dissertations	2	
		Softwares	3	
		New Methodologies	1	1
		Competencies Developed: Research Center		
		undergraduate	1	2
		master students	2	
		PhD students		1
		Masters Degree Thesis	1	
		PhD	1	1
		Competencies Developed: Enterprise		
		graduate	1	2
		undergraduate	2	
	TECHNOLOGY INNOVATIONS	Improved Materials		2
		Improved Products		1
		New Processes	1	
		Improved Processes		1
IMPACTS	ON THE ENTERPRISE	Proportion of sales increase	not available	not available
		Proportion of exports increase	not available	10% (approx.)
		Proportion of revenue increase	not available	not available
		Proportion of costs reduction	not available	10% (approx.)
		Increase of the technological capacity (Y or N)	Y	Y
		Use of advanced technologies (Y or N)	Y	Y
	SOCIAL	Use of cleaner technologies (Y or N)		Y
		Traineeships		2
		Trainings/Courses	1	
		Academic disciplines that use the developed knowledge	1	not available
		Other companies/institutions that used the knowledge or technology	3	not available
		New projects	1	1

Table 22.2: Other results of University Enterprise Interaction selected projects.

Reliability of Systems	Powdered Paints
Enterprise recognition in automotive industry	Improvement in University-Enterprise relationship
Improvement of the customers reliance on enterprise	The use of other training and equipment at University by the enterprise
Possibility of work at research group with practical questions	Possibility of best answers to customers
Possibility of testing new technologies in real applications for research group	Possibility of the use of developed techniques in other areas of the enterprise
Maturation and consolidation of research group	Contact of the research group with a big company

The use of this methodology was efficient. At the beginning there was a set of preliminary indicators. The identification of unexpected results caused an increase in the indicators list. Through the study of similar cases, we intended to get a more complete and efficient set of indicators for evaluation. Intangible results shall be found and should be presented because they characterize the complexity of benefits and impacts of this kind of project.

FINAL REMARKS

This proposition and the test of a set of indicators aim at moving forward the discussion about the evaluation of R&D projects financed by public institutions. The use of adequate indicators should enable conclusions not only about the results of financed projects, but also about the extent to which they affect the society. The impact indicators have this latter function. Product indicators demonstrate direct tangible results that are more narrowly connected to research center and associate enterprise. The Input Indicators quantify which resources have been used in order to achieve the presented results and impacts.

Many proposed indicators, especially those that have a financial character, could not be informed by the people involved in the cases studied. The enterprises have an idea of their extent, however they have no ways to precisely quantify them. This demonstrates that it is necessary to have a formal system of evaluation, so that there is control when the project is being developed, with the purpose of answering questions of this nature at the end.

Another aspect to be taken into account is the time that it takes for the appearance of an impact on the society, economy or the environment. Very often answers for some of the indicators can only be obtained a long time after the conclusion of the project. For instance, an innovation can bring long term profits after its launching; the benefits of a product or process ecologically correct that saves energy and doesn't produce residues can be felt for a long term. Besides, considering the gradual advancement of science, rarely a project represents a great advancement by itself. Thus it is important to consider the process of evaluation through indicators as one simultaneous picture. One of the questions still under discussion in this area is electing the best moment to take this picture.

Therefore more studies should be made in order to overcome the problems involved in setting indicators of results evaluation for Science and Technology projects. As stated earlier, there is no ideal system that works for all kinds of projects. It is necessary to take into account the specific nature of the project and the peculiarities of the policy that determine its objectives, as well as the span of time in which the impacts shall be perceived.

BIBLIOGRAPHY

Brazilian Academy of Sciences (1999). *Science In Brazil: An Overview*. Prepared for the World Conference on Science, Budapest, 26 June- 1 July .

Campos, André L. S. (1999) *Identificação de Impactos Econômicos a partir da Pesquisa Acadêmica: um Estudo de Projetos Temáticos da FAPESP*. Master Thesis . Instituto de Geociências / UNICAMP, Campinas - SP - Brasil.

Cozzens, Susan E. (2000) Assessing federally-supported academic research in the United States. *Research Evaluation*. Vol. 8, number 1, pg. 5-10. April.

FAPERGS . (1996). *Edital 01/96 – Edital Programa de Estímulo à interação de centros e grupos de pesquisa com o setor empresarial*. Secretaria de Ciência e Tecnologia: RS

FAPESP (1996). *Relatório de Atividades*. Secretaria de Ciência, Tecnologia e Desenvolvimento Econômico: SP.

Fracasso, Edi et al..(1998) "Indicadores e sugestões para avaliação institucional". *Relatório Preliminar*. FAPERGS: Porto Alegre, agosto.

MacLean, Marlie et al. (1998) Evaluating the research activity and impact of funding agencies. *Research Evaluation*. Vol. 7, number 1, pg. 7-16. April.

Maculan, Anne M., Meroni, José C. A. (1998). "Como avaliar a transferência do conhecimento na interação universidade-empresa?" *XX Simpósio de Gestão da Inovação Tecnológica*. São Paulo, 17 a 20 de novembro de 1998. *Anais...*

Martinez, Eduardo. (1998). "Glosario: ciencia, tecnología y desarrollo". In: Martinez, Eduardo, Albornoz, Mario (eds.) *Indicadores de ciencia y tecnologia: estado del arte y perspectivas*. Caracas: Nueva Sociedad.

Martinez, Eduardo, Albornoz, Mario. (1998a). "Indicadores de ciencia y tecnologia: balance y persperctivas". In: Martinez, Eduardo, Albornoz, Mario (eds.) *Indicadores de ciencia y tecnologia: estado del arte y perspectivas*. Caracas: Nueva Sociedad.

OCDE. (1998). "Manual de Oslo. La medición de las actividades científicas y técnicas. Principios básicos propuestos para la recopilación e interpretación de datos sobre innovación tecnológica", in:

Martinez, Eduardo, Albornoz, Mario (eds.) *Indicadores de ciencia y tecnologia: estado del arte y perspectivas*. Caracas: Nueva Sociedad.

OECD (1998a). "Consecuencias del programa de tecnología/economía para el desarrollo de indicadores". In: martinez, Eduardo, Albornoz, Mario (eds.) *Indicadores de ciencia y tecnologia: estado del arte y perspectivas*. Caracas: Nueva Sociedad.

Ohayon, Pierre. (1991). "Quadro metodológico para implementação de um sistema de indicadores da avaliação na FAPERJ – Fundação da Amparo à Pesquisa do Estado do Rio de Janeiro". *XVI Simpósio Nacional de Pesquisa em Administração* . 20 a 30 de outubro, Rio de Janeiro, P. E 81. *Anais*...

Sbraggia, Roberto. (1984) Avaliação do desempenho do projetos em instituições de pesquisa: um estudo empírico dentro do setor de tecnologia industrial. *Revista de Administração*. v.19, n.1, jan – mar, pp. 83-93.

Shelton, Joanna. (1997). "Opening Address". *OECD Conference on Policy Evaluation in Innovation and Technology*. Chapter 2, Paris 26-27, June.

Silva, Alberto C. (1999). *Presented at Seminário Internacional Universidade e Ciência na América Latina – A ciência apara o século vinte e um*. AUGM, ORCYT/UNESCO, IESALC/UNESCO e UFRGS. UFRGS, Porto Alegre, RS, Brasil. Nov. 18-19.

Street, Penny; Barker, Katharine.(1998) Evaluating the impacts of buildings energy research in the UK *Research Evaluation*. Vol. 4, number 4, pg. 171-179. December.

UNICEF. (1997). *A UNICEF Guide for Monitoring and Evaluation*. EUA, 1997.

Velho, Lea. (1994). "Indicadores científicos: aspectos teóricos y metodológicos". In: Martinez, Eduardo (ed.). *Ciencia, tecnología y desarrollo: interrelaciones teóricas y metodológicas*. Caracas: Nueva Sociedad.

Management of Technology
Copyright © 2003 by Elsevier Science Ltd.
All rights of reproduction in any form reserved.
ISBN: 0-08-044136-X

23

MANAGING SOFTWARE INNOVATION IN MULTI-COMPANY SETTINGS

Ian McLoughlin, The Business School, University of Newcastle, UK*
Christian Koch, Department for Civil Engineering, Technical University of Denmark**

SUMMARY

Software product development is becoming increasingly complex and increasingly occurs in multi-company alliances and networks. New product development in this setting can be seen as a political process. The aim here is to challenge and transcend the notion that political processes in innovation are merely a disruptive and even a counterproductive feature. We review the growing number of studies that highlight the political aspect of innovation and point to the way in which the mobilization of power – not just as a resource but as a relational and symbolic entity – are a central feature of sustained new product development and innovation. We report on a study conducted within the EU–TSER program. Drawing on intensive field studies in two constellations of enterprises - a dual collaboration and a complex innovation network - it is shown how the winning of resources, shifting positions of players and deeper structures such as culture and discourse are integral to and an inevitable feature of the product development process. This leads to an understanding of a networking paradox: in seeking to reduce political uncertainties of one type, actors engage with others and build collaborative relationships which themselves lead to other and new political issues which have to be tackled.

---

*   Ian McLoughlin is Professor of Management and Head of the University of Newcastle upon Tyne Business School.
**   Christian Koch is Associate Professor of management of production at the Group for Construction Management, Department of Civil Engineering at the Technical University of Denmark.

INTRODUCTION

Innovation is increasingly seen as a phenomenon best regarded as conducted through network relationships. Perspectives on innovation networks range from institutional and evolutionary economics on the one hand through organisational analysis/theory to sociologically influenced constructivist positions on the other. There have also been attempts to cross-fertilise between these apparently diverse positions in the study of innovation networks (Coombs et al.; 1996 Green et al., 1999). We wish to contribute to this development by seeking to apply a political process perspective to the analysis of innovation networks - especially collaboration between organisations engaged in software development. The political process perspective views organisations as 'fundamentally political entities' wherein organisational members pursue their own potentially conflicting interests (Pfeffer, 1992; Pettigrew, 1985; Dawson 1994; McLoughlin 1999; Buchanan and Badham 1999; Koch, 2000a). As such, the outcomes of technological change and innovation can be seen as shaped in significant ways by the exercise of power by participants as through building coalitions and negotiating with others. By examining coalition building within and between organisations when collaborating in new product development, we also broaden the traditional focus of the political process perspective, which has tended to focus on processes within the individual organisation. As Elg and Johansson (1997) note, networks of organisations can equally well be seen as structural arrangements fused by conflicting and mutual interests and, as such, a key dynamic of network development, will also be the desire to advance and defend self-interests on the part of participants.

The structure of our discussion is as follows. First we provide a brief overview of the treatment of political process as one factor shaping innovation networks and collaboration within and between organisations engaged in new product development. Here we suggest that the exercise of power through political activity is more central to innovation, collaboration and networks than is conventionally assumed. We then seek to demonstrate the role of political processes in collaboration to develop new products through a presentation of case study findings from a study of innovation networks in the UK, Denmark and Germany. Here we confine ourselves to a discussion of one of the UK and one of the Danish case studies. The discussion is developed over three dimensions of the political; winning resources, political processes, and the deeper structures such as cultures as a source for assigning meaning to the product development

The paper draws heavily on McLoughlin, Koch and Dickson (2001) as well as the work of the BiCoN research team (BiCoN is short for Building Collaborative Networks in innovation). The study was financed by the EU-TSER programme.[1]

THE ROLE OF THE POLITICAL IN INNOVATION STUDIES

The prevailing image in the literature on innovation networks is one of collaboration in new product development being built on values and relationships characterised by mutuality and trust (Weyer, 1997). The orthodox position would argue that conventional product innovation in 'mechanistic' firms in contrast is portrayed as difficult to sustain and one best characterised by adversarial relationships between functions, hierarchies, employer/employees, suppliers, customers and so on (Burns and Stalker, 1961). The mechanistic form is politicised, network is politics-free.

Brown and Eisenhardt (1995) find that many studies of new product development adopt a rationalistic perspective based on the assumption that 'a product that is well planned, implemented and appropriately supported will be a success' (1995:344) (including works like Souder & Sherman 1994). From this viewpoint there is little room for consideration of the political other than as a potentially disruptive barrier to innovation as noted above.

A second area of research identified by Brown et al however focuses more closely on the decision-making process and views successful product development as 'disciplined problem solving' (e.g. Clark and Fujimoto, 1991). This requires the exercise of 'subtle control' by senior management who must create a strong vision for a new product to ensure outcomes fit with corporate objectives but at the same time leave sufficient ambiguity for 'experiential improvisation' within the development team. The work of this balancing is ascribed to 'heavyweight' team leaders (Brown and Eisenhardt, 1995: 351). However, whilst suggestive of some kind of political process, as Brown et al point out, concepts such as 'heavyweight' team leaders remain vague and lack 'political realism' in the sense that such leaders are portrayed as almost 'superhuman'.

A final area of research identified in Brown et al's review stresses the significance of external communication to successful product development (including works like Allen, 1977). This goes further in highlighting political activity in some sense as a means of securing the resources required for successful product development. In particular, 'politically orientated external communication' is shown to increase the resources flowing to a product development team. In similar fashion, high levels of internal communication are seen to improve team performance.

---

[1] The project was funded by the European Commission under contract number PL97 – 1084 of the Targeted Socio-Economics Research Programme, Phase 2. Funding Period: January 1998 to December 1999.

In one of the studies which is more sensitive to political processes, Dougherty and Hardy (1996), argue that sustained new product development requires first the winning of resources (finance, technology, knowledge, information); second the creation of organisational processes and structures, which enable collaboration; and third the establishment of clear linkages between product development and overall organisational strategy. However these requirements are not easily fulfilled, especially in 'mature' organisations which have hitherto not been particularly innovative. In particular, problems may occur when trying to establish a smooth flow of resources. This requires project 'champions' to build effective coalitions of support; change existing organisational arrangements and routines which act as a constraint on effective collaboration; creating meanings which enable others to understand the strategic significance and value of a new product development. Indeed, from their own research Dougherty and Hardy suggest that, the most successful product innovators are those who were able to solve a *high proportion of the resource, change and creation of meaning problems* (see also Vendelø 1999).

Dougherty and Hardy are primarily concerned with internal collaboration and conducted research that focused on mature firms who hitherto had not engaged in sustained product innovation. Their analysis provides a number of pointers to the nature of the power-processes that may be involved in new product development in general, including those involving inter-organisational as well as intra-organisational collaboration. For example, they suggest that a focus on the personal power of individual managers to control resources (budgets, information, expertise etc.) 'only scratches the surface of power dynamics' (1996: 1147). They suggest that power also reside in the processes through which innovation occurs. Sustained innovation organisational systems are required which permit effective collaboration which is not dependent upon the actions of powerful individuals. Moreover, the power of the meaning supporting innovation is 'crucial' since without this the possession of resources 'easily unravels' (1996: 1148).

Midler (1993) studies the emergent, contingent and vulnerable character of the new product development process. Midler characterises the development of a new Renault car as a process of coalition building. Its proponents within the organisation seek support for the new car concept. This is presented as a complicated and 'incomplete' process where the project manager plays a core role in mobilising support. For our purposes, what is important here is the way in which the development of a new product can be seen as predicated on the building of a network of support through the enrolment of key supporters and interests. Our contention is that the majority of innovation processes can be construed in these terms, that is, as constituting internal and external processes of alliance building and negotiations.

This brings us back to a consideration of the manner in which collaboration is built, not just within, but also between organisations engaged in new product development. There is no reason to suppose that inter firm interactions should not be shaped by power-processes. Elg and

Johansson (1997), who develop upon earlier work by Frost and Egri (1991), take up this point. They examine decision-making processes in asymmetrical relationships in inter-firm networks. The proposition - based on resource-dependency theory – is that network participants will seek to influence the decision-making process, advancing their specific interests and enhancing their position within the network. For example, organisations with more powerful positions will seek to exploit and preserve this position whilst weaker organisations will seek to alter the conditions of their dependency. Network participants will seek potential sources of network support and then seek to control interactions within the network in order to use these supportive structures. Much of this will involve the 'observable' exercise of power by one party over another.

However, in a similar argument to Dougherty and Hardy, it is suggested that more subtle political activity will involve the non-observable 'hidden' exercise of power and the power embedded in 'deep structures' of 'taken for granted' norms, expectations and beliefs. In particular, the analysis of the distribution of power between network participants, which is provided by a resource-dependency model is seen by Elg and Johansson 1997 as too static. As Thomas (1994) notes, whilst adequate for a single decision-event at a particular point in time, when examining the unfolding pattern of a series of decisions over time, such notions of the structural sources of power are less realistic. For this reason, power processes should be examined by encompassing their relational characteristic and by recognising the importance of coalition building, enrolment and legitimation in mobilising and exerting power.

Summarising; innovation studies cover a range of different conceptualisations of political elements. We have argued for studying new product development as a political process exerted inside as well as across organisations using the most conceptualised versions, like Dougherty and Hardy, Elg & Johansson and Midler. From these studies we can derive a threefold focus on resources, the process of coalition building and the role of deeper structure such as culture as sources for creating of meaning. These dimensions can be further elaborated by drawing on research on organisational politics, which is done elsewhere (McLoughlin et al 2001).

SOFTWARE INNOVATION AS BUILDING OF COLLABORATIVE NETWORKS

The IT-sector and software development have experienced revolutionary growth and restructuring. The craft of developing software and ensuring its functionality and quality has therefore been significantly mingled with management, marketing and other corporate activities (Salzman and Rosenthal, 1994). Nevertheless, several forms of market and associated organisation of software development as product development continue to coexist. Two are significant for our concerns here:

1. Where markets require bespoke software solutions to specific business needs. These situations tend to be characterised by a dynamic of close collaboration between the supplier and the customer/end-user (Kyng and Mathiassen, 1997).

2. Where mass markets have emerged for software products (e.g. as for accounting and logistics software such as ERP, Koch, 2000b, Clausen & Koch, 1999). This typically involves a highly mediated relationship between the software supplier and the end-user.

In each case the imperatives for and dynamics of collaboration in internal and external networks tend to be different. Within the BiCoN-study a variety of collaborations were investigated. These included studies of specific artefacts as well as software development projects. They involved dyadic collaborations between firms, 'hybrid' network organisation, university-industry collaborations, and more complex multi-organisation networks. The two cases discussed below concern, first, the formation of the 'hybrid' network organisation and, second, a complex network involving a developer, intermediate developers/resellers, and a range of customers, where one participated in the development of the product studied. Both cases focus on software development. The research method included semi-structured interviews with nodal and other players, analysis of documentary material and more informal meetings and dialogue.

CASE 1: SOFTWARE DEVELOPMENT IN A HYBRID ORGANISATION: SOFTCO AND ELCO

SOFTCO's core business was information technology systems integration, applications development, outsourcing and 'business transformation'. A central activity was the application of arguably tailor-made 'state-of-the-art' IT systems to improve business processes in client organisations. Its rapid growth had been built around the establishment of partnerships with key clients in a number of industry sectors, including, financial services, health care, travel and, as we will see in this instance, the energy sector. The company targeted these sectors, because they were characterised by radical changes requiring organisations operating within them to fundamentally rethink business operations. This included in this case the other part of the hybrid organisation, an Electricity Company – Elco – which had been created by the privatisation of the UK energy market. In both cases the company names are disguised.

For Elco privatisation meant developing a strategic response to enable it to compete in the newly deregulated market. Like other supply companies, developing technological systems and infrastructure was identified as a key source of competitive advantage. The company did not see its computer systems as strategic and decided, in 1992, to embark upon a twelve-year outsourcing agreement with SOFTCO. This arrangement provided the basis for an extension of the collaboration between SOFTCO and Elco into two software systems development and modification projects.

SOFTCO had developed an approach to developing new software products which involved building organisational hybrids - joint temporary project organisations of mixed people from SOFTCO and Elco. The hybrids were built through a relatively systematic process of network building involving *inter alia*, pre-contract relationship building, 'body shopping' (a process of identifying and partnering key people in the client organisation with SOFTCO personnel) o support the mixing), and a change management team responsible for negotiating a formal collaboration agreement. The aim of 'organisational hybrids' was to 'bridge' management, operational and culture 'gaps' with potential partners where collaboration was conducted through client-specific organisational arrangements. The temporary project organisation was tasked with the required IT system development and business transformation. This quotation from a publication written by the chairman of SOFTCO spells out the managerial implications of this: "In a world where the lines between companies, industries, and even nations get blurred, a leader builds an effective organisation around values and work style. And a leader learns to define success in business as both producing financial strength and generating a team of people who support and nurture each other." (Chairman of SOFTCO, 1996).

The change management team of SOFTCO was involved once a contract agreement was imminent. The team worked independently of the pre-contract relationship building. This was a deliberate strategy to make sure that the inevitably adversarial nature of such negotiations did not impinge upon or deflect the building of high trust relations elsewhere. The change management team was also responsible for negotiating employment at the hybrid organisation with individual client personnel. The software development project was aimed at supporting customer management, in a deregulated setting where customers would be able to purchase electricity from any supply company. Early adaptation of business processes and information systems would allow Elco to enter the de-regulated market place ahead of many of its competitors and thereby capture vital new market share and extend its customer-base. Accordingly, the development of its information and computing systems were seen by Elco's Managing Director as a critical resource for the future. The outsourcing arrangement with SOFTCO was viewed as a means of reducing uncertainty by ensuring that this resource was available to the organisation. At the same time, it is envisaged that such an arrangement could be the basis for a joint venture that would create a new organisation able to market its services and expertise elsewhere in the energy industry. As in the case of most of its client partners, SOFTCO was very different in its way of organising, operating and in terms of its culture.

Elco was an organisation which had a history in the public sector and whose prior development had been based on a public service ethos, involved bureaucratic forms of organisation, management style, and collective regulation in industrial relations. In contrast,

SOFTCO was a small but rapidly growing organisation with a flat structure. It had an innovative approach to business development. This was manifested in an orientation towards the customer and membership of the organisation; an emphasis on flexibility and a willingness to take risks; and a strong encouragement to employees to take the initiative and to try new ideas. This 'cultural mismatch' called into question the effectiveness of SOFTCOs approach to building collaboration. This was manifested both within the new hybrid project organisation and between the project organisation and Elco, where employees and managers felt uneasy in many ways about the co-operation. The body shopping and the hybrid organisation were therefore accompanied with tensions and low trust in the co-operation. Despite these organisational problems, the 'hybrid' organisation began to make significant progress. Software was updated, new applications developed and the structure of Elco was simplified into a number of regional business units. The hybrid organisation expanded and a human resources function was established. This used recruitment and selection techniques to ensure a closer 'fit' between an individual's profile and the organisation's culture as additional staff were recruited. A major review of the collaboration after four years was influential in ensuring the continuation of the relationship between the two companies, despite the previous problems. Ironically, the application of newly-acquired commercial acumen - in part provided through the existing collaboration with SOFTCO - also allowed Elco to negotiate far more favourable terms than had originally been the case. This victory illustrated the extent of learning that had taken place at Elco. Its bargaining power had been enhanced by the recent recruitment of a new Finance Director and senior staff with IT knowledge, in a somewhat belated attempt to regain in-house technical knowledge and reduce the dependence on SOFTCO.

In 1998, six years after the signing of the initial outsourcing agreement, the hybrid organisation employed some 650 people. The workload in developing and revising software was now such that an SOFTCO subsidiary outside of Europe had been contracted to carry out development alongside other SOFTCO staff-based in its overseas headquarters. The 'hybrid' organisation became a multi company setting as development teams began to collaborate across three continents in what amounted to a 24 hour software development cycle.

In the late 1990s both Elco and SOFTCO experienced further changes in their business environments. Elco was the subject of a take over by another energy company. At the same time SOFTCO became a publicly quoted company. Elco, now under new ownership, gave notice of termination of the relationship with SOFTCO. The collaboration agreement ended five years short of the agreed 12 year arrangement. This was said by Elco to be the result of a 'strategic business decision', to 'return control of key elements of IT infrastructure and systems in house' and to 'provide the flexibility for IT to support [Elco's new owner's] strategy. This strategy was to 'acquire and merge with power companies in the United Kingdom, United States and world-wide'.

CASE 2: MASS PRODUCTION OF SOFTWARE: HANSEN AND ITS NETWORK

The company in the centre of the network is a software house named "Hansen" (a pseudonym). The software is a generic enterprise resource planning (ERP) package. This comprises customisable modules covering various aspect of business functionality (finance, human resources etc.). The installed base of these systems covers more than 50,000 customers within Denmark and more than 15,000 abroad. The system is sold in more than 20 countries.

The development, sale and implementation of this software involve a complex collaboration between Hansen itself and a network of value-added resellers (VAR-s) and a small number of major customers in the private and public sector. Many of the VAR-s had several times the turnover of Hansen itself and the network itself was continuing to develop with new entrants, existing members leaving and other restructuring effects (mergers between VAR-s and so on).

The VAR-s both co-operated and competed within this framework. Many had overlapping customer groups, whilst others focused on more restricted market niches. Within this framework a range of additional services had been developed and 'bundled' with the main software product, such as consulting, training and additional software modules. Within Denmark the network of VAR-s consists of over 100 companies. Internationally, there are approximately another 500 VAR-s linked to Hansen. These are legally independent companies with various types of formalised relationships with Hansen and 'end-user' customer enterprises.

It is important to note therefore that, in contrast to SOFTCO's close relationship with Elco in the above case, Hansen does not have a direct relationship with most of its customers. The development of the collaborative networks with the VAR-s was a consequence of a deliberate strategy. This sought to use such inter-organisational collaborations as a means of 'outsourcing' sales and implementation, whilst maintaining product development activities in house. However the larger and some of the more specialised VAR-s started developing additional software. The result was a distributed system of new product development. In this case we focus on the development of the third generation of the ERP system and a specific module within this. This project involved the development of collaborative networks within Hansen itself, which then interacted with the broader network of VAR-s and selected customers described above.

The software development process was initiated in the mid-90s. It is a clear example of 'classical product development' where innovations in the technical content of the product predominated building on experience of developing and using experience with the earlier generation of the product gained by the VAR-s and end-users. The overall business objective behind was to make the product more appropriate for use by middle sized (not just small) enterprises and to expand in the international market.

The organisation of the product development process was based upon the Microsoft Solutions Framework (MSF) (see Cusomano and Selby, 1995). This represented a shift from a traditional functional project organisation to a form of matrix organisation. This involved the decentralisation of decision making to product teams and the shortening of development cycles. The objectives behind were first a reduction in 'time-to-market'. Second a realisation that sustaining the growth of the company was dependent upon finding new ways in which to 'leverage' the skills, expertise and knowledge of programmers and system developers during the product development process.

The formation of teams for the software development broadly followed the MSF rules and procedures. One of the teams was followed in their work to realise one module of the package The team was particularly successful in negotiating with the overall project management an appropriate fit of its task to available resources. The team were able to limit the scope of the tasks they were required to undertake and were able to persuade the project management to take a task away from the team. Similarly, in the planning phase, the team was able to take the initiative in prioritising certain tasks and downplaying others. Subsequently the team was able to win additional human resources.

Internal communications within the team appeared to work effectively; as specified by MSF the team included a product manager, recruited externally, who had practical experience in the domain the software module was to address. In most of the MSF phases the team was able to agree internally most of its priorities and design and to resist 'interference' from outside. At 'post mortem' meetings held at the end of each cycle of the MSF, several activities were evaluated by the team. These included the internal collaboration within the team itself and how their respective roles were functioning.

The team established *external* communication about the customer requirement with the external intermediary network of VAR-s and significant major customers. In the first phase there were informal interactions between the team and the external VAR network. Here three VAR-s and one significant end user/customer were consulted. These largely informal linkages served to open up information and communication channels between the VAR-s (who had a more direct experience of customer requirements) and the team (who were also able to manage the VAR-s expectations as to what the new module would actually deliver). In a parallel process the VAR-s were more 'formally' consulted. A committee of VAR-s held three meetings before project management decided to halt the activity. This reflected a continuing debate within Hansen on the role of the VAR-s. Several different departments of Hansen articulated different views on this issue. Within the team studied, some members proffered an interpretation that 'listening to the customers is in contradiction with being ahead of the competitors'. The beta version of the module from this first cycle was released against the wishes of the team. This resulted in a heavy bombardment of telephone calls to the team from VAR representatives and others, who wanted specific details incorporated in the next cycle.

Two further forums served to facilitate the flow of information between Hansen and the VAR-s and between the VAR-s and end user/customers. These were monthly strategic meetings with both the Hansen distribution function and project management and project development workshops organised by the VAR-s for their customers which had in some instances resulted in joint specification of requirements. However from the point of view of the VAR-s network the overall development process posed a number of problems. Whilst all VAR-s were keen to inform and support the development of the new ERP-package, not all were convinced that the end product was superior to competitor offerings. In some cases VAR-s chose to develop their own additional modules in order to make their total offer more competitive from their viewpoint. Some VAR-s indicated that early product releases lacked the necessary quality and created problems with customers. By the end of our research period there were still some VAR-s who would not implement the main releases of the ERP-package because of perceived quality problems. Several VAR-s express consternation regarding infrequent releases of service packs for servicing the existing base, and some mentioned the lack of help from Hansen in creating sales arguments in relation to competing systems. To this end VAR-s used informal networks and contacts with software development project teams to gain product information of this type. In some cases these flows of information contradicted internal structures and procedures within Hansen.

Such tensions also highlight a differentiated landscape of VAR-s. Many are 'total systems solutions' providers where additional tailor made programming is a central offer. Some have a role as developers whereas others are mere implementers of a standardised system. If developers and total systems solutions providers flourish this is a problem for Hansen in the long term in so far as the company is primarily interested in branding its ERP product as a very flexible standard solution with little need of subsequent customisation.

DISCUSSION

Below we will discuss and compare the cases in terms of the following levels of power-processes identified earlier. First the role of resources, winning and maintaining them. Second the political process dynamics in the form of shifting relations between actors over time. Third the role of deeper structure. The two cases will be discussed and compared.

Mobilising and winning resources

One aspect of the political dynamic in network building is revealed by the insights offered by the resource dependency perspective. The winning of resources for new product development differ in the two cases since the Hansen management is very attentive towards continual product development and allocating the needed resources even to the extremely large development of the third generation of the product. Elco on the other hand demonstrate the 'ignorant' feature that can be seen as typical for mature organisations. Once the alliance between SOFTCO and Elco has been established however, the temporary project organisation is extremely successful in gaining resources. In the Hansen case the resource issue also occurs as a question of fit between the XAS-teams resources in the beginning of the development process and the task assigned to them. They thus successfully downgrade the task arguing that there is too little resource in the team for taking up a proposed task.

Political process dynamics

In the two cases it can be observed how the relative positions of the collaborators changed over time in the face of shifting contextual conditions and developments in the sophistication of the collaborators approach. The collaboration between SOFTCO and Elco and between Hansen and the VAR-s reflects the challenge of organising an alliance with partners while the actors strive to define their respective roles and, having done so, to build in a degree of control over the alliance. The development of the collaboration does seem to be characterised by a struggle for such control, which in the SOFTCO-Elco case ultimately was resolved by Elco's new owner through bringing IT-activities back in-house. In the Hansen-VAR case the struggle for control was resolved by varying and mediating social distance and closeness with the VAR representatives through formal and informal channels.

The commencing interactions between SOFTCO and Elco, quickly allowed SOFTCO to develop a position of considerable strength, through the appropriation of technological and business knowledge which Elco had viewed as non-core. Having achieved this SOFTCO was in a position of considerable influence in defining the development of the collaboration through the development of a 'hybrid' organisation. However, its success in this respect sharpened the sophistication of E's business strategy who sought to exercise greater control over the relationship with SOFTCO. This was done through tighter formal contractual controls and through introducing new managers as well as third parties to manage the relationship. Elco sought to gain control of the product development agenda by drawing upon new sources of support in the network. Thus, whilst the latter moves were resisted to some extent by SOFTCO, they had an effect by moving the collaboration into a position where the relative strength of each organisation was mutually accepted as complementary. However, this position was upset again by the broader changes of ownership, which resulted in Elco again redefining its perception of the relationship.

In the Hansen case, the nodal software house seems to have a non-contested leadership position. Hansen thus sets the agenda of the third generation of the ERP-software and sets out building the necessary internal and external supporting organisational arrangements. Some VAR-s however, do not need to wait for Hansen to develop their system and new modules but choose to start alternative processes of developing parallel modules and or other modules thus changing the relative importance of the Hansen development process. Moreover the internal network of Hansen around the MARK III and XAS does not stay aligned throughout the process. Rather sales and consulting representatives develop tensions internally in their quest for competitive advantage through early release of the new product.

Mobilising deeper structures

Finally a third level of power-processes, the 'deep structures' of power embedded in values, cultures and meaning is important. Innovation is not entirely dependent upon the actions of powerful 'resource-winners' or of power developed in political process. Power can also reside in organisational systems, which permit effective collaboration and in the 'power of meanings' supporting innovation. This seems to resonate with the new product development as 'disciplined problem solving' perspective discussed above, where strong visions and values link innovation to corporate objectives but leave sufficient ambiguity for 'experiential improvisation' within development teams. Hansen and SOFTCO's processes for organising software development work (such as the MSF-method and SOFTCO-s multi-team approach) and the culture through which they encourage sense-making can be seen as meaning systems which ensure 'product integrity'. In the SOFTCO case this constitutes a form of organizing for innovation suited for 'hybrid/agile' organisational forms. It blurs all manner of accepted boundaries and divisions in the interest of finding new ways to synthesise knowledge. The CEO-s understanding of values underpins the cultural side of the hybrid. The Hansen case on the other hand demonstrates more traditional ways of using organisational boundaries and procedures to enable the product development.

In contrast to this the role of teams in the Hansen case is more in the direction of a means to organise and compartmentalise a large and complicated product development task. Hansen mass produce software and the introduction of MSF is clearly a strong symbolic tool to balance out the need for creativity and teamwork with large scale project organising in a high speed and hyper competitive environment. MSF is used a tool for downplay tendencies of "over the wall" development enhancing cross disciplinary competency, done on the basis of the perceived success of and importance of MSF in the Microsoft context (Cusomano and Selby, 1995). The need for cultural underpinning of teamwork in the SOFTCO case mirrors the "one of a kind" organisation which similarly underpins the mass production element in the Hansen case.

CONCLUSION

Our analysis has demonstrated the emergent character and political dynamics of the software development process. In both cases operating across organisational boundaries in a multi company setting is the key characteristic of the innovation process. The arena for the political is thus broader and more complicated than traditional organisational politics studies would normally recognise. We have focused in particular on the issues of winning and mobilising resources, the process of changing actors' positions and developing coalitions, and the role of deeper structures of culture and discourse as a resource for ascribing meaning and direction to product development organisation. There are a number of examples of the importance of these issues. The findings from the two studies are further developed in the other BiCoN cases (BiCON 2000). In general, the BiCoN project points to what can be termed as the 'paradox of networking'. That is, technological (and indeed other forms) of collaboration are normally presented as based on intentions to seek a reduction in uncertainty in changing and unpredictable market and technological conditions. However, such behaviour exposes the organisation and its incumbents to new risks and uncertainties. These are associated with the complexities of forging collaborative relationships and the potentially novel (for the participants) organisational arrangements that may arise. Thus, whilst being a source of risk reduction, collaboration in innovation networks may expose collaborators to new vulnerabilities associated with building and managing network relationships and new organisational forms. As we have tried to show here, the building of collaborative networks is a political process and requires political action. It is not only a disruptive feature but an omnipresent element of product development and mastering that can be considered a central element of possible success for new product development.

REFERENCES

Allen, T. J. (1977). *Managing the flow of technology.* MIT press, Cambridge.

BiCON (2000): *Final Report in the BICON-project.* EU/TSER.The European Commission, Bruxelles.

Brown, S. and K.M. Eisenhardt (1995). Produce Development: past research, present findings and future directions. *Academy of Management Review.* 20 (2) 343 - 379.

Buchanan, D and Badham, R (1999). *Power, Politics and Organisational Change.* Sage, London.

Burns, T. and GM Stalker (1961). *The Management of Innovation.* Tavistock, London.

Child, J and D. Faulkner (1998). Strategies of Co-operation. Oxford UP.

Clark, K. and T. Fujimoto (1991). *Product Development Performance: Strategy, Management and Organization in the World Automobile Industry.* Harvard Business School Press, Boston

Clausen C. and C. Koch (1999). The Role of Occasions and Spaces in the Transformation of Information Technologies. *Technology Analysis and Strategic Management* vol. 11 no 3. 463-482.

Coombs, R.,A. Richards, P. Saviotti and V.Walsh (eds.)(1996). *Technological Collaboration: The Dynamics of Co-operation in Industrial Innovation.* Edward Elgar, Cheltenham.

Cusumano, M. A. and R.W. Selby (1995). *Microsoft Secrets: How the World's Most Powerful Software Company Creates Technology, Shapes Markets and Manages People.* Free press, New York.

Dougherty, D. and C. Hardy (1996). Sustained Product Innovation in Large Mature Organisations: Overcoming Innovation to Organisation Problems. *Academy of Management Journal*, 39 (5)

Elg, U and U. Johansson (1997). Decision-making in inter-firm networks as political process. *Organisation Studies*, 18 (3) 361 - 384.

Frost P and C. Egri (1991). The political process of innovation. *Research in Organisational Behaviour.* **13**, 229 - 295.

Green, K., R.Hull, A. McMeekin., V. Walsh. (1999). Construction of the techno-economic: networks vs. paradigms. *Research Policy.*

Koch, C. (2000a). "The Ventriloquist's Dummy ?- The Role of Technology in Political Processes", *Technology Analysis and Strategic Management.* Vol 12 no 1.119-138.

Koch, C. (2000b). ERP-software packages - between mass production communities and intraorganisational political processes   Paper prepared for the EGOS- colloquium: Subtheme 11 Technological Change and Organisational Action. Helsinki

Kyng M. and L. Mathiassen L (1997). *Computers and Design in Context.* MIT Press Cambridge, Massachusetts.

McLoughlin I. P. (1999). *Creative Technological Change: the shaping of technology and organisation.* Routledge, London.

McLoughlin I., C. Koch and K. Dickson (2001). What's this "tosh"? Innovation Networks and new product development as a political process. *International Journal of Innovation Management.* vol 5 no 3. 275-298.

Midler C.(1993). *L'auto qui n'existait pas.* Intereditions, Paris.

Miles, R.E. and Snow, C.C. (1986). Network Organisation: New Concepts for New Forms. *The McKinsey Quarterly*, Autumn.

Pettigrew, A. (1985). *The Awakening Giant.* Blackwell, Oxford.

Pfeffer, J., (1992). *Managing with Power: politics and influence in organisations.* Harvard Business Press, Boston.

Salzman H. and Rosenthal S. (1994). *Software by Design.* Oxford University Press, New York.

Senker, J. and Faulkner, W. (1992). Networks, tacit knowledge and innovation, in Coombs, R. Richards, A. Saviotti, P. and Walsh, V. (eds.) *Technological Collaboration: The Dynamics of Co-operation in Industrial Innovation,* Edward Elgar, Cheltenham.

Souder W.& Sherman J.(1994). *Managing New Technology Development.* McGraw-Hill. New York.

Thomas, R. (1994) *What Machines Can't Do.* University of California Press, Berkeley.

Vendelø, M. T.(1999). The Politics of Software Innovation. *Proceedings vol 2. PICMET-*conference. Portland USA.

Weyer, J. et al (1997*). Technik, die Gesellschaft schafft. Soziale Netzwerke als ort der Technikgenese.* Edition Sigma, Berlin.

Management of Technology
ISBN: 0-08-044136-X

24

MODELING MODULARITY OF PRODUCT ARCHITECTURES

Juliana Hsuan Mikkola, Copenhagen Business School, Denmark [ξ,*]
Oliver Gassmann, University of St. Gallen, Switzerland[**]

ABSTRACT

Modularity refers to the scheme by which interfaces shared among components in a given product architecture are specified and standardized to allow for greater substitutability of components across product families. It is also a new product development strategy for increasing product variety and customization. When interfaces of components or modules within a system becomes standardized, outsourcing decisions can be made accordingly with respect to a firm's long-term strategic planning of its NPD, manufacturing and supply chain management activities. This paper applies a mathematical model for analyzing the degree of modularity in a given product architecture by taking into account the following variables: components, degree of coupling, and substitutability of new-to-the-firm components. The application of the modularization function is illustrated with two elevator systems from Schindler Elevators of Switzerland: traction and hydraulic elevators. The comparative analysis of the elevators captures the sensitivity and dynamics of product architecture modularity created by three types of components (standard, neutral, and unique) and two types of interfaces (fundamental and optional).

[ξ] An earlier version of this paper was presented at the PICMET 2001 Conference.

[*] Juliana Hsuan Mikkola is Research Assistant at Copenhagen Business School, Denmark, Dept. of Operations Management. Email: jh.om@cbs.dk.

[**] Oliver Gassmann is Professor of Technology Management at University of St. Gallen, Switzerland, Institute of Technology Management. Email: Oliver.Gassmann@unisg.ch.

INTRODUCTION

Internationalization of markets, deregulation, more demanding customers, the advances in information and transportation technology contribute to the complexity of designing and managing supply chains (van Hoek *et al.*, 1999) as well as and the management of new product development (NPD) activities (Pine, 1993; Feitzinger and Lee, 1997; Fulkerson, 1997; Gilmore and Pine, 1997; Gooley, 1998). A growing number of high-tech firms (e.g., consumer electronics, automotive electronics) have embraced new approaches to the management of their NPD, manufacturing and supply chain management activities (Gassmann and von Zedtwitz, 1998, 1999; Boutellier *et al.*, 2000). In order to shorten NPD lead time, to introduce multiple product models quickly with new product variants at reduced costs, and to introduce many successive versions of the same product line with increased performance levels, many firms are pursuing modularization as a new product development strategy. Broadly speaking, modularization is an approach for organizing complex products and processes efficiently (Baldwin and Clark, 1997), by decomposing complex tasks into simpler portions so they can be managed independently[1]. Modularization permits components to be produced separately, or loosely coupled (Orton and Weick, 1990; Sanchez and Mahoney, 1996), and used interchangeably in different configurations without compromising system integrity (Flamm, 1988; Garud and Kumaraswamy, 1993; Garud and Kotha, 1994; Garud and Kumaraswamy, 1995). It can significantly reduce manufacturing processes and assemblies leading to increased product variety and customization.

Product configurations are rooted in product architecture designs, be integral or modular. In assessing modularity of product architectures, issues regarding to decomposability (i.e. modularization) as well as bundling of disparate components, into a new innovation (i.e. integration[2]) should be taken into consideration. At the heart of product architecture is the relationship shared among the components and respective interfaces, and the degree of modularity is dependent on: (a) the extent of economies of substitution of components across product families (Garud and Kumaraswamy, 1993, 1995); (b) whether the system can be disaggregated and recombined into new configurations, or mixing-and-matching (Garud and

---

[1] Decomposition of a complex system into smaller, more manageable parts has been well discussed in management and economic literature (e.g., scientific management principles with respect to standardized work designs and specialization of labor (Taylor, 1967), nearly decomposable systems (Simon, 1995; 1996), and Adam Smith's (1776) view on division of labor and task partitioning).

[2] Part integration is a common motive for integral product architectures (Ulrich and Eppinger, 1995; Ulrich *et al.*, 1993), and refers to (Ulrich and Ellison, 1999:647): "the combination of multiple parts into one contiguous part. [It] minimizes the use of material and space associated with component interfaces, and may improve geometric precision, but compromises the one-to-one mapping from functional elements to components."

Kumaraswamy, 1995; Sanchez and Mahoney, 1996; Schilling, 2000); and, (c) the degree to which a system achieves greater functionality by its components being specific to one another (Schilling, 2000).

Similar systems produced by different companies probably have different product architecture designs in terms of design choices and technologies used, suggesting that the composition of components is idiosyncratic to a particular product architecture design. The ability for a firm to develop and manufacture new products (be customized or standardized) is, to great extent, contingent on firm's NPD strategy and how its relationship with suppliers and customers is nurtured over time. If a firm is to invest time and money to develop new components for the product architectures, what are some alternatives to increase the value of these components? To what extent components and respective interfaces influence the modularity of product architectures? How sensitive is product architecture modularity to changes in component composition of newly developed components?

In order to address these questions, a mathematical model is applied for analyzing the degree of product architecture modularity by taking into consideration the following variables: components, degree of coupling, and substitutability of NTF components. The application of the modularization function is illustrated with two elevator systems from Schindler Lifts, the second largest elevator corporation in the world. The remaining of the paper is organized as follows. In the next section, our approach and methodology is introduced and compared with relevant literature. Then, a literature on measurement of modularity and product architecture is reviewed, followed by a brief discussion on the effects of components, interfaces, degree of coupling, and substitutability of NTF components in product architectures. Next, the modularization function is introduced and applied to assess two product architectures of Schindler Elevators: traction and hydraulic. Finally the paper finishes with a summary and suggestions for future research.

Approach and Methodology

In order to manage modularity of product architectures, firms should understand the fundamental relationships shared between components, respective interfaces, and substitutability of newly developed components. In this paper, the aim is to collect and analyze objective data of product architectures of complex systems in which modularity plays a special strategic role for firms. The methodology presented provides an integrated view of modularity management that includes strategic and new product design implications of product architecture designs.

Many studies on modularity are qualitative and exploratory in nature (c.f. Baldwin and Clark, 1997; Christensen and Rosenbloom, 1995; Garud and Kumarasmamy, 1995; Lundqvist *et al.*, 1996; Sanchez and Mahoney, 1996). There is also a great deal of quantitative studies on modularity that apply optimization models focusing mainly on manufacturing issues (c.f. Baker *et al.*, 1986; Dogramaci, 1979; Emmons and Tedesco, 1971). These studies have contributed greatly to our understanding of modularity but offer limited insights as to how firms can measure the degree of modularity embedded in product architectures. Nevertheless, there is a handful of studies that focus on measuring modularity. These approaches support and complement our approach, such as extracting information from bill-of-materials (BOM) to measure component standardization (Collier, 1981, 1982; Ulrich and Pearson, 1998), examining the variation in component sharing (Fisher *et al.*, 1999), designing product specific components (Ulrich and Ellison, 1999), and estimating the impact of design alternatives (Ulrich *et al.*, 1993). Architectural design decisions consider various trade-offs (described in the following section), and there are rarely optimal designs. Hence, we are not trying to find the optimal level of modularity in product architectures, but to gain a better understanding on the implications of the following elements of product architectures on modularization: components (standard and new-to-the-firm) and respective interfaces, degree of coupling, and substitutability.

PRODUCT ARCHITECTURE

The purpose of product architectures is to define the basic physical building blocks of the product in terms of both what they do and what their interfaces are with the rest of the device (Ulrich, 1995; Ulrich and Eppinger, 1995). Product architecture is often established during the product development process. This takes place during the system-level design phase of the process after the basic technological working principles have been established, but before the design of component and subsystems has begun. Product architectures can vary from modular to integral. Modular product architectures are used as flexible platforms for leveraging a large number of product variations (Gilmore and Pine, 1997; Meyer *et al.*, 1997; Robertson and Ulrich, 1998; Sanchez, 1996; Sanchez 1999), enabling a firm to gain cost savings through economies of scale from component commonality, inventory, logistics, as well as to introduce technologically improved products more rapidly. Modular architectures enable firms to minimize the physical changes required to achieve a functional change. Changes to product variants often are achieved through modular product architectures where changes in one component do not lead to changes in other components.

Conversely, in integral product architectures, changes to one component cannot be made without making changes to other components. Costs of customized components tends to be higher due to the integral nature of product architectures where an improvement in functional performance can not be achieved without making changes to other components. Integral architecture designs enhance knowledge sharing and interactive learning as team members rely on each other's expertise. Integral architectures are designed with maximum performance in mind, and the implementation of functional elements may be distributed across multiple physical elements (Ulrich and Eppinger, 1995). Some trade-offs between modular and integral designs are listed in Table 24.1.

Table 24.1. Trade-offs between modular and integral product architecture designs.

Benefits of Modular Designs	Benefits of Integral Designs
• Task specialization	• Interactive learning
• Platform flexibility	• High levels of performance through proprietary technologies
• Increased number of product variants	
• Economies of scale in component commonality	• Systemic innovations
• Cost savings in inventory and logistics	• Superior access to information
• Lower life cycle costs through easy maintenance	• Protection of innovation from imitation
	• High entry barriers for component suppliers
• Shorter product life cycles through incremental improvements such as upgrade, add-ons and adaptations	• Craftsmanship
• Flexibility in component reuse	
• Independent product development	
• Outsourcing	
• System reliability due to high production volume and experience curve	
Examples: Elevators, passenger cars, IBM PCs, Lego toys	***Examples:*** Formula One cars, Apollo Computers, satellites

Source: Cusumano and Nobeoka (1998), Fine (1998), Garud and Kumaraswamy (1995), Gilmore and Pine (1997), Hsuan (1999), Mikkola (2001), Meyer and Utterback (1993), Robertson and Ulrich (1998), Sanchez (1996), Sanchez (1999), Sanchez and Mahoney (1996), Schilling (2000), Ulrich (1995), Ulrich and Eppinger (1995), and personal interviews in software, electronics, and machinery industries.

Components

A *component* is defined as a physically distinct portion of the product that embodies a core design concept (Clark, 1985) and performs a well-defined function (Henderson and Clark, 1990). Product architecture defines the way in which components interact with each other. For many high-tech firms, components can be classified as either standard or new-to-the-firm (NTF), depending on whether the firms have had prior knowledge and application of these components in previous or existing product architectures.

Standard components refer to components that have been used in previous or existing architectural designs by the firm (i.e. carried over components) or components that are available from firm's library of components (i.e. qualified components). A subset of standard components is the commodity components, which are often off-the-shelf or generic parts. These components have well defined technical specifications that are generally accepted as industry standards, as many suppliers produce these components. These parts are often listed in catalogues with unit prices varying accordingly with the volume purchased. Due to previous experience with standard components, possible interface compatibility issues with other components can be assessed quickly without incurring expensive testing costs.

New-to-the-firm (NTF) components, on the other hand, refer to product-specific components (Ulrich and Ellison, 1999) that are introduced to the firm for the first time, such as with modular innovations[3]. Because prior knowledge about how NTF components interact with other components is limited, NTF components are assumed to contain higher technological risks than standard components. Interface compatibility issues with other components within the product architecture have to be tested and re-evaluated regularly, and sometimes this process can be costly and time consuming[4]. Often the risks are well justified by the technical superiority of these components, significantly improving the overall performance of the product architecture. The use of NTF components is strategic in nature because the integration of NTF components into product architectures prevents imitation by the competitors, thus creating competitive advantages for the firm, at least in the short-run. But too many NTF components may delay product development lead time and increase the technological complexity of the product architecture, as a system achieves greater functionality by the strong interdependence shared among components, or high synergistic specificity (Schilling, 2000).

Interfaces

Interfaces are linkages shared among components, and interface specifications define the protocol for the fundamental interactions across all components comprising a technological system. Modularity intentionally creates a high degree of independence between component designs by standardizing component interface specifications (Sanchez and Mahoney, 1996). Furthermore, the crystallization and development of interface specifications has a tremendous impact on setting worldwide industry standards (Link and Tassey, 1997; Tassey, 2000). The degree to which interfaces are standardized and specified defines the compatibility between components, subsequently the degree of modularity. Standard components have well specified and standardized interfaces, hence product architectures comprised of standard components are

---

[3]   Modular innovation is the introduction of new component technology inserted within essentially unchanged product architecture (Christensen and Rosenbloom, 1995). It changes only the relationships between core design concepts of a technology without changing the product's architecture (Henderson and Clark, 1990).

[4]   In a study of multi-project management in the automobile industry, Cusumano and Nobeoka (1998) found that developing components new to the firm requires extra time for concept generation, producing prototypes, and testing that companies can not do in parallel, hence requiring both a longer lead time and more engineering hours.

assumed to be modular. Conversely, interface specifications and hence interface compatibility issues of NTF components with other components of a given product architecture are not well understood. Consequently, introduction of NTF components into product architectures hinders modularity freedom. Interface specification of NTF components is dependent on technological innovation available in the market. For instance, if the NTF component is new to the world, its interface specification is most likely to be ill specified. However, when the NTF component is unique only to the firm, its interface specification is generally well defined within the industry, but not standardized within the firm. Only when the interface specification of NTF components becomes well specified and standardized within the firm that a NTF component becomes a standard component. According to Ulrich (1995), standardization arises when: (a) a component implements commonly useful functions; and (b) the interface to the component is identical across more than one different product.

Degree of Coupling

The product performance is governed by many component parameters that are related to one another in a complex, interdependent fashion. Components are typically characterized by many design parameters, which may need to be tuned arbitrarily in order to maximize overall product performance (Ulrich and Ellison, 1999). The way in which components are linked with one another creates a certain degree of coupling. A component that is dependent on interfacing with many components for functionality, in this context, impose high degree of coupling. For example, microprocessor (a component) in a motherboard (a PC sub-system) would be considered a critical part based on the number of interfaces shared with other components. In order for a microprocessor to function properly, it has to interface directly with a number of components, easily ranging from 56 to over 200 interfaces. Conversely, a capacitor would present a lower degree of coupling than microprocessors. Typically, capacitors require two interfaces for functionality, a cathode and an anode. We can imagine that a product architecture with a great percentage of critical components may not be easily decomposed. In Schilling's (2000) terms, product architectures with high degree of coupling among the components exhibit high 'synergistic specificity' as the strong interdependence shared among components inhibits recombination, separability, and substitution of components, hence preventing the architecture to shift into a more modular one. We estimate the degree of coupling [δ] as the ratio of the number of interfaces [k] per component [n] in a sub-system of a given product architecture. The empirical information on the number of interfaces can be gathered from product architecture schematics where specific linkages among components are laid out.

$$\delta_i = \frac{\sum k_c}{n_c}$$

For product architectures with multiple sub-systems, the aggregate degree of coupling value for these sub-systems, $\delta_{sub\text{-}system}$, can be approximated as the average of all δ_i, that is,

$$\delta_{sub-system} = \delta_{average} = \frac{\sum_{i=1}^{I} \delta_i}{I} \qquad \text{I = number of sub-systems}$$

Substitutability

Another crucial element of product architecture modularity is substitutability. Garud and Kumaraswamy (1993) use the term 'substitution' to suggest that technological progress may be achieved by substituting certain components of a technological system while reusing others, hence taking the advantages of economies of substitution. This has great implications for technological systems that are modularly upgradable. Economies of substitution (Garud and Kumarasmamy, 1995) exist when the cost of designing a high-performance system through the partial retention of existing components is lower than designing the system afresh. While standard components facilitate component reusability, NTF components improve the technological performance of the upgraded product architecture. The challenge is to design product architectures with desirable combination of standard and NTF components to gain from economies of substitution.

An aspect of substitutability is component sharing (i.e. using the same version of a component across multiple products) which is a product-based strategy that depends on the fact that families of similar products have similar components (Fisher *et al.*, 1999). Component sharing is viewed by firms as a way to offer high variety in the market place while retaining low variety in their operations. Component sharing of NTF components is especially critical. As articulated by Fisher *et al.* (1999:299): "Because each new and unique components must be designed and tested, component sharing can reduce the cost of product development. Each new and unique component generally also requires an investment in tooling or other fixed costs of production. Therefore component sharing may also reduce the required production investment associated with a new product." The managerial challenge is how to provide the high degree of uniqueness that seems necessary for competitive success while retaining the scale economies required for low cost.

The impact of substitutability of NTF components in product architecture modularity is captured through the 'substitutability factor' [s], which is estimated as the number of product families made possible by the average number of interfaces of NTF components [k_{NTF}] required for functionality:

$$s = \frac{no. \ of \ product \ families}{k_{NTF}(avg)}$$

For example, if a NTF component can be used in 10 families (or 10 times the same component), and two interfaces must be shared for functionality, then the substitutability factor of the product architecture is 5 components per interface. The greater the number of families that can use the NTF component, the higher the substitutability factor, hence higher degree of product architecture modularity.

THE MODULARIZATION FUNCTION

A simple mathematical model, termed modularization function *M(u)*, is derived to explain the degree of modularity in a given product architecture as a function of the following variables: components [*N* and *u*], degree of coupling [δ], and substitutability factor [*s*][5]:

$$M(u) = e^{-u^2/2Ns\delta} \qquad \text{Equation 2.1}$$

The sensitivity relationship of the modularization funtion, *M(u)*, with respect to the NTF component composition, *u*, is expressed as follows:

$$S_u^M = \frac{u}{M} \cdot \frac{dM}{du} = -\frac{u^2}{Ns\delta} \qquad \text{Equation 2.2}$$

M(u)	-	Modularization function	S_u^M -	Sensitivity function
u	-	number of NTF components	*N* -	total number of components
s	-	substitutability factor	δ -	degree of coupling

The modularization function shows that the combined effect of the variables varies exponentially with any set of NTF components. Every time the component composition *b* is altered (such as with incremental innovations) the degree of modularity also varies. In many cases, the introduction of NTF components requires changes to other parts of the product architecture as well, hence changing the values of *N* and δ. If we simply assessed the degree of modularity based on the number of components (be standard or NTF) and ignored the effects of interfaces (captured in δ and *s*) we may overlook the impact of interfaces on product architecture modularity.

The modularization function captures the complexity of product architecture designs that are often firm specific. It is one way of interpreting modularity of product architectures objectively. Although the information required for the assessment is often proprietary

---

[5]   The modularization function was first derived to analyze product architecture modularity of Chrysler Jeeps windshield wiper systems. Refer to Mikkola (2000) for the formulation and derivation of the function, and the application of the modularization function with two product architectures of Chrysler Jeeps windshield wipers controllers.

(especially with respect to NTF components), it is widely available within the firm (i.e. in databases, BOMs, schematic drawings, etc.). For managers, it can be used as a tool for communicating with the engineering, manufacturing, marketing, and purchasing functions. Changes in product architecture designs call for different strategies for managing production volume, manufacturing processes, amount of product variety, concurrent engineering, advertisement, etc. The modularization function can also be used to evaluate and compare competitors' product architectures through reverse engineering.

In deriving the modularization function, the following assumptions are made:

1. The functional specifications of components, including interface specifications, do not change over a period of time. This assumption allows the evaluation of the architecture's configuration and components composition independently from other sub-systems.
2. The product architecture is comprised of a combination of standard and NTF components.
3. It is argued that NTF components impose higher technological risks and greater interface compatibility issues with other components within the product architecture. Therefore, the lower the NTF components composition in a product architecture the higher the degree of modularity.
4. Product architecture comprised entirely of standard components can be easily copied by the competitors. Thus, it is assumed that there should be some amount of NTF components in the product architecture.
5. All standard components are equally critical.
6. All NTF components are equally critical.
7. All interfaces (i.e. electrical, logical, physical, etc.) are equally critical.

ROLE OF MODULARITY IN THE ELEVATOR INDUSTRY

Until the end of last century elevators have been characterized as typical products within the framework of Utterback's (1994) 'dominant design industry.' According to the elevator experts from Schindler Lifts, over capacities and cost competition has dominated the current market scene[6]. The product architecture of elevators has been stable over a long period due to regulations and relatively few innovations. In addition, the number of competitors has decreased dramatically during the last 15 years. Currently, a few large companies plus a large number of small local companies shape the elevator industry. Over 80 % of the world market share belong to seven global players. Modularity though standardized component interfaces has enabled smaller elevator companies to source from standard component manufacturers and therefore to benefit from economies of scale despite their small market share. Since the 1990s,

---

[6]   The information presented in this section is based on interviews with various experts from the elevator industry.

there has been a strong trend towards deregulation, similar to what has been taking place with the telecommunication industry. The induced innovation push has promoted radical new solutions with new product architectures such as 'machineroomless' elevators, self-propelling cars on self-supporting structures, and advanced traffic management systems.

According to experts at Schindler Lifts, newest technology developments in the elevator industry will have a big impact on the product architecture designs and subsequent degree of modularity. The leading elevator companies are developing new drive technologies, such as linear motors with integrated safety functions. This integration of technologies reduces the number of components and alters the interface relationships with other components, hence changing the overall degree of coupling and substitutability of these new components across elevator families. Furthermore, in industries with dominant design character, a strict interface management has to be applied in order to benefit from economies of scale and outsourcing potentials. These industries tend to change from proprietary solutions to common standards. Similar trends can be observed in the mobile telecommunication industry, where the global players like Nokia, Ericsson, and Siemens cooperate in order to set standards. Furthermore, the classical trade-off between optimizing manufacturing costs through integrated design and optimizing life cycle costs through modular design will shift towards the latter one. An enabler for this trend is the transparency of life cycle costs: the reusability of modules for product variants can lead to significantly lower life cycle costs. Drivers are economies of scale and scope, maintenance synergies (i.e., the benefits gained from modular components used for preventive maintenance to maximize passenger safety), and improved product quality.

In this paper we concentrate on analyzing the traditional elevator architectures and related component innovations, accounting for over 90% of the market. Based on the transmission principle, dominant elevator designs can be distinguished between: (1) the traction elevator (TR) with drive machine, ropes and counterweight, and (2) the hydraulic elevator (HY) with a hydraulic jack. According to market analysts at Schindler Lifts, there is a world market of 40,000 units of HY elevators and 160,000 units of TR elevators per year for Schindler, with an increasing demand towards TR elevators. In general, the elevator market is segmented into low-rise (less than 60,000 units), mid-rise (between 60,000 and 200,000 units) and high-rise (greater than 220,000 units).

Data Collection and Analysis

The data collection took place at Schindler Lifts and was conducted between 1997 and 2000. In *Phase 1* a detailed analysis on two principle types of elevators (TR and HY elevators) was carried out at Schindler Lifts. The description and analysis were accomplished with an object modeling technique called UML (Unified Modeling Language), originally developed for supporting object oriented software development. With the UML model, all components and respective interfaces were mapped and recorded into a database. In *Phase 2*, the assessment of

TR and HY elevators was supplemented by several follow-up interviews with elevator experts from R&D, system management, purchasing, and marketing. The main goal of these interdisciplinary sessions was to learn about the impact of modularity on the elevator industry as a whole, and to verify that our assumptions and interpretation of the data are accurate. Then in *Phase 3,* the modularization function (Equation 2.1) and sensitivity function (Equation 2.2) were applied for analyzing the degree of modularization in TR and HY elevators.

Comparative Analysis of Traction and Hydraulic Elevators

The basis for the analysis of the HY and TR elevators is supported by the product architecture data derived from the UML analysis, which provides a comprehensive database displaying various detailed information about several hundreds of components and respective interfaces of elevator architectures at different aggregate levels of analysis. The assessment of degree of modularization of HY and TR elevator architectures involved the following steps:

1. Define product architecture and its boundaries. The analysis of HY and TR elevator systems is carried out at two levels: sub-system level (transmission) and system level (elevator), as shown in Fig. 24.1.

2. Fig. 24.2. Decompose the product architecture into sub-units, so that each one of the sub-units can be assessed independently. Fig. 24.2. shows a partial product architecture of TR elevators. The classification of components into *'unique', 'neutral',* and *'standard'* was defined by an interdisciplinary group of R&D, purchasing, and market experts. *'Unique'* represents a NTF component[7]. *'Standard'* represents a component

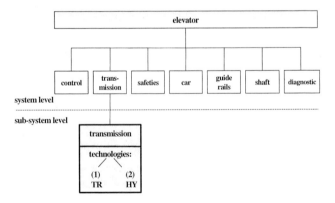

Fig. 24.1. The elevator and its sub-systems.

---

[7]   In order to be consistent with Schindler's terminology for components, 'unique' is similar to NTF components.

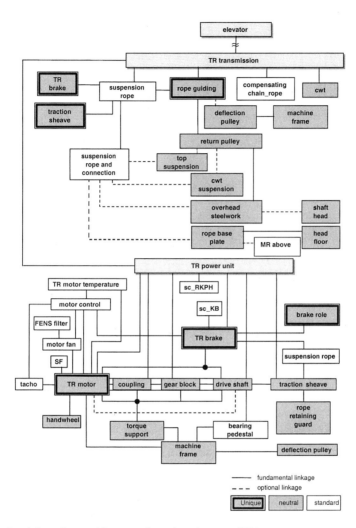

Fig. 24.2. *Partial product architecture of traction elevators (TR).*

that is not new to the firm. Depending on the application and customization requested by the customers, a *'neutral'* component can be considered either as a standard component or as a unique component. The linkage (or interface) shared between the components is characterized as *'fundamental'* and *'optional'*. While fundamental linkages exist for all elevator variants, optional linkages are only relevant for certain variants.

3. Assess the substitutability factor of the TR or HY transmission product architectures, approximated as the number of elevator families divided by the average number of interfaces shared by the NTF components comprising each transmission sub-systems.

4. Count the total number of components N comprising the product architecture, by adding the number of standard, neutral, and unique components.

5. Count the number of NTF components.

6. Count the number of neutral components. Because neutral components are considered unique components by some elevators (due to customization), but not all elevators, we allowed the neutral components to function as standard or as unique components. That is, in one extreme, all neutral components are counted as standard components, and on the other extreme, all neutral components are counted as unique components. This assumption changes the unique component composition, hence allowing us to see the maximum impact of unique components on modularity of HY and TR elevators. For instance, the deflection pulley is a neutral component that is linked to the machine frame with a fundamental linkage. In some TR elevator applications, these components are used as unique components and/or standard components. The optional linkage of deflection pulley to the rope guiding indicates this option.

7. Since both HY and TR elevators have fundamental and optional linkages as well as three classifications of components (unique, neutral, and standard), the basic evaluation starts with only components linked by fundamental interfaces. The maximum relationship shared among the components and respective linkages is achieved when the remaining components with optional linkages are added to the product architecture. This generates a different set of values of degree of coupling δ, substitutability factor s, unique component composition b, and the total number of components N in the analysis.

8. Compute the degree of coupling δ, or the average number of interfaces per component, for each of HY and TR transmissions, as formulated in Section 2.3. For the sake of illustrating the application of the modularization function at the system level, other sub-systems (i.e., control, transmission, safeties, car, guide rails, shaft, and diagnostic) are assumed to have the same degree of coupling value $\delta_{sub\text{-}system}$ as the transmission sub-system. Hence, $\delta_{sub\text{-}system}$ represents the average value of all sub-systems. However, a more robust analysis of the modularity would include systematic analysis of these sub-systems.

9. Plug these values into the modularization function (Equation 2.1) to calculate the degree of modularity inherent in the product architectures. A range of modularity levels can exist for the two elevators, with $M_{fundamental}(u)$ and $M(u)$ representing the basic and maximum modularity relationships respectively. A comparative analysis of HY and TR elevators is summarized in Table 24.2.

Table 24.2. A comparison of HY and TR Elevators.

HY ELEVATORS

2 families (low-rise, mid-rise)
$u = 3$ components
$n_{neutral} = 16$ components

fundamental linkages	**all linkages**
N = 37 components	N = 43 components
$b = 8\ \%$	$b = 7\ \%$
$k_{NTF}(\text{avg}) = 1{,}67$	$k_{NTF}(\text{avg}) = 1{,}67$
$s = 1{,}2$ components/interface	$s = 1{,}2$ components/interface
$\delta = 4{,}02$ interfaces/component	$\delta = 4{,}59$ interfaces/component
$M_{fundamental}(u) = 0{,}98$	$M(u) = 0{,}98$
$M(u)_{u+neutral} = 0{,}36$	$M(u)_{u+neutral} = 0{,}47$

TR ELEVATORS

3 families (low-rise, mid-rise, high-rise)
$u = 6$ components
$n_{neutral} = 19$ components

fundamental linkages	**all linkages**
N = 38 components	N = 42 components
$b = 16\ \%$	$b = 14\ \%$
$k_{NTF}(\text{avg}) = 4{,}67$	$k_{NTF}(\text{avg}) = 5{,}00$
$s = 0{,}64$ components/interface	$s = 0{,}60$ components/interface
$\delta = 4{,}83$ interfaces/component	$\delta = 5{,}01$ interfaces/component
$M_{fundamental}(u) = 0{,}86$	$M(u) = 0{,}87$
$M(u)_{u+neutral} = 0{,}07$	$M(u)_{u+neutral} = 0{,}08$

The graphical interpretation of modularization functions for HY and TR elevators are illustrated in Fig. 24.3.

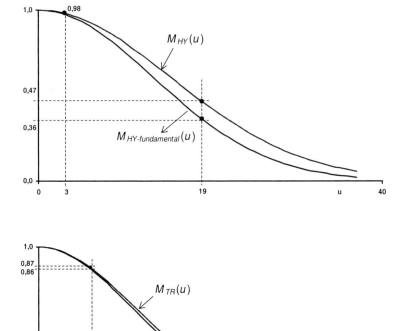

Fig. 24.3. Modularization functions of HY and TR Elevators.

Some preliminary findings of HY and TR elevators include the following:

1. Both elevators are highly modular from a unique component composition perspective, $M_{HY}(3) = 0,98$ and $M_{TR}(6) = 0,87$. These relative low values of u indicate that the basic product architectures of HY and TR elevators have components with standardized and well-specified interfaces, where cost savings advantages are gained. Suppliers can be specialized in developing specific capabilities for component development. This explains the decrease in the number of competitors and the emergence of a strong component supplier industry which is becoming increasingly important, similar to the computer

industry, as described by Fine (1998). In part it explains why market entry barriers for new elevator companies are relative low.

2. When all linkages are taken into consideration, HY elevators are slightly more modular than TR elevators due to higher substitutability factor (s = 1,2), lower unique component composition (b = 7%), and lower degree of coupling (δ = 4,59). Although the three unique components are shared by only two families (low-rise and mid-rise), HY elevators have higher substitutability factor which is attributed by the lower average number of interfaces of NTF components [$k_{NTF}(avg)_{HY}$ = 1,67 compared with $k_{NTF}(avg)_{TR}$ = 5,00)]. The degree of coupling of TR elevators (δ = 5,01) indicates that the components are more tightly coupled than HY elevators (δ = 4.59) exhibiting higher synergistic specificity. Graphically, the higher modularity of HY elevators are indicated by the relative slopes of the modularity functions, with $M_{TR}(u)$ much steeper than $M_{HY}(u)$. According to market experts at Schindler, HY elevators are considered commodity products with little differentiation potential, since these elevators are classified as low cost products. Generally, the components suppliers of the HY elevator tend to have more power than the suppliers of the TR elevator.

3. When neutral components are allowed to function as unique components, then TR elevators have more leverage in gaining modularity from neutral components. For instance, TR elevator has 6 unique components and 19 neutral components (that is a total of 25 units). When all the neutral components are treated as unique components, then modularity value of TR elevators, $M_{TR}(u)$, can range from 0,08 to 0,87, compared with the value of HY elevators, $M_{HY}(u)$, ranging from 0,47 to 0,98. This suggests that there are more opportunities for TR elevators to become more modular. HY elevators are so modular that even when all the neutral components are treated as unique components, the worst degree of modularity is 0,36 [for $M_{HY\text{-}fundamental}(u)$] compared to a value of 0,07 [for $M_{TR\text{-}fundamental}(u)$]. In most cases, however, neutral components are treated as standard components rather than unique components, but allowing the neutral components to function as unique components sets the worse case scenario for the degree of modularity in the TR and HY product architectures.

4. The modularity of both TR and HY elevators can be improved by increasing the substitutability factor s. This can be accomplished by incorporating NTF components across more number of elevator families or to reduce the average number of interfaces of unique components, $k_{NTF}(avg)$. Many innovations in the elevator technology are leading towards component integration rather than decomposition, which reduce the total number of components. The introduction of these innovations into the product architecture alters the interface relationship shared with other compohents and subsystems, consequently changing the overall degree of coupling and substitutability of these new components across other elevator families.

5. While component modularity is captured by the neutral components, the optional linkages capture interface modularity. When all linkages (fundamental plus optional linkages) are considered, HY elevators have considerably higher leverage for increasing degree of modularity than TR elevators. This is indicated by the larger differences between the modularization functions $M(u)$ and $M_{fundamental}(u)$, that is, $[M_{HY}(u) - M_{HY\text{-}fundamental}(u)] > [M_{TR}(u) - M_{TR\text{-}fundamental}(u)]$.

The modularization function also allows us to plot the sensitivity graphs for HY and TR elevators, as illustrated in Fig. 24.4. The sensitivity graphs reveal that TR elevators are more sensitive to increases in the number of unique components, u. This is indicated by the steeper slopes of both HY elevator sensitivity functions, $S_{fundamental}(M;u)$ and $S(M;u)$, compared with those of TR elevators.

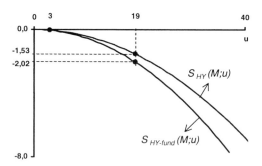

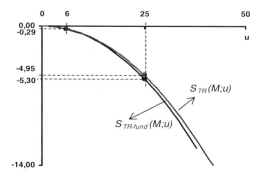

Fig. 24.4. Sensitivity graphs of HY and TR Elevators.

SUMMARY AND OUTLOOK

This paper analyzed modularity management of product architectures. It was argued that modularity takes place when interfaces shared among components in a given product architecture become specified and standardized to allow for greater substitutability of components across product families. Product architectures are comprised of a combination of standard and new-to-the-firm (NTF) components depending on the extent a firm had previous experience with the components, which reflect firms' strategic choices and idiosyncratic capabilities. Standard components have well-specified interface specifications and costs savings are gained through economies of scale. Organizational focus is preserved leading to task specialization and development of capabilities. NTF components, on the other hand, do not have standardized interface specifications and have higher technological risks and longer NPD lead times. However, they introduce product novelty, have superior performance, and prevent imitation from competitors. The way in which components are linked with one another creates a certain degree of coupling, indicating the degree of interdependence shared among components and whether they can be recombined, separated and substituted, hence affecting the technological path of the product architecture. Component sharing of NTF components to gain from economies of substitution is especially crucial when the cost of designing a high-performance system through the partial retention of existing components is lower than designing the system afresh. The challenge is to provide high degree of uniqueness that seems necessary for competitive success while retaining scale of economies required for low cost.

A mathematical model, termed modularization function, was introduced to analyze the degree of modularity embedded in product architectures by taking into account the following variables: components, degree of coupling, and substitutability of NTF components across product families. The application of the modularization function was illustrated with two dominant designs of elevator systems from Schindler Lifts for comparative analysis: traction (TR) and hydraulic (HY). One finding indicated that HY elevators are more modular than TR elevators due to higher substitutability factor, also illustrated by the relative slopes of the modularization functions. From interface management perspective, HY elevators have more leverage from the optional linkages than the TR elevators, indicated by larger gaps between the modularization functions. In both product architectures, modularity can be improved by increasing the substitutability factor, and this can be accomplished by incorporating NTF components across other elevator families or to reduce the average number of interfaces of NTF components. Finally, the sensitive analysis showed that TR elevators are more sensitive to increases in the number of NTF components, indicated by a steeper slope.

So far, the analysis presented in this paper merely provided an introduction as to how product architecture modularity and sensitivity analysis of elevators can be measured. Certainly a more extensive empirical work is called for in documenting the evolution of elevator product architectures over time. A more robust analysis would include the systematic analysis and application of modularization function to other sub-systems of HY and TR elevators (i.e. control, safeties, car, guide rails, shaft, and diagnostics). Although the application of the modularization function to these two distinct systems provide very preliminary findings on how the degree of modularity of product architectures can be assessed, nevertheless it can be a useful tool for illustrating the aggregated effect and impact of components and interfaces on modularity.

Modularity management of product architectures should not be in isolation of manufacturing strategy (Nevins and Whitney, 1989) and organizational designs, especially regarding to multi-project management (Cusumano and Nobeoka, 1998). We are aware that the benefits of economies of substitution depend on the production volume. For instance, it may not make sense for a firm to maximize on economies of substitution when production volume is low. It may make more sense for a firm to pursue an integral design strategy. Furthermore, as the majority of products sold in the market place involve many suppliers with distinctive knowledge and expertise, the design of product architectures should also take into consideration how it impacts inter- versus intra-firm learning and knowledge management (Fine and Whitney, 1996; Sanchez and Mahoney, 1996). It has been debated that outsourcing of non-core technical activities are enabled by the standardization of these non-core components with respect to the core technology (Fine, 1998; Fine and Whitney, 1996). Can decisions regarding to product architecture designs provide us insights to strategic decisions regarding outsourcing, manufacturing, and supply chain management? If so, how should firms design its organization to match such strategies with respect to its suppliers and customers? Other areas of great interest for research include, for example, the impacts of product architecture design choices (e.g., multiplexing and de-integration of components) with respect to cost and benefit analysis of modularity.

REFERENCES

Baker, K.R., Magazine, M.J. and Nuttle, H.L.W. (1986) "The effect of commonality on safety stock in a simple inventory model," *Management Science*, **32**(8), 982-988.

Baldwin, C.Y. and Clark, K.B. (1997) "Managing in an Age of Modularity," *Harvard Business Review*, (September-October), 84-93.

Boutellier, R., Gassmann, O. and von Zedtwitz, M. (2000) *Managing Global Innovation*, Uncovering the Secrets of Future Competitiveness, 2nd ed., Springer: Berlin, Tokyo, New York.

Christensen, C.M. and Rosenbloom, R.S. (1995) "Explaining the attacker's advantage: technological paradigms, organizational dynamics, and the value network," *Research Policy*, **24**, 233-257.

Clark, K.B. (1985) "The interaction of design hierarchies and market concepts in technological evolution," *Research Policy*, **14**, 235-251.

Collier, D.A. (1981) "The measurement and operating benefits of component part commonality," *Decision Sciences*, **12**(1), 85.

Collier, D.A. (1982) "Aggregate safety stock levels and component part commonality," *Management Science*, **28**(11), 1296-1303.

Cusumano, M.A. and Nobeoka, K. (1998) *Thinking Beyond Lean*. New York, NY: The Free Press.

Dogramaci, A. (1979) "Design of common components considering implications of inventory costs and forecasting," *AIIE Transactions*, **11**(2), 129-135.

Emmons, H. and Tedesco, A.R. (1971) "The modular growth design problem," *AIIE Transactions*, **3**(2), 104-114.

Feitzinger, E. and Lee, H.L. (1997) "Mass customization at Hewlett-Packard: the power of postponement," *Harvard Business Review*, (Jan-Feb), 116-121.

Fine, C.H. (1998) *Clockspeed – Winning Industry Control in the Age of Temporary Advantage*. Reading, MA: Perseus Books.

Fine, C. and Whitney, D.E. (1996) "Is the make-buy decision process a core competence?"Available from http://web.mit.edu/ctpid/www/Whitney/.

Fisher, M., Ramdas, K. and Ulrich, K. (1999) "Component sharing in the management of product variety: A study of automotive braking systems," *Management Science*, **45**(3), 297-315.

Flamm, K. (1988) *Creating the Computer: Government, Industry and High Technology*. Washington, DC: Bookings Institution.

Fulkerson, B. (1997) "A response to dynamic change in the market place," *Decision Support Systems*, **21**, 199-214.

Garud, R and Kotha, S. (1994) "Using the brain as a metaphor to model flexible production systems," *Academy of Management Review*, **19**, 671-698.

Garud, R. and Kumaraswamy, A. (1993) "Changing Competitive Dynamics in Network Industries: an Exploration of Sun Microsystem's Open Systems Strategy," *Strategic Management Journal*, **14**, 351-369.

Garud, R. and Kumaraswamy, A. (1995) "Technological and Organizational Designs for Realizing Economies of Substitution," *Strategic Management Journal*, **16**, 93-109.

Gassmann, O. and von Zedtwitz, M. (1998) "Organization of Industrial R&D on a Global Scale," *R&D Management*, **28**(3), 147-161.

Gassmann, O. and von Zedtwitz, M. (1999) "New Concepts and Trends in International R&D Organization," *Research Policy*, **28**, 231-250.

Gilmore, J.H. and Pine, B.J. (1997) "The Four Faces of Mass Customization," *Harvard Business Review*, (Jan-Feb), 91-101.

Gooley, T.B. (1998) "Mass Customization: How logistics makes it happen," *Logistics Management & Distribution Report*, (April 1st).

Henderson, R.M. and Clark, K.B. (1990) "Architectural Innovation: The Reconfiguration of Existing Product Technologies and the Failure of Established Firms," *Administrative Science Quarterly*, **35**, 9-30.

Hsuan, J. (1999) "Impacts of supplier-buyer relationships on modularization in new product development," *European Journal of Purchasing and Supply Management*, **5**, 197-209.

Lundqvist, M., Sundgren, N. and Trygg, L. (1996) "Remodularization of a Product Line: Adding Complexity to Project Management," *Journal of Product Innovations Management*, **13**, 311-324.

Meyer, M.H. and Utterback, J.M. (1993) "The Product Family and the Dynamics of Core Capability," *Sloan Management Review*, (Spring), 29-47.

Mikkola, J.H. (2000) "Modularization Assessment of Product Architecture," *DRUID Working Paper 00-4*.

Mikkola, J.H. (2001) "Modularity and interface management of product architectures," in the proceedings of *Proceedings of PICMET '01 – Technology Management in the Knowledge Era: Life in the e-World*, Vol. 2 (CD ROM), Portland, Oregon, USA, July 29 - August 2.

Nevins, J.L. and Whitney, D.E. (1989) *Concurrent Design of Products and Processes*. McGraw-Hill Publishing Company.

Orton, J.D. and Weick, K.E. (1990) "Loosely coupled systems: A re-conceptualization," *Academy of Management Review*, **15**, 203-223.

Pine, J. (1993) *Mass Customization – The New Frontier in Business Competition*. Boston, MA: Harvard Business School Press.

Robertson, D. and Ulrich, K. (1998) "Planning for Product Platforms," *Sloan Management Review*, (Summer), 19-31.

Sanchez, R. (1996) "Strategic Product Creation: Managing New Interactions of Technology, Markets, and Organizations," *European Management Journal*, **14**(2), 121-138.

Sanchez, R. (1999) "Modular Architectures in the Marketing Process," *Journal of Marketing*, **63** (Special Issue), 92-111.

Sanchez, R. and Mahoney, J.T. (1996) "Modularity, Flexibility, and Knowledge Management in Product and Organisation Design," *Strategic Management Journal*, **17** (Winter Special Issue), 63-76.

Schilling, M.A. (2000) "Toward a general modular systems theory and its application to interfirm product modularity," *Academy of Management Review*, **25**(2), 312-334.

Simon, H. (1995) "Near decomposability and complexity: How a mind resides in a brain," in Morowitz, H. and Singer, J. (Eds.), *The Mind, the Brain, and CAS*. SFI Studies in the Sciences of Complexity, XXII, Addison-Wesley.

Simon, H. (1996) The Sciences of Artificial. 3rd Edition, Cambridge, MA: MIT Press.

Smith, A. (1776) *An Inquiry into the Nature and Causes of the Wealth of Nations*. London, W. Strahan & T. Cadell.

Taylor, F.W. (1967) *Principles of Scientific Management*. New York: Norton.

Ulrich, K. (1995) "The role of product architecture in the manufacturing firm," *Research Policy*, **24**, pp. 419-440.

Ulrich, K.T. and Ellison, D. (1999) "Holistic customer requirements and the design-select decision," *Management Science*, **45**(5), 641-658.

Ulrich, K.T. and Eppinger, S.D. (1995) *Product Design and Development*. McGraw-Hill, New York.

Ulrich K.T. and Pearson, S. (1998) "Assessing the importance of design through product archeology," *Management Science*, **44**(3), 352-369.

Ulrich, K.T., Sartorius, D., Pearson, S. and Jakiela, M. (1993) "Including the value of time in design-for-manufacturing decision making," *Management Science*, **39**(4), 429-447.

Utterback, J.M. (1994) *Mastering the Dynamics of Innovation*. Boston, MA: Harvard Business School Press.

van Hoek, R.I., Vos, B. and Commandeur, H.R. (1999) "Restructuring European Supply Chains by Implementing Postponement Strategies," *Long Range Planning*, **32**(5), 505-518.

Management of Technology
ISBN: 0-08-044136-X

25

LINKING TECHNOLOGY SELECTION AND R&D PROJECT SELECTION IN INNOVATIVE PRODUCT DEVELOPMENT NETWORKS

Marko Torkkeli, Lappeenranta University of Technology (LUT), Lappeenranta, Finland[*,†]
Jouni Koivuniemi, Lappeenranta University of Technology (LUT), Lappeenranta, Finland[**]
Ville Ojanen, Lappeenranta University of Technology (LUT), Lappeenranta, Finland[***]
Markku Tuominen, Lappeenranta University of Technology (LUT), Lappeenranta, Finland[****]

INTRODUCTION

The era of New Economy has brought many changes to business logic, which is shaping decision making processes in companies. Fast technological changes and competitive dynamics in the market drive companies to consider technologies and R&D projects concurrently. New technologies are seldom developed by one company only because of the remarkable risks, needed resources, and time required to develop the technology. In the changing environment

---

[*] Marko Torkkeli is professor at the Department of Industrial Engineering and Management at LUT, located in Lappeenranta, Finland. Email: marko.torkkeli@lut.fi.
[†] This article is a part of a research project called *"5T - Product Development Management in the Networked Economy"*. The project is coordinated by Telecom Business Research Center (TBRC), Lappeenranta.
[**] Jouni Koivuniemi is project manager and researcher at the Department of Industrial Engineering and Management, and TBRC at LUT, located in Lappeenranta, Finland. Email: jouni.koivuniemi@lut.fi.
[***] Ville Ojanen is researcher at the Department of Industrial Engineering and Management, and TBRC at LUT, located in Lappeenranta, Finland. Email: ville.ojanen@lut.fi.
[****] Dr. Markku Tuominen is professor and Dean of the Department of Industrial Engineering and Management at LUT, located in Lappeenranta, Finland. Email: markku.tuominen@lut.fi.

competitive advantage can be gained with the help of collaboration that combines the competencies of different companies in a network. For these reasons, many companies are presently turning to collaborative product development (PD). The companies aspire for flexibility by sharing risks, generating new options and blending competencies through operating in PD networks. Networking and co-operation are important for the absorption of the knowledge needed for learning and for dividing costs (Cohen and Levinthal, 1990). In network environments there is a need to strengthen linkages between technology selection and R&D project selection decisions. Innovative product development has traditionally been considered as a rather isolated phenomenon, but today companies are more and more under the influence of other companies in the network. These influences in the form of R&D collaboration have been identified particularly during the actual development phases of new technologies and products. The relationship between technology selection characteristics and R&D project selection characteristics are so far not completely understood. However, the importance of these critical practices during the early phase management of innovation processes is largely recognized. What is relevant to both of these processes is a tendency towards more flexible and adaptable processes. As the market environment is rapidly changing, the processes need to change correspondingly.

The purpose of this paper is to define and analyze important linkages between technology selection and R&D project selection in innovative product development networks. The paper also aims to clarify the effects the selected technologies and R&D projects have on the other actors in the network. An R&D network is a group of companies and other stakeholders sharing a common interest to develop technologies and/or products/services together. The selection decisions of one party/actor have manifold effects on the other actors' decision making in the PD network. There are many types of collaboration in innovative PD networks. The focus of this study is on shared product development, which can be classified as a high intensity but informal network form of organization (White et al., 1996). The more formal types of network organization forms, like strategic alliances and contractual relationships are not emphasized in this paper. In this study we concentrate on the phenomenon of product development network especially in the light of collaboration between companies and other actors (e.g. competitors, partners, subcontractors, customers and/or research institutes) in order to develop technology and execute product development projects successfully.

Both technology selection and R&D project selection are regarded as complex technology management processes. The aim is to help the decision makers to identify the characteristics of selection processes in order to better manage product development in networks. There exist numerous relations, links, drawbacks, and causalities between the network actors, technology selection and R&D project selection. The starting point of causal chains in a network is often based on the decisions made by a large company. For example, if a large company makes a strategic decision to focus on a core technology (e.g. wireless application protocol, WAP), it encounters a selection situation between various possible R&D projects based on that technology. The selections finally made have manifold effects on the project selection decisions made by the other companies in the network. The number of links that have to be managed increases rapidly, when the number of technologies, joint R&D projects and actors in the network increases.

This paper offers guidelines for managing complex linkages between technology selection and R&D project selection in the network environment. The paper presents an analysis of the causal effects of these selection decisions on the network. With the help of these results companies can better select the right technologies and the right R&D projects to be carried out in order to achieve competitive advantage.

INNOVATIVE PRODUCT DEVELOPMENT NETWORKS

Product innovation has traditionally been considered as a rather isolated phenomenon. Recently especially the characteristics of dynamic and turbulent business environments, e.g. fast technological changes in the information and communication technology (ICT) industry have challenged the companies to collaborate and create innovative networks. While distributed innovation offers exciting possibilities for a firm to capitalize on the creativity of its partners and customers, its management requires the firms to re-examine the mechanisms they use to govern innovation (Sawhney and Prandelli, 2000). By nature, product development networks are more chaotic than traditional product innovation activities within a firm's boundaries. Several previous studies (e.g. Combs, 1993; Harmsen et al., 2000; Ingham and Mothe, 1998; Sawhney and Prandelli, 2000) addressing collaboration and networks in research and development have emphasized managing knowledge and information sharing, and organizational learning.

Networking as a concept is a new organizational form and a unique combination of strategy, structure and management. It is a dynamic process and it can need a variety of strategies to come into existence (Zeffane, 1994). Collaboration in networks can be informal (e.g. shared product development, which can be classified as a high intensity but informal form of network organization), or formal (e.g. strategic alliances and contractual relationships) (White et al., 1996).

The development of new technologies and new products, especially radical innovations, is expensive and time-consuming when done by internal R&D. Innovative networks are needed to build competence coalitions of focused actors in order to gain special synergy from the network. Quinn (2000) has presented several common reasons why companies of any size are increasingly benefiting from outsourcing particular aspects of innovation. The main reasons are 1) resource limits, 2) specialist talents, 3) multiple risks, 4) attractive talent, and 5) speed

(Quinn, 2000). In a highly turbulent environment companies invest significantly in technology and product development. Through networking the risks and costs involved in product development can be shared and the development becomes faster. This is very essential, since speed is everything and time-to-market is often the most essential measure of project effectiveness in dynamic markets. Technology acquisition is also a very significant reason for networking in technology intensive markets. The acquired technological competencies must fit the strategic technology portfolio of the company in the network. Through effective collaboration and defining the linkages between different selection processes, the development of new technologies and products becomes faster, and new business opportunities can be gained by mixing competencies sensibly.

TECHNOLOGY SELECTION

Concept and classification of technologies

Industrial companies use many technologies in their operations. Nowadays being wrong in technology investment is more expensive and crucial than earlier (Bayus, 1994). According to Betz (1998) some of these technologies are extremely important to the business and can be called core technologies for the company. The other technologies that the company uses can also be necessary, but may not be unique especially in the industry or network where the company operates. Core technologies are the most vital part of a company's competitiveness and survival in the long term.

In order to understand the requirements and criteria for the specific technology selection, technologies must be categorized in some way. Steele (1989) and Betz (1998), among others, have roughly classified technologies into three dimensions:

1. Product/service technologies = "product technologies"
2. Manufacturing/service-delivery technologies = "production technologies"
3. Information/operations technologies for management control = "information technologies"

This classification helps in understanding the technology specific requirements for the selection process and the supporting tools used in the process. When carrying out a real process, identification of company specific criteria is needed. Usually this involves the consideration of a variety of factors, such as business and technology strategy, availability of resources and competitive position and markets. Drawing from the appropriate literature, we have identified the common and most utilized criteria associated with the selection of different technologies.

Technology selection processes and used criteria

Many studies have been conducted about the selection of projects or products (see e.g. Stewart, 1991; Bard et al., 1988). According to Melachrinoudis and Rice (1991), the evaluation of technologies to be selected is a different task from the evaluation of products (or projects). First, because different evaluation criteria have to be used, and second, since technologies are usually very much broader in scope than project proposals, their evaluation is based on much more uncertain information. Mullins and Sutherland (1998) identify three levels of uncertainty that confront companies operating in rapidly changing markets: the customer cannot easily articulate his needs, uncertainty about how to turn the new technologies into products that meet the needs of the customer, and uncertainty about how much capital to invest, and when to invest. In addition, the technologies selected draw new R&D directions for the company, which will affect the contents of future product proposals.

Generally technology selection is based on a company's strategic goals and targets. The selection of technologies is a management process of making a choice between a number of distinct technology alternatives. It suggests the gathering of information about the alternatives from various sources, and the evaluation of the alternatives against each other or a set of criteria. Melachrinoudis and Rice (1991) have emphasized the fact that the task of comparing many competing technologies for the purpose of evaluating them becomes very complex due to the many subjective, partially contradictory and complex criteria involved, and the lack of information or uncertainty on the potential contributions of the technologies toward the criteria or objectives. This makes technology selection one of the most challenging decision making areas the management of a company encounters. One challenge, that Porter et al. (1991) state, rises from the effects of technology that may occur after a long period of time.

Farrukh et al. (2000) have defined a number of general criteria which should be taken into account in the selection of technologies for R&D programs, e.g. cost versus benefit, radical versus incremental, flexibility, risk assessment, make versus buy versus collaborate etc. Yap and Souder (1993) have emphasized that several characteristics of technologies should be taken into account in any technology selection model. These include the uncertainties of commercial and technical success, the funding history of the technologies, the resource requirements to develop technologies, the degree to which the technologies contribute to established missions, and the current life-cycle stage of the technologies. Besides, there can be many relationships between different technologies that must be taken into consideration. The selected technology must match the present technologies and systems of the company.

The selection factors that Fahrni and Spätig (1990) have defined include concentration on the most critical problem, the degree of quantification of relevant factors, the degree of interdependencies between projects (technologies), consideration of single or multiple objectives and the degree of risk. According to Arbel and Shapira (1986) there is a need for a systematic analysis of factors involved in the selection, considering the criteria and parameters leading to the evaluation and selection of an optimal choice. Their selection model focuses on two major groups of issues: benefit and cost. Piippo and Tuominen (1990) have emphasized the match of alternatives to the capabilities and strategies of companies and risks as major factors in the selection, in addition to benefits and costs.

R&D PROJECT SELECTION

The importance of R&D project selection

Selection of right R&D projects is vital for the successful development of new products. R&D is an investment that must compete for corporate support with other investment opportunities, such as new product advertising and market expansion. The purpose of R&D project evaluation and selection is to define projects which can succeed and contribute most to the objectives of the company. By definition, an R&D project is based on one or more technologies and aims at direct financial outcomes. R&D project selection should be seen as an essential part of the R&D management control system and examined as a continuous process (Twiss, 1986). R&D management is described as a systematic process in many companies. In order to be an effective part of the control process of R&D, project selection should also be handled as a process.

The traditional view of project selection

The R&D project selection process is a part of the early phase management of the innovation process. These phases are also often called the fuzzy front-end (Khurana and Rosenthal, 1997) or more recently the front end of innovation (Koen et al., 2001). Traditionally, the approaches companies use for project selection have been described as stage-gate systems, where the number of gates and stages varies between companies. The number of stages is generally lower in service processes than in the processes used for developing manufactured goods (Griffin, 1997). Commonly project selection processes include such stages as ideation, concept generation and concept screening and evaluation (Griffin, 1997; Cooper, 1999). Portfolio assessments can also be seen as a part of project selection processes: projects on different levels of completion should be periodically reviewed and re-evaluated with the possibility of termination at any time on the basis of additional information (Twiss, 1986). The project selection process should end up in a set of projects, which a) is aligned with the company strategies, b) is balanced in terms of defined parameters, and c) yields a maximum value in terms of defined company objectives (Cooper et al., 1998). Project selection processes are becoming cross-functional; R&D and marketing people select projects together (Cooper, 1999).

Many approaches to project evaluation and idea selection have been developed. These approaches include many different methods (e.g. Martino, 1995; Cooper et al., 1998), and systems (Iyigün, 1993; Liberatore and Stylianou, 1995). Several studies have compared developed selection methods and analyzed their benefits and restrictions (e.g. Baker and Albaum, 1986; Cooper, 1998; Danila, 1989; Fahrni and Spätig, 1990; Martino, 1995; Souder and Mankovic, 1986; Twiss, 1986). According to Higgins and Watts (1986) and the more recent studies by Martino (1995) and Cooper et al. (1998), the use of R&D project selection methods is quite low in companies, especially the use of complicated, mathematically oriented tools. However, simpler methods have been used more commonly, including financial methods, business strategy, bubble diagrams, scoring models, and checklists (Cooper, 1999). The best companies use several complementary methods at the same time (Cooper, 1999), which makes it possible to take into account both qualitative and quantitative criteria.

Towards more adaptive project selection processes

The rapidly changing, dynamic environment often brings about a chaotic picture of innovation management. A lot of new challenges to innovation management and project selection processes have arisen, including flexibility (Cooper, 1994), ability to respond to changes quickly (Miller and Morris, 1999), and a more explicit management of uncertainties (Mullins and Sutherland, 1998). As the environment itself asks for flexibility of the R&D project selection processes, the process has to include systematic elements as well. The following two subchapters discuss the systematic and flexible elements of R&D project selection processes in detail. These two approaches should not be thought of as contradictory, as they aim at the same overall goal, i.e. to enable an effective way of handling new product ideas, and to increase the likelihood of finding successful projects (commercially and/or in some other way successful) early enough.

Systematic elements

Basically, R&D project selection is about setting priorities between project candidates on the basis of uncertain information (three levels of uncertainties by Mullins and Sutherland, 1998)). The uncertainties and development flexibility related to the rapidly changing environment need to be managed explicitly (Iansiti and MacCormack, 1997). The systematic elements can be seen as a framework which sets overall boundaries for the selection process. More specifically, issues that describe the systematic side of project selection processes include the following:

- There exists an agreed procedure for project selection and priority setting (e.g. how new ideas are handled and put forward);
- Stages and gates are defined explicitly (certain tasks concerning all ideas and project proposals are needed);

- Links to business strategy and technology strategies have been identified;
- New ideas are systematically compared against available alternative technologies;
- Customers' present and future needs are identified and systematically incorporated in selection decisions;
- Relevant screening and evaluation criteria (must meet -criteria, should meet -criteria) are predefined and responsibilities for evaluation have been set (cross-functional task);
- People are committed to the project selection criteria;
- There exist mechanisms of transferring knowledge from previous projects (Verganti et al., 1998);
- The interrelations to other projects are identified ('Do not discover the wheel again');
- The early phases of the innovation process are emphasized to be able to reach the desired level of knowledge as early as possible (decreasing uncertainties);
- The R&D project portfolio is continually monitored and updated;
- The project selection process is supported by easy-to-use tools and methods.

Flexible elements

In the rapidly changing environment a very rigorous R&D project selection process will not work. Due to shortened product life cycles, competitive dynamics, emerging technologies and suddenly appearing market possibilities, the demand for more flexible elements in the R&D project selection processes is increasing. The issues of flexibility include:

- The R&D project selection process is continually adjusted to the changing needs; the process is fluid and adaptable (Davidson, 1999; Cooper, 1999);
- There exists a facilitator, who makes sure that the process works efficiently and effectively (Cooper, 1999), and who runs the adjustments to the process (Davidson, 1999);
- There exist different guidelines for handling different kinds of project proposals (e.g. product improvements, cost reductions, new products);
- There exist different criteria for different kinds of project proposals;
- Stages and gates are overlapping (parallel process);
- Stages and gates are conditional; the decision can be made in the absence of perfect information (Cooper, 1999);
- Stages and gates can be omitted in certain conditions;
- There exists a procedure for handling very promising ideas very quickly (for example a predefined "trigger" criterion such as a huge market potential);
- Customers are engaged in project selection processes (e.g. shared idea bank);
- Many complementary methods are in use;

Flexibility requires a willingness and organizational agility to integrate new approaches, while preserving the value of existing approaches (Davidson, 1999). In other words, flexibility means continually adjusting the process to the organization's needs and desires (Davidson, 1999).

LINKAGES BETWEEN SELECTION PROCESSES IN A NETWORK

Common features of selection processes

Technology selection and R&D project selection can both be regarded as decision making processes with many common features. Platts (1994) has presented some common characteristics of successful selection methodologies:

- *Procedure*: well defined stages, simple tools and techniques, producing written records
- *Participation*: individual and group, workshop style meetings, decision making leading to action
- *Project managing*: adequate resourcing, agreed timescales
- *Point of entry*: clearly defined expectations, ways to establish understanding, agreement and commitment.

The criteria and firm-specific aspects involved in selection decisions can vary quite a lot depending on the characteristics of the technology, the R&D project and the organization. Regardless of the criteria used, the selection process must meet some of the basic requirements listed above. Also, the systematic and flexible elements described in the connection with R&D project selection can be applied to technology selection as well. Furthermore, the network environment adds some new requirements for the selection processes. What is needed in a broader context, is a convergence of the innovation processes of the actors in the network. In that case, common stages of the process can be difficult to define, because every actor in the network has their own process with certain stages. Generally companies have their own specific tools and techniques, which can include or need classified sensitive information about the company that should not be shared with other companies. Commitment and mutual trust between the network actors are key issues in group participation in workshops. When a bigger group of people are collaborating, the implementation of decisions and putting them into action are extremely important aspects. Companies have more resources available in the network environment, which makes it quite difficult to agree on timescales. The network environment imposes turbulent and continuously changing requirements, which force the companies to assess the existing and new network actors carefully to ensure appropriate collaboration partners. The company's own and collaboration projects should be communicated as early as possible to the appropriate partners. Collaboration and communication within the network provide early warnings of technological developments. This helps the companies to incorporate new technology advances into their own products and processes.

The importance of selection decisions in the network

Fig. 25.1 describes a loop that emphasizes the existence of effective technology selection and R&D project selection processes. As mentioned earlier, there are many factors encouraging companies to collaborate in innovation management, e.g. shortened time-to-market. Time and resources are often wasted if a company develops technologies alone. By collaboration in technology development the companies in the network can concentrate on the utilization and development of specialized skills and resources with shared risks. Collaboration also brings about shorter development times - new technologies are ready earlier and also product platforms with new products and services reach the market earlier. Responses from the market can be absorbed from customers to provide signals for new products and services. New technologies need to be developed while the old ones mature. A company needs to face technology selection and R&D project selection decisions more often than it would probably have to do without collaborative relationships.

The cycle is re-enforcing, but there are factors that restrain the re-enforcement of the loop. These factors are for example technological barriers or unrecognized customer needs. This means that a company needs to have practices of identifying their customers' present and particularly future and latent needs, and practices to incorporate this information in the technology selection and R&D project selection decisions. The technology push cannot be utilized as the only way of setting development priorities.

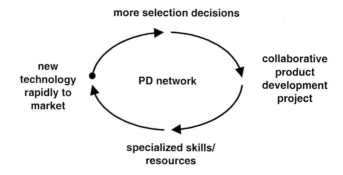

more selection decisions

new technology rapidly to market

PD network

collaborative product development project

specialized skills/ resources

Fig. 25.1. Collaboration leads to new selection situations quicker.

The role of actors in the product development network

Fig. 25.2 provides an example of a possible product development network from a larger company's perspective including relationships and links between different actors. The value chain of telecommunications services is also described in Fig. 25.2 in order to illustrate different roles companies have in the networks of this industry. This example concentrates on the main linkages between the big actor and its interest groups. In a product development network the amount of linkages can be extensive. The starting point for a company would be to recognize its own role (operator, service operator etc.) and position (linkages to other actors) in the network, as well as its customers', suppliers' and competitors' role and positioning. The dashed line illustrates important, but normally not systematically recognized linkages. For example a subcontractor can develop an extremely important technology that will change the whole platform of the larger company. In order to follow this development, the information flow within the network should be organized in an effective way.

In the network, the larger company has the role of a 'technology engine', meaning that it invests heavily in being a pioneer in many new technology-based business fields. The larger company has different types of relationships to the other actors in the network. For instance, it has strong bargaining power against some subcontractors in technology development decisions, but it has to have a more sensitive relationship to a critical partner (e.g. small organization - an SME) that has some critical competencies and completes its technology portfolio. The partners in the networks have distinctive objectives in co-operative product development projects, and therefore communication between the partners plays a very essential role already in the very early stages of co-operation.

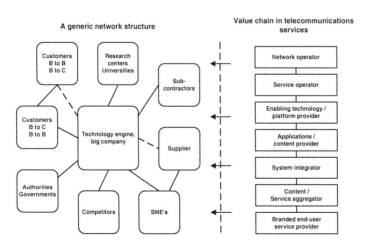

Fig. 25.2. Actors, roles and linkages in the product development.

The actors in the network should have situational flexibility, because fast changes can occur in the environment, and the development of networks as organizational forms is a continuous process. The formation of these types of product development networks is often triggered by common interests between companies to develop a technology or technological platform. Once started, the existing network then incubates new technologies and new projects.

Technologies and R&D projects affect not only the customers, but also their customers and other stakeholders within the network. It is important to see not only the customer, but also beyond the customer to its customers and other stakeholders when operating in a product development network. Future needs and trends can be predicted by networking closely with both b-to-b and b-to-c actors.

The 'technology engine' and its competitors can have mutual interests concerning important new technology. For example the 3rd generation mobile technology UMTS connects operators to buy licenses in a consortium and develop markets with the equipment manufacturers. The whole network has an equal interest to increase the size of the market as fast as possible. From the risk management point of view in the case of UMTS, (negative) network effects can be considered to affect the whole industry field strongly for a long period of time in the future. This illustrates the negative sides of PD networks where potential problems of big players can impede the business of other network stakeholders.

Research centers and universities do basic and applied research that produces useful and vital information for technology selection and R&D project selection. Authorities produce legislation and regulations that can have a negative effect on the usability of certain technology in a certain market area. For example the license fees of UMTS are quite high in certain markets, which will possibly delay market development.

Causal relations between technologies, platforms and products

Fig. 25.3 illustrates the linkages between technologies and R&D projects. The left side of the figure describes the platform concept, which can be defined here as 'underlying structures or basic architectures that are common across a group of products and services or that will be the basis of a series of products and services commercialized over a number of years' (definition adapted from Rosenau et al. (1996)). There exists different kind of platforms including technology, product and services platforms. The technologies themselves can be far from actual products and services. It is the use of the technology that matters more than the technology itself (Miller and Morris, 1999). Single technologies can be used to build up technology and product platforms on which new products and services, and probably also new technologies, are developed. The challenge to technology selection is which technologies to choose for the platforms. Platform thinking makes it possible to quickly develop new products and services after the platform has been established.

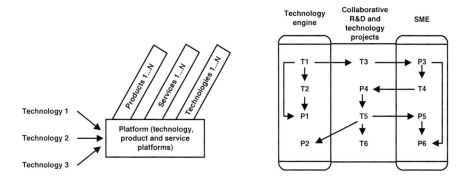

Fig. 25.3. Interrelated technologies, platforms and R&D projects.

The right side of Fig. 25.3 illustrates the causal effects the technology selections and project selections have on the actors in the network. The example is a simplification of Fig. 25.2, the relationship between a 'technology engine' (big company) and an SME. The 'technology engine' first develops (together with for example its competitors, as in the case of Bluetooth) or acquires technology T1 and selects T1 as a core technology. T1 seeds ideas for R&D projects and new technologies first of all inside the technology engine (platform development is omitted in Fig. 25.3 for simplicity), but also inside the SME. The technology engine and the SME have a mutual interest to develop T3, which enables the R&D project P3. In this case T1 is an enabling technology for the R&D project P1, but also for new technologies T2 and T3. The idea to start developing technology T4 in the SME is initiated from project P3. In the example the technology engine has found project P4 and technologies T3, T5 and T6 interesting enough to start collaboration in innovation management with the SME. In this case the R&D project P2 is not enabled until a long causal chain through T1-T3-P3-T4-P4-T5 is realized.

CONCLUSION

The purpose of this paper was to clarify the characteristics and linkages of technology selection and R&D project selection from the product development network point of view. Product development is critical for the long-term profitability of both a single company and companies networked in their R&D priorities. Identification and well organized management of the linkages between technology selection and R&D project selection plays an essential role in product development in the New Economy era by offering remarkable potential to increase the total value through the network. With the help of linkage description, companies adopt the value of networking by selecting the right technologies and the right R&D projects to be carried out by themselves or together with other players in the network in order to achieve competitive advantage.

Technology and project selection in the networked innovation environment is not radically different from the selection decisions made in a more traditional environment - explicit criteria and management commitment are needed to accomplish and maintain the best technology and project portfolios. The development of systematic and effective processes means the promotion of collaboration during the early phase management of innovation processes that is essential in order to identify weak signals from the market. Concrete ways of action in PD networks could include the use of shared idea banks with customers and partners, and the use of workshop-type evaluation and selection sessions.

A company operating in a network should first recognize its position in relation to the other actors. By identifying its role in the network a company can better forecast and prepare for new requirements and identify latent needs stated by customers' customers. Identification of the important linkages between technology selection and R&D project selection decisions, and between the actors, helps in the priority setting of the company's own technologies and projects. By managing the linkages the company can better identify its core technologies and projects that should be kept inside the company for competitive edge. Cause-effect relationships between technology selection decisions and R&D project selection decisions are complex. The technology and project decisions influence the company itself and the decision processes of other actors. The position of a company in the network is characterized by its strategic innovation management principles. The decisions of 'technology engines' have different effects on the network compared to the decisions made by technology adaptors or imitators. Companies can better understand and predict the effects of their own actions to the companies in the network by identifying the causal chains between the decisions.

Both technology selection and R&D project selection require flexibility and capability to react rapidly, especially in the turbulent market environment. When selection decisions are made in collaboration, the managerial attitudes have to be open-minded. A shortened total development time becomes even shorter when the planning of technology selection and R&D project selection overlap.

This paper has clarified the characteristics of the PD network and the decision making processes concerning technologies and R&D projects in a network at the conceptual level. Practical evidence and industry level characteristics in networked technology selection and R&D project selection can be provided by for instance a case study in ICT industry, where the dynamic environment and already strongly networked operations models incubate new technologies, products and services.

BIBLIOGRAPHY

Arbel, A. and Shapira, Y. (1986): A decision framework for evaluating vacuum pumping technology. *Journal of Vacuum Science & Technology*, A4, 2, 230-236.

Baker, K. and Albaum, G. (1986): Modeling new product screening decisions. *Journal of Product Innovation Management*, 1, 32-39.

Bard, J.F., Balachandra, R., and Kaufmann, P.E. (1988): An integrative approach to R&D project selection and termination. *IEEE Transactions on Engineering Management*, 35, 3, 139-146.

Bayus, B. (1994): Are product life cycles really getting shorter? *Journal of Product Innovation Management*, 11, 4, 300–308.

Betz, F. (1998): *Managing Technological Innovation*. New York, John Wiley & Sons.

Cohen, W. M. and Levinthal, D. A. (1990): Absorptive capacity: A new perspective on learning and innovation. *Administrative Science Quarterly*, 35, 128-152.

Combs, K.L. (1993): The role of information sharing in cooperative research and development. *International Journal of Industrial Organizations*, 11, 535-551.

Cooper, R.G. (1994): Third generation new product processes. *Journal of Product Innovation Management*, 11, 3-14.

Cooper, R.G. (1999): *Product Leadership: Creating and Launching Superior New Products*. Cambridge (MA), Perseus Books.

Cooper, R.G., Edgett, S.J. and Kleinschmidt, E.J. (1998): *Portfolio Management for New Products*. Reading (MA), Addison-Wesley.

Danila, N. (1989): Strategic evaluation and selection of R&D projects. *R&D Management*, 19, 1, 47-62.

Davidson, J.M., Clamen, A. and Karol, R.A. (1999): Learning from the best new product developers. *Research Technology Management*, July-August, 12-18.

Fahrni, P. and Spätig, M. (1990): An application-oriented guide to R&D project selection and evaluation methods. *R&D Management*, 20, 155-171.

Farrukh, C., Phaal, R., Probert, D., Gregory, M., and Wright, J. (2000): Developing a process for the relative valuation of R&D programmes. *R&D Management*, 30, 1, 43-53.

Griffin, A. (1997): PDMA research on new product development practices: updating trends and benchmarking best practices. *Journal of Product Innovation Management*, 14, 429-458.

Harmsen, H., Grunert, K.G. and Bove, K. (2000): Company competencies as a network: the role of product development. *Journal of Product Innovation Management*, 17, 194-207.

Higgins, J. and Watts, K. (1986): Some perspectives on the use of management science techniques in R&D management. R&D Management, 16, 4, 291-296.

Iansiti, M. and MacCormack, A. (1997): Developing products on Internet time. *Harvard Business Review*, September-October, 108-117.

Ingham, M. and Mothe,C. (1998): How to learn in R&D partnership? *R&D Management*, 28,4,249-261.

Iyigün, M.G. (1993): A decision support system for R&D project selection and resource allocation under uncertainty. *Project Management Journal*, XXIV, 5, 5-13.

Khurana, A. and Rosenthal, S. (1997): Integrating the fuzzy front-end of new product development. *Sloan Management Review* (Winter) 38:2, 103-120.

Koen, P., Ajamian, G., Burkart, R., Clamen, A., Davidson, J., D'Amore, R., Elkins, C., Herald, K., Incorvia, M., Johnson, A., Karol, R., Seibert, R., Slavejkov, A. and Wagner, K. (2001): Providing clarity and a common language to the "fuzzy front end". *Research Technology Management*, March-April, 46-55.

Liberatore, M.J. and Stylianou, A.C. (1995): Expert support systems for new product development decision making: a modeling approach and applications. *Management Science*, 41,8,1296-1316.

Martino, J.P. (1995): *R&D Project Selection*. New York, John Wiley & Sons.

Melachrinoudis, E. and Rice, K., (1991): The prioritization of technologies in a research laboratory. *IEEE Transactions on Engineering Management*, 38, 3, 269-278.

Miller, W.L. and Morris, L. (1999): *Fourth Generation R&D*. New York, John Wiley & Sons.

Mullins, J.W. and Sutherland, D.J. (1998): New product development in rapidly changing markets: an exploratory study. *Journal of Product Innovation Management*, 15, 3, 224-236.

Piippo, P., and Tuominen, M. (1990): Promoting innovation management by decision support systems; Facilitating new products' relevance to the corporate objectives, in Jürgen Allesch (eds), *Consulting in innovation: practice – methods – perspectives*, Holland, Elsevier Science Publishers, 267-292.

Platts, K. (1994): Characteristics of methodologies for manufacturing strategy formulation. *Computer Integrated Manufacturing Systems*, 7, 2, 93-99.

Porter, A.L, Roper, T., Mason, T., Rossini, F., Banks, J., and Wiederholt, B. (1991): *Forecasting and Management of Technology*. New York, John Wiley & Sons.

Rosenau, M.D., Griffin, A., Castellion, G. and Anschuetz, N. (1996): *The PDMA Handbook of New Product Development*. New York, John Wiley & Sons.

Quinn, J. B. (2000): Outsourcing innovation: the new engine of growth. *Sloan Management Review*, Summer, 13-28.

Sawhney, M. and Prandelli, E. (2000): Communities of creation: Managing distributed innovation in turbulent markets. *California Management Review*, 42, 4, 24-54.

Souder, W. and Mandakovic, T. (1986): R&D project selection models. *Research Management*, 29, 4, 36-42.

Steele L.W. (1989): *Managing Technology – The Strategic View*. New York, McGraw-Hill.

Stewart T.J. (1991): A multi-criteria decision support system for R&D project selection. *Journal of the Operational Research Society*, 42, 1, 17-26.

Twiss, B.C. (1986): *Managing Technological Innovation*. London, Pitman Publishing.

Verganti, R., MacCormack, A. and Iansiti, M. (1998): Rapid learning and adaption in product development: an empirical study of the Internet software industry. Paper presented at the 5th International Product Development Management Conference, Como, Italy, May 25-26.

White, J.E., Gorton, M.J. and Chaston, I. (1996): Facilitating co-operative networks of high-technology small firms: problems and strategies. *Small Business and Enterprise Development*, 3, 34-47.

Yap C., and Souder Wm. (1993): A filter system for technology evaluation and selection. *Technovation*, 13, 449-469.

Zeffane, R. (1994): Inter-organizational alliance and network dynamics, processes and technology. *Leadership & Organization Development Journal*, 15, 7, 28-32.

Management of Technology
Copyright © 2003 by Elsevier Science Ltd.
ISBN: 0-08-044136-X

26

NEW TRENDS IN AUTOMOTIVE SUPPLY: THE FULLY INTEGRATED SUPPLY CHAIN AND THE GENERAL MOTORS CASE IN RIO GRANDE DO SUL (BRAZIL)

Paulo Antônio Zawislak, Federal University of Rio Grande do Sul, Porto Alegre, Brazil [*]
Cristina Rodrigues de Borba Vieira, Federal University of Rio Grande do Sul, Porto Alegre, Brazil [**]

INTRODUCTION

The complexity of the production of an automobile and the relevance of this industry, in all economies, because of its capacity of creating jobs and income, as well as for the development of the management technologies, make the study of the automotive chain something very interesting.

Currently, the companies in this industry are producing in a very competitive environment, where cost reduction and increased productivity are the solution for those that intend to continue operating in the market. Competition, however, is not only amongst companies but especially amongst different chains. Each motor company (or O.E.M.) has been seeking to make a "perfect chain" working all along with suppliers.

[*]   Paulo Antônio Zawislak, Ph.D., Nucleus of Management of Technology / Administration School / Federal University of Rio Grande do Sul - Porto Alegre-RS/Brazil. Email: pazawislak@ea.ufrgs.br.
[**]   Cristina Rodrigues de Borba Vieira, M.Sc., Nucleus of Management of Technology / Administration School / Federal University of Rio Grande do Sul - Porto Alegre-RS/Brazil. Email: crbvieira@yahoo.com.br.

In this context of supply chain competition, more than a company, everything must be efficient and every activity must get the maximum possible value at the same time it tends to zero waste. In order to do this, the O.E.M.s focus their activities according to their core competencies. They do it with activities such as car design, final assembly and selling/marketing/financing, through which they can add more value to the final product, transferring to their suppliers a batch of less adding value activities. It is possible to recognize that some components may have a better quality and cost less whenever manufactured by specialized suppliers. This trend follows the lessons brought up by the so-called Toyota Production System – or lean production –, showing the change of auto parts' own competitive standards.

This new production process, which distributes the different productive activities of the same process, demands a huge flow reorganization effort, whether in terms of information or material. The different parts must work like a single unit of a perfect mechanism: The Fully Integrated Supply Chain.

The Fully Integrated Supply Chain means that the demands made by the O.E.M. to the system suppliers also are made by them to the second tier suppliers and so forth. However, the need of these companies to working with the same principles makes the suppliers' capacity to fulfil the demands of the head company mandatory. What we see is that the O.E.M., the system suppliers and the other level suppliers are getting much closer (Vieira and Zawislak, 2002).

The arrival of General Motors in Rio Grande do Sul, southern state of Brazil, with an innovative vehicle production project, is just the opportunity to check whether such supply changes between the O.E.M. and its suppliers are really being carried out.

The objective of this article is to make a few points about new standards of production and supply in the automotive industry, remarkably from the new General Motors Brazilian case on. Therefore, this article was organized in 5 sections, where the Fully Integrated Supply Chain concepts will be presented; the new supply forms that are coming out in Brazil and in the rest of the world; the GM project made for RS and the final discussions.

THE FULLY INTEGRATED SUPPLY CHAIN

The growing competition amongst automotive industry companies has been raising the interest for questions such as the building of efficient supply chains, the forms of chain management and logistics, the value adding and waste reduction. All these aspects are linked with the new ways of production that are being developed by the O.E.M.s.

This competitive environment demands that companies be clear in their business and the development of capabilities in the production chain. This means that companies need to be really sure about their targets in order to find a better position along the value chain (Pires, 1998).

The Fully Integrated Supply Chain is based on a relationship between the O.E.M. and its suppliers. This relationship is so closely knit that any change made in the product or process is noticed along the links of the chain. Unlike what happens in purchase contracts, the products are developed together by the client and the suppliers (co-design), as well as the (targeted) prices and its reduction rates (which might be in periods of up to 5 years) are agreed on together. Besides that, the supplier, at the client's own assembly line, and the production program are set through the EDI (electronic data system). The total interchange for the automotive chain means the emergence of a new form of industrial organization based on the maximum company interaction (Zawislak, 1999).

Supply Chain Management and Integrated Logistics

The Fully Integrated Supply Chain must work like a large firm and be managed efficiently in a synchronized way. The supply chain management is a robust toolbox for interchange flow of all chain links from the supplier to the final customer himself (Cooper and Ellram, 1993).

However, the supply chain management means that the increase of relationships and the number of guests must be followed by new co-operative relationships, with information and infrastructure sharing, and by concrete inventory reduction, either through just-in-time delivery or by using electronic interchange. Finally, it is necessary to make a competitive strategy for the whole chain (Furlanetto and Zawislak, 2000).

From this point of view logistics play a key role. It is said to be the process of planning, introducing and controlling value streams, where material flow and the related information goes further then just moving different parts and goods to the consumption areas. The emergence of a new logistic standard (Stock and Greis and Kasarda, 1998) is then possible. In this case, logistics does not happen amongst different companies but amongst different supply chains, and its competitive success depends more and more on the ability to co-ordinate and integrate the production activities geographically spread out.

To establish this chain management based on integrated logistics, companies need to work according to the lean production principles.

The Lean Thinking

The lean production, as introduced by Womack et al (1998), is based on the "Lean Thinking". According to Ferro,

> "the Lean Thinking is an operational philosophy or a business system, a way of specifying value, aligning in the best sequence the actions that produce value, performing these activities without interruption every time someone requests it and performing them more and more efficiently, that is, doing more and more with less and less (...) and, at the same time, getting

closer and closer to providing customers with exactly what they wish at the right time" (2000, p. 6).

It is a philosophy which is on the search for creating flow and adding value by reducing periods in between the crossing of a production step and, obviously, a generalized effort to eliminate all possible waste (including human effort, time, space, movement, transport, inventory, waiting, production, equipment, unnecessary activities, ultimately, everything that does not add any value). The use of management and quality techniques, such as value stream mapping, kanban, one-piece-flow, kaizen, is part of the process, which allows the reduction and the optimization of spaces, distances and time (Rother and Shook, 1999).

According to this idea, there should be a wide management system in the companies from production to top management, passing by every other strategic area of the company, form development to marketing. Likewise – and even most importantly – there should be an effort to find new ways of adding value.

By eliminating the most diverse forms of waste, as well as everything that does not add any value to the products, it should be possible to reach a perfectly lean process, that is, it should be possible to produce any product, pulled by customers, according to a continuous flow. The perfect "lean" world could be summed up as the one where, from nature (a source of any gross raw material) to the final customer (with its product containing that raw material in its essence), there would be a single large fully synchronized production line. It would be possible to precisely foresee the delivery time of the product to the customer.

However, as one knows, there are yet insurmountable physical and technological limits. This "perfect world" is then far from being reached. In the automotive industry, for example, it usually takes 3 days on average to assemble a vehicle, and the process should have started at least 45 days before the assembly so that the consumer can, some 45 days later, receive his/her product. So, whatever is technically and economically feasible is made lean.

Several tools have helped this process. Much has been heard of pull system, management and production team, cell layout, trouble-shooting teams, software for integrated management, use of quality norms and requirements, six sigma, etc. The use of these elements has been highly beneficial in a number of experiments.

But in the lean production world, the company being lean individually is not enough. So that the whole value stream (from the raw material to the final customer) be as efficient as possible, it is necessary that the whole value chain, i.e. the whole productive chain of a given product, be actually integrated. The productive chain "invaded" by the lean thinking generates what will be called "Fully Integrated Supply Chain".

Finally, it is with a lean chain that the relationship and the production of each one of the companies produce more with fewer resources.

NEW SUPPLY FORMS AND THE BRAZILIAN EXPERIENCE

The arrival of new motor companies in Brazil and the improvement made by existing O.E.Ms, during the late 90's[1], brings with them an entire new supply paradigm. In general, the O.E.M. started the changes in the standard relationships with its closest suppliers, which implies new supplying forms.

The system suppliers are companies that have capabilities that the O.E.M. itself may not have or may not be interested in developing. For this reason, they participate since the conception of the product and develop, for instance, quality programs together with the O.E.M., being able to incorporate different activities, which are not the ones from the beginning. As the system suppliers take part in the conception of the product, the development of new technologies and productive processes is encouraged. This process recognizes the fact that some components have a better quality and cost when manufactured by the suppliers rather than by the O.E.M.

Generally speaking it is possible to mark a world trend that leads to the creation of a supplier network. The O.E.Ms will turn their attention to the component system. The system suppliers are entitled to deliver the modules whose components were received by other less qualified suppliers. All this, however, implies different industrial arrangements.

New Industrial Arrangements

Applied to the new supply forms represented by the Fully Integrated Supply Chain, there are also revolutionary production organization forms with visible physical organization impacts. These impacts convey more efficiency to the lean production standards. The sites, as the production facilities are called, work aiming at a growing interchange between O.E.Ms and their system suppliers, global companies that manufacture whole modules (pivots, electronic systems, etc.).

This interchange is nothing but the evolution of classic industrial districts, where companies of a same sector, working at different levels of the production chain, get together to obtain external savings, like technical assistance and transport cost reduction for example (see Fig. 26.1).

At this level, however, the split parts are still visible. The ABC Paulista Region (São Paulo, Brazil) could be considered as an industrial district, although its spatial organization was not intended for that.

---

[1]   Form 1995 to 2001, Toyota, Honda, Chrylser, Mitsubishi, Mercedes-Benz Auto build new plants that have forced local established players, such as GM, Ford and VW, to dramatically improve their existing and even to build new ones (see Zawislak, 1999).

Source: Zawislak (1999)

Fig. 26.1. Industrial District.

Regarding another subject, there is what has been called modular consortium, where the VW's experience in Resende (Rio de Janeiro, Brazil) is far and away the best example. With this sort of physical logistic arrangement, the final assembly production operations are carried out by the module suppliers themselves inside a plant of the company that contracted them. (See Fig. 26.2) (Zawislak and Vieira and Irala, 2000).

What is different from one extremity to the other is, on one hand, the level of manufactured value adding made by the O.E.M. itself and, on the other hand, the physical proximity amongst companies. While in an industrial district the O.E.M's value adding level is high, in the modular consortium it tends to be lower. This is linked to external savings enabled by the proximity. There is a clear reduction in distances, times, losses linked to logistics in its classic meaning.

The intermediate level, in between the industrial district and the modular consortium, is the so-called industrial condominium (Fig. 26.3). It is known as the place where the main system suppliers (systemists) are within the O.E.M's site, which is still responsible for the final assembly.

Fig. 26.3 shows two different ways of arranging the industrial condominium; the "a" type, where the suppliers, event in the same site, are still fence-separate from the O.E.M. (this is the case of General Motors in Rio Grande do Sul, Brazil – which will be further detailed);

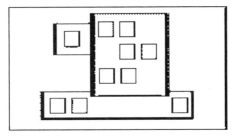

Source: Zawislak (1999)

Fig. 26.2. Modular Consortium.

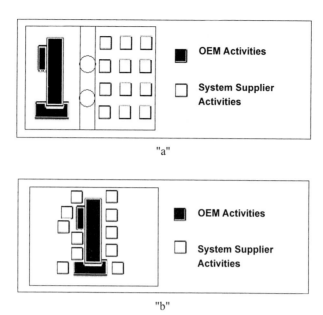

Source: Zawislak (1999)

Fig. 26.3. Industrial Condominium.

and the "b" type, where the suppliers, responsible for a specific system, are placed close to the O.E.M.'s exact consumption point (this is the case of Ford in Bahia, Brazil).

THE GENERAL MOTORS IN RIO GRANDE DO SUL, BRAZIL – THE BLUE MACAW PROJECT[2]

The new General Motors plant started being built up in 1997, in Gravataí (Rio Grande do Sul, Brazil). This industrial unit is part of a major project (Yellowstone Project), together with other new plants, where GM is aiming at the development of the new lean production model. From the Nummi Project (a joint-venture with Toyota) to the Blue Macaw, GM has accomplish a long 25 year's way to reach what is, according to a GM executive, "the world's most modern car-making plant and not only GM's" (A viagem, 1998, p.04).

The installation of the Gravataí Automotive Industrial Complex (CIAG), as the enterprise is known, costs around US$ 550 million. Of this, US$ 375 million was invested by

---

[2] Some information contained in this article was obtained by visiting the General Motors' plant and from lectures delivered by GM professionals.

GM and US$ 175 million by its system suppliers. The Government of the State of Rio Grande do Sul committed to invest approximately US$ 130 million[3].

It is the third GM plant in Brazil and the first one outside the state of São Paulo (Festa, 2000). The plant's project was especially designed to produce the Celta model, which was the automaker's first car having a fully Brazilian design. The new plant's product is a car deriving from Corsa (in a reduced platform[4]), where GM reduced the price (to approximately US$ 6,000) with a modern design, based on the Europeans Astra and Vectra models (Naiditch, 2001).

Besides the news involving the product, the company is bringing out new production organization concepts as well as concepts regarding supply and logistics, all based on the idea of the Fully Integrated Supply Chain. This unit represents what GM believes to be essential for making the new production system work. The car is produced in modules together with 17 system suppliers located on GM's site (see Fig. 26.4) and 91 off-site (23 imported).

In the same way, the target of this new industrial arrangement is to get the maximum value in all activities, reducing waste and cost and thus increasing profits.

The General Motors Site

The main change brought by GM to Rio Grande do Sul is the way it organizes its productive process. To get the maximum efficiency with the lean standards currently applied, the process physical arrangement itself gains fresh air. Unlike the modular consortium (see figure 9.2), in the GM industrial condominium the break up is still on despite the geographic proximity between the system suppliers individual plants and GM's.

According to Fig. 26.4, the system suppliers, located in one of the sides, produce very close to the GM assembly plant located on the other side. Anyway, that means a natural evolution of the production methods used by General Motors in São Paulo, which flows are performed by the supply relationships (sequence delivery, milk run, inner transport of materials) form companies located kilometers far from de GM's site.

Next are some details related to General Motors. They include its productive process and quality, its system suppliers and logistics, which really place the whole in a fully integrated relationship new standard.

---

[3]   For further details on the distribution of these investments among GM, system suppliers and the State Government, see FIERGS, 2000.

[4]   While in other plants, cars are built up with more or less 4.500 part numbers, in the Gravataí case, GM is working with only 843 different items on the Celta.

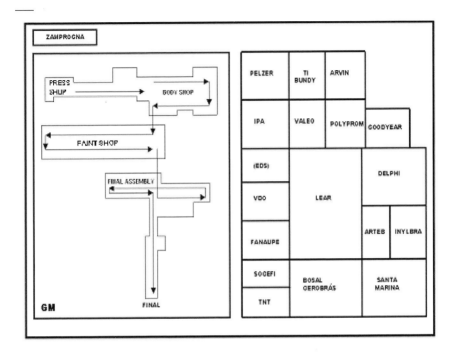

Fig. 26.4. The GM Site in Rio Grande do Sul (Source: GM release).

The GM Productive Process

Four basic steps are developed in the plant's assembly line[5]: press shop, body shop, paint shop and final assembly (see Fig. 26.4). The level of automation presented is amazing. There are 120 robots in all; the body shop for example, is 90% automated. There is software for monitoring the vehicle height during the assembly and every fastener machine is a powered unit, thus allowing reducing operators' physical effort.

The car assembly starts by receiving the metal blanks of the body of the vehicle, which are supplied by Zamprogna (the only system supplier located 30 minutes far from the site). These blanks are pressed and later they head to the body shop where the shaped components are soldered. In the body shop, 99 robots, fed by different cells, forming a "fish backbone" in a "U-shape", drive the one-piece-flow process.

---

[5] Much of the information on GM's assembly line was obtained from a special coverage made by Zero Hora, a local newspaper, on the day of the plant's inauguration (July 20, 2000) and also several visits made to GM site, from 1999 to 2001, by the Group of Studies of the Automotive Chain of Rio Grande do Sul (GCARS).

With the body of the vehicle set, the car goes to the highly automated paint area. Only in some inner parts, where the machines are not able to reach, the workers paint it out manually. The cars are produced in 5 colors (red, blue, green, silver and white), with the option of black.

After the paint, the vehicle body goes to the final assembly. Doors, bonnet and trunk cover are taken off to receive the overall finish. Meanwhile, the car receives the engine and the gear systems which are provided by GM São José dos Campos (São Paulo, Brazil) and the other components, provided by the other 16 system suppliers located in the CIAG's site.

When the vehicle is ready it goes to the test track, returning to the plant if any final adjustments are required and afterwards the car is available for the trucks.

This whole assembly process could take from 1.5 to 2 days (17 work hours). That is only possible because the plant must start the process with zero-inventory and the suppliers have 40 minutes to get the auto parts delivered at the exact place of the assembly. Hopefully, better than at any other place, GM is really reaching a low cost and high efficiency manufacturing process.

Quality

The Gravataí unit's philosophy is that of continuous improvement. This process is made through the kaizen shop – a place to discuss improvements, where employees make suggestions in order to shoot the problems. Employees of all levels must take part – from the shop floor to the management – and are awarded when the suggestion is carried out. Moreover, and to avoid mistakes, labor follows a standard and the employees get acquainted with every part of the process by rotation. In relation to the product quality control, the project sets the checklist before going to any other area. Not to mention the 3 quality gates – body shop, tapestry and assembly finishing.

The Gravataí plant's production works according to the andon system, where any employee is able to interrupt the production when a failure is noted during the process in order to correct any mistakes occurred before the end of the car manufacturing. But in case of being short in any auto parts of minor importance the car still will be assembled, being recovered only at the end of the line.

To keep the quality level of the auto parts received from suppliers, the O.E.M. has created the Supplier Quality Engineering Department. This department checks the first job lot before the delivery and also checks it during the production. If problems are noted, this department tells the supplier to check the reasons why. Suppliers are responsible for the guaranty and all of them must be always on time. The quantity and quality set by the O.E.M. must be complied with (Sistemistas, 2000).

The Supply to GM

Generally speaking, GM's main requirements to its suppliers – either system suppliers or tier suppliers – may be summarized in four words: technology, quality, price and service (Zawislak, 1999).

For that reason, the QS 9000 certification is very important. It allows any company to work always trying to improve the quality of the processes, products and services, using the most suitable technology available and keeping competitive prices. According to a comment made by a Delphi executive about the need of the company to get the QS 9000 certification: "the requirements have improved the quality of the product, process and chain management level. We have had the impact with the QS, which has helped us systematize our communication processes and scrap reduction" (Cadeia, 1999, front page).

For organizing its direct suppliers, the system suppliers, the company has adopted exactly the above-mentioned industrial condominium system. All the 17 system suppliers must work exclusively with GM using what they call an "on-line just-in-time system" and with a single logistics operator, TNT Logistics (see "Logistics" below).

The systemists themselves are globally supplying companies that are the O.E.M's partners in other countries, complying with their demands[6]. Besides the 17 system suppliers, GM has to work with other 114 second and third-tier companies that are supposed to supply directly to the systemists. However, General Motors negotiates with these suppliers in order to get better prices and paying terms rather than each system supplier making the order individually.

General Motors itself works with maximum 40-minutes stock in the consumption point, while systemists work with a 12-hour inventory for the external suppliers. For doing so, GM-systemists relationship works based upon the following management tools: "classic" kanban (for storage parts), electronic kanban (for on-site parts), electronic pull system (for body shop blanks), and many different visual controls spread-out by the plant.

However, the O.E.M. and the systemists are always trying to reduce the risks of running short of auto parts during the process by enhancing readiness and punctuality. This implies a strong logistic effort.

---

[6]   The suppliers and its systems are: Arteb – lighting; Arvin Meritor – exhaust systems; Bosal Gerobrás – tool kit; Delphi – suspension; Fanaupe – fixing elements; Goodyear – wheels and tires; Inylbra – tapestry and thermo-acoustic insulation; Lear – seats, finishes, doors and roof; Pelzer – plastic injected parts; Polyprom – pressed items; Santa Marina – laminated glasses; Sogefi – air filter; Soplast – fuel tank; TI Brasil – brake and fuel lines; Valeo – cooling systems; VDO – cockpit; Zamprogna – blanks.

Logistics

To make sure that the GM–system suppliers integration is carried out, there is a logistic strategy developed to work beyond what the company is doing by now. This supplying arrangement is basically split in three parts, all of them under the responsibility of TNT Logistics.

TNT is responsible for transporting the system supplier's products to the plant and for collecting the supplier's production outside the site. In fact, TNT could be called the "18th systemist", but instead of delivering tangible goods, it does a service, the in-bound and the out-bound logistics based on the whole production schedule.

The in-bound logistics are made to accomplish the on-time delivery sequence made for synchronizing GM and systemists production inside the CIAG. On the site, TNT works with the kanban and andon systems. Using the "classic" and electronic kanban system, the GM operator works with a module identification card (or sign) to order his replacements. The TNT employee collects the ordering cards (or receives the ordering sign) and seeks out (within a dolly or truck system) new modules within the system suppliers, placing the full package at the line point. Using the andon system, the GM employee detects a shortage of modules and orders a new package through a computer linked to TNT.

For the out-bound logistics there are two possibilities of collecting (see Fig. 26.5). In

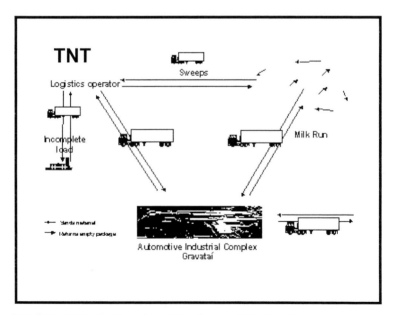

Fig. 26.5 GM – TNT – Out-Bound Logistics (Source: GM release).

the first one, called milk-run, TNT, based on an every day schedule, seeks the components with the suppliers, taking them, after loading a truck with different parts, directly to Gravataí. The company proceeds likewise with suppliers located in the states of Rio Grande do Sul, Santa Catarina and Minas Gerais.

In the second possibility, the sweep run, the components produced in São Paulo are collected and stocked up in warehouses where TNT is consolidated and, only at this point, are taken to the GM site following the production schedule.

All this logistics engineering is based on the intensive use of the electronic integration. Receiving the sale sign directly from the dealers, GM's information system allows the exchange of the production scheduling information (based on monthly, weekly, daily, hourly and, if possible, minute-by-minute data) amongst systemists, TNT and, in some cases, second tier suppliers. Such accuracy enables the delivery of a specific system, in the exact sequence of the GM production, which is somehow a pulled response to customer demand.

Some Results

After two years of CIAG's operation, the results are more encouraging so far for GM than for the State of Rio Grande do Sul itself. In terms of new jobs for example, CIAG generated some 3.000 new direct jobs and approximately the same amount of indirect ones.

Celta already speaks for 28% of the company's passenger car sales in Brazil, and it is responsible for 14% of GM's income in the country. (Celta, 2001). Additionally, it estimated that the Rio Grande do Sul plant has already reached sales of US$ 500 millions.

On October 29, 2001, the Celta number 100,000 was made, of which over 75% are orders deriving from sales over the Internet, even if these are made in 95% of the cases in kiosks installed at the authorized dealers.

Another interesting result that shows the plant's flexibility is the on-going increase of Celta's building combinations. While in July 2000 there were only 10 combinations (due to five color alternatives and a two model car for one only market) GM intends to reach 240 combinations in June 2002 by adding air-conditioning, three new markets and three and five door models.

FINAL DISCUSSIONS

This new industrial organization, based on the exchange of materials and information between the O.E.M. and the system suppliers, works in order to cut off waste and to get the maximum possible value. That might be the trend in the automotive industry in Brazil and in the rest of the world. "The full integration of the automotive chain means the emergence of a new form of industrial organization based on full integration amongst companies" (Zawislak, 1999, p. 14).

The way General Motors is working with its suppliers may be featured as a Fully Integrated Supply Chain model. According to what has been presented, the need of integration among the chain agents through the continuous information flow, synchronized work and partner relationships is remarkable. Hopefully, every link will perform the activities according to the standards set by the O.E.M.

The new production model, which is being developed by General Motors at the Gravataí unit, will be able to show a visible technological capability process. From a closer relationship, there is a learning point between the O.E.M. and the system suppliers that aims at reducing the engineering waste, time and product development cost. With this model, the O.E.M. not only "teaches" the system suppliers but also "learns" from them. It is possible, then, to develop the quality systems and the project together increasingly competitive.

In addition, it is possible to get over a few impacts in the Rio Grande do Sul local automotive chain through the dissemination of the Fully Integrated Supply Chain model outside the site itself. The local companies taking part in the General Motors Fully Integrated Supply Chain must get into a technological and cultural changing process. In fact, the most sensitive elements of this change can be summarized by the need to adopt lean production and quality concepts, as well as technological conditions for the relationship amongst the chain links (e-business).

The results should be noticed over a time period either because of the increasing number of clients or because of the new absorbed competencies. Therefore, this should mean more competition. Meanwhile, the greatest winners are GM and its direct in-site suppliers. Thus it is possible to affirm that the fully integrated supply chain is still must more dependent on GM's strategy than on the supply chain as a whole.

REFERENCES

A viagem da GM até os domínios do paradoxo (1998): Gazeta Mercantil. Porto Alegre, Fevereiro 2, Gazeta Mercantil Rio Grande do Sul, p 4.

CADEIA automotiva ganha qualidade (1999): Gazeta Mercantil. Porto Alegre, Dezembro 9, Gazeta Mercantil Rio Grande do Sul, front page.

CELTA já responde por 28% das vendas de automóvéis da GM (2001): Gazeta Mercantil Porto Alegre, Julho 20 to 22.

Cooper, M. C. and Ellram, L. M.(1993): Characteristics of Supply Chain Management and Implications for Purchasing and Logistics Strategy. *The International Journal of Logistics Management*, Vol. 4, n. 2, pp.13-24.

Ferro, J. R. (2000): Encontro mostrará aos gaúchos benefícios da produção enxuta. *Jornal do IGEA*, nº 11, Março, p. 6.

FESTA da conciliação na abertura da montadora (2000): Zero Hora, Porto Alegre, Julho 21, 2000.

Furlanetto, E. and Zawislak, P. A. (2000): Coordenação pela Cadeia Produtiva: uma Alternativa ao Mercado e à Hierarquia. *Anais... ENANPAD 2000.* Florianópolis, SC, 10-13 de setembro.

Naiditch, S. A Cidade da GM [on line] (2001): Available at: http://www2.uol.com.br/exame/ed716/mercado80.shl (consulted on July 22, 2001).

Pires, S. R. I. (1998): Managerial Implications of the Modular Consortium Model in a Brazilian Automotive Plant. *International Journal of Operations and Production Management,* Vol. 18, n. 3, pp.221-232.

Rother, M. and Shook, J. (1999): *Learning to See.* São Paulo: Lean Institute Brazil.

SISTEMISTAS participam do desenvolvimento do carro (2000): Gazeta Mercantil. Porto Alegre, Maio 18, Gazeta Mercantil Rio Grande do Sul, p.5.

Stock, G. N. and Greis, N. P. and Kasarda, J. D. (1998): Logistics, Strategy and Structure. *The International Journal of Operations and Production Management,* Vol. 4, n. 1, pp.37-52.

Vieira, C. R. B. and Zawislak, P. A. (2002): The Evolution of the Supply Capacity of some of the Auto Part Companies in the State of Rio Grande do Sul. *Proceedings... X IAMOT – International Conference on Management of Technology,* Miami, March 10-15.

Womack et al. (1998): *A Mentalidade Enxuta.* Rio de Janeiro: Campus.

Zawislak, P. A. (coord.) (1999): *Diagnóstico Automotivo. A Plataforma Tecnológica da Cadeia Automotiva do RS.* Porto Alegre: UFRGS/PPGA/NITEC/FIERGS.

Zawislak, P. A. and Vieira, C. R. B. and Irala, M. S. (2000): A Produção Enxuta e Novos Padrões de Fornecimento em Três Montadoras de Veículos no Brasil. *Anais... XXI Simpósio de Gestão da Inovação Tecnológica.* São Paulo, SP, 7-10 de novembro.

Management of Technology
Copyright © 2003 by Elsevier Science Ltd.
All rights of reproduction in any form reserved.
ISBN: 0-08-044136-X

27

CHANGING PROCESS MODELS TO IMPROVE DEMAND CHAIN PERFORMANCE

Jussi Heikkilä, Helsinki University of Technology, Espoo, Finland[*]
Olli Suolanen, Helsinki University of Technology, Espoo, Finland[**]

ABSTRACT

Case study research in the telecommunications industry indicates that there are significantly different customer needs and situations for a telecommunications technology manufacturer to satisfy when delivering cellular networks. The crucial question for a technology manufacturer is how to design the demand chain architecture to support these distinct customer needs and situations. The paper is based on a research project in which a tool was developed to support design and selection of alternative demand chain process models—together forming the demand chain architecture in cellular network building. We argue that the use of alternative demand chain process models improves the quality of decision making when choosing the right chain structure for particular customer situations and sets clear targets for the development of demand chain performance in individual customer – supplier relationships.

INTRODUCTION

The background of this paper is a business situation in which a major telecommunications technology company, Nokia Networks, implemented a demand chain efficiency improvement project with several of their customers. The company delivers equipment for their customers'

---

[*]   Dr. Jussi Heikkilä is Professor of Industrial Management at Helsinki University of Technology, Finland.
[**] Olli Suolanen is a Supply Chain Management Consultant at IBM Finland.

cellular telecommunications networks. The cellular network consists of switches, base station controllers and base tranceiver stations (more commonly known as base stations). Base stations are delivered in hundreds—sometimes in thousands—per year to telecommunications operators.

Nokia Networks implemented a demand chain improvement program called "Win-win" with several customers. The central elements of the "Win-win" program were funnel forecasting with the expectation that the customer could systematically improve its planning accuracy over time, removal of inventories between the base station factory and the customer, and assembling the final base station configurations in the factory for direct delivery to final destinations.

The results of the efficiency improvement projects initiated by Nokia Networks were mixed; success in some of them and failure in others. "Win-win" was a perfect fit for some of the customers, whereas in other cases there was a serious misfit between the support that the customer expected from their supplier-partner and the improvement program elements.

The resultant question for Nokia Networks was how to tailor the demand chain improvement program according to the distinct needs and characteristics of specific customer segments. The demand chain process architecture must be robust—in order to apply different demand chains in different customer situations.

BACKGROUND LITERATURE

Supply chain management means managing an entire value chain instead of focusing on local optima. Demand chain management means focusing on the customer needs as the starting point for defining the logic of a well-performing supply chain.

Stalk (1988) suggests improving supply chain efficiency by reducing time delays in the flow of information and materials throughout the chain. Holmström (1995) shows a positive correlation between speed and efficiency in manufacturing. Holmström suggests that inventory needs to be reduced so that demand distortion is diminished and synchronization of production with demand is enhanced, thereby speeding up operations and improving performance. There is no reason to disagree with these overall objectives to improve demand chain efficiency. But our case research findings indicate that reduction of inventory is challenging, and efforts to speed-up operations can fail with non-cooperative chain partners.

Towill, Naim and Wikner (1992) suggest that supply chain improvement is an evolutionary process, in which 'organizational aspects' between the organizations in the chain are gradually taken into consideration, in addition to the systems dynamics aspects. Our findings suggest that effectivenes and efficiency in a fast growing young industry largely depend on understanding the underlying differences between customer needs and situations, and being able to adapt a demand chain accordingly. A partnership type of relationship can have better demand chain effectiveness and efficiency than "arms-length" relationships. But developing partnerships usually takes time (Heide and John 1990; Monczka, Petersen, Handfield and Ragatz 1998). Initial demand chain structures need to be established according to existing relationships. Once the relationships develop, more advanced demand chain coordination mechanisms can be established.

According to Fisher (1997), supply chain design must understand the demand behavior in a particular industry and organize the chain to serve it accordingly. In gaining this understanding, the crucial flow of information is from the marketplace to the chain. It is important to cut lead-times to produce the product close to the time when demand materializes. The critical decisions about inventory and capacity are where in the chain to position inventory and available production and assembly capacity in order to have maximum flexibility to deal with fluctuating demand. Fisher suggests that selection of the supply chain structure primarily depends on the industry characteristics. We feel that this is too simple an approach. We suggest that several different chains are needed within a single industry to meet various customer needs and situations.

RESEARCH APPROACH

The research in this paper consists of the following two parts:

- Case research on the customer – supplier relationships in cellular network building and how relationship characteristics are related to demand chain effectiveness/efficiency.
- Simulation experiments to enhance understanding of the match between demand chain processes and specific customer characteristics.

The first part of the research aimed at characterizing various customer situations that Nokia Networks must satisfy as operators build and expand their cellular networks. Six different customer cases were studied as well as the demand chains best suited to each case. The second part of the research concentrated on further developing the match between demand chain management and distinct customer situations—through simulation studies.

CASE STUDY RESULTS

Case studies of six customer cases resulted in observations as to why the "Win-win" improvement project succeeded in some customer relationships and why it failed in others (Heikkilä 2000). The results produce the following two major categories:

- Arms-length relationships with weak results in implementing an improved demand chain structure.
- Successful direct delivery partnership demand chains.

Arms-Length Relationship Cases

The arms-length relationships were characterized by new or semi-established relationships between the customer and the supplier, and the customer being relatively new in the market. The customer's network building concentrated on geographic coverage or capacity increase, and both delivery volume and volume growth were high. The reliability of the planning information was clearly lower than in the direct delivery partnership demand chains.

Demand information was distorted because of consistent over-forecasting, long delays in the ordering process inside the customer organization, weekly order batching from the customer to the supplier's sales organization and from the sales organization to the factory. The actual material need often changed during the order-to-delivery process because of inaccurate planning and long delays.

There was a high quantity of information sharing in the customer – supplier relationship, but lower perceived quality of information sharing (reliability of the other party). The perceived benevolence of the other party varied, but was clearly lower than in the partnership relationships. The "Win-win" improvement project had been attempted in these cases. The results did not meet the targets set. The customers did not perceive clear gain from the improvement project.

The direct delivery demand chain structure proposed in the improvement program was low, because the structure did not match with the customer's planning capabilities. The customers were relatively new in the industry and their planning capabilities were not comparable to those of established customers in the direct delivery partnerships. Both the customers' and the supplier's sales organizations perceived that moving to direct deliveries would slow down the network building process. The customer was used to making order changes during the order-to-delivery process and perceived that they were served on short notice from the country warehouse. The improvement program proposed a structure in which the deliveries would be made in 30 days directly from the factory in full configuration, no changes allowed during the delivery time. However, the customer's reliable demand visibility was shorter than the delivery lead-time. Therefore, implementation of the improved demand chain structure was never completed but Nokia Networks's country organizations continued to deliver base stations from the country warehouses. A lot of reconfiguration work was done in the country warehouse to respond to the customer's last minute order changes.

Direct delivery partnership demand chains

These partnerships were characterized by established relationships between the customer and the supplier, the customer's in-depth knowledge of the industry and the market, and good experience of the employees working in the relationship interface. The customers were in advanced stages in their network building, focusing on optimization of their network and introducing new end-customer features. There was high quantity and quality of information sharing in the relationship and both the customer and the supplier perceived the partner as reliable and benevolent.

The customer and supplier co-operated well in the demand chain improvement project and implementation was carried out successfully. The result was significant simplification of the chain and removal of non-value adding steps from the chain. There was no consistently biased demand information provided by the customer. The customer placed orders daily.

Effectiveness of the demand chain was high in the direct delivery partnerships. The structure implemented in the improvement project met the customer situation and need. Customers had good competence and good experience of the industry and the market. Their planning capabilities were good. The direct delivery structure allowed removal of country warehouses with several months' of supply. Both customers perceived that flexibility increased.

Summary of the case study results

The direct base station delivery model implemented in the partnership cases matched well with the customers' situation and planning capabilities, making the demand chain structure effective. The direct delivery model implementation was attempted also in the "arms-length" cases. The implementation failed because of the poor match between the customer's planning capabilities and the attempted demand chain structure. This resulted in low effectiveness of the demand chain.

Based on these observations we designed a demand chain architecture consisting of several alternative process models to be adapted to different customer situations and needs. There is an evolutionary idea in this architecture in that the demand chain structure will be consistently developed when the customer – supplier relationship develops towards a partnership mode and the planning capabilities develop in the chain.

ALTERNATIVE DEMAND CHAIN PROCESS MODELS

The case research findings indicate that several alternative demand chain process models are necessary in the cellular network building with a large number of customers. The following priority for decisions is proposed in designing alternative demand chain process models for this industry:

1. Support the customer's network building process by delivery speed that matches the customer's planning capabilities.
2. Decide on the order-penetration point for equipment deliveries according to the delivery speed needed.

3. Create flexibility in the assembly capacity to meet the market uncertainty.

4. Optimize inventory within the constraints resulting from the criteria above.

The final equipment configuration needs to be done at an order penetration point where an inventory decouples the successive operations and where the equipment is assigned to a specific base station site. This means building a market responsive chain. This would allow buffering of the materials to a point where real uncertainty of the market is best known. This point is different in different customer situations and the location of it primarily depends on the quality of the planning information available and the execution capability of the supplier. It could be a country warehouse, distribution center serving several customers, or it could be the factory in which the main units of the base station site package are assembled.

Based on the case study findings, three demand chain process models were proposed to serve the different customer needs, see Fig. 27.1-3. These three demand chain process models were proposed to emphasize the importance of compatibility between customer situations/planning capabilities, and demand chain structures. Figure 27.1 shows the demand chain process model in which the configuration point is the country warehouse. Full base station configurations are made in the country warehouse and the country inventory is being replenished by equipment modules according to the deliveries realized. This model is proposed to be used when there is need for a highly reactive chain, the planning capabilities are not good, and there are long delays in the ordering process or disconnected information flows.

The demand chain process model with a distribution center as a configuration point shown in Fig. 27.2 is proposed to improve the demand chain efficiency from the country warehouse process model. The idea is that several customers would be served from one distribution center, enabling removal of several country warehouses.

The advantages of the distribution center model compared to the country warehouse process model are considerable inventory reduction through consolidation, effective buffering of the feeding chains of various base station site elements, better transparency over the inventory situation, and pooling of logistics capabilities.

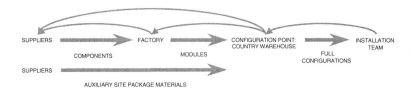

Fig. 27.1. Demand chain process model with the configuration point in the country warehouse.

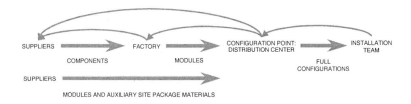

Fig. 27.2. Demand chain process model with the configuration point in the distribution center.

Figure 27.3 describes the most advanced demand chain process model with direct deliveries from the factory providing full base station configurations and auxiliary site package materials. This model was implemented in the partnership cases described above. The advantages of this direct delivery process model are lean and fast reacting demand chain, good transparency throughout the chain, disturbances being immediately visible, and the chain being quickly reconfigured to changing market, technology and product changes.

SIMULATION RESEARCH

To investigate alternative demand chain process models we built a simulation tool, using AutoMod as the simulation engine. Four different chain process models were built as basic scenarios, each with their own logic. The first process model illustrates the situation that was experienced in the "arms-length" relationships in which implementation of the direct delivery models did not succeed. The other three models are alternatives to be applied in different customer situations. In each of the alternative scenarios there is one factory manufacturing four product modules and the chain serves six different customers (each in a different country).

The simulation tool expects the following input variables to begin calculating the outputs:

• Requested delivery time by the customer.

Fig. 27.3. Demand chain process model with virtual configuration point and coordinated deliveries to the installation teams' material collection points.

- Buffer inventory as the starting situation in each of the country warehouses.
- Buffer inventory as the starting situation in the factory for each of the four modules.
- Replenishment logic: lot-for-lot or Kanban, and Kanban size if Kanban; and replenishment interval.

With these input variables the tool calculates the delivery accuracy and total average inventory for the last 25 days of the simulation run, combining the average factory inventory and the average country warehouse or regional distribution center inventory, depending on the demand chain process model used. The delivery accuracy is calculated so that if the right product is at the customer at the latest on the day it was requested, then the delivery is acceptable, otherwise not. The model does not penalize for early deliveries. Only deliveries of full configurations according to the order are acceptable.

Basic assumptions used in developing the simulation tool

The product modelled in the simulation consists of four different modules: a, b, c, and d. The product structure used in the simulation is shown in Fig. 27.4. There are six different types of modules a, module b is common to all the final products, and there are two different c-modules and three different d-modules. This product structure makes it possible to produce 36 different types of final products. This is a considerable simplification of the real base station configuration structure. Simplification was however needed to make the duration of the simulation computations practical. Despite this simplification, the differences in the dynamics of the different demand chain process models can be seen.

The total demand used in the simulation tool for all the end products fluctuates strongly from day to day. The daily peaks in demand for products in one country can be three times as high as the daily average demand. The overall demand is further divided into the specific end products following the 20/80-rule, 20% of the end products make up 80% of the total demand, which is fairly accurate compared to real life. The overall demand is first generated in the simulator, and then directly broken down to specific products and their associated modules.

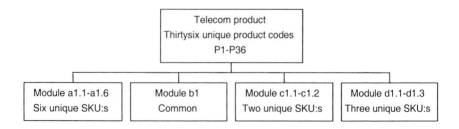

Fig. 27.4. Product structure.

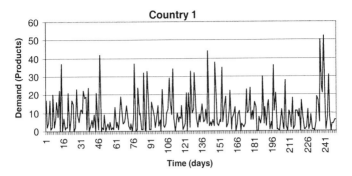

Fig. 27.5. Example of the demand fluctuation.

The module demand is, therefore, dependent of the end product demand. In Fig. 27.5 we can see an example of the demand pattern used in the model.

A major problem observed in the case studies was an increasing number of order changes made by the customers when the delivery lead-time became longer. This was included in the simulation model by building in an assumption of an increasing number of order changes when the lead-time to the customer increases. In Fig. 27.6 the share of order changes used in the model are depicted as a function of time elapsed.

Country warehouse model with configuration point in the factory

In the country warehouse model, there is a warehouse in each of the six countries to deliver the final product configurations to the base station sites, see Fig. 27.7.

Fig. 27.6. Order changes as a function of order-to-delivery lead-time elapsed (Five days in the simulator counts for one week in reality).

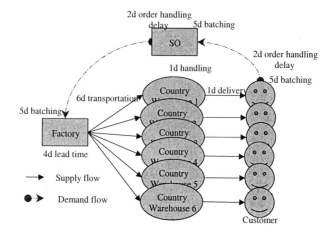

Fig. 27.7. Country warehouse model with configuration point in the factory.

The customer sends their orders to Nokia Networks's sales organization (SO) in five day batches. The SO sends their orders to the factory in five days batches as well. Also, the factory batches the orders they receive, and release them to production every five days. There is a two day order handling delay in both the customer organization and in the SO. It takes four days for the factory to assemble and test, and another six days to ship the final product configurations to the country warehouses. It takes one day to deliver from the country warehouses to the customers.

The agreed delivery time from the original customer order until delivery to the site is 30 days (six weeks). Full product configurations are delivered to the country warehouses. "Cannibalization", ie. reconfiguration of the products in the warehouse, becomes an important response mechanism because the long delivery lead-times in this demand chain process model result in an increasing number of order changes during the order-to-delivery cycle. If there is an order change then the existing country warehouse stock is checked against the new required configuration. If such an exact final product configuration cannot be found, then the particular product will be reconfigured (if possible) by disassembling one other product. In this case, the obsolete stock is increased by the leftovers, which cannot be reused. For the disassembled final product configuration a replacement order is made to the factory. The changed order is handled the same day in the country warehouse. If required parts are not available the procedure is repeated in following days until the order is filled. Simulation results are shown in Fig. 27.8.

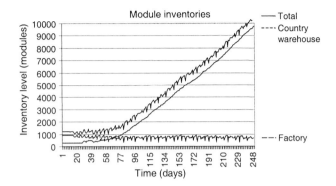

Fig. 27.8. Module inventories when full configurations are sent from the factory.

Country warehouse model with configuration point in the country warehouse

This model acknowledges that high responsiveness is needed when a customer has a short planning visibility and the planning information is not reliable. The main problem in the first model is the high number of order changes during the time from order to delivery, resulting in increasing obsolete inventory in the country warehouses. The way to improve the demand chain process performance in this case is to remove the full configuration testing in the factory (this was also implemented in practice by Nokia Networks), to improve individual module

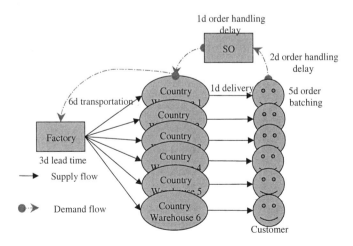

Fig. 27.9. Country warehouse model with configuration point in the country warehouse.

testing, and to ship modules to the country warehouse to be assembled as needed into the final product configurations in the warehouse. When the configuration point is moved to the country warehouse, the responsiveness of the demand chain improves. The requested delivery time from the order to delivery is reduced from 30 to 10 days. At the same time the order delays in the supplier part of the demand chain are reduced. The five day batches of orders are removed and the SO send their orders to the factory every day. No changes are required in the customer's way of working.

Removal of final configuration testing allows reduction of the processing time from four to three days in the factory. Transportation time to the country warehouses remains six days and the delivery time from the country warehouse to the sites is still one day. The "cannibalization" problem is solved when moving into this model and, therefore, the country warehouses do not collect obsolete inventory. Delivery accuracy improves radically. Simulation results are shown in Fig. 27.10. The average total inventory level in the six demand chains during the last 25 days of the simulation run is less than half compared to the first model.

Regional distribution center model with configuration in the regional distribution center

The regional distribution center (RDC) model assumes that all the six country customers are served from one distribution center, see Fig. 27.11.

The distribution center delivers directly to the subcontractor responsible for the installation works at the base station sites. The time to transport the final configurations to the customer increases from one to three days. If the ordering delay and the order batching remain

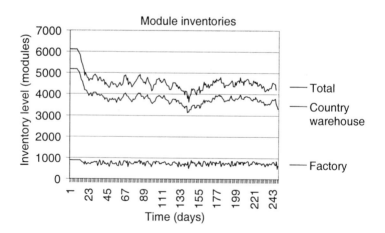

Fig. 27.10. Module inventories when full configurations are sent from the country warehouse.

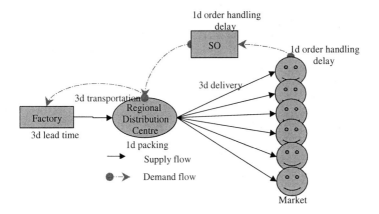

Fig. 27.11. Regional distribution center model with configuration point in the regional distribution center.

as before in the customer organization, the delivery lead-time would need to be increased. Therefore, if the customer's ordering practices do not change, there is no incentive for the customer to move to this model.

We assume that a demand chain can be moved from the country warehouse model to the RDC model when the customer can improve it's ordering practice, meaning that the order delays are removed in the customer part of the process. In the simulation model there is now only a one-day order handling delay at both the customer and the SO. This allows promising a lead-time reduction from ten to six days, making change to this model attractive to the customer.

The final configurations are assembled from the modules kept in stock in the RDC. The modules are replenished from the factory with three days packing and shipping time and three days transportation time from factory to the distribution center. Packing and shipping from the distribution center takes one day after the order is received. The delivery time from the distribution center to the sites is three days. Simulation results are illustrated in Fig. 27.12. Almost half of the total chain inventory can be removed compared to the previous model.

Direct delivery model

This is the model that was implemented in the "Win-win" partnership model observed in the case studies. There are no intermediate warehouses, which naturally results in a lower chain inventory than in the other models, see Fig. 27.13.

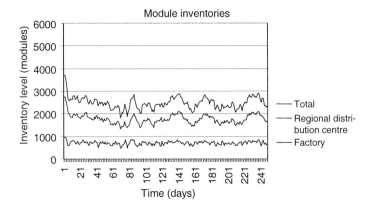

Fig. 27.12. Module inventories in the RDC model.

The advantages of this direct delivery process model are a lean and fast reacting demand chain, good transparency of the inventory situation in the chain, disturbances being immediately visible, and the chain being quickly reconfigured to changing market requirements, technology, and product changes. The requirements for implementing this model are flawless execution of the supplier's operations, good customer planning capabilities and ordering without delays. Simulation results are seen in Fig. 27.14. The results are inventory reduction of roughly two thirds compared to the regional distribution center.

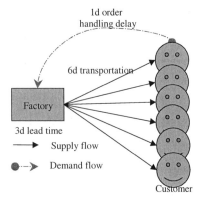

Fig. 27.13. Direct delivery model.

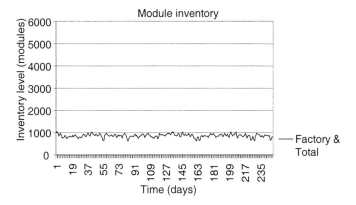

Fig. 27.14. Module inventories in the direct delivery model.

SUMMARY OF THE SIMULATION RESULTS

Table 27.1 compares the performance of the four alternative demand chain process models according to the simulation results. It also shows what would be the incentives for both the supplier and the customer to move from one process model to another model and the requirements to make this change.

The first process model describes the situation that Nokia Networks faced when trying to implement the direct delivery process model in the arms-length relationships with customers

Table 27.1. Comparison of the four alternative demand chain process models.

Performance and requirements/process model	Full configurations from facory via country warehouse	Configuration point in the country warehouse	Configuration point in the distribution center	Direct delivery of full configurations from the factory
Agreed delivery lead time, days	30	10	6	10
Maximum order handling delay	14	8	2	1
Delivery time to the point of need	8	1	3	6
Delivery accuracy, %	30 %	97 %	98 %	99 %
Total inventories in the chain, average number of modules during the last month of simulation run	9933	4477	2426	859
Incentive for the supplier to move to this model from the previous model		Reduced inventory cost, lower risk of obsolescence, order change problem minimized	Inventory reduction through consolidation, effective buffering of the base station modules	Lean and fast reacting chain with low inventory
Incentive for the customer to move to this model from the previous model		Improved delivery accuracy	Shared cost saving	Chain quickly reconfigurable to changing market, technology and product changes
Requirements for moving to this model from the previous model		Product structure enabling final configuration in the country warehouse	Removal of batching and order delays inside the customer organization	Mutually accepted longer delivery lead-time, reliable planning information

having poor planning capabilities. The planning visibility and the process performance did not match each other. The result was low delivery accuracy, a high number of order changes and high inventory, with a growing share of obsolete stock of high-technology equipment modules.

The second model shows that considerable performance improvement can be achieved even without the customer changing its behavior. The requirements for running this model are that the product structure can be changed to enable the final configuration to be done in the country warehouse. Also, order batching and order delays should be removed inside the supplier's sales organization. The incentives for the supplier to move to this model are reduced inventory cost, minimized order change problem and lower risk of obsolete inventory. The customer experiences delivery accuracy is being raised to a good level.

Consolidating all the final configuration deliveries from the country warehouses to one regional distribution center allows reduction of the supplier's inventory and effective buffering of the base station modules. However, this change requires an important change in the customer behavior. The customer should remove batching of orders and move to daily ordering, and they should also remove all the additional delays from their ordering process. This would allow shorter lead-time from original order until delivery. The cost savings are on the supplier side. In order to get the customer to change their behavior, sharing of the cost savings should be made explicit and attractive to the customer.

Direct delivery model is the most advanced of the models studied. It was successfully implemented in the partnership type of relationships in the case studies. Compared to the RDC model, the delivery time needs to be increased if the packing and shipping times of the modules and final configurations remain the same. The supplier's inventory cost can again be reduced when moving to this model from the previous model. But the main competitive benefit is the resulting lean and fast reacting chain in the fast changing competitive environment of a high-technology industry. The chain can be quickly reconfigured to the changing market, technology and product changes. The important requirements to be able to implement this model are good co-operation between the customer and the supplier, reliable planning information from the customer and a mutually agreed delivery lead-time.

CONCLUSIONS

Demand chain processes need to be designed to fit particular market conditions. A one-size-fits-all –approach was not appropriate for the environment found by the telecommunications technology company studied in this research. In order to increase chain effectiveness and efficiency, both supplier and customer need to change their processes. These changes need to be implemented collaboratively. This implementation to be successful, the benefits for both parties need to be explicitly understood and fairly shared.

REFERENCES

Fisher, M.L. (1997). What is the right supply chain for your product?, *Harvard Business Review*, 75, 105-116.

Heide, J.B. and G. John (1990). Alliances in industrial purchasing: the determinants of joint action in buyer-supplier relationships, *Journal of Marketing Research*, 27, February, 24-36.

Heikkilä, J. (2000). *Developing Demand Chain Management: Case Study on the Fast Growing Cellular Networks Industry*, Acta Polytechnica Scandinavica, Industrial Management and Business Administration Series, No. 8, The Finnish Academies of Technology, Espoo.

Holmström, J. (1995). *Realizing the Productivity Potential of Speed*, Acta Polytechnica Scandinavia, Mathematics and Computing in Engineering Series, No. 73, The Finnish Academy of Technology, Helsinki.

Monczka, R.M., K.J. Petersen, R.B. Handfield and G.L. Ragatz (1998). Success factors in strategic supplier alliances: the buying company perspective, *Decision Sciences*, 29, 553-573.

Stalk, G. (1988). Time: the next strategic advantage, *Harvard Business Review*, 66, 41-51.

Towill, D.R., M.M. Naim and J. Wikner (1992). Industrial dynamics simulation models in the design of supply chains, *International Journal of Physical Distribution and Logistics Management*, 22, 3-13.

Management of Technology
ISBN: 0-08-044136-X

28

GETTING HOLD ON THE DISAPPEARING WORKER? – MANAGERIAL ISSUES OF DISTANCE WORK

*Martine Buser, ILEMT, Federal Institute of Technology, Lausanne, Switzerland**
*Christian Koch, Department for Civil Engineering, Technical University of Denmark****

SUMMARY

This contribution deals with the IT-transformation of organisations in the direction of virtualisation, focusing especially on managerial issues related to distance work. Where the main discourse concentrates on the changes of work, management actually needs to adapt as well. Moreover there is a tendency to discuss distance work independently of the development of the "basis"-organisation, i.e. the organisation that the distance work relates to.

Drawing on case material from Swiss enterprises, the contribution discusses how management in practice is -and can be- exercised when the organisation is construed into a *space of flows*. The implications lead not only into the coaching of self-management, but also into rethinking the spatial aspect of management and the new boundaries of organisation. Ultimately the reconceptualisation of management needs to encompass networking with independent distance workers and understanding and mobilising features of regional and national labour markets.

---

* Martine Buser is a sociologist at the Institute of Logistic, Economic and Management of Technology at the Swiss Federal Institute of Technology in Lausanne.
** Christian Koch is Associate Professor of management of production at the Group for Construction Management, Department of Civil Engineering at the Technical University of Denmark.

INTRODUCTION

In this article we focus on managerial issues related to new forms of organisation related to the use of information and telecommunication technologies (ICT). Virtualisation is often used as term for these changes and this concept is used but also contested. A main point of the article is to analyse and argue for that managerial issues change with the new forms of organisation, but it is a gradual slide into new forms, which do not radically change management from one day to another. We thus use the term modest virtualisation.

We draw on case material from a Swiss study of small and medium size enterprises all handling information in some way (Buser et al 2000). We look at four managerial activities, design and execution of tasks, coordination, control and performance. Although the empirical material stem from SME, the role of size is not central in our discussion. SME-s are however viewed as central in contemporary economy. Several observers have argued that disintegration of the larger companies into smaller ones will be the hallmark of the new economy and or postmodern society (McGrath et al 1998). However a more modest position would be to point out that small enterprises have been prevalent in western economy –European and American for a long time. Moreover what might be even more important is the degree of integration with others enterprises in economic units or as supply chains and the like (Castells 1996).

We focus here on managerial options related to the development in the direction of virtualisation, which we define as the possibility to work together apart in time and geography. Virtualisation with information and communication technologies (ICT) offers new opportunities and challenges to management. Virtualisation implies that there is a change and enlargement of the repertoire and genres (Orlikowsky & Yates 1994) of collaboration and coordination options, although it should be noted that enterprises have been used to a broad set of cooperation- and collaboration- as well as communication-forms previously.

An important point is to look at the entire organisational transformation and not only on the external part such as distance work. Where the main discourse on new trends tend to concentrate on the changes of work, management actually needs to adapt as well. Moreover there is a tendency to discuss telework, mobile work and the like independently of the development of the "basis"-organisation, i.e. the organisation which these form of work relates to.

The article is structured as follows. The opening is the method, followed by some theoretical discussion on virtualisation and managerial tasks in organisations developing in that direction. These two elements then are analysed in cases of Swiss enterprises. Finally some implication about the management tasks and roles is discussed.

METHOD

The theoretical frame adopted is interpretative sociology. The Swiss study of telematics and new forms of work (Buser et al 2000) encompasses 20 enterprises in Switzerland. 17 of these are still practicing distance work. The organisations are engineering's consultancy, public services, insurance, translation services, data capture/ inquiries-services.

The study cover basic organisations (Swiss enterprises), and employees on contract base or other working at a distance. Even if the distance work is often seen as a way of getting self-employed, this was the exception in the study. Actually, in our sample two engineers started as freelancers before becoming employee of a company.

30 semi structured interviews were carried out, each of a duration of approximately 2 hours. The interviews were made in the company or at the home of the worker. The study provides a snap shot of new forms of work, but given the length and character of the study, it also have clear limitations. It is for example not possible to study the career prospect for distance employees "within" their company.

VIRTUAL ORGANISATIONS

In this section we provide a definition of virtual organisation, develop a concept for management of modest virtualised organisations and offer a typology of them, and continue with a discussion of the managerial issues. Finally we thematize the issue of spatiality.

Many authors have described the new emerging form of economy and society, which is based on information technologies. This shift in the ways the entire production systems are organised has been called among other the Information Society, The Information Age or the Networked Society (Castells 1996). At the enterprise level, we find notions as the flexible enterprise the knowledge-based firm and the networked enterprise (Castells 1996) or the virtual organisation (Jackson & Weilen 1998, Igbaria & Tan 1998, Harris 1998). These terms attempt to describe different elements in the process of change, but it can be said that at a general level they try to capture the same fundamental change in organisations.

The role of technologies in organisational change can be seen as a tool to allow but also to constrain transformation. In the 1980s most information technology was introduced in the departments and functions of the enterprises: word processing, accounting systems etc. Zuboff's (1988), analysis, from this period, pointed at the automation and informing capabilities of the technology. By the turn of the century however, this capacity has developed however. Castells observes that ICT enables work processes to be split up and pooled by new criteria. It is not geography but rather type of work that become central. For example the handling of planning information can be done in one geographical space for an entire network of companies. Human work will therefore be oriented towards the flows of information, which constitute new units of work different form classical geographical spaces: What Castells calls *the space of flows*. And it is not only new units of work but also new economic units and a new role of regions. Nevertheless it should not been forgotten that some organisations despite the availability of ICTs support, maintain their traditional structure (Koch 2000). Moreover changes of practices can happen independently from technological innovation and being then "extraordinarily enhanced" by ICTs (Castells 1996).

In this article, we will use the term of virtualisation focusing mainly, within the frame of time - space compression that ICT offer, (Harvey 1996) on working together apart in time and geography (Castells 1996). ICTs can be seen as assisting firms in the realisation of virtualisation by :

- bringing greater flexibility to production,
- speeding access to and processing information
- increasing the control over decentralised system
- creating a common informational axis
- handling information with greater sensitivity
- linking spatially separate activities.

Below we use "virtualisation" as shorthand for these tendencies. In the empirical material three types of virtualisation were studied: telecommuniting, distance work and satellite offices. We concentrate on the link between managers and distance employees.

MANAGEMENT IN ORGANISATIONS

The role of management in organisation can be discussed in three levels: The external environment (the spatial surroundings of the enterprise), the organisation in itself and the individual employee and manager (Daniels et al 2000). When we discuss distance workers and telecommuting, the distinction between the organisation and the individual becomes crucial, whereas below we discuss managerial issues for the organisation and the individual in one "go", followed by a discussion of the external environment.

We will not attempt here to offer neither an exhaustive discussion on the features of the organisation and the role of managerial activities nor a full theoretical obedience to the abundance of different organisation theoretical paradigms. The goal here is merely to get to the specifics of managerial tasks when the organisation is developed in the direction of virtualisation. The classical characteristic of an organisation was that the organisation like a physical organism had a well-defined physical boundary (Ortmann 1995), which enabled a set of management and employee practices, building on co-presence, to be developed (Giddens 1984). The organisation can be viewed as an assemblage of human tasks. These tasks need to be carried out, in order to realise a set of products and to maintain the organisation through the related administerial activities. Doing this means/meant organising people within a physical space. Organising people and designing a division of labour creates tensions between goals, tasks and personal intentions. The organisation also becomes a political arena.

Since the days of scientific management, there has been a strong belief in organisation that the management of and execution of tasks could or should be separated. This constitutes execution of tasks but also planning and coordination as managerial fields in some interaction with employees. Similarly bureaucracy theories would argue that responsibility, decision latitude, command and control mechanisms should be installed. Human relations and socio-technical approaches would argue for motivating and quality of working life aspects should be included. In contemporary discussions there is an inclination towards institutional, postmodern and cultural approaches. Drawing on the institutional argument our contention is that these recipes can all be mobilised, referred to or even contingent in contemporary organisational life without even being explicitly referred to (Scott & Meyer 1994). In this plethora we choose to focus on the following four aspect of managing an organisation: The design and execution of tasks, the coordination of activities, the control of activities and performance and reward (McGrath & Houlihan 1998) (see below for further discussion). There are political issues related to this, issues to be negotiated and/ or solved. Related to the managerial dimensions on can point at, drawing on Hildebrandt and Seltz (1989) work content, workload, work hours, forms of control and long term employability of the employees as well as the managers.

MANAGERIAL ASPECTS OF MODEST VIRTUALISATION

As presented above, one can choose a number of approaches to management of organisations with modest virtualisation. Below the chosen activities is discussed:

- designing tasks
- coordination
- control
- performance and reward

This means that we leave a number for other possible issues, management of information technology, security issues, the manager as teleworker him/herself and issues of innovation and product development in these organisations. We view the managerial issue as tasks themselves that can be carried out by one or several persons in the organisation in a process or even as a routine by employees themselves.

The moderate virtualisation implies that the organisation operates with a coexistence of "traditional" co-presence and communication technology based management forms (such as telephone negotiations) with a new repertoire of mediators of management. Orlikowsky & Yates (1994) discuss this coexistence as a glide and extension in repertoire of communication and cooperation forms. Some traditional, like memos, might be transformed to group-mailed messages in the e-mail system, whereas new ones like discussion groups and groupware based coordination of project work will be added to the genres and repertoire of organising and managing.

Looking at *designing and execution of tasks* it is clear that it becomes a managerial issue to have a necessary knowledge of the organisation in order to identify "bulks of work" which can be moved around and coordinated across geographical boundaries. The central issues are who decides what is taken home, done where in the organisation. The criteria for doing this might be perceived skills of employees, obtaining economy of scale by pooling tasks, free capacity etc. The coordination can be done through the use of ICT, which offers functionality for planning and coordination across geographical boundaries (e-mail, intranet, groupware). In the case section in this paper, this use of ICT will be developed further. The limitations of virtualisation of organisation lie, first, in defining a maintaining task boundaries and handling the related physical flows. Secondly, the embeddedness of knowledge in practices and objects and elsewhere will limit virtualisation; information might be entirely transportable, but knowledge is not (Wenger 1998).

The *coordination* activities are not merely to tune and synchronise current tasks solved by employees. More important is the handling of the political issues that emerges from different perspectives present in the organisation. Traditional coordination was exercised via co-presence organisational forms, such as meetings, one to one dialogue and informal dialogue ("orienterierungen", Hildebrandt and Seltz 1989). The synchronisation part of this coordination can be done through the use of ICT, which offers functionality for planning and coordination across geographical boundaries (e-mail, intranet, groupware, planning functionality within project management software and enterprise resource planning, ERP). The negotiative parts however can only partly be taken over by ICT-based coordination and it is necessary to develop a new set of communicative skills to exercise this, mirrored in the debate on email ethics (Igbaria & Tan 1998).

The *control activities* in traditional organisation often partly built implicitly on co-presence and mutual visibility. This understanding leads to the assumption that in virtualised organisations managers must seek to manage what they cannot see, by building relationships of trust. (Handy 1995). In contrast to this we would argue that trust-based control is but one form of possible control. In some forms of virtualisation ICT becomes closely embedded in work routines, meaning that the actual work and the registered screen activity are close to each other. In these cases, where call centre work is included, classical control activity can be enhanced. A process of recentralisation is also occurring in some organisations as a result of the increasing span of control, which ICTs allow (McLoughlin 1999), changing the degree of autonomy and distribution of responsibility. In other types of work it is on the other hand important to find new ways to exercise appropriate control over quantity and quality of work delivered. Within distance work it is likely to employ frame-oriented control or even to change to other payment for the performance. Finally it is widespread to try to exercise control with abuse of the ICT. The fear of use of e-mail and Internet browsers for private purposes seems to be widespread among managers both in traditional and moderate virtualised organisations. This exercise seems to enhance the development of adversarial relations between management and employees. Generally within the control oriented managerial task lies possibilities of mobilizing ICT as rigid control instrument as well as realizing enhanced autonomy and competence. Moreover, as with any other new development in the arena of industrial relations, virtualisation has attracted commentary on whether it represents the end of industrial disputes and conflict or will simply give rise to new forms of conflict and dispute that have previously been undetected or not acknowledged in the discourse. A number of authors actually picture virtualisation as intrinsically linked with high trust (Dalsgård and Bendix, 1996; Handy, 1995). Contemporary developments in organisations indicate that high trust continues to be but one model of virtualisation (Harris, 1998; McLoughlin 1999, Koch 2000), as the case studies below will demonstrate.

Measuring and rewarding the *performance* is closely related to the control issue. In a frame oriented control form based on trust, empirical results actually show that distance workers deliver a higher performance than previously, at least in working hours and flexibility (Empirica 1999). However as Standen in Daniels et al. (2000) point out, this is an one sided interpretation and he urges managers and distance worker to cooperate in setting boundaries between work and leisure. One of his arguments is that spill over of problems and tension might become a problem for first the teleworker and secondly for the enterprise.

SPATIALITY

Organisations are on the one hand typically bound to certain regional areas, but are at the same time using ICT to seek out new locations, in order to unlock assumed labour reserves:

ICTs are facilitating a redefinition of corporate structure within existing location parameters effectively allowing the geography of the firm to be reconstituted without involving relocation. At the same time however precarious work contracts and other temporary forms of organisation attaches the organisation to regional labour markets: Developing of team-working and networking both of which are facilitated by ICTs. These processes are happening within individual sites as well as across sites, sometimes on global scale. Finally but crucially organisations are using ICTs to access existing or new markets remotely, thus reconfiguring their spatial organisation and impacting upon worker and consumer mobility and travel.

There is thus a tendency that organisations dissolute into regional and global communities. Mobile workers, contracts workers and others and the organisation become mutually dependent. This dependency forms cluster-like spaces (Porter 1995).

SWISS STUDY OF TELEWORK

The study encompasses as mentioned three types of virtualisation: internal virtualisation (satellite offices), distance work and telecommuting. The virtualisation in the cases is modest, in central tasks and activities of the organisations only smaller elements are carried out in an integrated way over Internet and other communication means. There is thus very little integration of execution of tasks, a little integration of coordination enabled by e-mail, and the control of performance is not virtualised but rather reformulated. The case material represents a panel of different situations rather than an exhaustive list of practices. The material does not represent any one best way but many different situations developing, as enterprises capture opportunities.

All the enterprises we have seen belonged to services sector and are dealing with information or knowledge production. As we have already said it, we have found out many different ways of engaging in virtualisation of work. Nevertheless we should first draw a distinction between firms, which emerge form a traditional form into forms of virtualisation, from the one who have been created and designed on the basis of *distance work*. For the former, the will to involve into distance work can emanate or from the top management therefore employees have then to be convinced to invest in it, or it can be initiated by the employees themselves. Then they have to persuade the management to agree with their proposal. Level of commitment from both sides is often proportional to their motivation and involvement at the beginning of the process. The transition phases can therefore be difficult to deal with. The new firm does not have combine two different overlapping organisational systems and can concentrate on a coherent way of managing. The motivations followed by the firm have of course consequences on the way it is implemented. For the enterprises interviewed, they can be summarised as follows:

- To optimise human resources by making them more flexible and adaptable, teleworkers' output are known to be higher.
- To keep valuable employees who wish to have a more flexible time schedule
- To minimise the risk and costs when launching a new company
- To save on office and external costs
- To give out extra job or even to outsource some kind of activities.
- To increase the size of their recruiting field for specific competencies or lower salaries
- To step up their presence in remote area

We will come back to the two last aims in the part, which deals with spatial issues.

Design and execution of tasks

Design of tasks proved to be linked with the kind of work. Types of jobs forming our sampling are actives in relatively independent categories, which implies a rather low level of collaboration. We have divided them in three groups regarding job qualification and autonomy in execution. The first group, Group A, concern high qualified tasks done by people who, within a contractual frame, self-manage their task regarding how and when to do it, this definition applies to consultant, engineers, translators, and some computer scientists; The second group, B, can autonomously organise its time schedule, but has heavy constraints. They exercise routines regarding production aims, week- or month based. This characteristic applies to insurance agents and computer scientists. The third group, C, encompass low skilled people, with almost no autonomy since routines and daily production are clearly defined and should not be modified, it concerns activities like data capture for pharmacy. Borders between those groups could of course be discussed but it appears to be related to the way the managers have to tackle the flow of work and their employees. Indeed, the kind of management is radically different and required distinct qualifications.

An important issue is the division of working time between the company and the home. The *telecommuters* are mostly assuming themselves the consequences of being home one or two days a week. Their company, in the sample at least, do not modify the way the work is organised and distributed. But the fact that there is no changes in organisational level does not means that there is no informal adjustments made by the management: agreement on which day to be out and how and where to be reachable. In the cases is found a more or less tacit arrangement between workers and managers on which tasks should be done at home, mostly conception and writing job or in the office, mainly communication and coordination activities.

In the A group, the manager adapts the job to employees' competencies and qualifications; frequently the employee is taking part in the definition of the project he is going to be involved in, giving information of what he can or can not achieve. The project group or the manager estimates the conditions of realisation and sets the deadline together with the worker; meeting and coordination events are planned. Once the outcome is settled, the delivery is depending on the employee.

In the B group, the job description is independent of the person who has to complete it. Procedures and aims are well defined as part of the task definition within the job description. . But, in the case of the insurance company, the competences of the agent are recognised and valued at management level. Regular changes in job objectives or procedures are transmitted to the employee who can sometimes contest them.

Autonomy in job organisation is seen by the two group as the bigger advantage, even if all of them work over time mainly late in the evening and during the weekend. Single people who sometimes can feel out of social life see this as a danger. But it represents a big advantage for parents willing to take care of their children.

In the C group, tasks are fully described and there are no interpretation problems on how it should be done. The data files that have to be captured are divided at the enterprise level among the hundred people who have to treat them. The time they spend on doing so have no interest for the direction. The managers don't know personally most of their distant employees, what counts is that the files come back in due time and that they content as few errors as possible.

Coordination

For the A group, there is still a hierarchical control for coordination within the small group involved in the project. If the group generally doesn't meet big problems during the realisation phase, the manager is still in charges of gathering what has been done and has to function as a communication link between the different members of the team. When small problems occurs the manager but also the co-workers are tempted to address first the collaborators being present rather than to call the distance worker. They are two reasons put forward: the saving of time, they said it quicker and more convenient but also uneasiness in calling at home. This also underlines the differentiated use of ITC's means: phone when a quick answer is needed or matters have to be discussed, mails for a less urgent question, a request of information but also to avoid facing resistance or disappointment towards the demanded tasks. Some managers realise that the e-mails facilitate their communication to the point that they don't always realise how much there are asking for to employees.

Managers feel the necessity too include the distance employee by regular group meetings (one full day every three weeks or once a month) not so much for the work progress but for the person to feel really integrated in the company. To reinforce this feeling, they also try to give away all the information that could be of interest for the distance worker, even if they are not really relevant for his task.

In the B group, coordination is often already part of the job routine, as outcomes are automatically recorded. General meetings are used to transmit new objectives or explain the specificities of new products. As the employees are paid regarding the amount of tasks realised, they are reluctant towards too often meetings which are considered as a lost of time. Most of news is therefore sent by e-mails. The difficulty is then to be able to sort out what is really essential for the employee. When routine problems occur, there is a planed procedure to follow. If the problem is related to the worker productivity then face-to-face meetings are organised.

In the insurance company, some agents cope very well with being at home, when some others have rent together an office to recreate a common professional space drawing a clear line between private and working life. It is not so much to deal with the company but with the customers, which represents a problem for them. They have to coordinate both relationships.

The latter is said to be the heaviest one, as the customers seem to have more difficulties to respect private life than the managers.

In the group C, coordination is linked to the workflow rather than to people. Files are sent to the distance workers, treated, and come back to be sent further. The coordination regarding people which is made by one manager, concerns planning for holidays or in case of diseases. There is no official relationship among the distant workers, even if some of them have met for the training program.

Control

For the members of group A, trust is said to supplant control. It starts when negotiating contracts or projects and solidifies with respects of deadline and quality of outcomes. If these requirements are successfully reached, then control is said to be unnecessary by managers. The first trails are in that sense very important for the perpetuation of the work relationship.

For the group B, the meeting of objectives is the key requirement for control. ICTs tools are used to gather automatically all the information and record them in the central server. It is on this base that the wages are defined. For this reason, the time schedule of employees is not so much under control.

In the group C, the control is related to the quality of outcomes and respects of deadline. The management does not care of whom is doing the job as long as it is well done, they don't control the time the employees need as the task as been designed on an average base: to a x numbers of files correspond x hours which equal to x salary.

The companies provide most of the ICTs tools used by the distant employees. But in some cases, mostly telecommuters, the employee is supporting a part of the expenses mainly regarding mobile phone and phones lines. The rule is of course that tools should be reserved for professional purposes. The control is sometimes done without employees being aware of it. For example this employee who was training on a new computer, printing private letter on a Sunday afternoon, and was surprised to receive a mail asking if this letter should be kept in the central server of the company. But usually no specific control is done regarding private use of the material. However, in case of break down, if the computer contents extra-data or application, the employee is in charge of the reparation. This contractual clause is effective enough to prevent employee to let their children play with the company's computer. But the border between private and professional is still unclear as the company can find advantages too in the private surroundings of the worker. Often in case of technical problem, the home-worker relies first on people living close to him, relatives or friends, for help to fix it.

Performance

It quickly becomes clear to the managers if someone is able to cope with distance work or not. In some cases, after trials of 6 to 12 months, people reintegrated the office at least on a part time base. The lack of formal but mostly informal communication and social interaction has lead to a fall of stimulation and motivation For those who continue the distant relationship, the adaptation phase is nonetheless said to be a long learning process about how to separate professional occupation from private life. Some managers do recognise that they expect a bit more in term of availability form their distant workers regarding time schedule but try to respect the weekend as a free time. They also expect their employees to work in proper conditions and don't like so much to be confront with their private life for instance when a child is answering the phone.

For both groups A and B, the distance worker is reacting rather quickly to any external solicitation, mail, phone, fax. When the indoor employee would postpone it to the next day, the distant worker is willing to do a bit more it. This is seen as a way to show and prove that he is efficiently working. In case of disease, the distant worker is also more efficient. When being sick the indoor employee would stay in bed, the home based one will still try to work a little. Being the master of his own time and production, he is more demanding and severe regarding his own outcomes. But more autonomy, more freedom, and more responsibility lead also to more stress and the balance between job and leisure is not always is to easy to find. The management take of course advantage of this increased output, but should be also concerned by the longer-term prospect. No study as far as we know deals with this issue on a longitudinal prospect.

For group A, the performance of the workers is rewarded by involvement into new projects.

For the group B, as we already said their salary is based on their production, the lines they program, the contracts they sell or the customers they gather determine their income. The more they succeed in productivity the freer they are regarding their time occupancy.

Regarding group C, the performance is equal to control, as the management don't care on how they work as long as the productivity is meeting the requirement.

Regional aspects

Distance work has often been ascribed to be the answer to revitalise peripheral regions by provoking a large migration from the town centres. However we have to admit that this is not the case in this study where most of the concerned enterprises are located close to cities or town centres. None of the employees or managers interviewed has moved since he or she started to work at distance. People said they are well integrated where they live and don't wish to change it. The ICTs tools development is not sufficient to outbalance the deficit decentralised regions show compared to urban areas. Although they have financial advantages (lower taxes and prices) they are still unattractive for these enterprises. While none of firms has delocalised its previous settings however, some of them have used this new mode of collaboration to enlarge their scope of activities. Three of the 17 companies, belonging to group A, have hired people living in remote areas. In the first case, to engage new employees close to customers, having an existing network and arguably sharing the same cultural background, mainly regional dialect, was seen as a successful mean to broaden the firm activities. This company, which pays very much attention to local particularities, is also operating at international level. The two other examples deal with the opening of satellite centres in order to find effective and less expensive employees in Switzerland but also in France. For one of the companies, a trial to collaborate on the same base with Spain ended as a failure, which was accounted by too many cultural differences. Altogether, these three examples are said to be successful by the people involved at both managerial and employee's level.

DISCUSSION AND CONCLUSION

We have discussed trends towards virtualisation of enterprises. Although a bulk of literature seems to have fully virtualised organisational life, we find only modest and mingled models of working together apart. The managerial challenges are accordingly related to orchestrating an enlarged repertoire of communication and cooperation forms. And to design work which fits with the virtualisation. The design of bulks of work for teleworking is often the responsibility of the employee herself in the high skill group. On the other hand the low skilled group exhibit rather traditional managerial prerogatives in keeping detailed descriptions of work. Furthermore there seem to be at least two ways of getting hold of the disappearing worker: The first is the classical "modern" approach, which will use ICT to control performance. The second is likely to be the more efficient and built on self-management by the teleworker in combination with coaching and framesetting by the managers.

There seems to be a coexistence of formalisation and "deformalisation" in the cases: In some instances contracts with (new) temporary co-operators is made, whereas other cases show long-term network relationship with others (Schwarz 1999). In the latter informal cooperation is frequent.

The study does not show a strong localisation into peripheral regions. Distance work in these cases is first a new organisational form before being a change in firm localisation or an issue about regional delocalisation. It can be speculated that highly skilled employees belong to a life form, which adhere to the facilities of larger cities. Moreover it is likely that management still need to adjust to the idea of having such options at hand.

Our material shows changes in execution, communication and cooperation as well as control which goes in the direction of enhancing work forms where time and space is compressed. The notion of virtualisation has clear limits in describing these changes. While there seems to be a coexistence of work forms with and without distance and time difference, little indicates that work places are about to disappear and get non- physical. There is not much mysterious or high tech about cooperating by telephone, which was actually done a lot in the cases. In this way managers also have to get a hold on fanciful new terms for new forms of rationalisation, which more represent wishful thinking that everyday life of the organisation.

REFERENCES

Buser M., Poschet L, and Pulver B (2000). *Télématique et nouvelles formes de travail*. TA- report 35a. Conseil Suisse de la Science, Bern.

Buser M. and L. Poschet (2002) *Mobile Arbeit in Vielfältiger Ausprägung.* In L.Rey (ed). Mobile Arbeit in der Schweiz. VDF, Zurich, 77-125.

Castells M.(1996a). The rise of the network society. Blackwell Publishers, Cambridge Massachusetts.

Dalsgaard L and J. Bendix (1996*) Netværksorganisering. Etablering og ledelse af netværk som ny organisationsform.* Børsen, København

Daniels K, D. Lemond and P. Standen (2000). Managing telework. ITB Press, London.

Empirica (1999). Telework boom in Europe. European Commission

Giddens A.(1984). *The Constitution of Society*. University of California Press, Berkeley.

Jackson P. and Van der Wielen J (eds) (1998). Teleworking: International Perspectives. Routledge, London.

Handy, C. (1995), "Trust and the virtual organisation", *Harvard Business Review*, May-June, pp.40-50.

Harris, M. (1998), "Rethinking the virtual organisation", in Jackson, P., and Van der Wielen, J. (EdS.), *Teleworking: International Perspectives*, pp.74-92. Routledge, London.

Harvey D. (1996). *Justice, Nature and the Geography of Difference*. Blackwell, Oxford.

Hildebrandt E. and R. Seltz (1989) *Wandel betriebliche sozialverfassung durch systemische kontrolle*. Edition Zigma, Berlin.

Igbaria M and M. Tan (1998). *The Virtual Workplace*. IDEA-publishing, USA.

Koch C. (2000). Building Coalitions in an Era of Technological Change: Virtual Manufacturing and the role of the unions, employees and management. *Journal of Organisational Change Management*. Vol 13 no.3. 275- 288.

McGrath P and M. Houlihan M (1998). Conceptualising Telework. Modern or Postmodern. In Jackson, P., and Van der Wielen, J. (EdS.), *Teleworking: International Perspectives*, Routledge, pp.56-73

McLoughlin I.P. (1999). *Creative Technology Change*. Routledge, London.

Orlikowsky W and J. Yates (1994). Genre Repertoire: The structuring of Communicative Practices in Organizations. *Administrative Science Quarterly* 39. 541-574.

Ortmann, G. (1995), *Formen der Produktion; Organisation und Rekursivität.* Westdeutscher Verlag, Opladen.

Porter M.E.(1995). *Competitive Advantage of Nations.* McGraw-Hill, New York.

Schwarz H. (1999). *The Hidden Work In Virtual Work.* MIT, US (mimeo)

Scott W. & Meyer J. (1994). *Institutional Environments and Organizations.* Sage, Thousand Oaks.

Wenger E. (1998). *Communities of Practice.* Cambridge University Press, Cambridge.

Zuboff, S. (1988). *In the Age of the Smart Machine - the Future of Work and Power.* Basic Books, New York.

Management of Technology
Copyright © 2003 by Elsevier Science Ltd.
All rights of reproduction in any form reserved.
ISBN: 0-08-044136-X

29

INNOVATION AND CLUSTERING: A KOREAN CASE

Sunyang Chung, Institute for Technological Innovation (ITI), Sejong University, Seoul, Korea[*]

INTRODUCTION

According to experts, the 21st century will be characterized not only by knowledge-based economy (OECD, 1996a) but also by regionalization (Ohmae, 1995; Storper and Scott, 1995). Merging these two trends, a new concept of *regional innovation system* has been identified. Regional innovation system underlies that innovations are better fostered and utilized, when innovation activities are systematically clustered around a region (e.g., Meyer-Krahmer, 1990; Süss et al, 1992; Blöcker et al, 1992; Brazyck, Coocke and Heidenreich, 1998, Chung, 2000). It implies that a decentralized cluster approach is needed for regional and national development strategy. This approach is particularly relevant for innovation-oriented regional economic development because an innovation cluster can be easily established on a regional base.

Korea, a traditionally centralized country, has been adopting a regional cluster approach to technological and economic development especially since the middle of the 1990s. The importance of regional innovation cluster has been widely diffused among Korean regional governments and innovation actors. Some of regional governments are very active in promoting regional S&T activities. They established an organization for S&T promotion in their regional administration, increased R&D budget, and implemented a series of ambitious plans for developing regional economies in terms of enhancing technological and innovation capabilities (Chung, 1999a, 2000). Like the central government (Byun, 1989), Korean regional

---

[*] Dr. Sunyang Chung is Professor of Technology Management at School of Business Administration and Director of Institute for Technological Innovation (ITI), Sejong University located in Seoul, South Korea. Email: sychung@sejong.ac.kr.

governments are also very ambitious and aggressive in their efforts to increase S&T capabilities and to pursue economic development of their regions.

There have been many articles on regional innovation systems not only in Korea but also in other countries. In particular, as for the Korean analysis, there have been several analyses on regional innovation systems as a whole, especially by the author himself (Chung, 1999a, 1999b, 1999c, 2000; Chung et al, 1997, 1999a). However, only few analyses on a specific region itself have been made. Therefore, this chapter will deal with region-specific analysis on a representative regional innovation system in Korea. For this purpose, we identify two research questions. First, what are the specific characteristics of a representative regional innovation system in Korea? For this purpose, we select Kwangju as a specific region. From this analysis on the Kwangju Regional Innovation System we can identify very interesting characteristics of Korean regional innovation systems in general. The second question is what are strategic implications from the Korean regional innovation system? These implications could be applied to refine Korean regional innovation systems and those of other countries. This chapter is based on a series of our researches on regional innovation activities and systems in Korea. By indicating Korea-specific approach to regional innovation clustering, it could identify some interesting strategic implications that would be also interesting for foreign countries.

REGIONAL INNOVATION SYSTEM

Nowadays, the concept of regional innovation system has been gaining much attention from policy makers and researchers (e.g. Brazyck et al., 1998; De La Mothe & Paquet, 1998). Two streams of development study have influenced the concept: regional development theory and modern innovation theory (Chung, 1999a).

Since the middle of the 1980s, on the one hand, some economists have emphasized the role of region in economic progress over the widespread globalisation of economic activities in the world. They have also recognized the importance of technological innovation in regional economic development. As a result, *innovation-oriented regional policy* has been developed. For example, Meyer-Krahmer (1990) argues that regional policy should orient to innovation policy in order to effectively attain the objectives of regional economic development. Ohmae (1995) stresses that the nation-state has been losing its importance in a globalized economy and that the region-state has become a focal point of economic activities. In support of this, he argues that regions are more dynamic and reflexive than states in R&D and economic activities. Breschi & Malerba (1992) argue that regional cluster will result in industrial cluster in innovation activities. Florida (1995, 1998) argues that a region should become a *learning region* by appreciating the importance of knowledge and that public policy should not only target short-term economic competitiveness but also the long-term sustainable advantage of regions.

On the other hand, there has been a strong demand for the decentralization of S&T and innovation policy since the end of the 1980s (e.g. Hucke & Wollmann, 1989; Hilpert, 1991). This decentralization demand was met with regional development policy that had become conscious of the importance of technology. As a result, a *region-oriented innovation policy* has been developed (Meyer-Krahmer, 1985, 1990; Süss et al, 1992). The policy was oriented to the development of a region by increasing its internal technological capabilities (Kreibich, 1989). It aimed at establishing innovation-friendly industrial structures under the leading role of regional governments. Various efforts were taken, including financial support, education and training, institutional setting, and so on, to increase regional innovation capabilities.

In the end of the 1980s, in the area of S&T policy study, a new policy concept, national innovation system (NIS), has been raised for the efficient development of national economy in terms of accumulating technological innovation (e.g. Freeman, 1987; Nelson, 1993; Lundvall, 1992; Patel & Pavitt, 1994; Chung, 1996; Chung & Lay, 1997). Influenced by the importance of region in economic development, this concept has easily adopted the issue of regional innovation cluster, so that a concept off regional innovation system has been developed. In the discussion about national innovation system, we understand innovation to mean technological innovation and define a national innovation system as a complex of innovation actors and institutions that are directly related to the generation, diffusion, and appropriation of technological innovation and also the interrelationship between innovation actors. The major concern of this concept is how we can formulate an effective national setting of major innovation actors and how to motivate information flows among them in order to generate and appropriate innovation effectively. A national innovation system consists of four comprehensive actor groups around innovations: industry, public research sector, academia, and government.

All these studies emphasize that innovation can be better generated, exploited, and diffused, when innovation actors are regionally clustered. Based on these studies, the concept of national innovation system has been applied to regional level, so that a concept of *regional innovation system* has been developed. In this chapter, following the definition of national innovation system, we define a regional innovation system (RIS) as a complex of innovation actors and institutions in a region that are directly related to the generation, diffusion, and appropriation of technological innovation and an inter-relationship between these regional innovation actors. There are five innovation actor groups in a regional innovation system. Actual innovation actors, i.e., universities, firms, and public research institutes, compose of an *interaction platform*. In addition, regional government and the central government play a role of facilitator and coordinator. They support and direct innovation activities of region-based actors by setting the interaction platform through joint financing and responsibility.

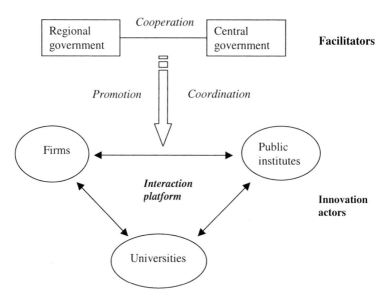

Fig. 29.1. General model of regional innovation system.

Figure 29.1 describes a general model of regional innovation system. Through trust and close interaction between regional innovation actors, a regional innovation system can generate its own *sectoral innovation system* (SIS). When a region doesn't have sufficient trust, the trust can be studied and accumulated to some extent. The main role of regional and central governments is to create this trust and promote interactive learning between major innovation actors in a regional innovation system. They should create relevant institutional settings and clusters that facilitate interactive learning and innovation activities in a region. As facilitators of networking, governments should create an effective interaction platform that could facilitates knowledge exchange and interactive learning between innovation actors, i.e. firms, public research institutes, and universities.

We argue that regional innovation systems (RIS) are very helpful for attaining effective sectoral innovation systems (SIS) and also a competent national innovation system (NIS). The concept of regional innovation system is easier to implement than sectoral innovation system (Chung, 2000). OECD (1999) also argues that such cluster approach is much better in promoting innovation activities than traditional sectoral approach. However, we argue that the regional innovation system can merge these two approaches, as national innovation system can be formulated by a matrix of regional and sectoral innovation systems.

KWANGJU REGIONAL INNOVATION SYSTEM

As a representative case of Korean regional innovation systems, we select Kwangju metropolitan city, based on a series of our analyses on Korean regional innovation systems. There are 16 regions in Korea and Kwangju is one of them. It is located in the southwestern part of Korea and, historically, it has been one of the most under-developed regions in Korea. However, it has been making a great effort to formulate and implement its own regional innovation system since the middle of the 1990s (Chung et al, 1999b; SERI, 1999). In particular, the regional government of Kwangju has been deliberately motivated its innovation actors to actively participate in the Kwangju Regional Innovation System. This region is very representative because its regional government is very late but very ambitious in its efforts of industrialization like the Korean central government in its history of industrialization. This region has been very eager to develop its regional economy.

As of 1999, the territory of Kwangju metropolitan city is about 501.15 km², which represents about 0.5% of the total territory of Korea. The total population of Kwangju is about 1,258 thousand people, which represents about 2.8% of the total Korean population. According to our analysis, the Kwangju's specialized industries are "other machinery and equipment manufacturing" from the perspective of value added and number of companies compared to population. However, the specialty based on value added can be found in "recycled material treatment", "rubber and plastic production", and "other electric machines and transfer equipment production" (Chung et al, 1999a).

For the first time in the Korean regional governments, in April 1999, Kwangju has been prepared its own *Five Year Plan for Promoting Science and Technology*. In this sense we selected this region as a representative case of Korean regional innovation system. Based on this plan it has been developing systematically photonics, information and telecommunication, and mechatronics industries (Chung et al, 1999b). In addition, it has prepared and implementing *A Comprehensive Plan for Developing Kwangju's High-tech Industries*. For effectively fulfilling these tasks, the Kwangju regional government established a *Department of Promoting High-tech Industries* in its administration.

In order to effectively analyse a regional innovation system, at least, we need three indicators on a region: R&D resources, innovation actors, and role of regional and central governments. From the first indicator, we can grasp a degree of interaction between innovation actors because these resources constitute soft infrastructure of a regional innovation system. The later two indicators describe a division of labour among important players in a regional innovation system. In this section, we will analyse the Kwangju Regional Innovation System in terms of these three indicators.

R&D Resources

As of 1997 R&D investment of Kwangju is only 129 billion won, which represents only about 1.06% of the total R&D investment in Korea. Its R&D personnel is about 4,775 people who amount to 2.11% of the total R&D personnel (MOST/STEPI, 1998). Among 16 regions in Korea, as a result, Kwangju is positioned at 13th place in R&D investment and 12th in R&D personnel (see Table 29.1). When we look at the number of innovation actors, i.e. the number of universities, public research institutes, and industrial companies, only 1.08% of total innovation actors are in Kwangju. It represents about there are about 15th among total 16 regions in Korea. As a whole, we conclude that Kwangju's R&D efforts are very weak compared to other regions. Therefore, Kwangju should increase R&D resources to a large scale in order to attain a competent regional innovation system.

However, we can see that universities in Kwangju show a relatively strong R&D potential.

Table 29.1. R&D resources in Kwangju (1997).

(Unit: %, order)

	Innovation actors* (Order)	R&D investment (Order)	R&D personnel (Order)
Academia	3.82(13)	4.78(6)	3.82(9)
Public research sector	1.23(15)	0.02(15)	0.17(15)
Industry	0.68(15)	0.76(14)	1.10(12)
Total	1.08(15)	1.06(13)	2.11(12)

Notes:
  1) % implies the share of the nation-wide total.
  2) Order means the position among 16 regions in Korea.
  * Number of universities, public research institutes and companies.
Source: MOST/STEPI (1998)

While the number of universities positioned at the 13th place among 16 regions in Korea, their R&D expenditures ranked at the 6th and R&D personnel at the 9th place. It indicates that Kwangju's universities show a very high degree of R&D intensity, compared to other actor groups. Therefore, universities should play an essential role in the Kwangju Regional Innovation System.

University Research

It deserves to look into individual innovation actor groups. First, as for academia, there are 13 universities in Kwangju, including colleges, which represents about 3.82% of the total number of universities in Korea. Universities in Kwangju have 35 research institutes, which are about

Table 29.2. Innovation potential of universities in Kwangju.

	Number of professors	Number of institutes
Information and communication technologies	151(4.4%)	3(3.3%)
Machinery and equipment	65(4.6%)	2(6.1%)
Construction and civil engineering	106(6.4%)	1(2.3%)
Metal and materials	29(4.9%)	-
Chemistry and chemical engineering	81(4.7%)	1(5.9%)
Environment	29(6.0%)	2(3.3%)
Natural resources and energy	26(7.2%)	1(4.2%)
Biotechnology, agriculture and forestry	107(4.4%)	3(2.9%)
Industrial design	71(6.8%)	2(8.7%)
Medical sciences	358(4.9%)	12(6.0%)
General support for industry	-	6(3.6%)
Basic sciences	58(3.3%)	2(2.1%)
Total	1,081(4.9%)	35(4.0%)

Notes:
1. Calculation is made around four-year engineering schools and school branch are dealt separately.
2. "General support for industry" means the interdisciplinary professors and institutes that cover several disciplines.
3. KAIST, ERC/SRC, RRC, and branches of the Korea Academy of Industrial Technologies are excluded.
4. % means the portion of the nation-wide total.

Source: Author's calculation based on the Korean University Press (1998).

4% of the nation-wide total. Among 16 regions, this number is positioned at the 13th place (see Table 29.2). The total R&D expenditures of the Kwangju's universities is about 61 billion won and its R&D personnel are 3,014 people. Among 16 regions, the academic sector in Kwangju positioned at the 6th in R&D expenditures and at the 9th in R&D personnel. It indicates that Kwangju's universities have a relatively strong level of R&D activities compared to other innovation actors.

According to the survey of MOST/STEPI (1998), about 46.4% of the Kwangju's total R&D expenditures are expensed by the university sector. Therefore, we can confirm again that universities are very important in the Kwangju Regional Innovation System. At nation-wide, the average portion of universities is about 10%. In this sense, universities should play an essential role in the Kwangju Regional Innovation System. By the same token, the role of private companies should be brought up, as their portion in Kwangju's total R&D expenditure is only about 53.4%, whereas the nation-wide average is about 73%.

When we look at the number of professors in science and engineering, there are 1,081 professors in Kwangju, which represents about 4.9% of the total number of professors in Korea. As for the number, medical sciences (358 professors), information and communication technologies (151 professors), biotechnology, agriculture and fishery (107 professors), and construction and civil engineering (106 professors) show relatively high degree of R&D potential. Looking into the relative share in the nationwide total, natural resources and energy (7.2%), industrial design (6.8%), and construction and civil engineering (6.4%) show a higher degree of innovation potential. As for the number of university research institutes, industrial design (8.7%), machinery and equipment (6.1%), medical sciences (6.0%), and chemistry and chemical engineering (5.9%) show relatively high degree of innovation potential.

It is difficult to identify which S&T fields are strong in the university sector of Kwangju. But we think that the number of professors represents better universities' R&D potential than that of universities' research institutes, as there are no sufficient research institutes in the university sector in this region. According to the number of professors, Kwangju shows relatively strong R&D potential in medical sciences, biotechnology, construction, and information technologies.

Public Research Institutes

As of 1997, Kwangju's public research institutes show a very weak R&D potential. Kwangju has only 3 public research institutes: two public institutes for experiment and testing and one government-sponsored research institute (see Table 29.3). In general, a public institute for experiment and testing is not actively engaged in R&D activities in Korea. Among 16 regions in Korea, Kwangju is listed at 15th place in the number of public institutes, at 15th in R&D expenditures, and at the 15th in R&D personnel. It implies that the innovation potential of Kwangju's public research institutes is the weakest in Korean regions except the Ulsan metropolitan city, which became a metropolitan city in 1998 and has no public research institute.

Kwangju's weakness in the public research sector is also confirmed by the fact that its portion of R&D expenditures and R&D personnel in the national total is much smaller than

Table 29.3. Innovation potential of public research institutes in Kwangju (1997).

	Number of innovation actors (number)	R&D expenditures (million won)	Number of research personnel (persons)
Public institutes for experiment and testing	2(1.96%)	127(0.03%)	35(0.51%)
Government-sponsored research institute	1(1.96%)	260(0.02%)	5(0.04%)
Total	3(1.23%)	387(0.02%)	40(0.17%)

Note: % means the share of the nation-wide total.
Source: MOST/STEPI (1998)

that of innovation actors, i.e. the number of public research institutes. It implies that public research institutes in Kwangju are not R&D-oriented, but they focus on simple experiment and testing. Therefore, in order to strengthen the innovation potential of the Kwangju Regional Innovation System, Kwangju needs research-intensive public research institutes. Based on the close cooperation with the central government, the Kwangju regional government should establish public research institutes or at least invite some branches of existing public research institutes that are concentrated on the Dae-Duck Science Park located in the center of Korea. In Korea, public research institutes have played an important role of bridge between academic research and industrial application. In addition, they have been major tools of governmental innovation strategy, as they can closely cooperate with the central and regional governments and governments can entrust them the role of coordination for R&D activities in region.

Firms' Innovation Activities

The total amount of R&D expenditures of Kwangju's industry as of 1997 is about 75 billion won, which represents about 0.85% of the total industrial R&D expenditures (MOST/STEPI, 1998). Most of all, Kwangju has a problem of shortage in industrial innovation actors. According to Table 29.1, the number of industrial companies is about 0.68% of the total companies in Korea. This is very small portion compared to that of other innovation actor groups. As a result, the Kwangju's industry is ranked at the 14th place in the number of industrial companies, at the 14th in the industrial R&D expenditures, and at the 12th in industrial R&D personnel among 16 regions. When we look at R&D expenditures according to industrial sectors, chemical industry (41.3%), transportation equipment (41.3%), and assembled metals (15.5%) are the most R&D-intensive sectors (Chung et al, 1999a). These three sectors represent about 99.3% of the total R&D expenditures of Kwangju. It indicates that other industrial sectors are very weak in their innovation activities.

As of the end 1998, there are only 37 private research institutes in Kwangju, which represents 1.0% of the total number of R&D institutes in Korea (see Table 29.4). Since the beginning of the 1980s, Korean enterprises have tried to enhance their competitiveness in terms of establishing and operating corporate research institutes (OECD, 1996b; Chung and Lay, 1997). There were 3,760 industrial research institutes in Korea as of the end 1998 and so Kwangju is severely lacking in industrial research institutes. As a result, Kwangju is ranked at the 13th place in the number of private research institutes among 16 regions in Korea. There are 8 institutes of big enterprises and 29 institutes of SMEs. Looking into industrial distribution, there are 14 institutes in machinery and metal sector, 12 institutes in electric and electronic sector, and 6 institutes in chemical sector. They represent Kwangju's strategic technology fields of industrial applications.

To summarize, Kwangju has very weak industrial innovation potential. It reflects that this region is one of the most underdeveloped regions in Korea. There are insufficient

Table 29.4. Private research institutes in Kwangju (1998).

(Unit: Number, %)

	Machinery and metals	Electric and electronics	Chemical sector	Food	Textile	Others	Total
Big enterprises	3(1.7)	3(1.3)	2(1.0)	(-)	(-)	(-)	8(1.1)
SMEs	11(1.6)	9(0.6)	4(0.9)	(-)	(-)	5(2.1)	29(1.0)
Total	14(1.6)	12(0.7)	6(0.9)	(-)	(-)	5(1.4)	37(1.0)

Note: % is the share of the individual item's total.
Source: KITA (1999)

industrial companies by having only 0.68% of the total industrial companies in Korea (see Table 29.1) and these existing companies are not technology-intensive. In this sense, Kwangju should invite technology-intensive companies from outside. In particular, it should motivate good scientists and engineers, who are relatively well qualified in this region, to start up their own venture companies that could effectively contribute to the development of regional economy. Considering that Kwangju has relatively many R&D-oriented universities and there has been a fever of start-ups all over Korea including this region, especially since the end of the 1990s, such technology-intensive start-up companies will play an important role in the Kwangju Regional Innovation System.

Role of Governments

Above we discussed innovation actor groups in the interaction platform, i.e. universities, public research institutes, and firms. In order to activate interaction between innovation actors, we need a role of promotion and coordination from the regional and central governments. According to our analysis, the role of Korean governments in promoting regional S&T activities is characterized by the close cooperation between the central and regional governments. In general, regional government invests a matching fund and implements region-specific programs based on the guidance of the central government (Chung, 1999b). There are few region-specific instruments for promoting regional innovation activities. It could be attributed to the short history of regional innovation strategy and also to the low level of self-sufficiency of regional governments' budget (Chung et al, 1997, 1999a). Korean regional governments have no sufficient money to initiate their own promotion schemes. Therefore, the matching fund of regional government is less than half of the central government.

Table 29.5 shows the major R&D programs in Kwangju and budgets of the regional government for promotion its regional innovation activities. Most programs have been initiated by the central government and the Kwangju regional government has implemented them and

Table 29.5. Major R&D programs and budgets of the Kwangju regional government (1999).

(Unit: million won)

Programs	1997	1998	1999
Consortium among Firms, Universities, and Public Research Institutes	400	320	400(9.2%)
Regional Research Center (RRC)	200	300	500(11.5%)
Technology Innovation Center (TIC)	100	100	100(2.3%)
Kwangju-Chonnam Technopark	-	5,757	2,910(67.2%)
Joint Technology Development between Industry and University	170	170	300(6.9%)
Business Incubating (BI)	-	-	100(2.3%)
International S&T Cooperation	-	20	20(0.5%)
Total	870	6,667	4,330(100%)

Source: MOST (1999).

also invested a certain level of matching fund. These programs have contributed a lot to strengthen the Kwangju Regional Innovation System. As a whole, Table 29.5 shows that the amount of Kwangju's investment in R&D programs has been increased dramatically from 870 million won in 1997 to 4,330 million won in 1999. It indicates that the recognition of the Kwangju regional government on the importance of science and technology in regional development has been increased to a large extent.

The most important program is the Kwangju-Chonnam Technopark Program, in which 67.2% of the Kwangju's R&D budget was invested. With a big distance, 11.5% was invested in RRC (Regional Research Center) program, and 9.2% in the Consortium among Firms, Universities, and Public Institutes. These three programs are quite important for this region, because the central government has invested quite a big money. It also makes the Kwangju regional government to invest a significant amount of budget as a matching fund.

Special characteristics of the major programs are as follows. First, Kwangju supports the establishment of the Kwangju-Chonnam Technopark to elaborate technological capabilities of existing industries and to develop new advanced technologies. As of 1999, Kwangju invested 29 billion won as a matching fund with the central government.

Second, there are two Regional Research Centers (RRCs) in Kwangju as of the end of 1999. The purpose of this program is, in terms of the joint financing by the Kwangju regional government and the central government, to activate R&D activities of universities in regions and so to promote the competitiveness of region-specific industrial sectors. Since 1995, "Regional Research Center for Transportation Machinery and Parts, and Factory Automation" in Chosun University has been supported. Since 1998, there is also "Regional Research Center for High-Quality Electric and Electronic Parts and System" in Chonnam National University.

As of 1999, 500 million won has been funded for both RRCs by the Kwangju regional government.

Third, Kwangju supports its innovation actors in terms of the program "Consortium among Firms, Universities, and Public Institutes". This program aims at solving bottleneck technologies at production site through utilizing innovation resources of SMEs, public research institutes, and universities in a region. A consortium was established around an university in a region and, as of the end of 1999, there were four consortia in Kwangju (Chonnam Univ., Chosun Univ., Honam Univ., and Kwangju Univ.), in which 70 SMEs were actively participating. Kwangju funded about 400 million won these consortia in 1999.

Fourth, there is a Kwangju-specific program for "Joint Technology Development between Industry and University". This program is to support SMEs to solve bottleneck technologies and promote SMEs' new technology development through activating network among SMEs, universities, and the Kwangju regional government. As of 1998, 170 million won has been supported for 30 projects in four research areas, i.e. design development, factory automation, new technology development, and supply of foreign S&T information.

Finally, there is a Technology Innovation Center (TIC) in Kwangju. Among 6 TICs in Korea, as of 1999, Kwangju has a "Parts Industry TechnoCenter". TIC's major activities are business incubating, technological and managerial support, and training and guidance in order to bring up region-specific industrial sectors and to develop new high technologies. Every year, the central government support the TIC 1 billion won and the Kwangju regional government 100 million won for the period of ten years.

CONCLUSIONS

In this chapter, we analysed a representative regional innovation system, Kwangju Regional Innovation System, in Korea. The reason why we call this system as representative is that almost every Korean regional innovation system has similar composition and characteristics. In particular, the Korean central government's measures to enhance interactive learning among regional innovation actors apply for all regional innovation systems. In this sense, some strategic implications identified here will be of importance for other regional innovation systems.

The Kwangju Regional Innovation System has 13 universities, 3 public research institutes, and 37 private research institutes. This regional innovation system is characterized by the close interaction between universities and private companies. The regional government of Kwangju, based on the strong support of the central government, has prepared for various policy measures for enhancing interaction between regional innovation actors, representatively, the Kwangju-Chonnam Technopark, Regional Research Centers, and Consortium among Firms, Universities, and Public Research Institutes.

The Kwangju Regional Innovation System is also characterized by the strong involvement of the regional government. The Kwangju's regional government has supported very strongly to refine its regional innovation system in terms of various policy measures. For example, it prepared for its *Five Year Plan for Promotion Science and Technology* for the first time in Korean regional governments (Chung, et al, 1999b) and established a *Department of Promoting High-tech Industries* in its administration in order to systematically support regional innovation activities and nurture advanced industrial sectors. In addition, it has strongly support the trust among regional innovation actors.

However, there are also some important problems in the Kwangju Regional Innovation System. In particular, this region has no sufficient technology-intensive enterprises due to the short history of industrialization. It has also a structural deficit of lacking public research institutes. However, universities in Kwangju have shown a very high level of innovation potential. Therefore, we can draw some important policy implications for Kwangju's regional innovation system. First, the Kwangju Regional Innovation System should be established and implemented especially around R&D-intensive universities in this region. Second, start-up companies, which are rapidly growing in this region, should play an important role in this regional innovation system. Third, a strong interaction should be activated between universities and start-up companies. Finally, public research institutes, especially government-sponsored research institutes, should be established in the long run and they should play a role of bridge in the regional innovation system. Constituted mainly by these young innovation actors, especially start-up companies and public research institutes, the Kwangju Regional Innovation System could become a very dynamic and prolific regional innovation system.

Since the end of the 1990s, the Kwangju Regional Innovation System has been targeting to nurture *photonics* industry, based on the strong involvement of the regional government and innovation actors. The Five Year Plan mentioned above identifies this industry as the most promising strategic industrial sector for Kwangju and there is a strong consensus about it among major innovation actors in this region. There are some obvious results in Kwangju's photonics industry. For example, the Kwangju-Chonnam Technopark has already incubating many photonics start-up companies and several competitive enterprises in this sector have been invited and settled. Therefore, we are convinced that the Kwangju Regional Innovation System could create a very effective Photonics Innovation System. Considering that the photonics are emerging technologies in the 21st century, we expect that *Kwangju's Photonics Innovation System* can make a great contribution to the development of Korea by strengthening the Korea's national innovation system as a whole.

BIBLIOGRAPHY

Blöcker, A., J. Köther and D. Rehfeld (1992). Die Region als technologiepolitisches Handlungsfeld? In: *Politische Techniksteuerung* (K. Grimmer, K. Häusler, S. Kuhlmann, S. and G. Simonis, eds.), pp. 183-201. Leske und Budrich, Opladen.

Braczyk, H. J., P. Cooke and M. Heidenreich (eds.) (1998). *Regional Innovation Systems*. UCL Press, London.

Breschi, S. and F. Malerba (1997). Sectoral innovation system: technological regimes, Schumpetarian dynamics, and spatial boundaries. In: *Systems of Innovation: Technology, Institutions and Organizations* (C. Edquist, ed.), pp. 130-156. Pinter Publishers, London, Washington.

Byun, H. Y. (1989). Industry. In: *The Korean Economy*. (H. Y. Byun, ed.) pp. 263-290. (Korean).

Chung, S. (1996). *Technologiepolitik für neue Produktionstechnologien in Korea und Deutschland*. Physica-Verlag, Heidelberg.

Chung, S. (1999a). Regional innovation systems in Korea. Presented at the *3rd International Conference on Technology Policy and Innovation*, University of Texas at Austin, Austin, Texas, August 30~ September 2, 1999.

Chung, S. (1999b). *Establishing Regional Innovation Systems*. Science and Technology Policy Institute, Seoul (Korean).

Chung, S. (2000). Regional innovation systems as building stones of a national innovation system. Presented at the Ninth International Conference on Management of Technology, held at Miami, Florida on February 20-25, 2000.

Chung, S. and G. Lay (1997). Technology policy between "diversity" and "one best practice" - a comparison of Korean and German promotion schemes for new production technologies -. *Technovation* **17**, 675-693.

Chung, S., J. Lee and J. Song (1997). *Regional S&T Annual Report*. STEPI/MOST, Seoul (Korean).

Chung, S., J. Lee et al (1999a). *Regional S&T Annual Report*. STEPI/MOST, Seoul (Korean).

Chung, S. J. Lee et al (1999b). *Five Year Plan for Promoting Kwangju's Science and Technology*. Science and Technology Policy Institute, Seoul/Kwangju.

De La Mothe and G. Paquet (eds.) (1998). *Local and Regional Systems of Innovation*. Kulwer Academic Publishers, Dortrecht, London.

Florida, R. (1995). Toward the learning region. *Futures*, **27**, 527-536.

Florida, R. (1998). Calibrating the learning region. In: *Local and Regional Systems of Innovation* (De La Mothe and G. Paquet, eds.), pp. 19-28. Kluwer Academic Publishers, Boston, Dortrecht, London.

Freeman, C. (1987). *Technology Policy and Economic Performance: Lessons from Japan*. Pinter Publishers, London, New York.

Hilpert, U. (ed.) (1991). *Regional Innovation and Decentralization: High Tech-Industry and Government Policy*. Routledge, London.

Hucke, J. and H. Wollmann (eds.) (1989). *Dezentrale Technologiepolitik?: Technikförderung durch Bundesländer und Kommunen*, Basel.

Korea Industrial Technology Association (KITA) (1999). *Trend of Establishment of Corporate Research Institutes 1998*, Seoul (Korean).

Korean University Press (1998). *Annual Report of University Education*. Seoul (Korean).

Kreibich, R. (1989). Innovationsstrukturpolitik: Chancen, Probleme, Zukunftsoptionen. In: *Technikgestaltung in der Stadt und Regionalentwicklung* (W. Schuchard, L. Hack and F. Naschold) Dortmund.

Lundvall, B. -A. (ed.) (1992). *National Systems of Innovation: Towards a Theory of Innovation and Interactive Learning*. Pinter Publishers, London.

Meyer-Krahmer, F. (1985). Innovation behavior and regional indigenous potential. *Regional Studies,*12, 523-524.

Meyer-Krahmer, F. (1990). Innovationsorientierte Regionalpolitik: Ansatz, Instrumente, Grenzen. In: *Wissenschaft, Technik und Arbeit: Innovationen in Ost und West* (H. E. Gramatzki et al, eds.), pp. 343-359, VWL-inform, Kassel.

Ministry of Science and Technology (MOST) (1999). *R&D Budgets of Regional Governments in Korea*. Internal Documents, Seoul (Korean).

Ministry of Science and Technology (MOST)/Science and Technology Policy Institute (STEPI) (1999). *Report on the Survey of Research and Development in Science and Technology*, Seoul (Korean).

Nelson, R. R. (ed.) (1993). *National Innovation Systems: A Comparative Analysis*. Oxford University Press: New York, Oxford.

OECD (1996a). *Knowledge-Based Economy*. Paris.

OECD (1996b). *Reviews of National Science and Technology Policy: Republic of Korea*, Paris.

OECD (1999). *Boosting Innovation: The Cluster Approach*, Paris.

Ohmae, K. (1990). *The Borderless World: Power and Strategy in the Inter-linked Economy*. Harper Business, New York.

Ohmae, K. (1995), *The End of the Nation-State: The Rise of Regional Economies*. The Free Press, New York.

Patel, P. and K. Pavitt (1994). The nature and economic importance of national innovations systems. *STI Review*, 9-32.

Samsung Economic Research Institute (SERI) (1999). *Plan for Photonics Industry in Kwangju*. Seoul (Korean).

Storper, M. and A. J. Scott (1995). The wealth of regions: market forces and policy imperatives in local and global context. *Futures*, **27**, 505-526.

Süss, W., R. Marx, S. Langer, S. and C. Scholle (1992). Regionale Innovationspolitik im Spannungsfeld von Europäischem Binnenmarkt und deutscher Integration, In: *Politische Techniksteuerung* (K. Grimmer, K. Häusler, S. Kuhlmann, S. and G. Simonis, eds.), pp. 154-181. Leske und Budrich, Opladen.

Management of Technology
Copyright © 2003 by Elsevier Science Ltd.
All rights of reproduction in any form reserved.
ISBN: 0-08-044136-X

30

IMPLEMENTING THE INTERNATIONAL RELOCATION OF PRODUCTION TECHNOLOGY

Erik J. de Bruijn, Technology and Development Group, University of Twente[*]
Harm-Jan Steenhuis, College of Business & Public Administration, Eastern Washington University[**]

ABSTRACT

Although the international re-location of production technology has been a widely discussed subject, the actual implementation of re-location of production has received limited research attention. The implementation is, in those instances where the entire process of production technology transfer has been identified, often only seen as one step in a total of six or more steps and the emphasis has been on strategic decision making. The actual re-location of production technology was investigated from one company to another company (in another country) for the reason that without a thorough understanding of implementation issues, strategic decisions can hardly be properly made. Based upon the analysis of four case studies, which were carried out in one type of industry (the aircraft industry) to allow in-depth understanding of the technology, an implementation model has been developed which incorporates the activities that have to be carried out during the re-location of production technology. Evidence from the case studies suggests that omitting some of these activities in the project plan results in serious time delays or extra cost.

---

[*] Erik Joost de Bruijn is Professor of Business Management in Developing and New Industrialising Economies at the Faculty of technology and Management of the University of Twente, Enschede, Netherlands.

[**] Dr. Harm-Jan Steenhuis is Assistant Professor of Operations Management at Eastern Washington University, Spokane, USA.

INTRODUCTION

As far back as 30 years ago, the re-location of production technology[1] was identified as crucial for countries and companies (Quinn, 1969). Gregory et al. (1996) identified that "The only way to gain lasting competitive advantage is to leverage your capabilities around the world so that the company as a whole is greater than the sum of its parts." An important part of the international manufacturing strategy is the manufacturing mobility: "the ability to access and orchestrate product design and technology development internationally, to take advantage of dispersed resources both within and outside the company" (Gregory et al., 1996). This involves the international re-location, or transfer, of manufacturing activities.

Although the international transfer of manufacturing activities has been a topic of research for a considerable time, the emphasis in this research has mainly been on the identification of important factors without considering the entire technology transfer process, see e.g. (Godkin, 1988; Madu, 1989; Reddy and Zhao, 1990; Cusumano and Elenkov, 1994; Tsang, 1994; Plenert, 1997). In instances where the process of technology transfer has been investigated in depth the emphasis has been on (strategic) decision making. For example Ramanathan (1999) and Nahar (1999) give respectively a six-phase and an eight-phase model for international technology transfer. Only one of these six respectively eight phases involves the implementation.

But how can managers be guided in their decision making if the entire process of technology transfer is not shown or if implementation issues are largely ignored? This research is, therefore, focussed on the implementation of international re-location of production technology.

METHODOLOGY

The aim of the research is to identify how international re-location of production is implemented at the company level. After theoretical and practical issues had been examined a choice was made to focus the study on the descriptive and explanatory level. In technology transfer technological characteristics have a major influence on the implementation, it was therefore decided to focus the study on one particular technology: aircraft production technology. This allowed gaining in-depth understanding of the technological characteristics. The in the literature general accepted view and in line with the practical findings considers a technology as having a core consisting of humanware, inforware and technoware. In these cases humanware includes the number of people necessary for producing the aircraft or aircraft

---

[1]   In this chapter the terms international re-location of production technology and international technology transfer are used synonymously.

part, their skills and their ability to use these skills. Inforware includes product specific information such as drawings, process planning sheets and bills of material, and it includes process specific information such as process specifications. Technoware includes the necessary floor area for producing the aircraft or aircraft part (i.e. factory space), product specific equipment (for example jigs) and general equipment (for example riveting machines). The technology has inputs (detail parts or subassemblies, materials, fasteners etc.), outputs (aircraft or aircraft parts with specific characteristics) and it is guided by management (a number of managers with certain skills and with certain abilities to use these skills).

To be able to build descriptive and explanatory theory a methodological approach conform Eisenhardt (1989) was followed after it had been found that the main alternatives, namely grounded theory (Glaser and Strauss, 1967; Strauss and Corbin, 1990; Glaser, 1992) and deductive case study research (Yin, 1994; Stake, 1995), were not suitable for these applications. Cases were chosen by using snowball sampling (Miles and Huberman, 1994; Verschuren and Doorewaard, 1999) to fill theoretical categories (Eisenhardt, 1989). Dubin (1978) and Bacharach (1989) were used in addition to Eisenhardt to determine criteria for theory; the outcome of theory building research.

Four case studies were carried out in the aircraft industry in which approximately 315 interviews were held with 45 people who were mainly involved in planning, implementing, and controlling the transfer. Triangulation and member checks were used to improve the construct validity. In addition, to increase the degrees of freedom (Swanborn, 1996), information was also obtained outside the case study companies, in the same type of industry. In quantitative studies there are a number of accepted techniques for data analysis, this is not the case for qualitative studies. This sometimes is considered as one of the weaknesses of qualitative studies leading to a 'problematic acceptance' of the validity of the research. In this study, however, the viewpoint of Miles and Huberman has been adopted. They state "as qualitative researchers, we need to keep sharing our craft – that is, the explicit, systematic methods we use to draw conclusions and to test them carefully. We need methods that are credible, dependable, and replicable in qualitative terms." (Miles and Huberman, 1994, p. 2). The data collected in the cases has been analysed by using causal network diagrams, see (Miles and Huberman, 1994, pp. 151) this technique helps to improve the internal validity. To increase the soundness of the research a case study protocol was used. A case study data base was developed with a chain of evidence thus enabling the derivation of evidence from initial research questions to case study conclusions and vice versa.

CASE STUDIES

Case 1

The first case study was a transfer of technology between the UK and Romania. The transfer started at the end of the 1970s and ended in the early 1990s. It involved the transfer of an aircraft manufacturing line. The aircraft was already being manufactured in the UK for approximately 10 years and it was therefore well established technology.

The technology that was transferred was the complete technology. The destination company initially received sub-assemblies from the source company. Later in the project more and more parts were manufactured by the destination company. People were trained at the destination company and in certain instances training was provided at the source company. Technical assistance was provided for almost the entire transfer period. Tools and equipment were to a certain extent provided by the source company others were manufactured by the destination company based on drawings provided by the source company. All necessary information, product and process, was provided by the source company and used (after translation) by the destination company. Management responsibilities were also transferred to the destination company. The destination company was responsible for selling the aircraft that it produced. In essence, the manufacturing in Romania was a copy of the manufacturing in the UK.

The transfer was faced with large delays (up to approximately 370 weeks) eventually leading to abandonment of the project. There were four major causes for the delays. First, the technology was very complex and large which led to difficulties with managing and controlling the transfer. Second, due to financial restraints, the Romanians decided to replace the UK supplies (approved) such as bolts and rivets with supplies that were produced in Romania. However, these Romanian supplies were not approved and therefor not acceptable for aircraft sold to other countries. Third, the UK company stopped production and withdrew from the project leading to difficulties with training and technical assistance. Fourth, the aircraft had to be produced according to UK production philosophies but it was quite a challenge for the Romanian company to accept, understand and apply these production methods. For example, when sealant is applied, a certain temperature is required. During cold days it turned out that the Romanian heating system was insufficient to reach the required temperature in the factory. To solve this problem plastic was put over the aircraft and heaters were placed within this covered area to get a locally acceptable temperature.

In the research the magnitude of the technology was considered to be very important and it was used for further case selection (Steenhuis, 1998a).

Case 2

The second case involved a technology transfer between Canada and Romania. The transfer started in 1996 and it involved the assembly of cockpits. The cockpit production had already taken place for years in Canada and the design was therefore well established. The present stage of the project is continuous production of the cockpits in Romania.

The technology that was transferred was not a complete technology. The destination company received all required inputs from the source company and only assembled the cockpit. Thus detail parts manufacturing was not part of the transfer. At the destination company people were trained and technical assistance was provided. Tools and equipment were manufactured or provided by the destination company based on the available information from the source company. All necessary information (product and process) was provided by the source company and used by the destination company. Although the destination company was responsible for production, management authority was not entirely transferred, a foreign representative was located on site in Romania to guide the project. Work at the destination company was essentially carried out the same manner as at the source company. After assembly by the destination company the cockpits were shipped to Canada for use in the final assembly line.

The technology transfer was successful to an extent that within the planned time frame the first article was produced and inspected and presently production is taking place. However, quality problems arose during the project and delays occurred. The quality problems were mainly due to inaccuracy of the information that was provided by the source company. Due to shopfloor at the source company practice (people at the shopfloor deviate from the design and produce a slightly different part or with slightly different processes), the information provided was not up-to-date. Delays were mainly caused by changing aircraft demand, inaccurate information, and a deteriorating motivation of the workforce. E.g. as a consequence of inaccurate information the wrong fasteners were supplied which had to be replaced causing delays.

The case study analysis showed (confirmed by checking with other transfer experiences) that older technologies are likely to have incorrect information. Therefore the age of technology was used as determining factor (selection criteria) for other cases (Steenhuis, 1998b).

Case 3

The third case study involved another transfer of technology from the UK to Romania. The transfer started in 1997 and during the research project the actual implementation was not completed. Presently continuous production is taking place in Romania. The technology that was transferred was the assembly of tail parts of a new aircraft.

Similar to the second case, only a partial technology was transferred. All required inputs were supplied to Romania from the UK and detail parts manufacturing was not part of the project. People were trained in Romania and in some instances in the UK and technical assistance was also provided. Tools and equipment were manufactured or provided by the destination company based on the provided information. Three to four foreign representatives remained on site in Romania to assist and help managing the project. All necessary information (product and process) was provided by the source company and used by the destination company in a similar way as at the source company. Both companies were using the same information by using electronic connections and the information was developed during the project based on lessons learned at either of the two companies. After assembly by the destination company the tail parts were shipped to the UK.

Besides customs problems, which affected the availability of parts, there were major problems with the accuracy of information. Since the aircraft was relatively new many modifications were made at the source company. As a result several drawings and planning sheets had to be changed and one of the major assemblies was seriously delayed because at the destination company it was not known what modifications were required.

Lessons from these three case studies indicated some particular problems caused by the environment of an industrially developing country, notably: lack of finances, poorly developed local industries, bad working conditions, and bad infrastructure and customs problems. To investigate to what extend these were typical issues for a 'developing country' the fourth case study was chosen in an industrially developed country (Steenhuis, 1999a).

Case 4

This study dealt with a technology transfer between Germany and the Netherlands. The transfer started in 1998. The implementation of the transfer was completed in 1998 and presently the Dutch company is engaged in continuous production. The technology that was transferred was the manufacturing of fuselage skin sections.

In this case, different from the second and third case, a 'complete' manufacturing package was transferred. One of the reasons that this could be realised was that the destination company was located in an industrially developed country and was experienced. The destination company was responsible for the inputs, detail parts production and end product. The source company did not have any influence on how the production was scheduled or managed. Training was not provided and except for a few rare instances technical assistance was also not provided. Because it was estimated that the level of the destination company was at such a level that this was not required. Tools and equipment were, with one exception caused by information problems, manufactured or provided by the destination company based on the information provided by the source company. The source company provided the destination company with the required product and process information. However, the destination company used different machines and followed a different production philosophy (used different production processes). Production scheduling and management was the complete responsibility of the destination company.

The major problem in this technology transfer was the accuracy of information. Both companies assumed that, because both were experienced aircraft and aircraft parts manufacturing companies, the information provided and the processes used were understood and accepted. However, since the destination company followed a different production philosophy which represented information in a different way misinterpretations occurred. These misinterpretations could have been prevented if one had been aware of those differences and training or technical assistance had been provided and one had been aware of interpretation differences. At the same time, some information was misinterpreted due to the different background of the companies. This occurred whereas it was completely unexpected that it was possible to interpret information in different ways. The mistakes that were the result of these misinterpretations and the extra time and cost required in order to get the alternative processes of the destination company accepted by the source company led to a budget overrun at the destination company of more than 120% (Steenhuis, 1999b)

IMPLEMENTING INTERNATIONAL TECHNOLOGY TRANSFER

These case studies show that the implementation of international technology transfer can be considered to contain four groups of activities: transfer of information; installing technology components (humanware, inforware, technoware and input); first article production; and packaging, transport, and delivery of the product. This is represented in Fig. 30.1.

The start of the implementation is with the transfer of inforware from the source company to the destination company. After this, the technology (humanware, inforware, technoware, and inputs) has to be brought to the required level at the destination company. The design information needs to be interpreted before the destination company can decide how to produce. After this the tooling designs have to be made or translated, and process specifications at the destination company checked. Planning sheets and a quality plan are developed and the systems database (material etc.) has to be set up. Once the technology is set up, the first article (batch) production and inspection takes place at the destination company.

During the implementation numerous delays can occur and the case studies showed that the critical path can differ for different technology transfer projects. Whether or not a delay is critical depends on the linkage of the activity for which the delay occurred, and the leeway that other activities have to make up for the delay. This depends on the overall leeway that was included in the project plan. The delays were greatly underestimated.

Some of the activities in Fig. 30.1 are interchangeable. E.g., it is possible for the destination company to produce the detail parts (this is mentioned under 'first article

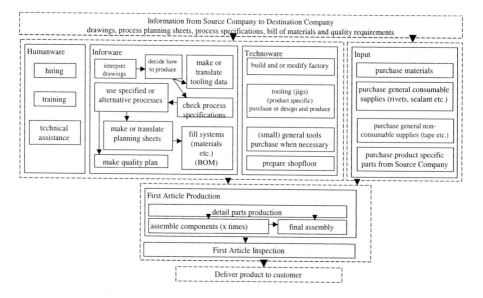

Fig. 30.1. Implementation activities.

production and was done in case 1 and case 4) but it is also possible that the source company supplies the detail parts (this is mentioned under input and was realised in case 2 and case 3).

CONCLUSIONS

The four cases that were analysed during the research project show that the implementation of international re-location of production technology requires a specific set of activities to be carried out. This set of activities has been represented in the model in Fig. 30.1. The model shows that the main group of activities concentrates on transferring the technology components. It is not necessary that all activities in the model are carried out because some activities are interchangeable. However, in order to avoid (unnecessary) delays and extra production costs companies need to carefully consider all activities and their potential impact on the production schedule.

REFERENCES

Bacharach, S.B. (1989). Organizational theories: some criteria for evaluation. *Academy of Management Review,* **14**, 496-515.

Cusumano, M.A. and Elenkov, D. (1994). Linking international technology transfer with strategy and management: a literature commentary. *Research Policy*, **23**, 195-215.

Dubin, R. (1978). *Theory building* (revised edition). The Free Press, London.

Eisenhardt, K.M. (1989). Building theories from case study research. *Academy of Management Review*, **14**, 532-550.

Glaser, B. (1992). *Basics of grounded theory analysis: emergence vs forcing.* Sociology Press, Mill Valley.

Glaser, B. and Strauss, A. (1967). *The discovery of grounded theory.* Aldine, Chicago.

Godkin, L. (1988). Problems and practicalities of technology transfer: a survey of the literature. *International Journal of Technology Management*, **3**, 587-603.

Gregory, M.J., et al. (1996). International manufacturing capabilities: a framework to support the assessment, development and deployment. in *Manufacturing strategy: operations strategy in a global context*. EurOMA 4th International Conference Proceedings (C. Voss, ed.).

Madu, C.N. (1989). Transferring technology to developing countries – critical factors for success. *Long Range Planning.* **22(4)**, 115-124.

Miles, M.B. and Huberman, A.M. (1994). *Qualitative data analysis, An expanded source book* (second edition). Sage publications, Thousand Oaks.

Nahar, N. (1999) IT-enabled effective and efficient international technology transfer for SMEs. in: Proceedings of the evolution and challenges in system development, pp. 85-98, Bled.

Plenert, G. (1997). Requirements for technology transfer to Third World countries. *International Journal of Technology Management.* **13(4)**, 421-425.

Quinn, J.B. (1969). Technology transfer by multinational companies. *Harvard Business Review*, **November-December**, 147-161.

Ramanathan, K. (1999). A normative model for the planning and implementation of international technology transfer. in: *Technology and innovation management*, PICMET '99 Portland International Conference on the Management of Engineering and Technology (Kocaoglu, D.F., Anderson, T.R., eds.).

Reddy, N.M. and Zhao, L. (1990). International technology transfer: a review. *Research Policy*, **19**, 285-307.

Stake, R.E. (1995). *The art of case study research.* Sage publications, Thousand Oaks.

Steenhuis, H.J. (1998a). *Manufacturing aircraft in East Europe to a West European standard, A case study on the transfer of technology,* Working paper no. 96. Technology and Development Group, University of Twente.

Steenhuis, H.J. (1998b). *Manufacturing North American aircraft parts in East Europe, A case study on the transfer of established production technology under a supply contract,* Working paper no. 97. Technology and Development Group, University of Twente.

Steenhuis, H.J (1999a). *Manufacturing West European aircraft parts in East Europe, A case study on the transfer of unstable production technology under a supply contract,* Working paper no. 98. Technology and Development Group, University of Twente.

Steenhuis, H.J. (1999b). *Manufacturing West European aircraft parts in West Europe, A case study on the transfer of established production technology under a supply contract,* Working paper no. 102. Technology and Development Group, University of Twente.

Steenhuis, H.J. (2000). *International technology transfer, Building theory from a multiple case-study in the aircraft industry,* Ph.D. thesis University of Twente, Enschede.

Strauss, A. and Corbin, J. (1990). *Basics of qualitative research, Grounded theory procedures and techniques.* Sage publications, Newbury Park.

Swanborn, P.G. (1996). *Case-study's, Wat, wanneer en hoe?.* Boom, Amsterdam, Meppel. In Dutch.

Tsang, E.W.K. (1994). Strategies for transferring technology to China, *Long Range Planning.* **27(3)**, 98-107.

Verschuren, P. and Doorewaard, H. (1995). *Designing a research project.* Lemma, Utrecht. (the same book was first published in Dutch: Verschuren, P., and Doorewaard, H. (1995). *Het ontwerpen van een onderzoek.* Lemma, Utrecht).

Yin, R.K. (1994). *Case study research, Design and methods.* Sage publications, Thousand Oaks. second edition.

AUTHOR INDEX